INTERNATIONAL LOANS, BONDS AND SECU

QUICK REFERENCE GUIDE

Chapter		Page
1.	Introduction	3
2.	Term Loans: Financial Terms	15
3.	Term Loans: Warranties, Covenants and Defaults	28
4.	Term Loans: Miscellaneous Clauses	54
5.	Term Loans: Governing Law and Jurisdiction Clauses, Waivers of Immunity	61
6.	Syndicated Loans	90
7.	Loan Transfers and Participations	104
8.	Bond Issues: General Principles	119
9.	Bond Issues: Special Types of Issue	144
10.	Bond Trustees and Bondholder Meetings	164
11.	Syndicate Agents and Bondholder Trustees as Fiduciaries	189
12.	Legal Opinions: Introduction	215
13.	Legal Opinions: Principal Contents	226
14.	Securities Regulation: Introduction	251
15.	Securities Regulation: Country Summaries	263
16.	Securities Regulation: Exemptions from Prospectus Requirements	282
17.	Securities Regulation: Misrepresentation and Non-Disclosure	301
18.	Securities Regulation: Regulation of Dealers	335
19.	Securities Regulation: Securities Frauds	347
20.	Securities Regulation: Extraterritorial Scope	361
21.	Securities Regulation: US Selling Restrictions in Eurobond Issues	367
22.	Bank Regulation: General Principles	377
23.	Bank Regulation: Basle Capital Adequacy	390

Appendix: Outlines and Precedents

I.	Loan Agreements	405
II.	Legal Opinions	485
III.	Bond Issues	493

LAW AND PRACTICE OF INTERNATIONAL FINANCE

INTERNATIONAL LOANS, BONDS AND SECURITIES REGULATION

AUSTRALIA
The Law Book Company
Brisbane ∗ Sydney ∗ Melbourne ∗ Perth

CANADA
Carswell
Ottawa ∗ Toronto ∗ Calgary ∗ Montreal ∗ Vancouver

AGENTS:
Steimatzky's Agency Ltd., Tel Aviv;
N.M. Tripathi (Private) Ltd., Bombay;
Eastern Law House (Private) Ltd., Calcutta;
M.P.P. House, Bangalore;
Universal Book Traders, Delhi;
Aditya Books, Delhi;
MacMillan Shuppan KK, Tokyo;
Pakistan Law House, Karachi, Lahore.

LAW AND PRACTICE OF INTERNATIONAL FINANCE

INTERNATIONAL LOANS, BONDS AND SECURITIES REGULATION

By

Philip R Wood

BA (Cape Town), MA (Oxon)

Solicitor of the Supreme Court

Visiting Professor, Queen Mary
& Westfield College,
University of London

LONDON
SWEET & MAXWELL
1995

Published in 1995 by
Sweet and Maxwell Limited of
South Quay Plaza, 183 Marsh Wall,
London E14 9FT
Computerset by Interactive Sciences, Gloucester
Printed in Great Britain by
Butler & Tanner, Frome and London

No natural forests were destroyed to make this product:
only farmed timber was used and re-planted

**A CIP catalogue record for this book is
available from the British Library**

ISBN 0 421 54310 8

All rights reserved.
UK Statutory material in this publication
is acknowledged as Crown copyright

*No part of this publication may be reproduced or transmitted
in any form or by any means, or stored in any retrieval system of
any nature without prior written permission, except for permitted
fair dealing under the Copyright, Designs and Patents Act 1988, or
in accordance with the terms of a licence issued by the Copyright
Licensing Agency in respect of photocopying and/or reprographic
reproduction. Application for permission for other use of copyright
material including permission to reproduce extracts in other
published works shall be made to the publishers.
Full acknowledgement of author, publisher and source
must be given.*

©
PHILIP R WOOD
1995

To my wife Marie-elisabeth, my twin sons
John Barnaby and Richard,
my daughter Sophie and my son Timothy

PREFACE

This book is one in a series of six works on international financial law which, taken together, are the successor to my *Law and Practice of International Finance* which was published in 1980 and which was reprinted eight times.

The works now cover a much broader range of subjects, with substantial additions in the fields of comparative law, insolvency, security, set-off, and title finance, as well as specialist subjects like netting, securitisations and swaps and derivatives. But the works have the same objectives as the original book. However great a gap there may be between the aim and the actuality, the objectives I have sought to achieve are to be practical as well as academic, to provide both a theoretical guide and legal source-book as well as a practitioner's manual, to be international, to provide serious comparative law information, to get to the point as quickly as possible, to simplify the difficulties, to find the principles underlying the particularity, to inform, and, most of all, to be useful.

The six works are separate but they are nevertheless related. Together the books are intended to form a complete library for the international banking and financial lawyer, as well as for specialists in related areas such as insolvency, leasing, and ship and aircraft finance. The topics covered by each volume are summarised on the inside of the front cover.

These books offer what I hope is a fundamentally new approach to comparative law in this area and, for the first time perhaps, provide the essential keys to an understanding of the world's jurisdictions, the keys to unlock the dark cupboard of financial law so that the light may shine in. These keys are not merely functional; they are also ethical and they are driven by history. The ideas are really quite simple, once discovered, but this should not obscure the difficulty of their application to the variety of circumstances. The core of the first book, entitled *Comparative Financial Law*, is a classification and snap-shot of virtually all the jurisdictions in the world – more than 300 of them – according to various financial law criteria. These criteria are developed in succeeding books in the series and applied to particular transactions. I believe that this also is the first time that a classification of this type has been done in this detail; but it has to be done because comparative law is no longer an academic luxury: it is a practical necessity if we are to have an orderly international legal regime.

My hope is that my voyage of discovery into what is really going on in world financial law will help to mitigate international legal surprises and legal risks and, in the wider context, that jurisdictions will be better equipped to make essential choices as to what their legal systems should achieve. This is particularly important in view of the fact that at least 30 per cent of the world's population live under legal systems which are still emerging and that the remainder live in jurisdictions divided into camps which often do not agree on basic policies. There is no reason why we should not agree on the basic policies: we do not have to have a muddle. The law is our servant, not our master. It must set us free, not tie us down. It must satisfy our sense of justice.

This book on international loans, bonds and securities regulation is largely a practical book with detailed commentaries on actual documents. It also contains an international survey of securities regulation and an orientational summary of bank regulation. I hope that the practical slant of this book will assist in showing how the theoretical doctrines discussed elsewhere in this series are applied in the real world.

A small amount of material from other works in the series is reproduced in this book so that the subject may be seen as a whole.

The books also contain lists of about 250 research topics in total which might be appropriate for further research and which I hope will be useful to prospective writers.

I am acutely conscious of the fact that, in writing about legal systems other than my own (which is England), I will often have committed some real howlers and I hope that my foreign colleagues will be tolerant of my ignorance. Obviously one must always confirm the position with competent local lawyers.

As regards style, I have endeavoured to be as economical as possible in these works. The citation is selective: there are now millions of cases and it is hopeless to try and list even a proportion of them. I am easily terrorised by footnotes and therefore, if material is good enough to go in the footnotes, it is good enough to go in the text: as a result there are no footnotes in these works. At least one does not have to read the text in two places at once. Tables of cases and statutes seemed less sensible in a work endeavouring to cover hundreds of jurisdictions where there is an avalanche of names and numbers and dates and acts and statutes and decrees, and, in view of this, I decided to omit them.

I have endeavoured to reflect the law round about the middle of 1994 based on the international materials then available to me, although some subsequent changes were introduced in the course of publication.

Philip R Wood
One New Change
London

Request for Information

Works on the law in the jurisdictions of the world must rely heavily on information from private sources. With a view to improving the information in any subsequent editions there may be, I would be very pleased to receive papers of all kinds on subjects covered by this and other works in this series – seminar papers, essays, articles, client briefings by law firms, memoranda, notices of book publications, and the like. Material should be sent to me at the following address:

Philip R Wood
Allen & Overy
One New Change
London EC4M 9QQ

Fax: 0171 330 9999

ACKNOWLEDGEMENTS

I owe to many a debt of gratitude in the help they gave me in preparing this work.

I am grateful to many partners and colleagues at Allen & Overy and to secondees from foreign firms for their advice and assistance. Jonathan Mellor read my chapters on bond issues and made many helpful suggestions. Geoff Fuller helped on trustee aspects of bond issues. Mark Welling and Catherine Husted assisted on bond issues materials; chapter 21 on US selling restrictions is based on a paper largely prepared by Edward H Murray. Alex Cameron, while a trainee, largely wrote the two chapters on bank regulation. James Aitken of Buddle Findlay in New Zealand provided materials on New Zealand securities regulation. I owe a particular debt to the authors of the works listed in the bibliography and of a very large number of articles and books not listed in this book or in the select bibliography without which it would not have been possible to write this book: if I have used their words, as I believe I often have, this is because they said it much better than I ever could. There are many others – practitioners, students, academics, bankers and others – who have contributed to this work in one way or another: it would be impossible for me to thank them all individually.

None of the above is of course responsible for the defects in this work.

I am most grateful to my secretary Sue Wisbey and to the Allen & Overy word processing department and checkers who laboured so magnificently to produce this work.

I am thankful to my publishers for their hard work and patience in bringing this work – and the other books in this series – to fruition and also for their support through all the years.

My brother John, my sister Melanie and my mother all encouraged me and were tolerant of my efforts.

My late father Leslie Wood, who was also a lawyer, first inculcated in me a fascination for the law while I was a boy in Northern Rhodesia, now Zambia.

Finally, I owe an enormous debt to my wife and children and can only express my affection for them by the token of dedicating this book to them.

CONTENTS

	Page
Preface	vii
Acknowledgements	x
Abbreviations	xxi

PART I: TERM LOANS AND BONDS

1. Introduction

	Page
General	3
International element	3
Term loans	4
Syndicated loans	5
London Eurocurrency market	6
Origins of the market	6
State insolvencies in 1980s	7
Subsequent developments	8
Project finance	8
Bond issues	9
Origins of the Eurobond market	9
Types of bonds	10
Regulation of international finance	11
Insolvency law	12
State loans	13
Legal opinions	14

2. Term loans: financial terms

	Page
Introduction	15
Agreement to lend	15
Conditions precedent	16
Drawdown of loans	19
Application of proceeds	19
Repayment	21
Prepayments and cancellation	21
Interest	22
Substitute basis clause	23
Multicurrency option	24
Payments by the borrower	25
Appropriations	27
Set-offs by borrower	27

3. Term loans: warranties, covenants and defaults

Representations and warranties

	Page
Usual warranties	28
Objectives of clause	29
Negotiation points	30
No warranties	31

Covenants

	Page
General	31
Objectives of corporate covenants	32
Remedies for breach	33
Lender liability	33
Negative pledge	34
Pari passu clause	41
Disposals	42
Financial covenants	43
Information	44
Other covenants	45

Events of default

	Page
Effects of defaults	46
Classification of defaults	46
Non-payment	47

International Loans, Bonds and Securities Regulation

Chapter	Page	Chapter	Page
Breach of other obligations	47	Applicable law in absence of express choice	66
Breach of warranty	47	Summary of international rules	67
Cross-default	48	State contracts	68
Creditor processes	49	Alternative or optional choices of law	68
Liquidation and insolvency proceedings	50	Depeçage	68
Actual insolvency	50	Incorporation of law	69
Material adverse change	50	Renvoi	69
Change of control ("poison pill")	51	Public international law	69
Subsidiaries and guarantors	52	Summary of scope of applicable law	69
Government loans	52		
Miscellaneous	52		
Acceleration	53	**Jurisdiction clause**	70

4. Term loans: miscellaneous clauses

		Purposes of forum selection	71
		Appointment of agent	73
		Mailing of process	73
Introduction	54	Venue	74
		Civilian practice	74
Margin protections		Exclusive and multiple jurisdiction clauses	74
Tax grossing-up	54	International jurisdiction rules	75
Increased costs	56		
Currency indemnity	56	**European Judgments Conventions**	76
Default indemnity	57		
Illegality clause	57	**Restrictions on judicial jurisdiction**	84
Other clauses		Arbitration	85
Assignments	58	**Waivers of sovereign immunity**	
Set-off	59		
Waivers	59	Terms of clause	87
Boiler-plate	60	State immunity	88
		Principles of waiver clauses	88

5. Term loans: governing law and jurisdiction clauses and waivers of indemnity

6. Syndicated loans

Loan syndication generally

		Introduction	90
Introduction	61	Mandate	90
Terms of clause	61	Functions of lead bank	91
Factors influencing choice of law	62	Summary of syndication principles	91
Insulation	62		
Limits on insulation	63	**Solicitation of participants**	
Rome Convention of 1980	64		
Express choice of applicable law	65		
Evasive choices of law	66	Information memorandum	92

Chapter	Page	Chapter	Page
International regulation of invitational material	92	**Marketing and distribution of bonds**	
Misrepresentation liability	93	Main methods of marketing and distribution	124
Relationship between syndicate members		London eurobond issues: structure	124
		London eurobond issues: documents	125
Severality	94	Issue procedures	127
Syndicate democracy	94	Stabilisation	127
Payment of loans to borrower	96		
Payments by borrower	96	**Listing of bonds**	
Pro rata sharing clauses	96		
		Stock exchanges	128
Syndicate agents		Advantages of listing	128
		Disadvantages of listing	128
Introduction	98		
Scope of agent's authority	99	**Tax considerations for bonds**	129
Agent is agent of banks not borrower	100	**Negotiability of bonds**	
Contractual duties of agent	100		
Agent as fiduciary	100	Meaning of negotiability	130
Exercise of agent bank's discretions generally	101	English law of negotiability	131
Monitoring duties	101	Bearer and registered bonds compared	132
Acceleration	102	Governing law of negotiability	133
Agent bank's right of indemnity	102		
Removal of agent bank	102	**Clearing systems**	134
7. Loan transfers and participations		**Terms of bonds**	135
Introduction	104	Face of bond	135
Participations by assignment	106	Incorporation of fiscal agency agreement/trust deed	135
Sub-participations	110		
Novations	114	Form and transfer	136
Risk participations	116	Covenants	137
Loan transfers and capital adequacy	116	Interest	138
		Redemption	139
Loan transfers and securities regulation	117	Payments	141
		Prescription	142
		Events of default	143
8. Bond issues: general principles		Miscellaneous	143
		9. Bond issues: special types of issue	
Comparison of bond issues and syndicated loan agreements			
		Equity-linked bonds	
Main differences	119		
Detailed comparison	120	Introduction	144

Chapter	Page	Chapter	Page
Convertible bonds generally	144	Advantages for bondholders	164
Bonds with share warrants attached	145	Disadvantages of trustees	166
Listing	146	Mandatory requirements for a trustee	167
Advantages of equity-linked issues	146	**Comparison of trustees and fiscal agents**	168
Exchange rate	147		
Loss of conversion privilege	147		
Legal aspects of convertible bonds	148	**Legal characteristics of the trust**	
Anti-dilution provisions	150	Divided ownership	169
Takeovers	152	What is the trust property?	170
Mergers and spin-offs	153	Civilian attitudes to the trust	170
Covenants of issuer	154	Fiduciary duties of trustees	172
Taxation	155		
Warrants to purchase bonds		**Eligibility to act as trustee or representative**	
General	156		
Securities regulation	156	Regulatory requirements	172
Warrants exercise procedure	157	Retirement of trustees	173
Bearer depository receipts		**Bondholders' meetings**	
Reasons for bearer depository receipts	157	Generally	173
Structure involving depository	157	Main issues for bondholder decision	174
Documenting the depository arrangements	158	Enforcement by trustees	175
		Organisation of bondholders	178
Secured issues	159	Issues on which majority can bind minority	179
Eurocommercial paper		Minority protection	180
Introduction	159	Trustee's unilateral power to waive and modify	182
Documentation	160	Bondholder communities: comparative review	182
Euro medium-term note programmes		**Bonds held by custodians**	185
Generally	161	**Governing law of trust deeds**	
Documentation	162		
10. **Bond trustees and bondholder meetings**		Contract between issuer and trustee	186
		Relationship between trustee and bondholders	186
Anglo-American bond trustees		Conflict with bondholder statutes	187
Introduction	164	Prescriptive jurisdiction	188

Chapter	Page	Chapter	Page
11. Syndicate agents and bondholder trustees as fiduciaries		Monitoring duties of trustees	198
		Confidental information	200
		Notification of defaults	201
Comparison of bondholder trustees and syndicate agents		**Chinese Walls**	
		Generally	203
Generally	189	Weaknesses of Chinese Walls	204
Differences	189	Case law on Chinese Walls	204
Conflicts of interests and secret profits		**Exculpation clauses**	
		Trust deed practice	206
General rule	190	Syndicate agent practice	206
Examples of potential conflicts	191	General effect of exclusion clauses: is there a duty?	207
Effect of conflict	192	Efficacy of exculpations	207
Regulatory controls of conflicts	192	Statutory limitations on exclusion clauses	209
Solutions for trustee or agent faced with conflict	195		
Secret profits	197		
Due diligence by the fiduciary		**Indemnity to fiduciaries**	
Due diligence generally	197	Trustees	211
Approval of documentation	198	Syndicate agents	211

PART II: LEGAL OPINIONS

Chapter	Page	Chapter	Page
12. Legal opinions: introduction		Persons entitled to rely on opinions	223
Generally	215	Lawyers as "experts"	223
Comparison with European notaries	215	Liability in tort	223
What jurisdictions should be covered?	217	**13. Legal opinions: principal contents**	
Scope of opinions	217		
Documents examined	218	**Foreign lawyer's legal opinion**	226
Assumptions	218		
Qualifications generally	219	Status	226
Opinion as to facts	220	Corporate powers	231
Foreign law	220	Due authorisation, execution and delivery	232
Whose lawyers give the opinion?	222	Execution and delivery	233
Opinions as to law of borrower's domicile	222	Legal validity	234
When is the opinion given?	222	Official consents	238

Chapter	Page	Chapter	Page
Non-conflict with laws, constitution of contracts	239	**Opinions on bond issues**	
Litigation	239	Securities regulation	244
Stamp duties	240	Prospectuses	245
Filings	240		
Legal form	241	**Opinions on security**	245
Taxes	241		
Pari passu ranking	241	**Opinion of principal lawyers**	
Enforcement of foreign judgments	242		
Immunity	242	Generally	247
No adverse consequences; qualifications to do business	243	Who is the client?	247
		Conditions precedent	247
Application of governing law	244	Expert's opinion	248

PART III: SECURITIES REGULATION

Chapter	Page	Chapter	Page
14. Securities regulation: introduction		EC Council Directives: summary	268
		EC Admissions Directive	268
		EC Listing Particulars Directive	269
Summary of regulation		EC Interim Reports Directive	272
		EC Mutual Recognition Directive	272
Introduction	251	EC Prospectus Directive	272
Heads of financial regulation	251	EC Second Mutual Recognition Directive	273
Policies of securities regulation generally	252	EC UCITS Directive	273
Excesses of regulatory regimes	252	EC Second Banking Directive	273
International approaches	254	EC Investment Services Directive	273
Degree of codification	254	EC Capital Adequacy Directive	273
Summary of securities regulation	255	Continenal European securities regimes	274
Meaning of regulated "securities"	257	Australia	274
		Japan	275
History of securities regulation		Canada	276
		New Zealand	276
The beginnings	259	Traditional English countries	277
United States in the 1930s	260	Russia	279
Spread of formal regulation	261	China	280
Continental Europe	262	Other countries	281
15. Securities regulation: country summaries		**16. Exemptions from prospectus requirements**	
Sources of law	263		
United Kingdom	263	Introduction	282
United States	265	Summary of main exemptions	283

Chapter	Page	Chapter	Page
Exemption for private offerings	283	**Prospectus contents**	
Exemption for secondary market trading	294	Strengths and weaknesses of disclosure codes	322
Shelf registration	295	Contents of corporate prospectuses	324
Guaranteed issues	295	Contents of bank prospectuses	327
Collective investment schemes	296	Contents of governmental prospectuses	328
Application of prospectus requirements to international bonds	298	**Continuing stock exchange disclosure**	329
Application of prospectus requirements to loan syndications	298	**Misrepresentation and conflict of laws**	

17. Securities regulation: misrepresentation and non-disclosure

		Governing law of torts	329
		Law of the courts (lex fori)	330
		Law of the place of the tort	331
Sources of law	301	Closely connected law of the tort	331
Summary of enhanced liability under regulated prospectuses	301	English law	332
Heads of general misrepresentation liability in England	302	Jurisdiction over tort claims for misrepresentation	332
Heads of misrepresentation liability in the United States	304		

18. Securities regulation: regulation of dealers

Authorisation of dealers

Aspects of general law of misrepresentation

		Licensing of investment businesses	335
Misrepresentor's knowledge of the misrepresentation	308	Authorisation in Britain	335
What is a misrepresentation?	310	Authorisation in the United States	338
True information subsequently becomes false	312	**Conduct of business**	
Access to information	313		
Inducement (reliance)	313	Regulation of conduct of investment business generally	338
Materiality	314	Conduct of business in the United Kingdom	339
Remedies	314		
Who can sue?	315		
Who can be sued?	316	Conduct of business in the United States	340
Misrepresentation liability of managing banks and co-managers	317	Protection of client assets	340
		Conflict of interest generally	341
Exclusion of liability by loan syndication managers	320	Self-dealing and secret profits	342
		Managing conflicts	343
Exclusion of liability by bond managers	320	Duties of skill, care and diligence	343
		Customer agreements	344

International Loans, Bonds and Securities Regulation

Chapter	Page	Chapter	Page
Remedies	344	Conflict of duties	358
Margin regulations	344	Negative profits	359
Cold calling	345	Intent	359
Financial regulation of dealers	345	Exemption for stabilisation	359
		Territoriality	360
		Other exemptions	360

19. Securities regulation: securities frauds

Summary	347
Market manipulation	347
Corners	347
False rumours	348
Scalping	348
Exemption for stabilisation	349
Churning	349

Insider dealing

Meaning of insider dealing	349
Insider dealing under the general law	350
Specific regulation of insider dealing	351
EC Directive on Insider Dealing	352
United States	354
Other countries	355
Main prohibitions	355
Inside information	357
Securities covered by the prohibitions	357
Sanctions	358

20. Securities regulation: extraterritorial scope

Internationalisation of securities markets	361
Territorial scope of criminal statutes	362
Enforcement of criminal statutes	362
Jurisdiction over civil wrongs	363
Principles of prescriptive jurisdiction	363
Comment on extraterritorial application	366

21. Securities regulation: US selling restrictions in eurobond issues

Introduction	367
Regulation S	367
TEFRA C and D	370
Rule 144A	372
Standard form selling restrictions	373

PART IV: BANK REGULATION

Chapter	Page	Chapter	Page
22. Bank regulation: general principles		Capital adequacy	
		Minimum capital	382
Introduction		Basle Agreement	382
Credit businesses	377	**Liquidity**	385
Authorisation of banks	378		
Restrictions on non-banking activities	379	**Large exposures**	386
Financial supervision generally	379	**Systems and controls**	388
Main heads of financial supervision	381	**Foreign exchange risk**	388

Chapter	Page	Chapter	Page
Ownership and management	389	Tier 2: Supplementary capital	391
		Deductions from total capital	392
23. Bank regulation: Basle capital adequacy		Limits and restrictions on capital	392
		Risk weights by category of on-balance-sheet asset	392
Introduction	390	Credit conversion factors for off-balance-sheet items	394
Tier 1: Core capital	390		

APPENDIX: OUTLINES AND PRECEDENTS

Part	Page
I. Loan Agreements	405
II. Legal Opinions	485
III. Bond Issues	493
Select Bibliography	528
List of Research Topics	531
Index	533

ABBREVIATIONS

ABGB	Austrian General Civil Code
Art	Article
BA	Bankruptcy Act
BC	Bankruptcy Code
BGB	German Civil Code
BL	Bankruptcy Law
c	chapter (of laws)
CC	Civil Code
CCP	Code of Civil Procedure
CO	Code of Obligations
ComC	Commercial Code
Conflicts Restatement	Restatement of the Law, Conflict of Laws 2d, by the American Law Institute
Dicey	Lawrence Collins (general editor), *Dicey and Morris on the Conflict of Laws* (12th ed 1993) Sweet & Maxwell
EISO	Philip Wood, *English and International Set-off* (1989) Sweet & Maxwell
IA	Insolvency Act
ICSID	International Centre for the Settlement of Investment Disputes
IR	Insolvency Rules (England)
Mann, Money	FA Mann, *The Legal Aspect of Money* (5th ed 1992) Clarendon Press, Oxford
Ord	Order
PILA	Private International Law Act 1987 (Switzerland)
Restatement	Restatement of the Law by the American Law Institute
RSC	Rules of the Supreme Court (England)
s	section
Sched	Schedule
UCC	Uniform Commercial Code (United States)
ZPO	Code of Civil Procedure (*Zivilprozessordnung*)
Zweigert/Kötz	K Zweigert and H Kötz, *An Introduction to Comparative Law* (2nd ed 1987)

Part I

TERM LOANS AND BONDS

Chapter 1

INTRODUCTION

General

This book deals primarily with international term loans, international bond issues and other issues of debt securities, and also with securities and bank regulation, and is one of a series of works on international financial law.

This chapter largely repeats introductory remarks in the first of the series of works – on comparative financial law – and is introduced here for the convenience of the reader so that the topics covered by this book may be seen as a whole.

International loans may be made by banks under the terms of a loan agreement or raised from other institutions (such as pension funds, large corporations, insurance companies or government agencies) which have funds to invest and which will normally expect to receive a certificate or bond recording the terms of their loan which they can transfer. In the case of these other institutions, the funds come from pension moneys or insurance premiums or other surplus moneys arising from their operations. They could deposit these moneys with banks but the interest rate on debt securities may be higher.

The borrowers are governments, state entities, international organisations (like the World Bank), provinces, municipalities, large industrial corporations and single-purpose project companies. They are not individual or small enterprises. We are not concerned with consumer credit or small business finance.

The credits may be unsecured or protected by security, such as a mortgage of land and buildings or a pledge of investment securities. They may be guaranteed as where a parent company guarantees a loan by a subsidiary. Asset protection may take other forms, of which financial leasing is a notable example. Security, guarantees and title finance are reviewed in other volumes in this series.

1–1

1–2

International element

The focus is on international transactions, not domestic finance. An international transaction is one which has contacts with more than one legal

1–3

jurisdiction. That international element may arise from the fact that a lending bank is located in one jurisdiction and the borrower in another, or that the bank lends in a foreign currency and not the domestic currency of the borrower, or that bonds are sold to foreign investors by an international syndicate of managers.

Since the credits have an international element, it is necessary to study how the differences between legal systems are resolved. For example, if a corporation is prevented from repaying an international loan by reason of an exchange control introduced by its home state, will foreign courts recognise that the borrower is relieved of its obligation, and will those foreign courts have jurisdiction over the borrower to order it to pay or allow it not to pay? Would foreign creditors be able to bankrupt the corporation in their own countries? If the corporation is a central bank owned by the state, will it be entitled to claim it is immune from the courts of another state because it is a sovereign creature?

This is the province of private international law and sometimes public international law. Hence regard must be had to the conflicts of law rules as to contracts and insolvency, as well as the jurisdiction of the courts to hear disputes and to enforce claims and the question of sovereign immunity. Some of the rules are alluded to in these pages and there is a chapter on governing law and jurisdiction clauses and waivers of sovereign immunity. But the topics are so large that a full treatment is also reserved for other works in this series.

Term loans

1–4 Bank credits are bank lending financed by deposits, primarily from other banks in money markets or from issues of negotiable certificates of deposit or from customer deposits. Borrowers require medium or long-term loans (e.g. three to 15 years) to finance capital investments and the like. But depositors are only prepared to lend to their banks by way of deposit short-term, e.g. six months or on demand. Banks therefore act as intermediaries and borrow short to lend long. Their gross profit is the spread or margin between the interest they pay to their depositors on the short-term deposits and interest they earn on the long-term loan, e.g. 1 per cent, not much in any event. Hence the floating rate term loan agreement – a contract which has been so frequently polished that it is now overlaid with an impressive, but nevertheless impenetrable, patina of tradition. The rate of interest which the borrower pays the bank changes periodically when the rate at which the bank borrows changes – it floats.

Because these loans last for a period of years before the borrower must repay in full, the lender expects protections in case something should go wrong in the meantime and prejudice final repayment. For example, the borrower must provide continuing information as to its financial condition, not dispose of all its assets or go into some other business. Hence, apart from the financial terms, loan agreements contain covenants regarding the management of the borrower's business in very limited areas crucial to the lender. If the borrower defaults in paying a principal or interest instalment or becomes insolvent or fails to comply with a term of the agreement, the lender can call in the loan immediately before its full term has expired and before it is too late, but not otherwise. These are the events of default.

Syndicated loans

Huge loans involve spreading the risk amongst a group or syndicate of banks who lend separate portions of the loan under the terms of a single agreement organised and administered by an agent bank. Hence the syndicated credit agreement. The amounts are usually in the region of $30 million to $200 million but can be much larger, e.g. $7 billion. Like bilateral term loan agreements, these multilateral contracts have also sacramentalised their own rites and in particular have produced much liturgy, by no means brief, as to the duties of the members of this little communion to each other and as to the role of their chief priest, the agent bank.

The syndicated loan was probably originally an American idea. In the nineteenth and early twentieth centuries British and Continental European banks tended to finance their industrial customers by single-bank credits. In England, enterprises would typically borrow from one bank which would provide a demand loan and take a fixed and floating charge over all the assets. Although the loan was on demand and therefore technically was unpredictable, banks of course did not call it in unless the position was hopeless and often long after the position was hopeless. The system worked well. But in the United States, the approach was different. The pattern there was for a group of banks to make the loan under a common agreement, to agree to lend for a fixed period determinable only on an event of default, and to lend unsecured but on terms that the borrower was prohibited from granting security to anybody else – the negative pledge.

These agreements are remarkable for their egalitarian emphasis on equality between creditors. They have a cross-default, which is an event of default sparking off on non-payment by the borrower of another loan, so that no creditor can steal a march on the others. They have the negative pledge, just mentioned, which enforces the equality principle that all creditors must be unsecured so that on insolvency the assets are equally divided. They have a pro rata sharing clause whereby the syndicate banks agree to share equally any individual receipts recovered by one bank in excess of those paid to the others – a romantic idea which has, however, been more honoured in the breach than the observance.

London eurocurrency market

1–6   The American style was imported to London in the 1960s with the growth of the London eurocurrency market, initially promoted by American banks, quickly joined by Canadian, Japanese, British and European banks, those from other nations and, after the oil price increases in the 1970s, by Arab banks.

The London eurocurrency market was, and is, a deposit market between banks. Banks borrow short-term deposits from each other – for one, three, six, nine or twelve months, but usually three or six months – to finance bilateral or syndicated medium term loans to foreign states, state enterprises and large industrial undertakings. The market was and remains primarily a US dollar market and other currencies were less commonly used for various reasons, including the importance of the US dollar as a reserve currency and the desire of central banks in Japan and Europe to maintain sovereignty over their own currencies, a desire expressed in exchange controls, statutory borrowing controls (Britain) and administrative guidelines (especially in Germany, Japan and Switzerland).

The term "eurocurrency market" was coined to describe this deposit market. Eurocurrency is not a special currency issued by banks in the form of notes and coins embossed with the head of Charlemagne. Eurocurrency is financial vernacular for a deposit payable at a branch of a bank outside the country of the currency. Thus a eurodollar is a US dollar deposit payable by a bank outside the United States – even if the bank is in Singapore. The term is apt because of course most money is now bank money, i.e. payable by a bank, as opposed to notes and coins.

Origins of the market

1–7   The London eurocurrency market originated from a variety of economic, political, legal and other factors.

The US dollar supplanted sterling as the prime reserve currency after World War II. US dollars were deposited by central banks, governments and others with banks abroad, partly as result of the US balance of payments deficit, partly because of the absence of US capital and exchange controls. Regulation D of the US Federal Reserve imposed reserve requirements on deposits taken by US banks, reducing the interest payable on US deposits so that depositors earned more in Europe. A reserve requirement is a requirement that a bank deposit moneys interest free with the central bank so that the depositing bank has sufficient liquidity to pay its own depositors if they should demand repayment in greater amounts than expected – a run on the bank.

Regulation Q of the Federal Reserve put a ceiling on interest payable by US banks on time deposits, so foreign banks in Europe could pay higher interest, thereby attracting US dollar deposits.

The growth was fed by the desire of major banks to expand their business internationally away from the limited market for domestic lending.

Sovereign depositors favoured UK political stability and non-interference. This was probably supported by the fear by communist governments of US seizures, such as the attempt in 1948 by the US Treasury to block the withdrawal of $20 million of Czech gold from the Federal Reserve. London was also favoured because it had a developed financial and legal infrastructure and because of the language.

An enormous fillip was given to the market by the petrodollar explosion after the 1973 oil cartel, followed by a doubling of the oil price in 1979–1980. Oil producers deposited oil profits in safe Western banks short-term. These banks lent medium-term largely to lesser developed countries to help them pay for oil and to develop their economies – a process sometimes referred to as "recycling" or "intermediation".

State insolvencies in 1980s

The result was catastrophic. The banks assumed that repayment by the less rich countries could always be made out of new loans. This was falsified by the inability of many lesser developed countries even to pay interest, leading to multiple state insolvencies in the 1980s, commencing with Poland and Turkey and ultimately gathering up in its dark chariot most countries in Latin America, Africa, communist central Europe and elsewhere, but not the leading industrial states.

A state is insolvent when it cannot repay its foreign currency debts – states can always pay debts in their own currency simply by printing more money (although this itself can have serious domestic economic consequences, notably inflation). To repay foreign currency, the state must be able to earn sufficient foreign currency, e.g. from exports. Many of these lesser developed states simply did not earn enough – an unfortunate circumstance with a history going back for centuries. Banks, together with governmental creditors through their informal committee known as the Paris Club, spent most of the 1980s rescheduling these massive defaulted bank loans: it took many years to restore bank balance sheets, aided by accounting manoeuvres which were as imaginative as they were necessary. It was only in 1988 that the leading central banks were able to require that banks maintain capital of 8 per cent to their weighted portfolios in the Basle Agreement of that year, a remarkable illustration of international cooperation.

Subsequent developments

1–9 In the meantime the market did not stay still. Eurocurrency markets sprang up elsewhere – Paris, Singapore, Hong Kong. The lending reverted to large corporate loans, some of them exploiting every imaginable type of facility that the financial mind could engender – short-term revolving notes, competitive tender panels whereby banks bid to lend on a revolving basis, acceptances (which are effectively guarantees by the banks of trade bills of exchange issued by the borrower so that the borrower can sell them). Hence the arrival of the multi-option facility, whose life was as short as its documentation long. A revolving loan is a short-term loan which is repaid out of the proceeds of a new loan – the loans turn over or revolve. In the same period, substantial loans were made to finance take-overs of companies, including take-overs by the existing management (management buy-outs). That cycle ended with yet more spectacular insolvencies in the late 1980s and early 1990s, this time of large industrial and property corporations, caught in a deep economic recession and high interest rates.

Project finance

1–10 Of particular persistence throughout this period, and growing in the 1990s, were bank credits to finance projects – the development of an oil or gas field, a mine, a toll bridge or tunnel, a refinery, a pipeline or an ordinary office or shop development. Many are stupendous industrial projects, like giant electricity power stations. The essence of project finance is that banks lend to a project company, owned by the project sponsors, to finance the development. The project company carries on solely the business of building and operating the project so that, if the project fails, the banks have no other source of repayment, except for whatever guarantees and the like they have been able to negotiate. As a result, project finance can be risky and requires close attention to structure, to the security available, to the commercial contracts and to any government concession.

Following the wave of privatisations in the 1980s and beyond, whereby governments sold state enterprises to the public or to private companies, and the dismantling of the ideology of state corporatism, many countries now seek to finance their infrastructure and industrial expansion by granting a lease or other property right to private sponsors who build the project, operate it and then transfer it back to the public sector after repaying the capital and reaping a profit for their efforts and expertise which are usually prodigious. By these "build-operate-transfer" projects, states harness private industrial enterprise and capital but without burdening the state budget. The foreign capital is often backed by finance or guarantees from export credit agencies supporting their national exporters of equipment for the project. Whether this project capital will enjoy better fortune than its forbears remains to be seen.

Project finance is studied in another work in this series, but many of the basic principles on syndicated term loans in this book will be the foundation of the superstructure of project finance.

Bond issues

Bond issues are lending in the form of negotiable debt securities subscribed by investors and payable to whoever physically has them – the bearer. Investment banks organise the issue and underwrite the initial sale but otherwise banks do not act as intermediaries. The investor carries the default risk, whereas in bank loans the bank carries the default risk. 1–11

The transaction is a loan, but the terms of the loan are set out in securities, each of which is in a relatively small amount, e.g. $1,000, so as to facilitate transfers by the investors. The main differences with bank loans are that the securities must be freely and easily marketable (banks do not usually trade loans), that the investors may be multitudinous and anonymous, that the terms of bonds tend towards greater standardisation and simplicity, and that the issue of the bonds attracts the adversities of securities regulation. Bond issues are generally listed on a stock exchange, such as London or Luxembourg, not to provide a market but to enlarge the number of potential investors: many institutions cannot, by choice or regulation, invest in unlisted securities because they are usually riskier. The market is known as the international capital market or the primary market – "primary" to connote new issues as opposed to the secondary market for trades in securities already issued.

Origins of the eurobond market

Although this is disputed, the first real eurobond issue was an issue by the Italian Autostrade in 1965. The essence of the transaction was that the US dollar bonds were listed in London, and that the issue was managed by European banks and sold to European investors. This was no more than a 1–12 revival of the numerous eighteenth and nineteenth century issues in Europe and latterly in the United States.

The market developed in London for a variety of reasons. First, securities regulation in Europe for issues to sophisticated investors was very liberal and avoided the cumbersome US requirements which insisted on the preparation and registration of a massive and time-consuming prospectus. Secondly, a US interest equalisation tax in 1963 imposed a tax penalty on US investors buying foreign bonds. Thirdly, US restrictions on direct overseas investment by US corporations in the late 1960s forced US foreign subsidiaries to borrow abroad. Other factors were that European fees were cheaper than in the United States and that there was a substantial European demand, e.g. in Switzerland, for private portfolio investment.

Types of bonds

1–13 The bonds may be foreign bonds, which are bonds issued by a foreign issuer and subscribed by investors in a single country, e.g. bonds issued by a Swedish company and purchased by Japanese investors. But more usually bonds are purchased by investors internationally in which event they are referred to as eurobonds, reflecting their birthplace, or as international bonds.

The investors are invariably sophisticated investors, not the general public. Typically they are governments, insurance companies, pension funds, investment companies or trusts, banks and large corporations. Although the Belgian dentist is famed as the archetypal eurobond investor, purchases of bonds by individuals is small, although individuals may invest in funds which hold bonds and of course individuals are the ultimate beneficiaries, however remote they may be from the actual holder. Hence the market is wholesale, not retail, and rules of law designed to protect innocent individuals from others and from themselves play, or should play, no leading role.

1–14 The bonds may be ordinary bonds evidencing a simple debt or they may be convertible into shares of the issuer or its parent or have attached to them warrants to subscribe for shares: these are equity-linked bonds. The bondholder will convert if equity shares will be worth more, or produce more income, than the bonds.

Bonds typically have maturities of between seven to 12 years, sometimes shorter, sometimes longer. But there are various other types of instrument of shorter maturities, such as medium-term notes and short-term revolving issues of commercial paper having maturities of less than a year and rolled over into a fresh issue on maturity.

Although the bonds are negotiable bearer securities, the investors do not put them under their mattresses. Instead they deposit them with a custodian to look after them in safe-keeping. When they desire to transfer them, all that happens is that the custodian debits the account of the seller and credits the account of the buyer. The bonds lie sleepily where they are, in a vault somewhere, often thousands of miles from the office of the custodian. Because of the vast amounts of these investment securities – more than $1,400 billion with one single custodian in Brussels – the system is convenient and safe. Indeed, if it were not for custodians, a mountain of paperwork would utterly crush the market and everybody in it. These custodians are therefore granaries or silos for intangibles. They are keepers.

Regulation of international finance

Then there is the question of regulation. The main objectives of regulation are to protect the public from incompetence and deceit, from their own imprudence or lack of sophistication, and from the insolvency of regulated institutions and debtors. The original regulation of money took the form of usury and gaming laws, primarily designed to protect over-optimistic individuals against debt and speculation and the miseries they can bring. Usury and gaming laws have been overtaken in importance over the last 60 years or so by securities regulation and bank regulation. Both have regimes requiring securities dealers and banks to be officially licensed and to show competence and honesty, both have elaborate regimes for official supervision and monitoring of the financial health of dealers and banks, and securities regulation has disclosure rules whereby investors are to be informed of the quantity of the investments that are offered.

1–15

Of course there is also consumer credit legislation, which is of minimal importance in our context, and also the various national restrictive practices in the form of exchange controls and borrowing controls. The latter two have been more or less dismantled in the main industrialised states, but exchange controls remain of significance.

There are marked differences between securities regulation and bank regulation. Securities regulation surprises the bystanding observer – a jumble of bizarre and gothic statutes bristling with such ferocious detail, often born of a deep moral anxiety about cheating, as almost entirely to bury the plain objectives which all sensible people subscribe to. Many states effectively erect a paper wall against access by foreign enterprises to local savings. By contrast, bank regulation on the whole is comparatively harmonious and sensible at the international level.

The reason for this disparity is probably that bank insolvencies could potentially be so damaging to the public, to world order and to prosperity that concerted action was essential. Other reasons are that the banking population is much less than the population of those involved in the securities business and so is more manageable, that there is less public involvement in securities than in banking and so a diminished public interest, that banks are supervised by a few regulators dominated by the central banks of a handful of leading industrialised countries, and that central bankers are less disposed to allow unsophisticated emotions about money to interfere with their judgment of what is necessary.

Insolvency law

1–16 In credit transactions, the main risk for the creditor is that he will not be paid because the borrower is insolvent. Hence much of the law and practice in this area is concerned with the insolvency risk.

Examples taken at random are:

1. the importance of guarantees, security, title finance and set-off in order to mitigate the insolvency risk;

2. covenants in term loan agreements and bonds, such as the negative pledge, pari passu clause, anti-disposal clause and financial ratios variously designed to protect the credit;

3. events of default in term loan agreements and bonds, such as a cross-default, intended to provide early warning of financial difficulties;

4. the appointment of bond trustees and bondholder representation of bondholders, in order to facilitate a debt restructuring where the issuer is in financial difficulties;

5. the potential liability of lead managers of syndicated loans and managers of bond issuers for inaccuracies in offering circulars if the borrower is insolvent and therefore unable to pay;

6. capital adequacy rules for banks and investment businesses whereby their solvency is subject to official supervision; and

7. disclosure rules imposed by securities regulation and stock exchanges in relation to prospectuses and the issuer's continuing financial condition so that credit risks are disclosed so far as practicable.

1–17 It is not easy for creditors to escape future insolvencies. One has only to take each 10-year slice of history since 1900 and examine what transpired in each decade. Those who woke, entranced by optimistic dreams, on the first day of each decade could hardly imagine the political and economic disasters, the upheavals, the catastrophes, that would strike down their hopes at some time during that decade – with only a few decades offering tolerable calm and peace. It is not therefore altogether a matter for reprimand, nor is it perplexing, that financiers who advance loans, which may have a term approaching that length of period, should find that prophecy is more difficult than history.

Of course most loans are repaid. If that were not so, banks would go out of business and their depositors could not safely deposit their money with them. Yet the risks are great.

The loss of a loan of $10,000,000 earning a net profit of 1 per cent requires a portfolio of $1,000,000,000 to replace it. Banking is not for amateurs. But we must have banks as keepers of people's means of exchange. And the solvency of these keepers must be safeguarded. Hence, bank regulation.

Jurisdictions differ fundamentally on their insolvency policies. The laws of one group assist creditors, usually the keepers, to escape insolvency, while others seek to enlarge the debtor's estate as much as possible. These opposing views, which are fiercely contested, are without doubt the key to unlock the comparative law of commerce and finance and are discussed in detail in another work in this series. But the threat of insolvency will be apparent from much of the law and practice in the areas covered by this book.

State loans

Historically a substantial part of international borrowing for centuries has been by states or their more recent creatures, a central bank or a state entity. States are special creatures of law, primarily because, although they can and do become insolvent, they cannot be subjected to bankruptcy proceedings. One cannot sell a state to pay its creditors, or, rather, one could (e.g. the sale of Louisiana by Napoleon), but politically it is usually out of the question. For long, states were protected by sovereign immunity whereby they could not be sued in foreign courts, but that has now been reduced and is invariably waived by contract in formal bonds or credit agreements. Hence they are technically unprotected by the freeze on creditor enforcement actions which is the main feature of municipal bankruptcy laws, but they are still protected by a range of defences, largely based on creditor consensus and mature conduct.

The issues raised by state loans are so large that this topic, too, is largely covered in a separate work although there is a brief discussion here of waivers of immunity in term loan agreements. Nevertheless state term loans and bond issues are fundamentally the same as those discussed in this book and much of what is said here will be relevant in the governmental context.

Legal opinions

1–19 Finally, there is the role of lawyers. Apart from drafting and negotiating documentation, they must plan and structure the transaction and hopefully facilitate it. Their task may range from the purely technical to strategic commercial advice and commonly includes the management of the transaction's documentation. Like the medieval notaries, they must advise on its legal effect and draw attention to legal difficulties which would not be obvious or which would defeat legitimate expectations. But they are also expected to give a formal legal opinion at the closing of a financial transaction. These opinions often do not say much, but they are part of the ritual which cannot be avoided. Hence the forms and conventions must be studied. This study forms subsequent chapters in this book.

CHAPTER 2

TERM LOANS: FINANCIAL TERMS

Introduction

Term loans are loans for a fixed term, cancellable only if certain conditions are not satisfied and repayable prematurely only on an event of default. By contrast, overdrafts or "lines of credit" are cancellable and repayable on notice from the bank. The object of a term loan is to improve the predictability of the finance. This and succeeding chapters will review the usual chief terms of term loan agreements. 2–1

Apart from financial terms, it is obvious that, if a bank agrees to make a loan for seven to 10 years, the protection of the credit requires that there should be some restraint on prejudicial management of the borrower's business, e.g. a sale by the borrower of all of its assets, and some provision for early termination if the borrower does not comply with the terms of the agreement or events happen which make it highly likely that the borrower will not be able to perform, e.g. the borrower becomes insolvent. In practice, therefore, much of the negotiation of non-financial terms tends to centre on the covenants and events of default.

All the clauses cited in these chapters are in summary form only. A full form of syndicated term loan agreement appears in the Appendix to this book.

Agreement to lend

The clause provides in outline: 2–2

> "The bank will make loans up to its specified commitment during the commitment period."

Drawdowns may be in a single amount or in instalments, and must usually be in minimum and rounded amounts. There is always an expiry date on the period during which the bank will lend – commonly called the commitment period.

The loan may be "**revolving**", i.e. the borrower can borrow, repay and re-borrow up to the stated maximum commitment of the bank.

Conditions precedent

2–3   Loan agreements provide that the bank is not obliged to lend unless certain conditions are satisfied – the "conditions precedent".

First, there are conditions precedent to all loans. These are to ensure that all legal matters are in order and that the security is in place. The clause provides in outline that the bank is not obliged to make any loans until the bank has received:

- any guarantees for the loan
- constitutional documents of the borrower and its authorisations, e.g. board resolutions, and signature lists
- official consents, e.g. exchange control consents
- process agency appointment under a forum selection clause
- legal opinions as to the validity of the documentation and other matters

2–4   If the loan is secured the conditions precedent may also include (depending on the collateral):

- a transfer of the asset being financed, e.g. conveyance, bill of sale, and deposit of title deeds, share certificates or any other paper representing the collateral
- valuations
- evidence of good title to land, ship, aircraft, etc. and evidence that the asset is free from encumbrances
- registration of title to the asset if there is an ownership register, e.g. land
- perfection of the security, e.g. its registration or filing in a public bureau (companies registry, state filing office, mercantile register), or registration of the bank as pledgee in the books of the issuer of securities
- insurances are in place (notice of assignment to insurers, brokers' undertakings, loss payable clauses
- notice of assignment of contracts, charterparties, and leases, and consents to assignment.

Secondly, there are conditions precedent to each loan separately. The clause provides in outline:

- the bank is not obliged to make a loan unless, at the time of the request for the loan and the borrowing of the loan, and immediately after the loan is made:
    - the representations and warranties are true on up-dated basis;
    - no event of default or event which with giving of notice, lapse of time or other conditions would constitute an event of default has occurred;
    - (sometimes) no material adverse change in the borrower's financial condition;
    - borrowers certificates as to the above, if the bank so requests.

As to the warranties, see para 3–1 *et seq*. As to events of default, see para 3–37 *et seq*.

The conditions to each loan separately are to ensure:

- That all legal and financial matters are still in order prior to each separate borrowing. Hence the warranties must continue to be correct as if repeated. A bank should not be liable to lend if a subsequent legal defect has arisen, e.g. the introduction of an exchange control prohibiting the borrower from making payments to foreign creditors.
- That the bank is not obliged to lend if it is only a matter of time before a default occurs (the borrower must not rob Peter to pay Paul) and to reduce the possibility of throwing good money after bad. Hence there must be no event of default or *pending* event of default. Grace periods are removed from the events of default for this purpose. For example, if the borrower has failed to pay interest and there is a grace period before a default can be declared, the borrower should not be able to borrow a new loan in that grace period since the non-payment of the interest is likely to be an indication that the borrower is insolvent so that the new money will be lost. If the borrower has breached a financial ratio or granted security in breach of a negative pledge prohibiting the security and has a 30-day grace period to remedy the default, the new money should be blocked. Whether other relaxations in the events of default should be stripped for the purpose of the conditions precedent is a matter for negotiation, e.g. materiality tests, and amount thresholds in cross-default or creditor executions: this tightening up would be less usual. Materiality tests in the events of default which are imported into the conditions precedent can be problematic because often the bank has insufficient information and is exposed to a damages risk if it should

wrongfully refuse to make a loan. But some ambiguity is often inevitable in order to achieve a fair balance.

Note that the condition precedent suspends the obligation to make the loan, but does not cancel the facility: cancellation requires a full event of default.

2–7 The above conditions must be satisfied if the loan is made. For example, a loan may cause a borrowing limit in another agreement to be violated, thereby causing a default which might bring the house down.

It is sometimes stated that fulfilment of the conditions precedent is to be "satisfactory" to the bank. Case law variously interprets phrases of this type as "reasonably satisfactory" or, contrarily, as "satisfactory in its complete discretion". See the standard works on contract. It is best to state which one means, if the point is considered important.

If there are no conditions precedent, the bank is obliged to lend in accordance with its agreement, unless the borrower has defaulted and the default is sufficiently serious to entitle the bank to cancel in accordance with ordinary contract law. Thus insolvency will generally constitute an anticipatory repudiation by the borrower.

2–8 **Remedies for bank default** The liability of the bank for failure to lend is often material, e.g. if the borrower is in difficulties and it is unclear whether the bank is obliged to lend. It may, for example, be unclear whether an event of default covering a material adverse change in the borrower's financial condition has occurred, and the bank might be throwing good money after bad.

Under English law, a borrower cannot obtain specific performance if the bank fails to lend: *South African Territories v Wallington* [1898] AC 309. The borrower's remedy is solely for damages.

The damages payable by the bank are:

– Reasonably foreseeable losses, e.g. extra interest and costs incurred by the borrower in arranging another loan: *Prehn v Royal Bank of Liverpool* (1870) LR5 Exch 92. But the lender is not responsible for extra costs of a new loan which are attributable to a decline in the borrower's credit in the meantime: *Bahamas (Inagua) Sisal Plantation v Griffin* (1897) 14 TLR 139.

– Specially contemplated losses, e.g. inevitable default by the borrower on a contract being financed by the loan, or loss of profit on that contract but only if the bank is expressly on notice that the loan is to be used for that contract and of the potential consequences: *Manchester & Oldham Bank v Cook* (1883) 49 LT 674; *Wallis Chlorine Syndicate Ltd v American Alkali Co Ltd* [1901] TLR 656. The borrower must endeavour to mitigate his losses, e.g. by borrowing elsewhere.

Lender liability risk in this context is discussed further in another work (on the principles of international insolvency) in this series on international financial law.

Remedies for borrower default in borrowing This question is usually irrelevant because the borrower generally has the option to borrow but does not commit to borrow. Banks do not force people to borrow.

Under English law, an order for specific performance is not available to compel a borrower to borrow if the borrower is committed. The lender has only a right to damages which are its reasonably foreseeable losses plus specifically contemplated losses: *Rogers v Challis* (1859) 27 Beav 175.

2–9

Drawdown of loans

This sets out procedures: the time and form of the notice of borrowing to be given by the borrower to the bank, the place of payment of the loan proceeds, payment on business days in the country of the bank and the country of payment, and the funds of payment, e.g. immediately available funds. Foreign currency loans are invariably credited to a bank account of the borrower in the chief financial centre in the country of the currency, e.g. New York for US dollars, London for Sterling, Tokyo for Yen, Frankfurt for Deutschmarks. All currency payments for credit to a bank account must usually be made through the clearing system in the country of the currency: any delays, expenses and risks in transferring the proceeds to the borrower's country are a matter for the borrower.

2–10

Immediately available funds are those which the borrower can draw immediately from the bank account to which they are credited. Thus they must not be conditional on the clearing being completed.

It is usually stated that the borrower is liable for the bank's breakage costs if it fails to borrow after service of a borrowing notice, e.g. if the bank has financed the loan by a deposit in the market and must reapply the deposit at a lesser interest rate compared to that at which it took the deposit. The advance of the loan may be forestalled at the last moment because of a sudden default or other right to suspend the loan.

Application of proceeds

The clause provides:

2–11

> "**The borrower will apply the proceeds of the loan towards** [stated purpose] ...".

Control of proceeds serves a credit purpose – the borrower should apply the money for the intended purpose, e.g. purchasing a factory which will improve the borrower's business. But often the purpose is general, e.g. "working capital purposes".

2–12 **Loans for an unlawful purpose** Examples of loans for an unlawful purpose are: loans contrary to prohibited financial assistance by the company for the purpose of acquiring its own shares; loans to pay dividends which are unlawful because the borrower is insolvent; loans to purchase shares in a specially protected sector (banks, media, national resources, insurance companies) where the purchase is illegal unless an official consent is obtained; and loans to pay a bribe to an official to procure a government contract. Except for unlawful financial assistance under the Companies Act 1985 s 151 and parallel provisions elsewhere, illegality problems appear to be rare.

If the contract *necessarily* has an unlawful purpose, it is unenforceable even if the bank did not know of the illegality: *Allan Merchandising v Cloke* [1963] 2 QB 240. But ignorance of foreign law is likely to be treated as mistake of fact, not law. If the contract does not necessarily involve an unlawful purpose, the bank's position generally depends on whether the bank participated in the illegality, i.e. depends on whether the bank knew of the illegal purpose before it made the loan. A loan to pay off an illegal loan may itself be tainted with illegality: *Spector v Ageda* [1973] Ch 30.

If the loan is lent for a specific purpose, e.g. to finance a contract, and the purpose fails or the borrower fails to apply it for that purpose, in common law countries (but not other countries) the lender may have a proprietary claim on the borrower's insolvency for restitution of the proceeds if they are traceable: *Gibert v Gonard* (1884) 54 LJ Ch 439 (misapplied loan to purchase property to be mortgaged to lender); *Barclays Bank Ltd v Quistclose Investments Ltd* [1970] AC 597, HL. Otherwise the bank is left with a mere event of default for breach of a term of the agreement and an unsecured claim. These proprietary claims and tracing generally are reviewed in another work (on the principles of international insolvency) in this series on financial law.

2–13 If the loan agreement is governed by English law, the bank will not be obliged to lend if the advance of the loan is illegal by the law of the place where it must be advanced, e.g. if an embargo is introduced at that place prohibiting payments to an entity in the borrower's country. For example, if a US dollar loan is to be made to a Ruritanian entity by credit to an account in New York and if the US freezes payments to Ruritanian entities under trading with the enemy legislation, the English courts will not compel the bank to lend. But this is so only if the bank must make payments in the country where the payment is illegal. If by the contract the payments could be made to an account in another country where the payment is not illegal, then the bank must lend. See *Ralli Bros v Cia Naviera Sota y Aznar* [1920] 2 KB 287, CA (payment of freight over a certain amount illegal under law of Spain where the freight had to be paid); *Libyan Arab Foreign Bank v Manufacturers Hanover Trust Co (No 2)* [1989] 1 Lloyds Rep 608 (payment by bank of US dollar letter of credit issued by London branch of bank illegal under US law because of US embargo against Libya. But the payment could by the contract be made in London so the bank was obliged to pay).

If the loan involves a gross violation of the laws of a friendly foreign country when the agreement is entered into, the agreement is invalid in England on grounds of public policy: see *Foster v Driscoll* [1929] 1 KB 470, CA. But this is not so if the illegality arises subsequently, such as an exchange control: see, e.g. *Kleinwort Sons & Co v Ungarische Baumwolle Industrie A/G* [1939] 2 KB 678, CA. In this case it must be shown that the payment is illegal under the laws of the country where the payment must be made by the contract in accordance with the rule described in the previous paragraph.

These rules are examined in more detail elsewhere in this series of works, including the position under the laws of other jurisdictions.

Repayment

Repayment may be by instalments or in a single amount ("bullet"). 2–14

Prepayments and cancellation

> A clause sets out procedures for prepayments, e.g. prepayments may be made only at end of interest periods; minimum and rounded amounts; the application of prepayments to repayment instalments in inverse order of maturity, and the cancellation of the bank's commitment to lend on notice from borrower

2–15

In bank floating rate loans, prepayments are generally permitted at the end of interest periods: contrast bond issues where the restriction on prepayment is to protect the bondholder against falls in interest rates and hence loss of his higher fixed rate earned on the bond. As to the position where there is no express right of prepayment, see para 8–49.

Prepayments should be applied against the repayment instalments in the inverse order of their maturity so as to shorten the life of the loan: this is usual banking policy. If not so provided, many jurisdictions confer on the debtor a first right of appropriation. But, as a matter of construction of the particular contract, it may well be found that, where a borrower has agreed to repay a loan by stated instalments, those instalments must be paid as stated until the loan is fully discharged so that in effect the prepayment would be applied in inverse order.

Prepayments are generally allowed only at the end of interest periods to avoid breakage costs. Thus if the interest period is six months and the bank borrows a funding deposit at 10 per cent, is prepaid after four months and can re-lend the proceeds in the market only at 8 per cent, the bank suffers a loss of 2 per cent for two months.

Premiums on prepayments are unusual, but are sometimes found to compensate the bank for its trouble, especially in project loans. As between commercial parties, small premiums, of, say, $\frac{1}{4}$ per cent to one per cent are valid in England; to be upset, they must be grossly unfair and unconscionable.

Generally the borrower must pay a commitment fee (e.g. $\frac{1}{4}$ per cent) on the unused amount of the bank's commitment during the commitment period, payable quarterly or semi-annually and on cancellations by the borrower.

Interest

2–16 The clause provides in outline:

> "The borrower will pay interest at a percentage margin, e.g. 1 per cent above LIBOR, namely, the rate at which the bank is offered deposits matching as to currency and maturity in the London interbank market (or at a market rate shown on a market screen) – usually at 11.00 a.m. local time in the funding market two business days before the interest period concerned.
>
> The borrower chooses interest periods of (generally) 1, 3 or 6 months (and sometimes 9 or 12 months).
>
> 365-day year basis for sterling (unless euro sterling); 360 day year basis for all other currencies.
>
> The borrower will pay default interest at (usually) 1 per cent plus normal margin plus higher of existing rate and new LIBOR.
>
> Default interest is payable as well after as before judgment and overdue interest (interest on interest) is capitalised."

2–17 In floating rate loans, the interest rate changes periodically. The bank funds the loan by a short-term deposit in the inter-bank market for the chosen period and on-lends to the borrower plus the margin or spread, which is the bank's gross profit. At the end of each interest period, the bank repays its funding deposit in the inter-bank market and borrows another deposit for the next interest period. The borrower does not repay. The bank borrows short to lend long. Of course the bank may have funded from other sources. In substance floating rate loans are "cost of funds" loans, plus the spread, and anything which increases the cost of funds to the bank or reduces the interest is for the account of the borrower, e.g. increased costs due to reserve requirements or deductions for withholding taxes. For various forms of interest clause, see the Appendix.

Other interest bases are common, e.g. UK bank base rate, US bank prime rate, US Treasury bill rate, etc. The loan can of course be at a fixed rate throughout.

There are no **usury laws** in England (except for consumer transactions and rules in the Insolvency Act 1986 for setting aside extortionate credit bargains on insolvency), but usury laws are common in other jurisdictions, especially in Islamic countries.

The question of enforceability of **penalty interest on overdue sums** is not a major commercial problem: a small increase in rate is unlikely to be a penalty because it is not unconscionable. But compound interest (interest on interest) is problematic in some jurisdictions (not England), notably in relation to secured loans.

English **judgment debts** carry interest at the prescribed rate: Judgments Act 1838 s 17. But this may be lower than the market rate and so the default rate is generally expressed to apply also after judgment. The Apportionment Act 1870 apportions interest.

Post-insolvency interest is usually irrecoverable as a non-provable debt: IR 1986, r 4.93. This is so in many other countries.

Substitute basis clause

The clause provides in outline:

> "If the bank determines that funding deposits are not readily available in the specified deposit market, then:
>
> — version 1: further drawdowns are suspended and the bank can call for mandatory prepayment of existing loans (with interest at a rate certified by bank) unless otherwise agreed — snatch-back
>
> — version 2: bank and borrower negotiate for 30 days but if they do not agree, the bank conclusively determines the new interest basis — bank is locked-in, albeit on its own terms."

This is a disaster or force majeure clause to protect the bank if the funding market is disrupted. The main object is to give the bank sufficient contractual bargaining power to negotiate new terms in the event of severe market disruption leading to non-availability of deposits to the bank to fund the loan. Because of the general availability of funds, the clause is much less important than it used to be in the case of major currencies funded in major markets, but is still significant for loans in minor currencies. The clause was used during the 1989 Iraq invasion of Kuwait for loans in Kuwaiti Dinars.

2–20   In the absence of the clause, if the interest cannot be fixed as provided by the interest clause, the possibilities are:

– No interest is payable (unlikely).

– The court might apply the nearest alternative to give business efficacy to the contract.

> In *First National Securities v Onwuegbuzie* (1976) CLY 133, Lambeth County Ct, interest was calculated at the official Bank of England bank rate. This was abolished. *Held*: the court would apply the nearest equivalent.

– The court might award interest as a matter of equity (but at what rate?)

– The contract might be frustrated, perhaps leading to immediate repayability of the loan under the Law Reform (Frustrated Contracts) Act 1943.

Multicurrency option

2–21   Multicurrency loans are less popular than they used to be in the 1970s and 1980s. The clause provides in outline:

> "The borrower may prior to each interest period select the currency of the loan. If the bank is satisfied that the new currency is readily available, the borrower repays the old currency and the bank readvances the new currency. The amount of the new currency is calculated by reference to the spot rate of exchange between the base currency and the new currency two business days (usually) before the interest period."

The object of the clause is to enable the borrower to borrow other currencies at a lower rate of interest, but the borrower takes the risk of depreciation in that currency against the reference currency.

The calculation of the amount of the loan in an alternative currency amount is always by reference to the base currency at the time of the conversion. Thus:

- If a loan is in US dollars with a multicurrency option and the borrower switches from dollars to DM, then at the end of the interest period the borrower repays dollars and the bank advances DM calculated on the basis of the spot rate of exchange two business days before the beginning of the next interest period.

- If the borrower continues for the next interest period in DM, the borrower repays the old DM and the bank advances DM in an amount calculated on the basis of the spot rate of exchange for the purchase of DM with dollars two business days before the next interest period. This could be more or less.

- If the borrower continues for the next period in Swiss francs, the borrower repays DM and the bank advances Swiss francs. The amount of Swiss francs is calculated by reference to the new US dollar spot rate, not the rate of exchange between DM and Swiss francs.

The above is to make sure that the currency amount is brought back into line with the base currency of US dollars at the beginning of each interest period. In some jurisdictions (not England), roll-over loans may discharge the security on the ground that security can only secure existing debt.

The conversion involves actual advances and so each advance must be subject to the conditions precedent described in para 2–5, e.g. the new advance may contravene a borrowing limit.

For a form, see the Appendix.

Payments by the borrower

The clause provides in outline:

2–22

> "Borrower will make all payments in the specified currency, in immediately available funds, to the specified bank account in the country of currency."

The borrower is usually required to make payments in the financial centre in the country of the currency (e.g. US dollars in New York City, sterling in London, deutschmarks in Frankfurt, yen in Tokyo). The main reason is that payments are conveniently made through a clearing system in the country of the currency. Also payment in the currency centre helps:

- To avoid rules in other countries enabling the borrower to pay in local currency. These would be unusual if it is clear that only the foreign currency is contractually payable. Under English law, debtors can pay foreign currency debts payable in England in sterling unless otherwise agreed.

2–22 TERM LOANS: FINANCIAL TERMS

- To avoid transfer risks (exchange controls, freeze orders) and transfer expenses.
- To avoid problems over time differences.

Payment systems are reviewed in another volume in this series of works on international financial law.

2–23 **Legal significance of place of payment** Some of the legal implications of the place of payment are as follows:

(a) Where there is no express choice of a governing law of the contract, the place of payment, as the place of performance of the most important obligation under the loan contract, may be a pointer to the law of that place as the governing law. The courts of some countries may regard the place of payment as decisive. If the contract is impliedly governed by English law, the English court may claim jurisdiction under the English long-arm jurisdiction set out in RSC Ord 11, r 1.

(b) The English courts will not enforce a contract (at least if it is governed by English law) to the extent that performance is illegal at the place of performance. Examples of laws rendering performance illegal are exchange controls, freeze orders and usury laws. If payments are to be made in the borrower's country, this might defeat the insulation sought to be achieved by a choice of an external governing law.

(c) A debtor may be permitted to discharge a debt expressed in foreign currency in the local currency of the place of payment under local legal tender rules.

(d) The law of the place of payment may decide matters of the detail of performance, e.g. the time and method of payment.

(e) Courts may assume jurisdiction if there is a breach of the debtor's obligation to make payments and these payments are required to be made within the court's country.

(f) Under the State of Immunity Act 1978, subject to exceptions, a state is not immune as respects proceedings relating to an obligation of the state which by virtue of the contract falls to be performed wholly or partly in the United Kingdom. The fact that payments are to be made in the United States may assist in satisfying the jurisdictional requirements for the deimmunisation of foreign states and related persons under the US Foreign Sovereign Immunities Act of 1976.

(g) The place of payment may have taxation and stamp duty consequences under the laws of the jurisdiction concerned, e.g. withholding taxes.

(h) If a debt is properly recoverable in England, it may be garnished in England. Thus the location of the debt may decide whether or not a judgment creditor of the payee (e.g. a creditor of the borrower purporting to garnish the proceeds of a loan to be made by a bank) can attach the debt. Generally, however, under English law a simple debt is located where the debtor carries on business or resides as opposed to the place where the debt is payable.

The rules of conflict of laws and of jurisdiction briefly alluded to above are reviewed in more detail in another book in this series on financial law.

Time when payment is made The time when payments are deemed to be made if they are made by credit transfer is relevant to the question whether a default has occurred, whether the payment is made before a freeze order or embargo is imposed, and whether the payment is made before insolvency proceedings have commenced which freeze further payments by the debtor. 2–24

Appropriations

A clause generally permits the creditor to appropriate partial payments as it sees fit, e.g. to costs or interest before principal. Normally debtors have the first right of appropriation or imputation. In the absence of contract or appropriation by either debtor or creditor, various presumptions may apply, such as imputation to the debt most burdensome to the debtor, or to expenses, interest and principal in that order, or to the oldest debt in a current account. See, for example: France CC Arts 1253–1256; Germany BGB ss 366, 367; Japan CC Art 489 *et seq*; Korea CC Arts 476 *et seq*; Colombia Com C Art 881. 2–25

Set-offs by borrower

"The borrower will pay without set-off or counterclaim." 2–26

The reasons for a prohibition on set-offs by the borrower are the maxim "pay now, litigate later" and the cash-flow principle: the bank uses payments to repay underlying deposits.

Contracts not to set-off usually are valid if between solvent parties, but are ineffective upon an English insolvency, regardless of the governing law (because the insolvency set-off clause in r 4.90 of the Insolvency Rules 1986 is mandatory). But naturally the bank would then wish to be able to set off so as to be paid. International set-off is discussed in detail in another volume in this series of works on international financial law.

CHAPTER 3

TERM LOANS: WARRANTIES, COVENANTS AND DEFAULTS

Representations and warranties

3–1 This chapter deals with clauses which, apart from the financial terms, are the contractual heart of the agreement and which commonly absorb most of the negotiating time: the representations and warranties, the covenants of the borrower, and the events of default.

Usual warranties

The clause provides in outline as set out below.

Banking practice distinguishes between legal warranties and commercial warranties (asterisked). Legal warranties basically deal with the legal validity of the agreement. Commercial warranties deal with the borrower's financial condition and credit-standing.

"Borrower warrants:

- legal status of borrower, e.g. duly incorporated company;
- powers of borrower;
- authorisations of borrower;
- all consents to performance of borrower's obligations have been obtained (e.g. exchange control consents);
- the loan agreement does not conflict with laws or the borrower's constitutional documents or contracts (borrowing limits, negative pledges);
- legal validity and enforceability of borrower's obligations;
- pari passu ranking of loans with other unsecured debt;

REPRESENTATIONS AND WARRANTIES   3–2

- in secured loans, title to secured assets, first priority of security, validity on insolvency and against third parties, non-revocability as a preference;

- no litigation, actual or known to be threatened (material on group basis)*;

- borrower's last (group) accounts materially correct*;

- information memorandum materially correct and not misleading, projections reasonably based, no material omissions (to best of borrower's knowledge and belief);

- no material adverse change (group) in financial condition since date of last accounts*;

- (sometimes) ownership of properties and businesses lawfully carried on;

- no (material) default on contracts or other debt*;

- others, e.g. no stamp duties, no withholding taxes, enforcement of foreign judgements locally, valid choice of law, no immunity.

*These are commercial warranties. The others are legal.

Objectives of clause

The reasons for the clauses are: 3–2

1. The warranties set out the contractual basis on which the loan is made, i.e. the obligations are valid and the borrower's financial and business condition is as stated in the warranties, in its financial statements and any information memorandum issued in connection with the loan.

2. The warranties are investigatory in practice – hopefully to flush out problems in advance.

3. There is an express event of default if a warranty is incorrect: para 3–41. This is because the loan is made on the basis of validity of the documents and the borrower's disclosed financial condition. This may not of itself cure the defect, e.g. a warranty will not validate a loan which is legally invalid. But the bank remedy of acceleration under the events of default clause gives the bank bargaining power to readjust the documentation to meet the problem, if possible.

4. The bank can suspend drawdowns under the "conditions precedent" clause: para 2–5 *et seq*.

Negotiation points

3–3 As a drafting technique, warranties are often expressed to remain true (at least the legal warranties so that the borrower takes the risk of future legal changes): these are sometimes termed in banking vernacular as "evergreen" warranties. The rationale is that the borrower has the money, but the bank only has the piece of paper: hence the borrower should warrant that the piece of paper remains valid, even if this is beyond its control. Examples of subsequent changes are: the introduction of exchange controls, a moratorium or an embargo, a change in insolvency law introducing priority creditors or subordinating security to super-priority rehabilitation loans. The borrower is exposed if the commercial warranties are evergreen, e.g. a warranty as to no material adverse change in financial condition. This is because a breach of warranty is an event of default and hence an evergreen warranty inserts a "material adverse change" as an event of default.

Materiality and group tests may be introduced, especially in the commercial warranties. Materiality is unsuitable for legal warranties. In other cases, a definition of materiality as impinging on ability to perform is inappropriate since this might involve proof of insolvency and hence remove the sanction of the warranty. Apart from this, one cannot do much about the inherent vagueness of materiality tests. Legal warranties should not be subject to the exceptions in the legal opinions since the borrower should be expected to confirm validity even if this cannot be checked in all relevant jurisdictions, but obviously specific exceptions should be inserted if the warranty is incorrect in unqualified form, e.g. the obligations are not pari passu, but subject to priority creditors on insolvency. A general exception that validity is subject to bankruptcy laws should be approached with care since it is on bankruptcy that the lender most seeks validity. The calling of a default on the ground of breach of a legal warranty has been extremely rare. For the interpretation of legal warranties and a more detailed discussion, see chapter 29.

Normally warranties should not be to the best of the knowledge and belief of the borrower, except perhaps as to an information memorandum: the borrower's knowledge is irrelevant to the fact.

But naturally borrowers may take a different view on all these points and these are all matters for negotiation in the circumstances of the case.

Warranties as to the validity of performance may be limited to the borrower's performance, not the bank's.

No warranties

If there are no express warranties, the general law relating to misrepresentations of fact inducing a contract applies to loan contracts in the same way as it applies to any other contract. Thus, where a misrepresentation is made which induces the loan contract the lender may, even in the absence of express stipulation in the loan contract itself, have remedies of damages and rescission. The Misrepresentation Act 1967 (as amended by the Unfair Contracts Terms Act 1977) may be relevant. Damages do not generally add anything to the claim for the debt itself.

Covenants

General

The theory is that a lender providing capital acquires an interest in the preservation of that capital, thereby conferring an entitlement to some voice, however muted, in the management of the business in order to protect that interest. Unlike equity shares, debt does not have a right to vote for management. That "vote" is conferred by covenants, the breach of which results in the sanction of an event of default, thereby encouraging compliance.

Notwithstanding the traditional English meaning of "covenant" as an undertaking under seal, the market habitually refers to these obligations as covenants, no doubt to distinguish them from payment obligations.

The scope of covenants depends upon the circumstances, for example:

(a) The degree of risk undertaken by the lender. Thus the covenant protection in a project loan, where lenders take risks akin to equity shares, will be much greater than in the case of a small loan to a substantial international corporation.

(b) The nature of the borrower. Thus the covenants in a loan to a government will plainly be different from those in a loan to a corporate borrower.

(c) Whether the loan is secured or unsecured.

The usual basic standard covenants in corporate loans are: (1) supply of information; (2) negative pledge; (3) restriction on disposals; and (4) pari passu clause.

The others are case-by-case.

Objectives of corporate covenants

3-6 The primary functions of covenants in an unsecured term loan agreement with a corporate commercial borrower might include the following:

(a) To preserve the **equal ranking** of the claim against the assets on the insolvency of the borrower and to prohibit subordination or discrimination. These undertakings primarily include the negative pledge, the pari passu clause and the clause restricting disposals.

(b) To preserve or test **asset quality** so as to protect the earnings potential of the borrower and the break-up value of the assets. Such covenants include a restriction on disposals, obligations to repair and insure, restrictions on the leasing of assets, on the making of investments, on loans to third parties, and on capital expenditure, and various financial tests.

(c) To preserve or test **asset quantity and solvency**, and in particular to control the incurring of excessive liabilities. These covenants include financial ratios, such as a debt-equity ratio, a net worth minimum, a current ratio (the ratio of current assets to current liabilities) a working capital minimum (current assets less current liabilities), a ratio of interest payable to net profits, and a restriction on dividends and other distributions. Restrictions on disposals, on leases, on capital expenditure and on the incurring of contingent liabilities and a borrowing limit are also directed to this end.

(d) To test the **liquid assets** out of which the obligations can be serviced without resort to the sale of capital assets on which the earning power is based. Such covenants include a restriction on borrowings and on the incurring of contingent liabilities, and various financial ratios.

3-7 (e) To preserve the **type of business** being financed. The credit analysis of a computer manufacturing business is different from that of a pig-breeding operation. Appropriate covenants include restrictions on substantial changes in business and restrictions on substantial acquisitions of companies or business.

(f) To control an **excessively rapid growth** which cannot be sustained by financial resources or management availability. Covenants in this area include restrictions on mergers and the making of investments, limits on borrowings and on capital expenditures, and a restriction on substantial changes of business.

(g) To enable the lender to **monitor** the condition of the borrower and the terms of the loan. These covenants include an obligation to provide financial information and accounts together with certificates as to compliance with the loan agreement and the absence of events of default.

(h) To preserve the **identity** of the borrower. Such covenants include restrictions on amalgamations, and undertakings to pay all necessary corporate franchise taxes (necessary in some jurisdictions to qualify the corporation to do business), to keep corporate status in good standing, and to renew corporate charters in those jurisdictions where the corporation does not have eternal life.

Remedies for breach

The potential remedies for breach include: 3–8

- an express event of default, acceleration of the loan and cancellation of the commitments to lend: para 3–40
- suspension of new loans under the conditions precedent clause: para 2–5
- injunction, if available, to restrain a threatened breach: this could be relevant for the negative pledge and the restriction on disposals, but the bank must take action before the breach
- specific performance, if available (usually unimportant in practice)
- damages: but generally this will not add to the claim for the loan itself and is usually irrelevant in practice
- a claim in damages against a participating third party for the tort of procuring a breach of contractual relations, e.g. where a third party takes security in breach of a negative pledge and the third party knows of the negative pledge: para 3–22 *et seq.*

Lender liability

Under insolvency law, directors may be personally liable for the debts of a 3–9 company if they knowingly or recklessly incur those debts when the company is insolvent (fraudulent trading) or if the company is likely to go into insolvent liquidation and the director fails to take all necessary steps to minimise the loss to creditors (wrongful trading); or for negligent management. The scope of the liability depends on the jurisdiction.

A director usually includes a de facto manager of the company and hence a bank which controls and directs management may become a de facto director and be liable accordingly. It is generally true that only in the case of exceptionally intrusive interference in management could a bank be a "shadow director" and the mere monitoring of normal covenants will not be enough. The problem tends to arise only in default negotiations if a bank effectively takes over the management. This large topic is discussed elsewhere in this series of works on financial law.

Negative pledge

3–10 The negative pledge is the most fundamentally important covenant in an unsecured term loan agreement. The clause provides in outline:

> "The borrower will not create or permit to exist any security on its assets or those of its subsidiaries."

3–11 **Purposes of clause** The reasons for the clause are:

- Security (e.g. a floating charge) granted by the borrower to another creditor effectively subordinates the bank's unsecured loan and leaves no assets for the bank as unsecured creditor: it destroys the credit analysis which assumes pari passu payment. This is especially important if the borrower is in difficulties when it can only raise credit on security which is the very time the bank wishes to ensure it ranks pari passu.

- It enhances equality between creditors.

- It operates as an indirect control on the incurring of excessive liabilities (but a specific borrowing restriction is more effective).

- In secured transactions, it prevents problems caused by a second mortgagee: see para 3–21.

- In government loans, it controls the allocation of foreign reserves (currency, bullion, investments) to another creditor.

3–12 **Security covered** The prohibition should apply also to **existing security** so as to catch security granted prior to the entry into of the loan agreement: admittedly the sanction is only an event of default. This point is covered by the language: "not permit to exist".

The reference to security should include all forms of **security interest**, e.g. mortgage, lien, charge, hypothecation, pledge and all other forms of security interest in a sweep-up.

In England pledges (where the asset must be actually or constructively delivered into the possession of the pledgee) and liens (generally personal rights depending on possession of the asset and arising by operation of law) are distinguishable from mortgages which do not depend upon possession. However, "mortgage" and "charge" are often used generally for all classes of security. Under the Law of Property Act 1925 "mortgage" has been held to include a charge and vice versa: see *Re Bernstein* [1925] Ch 12. "Charge" in s 396 of the Companies Act 1985 covers all manner of security within its ambit. See Willes J in *Halliday v Holgate* (1868) LR 3 Exch 299 at 302 for an English classification of security interests.

The prohibition should not be limited purely to security for borrowings or guarantees of borrowings; financial credits can often be structured in such a way as not to constitute a borrowing, e.g. a purchase money credit.

Interpretation The interpretation of terms like "lien" and "security interest" is generally determined by the governing law: see Art 10(1)(a) of the Rome Convention on the Law Applicable to Contractual Obligations of 1980 implemented in the UK by the Contracts (Applicable) Law Act 1990. See also the US Conflicts Restatement s 204. Generally, but not necessarily, this means that technical terms tend to be given the meaning ascribed to them by the system of law which governs the contract.

3-13

Title finance Some clauses extend the meaning of security to title finance or quasi-security transactions which have the commercial effect of security but are not security in form, e.g. recourse factoring, sale and lease-back, financial leasing, set-off arrangements, hire purchase, title retention (conditional sale), stock borrowings and sale and repurchase ("repos"). But it is difficult to limit these to financial avoidance transactions and to exclude ordinary trade transactions. These transactions are reviewed in detail in another volume in this series of works on international financial law.

3-14

Title finance can be specifically controlled, e.g. by contractual restrictions on finance leases, sale and repurchase, sale and lease-back and factoring, whether or not on a recourse basis.

But it is often impracticable (although theoretically possible) to restrict the following:

— set-offs (because this would prevent the borrower from being indebted to a creditor who owed money to the borrower)

— title retention (because these are routine in sale of goods contracts) or hire purchase (also routine)

— ordinary leases (because leases of land, computer equipment etc. are routine).

Sometimes the prohibition in the negative pledge extends to "arrangements having the effect of security". This might prohibit the above forms of title finance, and possibly even a contractual set-off.

3–15   In many cases, these quasi-security transactions have been developed to avoid, e.g. registration of charges; non-availability in some countries of non-possessory mortgages; restrictions in some jurisdictions on mortgage enforcement (especially no private sale or absence of possession/receivership remedy or foreclosure); usury laws; borrowing restrictions; and balance sheet capitalisation. Some are now adopted for tax reasons, especially financial leasing (capital allowances). Some jurisdictions may recharacterise some of these transactions as secured loans for some purposes, e.g. registration of charges. English law generally does not recharacterise but gives effect to the form unless the transaction is a sham.

3–16   **Subsidiaries** The clause should be extended to security by subsidiaries and governmental entities, e.g. where a holding company borrower arranges for its subsidiaries to charge their assets as collateral security for an unsecured borrowing by the holding company. The effect is that the group can raise money when perhaps it should not be doing so, because its credit status allows only secured borrowings. This is the time the control should bite. The borrower could downstream assets to subsidiaries: see the New York case of *Re Associated Gas & Electric Co*, 61 F Supp 11 SDNY, 149 F 2d 996 (2d Cir 1045) where downstreaming of nearly all the parent's assets to a subsidiary, which charged them to secure debentures in favour of other lenders, was held to be a breach of the *parent's* negative pledge.

3–17   **Exclusions** Possible express exceptions include:

- Security with majority bank **consent** ("not to be unreasonably withheld" would be too vague). Materiality tests are generally regarded as too vague in this context.

- **Liens** arising by operation of law if discharged within a grace period, e.g. 30 days (the usual grace period for trade debt). This covers, e.g. vendor, custodian and repairer liens which arise automatically until the debt is paid. Without an exception, most companies would be constantly in default. The exception may be extended to liens which are contractual to the extent they would have arisen by operation of law in the absence of contract, e.g. liens by custodians of investment securities. Many standard trade forms reinforce liens by express contract. But this exception may not cover other trade liens, e.g. a transportation lien.

3–18
- Security if the bank is **equally and ratably secured** on the same or equivalent assets. This may lead to loss of control to the other secured creditor. Voting and management of the security by the two creditors would be an issue: the other creditor's debt may be so great that it dominates the bank so that there is no real equality, except in terms of priority over unsecured creditors. Also the bank's share would be security for pre-

existing debt and therefore vulnerable as a preference: the borrower is likely to use the exemption when it is in financial difficulties. But nevertheless the exception is common.

– Existing security on assets of **after-acquired subsidiaries** (if not created in contemplation of the acquisition and, if allowed, only up to the amount then secured). This enables the borrower to acquire a company which has existing security.

– Security on **after-acquired** assets to secure finance to acquire the asset or to secure the purchase price plus interest. This allows the borrower to purchase new assets and mortgage them for the price. But the exception might result in a progressive diminution of the borrower's unsecured assets as old assets are replaced by new secured assets. There could be limits related to the type of eligible asset (e.g. goods only), or to the amount of the secured finance (e.g. 80 per cent of the net acquisition cost) or to the total debt secured.

– Security over goods, bills of lading, proceeds, insurances etc. in the **ordinary course of trading**, e.g. import finance by letters of credit where the financing bank usually takes a pledge of the documents of title to the goods. These pledges are routine in import transactions.

– Security over investment securities required by a clearing house or organised exchange in connection with trading on the exchange, e.g. margin collateral for futures and options trading.

– Security over claims to the extent there would be a right of set-off between the claim and the secured debt in the absence of security such as a charge over a deposit back to the bank which owes the deposit.

– Security over listed investment securities in favour of an organised exchange or banks in connection with transfers of the securities. Exchanges or financing banks may have security over investment securities which are transferred on the exchange when actual transfer to the buyer follows payment to the seller, as is often the case.

– **Basket**, e.g. a *de minimis* amount for special cases not otherwise covered, e.g. a (small) percentage of tangible net worth.

– Substitutions for any of the above on the same asset and for not more than the amount outstanding and secured at the time of the substitution.

For a fuller list, see the Appendix.

In negative pledges given by states, the covenant is generally limited to external indebtedness. This may be defined as debt which is payable or optionally payable in or calculated by reference to any foreign currency or owing to non-residents. Such a limitation is generally acceptable to banks since governments are not normally disposed to charge their assets to secure domestic obligations.

Banks may need to deposit collateral in connection with clearings to secure overnight positions with their central bank.

3–21 **Second mortgages in secured loans** In secured loans (unless there is a proper subordination agreement), the clause should prohibit second-ranking security because:

- A second mortgage is restrictive of management of a default or a restructuring, e.g. if the senior creditor wishes to lend new money and add it to the existing security and the junior creditor can veto this. By withholding his consent, the junior creditor might attempt to harass the senior creditor into paying out the junior creditor.

- The junior creditor may have an independent right of enforcement at an inopportune time.

- The prohibition is essential in floating charges to prevent the junior creditor from obtaining priority of his fixed charge.

Subordinated debt and junior security are discussed in another volume in this series of works on international financial law.

3–22 **Scope and efficacy of negative pledge** There are limitations on the scope and efficacy of negative pledge.

- The negative pledge is not equivalent to security because the negative pledge does not restrict other unsecured liabilities ranking equally with the loan or allocate specific assets to the loan.

- The ordinary negative pledge often does not restrict transactions having a similar effect to security – quasi-security or vendor/lessor title finance: para 3–14.

- It is a contractual restriction only, so it is weak if the borrower disregards it. The breach may be an event of default, but the third party has the security. In practice, most international borrowers honour their agreements.

A third party creditor taking the security might be liable in damages for the tort of procuring a breach of contractual relations. Generally the third party must know of the restriction or recklessly shut his eyes if he is to be made liable: see especially *Swiss Bank Corpn v Lloyds Bank Ltd* [1979] Ch 548, reversed on different grounds [1982] AC 584.

3–23 English law has been primarily developed in relation to trade disputes but applies to all types of contract: see for example, *Lumley v Gye* (1853) 2 E & B 216 (inducing opera singer not to perform contract); *British Motor Trade Associations v Salvadori* [1949] Ch 556 (purchase of car in knowing breach of restriction on seller's right to sell); *Esso Petroleum Co Ltd v Kingswood Motors (Addleston) Ltd* [1974] QB 142 (agreement not to dispose of service station premises); *Law Debenture Trust Corpn plc v Ural Caspian Oil Corpn Ltd, Independent* March 10, 1994, CA (sale of shares). See also the charterparty cases involving conflict between a shipping mortgage and a charter and culminating in *The Myrto* [1977] 2 Lloyds LR 243.

The claim against the third party may only be an unsecured claim for damages, not avoidance of the security.

> But in the California case of *Coast Bank v Minterhout*, 61 Cal 2d 311, 292 P 2d 265, 38 Cal Rptr 505 (1964), the bank with a negative pledge was given a lien on wrongful security granted to a third party. This would probably not be followed in England.
>
> In *Re Associated Gas and Electric Co*, 61 F Supp 11 (SDNY 1944); affirmed 149 F 2d 996 (2d Cir 1045), cert denied 326 US 736 (1945), in the course of reorganisation a parent company transferred nearly all its assets to a newly-formed subsidiary. The subsidiary immediately issued debentures charged on those assets. *Held*: this was violation of the negative pledge on the parent because in essence the transaction amounted to a charge on the parent's assets for the benefit of the subsidiary's debenture holders. See also *Kelly v Hanover Bank*, 11 F Supp 497 (SDNY 1935), reversed 85 F 2d 61 (2d Cir 1936).

In England – and indeed many countries – a transfer of assets to evade creditors may be unsuccessful and lead either to a piercing of the veil of incorporation or a recapture under rules relating to insolvency preferences.

3–24 **Automatic security clause** Some agreements provide that if the borrower creates violating security, then the bank is **automatically** deemed to be equally and rateably secured on the same asset as was mortgaged to the other creditor. A number of questions arise on the efficacy of this clause.

The security may fail in some jurisdictions because the asset is future and has not been presently identified. It is sufficient in England if the asset is identified at the time the security is intended to grip since an agreement to grant security over a future asset binds that asset automatically when it comes into existence and if at that future time it can be identified as being the subject of the agreement – prior specificity is not necessary: *Tailby v Official Receiver* (1888) 13 AC 523; *Syrett v Egerton* [1957] 3 All ER 331; *Holroyd v Marshall* [1862] HL Cas 191. Many foreign jurisdictions, notably in the Franco-Latin group, will not allow this on the ground that the asset must be specifically identified at the time of the agreement and security over future assets is ineffective to bind that asset when it comes into existence.

But in England the bank could in any event not claim to be secured if the clause provided for the grant of matching security on **equivalent** assets, because no property interest can be created over an asset which cannot be specifically identified when the property interest is intended to attach.

3–25   The third party may not be affected if he has no notice of the clause. If so, one question is whether the bank would achieve a second-ranking security.

The security may fail for non-compliance with foreign formalities, e.g. notarisation, or because the mortgagee must be identified in the document, or because a maximum limit of secured debt must be stated, or because there can be no security for foreign currency, or no non-possessory security over goods, or because there has been no notification to the debtor of assigned receivables (required in some jurisdictions for validity) or no registration of the bank as pledgee in the books of the issuer of pledged securities (this is required in some jurisdictions).

The security may fail for lack of **registration** or filing, e.g. British Companies Act s 396, the US UCC Art 9, or a land registry.

3–26   The security may fail as an insolvency preference if it arises in the suspect period (security for existing debt). In *Re Eric Holmes* [1965] Ch 1052, a prior agreement to grant security on request did not save the security from being a preference. Many jurisdictions avoid security for pre-existing debt if granted in the suspect period prior to the debtor's insolvency and if the debtor was insolvent at the time.

On the other hand, the virtue of the clause is that it may improve the remedies of a lender if the negative pledge should be breached since specific performance of an agreement to give security is potentially available in the discretion of the court: see for example, *Hermann v Hodges* (1873) LR16 Eq 18.

There is some authority in the United States whereby an affirmative covenant to secure when other debt is secured was held to create an equitable lien on the assets concerned in the particular circumstances.

> In *Commercial Co v New York NH & HRR Co*, 94 Conn 13, 107 A 646 (1919) bonds issued by a railroad company contained a covenant that if the company should thereafter mortgage any of its presently-owned property, the bonds would participate equally in the security of such mortgage. *Held*: no valid mortgage could be effected on terms that would prevent the bondholders from sharing in the security. The majority *held* further that the bonds created an equitable lien forthwith in the property owned by it at the date of issue: the covenant was an affirmative one and moreover related to specific and identifiable property.

COVENANTS 3–28

In *Kaplan v Chase National Bank*, 156 Misc 471, 281 NYS 825, the covenant stated that the company would not create any lien on or pledge of the stock of its subsidiaries without rateably securing the debentures. The bank trustee lent money to the company and received stock on the securities without rateably securing the debentures. *Held*: the bank must treat the pledged collateral as though such a provision had been made. But clearly this was a conflict of interest case.

The law of preferences voidable on insolvency and the principles of international mortgages and security are discussed in other volumes in this series of works on international financial law.

Pari passu clause

The clause provides in outline: 3–27

"The Borrower's obligations under the loan agreement will rank pari passu with all its other unsecured liabilities."

The clause requires the equal ranking of unsecured claims on a forced distribution of available assets to unsecured creditors, primarily on insolvency. It does not require concurrent or equal payment prior to that time. It undoubtedly does not restrict guaranteed loans (e.g. loans to a subsidiary guaranteed by the parent) or set-offs.

In some states, especially Spain and related jurisdictions, unsecured creditors may rank ahead of other unsecured creditors if their credit document is notarised in the prescribed way (*escritura publica*).

Note also that in many jurisdictions certain claims rank ahead of ordinary unsecured debts on insolvency, e.g. bank depositors, insurance company policy-holders and (invariably) priority claims on liquidation, e.g. taxes, wages and liquidation costs. Consider also super-priority moratorium loans which are permitted in some jurisdictions in the case of corporate rehabilitation proceedings, e.g. the US Chapter 11 of the Bankruptcy Code of 1978 and the French *redressement judiciare*. 3–28

In government loans, the clause is probably to be construed as a general non-discrimination clause prohibiting, e.g. the allocation of insufficient assets to one creditor if the state is effectively bankrupt. There appears to be no case law.

The ranking applies only to *unsecured* liabilities. If the clause requires that the loan ranks pari passu with *all* liabilities of the borrower, including secured liabilities, the clause would be a concealed negative pledge.

The clause cannot alter the ranking prescribed by law, e.g. on liquidation.

The remedy for a breach is purely an event of default. If the borrower is already subject to insolvency proceedings, it is too late.

Disposals

3–29 The clause provides in outline:

> "The Borrower will not (and will procure that each of its subsidiaries will not) dispose of all or a substantial part (by one or a series of transactions, related or not) of its respective assets."

The reasons for the clause are:

1. It prevents **asset-stripping** of the borrower (on takeovers in particular), i.e. a sale of the borrower's assets on credit to an associated company so that the real productive assets of the borrower are converted into a claim on a possibly worthless company.
2. It prevents a creeping **change of business**.
3. It prevents **large-scale disposals** by the borrower to pay other pressing creditors if the borrower is in financial difficulties, thereby disturbing the equality of treatment between creditors.
4. It limits large-scale **evasion of the negative pledge** by quasi-security title finance devices, such as sale and lease-back, and factoring of receivables. See para 3–14.

3–30 As regards intra-group disposals, a disposal by the borrowing company to a subsidiary commercially subordinates the bank even though the assets are still in the group because the claim of the bank is against the parent, not the subsidiary. Therefore some clauses impose specially tight controls on the borrower as opposed to subsidiaries.

As to the meaning of "substantial", cumulative disposals of 10 to 15 per cent may be substantial: see *Commercial Union Assurance Co Ltd v Tickler Ltd*, March 4, 1959, unreported.

The restriction may be extended to the leasing or licensing of assets by the borrower as lessor in addition to outright disposals. A lease could put the asset beyond the reach of creditors just as much as an outright disposal, e.g. a 1,000-year lease of land and buildings for a large initial premium has a similar economic effect to a sale.

3–31 **Exclusions** Possible exclusions include:

– Disposals with majority bank consent. Banks generally resist "not to be unreasonably withheld" as being too vague.

Other covenants

There are many other possibilities. Examples are:

No mergers or amalgamations, i.e. no fusion of companies leading to a different credit. Contrast acquisitions of shares of other companies on a takeover which do not result in a fusion. These would have to be covered by a specific clause forbidding acquisitions by the borrower. For takeovers of the borrower's shares resulting in a change of control of the borrower, see para 3–50. Under private international law, universal successions by the law of the place of foreign incorporation may be recognised in England: *National Bank of Greece and Athens v Metliss* [1958] AC 509.

No guarantees by third parties of other loans to the same borrower. This is intended to prevent a new parent of the borrower or a government from guaranteeing other creditors but not this loan. The motive is equality of treatment. The clause is usually extended to other assurances against financial loss and collateral security.

Maintenance of consents, especially exchange control consents

No substantial change of business on group basis (the type of business being financed is important e.g. manufacturing, not bee-keeping)

Maintenance of status, licences and franchises (identity and existence of borrower)

Consider also:

— **environmental compliance**
— **payment of taxes**
— **(material) compliance with laws**
— **prudent and safe operations**
— **insurance** (risk)
— **repair** (asset quality)
— **no redemption of share capital** (asset leakage: shareholders should not be paid before creditors)
— **control of acquisitions, joint ventures, subsidiaries and other investments** (too rapid expansion, change of business, exposure to insolvency of others)

- **control of guarantees and the like** (exposure to insolvency of others)
- **control of loans and credits to others** (exposure to insolvency of others, leakage of cash assets)
- **control of capital expenditures** (too rapid expansion, financing risks).

Many of these are more typical of project finance.

Events of default

Effect of defaults

3–37 Events of default commonly have four effects by the express terms of the loan contract:

- an event expressly permits the bank to accelerate outstanding loans: para 3–54
- an event expressly permits the bank to cancel its obligations to lend further loans: para 3–54
- an event expressly enables the bank to suspend further loans under the "conditions precedent" clause: para 2–5 et seq. In this case it is usually provided that a pending event of default is sufficient, e.g. breach of covenant although a grace period has not expired.
- an event may constitute a default under other credit agreements of the borrower under a cross-default clause.

Calling a default is a last resort and will usually lead to the immediate demise of the borrower (cross-defaults; directors must stop trading if the company cannot pay its debts as they fall due by reason of wrongful or fraudulent trading because of personal liability in insolvency statutes). Most credit institutions are not rapacious money-lenders waiting to pounce. The *ability* to call a default is primarily to provide a sanction and to strengthen the hand of the bank in restructuring negotiations unless the case is hopeless.

Classification of defaults

3–38 There are three types of default:

(a) actual – non-payment;

(b) non-compliance with a non-monetary clause – because it might prejudice payment, e.g. breach of negative pledge, breach of warranty;

(c) early warning or anticipatory – the warning light, e.g. if the borrower is in liquidation, the bank should not have to wait until the next payment is dishonoured.

Non-payment

This covers: 3–39

> Non-payment on due date, at the required place, in the required currency, in the required funds.

Grace periods may be agreed with or without a bank notice. The grace period may apply only in the case of technical inadvertence or error (to isolate financial difficulties).

Breach of other obligations

This covers breach of obligations other than the payment obligations, e.g. the covenants, any prohibition on assignments, or failure to apply the loans to the intended purpose. 3–40

A materiality test is unwise from the point of view of the bank because the breached obligation would have weak sanctions since the bank might have to show that the default affects the borrower's ability to pay. This involves a credit analysis which is subjective and difficult to prove.

Grace periods are common, e.g. 30 days after written notice of default or 30 days after the borrower becomes aware of the default (but only if the default is curable in 30 days). Sometimes no grace periods are allowed in the case of identified major covenants, e.g. the negative pledge.

Breach of warranty

The representations and warranties are the basis upon which the loan is made: para 3–1 *et seq*. 3–41

Materiality of the incorrectness is often agreed as a matter of market practice, although admittedly vague.

If the warranties must remain continually true ("evergreen" warranties), this may be limited to legal warranties (plus a grace period to procure corrections) – since the bank is entitled to expect that the claim for the loan is valid. But the borrower is significantly exposed if the commercial warranties are evergreen, e.g. this may import a hidden material adverse change clause: para 3–48.

Cross-default

3–42 This provides:

> "Event of default if the borrower fails to pay other debt when due, or other debt is accelerated, or commitment to lend other debt is cancelled, an event of default or pending event of default occurs in relation to any other debt, or collateral security becomes enforceable or is enforced."

This is a fundamentally important clause. It is the leading anticipatory event of default: if the borrower has defaulted on another loan, it may only be a matter of time before the borrower defaults on this loan. It establishes equality in the race to the court-house door. It gives the bank the ability to be present at the table in debt restructuring negotiations (because the bank has the sanction of acceleration to bring the house down). It seeks to establish non-discriminatory treatment, e.g. the clause in practice limits preferential payments to other overdue creditors since each creditor can accelerate and hence stop the business. In practice, the cross-default has an inertia effect. If everybody can accelerate, nobody can since this spells bankruptcy. In the words of the old song: "If everybody is somebody, then nobody is anybody" (Gilbert & Sullivan, *The Gondoliers*). The clause has been called a lazy clause, because the creditor absorbs the protections of other creditors without negotiating them itself: this is not a complete view.

The extension to collateral security (where the borrower gives security without personal liability) – if indeed this is permitted under the negative pledge – is to catch the erosion of assets: but the borrower itself is not in default.

3–43 **Express limitations** Express limitations on the clause which borrowers may seek to negotiate may include:

(a) **Debt** may be limited to borrowings and guarantees of borrowings (but this will exclude acceptances, deferred purchase considerations, such as loan stock issued for shares on takeovers, financial leases, hire purchase, sale and repurchase, sale and lease-back, factoring of debts). This is not usually fatal since loans and guarantees generally collapse first. The clause does not usually apply to trade debt because otherwise many borrowers would always be in default.

(b) The debt may be limited to a **threshold amount**. From the bank's point of view, a missed principal instalment of more than $1,000,000 and a missed interest instalment of more than $100,000 would often be regarded as serious; hence any threshold tends to be different for principal and interest. Some thresholds relate to defaults of any amount pro-

EVENTS OF DEFAULT 3–45

vided that the principal of the other credit is more than a specified amount so that the cross-default only applies to big credits, regardless of the amount in default. Sometimes the debt excludes short-term debt and applies only to debt of original maturity of more than one year.

(c) The debt may be limited to **external debt**, i.e. a debt payable to a foreign creditor in (or optionally in) a foreign currency. This is common in governmental loans but very rare in corporate loans.

(d) The default may be limited to **actual acceleration** of other loans, not mere occurrence of a pending default or event whereby other debt is capable of being accelerated. Sometimes this version is called "cross-acceleration" as opposed to "cross-default". If a pending event of default (e.g. a breach of covenant which will be a default on expiry of a grace period) in another agreement is a cross-default in this agreement, the bank has the benefit of all the covenants in the other agreement and could accelerate for a technicality, even though the other creditor has agreed a grace period or waiver. In effect, all grace periods, materiality tests and the like are removed and, because the other creditor may have a similar cross-default, the grace period protections in the borrower's debt instruments are nullified: this has a domino effect. Banks sometimes maintain that the occurrence of a default in another agreement gives the creditor concerned the power to negotiate a preferred payment under threat of acceleration, thereby offending commercial pari passu treatment of all creditors.

3–44

(e) The premature acceleration may be limited to those caused by defaults, not, for example, those under a change of control clause, a maintenance of collateral value clause, an illegality clause (para 4–8) or a clause providing for cancellation if the interest cannot be fixed as contemplated (para 2–19). But the impact of a bank calling in an overdraft or line of credit should be the considered, as should the cancellation of undrawn amounts on uncommitted lines.

(f) Sometimes there is a grace period or an exclusion for defaults reasonably contested in good faith.

Creditor processes

This covers:

3–45

"Execution, attachment etc. against borrower's assets."

Creditor executions are generally a sign of financial difficulties. Possible relaxations are: (a) long grace period, (b) threshold amounts for the asset or debt concerned, and (c) the event applies only after the final judgment, so as to exclude unjustified prejudgment seizures, such as the Mareva injunction in England.

Liquidation and insolvency proceedings

3–46   This covers:

> "Liquidation, cessation of business, receivership, custodianship, administration, rehabilitation, insolvency proceedings, dissolution, arrangements or compositions."

These events are the stroke of midnight. A typical negotiation point is whether the clause should crystallise on mere petitions or applications by other creditors, since these may be unfounded. But the clause generally crystallises on voluntary petitions and applications or resolutions by the borrower itself or its shareholders.

In secured loans in England where there is a floating charge, the clause should also spring on an application or petition for an administration order, since the blocking of the administration order depends on the ability to appoint an administrative receiver before the order by a person who has security over all or substantially all of the assets of the company including a floating charge: see IA 1986 ss 9 and 10. There should be no grace period.

Actual insolvency

3–47   This covers:

> "Admission of or inability to pay debts as they fall due; insolvency as defined in any applicable insolvency legislation; moratorium, declared or de facto."

Grace periods and materiality tests are generally inappropriate.

Events relating to creditors' processes, liquidation and actual insolvency are usually extended to analogous events in other jurisdictions.

Material adverse change

3–48   This clause provides:

> "Event of default if any change occurs, financial or otherwise, which affects the borrower in a manner which in the opinion of the bank is materially adverse."

The material adverse change clause is important in practice and is often relied upon by banks, particularly to stop new loans under the conditions precedent clause. There are variations of wording. Obviously the clause is vague and subjective.

Sometimes there is a double test: "adverse change" and "the change affects ability of borrower to perform". From a bank's point of view, the clause should apply to significant deteriorations . If the change must also affect ability to pay, the clause is weak because this could amount to proving insolvency. One negotiating issue is whether the inability and its effect should be certain or probable or merely possible.

Banks often seek a discretion ("in the bank's (reasonable) opinion") because of the difficulty of proof and the absence of up-to-date information.

3–49

Borrowers commonly object that this clause converts a term loan into a demand loan and this removes the objective of term lending. Precise financial tests confer greater predictability for both sides: see para 3–32 *et seq*. Some clauses attempt specific tests, e.g. fall in profits or assets, or a drop in rating by a rating agency.

The clause is not standard in corporate loans, but is very common. The clause is very common in governmental loans and is intended to cover economic and political disasters which it would be undiplomatic to mention expressly – the clause is a substitute for corporate liquidations, etc. A version of the clause is standard in the loan agreements of the world and regional development banks.

The clause may be on a group basis.

Change of control ("poison pill")

This provides:

3–50

- **Event of default if a single person (or persons acting in concert) acquire control of borrower**
- **Existing controllers of the borrower lose control**

These clauses are not standard.

If the borrower becomes controlled by a single shareholder, e.g. on a take-over, it is easier for the new controller to manipulate the assets than if the borrower remains a public company. The legal safeguards for creditors of private companies are not as great as for public companies (e.g. easier reduction of capital, grant of financial assistance to purchase one's own shares, lesser company law, stock exchange and investor protections). The result is that the borrower may become responsible by a guarantee for the huge borrowings of the acquiring company raised to finance the take-over of the borrower. But the requirement for consent under this "poison pill" clause could place the bank in an invidious position since it might be seen to be taking sides in a take-over battle.

If the borrower is currently controlled by a strong shareholder or government, an event of default if there is a change of control may have limited embarrassment value in practice (because shareholders are not liable for debts of the company) and ideally a guarantee should be taken instead.

Subsidiaries and guarantors

3–51 **Subsidiaries** Subsidiaries are often included in appropriate events of default, e.g. cross-default and insolvency. Although a parent is not liable for the debts of its subsidiaries, the default of a subsidiary often means that the parent is in trouble. The default of a central bank is an indication of the insolvency of the government.

Guaranteed loans The events of default should apply also to any guarantor and to the guarantee. If the guarantor defaults, then the bank must be able to call in the loan under an event of default in the loan agreement before it can call the guarantee. Defaults by the guarantor or defects in the guarantee should have a sanction.

Government loans

3–52 Government loans generally include events covering non-payment, non-compliance, breach of warranty, cross-default, steps to reschedule, stopping of foreign currency payments, creditor processes, and material adverse change. There may be a default if the government ceases to be a member of the IMF, or ceases to be eligible to use its resources or there is a suspension of payments under a standby or non-observance of performance criteria in a standby, or a standby ceases to be in effect. The IMF is a lender of last resort. Standbys are mainly emergency loans, drawdowns under which are generally linked to economic performance criteria ("conditionality"): note that they are not legally binding and the drafting of any event of default should reflect this.

Miscellaneous

3–53 There are special events of default in:
- project loans
- ship and aircraft loans
- financial leases

These are discussed in other works in this series on international financial law.

Acceleration

If an event of default occurs, the agreement states that the bank may immediately accelerate outstanding loans plus accrued interest and cancel its commitment to make further loans.

3–54

In English law acceleration is not a void penal forfeiture. The English courts will not relieve against the "forfeiture" of acceleration, even if a payment is only a day late: *The Brimnes* [1974] 3 All ER 88, CA (forfeiture of ship charter); *The Laconia* [1977] AC 850 (forfeiture of ship charter); *Sport International Bussum BV v International Footwear Ltd* [1984] 1 All ER 376, CA (forfeiture of licences); *The Chikuma* [1981] 1 All ER 652, HL (forfeiture of ship charter); *The Angelic Star* [1988] 1 Lloyds Rep 122, CA (acceleration of shipping loan). If a debt is payable on demand, the English courts may construe this as no more than a few hours to obtain the money: *Cripps Pharmaceuticals v Wickenden* [1973] 2 All ER 606. This follows the English policies of predictability and freedom of contract: the borrower can negotiate grace periods.

Very few countries nullify acceleration clauses on insolvency rehabilitative proceedings. France is a country which does.

Where a contract contains a provision for its termination or acceleration by notice, notice must be given strictly in accordance with the terms of the contract: see *Re Berker Sportcraft Ltd's Agreements* (1947) 177 LT 420.

CHAPTER 4

TERM LOANS: MISCELLANEOUS CLAUSES

Introduction

4–1 This chapter deals with a variety of miscellaneous clauses which commonly appear in international term loan agreements. They are:
- margin protections, namely the tax grossing-up clause, the increased cost clause, a currency indemnity, and a default indemnity;
- the illegality clause;
- a number of other clauses, notably those regarding assignments, set-off and waivers.

Margin protections

4–2 These are clauses designed to protect the margin or spread payable to the bank which is the bank's gross profit, or the whole of the interest.

Tax grossing-up

The clause provides in outline:

> "If the borrower must deduct taxes, the borrower will pay extra so that the bank receives the full amount."

Grossing-up is principally to protect the bank against withholding taxes on interest and ensures that the bank receives 100, not, say, 75. "Grossing-up" means that borrower will pay extra so that, after all tax deductions, the bank receives the full amount on the due date as if there had been no deduction. Even if the bank will obtain a tax credit for the deduction, this will take time and the bank in the meantime suffers a cash flow loss. In a "cost of funds" loan, withholding taxes are a borrower's risk.

If a withholding tax is imposed, this is generally mandatory and cannot be overridden by contract: hence the need for gross-up. A foreign withholding tax deduction may not be recognised under the governing law of the contract in which event the borrower would have to gross-up in any event even in the absence of a specific gross-up clause to avoid a default: *Indian and General Investment Trust Co Ltd v Borax Consolidated Ltd* [1920] 1 KB 539. Sometimes grossing-up clauses are prohibited locally.

The clause may be extended to an indemnity for taxes relating to the loan and collected by direct assessment on the bank's branch in the borrower's country instead of by withholding ("effective connection" doctrine). But these might be caught by the increased cost clause: para 4–5.

The clause may be extended to any tax deductions on payments by an agent bank to syndicate members (this is not a deduction by the borrower).

Return of tax credits The clause may contain a qualified obligation on the bank to return any tax credits, i.e. where the bank can deduct the tax withheld from its tax liability on income by reason of the fact that it has already suffered the tax by withholding. The availability of tax credits depends on local tax law, including double taxation treaties. The borrower is usually required to supply certificates of tax deduction to enable the bank to obtain the tax credit from its revenue authority. Some banks prefer a woolly consultation clause because the bank is exposed to discovery of its tax affairs by the borrower, the payment of tax credits may itself have tax effect, there is a difficulty in allocating tax credits to particular loans, and a difficulty of determining when the benefit of a tax credit is actually received, or simply because the clause is administratively inconvenient.

Drafting Protections for the borrower are often negotiated. For example, the borrower is given an express right to prepay the bank if tax must be deducted from payments. The bank is obliged to endeavour to mitigate, e.g. by transferring the loan to another branch provided the bank is not prejudiced (and the transfer is not against the commercial policies of the bank). The clause allowing assignments and changes of lending office by a bank may state that these are not to give rise to an increased liability on the borrower under the grossing-up clause. For a form, see the Appendix.

There may be a limitation to taxes of the borrower's country. Banks resist since taxes may be levied, e.g. at the place of payment or at the branch office of the borrower or by the country through which the payment is made or on payments by an agent bank to syndicate members. There may be an exclusion of taxes on net income. Banks usually resist this because most withholding taxes are taxes on net income although collected at source. The name of the tax is immaterial if there is a deduction.

Stamp duties The borrower is generally obligated to pay any documentary taxes on the agreement.

Increased costs

4–5 The clause provides in outline:

> "If any law or official directive increases the bank's underlying costs, the borrower must compensate as certified by the bank."

This is a protection against erosion of the bank's return. Central bank reserve requirements, special taxes, capital adequacy rules and liquidity requirements may impose costs on the bank which are attributable to the loan but which are not reflected in the cost of funding deposits. See chapter 22. A "cost plus margin" loan is cost of funds and anything which increases that cost is to be passed to the borrower and is a borrower risk. The clause is not usually necessary in base rate or prime rate loans because these rates already reflect reserves and the like. The clause may also apply to costs imposed on the bank's holding company.

The weakness of the clause is the practical difficulty of allocating certain costs to particular loans and also the commercial acceptability of passing on some costs, e.g. the cost of compulsory increases in the bank's equity base because of capital adequacy rules.

Express protections for borrower often include: (a) the borrower has a right to prepay the bank immediately; (b) the bank must take mitigating action, e.g. by a change of lending office provided the bank is not prejudiced or the transfer is acceptable (the bank may not wish to transfer its loan to its Kiribati branch); (c) assignments and changes in lending office by the bank must not give rise to increased liability under this clause; (d) the clause is limited to changes in law or directive, so as to exclude existing requirements. But some requirements are already in place and the imposition of the cost may depend not on a change of law but, for example, on the bank's circumstances (e.g. if it loses capital or goes over a lending threshold); (e) an exclusion of taxes on the overall net income of the bank; and (f) the borrower must be notified as soon as the cost arises. For a form, see the Appendix.

Currency indemnity

4–6 The clause provides:

> "If the borrower's payments are converted into a non-contractual currency, the borrower will pay extra to ensure the bank receives the full amount in the contractual currency, plus costs of exchange."

In some jurisdictions, judgments for foreign currency debts are converted into local currency (at the due date or judgement date, not the date of receipt of enforcement proceeds). In most developed jurisdictions, insolvency proofs are converted into local currency at the date of insolvency. If the local currency depreciates, the loan depreciates correspondingly in value

English courts will give judgments in foreign currency but convert at the latest possible time, generally on execution order. This is also the general position for enforcement of foreign judgments and under various reciprocal enforcement conventions. On insolvency, foreign currency proofs are converted into sterling on insolvency order: IR 1986, r 4.91.

The clause may be ineffective. In England, top-up on insolvency is almost certainly invalid as offending the pari passu insolvency principle.

Default indemnity

The clause provides: 4–7

> "Borrower will pay losses (including breakage costs) resulting from the occurrence of an event of default or acceleration."

If the borrower or guarantor pays in mid-interest period, a bank may suffer a loss on account of funds borrowed (because the rate at which it can relend the returned funds may be less than the rate it is paying on the deposit it borrowed in the market to fund the loan).

Illegality clause

The clause provides: 4–8

> "If it becomes illegal for a bank to (a) make the loan, (b) fund the loan in the market as contemplated, or (c) have the loan outstanding, the bank can cancel and the borrower must prepay."

The reason for this force majeure clause is that the bank may be prohibited by a change of law in one jurisdiction, e.g. the country of its head office, from continuing the loan, but be contractually obliged to lend under the governing law of the contract, resulting in a limping contract. For example, under English conflicts rules (reflected in the 1980 Rome Convention), validity is governed by the governing law unless performance of an English law contract is illegal in the place where it must be performed, i.e. where the bank must make payments to the borrower or there is some other public policy objection. The rules are reviewed in another volume in this series of works on financial law.

Originally the clause was a protection against trading with enemy legislation, freeze orders and blocking orders. It could now also be relevant to regulatory prohibitions on a bank's activities.

The clause has been rarely used. The borrower's protections may include a qualified obligation on the bank to switch its lending office if the illegality arises, and a grace period.

Other clauses

Assignments

4–9   The clause provides:

> "The borrower may not transfer any of its obligations or assign any of its rights.
>
> The bank may assign all or any of its rights.
>
> The bank may change its lending office.
>
> The bank may disclose information to a proposed assignee or sub-participant."

There should be an absolute prohibition on assignments by the borrower of its rights (e.g. its rights to borrow) or its obligations. Naturally a borrower could not in any event transfer its obligations without agreement.

Banks may wish to assign in order to lay off risk; because of internal or official ceilings (too much exposure to the obligor); capital adequacy; taxation or reserve problems; or a desire to secure jurisdiction.

4–10   Protections for the borrower may include:

(a) the bank may not assign without the consent of the borrower (not to be unreasonably withheld or delayed except in the case of transfers within the group). This is inspired by "know thy lender". Banks sometimes exclude the requirement for consent if there has been an event of default to enable the bank to sell a defaulted loan without consent from the borrower

(b) the borrower's liabilities are not to be increased as a result of an assignment or change of lending office, e.g. under the tax grossing-up or increased cost clauses.

Set-off

The clause provides in outline:

4–11

"Bank may set off any matured obligation owed to the bank under the credit facility against any obligation owed by the bank to the borrower."

Solvent set-off is available in most jurisdictions for matured and liquidated debts, for current accounts, and for transactionally related claims. Many states permit set-off on the insolvency of the debtor (e.g. England and associated jurisdictions – where it is compulsory – also Japan, the Netherlands, Germany, Italy, Scandinavia, Switzerland, Austria). But some jurisdictions forbid insolvency set-off and a private contract cannot override this rule (e.g. France, Luxembourg, Belgium, Spain, Greece).

The clause might improve solvent set-off of the loan against deposits owed by the bank to the borrower, e.g. by dealing with the following: (a) multicurrency set-off; (b) exclusion of implied contracts not to set-off; (c) global set-off between international branches; (d) an improved set-off priority against assignees and creditors attaching deposits.

As mentioned, it is usually not possible to improve or create English insolvency set-off by contract.

Non-mutual set-off across legal entities, e.g. subsidiary of bank or subsidiary of borrower, is generally ineffective on insolvency because there is no mutuality.

Set-off is discussed on a comparative law basis elsewhere in this series of works.

For jurisdiction clauses, see para 5–24 *et seq*. For waivers of immunity, see para 5–63 *et seq*.

Waivers

A clause sometimes purports to limit waivers specifically to their terms (an odd provision) or requires waivers to be in writing. An actual waiver by a bank of a default by the borrower may be deemed to override a waiver clause, e.g. one which requires waivers to be in writing. The bank may be deemed to have waived a breach or event of default if by its conduct it leads the borrower to believe that the bank will not enforce its rights.

4–12

Examples of implied waivers are lending a new loan or substantial lapse of time if the bank knows of the breach (although mere delay is not usually a waiver but may be supporting evidence). Acceptance of commitment fees or principal or interest in arrears is not usually a waiver. The waiver must be unequivocal, so mere negotiations are usually not enough. Voluntary waivers where the borrower has not irrevocably changed his position in reliance on the waiver are generally revocable on reasonable notice. Best practice if there is a default is for the bank to reserve its rights in a "no-waiver" letter to the borrower pending negotiations on what to do.

Boiler-plate

4–13 Apart from useful administrative clauses as to notices and language, and a marginally useful clause to the effect that remedies and rights at law are not excluded (so that the remedies are not limited to those in the agreement) loan agreements generally end with a hotch-potch of somewhat meaningless provisions which continue to appear by force of habit. Thus one finds a provision purporting to sever illegal or invalid terms without prejudicing the entire agreement, and a provision that the agreement can be signed in counterparts and each is an original. These do not add up to much, at least under English law.

CHAPTER 5

TERM LOANS: GOVERNING LAW AND JURISDICTION CLAUSES; WAIVERS OF IMMUNITY

Introduction

Summary This chapter reviews (1) the choice of governing law clause, (2) jurisdiction clauses selecting a court or courts for the purpose of resolving disputes and the enforcement of the agreement, and (3) waivers of sovereign immunity. 5–1

The private international law of contracts, the scope of the jurisdiction of courts world-wide and the comparative law of sovereign immunity are immense topics which are studied in other works in this series of books on financial law and hence only a few selected aspects are summarised here. This chapter repeats material in other volumes, but in outline form, for the convenience of the reader.

Terms of clause

The clause provides: 5–2

"This Agreement is governed by English law."

Every legal issue under a financial contract must be determined in accordance with a system of law. An aspect of a contract cannot exist in a legal vacuum.

In England and in most developed countries the parties to a contract may normally choose the governing or proper law of the contract which will govern many of its aspects. This law may, for example, be the law of the borrower's country, the law of the creditor's country, the law of the market, such as the London Eurocurrency Market or the market in which the bonds are issued, or a neutral system of law.

Strictly the law chosen is that of a judicial district: there are seven legal systems in the British Isles of varying degrees of distinctiveness: England,

Scotland (anglicised Roman Law), Northern Ireland, Isle of Man, Jersey, Guernsey, and Alderney/Sark. Each state of the United States is a separate jurisdiction. But France and Japan have a unitary system of law.

English and New York law are common choices for international loan agreements.

Factors influencing choice of law

5-3 Factors which influence the choice of law for a financial contract include:

1. Non-legal preferences, such as patriotism, tradition, familiarity and convenience

2. Avoidance by the lender of a detailed investigation into an unfamiliar system of law

3. Commercial orientation, stability and predictability of the chosen legal system

4. The desire to coincide the governing law with the law of the enforcing forum (which may be external) – legal unpredictability may result if the court is called upon to apply a foreign law with which it is not familiar

5. The ability to use lawyers who have special experience in the type of financial contract concerned

6. Language

7. Insulation

Insulation is important and requires further examination.

Insulation

5-4 Insulation of the loan contract from legal changes in the borrower's country is perhaps the most important reason for the choice of an external system of law – it does not matter which law, so long as it is external. Historically the most common changes protecting national debtors have been (a) legislation imposing and moratorium on foreign obligations, (b) reduction of the interest rate by legislation, (c) requirements that repayment must be made in local currency to a local custodian, and (d) exchange controls. The risk may be increased where the borrower is a state or is state-related or is nationally important. These interferences often arise either because of political upheavals or because the state is insolvent – both of which are events against which the private contractor seeks some defence.

If the borrower's system of law is chosen a lender may be subject to changes in the local law. This conclusion flows from the rule that the proper law applying to the agreement is the law as it exists from time to time: *Re Helbert Wagg & Co Ltd* [1956] Ch 323. As the House of Lords stated in *Kahler v Midland Bank* [1950] AC 24, [1949] 2 All ER 621 "the proper law, because it sustains, may also modify or dissolve the contractual bond".

The point is illustrated by two contrasting English cases.

> In *Re Helbert Wagg & Co Ltd* [1956] Ch 323, a subsequent German moratorium law required a German borrower to make loan payments under a loan contract governed by German law to a government agency in Berlin in German marks instead of in pounds sterling. *Held*: the German law was effective to discharge the borrower. The German moratorium law arose under a German contract.
>
> On the other hand in *National Bank of Greece and Athens S A v Metliss* [1958] AC 509, HL, a Greek decree reduced the interest rate on bonds issued by a Greek bank and subject to English law. *Held*: the Greek law was disregarded and the borrower was liable to pay arrears of interest. The English governing law insulated the contract from changes in Greek law.

The result is that in England the lender can, by choice of external law, have complete certainty in knowing that the borrower's country cannot unilaterally alter the obligations by a change of local law. The piece of paper, at least, is inviolate and retains its bargaining power: that piece of paper, whether a credit agreement or bond or whatever, is all the creditor has to represent the money and plainly his position is somewhat unhappy if that too is destroyed.

It is not possible by contract to stabilise the law, e.g. that the governing law is that at the time of the contract. The fluctuating governing law must still be ascertained and will apply to this term of the contract. A change in the governing law will override. But a contract can provide that an invalidating change of law will constitute an event of default (although the change of law might override the ability to recover or the event of default itself).

Limits on insulation

Amongst the limits on the insulating effect of the choice of external law are:

1. There may be **no external assets** capable of attachment to satisfy a judgment against the borrower. If the action were brought locally, the local courts might ignore the foreign proper law to the extent it conflicted

with local overriding law, including perhaps the very laws (such as an exchange control) against which the lender sought to be insulated. But it is preferable for a creditor to have a legal claim, even if futile, than no claim at all.

2. A subsequent exchange control in the borrower's country, e.g. rationing payments, may, if that country is an IMF member, in certain circumstances achieve recognition in a few IMF states under **Art VIII 2(b) of the Bretton Woods Agreement**.

3. Local **insolvency proceedings** are in the main governed by local insolvency law.

Rome Convention of 1980

5–7 In member states of the European Union most conflicts rules in contract are governed by the 1980 EC Rome Convention on the Law Applicable to Contractual Obligations, implemented in the United Kingdom by the Contracts (Applicable Law) Act 1990. The Convention makes few major changes of substance to previous English case law on the subject and hence is largely a codification – at least so far as our subject is concerned. A Brussels Protocol of 1988 to the Rome Convention enables national courts to refer issues to the European Court. The Convention has been ratified by most EU states.

5–8 Other major statements are:

– The US Restatement on Conflicts of Laws (1971) produced by the American Law Institute

– The Swiss Act on Private International Law of 1987 ("Swiss PILA 1987"). See *Switzerland's Private International Law Statute* 1987, annotated translation by Karrer and Arnold (1989) Kluwer. See also the unannotated translation, Symeonides "The New Swiss Conflicts Codification: An Introduction" 37 *Am J Comp Law* 187 (1989).

– Dicey & Morris, *The Conflict of Laws* (11th ed 1987) Sweet & Maxwell, whose rules are effectively an elaborate code of English law prior to the Rome Convention and which may continue to be persuasive authority for English-influenced jurisdictions. The 12th edition reflects the Rome Convention.

There are conflicts codifications in a number of states, e.g. Turkey (1982), Austria (1979) and Hungary (1979), as well as the Bustamente Code applying in a number of Latin American states. Codes in codified countries usually contain basic rules.

Express choice of applicable law

5–9 **Rome Convention** As to freedom of choice, the primary rule is stated in Art 3(1) of the 1980 Rome Convention: "a contract shall be governed by the law chosen by the parties. The choice must be expressed or demonstrated with reasonable certainty by the terms of the contract or the circumstances of the case. By their choice the parties can select the law applicable to the whole or part only of a contract". Connection with the applicable law is not necessary.

This reflects English common law which allows virtually complete party autonomy in choice of law. Party autonomy is accepted now in most, if not all, developed systems, although in the US there must usually be some connection.

5–10 **United States** Section 187 of the US Conflicts Restatement confirms that the law chosen by the parties will be applied unless either (a) the chosen state has no substantial relationship to the parties or the transaction and there is no other reasonable basis for the parties' choice, or (b) the application of the law of the chosen state would be contrary to a fundamental policy of a state which has a materially greater interest than the chosen state and the determination of the particular issue and which, under an objectively ascertained governing law under s 188, would be the state of the applicable law in the absence of an effective choice of law by the party. The comments make it clear that the old objection that freedom of choice is tantamount to enabling parties to be legislators is now obsolete and further there does not have to be any connection provided there is some reasonable basis for choosing an unrelated system of law, e.g. because the parties wish to refer their contract to some well known and highly elaborated commercial law. Naturally any choice of law must be subject to the public policy of the forum, provided that policy is fundamental.

In 1984 the New York General Obligations Law was amended to enable parties to choose New York law for transactions of more than $250,000, whether or not the contract bears a reasonable relationship to New York: NY General Obligations Law s 5–1401.

5–11 **Switzerland** Article 116 of the Swiss Private International Law Act of 1987 provides that contracts are governed by the law chosen by the parties if explicit or clearly evident from the agreement or from the circumstances.

5–12 **Variation of governing law** Article 3(2) of the Rome Convention allows the parties to choose an applicable law either at the time the contract is concluded or at an earlier or later date. This allows the parties to amend a choice of applicable law previously made.

5–13 **No foreign element** Article 3(3) of the Rome Convention provides that where the parties have chosen a particular foreign law but all the other elements relevant to the situation are connected with another country, the express choice shall not prejudice those rules of that other country which cannot be derogated by contract (i.e. mandatory rules). Article 3(3) is of limited importance because all the elements must be connected with another country. The provision is intended to prevent the use of an artificial applicable law in order to avoid otherwise mandatory rules and is probably redundant.

Evasive choices of law

5–14 Pre-Convention it was said that the English courts will not uphold an express choice of law if the choice is made with a view to evading a mandatory rule of law which would have applied to the contract if an "objectively connected" proper law had been chosen, e.g. validating a loan which would be void or illegal under the legal system which would otherwise have applied. In *Vita Food Products Inc v Unus Shipping Co Ltd* [1939] AC 277, it was said that the choice must be "bona fide and legal".

The Rome Convention endeavours to give certainty to choice of law. The "evasive" rule – which has not been applied in England – is probably covered in any event by the overriding mandatory law/public policy rules in Arts 7(2) and 16.

Applicable law in absence of express choice

5–15 **Generally** Parties to a formal loan agreement or a bond issue usually make an express selection of governing law in the instrument itself. However, there are occasions when no express choice is made, e.g. because the loan is informally documented or because a governmental borrower on grounds of national prestige or some constitutional prohibition is not willing to submit expressly to a foreign law. The absence of an express choice of law is often, for similar reasons, accompanied by the absence of an express choice of forum. The English courts claim power to exercise a "long-arm" jurisdiction if the contract is expressly or impliedly governed by English law (see

RSC Ord 11, r 1(1) d) so that in such a case the potential availability of the English court could hinge entirely on a favourable determination that English law applies.

Summary of international rules

Municipal rules vary widely in the manner of determining the governing law in the absence of an express choice. Internationally the main theories might be summarised as follows:

1. Tacit or **implied choice,** e.g. choice of forum
2. **Centre of gravity** (sometimes called "presumed intention", "substantial connection", "dominant contacts", "most significant relationship"): the flexible English common law position and, prior to the Rome Convention, the principles followed in most Continental European states, except Italy. Under the Rome Convention, where the parties have not chosen an applicable law "the contract will be governed by the law of the country with which it is most closely connected": Art 4(1). There are various presumptions, but by Art 4(5) these are overridden "if it appears from the circumstances as a whole that the contract is more closely connected with another country. This is similar to the English common law rule, still prevailing in many English-based states, that the contract is governed by the legal system with which it has its closest and most real connection.
3. **Policy interests,** notably those promoted initially by American academic writers, such as "governmental interest analysis" which weighs the interests of the states concerned in having their own law applied; see the US Conflicts Restatement
4. (In the absence of a tacit choice) **rigid presumptions,** such as common nationality or common residence or the law of place of contracting or performance (mainly French and Spanish-influenced states)
5. Rome Convention – **mixture** of tacit choice, centre of gravity and presumptions, but mainly centre of gravity
6. **Law of the forum,** i.e. the courts apply their own law (non-commercial jurisdictions, e.g. some Arabian Gulf states)

In many commercial jurisdictions, the courts first see whether there is a tacit choice and, if there is not, they follow one of the other theories, either a flexible view (such as centre of gravity) or an inflexible rule (such as place of contracting). The rules are reviewed elsewhere in this series of volumes on international financial law.

State contracts

5-17 There are no special rules applying to state commercial contracts. It does not follow that the law of the state is applied. "It is an element of weight to be considered, but it is no more than that": *R v International Trustee* [1937] AC 500 at 557. In this case dollar bonds linked to the value of gold were issued in New York by the British Government. Subsequently the American Joint Resolution of 1933 abrogated gold clauses. The court applied New York law so that the gold clause was unenforceable.

Alternative or optional choices of law

5-18 A clause may state that if proceedings are taken in the courts of the borrower's jurisdiction, those courts will apply their own law. The principal difficulty is that there must be a governing law of a contract from the outset and this cannot be determined retrospectively by some uncertain event in the future: *The Amar* [1981] 1 All ER 498, [1981] 1 WLR 207. If the governing law is dependent upon an action being brought in a particular court, then the parties will not know what legal system governs their obligations until action is brought. See also *The Iran Vojdan* [1984] 2 Lloyds Rep 380 where the carrier's option to choose forum and governing law in Tehran, Hamburg or London was ineffective as a choice of law.

Probably under the Rome Convention, in such a case the applicable law must be determined in accordance with the rules applying if there is no express choice, until a party exercises his option to choose when this should be a permissible variation and effective choice under Art 3(2) – this provides that the parties may vary the governing law. Parties could therefore validly choose a governing law and provide for a different law to be applied according to the place of enforcement.

Depeçage

5-19 The Rome Convention allows the parties to choose different governing laws for different parts of a contract: Art 3(1). This reflects previous English common law. One can therefore state, for example, that the contract will be governed by English law, but that a waiver of immunity will be construed in accordance with New York law: *Forsikrings A/S Vesta v Butcher* [1989] AC 852, HL. This would be odd.

Incorporation of law

One should distinguish between the selection of the governing law of a contract and the incorporation of some of the provisions of a foreign law into the contract. Thus if the contract defines a "subsidiary" by reference to the definition in a Companies Act or incorporates certain provisions of the Uniform Commercial Code, then this is merely a shorthand method of setting out the incorporated terms in full and the English courts will construe the contract by reading in the incorporated terms.

A significant distinction between incorporation of foreign law and express choice of governing law is that, in the case of an incorporation of law, the law is incorporated as it stands at the date of the contract notwithstanding a subsequent change in law. Thus a statute is fixed at the time of the contract notwithstanding its subsequent amendment or repeal (unless otherwise provided). However the governing law applies as it exists from time to time. If during the subsistence of the contract the governing law changes, then the contract changes with it. Incorporation is frozen law: governing law is liquid law.

Renvoi

The governing law is the domestic law of the jurisdiction concerned, not its conflict of laws doctrines. There is no room for renvoi in the law of contract; one could go backward and forward like a yo-yo. This is confirmed by Art 15 of the Rome Convention. See also the US Conflicts Restatement s 187(3).

Public international law

Choice of public international law as governing law It may sometimes be the case that the parties to a financial contract prefer to choose public international law or one of its off-shoots instead of a municipal system of law as the governing law of the contract. The availability and implications of such a choice are reviewed elsewhere in this series of works on financial law.

Summary of scope of applicable law

The governing law of a loan contract does not by any means cover all aspects of the contract. Under the Rome Convention (and indeed under many other sophisticated systems of private international law) the applicable law primarily governs:

5-23 TERM LOANS: GOVERNING LAW AND JURISDICTION CLAUSES

— the existence and validity of the contract;

— formal validity, subject to exceptions;

— interpretation;

— performance, but not the detail of performance;

— the consequences of breaches;

— the extinguishing of obligations, including prescription and limitation.

The main issues in our context *not* covered by the applicable law relate to the following:

— mandatory statutes and public policy (law of the forum);

— corporate constitution, powers, and authorities (local law of the corporation);

— aspects of security (complex rules);

— corporate insolvency (complex rules);

— procedure (law of the forum);

— overriding conventions (law of the forum).

The voluminous law on these topics is reviewed in detail elsewhere in this series on international financial law.

Jurisdiction clause

5-24 A short-form clause may provide:

"For the benefit of the Bank, the Borrower agrees that the English courts shall have jurisdiction in connection with this Agreement, and appoints [   ] as its agent in England for service of process for this purpose. The jurisdiction of the English courts does not exclude any other court of competent jurisdiction."

5-25 In practice enforcement jurisdiction in this context tends not to be greatly used since the preferred method of debt recovery is by a consensual debt restructuring agreement. If that fails, the alternative is either a judicial rehabilitation proceeding or liquidation. Attempts by creditors to enforce by suit and execution is almost invariably met by insolvency proceedings, initiated either by the debtor or other creditors, which freeze further individual actions so that one creditor does not get ahead of the others. This does not apply to states since they cannot be judicially bankrupted, and this explains the greater emphasis placed on jurisdiction clauses in state loan contracts.

Nevertheless, the availability of court action is a basic sanction. Contracts without sanctions, even if the sanctions are not used in practice, have no value.

Purposes of forum selection

Most major term loan contracts contain an express forum selection clause, so that the general grounds on which courts exercise jurisdiction are of less relevance. Forum selection clauses cannot in practice be universal so that the jurisdiction of other courts to which an obligor has not expressly submitted may be relevant, e.g. if there are local assets. 5–26

Additional forum The first purpose of an express forum selection clause is to provide an additional forum outside the borrower's country for enforcement and the adjudication of disputes. The creditor therefore has the option of proceeding locally or, if a local action would be barred or futile for some reason, bringing the suit in the external forum. Because many international borrowers have worldwide assets, the absence of a local judgment is not necessarily fatal. Further, other courts may be prepared to enforce foreign judgments locally, a topic which is examined elsewhere.

Insulation The choice of an external forum in international finance helps to protect the insulation achieved by the choice of an external governing law. It has already been seen that the application of an external governing law can to some degree shield the obligations from adverse legislation introduced by the government of the borrower's country, e.g. exchange control or moratorium legislation, as discussed above. This objective might be defeated if the only available forum for enforcement were the courts of the borrower's country since those courts might either ignore the governing law altogether or apply it only to the extent that it is consistent with local laws. 5–27

Forum and governing law While it is true that governing law and jurisdiction are theoretically separate in the sense that the courts of commercial countries will not decline to adjudicate on a contract merely because a foreign system of law applies, it is desirable that the forum should follow the governing law in order to confer a greater predictability. At the most basic level, the courts of the country of the governing law, being familiar with their domestic law, are more likely to arrive at the expected result. Further, as a matter of convenience, no delays or expense will be involved in calling expert evidence as to the interpretation of another legal system. 5–28

More importantly, a foreign court may not give the governing law the scope that was intended. Courts almost invariably apply their own rules of private international law in matters of contract. The rules of the governing law may be overridden by a local statute which is directly applicable to the issue in question or by considerations of public policy.

5–29 **Standards of the courts** A material consideration in the choice of forum is the standards of the court concerned. The desired characteristics are: (1) a judiciary experienced in international investment disputes, (2) impartiality in the sense that undue preference is not given to local interests and policies in international matters; and (3) commercially-orientated court procedures.

Significant procedural considerations are the accessibility of the court and the length of the queue to get the matter heard, court costs and security for costs, whether summary enforcement procedures are available, the ability to attach assets prior to judgment to prevent them being removed from the jurisdiction thereby frustrating a judgment, the attitude of the courts to sovereign immunity, the absence of technical evidential obstacles in proving the claim, and the availability of effective enforcement procedures.

Immunity Where the borrower is a state or a state-related institution, then, even if the local courts are prepared to entertain an action against the home government, it is almost universally true that no enforcement proceedings will be permitted. The position may be different if the action is brought externally. Most commercial countries (including the United Kingdom and the United States) are prepared to give effect to express waivers of immunity from enforcement, thereby allowing attachment of assets which come within the jurisdiction.

5–30 **Foreign recognition** An express submission greatly enhances the eligibility of a judgment of those courts for recognition and enforcement in foreign countries which might not be prepared to enforce judgments based on a more tenuous jurisdiction.

Forum non conveniens In international loan transactions the ability of a borrower to complain that the specified court should not exercise jurisdiction on the grounds of the forum non conveniens doctrine is reduced almost to vanishing point where the borrower has expressly consented in advance to the jurisdiction of the stated court; he must be regarded as having taken into account questions of convenience at the time of the contract: see, e.g. *Scherk v Alberto-Culver Company*, 94 S Ct 2449 (1974), 417 US 506 (1976).

European Judgments Convention Where the borrower is located in a country which has ratified a European Judgments Convention a written agreement to confer jurisdiction on external courts is essential to contract out of the general rule that, subject to exceptions, the courts of the borrower's domicile are to have sole jurisdiction. This is discussed below.

Appointment of agent

5–31 The appointment of an agent for service of process serves two functions in common law jurisdictions.

In countries such as England the appointment of an agent within England to receive the writ is essential for the English courts to accept their virtually compulsory jurisdiction: RSC Ord 10, r 3. If the borrower were merely to submit and the writ could not be served on the borrower in England, then it would be necessary to apply to the court for leave to serve the writ outside the jurisdiction. While the grant of leave would be probable in the normal case where there is a submission, this is not a foregone conclusion. The second function of the appointment of an agent is to comply with due process requirements. An agent for service of process is not necessary for cases within the European Judgments Conventions (see below), but remains desirable to strengthen the availability of the judgment for enforcement in non-Convention countries.

In England the agent can be anybody. The preferred practice is to appoint an independent institution which performs these services. In state loans, it is desirable not to appoint the state's ambassador because of possible diplomatic immunity.

The clause sometimes includes a requirement that the borrower maintains an agent within the jurisdiction at all times in case the appointed agent should disappear. If the borrower should fail to do so, one imagines that the English courts would show readiness to allow service of the writ outside the jurisdiction.

It is generally expressed to be a condition precedent to the draw-down of loans that the agent bank for lenders receives a copy of the acceptance by the process agent of its appointment. While it seems to be open whether an effective agency contract between the borrower and the agent is strictly necessary in England, foreign enforcing courts might be less inclined to approve the jurisdictional basis of the judgment in the absence of the agent's acceptance of his agency.

Mailing of process

5–32 A provision for the simultaneous mailing of service of process is often inserted and intended, from the creditor's side, to place due process beyond peradventure and, from the debtor's side, to protect him against delays or loss. While it is usually expressly stated that the mailing of process is optional and that failure by the borrower to receive notice of process is no defence, lenders would be prudent to ensure that the proceedings are actually brought to the attention of the borrower so that it cannot be said that he did not have an opportunity to be heard.

Venue

5–33   A distinction must be drawn between jurisdiction and venue. Jurisdiction refers to the powers of the courts of a country generally to hear an action. Venue denotes the particular court in that country which will be seized of the dispute. Venue depends upon such matters as the location of the defendant, the amount of the claim and, in federal systems, the division of functions between the federal and state courts. In England it is not necessary to specify the particular court which will be the venue for the dispute since venue is exclusively decided by procedural rules. In New York it is useful to specify courts which have greater experience in investment disputes.

Civilian practice

5–34   Civilian jurisdiction clauses normally cover (a) an express submission to the non-exclusive jurisdiction of named courts, (b) the designation of a court of venue, e.g. the court of Frankfurt am Main and (c) the appointment of an agent (or election of domicile) for service of process within the jurisdiction.

French cases have held that the mere election by the borrower of a domicile within the jurisdiction may be construed not as a choice of forum but rather as an address for service of process: see *Enterprise Generale Transshipping v Etablissements Billiard*, Cass June 18, 1958, Rev Crit Dr Int Pr 1958 754 and *Cie Luxembourgoise d'Assurances Le Foyer v Dulac*, Cass November 13, 1957, Rev Crit Dr Int Pr 1958, 735.

Exclusive and multiple jurisdiction clauses

5–35   An occasionally controversial issue between lenders and borrowers is whether the rights of the lender or the bondholders to bring an enforcement action should be limited exclusively to the courts of a particular country. The view of lenders may be that default remedies should on no account be limited in any way. On the other hand a borrower may argue that he has a legitimate interest in the identity of the courts. Unless the forum is exclusive he could be exposed to litigation in a possibly hostile country. There could be language problems. In bond issues and large syndications, he may be exposed to a multiplicity of actions in a great many countries and to "forum shopping" whereby the investor seeks a jurisdiction most favourable to his case and disadvantageous to the borrower and it is therefore unreasonable to limit the possibilities of enforcement. In practice the lender's view generally prevails for the simple reason that in most financial contracts there is no dispute or complex factual or legal issue, but merely a non-payment.

The clause should state that the choice of forum is non-exclusive lest it be construed as limited to the named court.

But if an exclusive clause is agreed, then in England, France, Belgium and Germany the courts are, as a general rule, liberal in upholding derogations from their jurisdiction in favour of foreign courts. The international position is briefly reviewed in another volume. As to the position under the European Judgments Conventions, see below.

International jurisdiction rules

Generally Traditionally, the extent of a court's jurisdiction – at least in common law countries – is associated with the territory over which the government of the country concerned has sovereignty so that if the defendant is within the domain of a court and can be served with due process the court can hear the action. The state has power over the defendant. However states have developed "long-arm" rules whereby their courts can claim jurisdiction merely where one of the parties or the transaction has some connection with the country of the courts. The nexus with the jurisdiction is said to justify the exercise of judicial power. Because the connection can be somewhat tenuous, many countries have developed self-imposed restraints on the exercise of jurisdiction where such exercise would be unjust. The jurisdictional enquiry therefore has two stages; first whether the courts have the *power* to claim jurisdiction and secondly whether they will be prepared to *exercise* this power. 5–36

One is concerned here solely with civil jurisdiction in connection with actions in personam on loan contracts. The jurisdictional rules relating to insolvency, to admiralty actions to claims in tort (such as actions for negligence or misrepresentation) and those relating to security interests over assets, are different.

The following rules must be read subject to the European Conventions on Jurisdiction and Judgments in Civil and Commercial Matters, which are in force between most European states: see below.

Universal bases of jurisdiction It is thought that all commercial states claim the power to exercise jurisdiction in the following cases: 5–37

– the defendant **agreed to submit** to the jurisdiction by advance contract or, of course, actually appeared in the action, otherwise than (sometimes) solely to contest jurisdiction;

- the corporate defendant is **incorporated locally** or has a principal place of business locally;
- the defendant has a **local branch**, although sometimes the action is limited to transactions arising in connection with the branch. In many countries, local branches must register themselves at the local companies or commercial register and designate a person on whom process can be served, see e.g. the British Companies Act 1985 s 695.

5-38 **Summary of long-arm jurisdiction** There is substantial disparity between nations as to the exercise of jurisdiction on the basis of more fleeting connections with the forum – often called the long-arm, or extended, or exorbitant or excessive jurisdiction.

The main heads of long-arm jurisdiction are:

1. Transient presence locally of an individual debtor (England, US states), but the presence of a director is not enough to confer jurisdiction over the company.

2. The debtor does business locally, e.g. through an agent.

3. The transaction sued on has local connections, e.g. was made locally (England, but not New York), or the contract is expressly or impliedly governed by local law (England, but not New York – *Hanson v Denkla*, 357 US 235(1958)), or is to be performed locally.

4. Local nationality of plaintiff (France, Luxembourg – CC Art 14) and Italy (subject to reciprocity – CCP Art 4(4)), but not England, nor most US states.

5. Domicile of plaintiff, regardless of nationality: the Netherlands (CCP Art 126(3)) and Belgium (subject to reciprocity in the case of Belgium). Not England, not most US states.

6. Local assets of the defendant, however small – the "toothbrush" jurisdiction: Germany (ZPO Art 25), Austria (para 99 (1) of *Jurisdiktionsnormen*), Japan, Denmark, South Africa, Sweden.

European Judgments Conventions

5-39 **Introduction** The Brussels and Lugano Conventions of 1968 and 1988 respectively on Jurisdiction and the Enforcement of Judgments in Civil and Commercial Matters (plus the various accession and other protocols) are of great importance for European litigation and have a major impact on both Convention and non-Convention parties. The Conventions were implemented in the United Kingdom by the Civil Jurisdiction and Judgments Acts 1982 and 1991. These Conventions are discussed in another work in this series on financial law and only a few selected aspects are discussed here.

Countries covered The Brussels Convention applies to:

Belgium	Italy
Denmark	Luxembourg
France	Netherlands
Germany	Portugal
Greece	Spain
Ireland	United Kingdom

It may be extended to affiliated states, e.g. the Netherlands Antilles, the Faeroes, the Channel Islands and Gibraltar.

The Lugano Convention of 1988 extends the jurisdiction and enforcement rules of the 1968 Convention to European Free Trade Association states:

Austria	Norway
Finland	Sweden
Iceland	Switzerland

The Lugano Convention will presumably fall away for states in this group which join the European Union.

The implementation of the Conventions in each state should be checked, namely, whether they have the the force of law locally and whether they have been modified.

The Conventions are in similar, but not identical form. The differences are not likely to be material to international finance.

Basic principles The Conventions effect fundamental changes to normal jurisdiction bases. The first basic tenet of the Brussels Convention is that, subject to exceptions, "persons domiciled in a Contracting State shall, whatever their nationality, be sued in the courts of that State": Art 2. The second tenet is that, generally speaking, a judgment of a court in a Contracting State in accordance with the Convention is to be enforced universally in the entire Community, subject only to a public policy exception: Arts 26, 31. The Conventions apply only to civil and commercial matters and do not apply to arbitration or bankruptcy proceedings: see Art 1.

Non-domiciliaries are subject to the long-arm rules of each Contracting

State and judgments on the basis of those rules are enforced in all other states. Although the Contracting State where the action is first brought will generally have exclusive jurisdiction, the position in other Contracting States can be preserved by the wide availability of pre-judgment preservation measures, e.g. the Mareva injunction in England or the *saisie conservatoire* in France. The group of 18 Contracting States therefore operates as a monolithic jurisdictional unit with the widest conceivable long-arm jurisdictional rules available to a creditor of a debtor in a non-Convention state, e.g. Japan or the United States.

In the case of a Convention domiciliary, where it is desired to confer jurisdiction on another Contracting State, the creditor should take care to comply with the contracting-out provisions of Art 17. This Article is not without its difficulties. Again the position in other Contracting States can be protected by local preservative measures while the exclusive action continues in the chosen court.

Subject to exceptions, Scotland and N Ireland are treated as separate jurisdictions and are therefore in a similar position vis-à-vis England to Italy.

5–41 **Only Convention countries** It seems that a party can sue a Convention domiciliary in a competent non-Convention court, e.g. New York or Japan. This is important for loans to Convention domiciliaries where it is desired to confer jurisdiction on the courts of a non-Convention state (as is often the case).

> In *Re Harrods (Buenos Aires) Ltd* [1992] Ch 72, CA, it was held that the Convention was intended to regulate jurisdiction only as between Contracting States and the jurisdictional rules did not apply in a case involving a conflict of jurisdiction between the English courts and a non-Contracting State. In that case, it was argued that the defendant, an English company, had to be sued in England in accordance with the basic jurisdictional rule in Art 2, notwithstanding that Argentina might be the more convenient forum. The Court of Appeal held that, as a non-Contracting State was involved, i.e. Argentina, the English court retained its discretion to decide which jurisdiction was more appropriate and in this case Argentina was more appropriate. Under the Convention, the court could not have applied the forum non conveniens principles.

5–42 **Alternatives to domicile: Arts 5 and 6** There are a number of cases where a plaintiff can take proceedings otherwise than at the domicile of a debtor, assuming the courts are competent under their normal jurisdictional rules. In the context of financial transactions, the most important additional possibilities relate to: **contractual suits** ("courts for the place of performance of the obligation in question"); disputes arising out of the operations of **a branch, agency or other establishment** ("courts for the place in which the branch, agency or other establishment is situated"); **third party actions**, e.g. guarantees: ("court seized of the original proceedings, unless these were instituted solely with the object of removing [the third party] from the jurisdiction of the court which would be competent in his case"); **torts** ("place where the harmful event occurred"); **trusts** (where "the trust is domiciled"); **actions against more than one defendant** ("place where any one of them is domiciled"); **certain counterclaims**: ("the court in which the original claim is pending") and actions on a contract related to an action against the same defendant *in rem* arising out of **immovable property** (where "the property is situated").

Exclusive jurisdiction: Art 16 The courts of a Contracting State have exclusive jurisdiction in certain cases, including *in rem* suits relating to **immovable property**, presumably including mortgage actions (usually where the property is); the validity of the constitution, the nullity or the dissolution of **legal associations** or the decisions of their organs (where the seat is); and the validity of entries in **public registers**, e.g. land, commercial and ship registers (where the register is kept). 5–43

Insurance and consumer contracts There are separate provisions regarding insurance contracts and certain consumer contracts. Broadly speaking, their effect is that the policy holder or consumer must be sued in the courts of his domicile. A bank loan or bond issue would generally be outside the consumer provisions except in the case of credits made to finance the sale of goods: Art 13(2). 5–44

Forum non conveniens Where a Convention court has jurisdiction, the doctrine of forum non conveniens does not apply. 5–45

Protective measures Provisional and protective measures, such as Mareva injunctions, *saisie conservatoire* and their equivalent, may be sought in the courts of any Contracting State in accordance with their own rules notwithstanding that the courts of another Contracting State have jurisdiction as to the substance of the matter: Art 24. This is a potent provision because it enables scattered Convention assets to be preserved in accordance with local rules while the main action is proceeding elsewhere. 5–46

Concurrent and related actions: Arts 21 and 22 A principle of the Conventions is that only one Contracting State should exercise jurisdiction. Concurrent jurisdictions are possible, e.g. where Contracting States apply different domicile tests or an action is available in an alternative forum under the rules noted above. The basic rule is that the court first seized of the matter is to exercise jurisdiction. Related actions can be consolidated in 5–47 the court first seized. Hence banks seeking a favoured court must act quickly.

5–48 **Non-Convention defendants: Art 4** The Conventions are dangerous for obligors who are non-Convention domiciliaries, e.g. borrowers in the United States and Japan. If the defendant is not domiciled in a Contracting State, the jurisdiction of the courts of each Contracting State is, subject to the exclusivity provisions in Art 16 (e.g. proceedings relating to land or regarding corporate authorisations), to be determined by the law of that state. It follows that a non-Convention defendant is subject to the long-arm jurisdictional rules in each Contracting State and judgment obtained against him in one Contracting state will then have full faith and credit in all of the other Convention States. Thus a United States borrower could be sued in a Convention State on the basis of one of the following long-arm rules (these may be subject to forum non conveniens qualifications): (a) contract expressly or impliedly governed by English law (England); (b) the "toothbrush" jurisdiction, i.e. assets of the borrower located in the jurisdiction of the courts (Austria, Germany, Scotland, Denmark, Sweden); (c) nationality of plaintiff (France, Luxembourg); (d) (sometimes) residence of plaintiff (Belgium, the Netherlands, Italy).

Article 59 allows Convention states to agree individually, in reciprocal enforcement conventions with third states, not to recognise exorbitantly-based Community judgments in certain cases. The proposed United Kingdom/United States Convention on this topic is in abeyance. The United Kingdom entered into a convention with Canada on this topic in 1984: SI 1987/468.

5–49 **Contracting-out: Art 17** Article 17 is fundamentally important since financial agreements often contract out of the forum of the obligor, e.g. to achieve insulation. The Article is somewhat grudging in permitting derogations – an illiberal view. At that time, the United Kingdom was not a member of the EEC and could not influence the drafting. Article 17 provides as follows:

> "If the parties, one or more of whom is domiciled in a Contracting State, have agreed that a court or the courts of a Contracting State are to have jurisdiction to settle any disputes which have arisen or which may arise in connection with a particular legal relationship, that court or those courts shall have exclusive jurisdiction. Such an agreement conferring jurisdiction shall be either:
>
> (a) in writing or evidenced in writing, or
> (b) in a form which accords with practices which the parties have established between themselves, or
> (c) in international trade or commerce, in a form which accords with a usage of which the parties are or ought to have been aware and which in

such trade or commerce is widely known to, and regularly observed by, parties to contracts of the type involved in the particular trade or commerce concerned.

Where such an agreement is concluded by parties, none of whom is domiciled in a Contracting State, the courts of other Contracting States shall have no jurisdiction over their disputes unless the court or courts chosen have declined jurisdiction.

The court or courts of a Contracting State on which a trust instrument has conferred jurisdiction shall have exclusive jurisdiction in any proceedings brought against a settlor, trustee or beneficiary, if relations between these persons or their rights or obligations under the trust are involved.

Agreements or provisions of a trust instrument conferring jurisdiction shall have no legal force if they are contrary to the provisions of arts 12 [insurance] or 15 [consumer contracts], or if the courts whose jurisdiction they purport to exclude have exclusive jurisdiction by virtue of art 16 [e.g. land, corporate constitutions, public registers].

If an agreement conferring jurisdiction was concluded for the benefit of only one of the parties, that party shall retain the right to bring proceedings in any other court which has jurisdiction by virtue of the Convention."

Points on this are:

5–50

1. **Non-Convention courts** It seems that a Convention domiciliary can agree that a non-Convention court can have jurisdiction, e.g. an English company can in a credit agreement agree that the courts of New York or Tokyo shall have jurisdiction. But the French courts have held that a Convention domiciliary cannot confer jurisdiction on the courts of a non-Contracting State: *Bruno v Soc Citibank*, Court of Appeal, Versailles, 1991, 1992 Rev Crit 333. See also para 5–41.

2. **More than one Convention court** It seems that the parties may choose more than one Convention court in which neither party is domiciled, and that a non-exclusive choice of a non-domiciliary Convention court does not prejudice the Art 17 choice of a named court. This is supported by *Meeth v Glacetal Sàrl* [1978] ECR 2133, [1979] 1 CMLR 520.

   The contract provided that if the German buyer sued the French seller, the French courts alone would have jurisdiction. But if the French seller sued the German buyer, the German courts alone would have jurisdiction. The French seller sued the German buyer in Germany. *Held* by the European Court: Art 17 allowed the parties to agree on two or more courts. But note that they were domiciliary courts.

5–50   TERM LOANS: GOVERNING LAW AND JURISDICTION CLAUSES

This view that a non-exclusive clause does not forfeit Art 17 has been confirmed in *Kurz v Stella Musical Veranstaltungs GmbH* [1992] 1 All ER 630, in which the court held that a non-exclusive choice of jurisdiction clause did not offend Art 17. Parties are free to choose any number of jurisdictions, subject only to the mandatory provisions in Arts 12, 15 and 16. The Court of Appeal, Paris, reached a similar conclusion in *Hantarex SpA v SA Digital Research* (1993) IL Pr 501.

In *Belle Vue Mauricia Ltd v Canmaga Trade Corp*, Court of Appeal, Paris, 1990 (1991) I L Pr 455, a clause providing for the jurisdiction of the courts of Vaduz or Paris at the plaintiff's option was held valid. In *Soc Lyle & Scott v Soc Lisa Frey*, Court of Appeal, Paris 1989 (1990 Clunet 151), a clause that the vendor could designate jurisdiction of any court, in England or elsewhere, was held ineffective. The matter awaits clarification by the European Court.

3. **Assignees** In order to satisfy Art 17, the contracting-out must be the result of a consensus between the "parties". Consensus is necessary only as between the original banks parties to the loan agreement or the original parties to the bond issue, i.e. assignees and transferees should be bound and a borrower should not be able to object to the clause being invoked by an assignee of one of the banks or a transferee of a bond on the ground that the assignee or transferee was not a party to the Art 17 agreement: see para 19 of the Judgment of the Third Chamber, ECJ in Case 201/82, *Gerling Konzern Speziale Kreditversicherung AG v Amministrazione del Tesoro dello Stato* [1983] ECR 2503; Case 71/83, *The Tilly Russ* [1984] ECR 2417.

5–51   4. **Disputes** Although Art 17 refers to agreements "to settle any disputes" it is thought that any action for judicial remedies (including summary proceedings), even where there is no contention, should be a dispute within the provision.

5. **Benefit of one party** The domicile court can also be retained in certain cases. Thus if the jurisdiction agreement has been concluded for the benefit of only one of the parties, that party retains the right to sue in any other court which has jurisdiction under the Conventions: see Case 22/85, *Anterist v Credit Lyonnais* [1986] ECR 1951, ECJ. It is desirable to state that the clause is for the benefit of the desired party.

If there is more than one lender, e.g. as in a syndicated loan, then strictly the "benefit" provision is not satisfied since Art 17 states that, to permit additional jurisdiction in other Convention courts having jurisdiction under the Conventions, the agreement conferring jurisdiction must be concluded "for the benefit of only one of the parties". There is more than one party benefiting. It is considered that in multilateral loan agreements, "one of the parties" can be construed to mean all of the parties other than the borrower, i.e. one can divide the parties into two sides or teams, or alternatively, "one of the parties" might be capable of meaning all those parties for whose benefit the agreement as to jurisdiction was concluded. The matter has not been decided.

6. **Limits on contracting out** Contracting-out is subject to the insurance and consumer contract requirements (Arts 12 and 15) and to the exclusive jurisdictions in Art 16.

7. **No discretion** Where Art 17 applies, the chosen court has no power to override the jurisdiction agreement.

8. **Agent for service to process** An English agent for service of process is strictly not necessary in the case of a Convention defendant, but is often inserted to facilitate process.

9. **Writing** The clause must be in writing or evidenced in writing, or in international trade or commerce in a form which accords with usage in that trade, etc. Jurisdiction clauses in a bond issue, trust deed or other accompanying bond documentation should be specifically referred to in the bond so as to support consensus on jurisdiction.

10. **Non-Convention domiciliaries** If English jurisdiction is required, Art 17 contracting-out is advisable even for non-Convention companies, e.g. Japanese and US companies. This is because a company can subsequently move its domicile into a Convention state, e.g. by moving its central management. Although undecided by the European Court, it seems that Art 17 does not require Convention domicile at the time of the jurisdiction agreement.

11. **Luxembourg** For Luxembourg obligors it is necessary that there should be separate clauses exclusively devoted to jurisdiction whereby the Luxembourg obligors specifically and expressly agree to the jurisdiction clause by signature: see Art 1 of the Annexed Protocols to the Conventions. Signature of bond issue documentation containing the clause is apparently not enough for this purpose: the clause must be signed. See Case 784/79, *Porta-Leasing GmbH v Prestige International SA* [1980] ECR 1517.

12. **Non-Convention borrowers** If the borrower is a non-Convention domiciliary, but the trustee of the bonds, or any bondholder or any lending bank are Convention domiciliaries, a jurisdiction clause within Art 17 has the effect of vesting exclusive jurisdiction on the chosen Convention courts vis-à-vis other Contracting States. In other words, even if the issuer is non-Convention domiciled but any other party is Convention-domiciled, Art 17 contracting-out appears to override the provisions of Art 4 which allow each Convention State's exorbitant

jurisdictional bases to be relied upon in actions against non-Convention domiciliaries.

It is considered that the effect of an Art 17 prorogation is determined at the time of the agreement and is not affected by subsequent events, e.g. an assignment from a non-Convention domiciliary to a Convention domiciliary.

5–54 **Mutual recognition and enforcement of judgments** All "judgments" are enforceable under the Conventions including non-money judgments and interim orders, orders providing for periodical payment, orders freezing assets and injunctions, and no special procedure is required: Arts 25 and 26. A foreign judgment may not be reviewed as to its substance: Art 29.

The courts have no right, except within very confined limits, to investigate the jurisdiction of the court which gave the judgment: Art 28. The jurisdiction of the foreign court may only be investigated if the case falls within s 3 (insurance), s 4 (consumer contracts) or s 5 (exclusive jurisdiction) of Title II to the Conventions: Art 28. Even in these cases the English courts are bound by findings of fact on which the foreign court based its judgment: Art 28.

There are a limited number of exceptions to the universal recognition principle. The most significant relate to public policy (Art 27 (1)); judgments given in default of appearance if the defendant was not properly served in good time (Art 27(2)); where the judgment is irreconcilable with a judgment given in a dispute between the parties in the state in which recognition is sought (Art 27(3)); where the judgment is irreconcilable with an earlier judgment given in a non-Contracting State involving the same cause of action between the same parties and recognisable in the state addressed: Art 27(5).

Enforcement of a judgment in England under the Conventions is by way of registration. There are detailed rules concerning judgments subject to appeal and appeals from enforcement. A creditor cannot bring an action on the original cause of action.

Restrictions on judicial jurisdiction

5–55 **Forum non conveniens** Theoretically a debtor could be subject to actions in a multitude of countries at the instance of bank lenders and bondholders. In practice however long-arm jurisdictional statutes have been tempered by self-imposed restraints on the exercise of the jurisdiction. The courts in developed jurisdictions have paid liberal regard to the doctrine known as forum non conveniens whereby the courts may refuse jurisdiction if they consider that they are not the most convenient and natural forum for the hearing of the dispute.

In practice the doctrine of forum non conveniens is of lesser importance in relation to financial agreements or bond issues for two reasons. First, international borrowers generally have the resources to litigate anywhere in the world and cannot complain of mere inconvenience. Second, where a borrower submits to the jurisdiction of specified courts, he will usually be effectively barred from raising a forum non conveniens defence since it is likely to be presumed that he took into account convenience at the time of the contract. The doctrine is examined elsewhere in this series of works. When the case falls within the scope of the European Judgments Conventions, the power to refuse jurisdiction on forum non conveniens principles is curtailed in a number of respects.

It is thought that it would be virtually impossible in England for a debtor who has submitted to the jurisdiction of the English courts and appointed an agent for service of process there on whom process is duly served to claim subsequently that injustice would result from the exercise of that jurisdiction. He will be taken to have agreed in advance that those courts are convenient.

In New York, the General Obligations Law s 5–1402 provides that, if a contract with a foreign party choosing New York law involves at least $1 million, the choice of a New York forum for the adjudication of disputes under the contract must be given effect by the New York courts. This overrides the ability to dismiss on forum non conveniens principles. The statute was applied in *Credit Français International SA v Sociedad Financier de Comercio CA*, 490 NYS 2d 670 (S Ct NY Co 1985).

Multiple actions (lis alibi pendens) A multiple jurisdiction clause may enable a lender to take simultaneous default proceedings in a number of countries. A lender might wish to do so, for example, because of the availability of assets in several jurisdictions, because it is uncertain which claim can be more speedily pressed to conclusion or because there is a possibility that an action might succeed in one country but not in another. The principles are also examined elsewhere in this series.

Arbitration

Suitability of arbitration for financial contracts Arbitration as a method of settling disputes is not generally favoured by commercial financiers and this section does no more than indicate why this should be so. However, arbitration is sometimes (though very rarely) resorted to in the case of governmental loans where the state borrower is constitutionally prohibited or is unwilling to submit to the jurisdiction of foreign courts, e.g. Brazil.

5–57   TERM LOANS: GOVERNING LAW AND JURISDICTION CLAUSES

Arbitration is sometimes employed by international development banks which have a different attitude to enforcement sanctions.

5–58 **Finality** A general feature of arbitration laws is to exclude appeal from the arbitrator's award except on very limited grounds such as absence of jurisdiction or fraud. This principle is espoused by arbitration statutes in the United States, many Continental European countries, Japan and in England but at the option of the parties: Arbitration Act 1979 s 3.

Finality can be important in, say, construction contracts where it is desirable that a decision be handed down one way or the other so that the work can proceed. Such considerations do not generally apply to financial contracts.

5–59 **Is expert adjudication required?** Where a contract involves complicated technical or factual matters, it may be an advantage for disputes to be heard by experts who do not have to be educated in the field concerned. However disputes on financial agreements do not generally involve technical questions of fact and the proceedings are commonly brought to enforce payment or to decide the law rather than to resolve factual matters. Further, the commercial courts of internationally orientated jurisdictions are well equipped to settle complex investment contests.

Privacy The privacy and confidentiality of arbitration may be inimical to the interests of lenders since arbitration weakens the sanction of adverse publicity which a defaulting borrower might wish to avoid.

5–60 **Condition precedent** Arbitration of the dispute is generally a condition precedent to enforcement through the courts. Parties who agree to submit disputes solely to arbitration will generally be bound by their agreement: *Scott v Avery* (1855) 5 HL Cas 811; Arbitration Act 1979 s 1. In view of the time which it can take to set up the arbitral tribunal, the inability of a lender to proceed to summary judgment in municipal courts where there is nothing seriously in dispute can be a significant disadvantage. It follows that the arbitral tribunal is the exclusive forum unless otherwise agreed.

Procedure Generally speaking the rules of evidence and procedure established by arbitration tribunals are (often intentionally) less developed than court procedures. The result is that the course of the arbitration can be unpredictable and rapid resolution blocked if one of the parties is not prepared to cooperate. The absence of formal procedures confers a useful flexibility in construction disputes but not generally in financial contracts.

5–61 **Enforcement** Arbitration is often held in some neutral country where neither party is situate or has assets. It will almost invariably be necessary to implement the arbitration award by further proceedings for enforcement in other jurisdictions. The court may be slower to recognise a foreign arbitral award and more inclined to investigate its validity than in the case of a judgment of a foreign court. The position has however been improved by the New York Convention on the Recognition and Enforcement of Foreign Arbitral Awards of 1958 which has been ratified by a great many countries including some European countries (including Austria and the United Kingdom), Finland, Greece, Japan, Mexico, Nigeria, Norway, Philippines, Poland, Sweden, Switzerland and the United States.

Public contracts In some countries the arbitrability of state or public contracts may be subject to restrictions which might avoid the arbitration clause altogether or prevent effect being given to an arbitration award when enforcement is sought in the prohibiting country. An example is a Venezuelan Law of July 1967.

Jurisdictional disputes Unless the arbitration clause is carefully drafted, there can be an initial dispute as to its validity and interpretation and as to whether the tribunal has jurisdiction at all. Jurisdiction clauses, which do not have to develop the methods of choosing the arbitral tribunal or the matters which may be subject to proceedings, are inherently less susceptible to this difficulty.

5–62

Expense and delay It is not necessarily the case that arbitration is speedier and less expensive than process though commercially orientated courts. Unlike judges, arbitrators have to be paid. A venue has to be arranged and paid for.

Decision ex aequo et bono It is possible that arbitrators are more inclined to make compromise awards or to apply general equitable principles than to determine the matter in accordance with strict principles of municipal law. This is not necessarily a disadvantage in, say, construction contracts where compromise solutions may not be unacceptable but in financial contracts predictability is vital. Much of course depends upon the constitution of the arbitral tribunal, the law under which the arbitration is to be conducted, and the expertise of the arbitrators.

Waiver of sovereign immunity

Terms of clause

In loans to borrowers which are foreign states or political sub-divisions or state-owned corporations, a waiver of immunity might read:

5–63

"The borrower irrevocably waives all immunity to which it may be or become entitled in relation to this Agreement, including immunity from jurisdiction, enforcement, prejudgment proceedings, injunctions and all other legal proceedings and relief, both in respect of itself and its assets, and consents to such proceedings and relief."

5–64 **State immunity** Sovereign states have long been privileged subjects of international law. Before the twentieth century hardly any country in the world would permit its courts to entertain actions brought by a private citizen against foreign sovereigns. The traditional view is illustrated by Lord Campbell's strictures in the English case of *De Haber v The Queen of Portugal* (1851) 17 QB 171, 207: "to cite a foreign potentate in a municipal court ... is contrary to the law of nations and an insult which he is entitled to resent."

The immunity which one sovereign accorded to another in his own courts has been justified on doctrines of independence and dignity, but in practice was probably based on the expedient of gaining reciprocity and because judicial actions caused diplomatic antagonisms. However as states became increasingly involved in ordinary commercial activities, the maintenance of sovereign immunity has resulted in substantial injustice to private contractors. Most commercially significant jurisdictions now hold that if the sovereign descends to the market place, he must accept the sanctions of the market place – this is known as the restrictive doctrine of immunity. Distinctions are to be made between foreign governments and the home government, between governmental and commercial acts, between the position of states, political sub-divisions and state-owned corporations, and between immunity from judgment and immunity from enforcement as well immunity from prejudgment attachments: all are treated differently. The rules are reviewed in another volume in this series of works on international financial law.

The degree to which immunity has been restricted varies greatly amongst the several jurisdictions. A degree of statutory deimmunisation has been achieved by the US Foreign Sovereign Immunities Act of 1976, the UK State Immunity Act of 1978, the Singapore State Immunity Act of 1979, the South African Foreign States Immunity Act 1981, the Canadian State Immunity Act of 1982, the Pakistan State Immunities Ordinance 1981, and the Australian Foreign State Immunities Act 1985. By contrast, in other countries, deimmunisation of commercial transactions has been achieved by case law, e.g. Belgium, France, Germany, Italy and Switzerland.

Principles of waiver clauses

5–65 It appears to be universally recognised in most industrialised states that a state may irrevocably waive immunity by express contract in advance and there is some support for the principle that a waiver from jurisdiction is not a waiver from enforcement.

The practice in financial agreements where a state or state entity is the borrower is to set out an elaborate waiver of immunity clause whereby the borrower:

- waives immunity from jurisdiction in relation to the agreement (often not necessary because the act is commercial);

- waives immunity from enforcement, execution and attachment of its assets as regards any judgment in relation to the agreement. In many industrialised countries, commercial assets are deimmunised in any event, but the position as regards embassy bank accounts is complex. In the United Kingdom, but not the United States, this waiver will deimmunise military assets such as defence contracts;

- waives immunity from prejudgment proceedings, relief and attachment in relation to its assets such as Mareva injunctions or other prejudgment injunctions or attachments. An express written consent is necessary in both the United States and the United Kingdom;

- appoints an agent for service of process within the jurisdiction so as to avoid the slow-moving procedures for diplomatic process under relevant immunity legislation (UK, US) and to confer relatively automatic jurisdiction.

In the case of both the US and UK legislation, an express waiver of immunity from enforcement is required in the case of a central bank, i.e. its assets are, generally speaking, deemed to be governmental as opposed to commercial and therefore immune from suit in the absence of an express waiver.

CHAPTER 6

SYNDICATED LOANS

Loan syndication generally

Introduction

6–1 Large loans lend themselves to syndication amongst a number of banks since a single bank may not on its own be willing or able to advance the whole amount. The essence of syndication is that two or more banks agree to make loans to a borrower on common terms governed by a single agreement between all parties. The number of banks may be very small, sometimes called a "club loan" or very numerous and, exceptionally, may run into hundreds of lenders.

Mandate

6–2 The syndication is generally initiated by the grant of a mandate by the borrower to a managing bank or group of banks setting out the financial terms of the proposed loan, authorising the managing bank(s) or "lead bank" to arrange syndication and confirming that the mandate is exclusive. The financial terms are set out in a **"term sheet"** which states the amount, term, repayment schedule, interest margin, fees, any special terms and a general statement that the loan will contain representations and warranties, covenants, events of default and other usual clauses. For a form, see the Appendix.

The managing banks may agree to **underwrite** the whole loan, i.e. agree that they will lend the whole amount if they are unable to find other participants. This underwriting "commitment" is often expressed to be subject to material changes in market conditions prior to the signing of the formal loan agreement.

This mandate is (or should be) expressed as a **non-legally binding** commitment which is subject to contract: it operates as a commercial understanding between the parties until the formal loan documentation is entered into so as to enable the parties to proceed with arranging the loan. On normal principles of contract law, there is a presumption that commercial arrangements are intended to be legally binding and hence, if the mandate were not expressed to be subject to contract, the managers might be committed to its terms if sufficiently precise. There can be a contract even though not all the terms have been agreed and even though it is intended to enter into formal documentation later: see, e.g. *Branca v Cobarro* [1947] KB 854.

Functions of lead bank

6–3 The functions of the lead or managing bank are (a) to prepare an information memorandum about the borrower and the loan in conjunction with the borrower for despatch to potential participants, (b) to solicit expressions of interest from banks, and (c) to negotiate the loan documentation.

Summary of syndication principles

6–4 **Several commitments** Each bank agrees in the loan agreement to make a separate loan to the borrower up to its stated commitment. The commitments are several: the banks do not underwrite each other in normal syndication practice. Contributions to loans are made by the banks in proportion to their commitments and payments by the borrower are, generally speaking, divided between the banks in the same proportion.

However, all the loans are made on precisely the same terms.

Agent bank For convenience of administration, one of the banks is appointed agent of the syndicate through whom payments and communications are channelled. The agent is an administrative agent and rarely has significant management functions. The agent is agent of the banks, not the borrower.

Syndicate democracy The banks may agree between themselves to delegate limited decisions to majority control, e.g. certain waivers of non-payment obligations and the right to accelerate the loan on an event of default.

Pro rata sharing The banks may also establish a degree of communality by virtue of a pro rata sharing clause designed to ensure that receipts by syndicate members arising from set-offs, litigation proceeds and the like are shared proportionately without discrimination.

Solicitation of participants

Information memorandum

6-5 A lead bank mandated to arrange a syndication of a loan will approach other banks in the market to see whether or not they would be willing to participate. Common practice is for banks who express interest to be sent an information memorandum giving financial and other information about the borrower which has been prepared in conjunction with the borrower by the managing bank.

The information memorandum generally contains: (a) the term sheet giving details of the loan; (b) details of the history and business of the borrower; (c) details of the management of the borrower; and (d) the borrower's financial statements.

International regulation of invitational material

6-6 Many commercial jurisdictions have introduced legislation regulating the circulation of information to the public inviting investment in securities in order to protect the public from fraud. Generally speaking, if an information memorandum is a prospectus which is regulated by domestic legislation, then (a) it may have to contain **prescribed information**; (b) it may have to be **registered** with a Securities Commission, a Registrar of Companies or some other authority; and (c) the liability for **misrepresentation** may be more onerous, e.g. by throwing the onus of proof on to the defence and by avoiding exclusions of liability for misrepresentation.

It will almost invariably be found however that the information memorandum will benefit from an exemption, notably:

1. The circular constitutes a **private** offering and not an invitation to the "public". But the scope of the meaning of public may involve a small group, e.g. 30 or 40 persons.

2. It is issued only to **sophisticated investors** or professional investors or experts who can be expected to look after themselves.

3. The borrower is a **government** or a government instrumentality or a municipality.

4. The participations in the loan agreement do not constitute **"securities"** or **"debentures"** within the securities legislation.

5. The circular is issued externally to **foreign** residents and, as a matter of construction, the statute is territorially limited.

In the United Kingdom and the rest of Europe the circulation of offering material to sophisticated investors is generally permitted although the UK position under the Financial Services Act 1986 is complex. But in the United States, the Securities Act of 1933 and the Securities Exchange Act of 1934 contain provisions which are more restrictive. In particular, offerings to professional dealers in securities in the United States and private offerings have to satisfy stringent terms. Nevertheless, the US courts have in effect exempted bank loan agreements and the grant of participations from the scope of the Securities Acts in the normal case by exalting the remedial purpose of the legislation over the literal meaning of the words. The courts have held that the Securities Acts are only intended to protect those purchasing securities. Generally, a "note" is not a "security" regulated by the legislation if used in relation to a commercial loan but is a "security" if it represents an investment: see generally para 16–24 *et seq.*

6–7

Misrepresentation liability

The potential liability for misrepresentation in relation to the solicitation of participants is important to both borrower and the lead bank.

6–8

If the borrower induces the loan by misrepresentation, e.g. as to the borrower's financial status, then the borrower may be liable to an action for rescission of the loan contract or be liable in damages. There will also usually be an express event of default based on a warranty as to the correctness of the information memorandum. In the normal case, a damages claim will not add anything to the claim for the loan itself, but there are exceptional circumstances where it could do so, e.g. limited recourse loans where the rights of the banks to recover the loan are limited to the cash flow from the project and the benefit of the security.

From the managing bank's point of view, the risk of misrepresentation could result in serious consequences since, if the borrower is insolvent, participants induced to enter into the loan agreement by misrepresentation for which the managing bank is responsible may turn to the managing bank as the only pocket left to pay.

For the main heads of criminal and civil liability in relation to misrepresentation and for the scope of misrepresentation law, see para 17–1 *et seq.* For the potential misrepresentation liability of borrower, managing banks and co-managers, see para 17–24 *et seq.*

Relationship between syndicate members

Severality

6–9 Syndicated loans provide that:

(a) Each bank will make loans up to its specified commitment during the commitment period.

(b) Each bank's obligations are several.

(c) Each bank's rights are divided rights.

Normal syndications are not a partnership because there is no sharing of net profits: see s 1(1) of the Partnership Act 1890. Partnership would, e.g. lead to fiduciary duties between parties (such as full disclosure and avoidance of conflicts of interest), reciprocal indemnity liabilities, and special insolvency and tax regimes.

The obligation of each bank to lend is stated to be several. Banks do not underwrite each other or guarantee to the borrower that other banks in the syndicate will remain solvent. Hence the technical rules of joint liability are unimportant in practice.

6–10 The agent bank similarly does not guarantee that a bank will lend. Agents do not usually agree to procure a substitute for a failed bank and are pure agents who, in accordance with agency law, are not personally liable for the obligations of their principals. If a bank fails to lend, the borrower has a right to claim damages from that bank (generally the extra cost of alternative finance plus any specially contemplated damages).

The rights of the banks to the loans and under the agreement are generally expressed to be divided rights, i.e. owed to each bank individually. This is to underline that separate loans are owed to each bank individually, to avoid joinder of bank actions and to facilitate individual bank set-offs: a bank may not be entitled to set off a loan due to it against a deposit if it owns the loan in undivided shares with the other banks: *Bowyear v Pawson* (1881) 6 QBD 540. The technical rules concerning joint rights are in practice unimportant.

Syndicate democracy

6–11 **Usual practice** Many syndicated term loan agreements contain provisions for decision-making by the banks. Votes are generally measured according to the amount of the banks' participations. Majorities are usually either 50 per cent or $66\frac{2}{3}$ per cent.

Invariably the powers vested in the majority banks are not nearly as extensive as those which may be vested in bondholders or bond trustees since banks are sophisticated institutions with substantial commitments in the loan and are not willing to delegate management to a majority. Further there is usually no need to protect the general interest against the quiescent or maverick bondholder who might otherwise obstruct a beneficial arrangement.

The usual powers of majorities include: 6–12

(a) waivers of breaches of **covenant** or consents to the relaxation of covenants, such as the negative pledge;

(b) determining whether an incorrect representation or an adverse change in financial condition is **material** for the purposes of the events of default;

(c) directing the agent bank to **accelerate** the loans following an event of default. Generally 50 per cent or $66\frac{2}{3}$ per cent of the banks by value can dictate, but the agent may also have an express **discretion** to accelerate without prior reference to the banks (to cover emergencies).

Generally the following amendments by majority are not permitted:

— **Waiver of the conditions precedent** to the advance of loans. Hence each bank can unilaterally suspend its obligations to advance new money if a condition precedent is not fulfilled. But in project finance this waiver may be subject to majority control since all the banks might suffer from a decision by one bank not to lend.

— Power to extend maturities or reduce the amount of **payments** or the interest rate or to change the currency.

No-action clauses No-action clauses in bond trust deeds give the trustee the sole right to take proceedings, thereby excluding the individual rights of bondholder unless, e.g. a specified proportion of the bondholders instruct the trustee to take action and the trustee fails to do so: para 10–23. Apart from project finance, these clauses do not appear in syndicated loan agreements. Hence banks can individually sue for unpaid amounts (but may have to share under the pro rata sharing clause). 6–13

Validity of majority control Powers of the majority to bind a minority have been considered in several decisions involving bondholders and trustees for bondholders. See para 10–27 *et seq*.

Payment of loans to borrower

6–14 In syndicated loans, banks make the loans proceeds available to the agent bank who pays them to the borrower. Banks take the risk of an agent bank insolvency, i.e. if the agent becomes insolvent after receiving the proceeds of the loans from the banks but before paying them to the borrower (because the agent is agent of the banks) unless it can be shown that the proceeds are impressed with a "special purpose" trust and are traceable: these common law trusts are examined elsewhere in this series of works on financial law. In practice, the risk is small.

Payments by borrower

6–15 In syndicated loans, the borrower makes payments to the agent bank who distributes them to the banks pro rata. In law, the borrower is discharged after paying the agent even if the agent fails to pay the banks. This is because the agent is the agent of the banks and payment to an agent is payment to the principal.

It is usually provided that if the agent bank distributes payments to the banks or borrower without having received funds from the payer, the recipient will refund the payment plus interest. This claw-back is to cover the risk that the agent may pay out without being able to check that it has received corresponding cleared funds. If the amounts are very large, the clause may provide that the agent need not distribute funds unless it has been able to check that it has received corresponding cleared funds. Payment systems are reviewed in another work in this series.

Pro rata sharing clauses

6–16 The clause provides in outline:

> "If any bank receives a greater proportion of its share, it must immediately pay the excess to the agent, who redistributes to the banks pro rata and the paying bank is subrogated to the claims of the banks who are paid."

The clause appears only in syndicated loans. The provision is a syndicate equality clause designed to share individual receipts by one bank but not the others, such as receipts by set-off, proceeds of litigation, individual guarantees, or direct payment by the borrower. One practical effect is to discourage unilateral action by one bank because it will only have to share litigation proceeds, unless these are exempted, which they often are. The result is to build in a degree of inertia which enhances creditor consensus and is an indirect protection for the borrower. The clause is important in government loans, because there is no mandatory pari passu treatment of creditors on bankruptcy and no fraudulent preference doctrine. It is standard in debt restructuring agreements.

The clause may allow "double-dipping". For example, a bank has 140 deposit and 100 loan. On default by the borrower, the bank sets off against 100 of the deposit, leaving 40 of the deposit. Since the bank has now received 100 more than the other banks, it must pay 100 to the agent for distribution to all the banks pro rata. This payment is out of its own funds. As a result it acquires additional debt from the other banks by subrogation to the extent of the payments to them. Hence the borrower remains indebted to that bank which then sets off against the remaining 40 of the deposit. This itself gives rise to a fresh duty to pay the other banks. The process goes on until the whole deposit is used up, so that the effect is as if the deposit had been charged to secure the participations of all the banks.

The transfer of claims to acquire set-offs is not unusual and should be effective if the contract so provides. But a building up of set-offs in the suspect period prior to insolvency is restricted in those jurisdictions which allow insolvency set-off. A second set-off after the commencement of insolvency proceedings by reason of a post-petition assignment or subrogation by contract is doubtful, but the first set-off by reason of a post-petition subrogation pursuant to a pre-petition commitment should succeed in England.

The bank which shares should be expressly entitled to be subrogated to the receiving banks to the extent the bank pays the receiving banks. Some clauses provide for express assignments, but these are cumbersome, especially in those jurisdictions which prescribe special formalities, e.g. compulsory notice to the debtor as in France and many related countries. The clause may also cover the following:

- The sharing is unwound if the initial receiving bank is obliged to repay the excess payment to the borrower's liquidator, e.g. because it was a fraudulent preference.

- Judgment proceeds received by a bank which individually sues the borrower may be excluded from the duty to share – this allows a reward to the diligent.

- Any obligation to set-off so as to produce a recovery eligible for sharing may be expressly negatived. The bank may not wish to set-off. Whether there would be a legal duty on a bank to use a set-off so as to advantage the other banks is considered most unlikely in the normal case. Consider the doctrine of marshalling of securities.

- Sharing may be excluded if the receipt is from a third party, e.g. a private guarantee given to one bank only.

- In government restructuring loans, payments in local currency and transactions comprising debt/equity swaps may be excluded. The latter would allow banks to convert defaulted debt of an insolvent state into equity participations in local companies.

6–18 The clause has had a mixed success. The main problem has been unwillingness of banks to share. Thus the clause is one where the lawyers are commanded to compose the music, but when the band starts up, nobody wants to dance. The most celebrated instances of vain attempts by disappointed banks to persuade their colleagues to share arose when some banks set off Iranian loans against deposits at the time of the Iranian revolution of 1979 and when Argentina paid all but British banks during the Falklands crisis in the early 1980s.

Outside government loans, there is no pressing reason why banks should share just because they happen to lend under the same terms, but the romantic impulse of creditor equality, springing from a common agreement, is extraordinarily potent.

Syndicate agents

Introduction

6–19 In syndicated loan agreements one of the banks is appointed as agent of the banks for the convenience of the administration of the loan.

Two commercial features of the agent's role are of key importance in contemporary practice:

(a) Agent banks are generally unwilling to assume powers to manage the loan on behalf of the banks. Their remuneration, in the form of agency fees payable by the borrower, is usually very modest – often only enough to cover telexes and out-of-pocket expenses. Risks of maladministration are therefore not paid for.

(b) The banks themselves are generally not willing to delegate large management functions to an agent bank and wish to take their own decisions.

In the result, the agent bank's functions are defined precisely, are narrow in scope and impose administrative duties: the agreement does not confer large powers. In this light, many judicial decisions on general agents and trustees who have wide discretions in the conduct of their principal's business (e.g. trading or shipping agents) should be applied with caution in the syndication context. It follows too that agent banks themselves seek elaborate protections against risks which might otherwise arise.

Most aspects of this topic are dealt with in chapter 11.

Scope of agent's authority

The duties and powers usually delegated to the agent by the loan agreement are of two kinds: 6–20

(a) Some are **duties** so that they are contractual obligations.

(b) A few are **powers** attracting the rules as to the exercise of discretions, i.e. duties of due diligence and fiduciary duties. Fiduciary duties include a duty not to act in conflict of interest and not to take secret profits.

Typically, the main functions of the agent bank are: 6–21

1. **Paying agency duties** To receive centrally the proceeds of advances made by the banks and to disburse them to the borrower; to receive payments of principal, interest and other amounts in respect of the loan from the borrower and to distribute them to the syndicate pro rata.

2. **Conditions precedent duties** To examine the authorisations, official consents, legal opinions and other documentation furnished as a condition precedent to the advance of the loan to see that they comply with the requirements of the agreement.

3. **Receipt of notices** A duty to act as representative of the syndicate for the receipt of notices from the borrower for the borrowing of loans, the selection of interest periods, prepayments and the like, and to notify the banks accordingly.

4. **Banking duties** A duty (in floating rate loans) to determine the interest rate on the basis of the quotations of reference banks and to certify the rate to the borrower and the banks.

5. **Monitoring duties** A *duty* to the banks to forward financial and other information received from the borrower under the loan agreement; a *power* to call for compliance certificates and other information from the borrower in order to monitor the progress of the borrower and its observance of the agreement.

6. **Default duties** A duty to inform the banks of actual or impending events of default of which it becomes aware; a power to *accelerate* the loan on the occurrence of an event of default (often coupled with a duty to do so if so instructed by a specified proportion of the banks). Note that the *power* to accelerate at the agent's own initiative is intended to enable the agent to act in an emergency – generally an agent will have time to consult the syndicate. There will not usually be a power to enforce the loan agreement by the taking of legal proceedings: banks prefer to retain the right to take their own individual action once the loan has been accelerated.

Agent is agent of banks not borrower

6–22 The agent bank is invariably the agent of the *banks* and not of the borrower. Except as the contract otherwise provides, an agent generally owes no duties to anyone other than his principal. Hence an agent bank could not be sued by the borrower for default by a member of the syndicate in making the loans; payments by the borrower to the agent will discharge the borrower, and payments by the banks of loan proceeds to the agent will not discharge the banks if the agent becomes insolvent and fails to pass on the proceeds.

In the case of payments, the banks take the risk of their own agent. The banks *might* be able to recover the funds in the agent's liquidation under Anglo-American law (but not in most other countries) but only if they were clothed with a "special purpose" trust and were traceable: see *Barclays Bank v Quistclose Investments Ltd* [1970] AC 567, HL.

Contractual duties of agent

6–23 The duties of the agent towards the syndicate are primarily determined by the express terms of the agency contract. An agent bank must perform its contract in accordance with the normal rules of contract law. An agent bank has no discretion to disregard the contractual instructions even though it may reasonably believe that in departing from them it would be promoting the syndicate's interests.

Agent as fiduciary

6–24 Since an agent is a fiduciary, in theory the syndicate agent is subject to general rules applying to fiduciaries, in particular:

(a) **No conflict of interest** An agent should not put himself in a position where his duty conflicts with his self-interest or a duty to another principal unless the principal has given his fully informed consent. See para 11–3 *et seq.*

(b) **No secret profits** An agent may not make a secret profit out of his agency, e.g. where the agent secretly gains some financial advantage for himself from his position. The taking of secret profits will justify dismissal of the agent, negative any right to remuneration or indemnity and render the agent liable to the principal for the full amount of the profits. See para 11–2.

(c) **Due diligence** in the exercise of his powers and discretions.

Exercise of agent bank's discretions generally

6–25 The usual practice is to limit the agent bank's discretions so as to protect the agent bank and, in the interests of the banks, to reserve management of the loan to themselves. Nevertheless many syndicated loan agreements confer some discretionary powers on the agent bank. These often include a power to call for compliance certificates and financial **information** from the borrower, a power to approval the legal formalities required as a **condition precedent** to the making of loans; and a power to **accelerate** the loans on a default.

The general rule is that every commercial agent is bound to exercise such skill, care and diligence in the performance of his duties and the exercise of his powers as is reasonably necessary for the protection of the principal. If this standard is maintained, the agent bank will not be liable for negligence even though the bank has made a mistake or error of judgment.

An agent bank in doubt should obtain instructions from the syndicate.

Monitoring duties

6–26 This is part of the duty of due diligence. Whether an agent is under a positive duty to monitor the financial condition of the borrower so as to ensure that the interests of the syndicate are protected must depend upon the express and implied terms of the agency contract. Where an agent bank has express powers, e.g. to call for financial information and compliance certificates from the borrower, the frequency with which and the circumstances in which such powers are exercised should be tested in the light of the terms of the contract, and in the absence of express provisions, the general duty of an agent to act with care, skill and diligence with the interests of the banks in mind. Normally agent banks call for compliance certificates at fixed intervals depending on the complexity of the loan, e.g. semi-annually or annually, and may do so additionally if it appears that an unnotified default may have occurred. Accounts and other formal notices received from the borrower should be passed on to the syndicate without delay.

Many syndicated loan agreements specifically state that the agent bank has no duty to monitor compliance by the borrower and provide that the agent bank need not act unless directed to do so by the majority.

This is discussed at para 11–13 *et seq*. As to the notification of events of default: see para 11–18.

Acceleration

6–27 Most loan agreements provide that the loan may be accelerated only if a majority of the banks direct the agent to do so. But sometimes the agent also has an individual discretion to cover emergencies. Whether the agent is liable for non-acceleration would depend on the facts and agency duties of due diligence. It would require exceptional circumstances for a syndicate to be better protected by an acceleration – normally this has adverse consequences and threatens an orderly debt reorganisation, e.g. it may spark off cross-defaults and oblige the directors to cease trading and cause them to apply for insolvency proceedings.

Normally loan agreements provide that an agent can refrain from exercising a power unless directed to do so by the majority banks. In any event an agent can seek the instructions of the syndicate.

Agent bank's right of indemnity

6–28 Unless otherwise provided a principal must, as a general rule, indemnify his agent against losses, liabilities and expenses incurred in the proper performance by the agent of his functions carried out within the scope of his authority unless he is negligent.

This rule of law is commonly buttressed by an express clause whereby the banks indemnify the agent against agency liabilities unless caused by the agent's wilful misconduct or gross negligence.

Removal of agent bank

6–29 The general rule is that the authority of an agent, whether or not expressed to be irrevocable, is revocable in the sense that, if an agent is removed contrary to the contract, the courts will not reinstate him by an order for specific performance. The banks may however have a claim for damages for losses suffered (if any). However, the syndicate could not revoke the agency so as to avoid an obligation to indemnify the agent.

An agent can resign and usually there is express provision for resignation subject to a successor agent being appointed. An agent bank may sometimes choose to resign if there is a conflict of interest.

CHAPTER 7

LOAN TRANSFERS AND PARTICIPATIONS

Introduction

7–1 This chapter discusses aspects of the grant of participations by the lender (the "lead bank") to another bank (the "participant") in a loan or other credit facility already entered into.

Reasons for loan transfer Under the usual method of syndication, all the banks sign the loan agreement. But an original bank may wish to transfer a loan subsequently, e.g. because there was no time to syndicate, to avoid over-exposure to a borrower, to diversify a loan portfolio, to make a profit out of trading loans, e.g. by retaining part of the margin, or to remove assets which might attract a capital adequacy requirement: para 7–37.

7–2 **Main methods** The main methods of granting participations are as follows:

1. **Assignment** The lead bank assigns a portion of the loan to the participant, or otherwise transfers a proprietary interest, e.g. by declaration of trust.

2. **Sub-participations** The lead bank agrees to pay to the participant amounts equal to the participant's share of payments received by the lead bank from the borrower.

3. **Novations** The lead bank, the participant and the borrower agree to novate a portion of the loan agreement to the participant.

4. **"Risk participations"** The participant gives a guarantee to the lead bank of part of the loan.

Securitisations Securitisations, such as home loan repackaging schemes, are much more complex. These usually involve the sale of numerous loans to a vehicle company which issues debt securities to investors secured on the loans and are discussed in another volume in this series of works on international financial law.

Terminology Often the lead bank and the participant are referred to loosely as "seller" and "buyer". Strictly only an assignment involves the sale of an asset. Some loan agreements set out procedures for the transfers and forms to be used – at one time called transferable loan certificates or transferable loan instruments. This terminology is not used now.

Agency A participant cannot acquire a direct claim against the borrower by appointing the lead bank as agent of the participant *after* the loan agreement has been signed. A principal to a contract cannot afterwards convert himself into an agent: the appointment must be made before the contract is entered into: see for example, *Keighley Maxted & Co v Durant* [1901] AC 240, HL. But in England a bank may enter into a credit agreement apparently as principal but in reality as agent on behalf of undisclosed principals provided the principals have authorised the agent to do so prior to signature of the credit agreement.

Main points in summary The main points to consider in relation to each method are:

1. **Restrictions** on the transaction, e.g. express restrictions, or an implied restriction arising from the banker's duty of confidentiality

2. Transfer of the **benefit of the loan agreement,** e.g. the tax grossing-up and increased cost clause

3. Transfer of the lead bank's continuing **commitments to lend,** e.g. under a revolving credit

4. **Set-off**

5. **Solicitation** risks on the lead bank, e.g. for misrepresentation. The basic principles discussed at para 7–1 *et seq* also apply to assignments, sub-participations and novations.

6. Transfers of **secured** and guaranteed loans

7. **Appropriation** of payments

8. Participant's **recourse** to the lead bank

9. **Rescheduling** liability for new money

10. **Management** of the participation

11. **Capital adequacy** treatment

12. **Securities regulation**

7–5　　Tax and stamp duty are outside our scope.

The articles in legal periodicals on loan participations probably run to a several dozen pieces. There are a number of US cases which have mainly been concerned with set-offs by the borrowers against the bankrupt lead bank – a question which in turn has depended initially on whether the participation was intended to be an assignment (or trust) of part of a loan, or was intended to be a sub-participation which did not give the sub-participant a proprietary interest in the loan to the borrower: often the participation was tersely documented. Many of the cases turned upon a construction of the particular agreements and the circumstances. Some of the leading US cases are: *Re Yale Express System Inc*, 245 F Supp (1965) (no set-off mutuality between borrower and sub-participant); *Federal Deposit Ins Corp v Mademoiselle of California*, 379 F 2d 660 (9th Cir 1967) (borrower could set off debt owed by insolvent lead bank against participant who acquired proprietory interest in loan – result correct in substance, but reasoning difficult to follow); *Stratford Financial Corp v Finex Corp*, 367 F 2d 569 (2d Cir 1966); *Re Alda Commercial Corp*, 327 F Supp 1315 (SDNY 1971); *Chase Manhattan Bank NA v FDIC*, 554 F Supp 251 (WD Oklahoma 1983) (set-off case involving borrower set-off on insolvency of lead bank – one of the Penn Square Bank cases following its insolvency in 1982, having hugely participated its book); *Hibernia National Bank v FDIC*, 733 F 2d 1403 (10th Cir 1984) (Penn Square set-off); *Seattle First National Bank v FDIC*, 619 F Supp 1351 (WD Okla 1985) (Penn Square set-off); *Northern Trust Co v FDIC*, 619 F Supp 1340 (WD Oklahoma 1985) (Penn Square set-off); *Franklin v CIR*, 683 F 2d (5th Cir 1982).

For English cases on the topic (which has been frequently litigated in the US) of whether the borrower could set off a deposit against a participated loan on the insolvency of the lead bank, see, for example, *Re City Life Assurance Co Ltd, Stephenson's Case* [(1926)] Ch 91, CA; *De Mattos v Saunders* (1872) LR 7 CP 570; *Boyd v Mangles* (1847) 16 M&W 337. See also *Re Galt-Canadian Woodworking Machinery Ltd* (1982) 43 CBR 228 (Ontario S Ct).

Participations by assignment

7–6　**Transaction**　Under this transaction, the lead bank assigns to the participant all or part of its rights to loans under a loan agreement, plus the pro rata benefit of the loan agreement. The assignment may be notified or unnotified. The transfer could be by way of declaration of trust or a transfer of proceeds – the fruit, but not the tree.

Some credit facilities provide for assignments by means of prescribed certificates exhibited to the loan agreement and registered with the agent. In practice, they are similar to ordinary transferable debentures which are brought into being whenever a bank wishes to transfer a loan. Most transfer certificates are now novations: see para 7–28.

It is not practicable to review the voluminous law of assignments and our object is merely to indicate the leading points. The assignment is usually of part of a debt and there is no objection to this: *Re Steel Wing Co* [1921] 1 Ch 349.

Restrictions in loan agreement: assignability The first question is whether there are any express or implied restrictions on assignability. Usually only an express prohibition will restrict disposals of debts, since the law favours free marketability of assets. But an assignment which increases the borrower's liability (such as under a tax grossing-up or an increased cost clause) might be implicitly prohibited: see *Tolhurst v Portland Cement* [1902] 2 KB 660. If there is a restriction, the participation must generally be by way of a sub-participation unless the borrower's consent is obtained.

In England an assignment contravening a prohibition is void: see *Linden Gardens Trust Ltd v Lenesta Sludge Ltd* [1993] 3 All ER 417, HL. The assignment will not be treated as a clean transfer for capital adequacy purposes: para 7–37 *et seq*.

An assignment may conflict with the banker's duty of confidentiality. Express assignability should usually be an implied waiver of this duty in favour of assignees.

Benefit of loan agreement As assignee, the participant acquires direct rights against the borrower under the loan agreement and therefore has the benefit of the whole of the loan agreement, e.g. of the tax grossing-up clause, the increased costs clause and the like.

However an assignee may be expressly excluded from the benefit of the tax grossing-up clause and the increased cost clause. As discussed in chapter 4, many credit agreements provide that assignments by the banks must not increase the liabilities of the borrower under these clauses.

Transferability of lead bank's obligations By an assignment of rights, the lead bank does not transfer obligations to the borrower so as to be released from them, notably obligations to make new loans, as in the case of a revolving credit.

The participant will agree to pay its share of new advances against a deemed assignment of the new loan: a written assignment each time is not usually necessary in Anglo-American and Germanic jurisdictions. This payment is not a loan by the participant to the borrower but a payment of the purchase price by the participant to the lead bank for the sale of a loan made by the lead bank to the borrower.

The lead bank takes the risk that the participant might default in which case the lead bank will, as against the borrower, be obliged to lend the defaulted portion.

If there are continuing commitments to lend, the lead bank's exposure to the *participant* will generally be included in the lead bank's risk asset ratio: para 7–37 *et seq*.

7–10 **Notice to debtor** Notice to the borrower and other debtors (e.g. guarantors) is desirable to bind the debtor to pay the assignee (but in syndicated loans, payments are in any event routed through the agent); to preserve priority against competing assignments (assignments generally rank according to date of notice to the debtor); to exclude new **set-offs and defences**; (in English-based jurisdictions) to convert the assignment into a **legal assignment** (but this is normally unimportant because the main advantage of a legal assignment is non-joinder of the assignor in an action by the assignee against the borrower – which is a formality); to prevent the debtor and assignor from agreeing **variations** without the consent of the participant; to improve the **capital adequacy** treatment (a non-notified assignment will usually be regarded as a clean transfer for this purpose but this is subject to detailed conditions: para 7–37); and to reduce the commercial risk that the lead bank as lender of record will be pressured into lending **new money** on a rescheduling of the borrower's debt: para 7–16.

Participants from responsible lead banks are generally perfectly content to take most of these risks and to rely on the integrity of the lead bank.

Notice to the debtor is not necessary to transfer beneficial ownership from seller to buyer in Anglo-American and Germanic jurisdictions. A loan ceases to be an asset of the lead bank (attachable by its creditors or available to its creditors on its insolvency) once the beneficial ownership is transferred, even if notice is not given to the debtor.

But in certain Napoleonic states (e.g. France, Luxembourg, and other states in the Franco-Latin group, but not Belgium) or in Japan, South Korea and certain others, the beneficial ownership of the loan is not deemed transferred from the lead bank unless the borrower consents to the assignment in prescribed form or (sometimes) a translation of the assignment is served on the borrower by an official, e.g. the French *huissier*. Without this, the assignment is void on the lead bank's insolvency and can be attached by the lead bank's creditors. The transfer will also be ignored for capital adequacy purposes. See para 7–37 *et seq*.

As to conflict of law rules on assignments, see Art 12 of the 1980 Rome Convention on the Law Applicable to Contractual Obligations.

7–11 **Set-off** The borrower may set off, as against the assigned loan, certain cross-claims owed to the borrower by the lead bank (e.g. a deposit). The position is colossally complex and is reviewed elsewhere in this series of works on financial law under the general concept of set-off against interveners, e.g. assignees and attaching creditors. However generally the borrower will have agreed in the loan agreement not to raise set-offs and this is usually effective to prevent set-offs against the participant as assignee.

The lead bank should warrant to the participant that there are no set-offs and agree to compensate the participant for set-offs exercisable by the borrower against the assigned loan.

The assignment destroys set-off mutuality between the lead bank and the borrower as regards the assigned portion, but mutuality between borrower and lead bank should remain as regards the non-assigned portion retained by the lead bank. But in principle there is set-off mutuality between the participant and the borrower for the assigned portion, e.g. if the participant owes a deposit to the borrower, even if (in England) the assignment is not notified and (probably) even if there is no language severing the portions. But the US cases on this point are difficult to follow: para 7–5.

Solicitation All sales are subject to the normal fraud and misrepresentation rules, e.g. half-truths, misleading statements, failures to correct known inaccuracies. 7–12

The lead bank generally excludes liability for credit information and validity of the loan documentation. Exclusion clauses are subject to the usual limitations.

Secured and guaranteed loans If the loan is secured or guaranteed, one should check that the security and guarantees are assignable and assign them as well: often an assignment of the loan will be construed so as to include securities for the loan but not necessarily. Any assignment of security may have to be registered in an asset register, e.g. for land or ships. But there is no objection in Anglo-American jurisdictions if the lead bank remains the trustee of the whole of the security. 7–13

Appropriation of payments Partial payments by the borrower to the lead bank should be expressly appropriated pro rata between the lead bank's retained portion and the participant's portion. 7–14

Recourse to seller Although assignors are not liable for the payment of the debt assigned unless so agreed, the agreement should specifically exclude any recourse of the participant to the lead bank if the borrower fails to pay. For capital adequacy purposes, the Bank of England requires that the seller "has given notice to the buyer that it is under no obligation to repurchase the loan nor support any losses suffered by the buyer and that the buyer has acknowledged the absence of obligation": para 7–37 *et seq.* 7–15

A lead bank may however be liable for the invalidity of the asset sold by virtue of an implied warranty. This liability is usually expressly excluded.

International Loans, Bonds and Securities Regulation

7–16 **Rescheduling and new money clause** If the assignment is notified, the participant should normally be the lender of record for new money on rescheduling (especially in the case of sovereign loans) and thus potentially be subject to official and other pressures to reschedule and to advance further loans. The pressure to lend new money is extra-legal since there is no legal obligation on an assignee to make new advances to a borrower in financial difficulties.

If the assignment is not initially notified, in order to protect the lead bank from the commercial point of view, the assignment should be notified if the borrower reschedules and the participant should confirm that it is the lender of record for rescheduling and new money. Throwing rescheduling risks on to the participant is also a Bank of England requirement for capital adequacy purposes: para 7–37.

7–17 **Management** If the assignment is unnotified, consider whether the lead bank should have power to manage the participation – vote, give consents and waivers, agree variations, enforce. A lead bank may wish to appear to control the whole loan in accordance with its policies so as to maintain its relationship with the borrower, but is then exposed to maladministration risks. A participant should aim to control its portion.

Lead banks generally exclude responsibility for continuing disclosure or monitoring by an agency-type clause on the lines found in syndicated agreements. The lead bank is in the position of a fiduciary or trustee. The usual limits on exculpations will be relevant.

Sub-participations

7–18 **Transaction** Under this transaction, the participant places a deposit with the lead bank in the amount of its participation and the lead bank agrees to pay to the participant *amounts equal* to the participant's share of the receipts by the lead bank from the borrower when and if received. Payments of the sub-funding loan are conditional on the lead bank receiving corresponding amounts from the borrower.

A contract whereby a creditor agrees that his debtor need not pay him if the debtor does not receive payment from a third party is considered to be effective under English insolvency law. This is not a forfeiture – it would only be a forfeiture if the creditor agreed that he would not be paid on the creditor's insolvency since in that case the creditor is deprived of an asset of his insolvency. The substantive effect of the conditional debt is similar to a guarantee or collateral charge by the participant-creditor of the third party's debt and hence should be tested against the usual preference rules avoiding gifts and transactions at an undervalue by an insolvent party in the suspect period.

For an outline, see the Appendix.

Participant has double-risk The lead bank does not assign or declare a trust of any part of the original loan in favour of the participant. The participant is a creditor only of the lead bank and not the borrower. If the lead bank becomes insolvent, the participant is an unsecured creditor of the lead bank and has no direct claim against the borrower (the participant is not an assignee). Therefore the participant has a double risk – the risk of the borrower and the risk of the lead bank. 7–19

This risk could be avoided if the lead bank were to charge the loan agreement to the participant. But charges are not generally acceptable to banks. A charge might infringe negative pledges and require registration or filing. The granting of a charge is rare in international practice.

An agreement to grant a charge in the future is usually poor protection since the call might in practice fall in the lead bank's suspect period for preferences voidable on insolvency.

Purpose of sub-participations The purpose is generally to transfer the risk in the loan from the lead bank to participant and for the participant to pay for his share, but without an assignment. An assignment may not be possible because of, e.g. restrictions on assignment in the loan agreement, stamp duty, or withholding tax on interest payments to the participant if he is an assignee. But sub-participations have major disadvantages, mainly for the sub-participant. 7–20

Loan agreement restrictions It would be necessary to investigate whether there are any restrictions in the loan agreement on the transaction – it is not an assignment. 7–21

Apart from the usual results of breaches of contract, the forbidden sub-participation would fail for Bank of England capital adequacy purposes: para 7–39.

Unless the loan agreement or the borrower authorises the lead bank to disclose the loan agreement and information about the borrower to prospective and actual sub-participants, the sub-participation may contravene the banker's duty of confidentiality. An implied waiver might be easy to find, e.g. if the loan has been publicised with the borrower's consent.

Benefit of loan agreement The participant is not an assignee and therefore does not obtain the benefit of the loan agreement, including compensation clauses (tax grossing-up, increased costs), an illegality clause, an interest substitute basis clause or the right to vote, give consents or manage the loan. 7–22

Obligations under the loan agreement The lead bank is not released from any of its obligations owed to the borrower under the loan agreement, notably obligations to make further advances.

If the lead bank has a continuing commitment to lend, the lead bank's exposure to the *participant* (for failure to place a corresponding deposit) will be included in the lead bank's risk asset ratio: para 7–37 *et seq*.

7–23 **Set-off** The participant is not a creditor of the borrower so there is no set-off mutuality between borrower and participant: See, e.g. *Re Yale Express System Inc*, 245 F Supp 790 (1965) and para 7–5.

The lead bank is a creditor of the borrower for the whole amount and hence there is set-off mutuality between lead bank and borrower. Any set-off should expressly trigger an obligation on the lead bank to pay the participant an amount equal to the participant's share of the amount set-off as if it were a payment by the borrower.

Solicitation As to solicitation of the participant, the transaction is subject to normal fraud and misrepresentation risks, e.g. half-truths, misleading statements, etc.

7–24 **Secured and guaranteed loans** Since the transaction is not an assignment, any security or guarantee is not transferred to the participant. Instead the participant gains the benefit of these indirectly since the proceeds of a guarantee or realised security received by the loan bank should crystallise the lead bank's obligation to pay the participant proportionally. The participation agreement should so provide.

Appropriation of payments Partial payments by the borrower should expressly be notionally appropriated pro rata between the lead bank's portion and the participant's "portion" to determine if the lead bank must account to the participant.

Partial payments should also expressly be appropriated in a specified order (to the extent the lead bank has a right of appropriation), e.g. costs, interest, principal.

Recourse to lead bank For capital adequacy purposes, the Bank of England requires that the lead bank must have given notice to the participant that it is under no obligation to support any losses suffered by the participant and that the participant has acknowledged the absence of obligation: para 7–37 *et seq*.

7–25 **Rescheduling and new money** If the borrower reschedules its debt by reason of financial difficulties, the lead bank as lender will often as such be pressured into rescheduling and advancing new money. The agreement should if possible commit the participant to a corresponding rescheduling which matches that agreed by the lead bank and oblige the participant to advance its share of new moneys to the lead bank. Without such a commitment, the lead bank may not be able to vary the original loan, or permit its novation to a central bank (in the case of sovereign reschedulings), or require the participant to contribute. The lead bank may also be obliged to repay the participant if the rescheduling involves a technical replacement of the defaulted debt by new debt (because the lead bank has been "paid").

A similar problem arises if the lead bank agrees to convert its debt into equity — as where the borrower is insolvent and the conversion is necessary to re-establish the solvency of the borrower and hence avoid insolvency proceedings. The set-off of the loan against the subscription price for the shares may be a recovery which sparks off the duty of the lead bank to pay the participant. If the consideration for the shares is the cancellation of the loan, there may be a question as to whether under the terms of the participation the lead bank is authorised to cancel the loan. The whole object of the participation is that the participant should bear the risk of the borrower's insolvency and this would be defeated if the conversion either gave rise to an obligation on the lead bank to pay the participant in full (on set-off) or if the participant could veto the conversion (on a cancellation). The contract could by appropriate language compel the participant to accept the conversion and switch the loan participation into a corresponding participation in the shares.

Similar issues arise on debt/equity swaps on state insolvency.

7–26 It is theoretically possible, but commercially difficult, for a clause completely to protect the lead bank. The result is that the position depends on negotiation. If the participant refuses to allow the lead bank to agree a debt restructuring, then this might lead to the liquidation of the borrower, with resultant loss to the participant. But a great weakness of sub-participations is that the basic purpose of passing the insolvency risk to the sub-participant can be threatened by the fact that contractual clauses acceptable to sub-participants often do not protect the lead bank completely when it matters most.

To achieve the required capital adequacy effect, the Bank of England requires that "the documented terms of the transfer are such that, if the loan is rescheduled or renegotiated, the buyer and not the seller will be subject to the rescheduled or renegotiated terms": para 7–37 *et seq.*

7–27 **Management** Consider whether the participant will have any control over management of its portion — vote, give consents and waivers, agree variations, control the conduct of enforcement. Generally lead banks aim not to yield any control, but they may incur maladministration risks. The scope of the lead bank's implied duties to participants is unsettled but common sense indicates that wherever one person has the power by contract to alter the economic position of another, the person with the power is subject to an implied duty of due diligence. In other words, it is not unreasonable to apply agency principles by analogy.

Lead banks generally exclude responsibility for continuing disclosure or monitoring by a clause on the lines of an agency clause in a syndicated loan agreement.

Novations

7–28 **Transaction** By a novation agreement, the lead bank, the participant and the borrower agree that the participant will be substituted for the rights and obligations of the lead bank according to the participant's share and that the lead bank will be released from its appropriate share of those obligations. In effect the participant becomes a new party to the loan agreement having both rights and obligations as a bank. The lead bank is repaid out of the new loan by the participant.

7–29 **Substitution certificates** As a matter of contract law, all parties to the loan agreement must usually be a party to a novation including the borrower and any syndicate agent and all other syndicate members.

Some loan agreements provide for the novation to be carried out by the execution of a prescribed form exhibited to the loan agreement. The loan agreement provides that when this has been signed by the lead bank and the participant it can be signed by the agent on behalf of all the other banks and on behalf of the borrower so as to bind all parties.

Alternatively arrangements can be established whereby, for some nominal consideration, the borrower makes an irrevocable offer to future participants to accept novations which are accepted by submission of the form of novation to the agent for signature: this relies on the contractual principle of acceptance by prescribed conduct, instead of by communication of the acceptance.

7–30 **Transfer of obligations and benefits** The principle advantage of a novation is that continuing obligations of a lead bank, e.g. to make fresh advances or to indemnify the agent, are transferred to the participant and the lead bank is released, i.e. does not underwrite the participant if the participant fails to perform. Further, the participant has all the benefits of the loan agreement as a bank, e.g. the tax grossing-up clause, the illegality clause, and the increased costs clause. There is no need for notice to close out set-offs and the like. There are usually no problems over the bankers duty of confidentiality because the borrower has consented to the novation.

Set-off There will be normal set-off mutuality between the participant and the borrower as if the participant were an original bank.

Solicitation Usual misrepresentation and fraud rules will apply. Exclusion clauses are standard.

Secured and guaranteed loans The novation operates as the creation of a new debt in favour of a new creditor – the participant who was not identified at the time the loan agreement was originally entered into. The old debt is cancelled. Hence any guarantee or security might lapse.

7–31

The obstacle can be avoided by initially granting the security and the guarantee in favour of a trustee to secure a parallel obligation from the borrower to the trustee to pay the debt and on terms whereby the trustee holds the benefit of the security for a class of beneficiaries which includes the original banks and any persons who may become banks pursuant to the novation procedure. There is no objection in Anglo-American law to a trust for a class of future unascertained persons provided that the identity of the beneficiaries can be ascertained when the trust property vests.

The trust device is not usually available if the secured assets are situate in countries which do not recognise the trust. This is because mortgages over land, for example, must be registered in the name of the actual creditor – not the trustee.

Special points to consider Since a novation creates a new debt in favour of a new lender, it should be considered whether the new debt contravenes a borrowing limit of the borrower (e.g. if it has in the meantime used up any remaining room under its borrowing limits), whether any exchange control consents are required for the new debt, and whether any new registration of security is required: this is not necessary in the case of original security granted to a trustee so far as English law is concerned.

7–32

Appropriation of payments The point does not arise because the agent bank pays the participant directly in place of the lead bank.

Recourse to seller The participant has no recourse to the lead bank under a normal novation.

7–33

Rescheduling clause The participant is lender of record for rescheduling purposes.

7–34

Management The participant becomes a bank for the purposes of syndicate voting, the right to recover direct from the borrower and the right to manage its participation.

Risk participations

7-35 **Transaction** This is financial vernacular for a routine transaction. The participant gives a guarantee to the lead bank of a portion of the obligations owed by the borrower to the lead bank – a partial guarantee.

The main difference with the other forms of participation is that the participant does not provide funding to the lead bank. The participant merely takes the risk.

The transaction is a partial guarantee and therefore attracts ordinary guarantee law.

This method is usually inadvisable if there is a pro rata sharing clause in the loan agreement which applies to payments of the lead bank's participation from any source, not just from the borrower; the lead bank would have to share payments under the guarantee. The impact of the pro rata sharing clause might cause the participant to guarantee the entire syndicate.

7-36 **Benefit of loan agreement** The participant does not have any of the benefits under the loan agreement until subrogated. Hence the participant will not benefit from compensation clauses (tax grossing-up, increased costs), the illegality clause, or the substitute basis clause. It follows, that, for example, if an increased cost is imposed on the participant in relation to its guarantee it cannot look to the borrower for compensation.

Loan transfers and capital adequacy

7-37 **Basle Agreement** Most of the leading central banks have adopted the 1988 Basle Agreement whereby they agree that banks must maintain capital (equity plus disclosed reserves plus some types of subordinated debt) of at least 8 per cent of their assets and exposures. The various categories of assets etc. are given a risk-weighting which is a broad-brush method of determining their riskiness. Thus bank claims on OECD central banks have a zero risk weight, residential mortgages a 50 per cent risk weight, and ordinary loans to the private sector a 100 per cent risk weight, i.e. for each private sector loan the bank must have $8 capital for every $100 lent. See chapter 22.

7-38 **Loan transfers** A bank may wish to reduce its capital requirement by transferring loans to a participant. The question then is whether the bank has effectively transferred the risk so that it is no longer exposed to the borrower and hence need not maintain capital against this exposure.

The Bank of England's Notice on Loan Transfers and Securitisation of February 1989 amended in 1993 sets out rules for the capital adequacy treatment of loan transfers. The main object is to see that the lead bank legally and commercially transfers the risk (both rights and obligations) to the participant so that the loan is no longer a loan by the lead bank for capital adequacy purposes. This Notice does not apply to banks not regulated by the Bank of England.

If the transfer is not a "clean transfer", the Bank of England may treat the seller as continuing owner of the loan which will attract a risk weight and therefore a capital requirement.

General conditions In all cases (assignments, sub-participations, novations) the following main conditions (in summary) must be satisfied if the transfer is to qualify for Bank of England capital adequacy treatment of loan transfers: 7–39

1. The transfer does not contravene the terms and conditions of the underlying loan agreement and all the necessary consents have been obtained.
2. The buyer has no formal recourse to the seller for losses and the seller is not obliged to repurchase the loan.
3. The documented terms of the transfer are such that, if the loan is rescheduled or renegotiated, the buyer and not the seller would be subject to the rescheduled or renegotiated terms.

Detailed conditions There are detailed additional requirements according to whether the participation is a notified or non-notified assignment or a sub-participation. 7–40

If there are continuing commitments on the lead bank to continue lending to the borrower, then the lead bank will have an exposure to the *participant* which will attract a risk weight. But this does not apply to a novation because the lead bank's commitment to lend is transferred to the participant.

Loan transfers and securities regulation

If a loan transfer is an "investment" within the Financial Services Act 1986 or a "security" within the US securities legislation, then it may attract a requirement for the participants to be authorised, prospectus filing requirements, the furnishing of prescribed information and various anti-fraud rules. 7–41

Generally loan transfers will not be caught, e.g. a bank loan is not a "debenture" or a "security" or the sale is to an exempt sophisticated investor. In addition there are specific exemptions under the Financial Services Act 1986 which were promulgated for the avoidance of doubt, especially since some lawyers feared that some bank loans may technically be "debentures" which are investments regulated by that Act.

Securities regulation is discussed generally in chapters 14 to 21, and bank loans and participations at para 16–24 *et seq*.

CHAPTER 8

BOND ISSUES: GENERAL PRINCIPLES

Comparison of bond issues and syndicated loan agreements

Main differences

8–1 Bond issues are issues of transferable debt securities by a borrower to investors who may be limited in number or to the public at large in return for a subscription price.

International issues are issues of bonds to international investors. The chief differences with issues of debentures in a domestic market are that international bonds are negotiable bearer instruments, not registered, and, since they are issued to sophisticated investors, they can usually be issued without compliance with rules for the prescribed contents and filing of prospectuses.

These chapters are concerned only with international bonds, not domestic issues.

8–2 Some of the key differences between bond issues and loan agreements are:

1. **Transferability** Bonds must be easily transferable and must usually be negotiable. Banks do not usually trade in loans.

2. **Character of investors** Syndicated bank loans are made by sophisticated institutions, well able to analyse the credit risks involved. Bond investors may ultimately be the public at large who are not in a position to assess credit risks or the value of the securities. The law has therefore intervened to protect the public, e.g. by prospectus disclosure requirements. But in practice most international bondholders are also sophisticated institutions – insurance companies, banks, governments, large corporates, pension funds, investment funds. Hence international bonds usually benefit from "sophisticated investors" exemptions in relation to prospectus requirements.

3. **Number and anonymity of investors** International investors in bonds

are numerous and often anonymous because the bonds are bearer instruments. One result is that it is difficult to organise bondholders to approve modifications, to waive defaults or to agree a restructuring plan in the event of financial difficulties. Provisions in a trust deed or in corporate legislation whereby bondholders can vote on proposals affecting the bonds ameliorate this obstacle, but in practice modifications are much more difficult than is the case with bank loans where only a few banks need to be consulted. As a consequence, the covenants and events of default in bonds are much less rigorous than in syndicated loan agreements.

4. **Issue mechanics** Syndicated bank loans can make provision for a revolving credit, a standby facility, multicurrency options, complex project security arrangements and the like. They are a highly flexible form of financing which can be tailored to meet the needs of a particular transaction. Bond issues, on the other hand, do not enjoy this flexibility. The bonds must be sold to the market when there is a suitable "window". The issue mechanics can be cumbersome by reason of the marketing arrangements, the need for a formal offering circular, the desirability of listing and the impact of securities regulation. But these disadvantages can be mitigated in the case of debt issue programmes employing framework agreements and in practice the procedures in other cases are streamlined.

Detailed comparison

The following are some detailed similarities and differences between bonds and syndicated credits. Obviously the contractual variety is immense and this short review limits itself to typical terms only. The clauses mentioned below are explained elsewhere in this work.

Disclosure requirements Syndicated loans are usually exempt from prescribed disclosure and prospectus registration requirements. Bonds issued outside the United States can be structured so as to be exempt from disclosure and prospectus registration requirements. There are stock exchange disclosure requirements if the bonds are listed.

Information memoranda for syndicated loans are informal and not detailed. Bond issue offering circulars are sometimes more formal – usually because of stock exchange requirements – but short forms are used in the case of established issuers who are subject to stock exchange continuing disclosure requirements so that the information is already publicly available.

High disclosure standards apply in both cases, but contracting-out by managers is usual, again in both cases.

Documentation For syndicated loans, the marketing documents are informal, e.g. telexes to prospective participants and an information memorandum. For bonds, the marketing documents are more elaborate, e.g. formal invitational telexes, subscription agreement, (sometimes) underwriting and selling agreements, and a formal offering circular. But many of the documents are standardised and the documentation can be further reduced by the use of master forms covering future issues under debt issue programmes.

Syndicated loans are evidenced by a loan agreement. For bonds there are a trust deed or fiscal agency agreement and paying agency agreements. The issue is evidenced by bonds which are security printed, because they are bearer securities.

Advance of funds Syndicated loans are made on request by the borrower during a commitment period which allows multiple drawdowns and flexibility of timing.

Bonds are issued in a single advance. Two or more instalments are possible but cumbersome. Market conditions limit flexibility on timing. But the use of master agreements enhances the ability of the issuer to issue bonds quickly at intervals.

For syndicated loans, revolving and standby credits are available. Bonds can approximate to this by "tap" issues. As mentioned, under dealer programmes the issue mechanics can be reduced to the minimum in the case of pre-standardised framework documentation. For example, the procedures can be limited to an exchange of telexes followed by an issue of notes by the agent on behalf of the issuer.

Currency conversion Loans can be converted into other currencies periodically. For bonds, periodic currency conversion is impracticable.

Interest Loan interest is usually floating. The borrower can select different interest periods. Bonds have fixed or floating interest rates. The interest periods for floating rate notes are fixed and the issuer has no right of interest period selection.

Default interest on loans usually is at an increased penalty rate, but this is not the practice for bonds.

Repayment For loans, anything may be agreed, e.g. bullet, instalments, or variable according to project cash flows. For bonds, there is limited flexibility – the redemption is usually bullet or by fixed instalments. Sometimes there is a purchase fund.

Voluntary prepayment For loans, full or partial prepayments on interest payment dates are usually allowed. Prepayment premiums are unusual. In bonds, prepayments are usually not permitted. Sliding scale premiums on voluntary prepayments have been seen, but are rare in the eurobond market. As in the case of loans, prepayments are invariably allowed without premium if a withholding tax is imposed.

For loans, prepayments are made pro rata between the banks. For bonds, prepaid bonds are selected by lot so that chance decides if a bondholder is prepaid.

8–8 **Margin protections** Loans have increased costs protection but this is not so in floating rate notes. Both have tax grossing-up, but the tax grossing-up in bonds is more protective of the issuer.

Loan agreements contain an illegality clause, but bonds do not.

8–9 **Payments and equality** Payment of loans is made through an agent bank who is agent of the lenders. Payment of bonds is made against presentation of bonds and coupons at paying agents (choice of several). Paying agents are agents of the *issuer*. In practice bonds are usually held by custodians for the bondholders (Euroclear or Cedel) and it is the custodians who present them for payment.

Loan agreements contain a pro rata sharing clause but there is no pro rata sharing in bonds. The pari passu clause primarily insists on pro rata payment on insolvency which is the law in any event, but might possibly require non-discrimination before actual insolvency. However, if a trustee is appointed, the trustee generally distributes pro rata after a default, but the double-dipping effect of a pro rata sharing clause is not available.

There is a set-off clause in loans, but not in bonds.

8–10 **Warranties** Loan agreements contain elaborate warranties. Breaches are an event of default entitling the banks to suspend drawdowns, to cancel the commitments and to accelerate. Evergreen warranties, which must be continuously true, are common. In bonds, the only warranties are in the subscription agreement with the managers entitling them to cancel issue. Breach of warranty is not an event of default in bonds, so there is no acceleration for breach of warranty unless rescission is available as matter of law, e.g. for misrepresentation.

8–11 **Covenants** Loan agreements contain detailed information requirements, a negative pledge, a pari passu clause, an anti-disposal clause, and controls on changes of business. Financial ratios are common. There are often other covenants relating to the maintenance of exchange control consents, the maintenance of corporate status, and other matters. Project and secured credits bristle with covenants.

In bonds, information requirements are laconic, such as the provision of accounts or as required by the listing undertaking with the stock exchange. The negative pledge is very limited but a pari passu clause is standard. Sometimes an anti-disposal clause is an event of default. Usually there are no other covenants. The trust deed, if any, may contain reporting requirements and covenants as to the maintenance of exchange controls, corporate status, etc.

Events of default In loans, the defaults can be elaborated. A material adverse change clause is common. Breach of warranty is a default.   8–12

In bonds, the defaults are less stringent; there are less of them and longer grace periods. A material adverse change clause is very rare. Breach of warranty in the subscription agreement is not an express default.

In loans, accelerations require a majority bank consent but banks can individually suspend drawdowns on a default. Usually individual enforcement rights for sums unpaid are preserved. In bonds, acceleration and enforcement by individual holders is typical, but if there is a trustee then, by virtue of a no-action clause, only the trustee can accelerate and enforce, subject to ultimate bondholder control.

Modification In loans, unanimity is usually required for changes to the financial terms. Majority bank waivers are required for non-financial matters. In bonds, individual bondholder consent is required unless there is a provision in the bonds or a trust deed or under corporate law for bondholder meetings. These usually allow changes to the financial terms by specified majority resolutions.   8–13

Transfer Loans are assignable, sometimes subject to restrictions, e.g. borrower consent and no extra costs to be thereby incurred. Novations are usually contractually sanctioned. Bonds are negotiable and so are freely transferable.

Prescription There is no express provision in loan agreements. Hence the statutory limitation periods apply, e.g. six to 12 years.   8–14

In bonds there is a contractual cancellation of unpresented claims at the expiry of the stated period. The statutory periods may be contractually shortened.

Governing law, forum, waiver of immunity These are standard in both loans and bonds.

Marketing and distribution of bonds

Main methods of marketing and distribution

8–15 Broadly, the marketing method varies according to (a) the need or otherwise to test market response by a preliminary prospectus, and (b) the identity and range of the proposed investors, e.g. private, sophisticated or public. The main techniques may be summarised as follows:

1. **Private placements** A manager or group of managers subscribe for the whole issue and place the issue with selected private clients or even a single private investor. These issues are not usually listed, but may be.

8–16 2. **Preliminary prospectus offerings** The purpose of this method is to test the market before the managers fix the interest rate and any discount (or premium) on subscription. The managers contact a group of selected financial institutions with brief details of the issue and the issuer and an indication of the likely issue terms. The managers also send out a preliminary prospectus which omits the issue terms and is stated to be subject to amendments – the "red herring" or "pathfinder" prospectus. In the light of the response, the managers agree the interest rate with the issuer, arrange for the issue to be underwritten and then offer the bonds to the interested financial institutions. These institutions hold the bonds themselves or in due course on-sell to their clients or to the public, if permitted by securities regulation.

This is the traditional method followed in the case of an international eurobond offering and US and Canadian domestic offerings. But many eurobond issues are now "bought" deals: the managers dispense with the preliminary prospectus, buy the entire issue themselves and then on-sell to dealers.

3. **Impact day offerings** In this case the managers fix the issue terms with the issuer and announce the offering by public advertisement on an impact day. The public can apply on application forms for the securities within a stated period. The disadvantage of this method is that the managers are not able to fix the issue terms in the light of an initial market response and must hope the terms they decide on will attract sufficient investor interest. This is the method used for UK domestic offerings. It has never been used for eurobonds.

Many permutations of these three basic methods are possible in the various capital markets.

London eurobond issues: structure

8–17 The following describes the marketing techniques for a London eurobond issue.

The classical London eurobond structure involves the establishment of a hierarchy of three groups: (a) the **managers** (between three and, say, 12) who arrange the issue; (b) the **underwriters** comprising a larger group of financial institutions who agree to underwrite the issue in case investors do not subscribe; and (c) the **selling group**, comprising professional dealers in securities who place the bonds with their clients.

Often, there may only be two groups (managers and underwriters) or, more commonly nowadays, even only one (the managers). Administratively one lead manager is usually charged with organising the issue and preparing the documentation.

London eurobond issues: documents

The principal documents for a eurobond issue would include: 8–18

> The **prospectus** or **offering circular** giving information about the issue and the issuer and furnished to the selling group.
>
> A **subscription agreement** between the managers and the issuer setting out the terms upon which the managers agree to purchase or procure purchasers for the bonds: see the form in the Appendix. These terms may be summed up as follows:
>
> — **Subscription** The issuer agrees to issue and the managers agree to subscribe for, or procure subscribers for, the bonds in return for a commission, and subject to listing, execution of the documents, and the warranties remaining true until the issue is made. In English practice, the liability of the managers is joint and several, i.e. each manager is liable to subscribe the whole issue if the selling group, the underwriters and the other managers all fail. In US practice, the commitments of the managers (usually called underwriters) are several.
>
> — **Warranties** The issuer gives warranties on the lines of those in term loan agreements – see para 3–1 *et seq*. But there is a more elaborate warranty as to the accuracy of the offering circular. These warranties are given only to the managers – not investors. Breach is not an express event of default in the bonds.
>
> — **Market disruption** The managers are permitted at their discretion to terminate the agreement at any time prior to closing in the event of market disruption. The usual clause allows this "if, in the opinion of the managers, there shall have been such a change in national or international financial, political or economic conditions or currency exchange rates or exchange controls as would in their view be likely

to prejudice materially the success of the offering and distribution of the bonds or dealings in the bonds in the secondary market". Since the time between signature and closing is often no more than a few days, this clause is rarely used and it is probably not worth spending too much time on it, especially as all parties have a commercial interest to complete the issue, unless there really is a good reason to "pull" it.

– **Miscellaneous** The agreement contains miscellaneous clauses as to expenses, stabilisation, compliance with securities regulation, jurisdiction, waiver of immunity and governing law.

Underwriting agreements between the managers and the underwriters setting out the terms upon which the underwriters agree to underwrite the issue in specified proportions in return for a commission.

Selling agreements between the managers and the selling group members setting out the terms upon which members of the selling group agree to sell the bonds. The main purpose of this agreement is to throw the onus upon selling group members to comply with securities regulation and it therefore contains elaborate selling restrictions, e.g. not sell the bonds into, or deliver the offering circular or other invitational material into, jurisdictions where the distribution would be unlawful, in particular the United States.

A managers' agreement between the managers delegating the organisation of the issue to the lead manager and providing for the division of the management commission and the underwriting shares. The London market has a standard form agreement developed by a market association which is deemed to be signed when the subscription agreement is signed.

A trust deed (if there is a trustee) between a financial institution as trustee and the issuer whereby the trustee is appointed trustee for the bondholders to protect their interests.

A fiscal agency agreement (or, where there is a trustee, **a paying agency agreement**) between the issuer and a bank whereby the issuer appoints a fiscal or paying agent and sub-paying agents (always banks) in various international centres to make payments to the bondholders.

A global bond, pending printing of the definitive bonds.

The **bonds** themselves issued by the issuer and containing the terms of the loan.

Issue procedures

The traditional procedure is as follows. The lead manager arranges for the documents to be prepared. On the "launch", the lead manager sends an invitational telex to prospective underwriters and selling group members (if there are any) setting out brief terms of the issue (except the subscription price and coupon) and (in the case of a first-time issuer) a summary of the issuer's business and accounts. The lead manager sends the preliminary offering circular to the same people. The managers and issuer then agree the interest coupon and subscription price (i.e. par, discount or premium) and the underwriters agree to underwrite. Following this agreement, the subscription agreement is signed by issuer and managers. The managers are now legally committed. The final prospectus is despatched to buyers. The selling group members or other buyers settle how many bonds they are prepared to buy. The trust deed/fiscal agency and paying agency agreements are signed. The listing is confirmed by the stock exchange. At the closing, the issuer delivers the conditions precedent documentation and delivers the global bond to a common depository (custodian) for the clearing system (either Euroclear or Cedel) and the selling group members or other buyers of the bonds pay the lead manager the subscription price and the lead manager transfers the proceeds of subscription to the issuer. The common depository may be used as agent to pay the issuer against receipt of the global bond. In due course the definitive bonds are issued when printed.

The whole procedure usually takes between a week and three weeks.

Nowadays, most issues are "bought" deals. There are no underwriters and no formal selling group. The issue is announced to the market via a dealers screen, at which time the terms are fixed, and telexes are then despatched. The managers agree with the issuer to subscribe the whole issue themselves and they sell the bonds to their clients and other dealers.

Stabilisation

The managers are usually authorised by the issuer and underwriters to stabilise the bonds. Stabilisation is a procedure whereby the managers over-allot or under-allot to limit or create demand during the initial distribution of the bonds. Stabilisation is generally regarded as necessary to maintain an orderly distribution – otherwise the price might fluctuate wildly according to speculative dealings not related to the quality of the paper. For example, dealers wishing to make a quick profit on the selling commission will push up the price by their demands and the price may then collapse as they dump the bonds in the market. Stabilisation may conflict with rules as to market-rigging, insider trading and short-selling and accordingly has to be specially exempted by securities regulation (it is so exempted in the UK and US, subject to very detailed conditions).

Listing of bonds

Stock exchanges

8–23 Bonds which are intended to reach a large number of investors are generally listed on a stock exchange. For eurobond issues the most common stock exchanges are the London and Luxembourg stock exchanges. Other stock exchanges include Singapore, Frankfurt and Zurich depending on the target investor market. New York is not available for eurobond issues because SEC requirements make this impracticable.

Advantages of listing

8–24 The main advantage of listing is access to investors: listing enlarges the number of investors to whom the bonds can be sold. For example, many institutions such as pension funds, insurance companies and banks are for prudential reasons prohibited by law, official guidelines or their own self-imposed policies from investing in unlisted securities. Sometimes exchange controls may limit investment in unlisted securities but allow the holding of listed portfolios. Hence, listing greatly improves marketability.

A secondary advantage is that the stock exchange quotes the current price of the bonds based on prices at which the securities have changed hands so that investors benefit from a reasonably objective assessment of the current price. In practice very little trading of eurobonds is effected on stock exchanges since most dealings are carried out in the "over the counter" market, i.e. between dealers on behalf of their clients.

Disadvantages of listing

8–25 There are some disadvantages of a listing. The issuer must comply with the stock exchange disclosure requirements. The issuer must usually enter into a listing undertaking or its equivalent with the stock exchange whereby (inter alia) it commits itself to produce continuing information and to notify events which may lead to a false market in the securities, e.g. adverse changes which are not public knowledge and which may significantly affect the issuer's ability to meet its obligations. A stock exchange's listing requirements may change during the currency of securities and impose more onerous disclosure obligations. The issuer may be limited by the terms of the subscription agreement from de-listing or listing elsewhere. Listing may impede a rapid issue to take advantage of a "window" in the market. This is because stock exchange authorities may require listing particulars (offering circular, constitutional documents, issue documents, authorising resolutions etc.) to be submitted in advance of the issue of the securities, so that they can check them, although European stock exchanges often streamline their requirements so as to reduce this disadvantage in the case of euro issues.

Most stock exchanges require a paying agent to be located within the jurisdiction (not so in London or Luxembourg). Finally, the stock exchange may require a trustee to represent the bondholders and to monitor the issue (not so in London or Luxembourg).

Tax considerations for bonds

The ability of an issuer to make a bond issue and the structure of the bond issue are vitally affected by tax considerations. The two basic tax requirements are as follows:

1. The issuer must be able to pay interest free of withholding tax to investors. Investors are not willing to invest in bonds where the interest is reduced by taxation at source so that for every 100 of interest they receive only, say, 70. Bonds invariably contain a grossing-up clause which would make it prohibitively expensive to pay the interest plus the amount equal to tax. For grossing-up clauses, see para 4–160 *et seq*.

    If there is a withholding tax at source, then it may be possible to avoid the tax by structuring the issue differently. For example, the issuer could arrange for the bonds to be issued by an overseas finance vehicle located in a jurisdiction which does not impose a withholding tax. The parent guarantees the issue. The finance vehicle issuer on-lends the proceeds of the issue to the parent. All this increases the cost because a finance subsidiary must be set up and administered in accordance with local corporate law, and nominee directors must be appointed, paid and protected. Various tax haven states compete for the market by proffering the lowest common denominator of corporate formality and disclosure; they can be thwarted only by tax penalties by other states imposed on the parent to whom the proceeds are on-lent. The local jurisdiction might require a small taxable profit to be made locally which will necessitate a spread between the bond interest and the on-lending interest: their object is effectively to charge a small fee for the service, levied in the form of tax. In the past, both the Netherlands Antilles and the Netherlands were useful tax havens for this purpose by reason of a satisfactory network of double taxation treaties, but many developed countries have dismantled withholding taxes on eurobond issues so that their business enterprises can borrow in the international capital markets. Alternatively, it may be possible to use the bearer depository receipt structure discussed at para 9–27 *et seq*.

2. The issuer must be able to deduct interest payments for the purposes of determining liability to tax on its income. If the issue is by a finance subsidiary, the company to which the proceeds are on-lent must be able to deduct the interest on the on-lending. The rules depend upon the jurisdiction.

8–27   In the United States the US Tax Equity and Fiscal Responsibility Act of 1982, as amended (TEFRA), is designed to discourage the avoidance of US tax by the holding of anonymous bearer instruments. It does this by imposing tax sanctions on an issuer (e.g. an excise tax and denial of interest deduction) and on the holders of bonds, unless the bond is in registered form. Hence, if it is desired that the securities should ultimately be available in the secondary market to US investors, then the bond should provide for a registered option so that a US tax-paying investor can exchange his bearer bond for a registered bond. There are detailed protections for off-shore issues of eurobonds to protect issuers from unwittingly being exposed to tax sanctions if a US person buys a bearer bond. For the detail, see chapter 21.

In the United Kingdom, interest payments by a UK company on eurobonds can qualify for exemption from deduction of UK tax at source under s 124 of the Income and Corporation Tax Act 1988 if the bond is a *bearer* security quoted on a recognised stock exchange.

Negotiability of bonds

Meaning of negotiability

8–28   International debt instruments must be freely transferable. In practice they are usually negotiable, e.g. bearer bonds transferable by delivery, certificates of deposit or promissory notes. If they are non-negotiable they will commonly be transferable only by written instrument: the name of the holder is noted in a register maintained by registration agents of the issuer.

Negotiability must be distinguished from mere transferability or assignability. The main characteristic of negotiability is that the holder in due course acquires the property in the instrument and all rights under it free of any defects in title of a prior holder or defences available to the issuer against a prior holder. See below.

English law of negotiability

As regards English law, there are only two ways in which an instrument can acquire the characteristic of negotiability: by statute or by mercantile usage in the English mercantile world. An instrument cannot become negotiable by agreement between the parties or by custom which is not general. 8–29

As to statute, the Bills of Exchange Act 1882 recognises the negotiability of bills of exchange, promissory notes and cheques. But the requirements set out in the Act as to certainty of amount and unconditionality will almost never be satisfied by bearer bonds in the form encountered in international bond issues. Thus an instrument with a floating rate of interest or a currency indemnity is uncertain. If it has events of default, it is conditional.

As to mercantile usage, it has been firmly established in England and indeed in many other jurisdictions that a debt instrument may become negotiable if the financial community treats it as such. Thus in *Goodwin v Robarts* (1876) 1 App Cas 476 scrip issued by the Russian Government was held to be negotiable because merchants in England so regarded it. On the other hand in *Picker v London and County Banking Co* (1887) 18 QBD 515, CA, bonds issued by the Prussian Government were treated as negotiable in Prussia but not in England, and it was held that they were not negotiable. The London certificate of deposit acquired negotiability by custom in England in 1966. Others are various forms of bearer depository receipts and bearer participation certificates. The custom need not be long-standing since the test is the frequency of transaction. However, outside the Bills of Exchange Act 1882, only *bearer* instruments have been treated as negotiable: registered or nominative instruments do not qualify.

The law shows a benign disregard for theories defining rigid attributes necessary to qualify a bearer document as negotiable. In *Edelstein v Schuler* [1902] 2 KB 144 (following the leading case of *Bechuanaland Exploration Co v London Trading Bank* [1898] 2 QB 658) Bingham J said: 8–30

> "In my opinion, the time has passed when the negotiability of bearer bonds, whether government bonds or trading bonds, foreign or English, can be called into question in our courts. The existence of usage has so often been proved and its convenience is so obvious that it might be taken now to be part of the law."

In *London Joint Stock Bank v Simmons* [1892] AC 201, Lord Macnaghten said:

> "In a matter of this sort, it is not, I think, desirable to set up refined distinctions which are not understood or are uniformly and persistently ignored in the daily practice of the Stock Exchange."

Bearer and registered bonds compared

8-31 A comparison of some of the differences between a bearer negotiable bond and a registered non-negotiable bond will indicate some of the reasons that registered instruments are inconvenient in the international markets.

Notification to issuer Under the laws of some jurisdictions, the sale of a debt is *invalid* on the bankruptcy of the *seller* and as against execution creditors of the seller if the debtor has not been notified, often in prescribed form, e.g. France, Luxembourg, Italy, Japan, S Korea. Hence the debt still belongs to the seller and goes to his creditors on his insolvency.

In other countries, notification is desirable (e.g. for priorities), but does not affect validity on the bankruptcy of the seller, e.g. England, most US states, Germany.

In England, if notice is not given, the transferor must be joined in any action against the debtor, although the debtor can waive this. The holder of a negotiable bond can sue in his own name.

Anonymity Bearer bonds preserve anonymity, a feature desired by some international investors.

8-32 **Transfer** A bearer bond is transferable by delivery. A registered bond requires the filing of an instrument of transfer together with the bond certificate with the registration authority, possibly in a distant country. Payments are made to those on the register on a record date, e.g. 15 days before the interest payment or redemption date to enable the issuer to prepare and post the payment orders for interest to the registered holder: this gap is inconvenient. On the other hand bearer bonds carry with them the risk of theft or fraud. This risk is greatly reduced by depositing the bonds with custodians

8-33 **Title** The purchaser of a bearer bond who becomes a holder in due course can acquire a better title than the person he took it from. This enhances certainty and hence marketability. In the case of a non-negotiable registered bond, a transferee acquires no title if he takes a transfer from a thief who has stolen the original certificate and forged the owner's signature on the transfer: *Barton v London & North Western Railway* (1889) 24 QBD 77, CA.

Priorities The purchaser who becomes a holder in due course of a negotiable bond will normally take free of other interests, e.g. the claim of a third party to whom the bond has been hypothecated or the claim of a beneficiary for whom the bond is held in trust. The position of the purchaser of a registered bond is less secure. The English priority rules are complex but in broad terms the purchaser of a registered instrument will take free of these earlier competing interests only if he is not on actual or constructive notice of the prior interest and secures registration first: see, e.g. *Fry v Smellie* [1912] 3 KB 282, CA; *Peat v Clayton* [1906] 1 Ch 659, and generally on the subject *Colonial Bank v Cady* (1890) 15 App Cas 267, HL.

Set-offs and other defences of issuer In principle the transferee of a registered bond is subject to rights of set-off which the issuer could claim and which arise out of most claims contracted before the issuer has notice of the transfer. However, it is usually provided that registered debentures are to be transferable free from any claims which the issuer could set up against the original or any intermediate holder and in England such a provision is effective: *Re Blakely Ordnance Co* (1867) LR 3 Ch App 154. Negotiable bonds are in any event free of this difficulty: see Wood, *English and International Set-off* (1989) Sweet & Maxwell, para 12–68 *et seq*. The possibility of unknown set-offs would inhibit marketability.

Governing law of negotiability

In conflict of laws, negotiable instruments tend to be treated like chattels and are not governed by the rules which apply to ordinary assignments of claims. They are like chattels because, in contrast to an ordinary debt signified by a mark in a book, the whole claim is represented by a tangible document which has to be produced to be paid. Further the essence of negotiability is certainty and predictability which requires simple hard and fast rules so that a purchaser can know which law he has to look to see whether he gets good title. Generally, therefore, apart perhaps from the legal effect of transfers between the immediate parties, negotiability and its consequences tend to be determined according to the law of the place where the negotiation takes place, namely, where the instrument is at the time of delivery: see Dicey Rule 193; s 216 of the US Conflicts Restatement; *Lloyds Bank v Chartered Bank of India* [1929] 1 KB 40, CA. The rationale, originating from pre-telex days, is that this is the law which the holder would be most likely to consult in the case of questions. The Rome Convention on Applicable Law of 1980 does not apply to negotiable instruments to the extent that the obligations arise out of their negotiable character: Art 1(2)(c).

Clearing systems

8–37   Most negotiable eurobonds are deposited with one of two custodians known as Euroclear or Cedel located in Brussels and Luxembourg respectively.

The main objects of these custodians are to safeguard the bonds, to collect payments, and, most importantly, to facilitate transfers: if all the bonds are with same custodian or there are special arrangements between custodians (which there are between Euroclear and Cedel), there is no need to deliver the physical bond on a transfer. All that is necessary is for the custodian to debit the seller's account and to credit the buyer's account. The bonds stay where they are in some vault somewhere. To achieve the maximum reduction of paperwork, the bonds must be fungible, i.e. of the same issue so that one bond is identical to another and there is no need to transfer specific bonds. Without this facility, trading in bonds would come to a halt and the paperwork would crush the market.

8–38   In practice, there are tiers of custodians. A bondholder may deposit with his bank which deposits with Euroclear or Cedel which deposits with a local custodian in the country of the currency which deposits with a local clearing system, perhaps. Sales and pledges of the bond by the bondholder are replaced by sales or pledges of intangible claims against the head custodian: these intangible claims may be proprietary claims or debt claims. The legal technology is considered in another work in this series on financial law, in a section dealing with security over investment securities located with custodians. That section also describes Euroclear and Cedel in more detail. The asset dealt with is not the bond, but a claim against a custodian.

In addition, many securities are now dematerialised, i.e. not represented by any paper, for example government domestic currency debt securities (US Treasuries, UK Gilts). They are transferred or pledged by entry in the register maintained by or on behalf of the issuer.

The result of those remarkable developments is that the mountain of case law on negotiability is rapidly becoming of historical interest. But it must not be forgotten that negotiability was vital in the development of financial law to free the law from the shackles of obsolete rules inhibiting the transfer of intangible claims. Unhappily this development is by no means complete: para 8–31.

Terms of bonds

8–39 This section summarises the terms commonly found in international bonds. For a form, see the Appendix.

Face of bond

The face of the bond states that, the issuer, for value received, promises to pay to the bearer the amount of the bond and to pay interest at the prescribed rate in accordance with the detailed terms and conditions endorsed on the back of the bond.

Attached to fixed rate bonds are coupons, each for an interest payment in a fixed amount. Coupons are detachable and separately negotiable.

Incorporation of fiscal agency agreement/trust deed

8–40 The bonds state that they are issued subject to and with the benefit of the specified fiscal agency agreement (or trust deed if there is one) available for inspection at any of the paying agents and that the bondholders and couponholders are bound by and deemed to have notice of their terms.

There is no objection in English law to binding a bondholder to terms by reference, but firstly this term should not be misrepresented in any offering material even if the bondholders had a right of inspection, and secondly one must bear in mind the varying international position on surprise clauses incorporated by reference (bus and laundry ticket cases) and the attitude to unfair contract terms and terms imposed by standard contracts.

Rules are found in most, if not all, of the developed jurisdictions whereby exculpation clauses and harsh provisions in contracts with parties of little sophistication or weak bargaining power are subjected to close judicial scrutiny and may be nullified. Many of these are now encapsulated in consumer statutes or apply only to contracts involving consumers, but this is not always the case. The contracts particularly under attack are standard terms of business imposed on a party who had neither the bargaining power nor the sophistication to resist their terms. In such a case it could not be said that freedom of contract exists. In many countries, the courts limited the impact of these clauses by covert means, e.g. that a party is not bound by surprise terms contained by reference in his contract which he could not expect, e.g. an exclusion clause in a laundry ticket or bus ticket, and by rules whereby exclusion clauses are construed strictly against the party relying on them, e.g. by insisting that negligence or liability for a fundamental breach which goes to the root of the contract cannot be excluded except by very clear words, perhaps drawn to the attention of the other party.

For example, in Germany the Act for the Control of the Law of General Conditions of Business of April 1, 1977 contains a number of rules applying to standard terms even if they are between merchants so that the Act is not exclusively concerned with consumer protection. The British Unfair Contract Terms Act 1977 is to the same effect and there is a provision in s 27 which limits the ability to contract out in an international setting. In Austria Art 839 of the ABGB renders void any contract prohibited by law or in conflict with good morals, and a new provision (Art 879 para 3) provides that collateral agreements contained in general conditions of business or contractual forms are also void if, in view of all of the circumstances of the case, they are "grossly" disadvantageous to one of the parties. There is also a provision striking down unusual surprise clauses: see Art 864A. Both the French and Italian courts as well as the Swiss courts, have policed exemption clauses and sometimes invalidated them. The same tendencies are to be found in the United States: see ss 203, 206, 211 of the Restatement of Contracts (2nd). See also Art 36 of the Swedish Contract Acts of 1976. For a general review, on which the above paragraph is based, see Zweigert/Kötz, vol 2 chapter 1.

Attacks are more likely to happen in relation to bonds which are bought by members of the public, as opposed to sophisticated investors (the usual purchasers of bonds) who are well able to look after themselves.

As to conflict of laws, validity is normally governed by the governing law of the bond, and an "unfair" contract would usually only be capable of being struck down if it is within a public policy exemption or violates a mandatory rule of the forum. Conflicts of law are discussed in another work in this series on financial law.

In any event, the best policy is that any unusual or adverse terms should be reflected in the bonds themselves.

Form and transfer

8–41   The bonds state that they are issued in bearer form and that title thereto will pass by delivery. In other words, they are negotiable. See para 8–28 *et seq*.

Covenants

Detailed covenants are rare. The reason is that it would be impracticable for the issuer to negotiate modifications of over-rigid covenants with numerous bondholders if circumstances changed. More extensive covenants may be found if the bond is constituted by a trust deed since a representative is available to monitor the covenants on behalf of the bondholders.

Pari passu clause This usually states:

> "The Bonds are unsecured obligations of the Issuer and rank at least pari passu, without any preference amongst themselves, with all other outstanding, unsecured and unsubordinated obligations of the Issuer, present and future."

This statement contains two limbs: pari passu equality between bonds, and pari passu status with other unsecured debts.

For the effect of the pari passu clause generally, see para 3–27.

The inter-bond equality provision contracts out of any rule there may be that bonds rank according to the date of their creation: such a rule would be unusual but might apply, e.g. to a secured bond and also applies to formalised securities in some Spanish-influenced jurisdictions. The statement may also constitute a covenant that the issuer will not discriminate between bondholders although it is not clear if this applies only on competition between creditors, i.e. actual insolvency, even though not yet judicially ordered. It may prevent compromises whereby more favourable terms are made available to some but not all the bondholders. Listing codes and the general law may in any event require bondholders to be treated equally.

Negative pledge Most bonds will contain a negative pledge. For negative pledges, see para 3–10 *et seq*.

Negative pledges in bonds are traditionally without teeth: usually they only prohibit the grant of security for *comparable securities*, e.g. listed external debt of more than one year maturity. The issuer can secure non-listed debt, e.g. bank borrowings. These negative pledges are not designed to prevent the subordination of the bondholders by the creation of security by the issuer in favour of other creditors, but rather to prevent the issue of comparable secured debt whose existence might prejudice the relative value of the unsecured bonds and thereby directly affect bondholders' interests: investors might be more likely to purchase the secured bond. Hence the negative pledge is primarily intended to provide market support for the price of the bonds. But the romantic "same paper, same treatment" motive is also present. As a control on the grant of security by the issuer, the bond negative pledge is useless.

Information There is usually an obligation upon the issuer to furnish annual accounts for inspection at the offices of paying agents. This is also usually a listing requirement.

Interest

8–44   The following are some examples of the usual methods of fixing the interest rate:

Fixed rate A fixed interest rate bond states that the bond bears interest at the specified rate per annum payable annually in arrears on a specified date. Bonds cease to bear interest from their due date for redemption, unless not paid on due presentation. Interest stops on the due date for redemption because, if not so provided and if the holder delayed presentation, interest would continue to run: *Fowler v Midland Electricity Corporation* [1917] 1 Ch 526 and 656, CA. The clause encourages diligence by bondholders.

Unlike bank loans, there is usually no provision for an increased rate of default interest to discourage delayed payment.

8–45   **Floating rate** Floating rate bonds (generally called notes) are common because of their appeal to bank investors who are not willing to take the risk of a fixed rate.

The issuer appoints a bank as reference agent to fix the rate periodically, usually every three or six months, by reference to a market rate: this is usually the London interbank offered rate (LIBOR) because of its international acceptability, although local IBORS, e.g. in Hong Kong or Singapore, have been used, primarily for floating rate certificates of deposit. The rate should be one which would be acceptable to the investors for whom the notes are designed. The rate is announced in the financial press periodically after each fixing. Unlike loan agreements the issuer cannot select interest periods: bondholders desire certainty and the minimum of fuss.

There is no increased cost clause: for these, see para 4–5.

8–46   **Zero coupon (deep discount bonds)** These are bonds which do not carry any interest at all but are issued at a deep discount, e.g. 30 per cent below par. The return to the investor is the capital appreciation realised on sale or redemption. One advantage is an improved cash flow for the issuer – the issuer does not have to pay interest which is effectively "rolled-up" until final redemption. The investor's tax position may be improved since it may not be liable to pay income tax on the discount so that the earnings are free of tax, at least until redemption. But this depends upon the tax laws in the jurisdiction of the investor and the issuer. The other main questions are (i) whether the issuer will obtain tax relief on the accrued discounts over the life of the security, (ii) whether the investor is taxed on disposal or redemption as though it had received income equal to the accrued discount, and (iii) whether any capital gains will be charged on the discount.

If the bonds become prematurely due, e.g. the issuer redeems voluntarily when a tax law change imposes a withholding tax on interest on the bonds or if an event of default occurs, the investor receives compound returns up to the redemption date equal to the proportion of the return he would have received if the bonds had remained outstanding until final redemption.

Other questions are whether, in the event of the insolvent liquidation of the issuer, the usual prohibition on interest running in a liquidation will apply to the discount element and whether any borrowing limits would apply to the full principal amount, i.e. by treating the discount as capital.

Swaps The interest on the bond is often the subject of an interest swap. Swaps are reviewed in another volume in this series on financial law.

Redemption

The terms of repayment ("redemption" in bondese) are diverse. The following are some examples:

Bullet The bonds are repayable in one instalment.

Instalments The bonds are repayable by fixed periodic instalments. Normally the bonds for redemption are selected by drawings by lot by the fiscal agent. The bondholder is exposed to the whims of fortune.

Purchase fund The issuer is required to appoint a purchase agent who, by the terms of the bonds, must endeavour to purchase bonds during specified periods up to a specified total amount at a stated maximum price, normally par. The purchaser need not buy at par but can buy at below market prices. A purchase fund theoretically gives willing bondholders an opportunity to be "redeemed" and also, perhaps more importantly, provides market support for the bond: the demand created by the purchase agent theoretically pushes up the price. The disadvantage is that the "redemption" can be at less than par and, in practice, it is difficult to enforce impartiality in the purchase of bonds by the purchase agent. Purchase funds are now rare in the eurobond market.

8–48 **Perpetual bonds** A perpetual bond is one which is not redeemable by the issuer except upon default or if a withholding tax is imposed. Corporate irredeemables have been known in domestic markets for many years and in England statutory recognition is now given to them by company legislation, even if they are secured, i.e. the objection to clogs on the equity of redemption of mortgaged assets does not apply.

The defaults are generally limited to non-payment and winding-up.

Perpetuals are usually subordinated to all other creditors of the issuer. One purpose of a perpetual is to approximate the bond to preference share capital while preserving its status as debt. The reason may be that interest is tax deductible but preference dividends are not, but the effect of equity is required, e.g. for bank capital adequacy purposes. Subordinations are discussed in another work in this series.

8–49 **Early voluntary redemption** Investors generally prefer that issuers should not be able to voluntarily redeem the bond before its maturity because this results in a loss of the investment, e.g. the higher interest rate on the bonds if market rates are lower.

If a voluntary prepayment right is conceded, then a premium may be payable on a sliding scale commencing at, say, 105 per cent in the early years and dropping by, say, $\frac{1}{2}$ per cent for each subsequent semi-annual period. Prepayments and sliding scales are now unusual in the eurobond market. In England a prepayment premium is not a void penalty unless it is unfair or unconscionable or is payable on a default: see *Multiservice Bookbinding v Marden* [1978] 2 All ER 489 (a mortgage loan).

The bond generally provides that the bonds prepaid are selected by lot and for the application of prepayments towards any redemption instalments in inverse order, i.e. the compulsory redemption instalments continue in the full amount notwithstanding the early prepayment until the bonds are fully redeemed. Thus the life of the issue is shortened. Bank loan practice is the same.

Normally it will be clear from the language of the bond that an issuer does not have a right of early redemption if no express right is conferred by the bond. It was held in *Hooper v Western Counties and South Wales Telephone Co Ltd* (1892) 68 LT 78 that debentures are not redeemable before the stated fixed date unless otherwise provided. An Australian court has delivered a similar opinion in relation to a loan: *Hyde Management Services (Pty) Ltd v FAI Insurances* (1983) 144 CLR 541.

In the absence of an express provision as to application of partial prepayments towards instalments in inverse order, the issuer could probably not choose which instalments to apply the redemption amount against but must continue to pay in accordance with the fixed redemption terms of the bonds so that the prepayment shortens the life of the issue: but this depends on the terms of the bonds and any applicable rules as to rights of appropriation.

Early redemption for tax Almost invariably an issuer can voluntarily redeem the bonds if a withholding tax is imposed which gives rise to an obligation upon the issuer to pay additional amounts under the grossing-up clause in the bond. If this were not the case, the issuer would theoretically be subject to potentially unlimited liabilities at the hands of the tax legislature. Redemption in such a case must generally be on interest payment dates, in whole, and at par. Hence no discrimination between bondholders is permitted. This right of redemption is not usually allowed in issues by sovereign states since they control their own tax laws.

Purchase of bonds by issuer Unlike share capital, there are generally no legal restrictions on an issuer purchasing its own debt and even re-issuing it. In some jurisdictions, the acquisition of the debt instrument by the debtor may cause the debt to be extinguished automatically. In England the Companies Act 1985 allows debentures purchased by a company to be reissued with the original priority if they are secured.

Some bonds allow the issuer (or its subsidiaries) to purchase its own bonds provided:

- If made by tender, the tender is available to all bondholders alike (to prevent discrimination).

- The purchased bonds are cancelled. They must not be reissued or resold. Reissues would, for example, potentially run into securities regulation problems.

- Purchased bonds are credited towards any subsequent compulsory redemption instalments.

A purchase is therefore similar to a prepayment except that (i) the transaction requires a willing seller, (ii) the issuer need not purchase at par, and (iii) no prepayment premium is payable.

Payments

Bearer bonds Payments on bearer bonds are made against surrender of the bonds or coupons at the specified offices of the specified paying agent. Generally it is a custodian or sub-custodian who collects.

Payment is generally made either by cheque drawn on or by transfer to an account maintained by the payee with a bank in the country of the currency.

Payment is generally expressed to be subject to all applicable laws or regulations at the place of payment – meaning the office where the bond or coupon is presented. Hence, if taxes or exchange controls are imposed in one place, the bondholders can present their bonds at another paying agent. For the impact of exchange controls and illegality at the place of payment, see the relevant chapters in another work in this series.

The amount of any missing, unmatured coupon must be deducted from a payment of principal and is payable against surrender of the missing coupon. The reason is that the coupon is a bearer instrument and so can subsequently be presented for payment notwithstanding that the bond itself had been prepaid prior to the maturity of that coupon. Floating rate coupons are void if separated from the note.

8–53 **Paying agents** Generally the issuer can change the paying agents and appoint additional paying agents. Bonds normally require that the issuer maintain paying agents in a convenient jurisdiction for bondholders and also in the country where the bonds are listed (if the local stock exchange so requires, which it usually does). It is often not the case that a paying agent is maintained in the country of the currency; a paying agent in the US for US dollar issues would cause problems under US securities regulations which seek to prevent unregistered issues from coming to rest in the primary distribution in the US. For more detail on fiscal and paying agents, see para 10–9.

Prescription

8–54 A prescription clause in a bearer bond having a registered option provides that the bonds and coupons become void unless presented for payment within periods of usually 10 years and five years respectively of the due date (assuming the issuer places the funds with the fiscal agent).

Statutory periods Without a prescription clause, if a bondholder omitted to present a bond or coupon for payment, either through inadvertence or because of some disability, the issuer's liability to pay and the continuance of the covenants in the bond could endure almost indefinitely, subject only to the various statutes of limitation.

Contractual alterations It is usually not possible to extend the limitation period by private contract. However local laws vary as to whether contractual shortenings are permitted. In France, England and Germany there is no objection. However local stock exchanges may prescribe a minimum period in order to prevent issuers from fixing unduly short limitation periods to the prejudice of bondholders.

Events of default

Events of default are discussed generally at para 3–37 *et seq*. 8–55

In the case of bonds, the events of default are generally less stringent than those appearing in term loan agreements. The reasons are: the terms of the bonds are generally longer than medium-term loan agreements so there may be greater changes of circumstances; it is less easy to arrange modifications or waivers of non-material defaults than is the case with bank loans (and which are often impossible if there is no provision for meetings of bondholders or no trustee); and complex events of default requiring the exercise of judgment, e.g. as to materiality or those which require monitoring such as financial ratios, are not appropriate in the case of scattered bondholders even where there is a trustee. Trustees are generally unwilling to take on too wide a discretion.

The events of default normally included are non-payment, non-compliance, cross-default, insolvency, bankruptcy, dissolution, creditors' processes and sometimes substantial disposals.

Acceleration and enforcement If there is no trustee, then each bondholder can accelerate and enforce his own bond. For the position where there is a trustee, see para 10–21. If there is a trustee, the bonds will generally refer in outline terms to the no-action clause, the ability of the trustee to waive breaches, approve non-material modifications and approve mergers and transfers of the undertaking of an issuer in certain cases, meetings of bondholders and the ability of bondholders' resolutions to modify the bonds; and the indemnity in favour of the trustee. This is to avoid surprise clauses which might entitle the bondholder to claim he was not bound: see para 8–40.

Miscellaneous

Notices Notices are stated to be valid if published in a specified leading financial newspaper. 8–56

Governing law, forum and waiver of immunity These matters are briefly summarised in chapter 5.

Chapter 9

BOND ISSUES: SPECIAL TYPES OF ISSUES

Equity-linked bonds

Introduction

9–1 This chapter deals with various special types of issues of debt securities, namely:

- equity-linked bonds, either bonds convertible into shares or having warranties attached to them which entitle the holder to shares
- warrants to purchase bonds
- structures involving bearer depository receipts
- secured issues
- eurocommercial paper
- medium-term note programmes.

Convertible bonds generally

9–2 Convertible bond issues are issues of bonds by a company, the terms of which allow the holder to exchange his bonds for shares of the company or of the company's parent or subsidiary.

Conversion price The bond specifies the conversion price at which the shares may be acquired. This price may be the same for the entire conversion period or (very unusually in the eurobond market) it may be stepped-up at specified intervals. On conversion, no consideration is payable: the subscription price is paid by set-off of the principal amount of the bonds, which are surrendered for conversion, against the obligation to pay this price. For example, if the conversion price is $25 per share, then the holder of a $1,000 bond would, on conversion, receive 40 shares (i.e. 1,000 divided by

25) in exchange for his bond. The effect, from the company's point of view, is that what was loan capital now becomes equity capital so that the company's gearing is improved.

Conversion premium The conversion price is more than the market price of the underlying shares at the time of issue of the bonds, the difference being called the conversion premium. The amount of the premium is determined by such factors as the company's prospective rate of growth and the relative need to attract investors. The bondholder therefore speculates in the hope that the share price will eventually exceed the conversion price so that he can acquire shares cheaply. If the share price drops, he still has his fixed income bond. If he converts, he receives discretionary dividends (which may be taxed at source). But interest is mandatory and usually payable without deduction of tax at source.

Bonds with share warrants attached

Bonds may be issued to which are attached warrants which give the holder an option to subscribe a specified amount of cash for shares of the company or of its parent or subsidiary at a specified price. Warrants are usually detachable and can therefore be traded separately from the bonds.

On exercise of the option, the holder will normally have to pay for the new shares comprised in his warrant. For example, if the subscription price is $50 per share, and the warrant entitles the holder to subscribe $5,000, he would receive 100 shares (i.e. 5,000 divided by 50) on the exercise of his option and the payment of $5,000. The company's equity capital will therefore be increased without any change in its loan capital. However, if the company applies the funds received from the exercise of the options in redeeming or purchasing the original bonds, its position will be substantially the same as if it had issued convertible bonds and the conversion rights had been exercised, i.e. loan capital will be replaced by equity capital.

The subscription price is normally set above the market price of the underlying shares at the time of issue of the bonds and warrants. The holder, like the holder of a convertible bond, speculates in the hope that the market price of the underlying shares will rise above the subscription price, but is cushioned against poor share performance by the fixed income element of the bond. However, once the warrant has been detached and sold, its holder speculates solely on the share price going over the subscription price by a sufficient margin to reflect the fact that in the meantime, unlike a shareholder, the warrant holder does not receive income on his warrant.

Listing

9–4 Equity-linked bonds may be listed on a stock exchange just as may straight issues and, in the case of bonds with warrants, three separate listings may be obtained, namely for the bonds, the warrants and the bonds with the warrants attached. In particular, the shares must also be listed.

Because of the equity, and therefore more speculative, element, stock exchange requirements for equity-linked bonds are generally more stringent than for straight bonds, e.g. by requiring more information to be included in the offering circular.

Advantages of equity-linked issues

9–5 The attraction to the investor of an equity-linked bond is that, irrespective of the performance of the underlying shares, the bond provides a fixed rate of income (albeit a lower rate than on an otherwise similar non equity-linked bond) and is relatively secure, while at the same time giving the holder an option to convert into or subscribe for shares at a fixed price, and thereby benefit from any increase in the market value of the shares above that fixed price. The package provides safe debt plus speculative equity.

9–6 An issuer may have a number of reasons for issuing equity-linked bonds, including the following:

(a) **Terms** Since the equity element of the bonds is of value to the investor, the company will usually be able to negotiate better terms for itself, principally in the form of a lower interest rate, but also in the form of less restrictive covenants or the subordination of bondholders' claims to those of other unsecured creditors. But eurobonds nearly always contain a put option entitling the investor to call for repayment from, say, year 5 at, say, 120 per cent to give the investor a better rate of return and to put him (almost) in the position he would have been in if the bond had yielded a normal interest rate. This helps to remove the risk of a fall in the value of the shares.

(b) **Maturity** Since the option may be worth more to the investor the longer the period during which it may be exercised, the company may successfully issue bonds with a longer maturity than might otherwise be acceptable.

(c) **Access to investors** Institutional investors and trustees and other fiduciaries may be prohibited from investing directly in shares or warrants, but may nevertheless be permitted to invest in equity-linked bonds because of the back-stop protection afforded by the fixed income on the bonds.

(d) **Deferred equity financing** Equity-linked bonds are often regarded as a method of deferred equity financing. Where the issuer considers that the present market price undervalues the company's shares, equity-linked bonds may be issued, with the conversion/subscription price set at a level that reflects the issuer's view of the company's true worth. If and when the market price rises above that fixed price, investors will, at least in theory, exercise their options in respect of the company's shares. The company will thereby have increased its equity base by issuing shares at a higher price than it could have done at the time of the issue of the bonds and without having to wait. The increase in the equity base will improve the company's balance sheet and enable it to raise further loans.

But, since in practice investors do not convert or subscribe until the market price is well above the conversion or subscription price, the company will on conversion/subscription be issuing its shares at below, and possibly considerably below, current market price, thereby diluting the value of existing shareholdings in the company.

Exchange rate

If the bonds and the underlying shares are denominated in different currencies, e.g. the bonds in US dollars and the shares in the domestic currency of the company, it is necessary to specify the exchange rate that will apply on exercise of the conversion right. It is normally provided that the exchange rate prevailing at the time of issue of the bonds will apply throughout the conversion period. This provides a further element of speculation to the investor in a convertible bond: he stands to gain if the bond currency subsequently depreciates against the share currency and to lose if it appreciates.

This speculative element is absent in the case of warrants because the subscription price for shares on exercise of the option is generally expressed in the currency of the shares. To exercise the option, the holder may therefore have to buy the currency in question at the then prevailing exchange rate.

9–7

Loss of conversion privilege

In a number of cases the conversion privilege may be lost or prematurely determined either by issuer action or by third party action. This loss can be detrimental to bondholders because the bondholder originally received less benefits on his bond (e.g. a lower interest rate) in return for the conversion privilege. The main events which result in the destruction or premature acceleration of the conversion rights are:

9–8

(a) Forced conversions by virtue of an issuer **prepayment** option. But usually the issuer cannot redeem (except in the case of withholding taxes) unless the price of the shares is well above the conversion price, e.g. 130 per cent. Generally, this right, even if given, does not apply at all during the first few years.

(b) Expiry of the conversion period on an **acceleration**. This is a bondholder risk. They are unlikely to wish to convert on a default.

(c) Expiry of the conversion period on a **liquidation** or dissolution. Again, this is a bondholder risk (they will not wish to convert in any event since the shares will be valueless). The bonds may prevent the issuer from instigating a voluntary solvent liquidation except in the context of reorganisation where there is a carry-over of the conversion privilege.

(d) **Take-over** of the issuer for cash or where there is no carry-over of the conversion rights into the securities of the purchasing company (as there usually is).

(e) An **amalgamation** of the issuer or a reorganisation where there is no carry-over of the conversion rights into any new securities issued on the restructuring (as there usually is).

Legal aspects of convertible bonds

9–9 **Issue of shares at a discount** In most countries the policy of maintenance of capital requires that shares must not be issued at a discount. Thus in England the issue of £1 debentures at a discount with a provision that they may be exchanged immediately into fully paid £1 shares is unlawful, because the shares would be issued at a discount: *Mosely v Koffyfontein Mines* [1904] 2 Ch 108, CA. By the Companies Act 1985, the contract is void and allottees and (subject to certain defences) subsequent purchasers of the shares are jointly and severally liable to pay the discount plus interest.

In practice, the problem rarely arises because the market price of the shares is generally well above the par value and the conversion price is above the market value.

9–10 **Pre-emption rights** Commonly, corporate codes and stock exchanges require new shares to be offered to existing shareholders pro rata. A shareholders' meeting may have to be called to exclude this right and, if so, the timing of the issue may thereby be delayed. In addition to the pre-emption rights in the Companies Act 1985, the London Stock Exchange requires a shareholders' approval but may waive it for foreign issuers. UK public companies often pass annual resolutions at their AGM disapplying the Companies Act pre-emption rights and this satisfies the Stock Exchange requirement that the resolution should not be more than 15 months prior to the issue. Informal investors committees (e.g. the Investors' Protection Committee in Britain) may seek to limit the number of shares issued on a non-pre-emptive basis.

Securities regulation generally An equity-linked bond contemplates two separate issues of securities – first the bonds, and then the shares. In many countries the exchange of one security for another of the same issuer is not a public offer of securities attracting prospectus disclosure and registration requirements. The rationale for the rule is that existing security holders are supposed to know about the issuer or, alternatively, the requisite disclosure requirements were met at the time of the initial issue, as supplemented by continuing disclosure requirements. But the "exchange" exemption may not apply if the bonds are convertible into shares of another entity such as a parent guarantor. Thus the exchange exemption does not apply in such a case under the US Securities Act of 1933.

The position as regards warrants is more complex. There may be an exemption in favour of issues to existing security holders. The point is discussed at para 16–13.

Foreign investment restrictions Local laws directed against the foreign acquisition of local enterprises may prevent foreigners from acquiring control of more than a specified percentage of local companies – this can be quite low, e.g. 10 per cent. This plainly could affect a converting bondholder if exercise takes him over the threshold.

Compulsory takeover offers Some corporate codes provide that where a person acquires more than a threshold percentage of the equity of a company (30 per cent under the UK Takeover Code) he must make an offer for the remainder of the shares. Again, bondholders going over the threshold on conversion will be affected. Generally, convertible issues will involve a small proportion of the equity so that the rule will bite only if the bondholder is also independently a large shareholder.

Exchange controls Naturally there must be no exchange controls at the time of the issue of the bonds preventing foreign shareholders from subscribing for shares. If subsequent exchange controls are introduced before conversion or subscription, the bondholders rights may be defeated. Notwithstanding that the conversion or subscription rights are governed by foreign law (which usually insulates against local exchange controls in the case of debt obligations), the English courts will not enforce an obligation which is illegal where it has to be performed if the contract is governed by English law: see para 2–13. This could apply to the obligation of the issuer to issue and register new shares, an obligation which is presumably performable where the company is located. The result is that the bondholders take the risk of local exchange controls or other prohibitions. Many convertible bonds expressly throw this risk on to the bondholders, e.g. by a provision that conversion or subscription is subject to all applicable laws and regulations.

Stock exchange limits Stock exchanges may impose limits on the amount of equity capital that can be subscribed under convertible issues. The stock exchange in London has a 20 per cent limit (excluding employee share schemes) but can vary this for foreign issuers.

Anti-dilution provisions

9–14 **Generally** In the absence of express provision, the value of the right to convert into or subscribe for a company's shares could be severely eroded by action on the part of the company over which the bondholder has no control. For example, if the conversion price is $12 and a company subdivides its shares by converting $10 shares into two $5 shares, the market value of each share would be halved. In such a case, the conversion price should also be halved, i.e. $6. The anti-dilution provisions therefore provide for an appropriate adjustment to the conversion price.

In all cases except consolidation of shares, the application of the anti-dilution clauses results in a reduction in the original fixed conversion price to take account of the dilution and in effect entitles the bondholder to extra shares. For example:

1. If the company issues bonus shares, the number of shares representing the net assets of the company has simply been increased without the company receiving new moneys so that the value of each share is correspondingly diminished. The conversion price should be reduced proportionately.

2. If the company makes a rights issue below the current market price of the shares (as is almost invariably the case), the market price of the shares will in practice drop because full value has not been received and so the conversion price should drop proportionately, taking into account the fact that the company has received some proceeds.

3. If the company grants its shareholders pre-emption rights to buy other securities, e.g. loan stock, then although the market price of the shares is not affected, the bondholders are deprived of an advantage given to other shareholders and should be compensated.

EQUITY-LINKED BONDS 9–18

It will therefore be seen that the reasoning for adjustment varies according to the anti-dilution provision. For example: 9–15

(a) Mere mathematical adjustment, such as sub-divisions of shares.

(b) Genuine dilutions in the market value of the shares, such as bonus issues and rights issues at less than market value. Here the shareholders would otherwise receive a benefit at the bondholders' expense.

(c) Pari passu treatment of bondholders, such as rights issues of other securities. This ground for an adjustment is based on the equality motive and is of more debatable merit than the others.

Case law on dilution If there are no anti-dilution protections, then it may be that the bondholders could not look to the courts to protect them. US case law supports this approach. 9–16

> See, e.g. *Parkinson v West End Street Railway*, 173 Mass 446, 53 NE 891 (1899) (consolidation); *Pratt v American Bell Telephone Co*, 141 Mass 225, 5 NE 307 (1886) (rights offering); *Gay v Burgess Mills*, 30 RI 231, 74 A 714 (1909) (stock split; stock dividend); *Broad v Brockwell International Corp*, 642 F 2d 929 (572 Cir) (1980) (en banc), cert denied, 454 US 965 (1981); *Kesslar v General Cable Corp*, 92 Cal App 3d 531, 155 Cal Rptr 94 (1979).

While the cases are less likely to be relevant because of the universality of anti-dilution clauses, the principles could still hold good for those cases where residual risks are not covered. Much of the recent US case law has been concerned with the position of equity-linked bonds in the case of mergers and tender offers. The Stock Exchange in London has specific requirements for anti-dilution clauses.

Warrant issues There are two ways of dealing with the anti-dilution provisions on warrants attached to bonds. The first method is to reduce the warrant price according to the extent of the dilution. If this method is followed, the warrant-holder ends up with a smaller amount of the equity. The second method is to increase the number of shares which can be subscribed for. If this method is followed, then the warrant-holder acquires the same proportion of the equity notwithstanding the dilution. 9–17

No adjustment on dividend payments No adjustment is made if shares are issued to shareholders in lieu of a normal cash dividend, because the payment of a dividend, whether in cash or in specie, should not be an event that triggers the adjustment provisions. Bondholders do not qualify for share dividends until they convert: they receive interest instead. 9–18

The result is that the bondholders are prejudiced by large extraordinary

International Loans, Bonds and Securities Regulation

cash dividends to the shareholders. One form provides for notice to bondholders in the event of dividends paid otherwise than out of earned surplus. Convertible eurobonds often provide for adjustment in the case of all exceptional dividends. Corporate rules may in any event prohibit dividends out of capital. Theoretically a dividend limitation could be imposed, but this is not generally attractive to issuers.

> In *Harff v Kerkorian*, 324 A 2d 215 (Del Ch 1974), reversed, 347 A 2d 133 (Del 1975), a group of convertible bondholders challenged a large cash dividend by the issuer as a breach of fiduciary duty. *Held*: the bondholders assumed the risk of an issuer's dividend policy designed to destroy conversion value unless this amounted to fraud. The bondholders' challenge was unsuccessful.

As mentioned, an adjustment will be made if bonus shares are issued in an amount per share which is less than the market price per share prior to the declaration of the dividend.

Takeovers

9–19 If a third party takes over the issuing company by the purchase of all of its shares pursuant to a tender (takeover) offer, then some of the consequences are:

1. The bond/warrant holders are more vulnerable to **adverse action** by the new owner, e.g. asset-stripping which may not be covered by covenants in the bond; they may not be protected by the general law controlling abuse of minority shareholders (the bond/warrant holders are not shareholders).

2. The bondholders can still convert during the conversion period thereby **diluting the control** of the new owner.

3. Limited trading may render it impracticable to determine **a fair market price** of the shares upon which many of the anti-dilution clauses depend.

4. Although the issuer may still be obliged by the bond to maintain the listing of its shares even after the takeover, the stock exchange may **de-list** the shares where their controlling ownership prevents there being an adequate market in the shares.

9–20 Some forms accordingly provide that if a takeover or tender offer is made to all shareholders, the issuer will endeavour to procure that a like offer is extended to bondholders converting during the offer period. Theoretically this may be beyond the control of the issuer particularly in a contested bid, but in practice the fact that the de-listing of the shares may result in a default under the bonds and the fact that bondholders are still entitled to convert and thereby dilute the new owner's control provide an incentive to the new owner to make arrangements in the initial offer which deal with the rights of convertibles, e.g. by making them a comparable offer on the basis that the bondholders have converted.

The bondholders' position might be strengthened if their exclusion from the benefit of an offer were an event of default.

Securities codes and stock exchange regulations may themselves require the offeror to treat converting shareholders equally with existing shareholders: see for example the UK City Code on Takeovers and Mergers.

Unfortunately for the bondholders, a successful takeover effectively marks the end of the conversion rights so far as the issuer is concerned although they may be compensated by corresponding rights to convert into the shares of the new owner.

Mergers and spin-offs

If one company merges with another, i.e. there is a fusion, then, unless the issuer is the continuing corporation, the bondholders' rights will be in question. One form provides that in such event a trustee for the bondholders can require the issuer to procure that the surviving company grants rights to the bondholders to convert on a similar basis and with similar anti-dilution clauses into the securities of the new company.

Where a merger is achieved by the disposal of all or nearly all of the issuer's undertaking and assets to a new company in return for the issue to the old company's shareholders of shares in the new company, then a usual clause provides that the trustee for the bondholders can require the old company to procure that the new company grants similar rights to bondholders enabling them to convert into the securities of the new company.

If subsidiaries are spun off on the basis of issues of shares to the shareholders of the parent, the bondholders should have rights to convert into these new securities as well.

In these cases therefore there is a carry-over of the conversion privilege into the new securities.

> In *Broad v Rockwell International Corp*, 614 F 2d 418 (5th Cir 1980), vacated, 642 F 2d 929 (5th Cir) (en banc), cert denied, 454 US 965 (1981), there was a cash merger and the question was whether cash was "other property" within the meaning of a US standard clause providing for carry over of conversion rights into the "stock, securities or other property" receivable in the merger by the underlying common shares. *Held:* cash was included.

In *BSF Co v Philadelphia National Bank*, 42 Del Ch 106, 204 A 2d 746 (Sup Ct 1964), the issuer sold 75 per cent of its assets for cash. The issuer had issued convertible bonds. The purchaser of the assets did not grant conversion rights into its stock, even though the trust indenture provided that in case of the sale of assets or merger the bonds would be converted into common shares of the issuer or common shares of the acquiring company. *Held*: the language was unambiguous and would apply only in a case where stock of the purchaser was consideration for the assets. Since the issuer added the cash consideration to its asset base and the bondholder could participate in it by converting into common stock, the transaction did not prejudice the holder.

Covenants of issuer

9–22 The usual covenants of an issuer in an equity-linked issue are as follows:

(a) **Availability of sufficient shares** The issuer agrees to maintain sufficient authorised but unissued capital to cover the conversion and subscription rights in full.

(b) **Ranking of shares** The issuer agrees not to modify the rights attaching to the shares or to issue senior or more favourable share capital. This is to maintain the ranking and value of the conversion shares. If, say, the company were to issue new preferred shares on a rights basis, the dividend rate on the preferred shares would diminish the dividend potential on the ordinary (common) shares and hence reduce their value and the conversion privilege.

In *Russell v Northern Bank Dev Corpn Ltd* [1992] 3 All ER 161, HL, it was held that a provision in an agreement is void to the extent the company undertakes to limit powers reserved by the Companies Act to the members of the company. This would affect many undertakings in convertibles. As a result, the non-compliance event of default in bonds issued by UK companies provides that the event of default applies even if the undertaking in the bond is void.

(c) **Notification** The issuer agrees to notify changes in the conversion price by prescribed methods of publication. The issuer may also be required to notify other events which may affect the bondholders' rights, e.g. dividends (otherwise than out of earned surplus), rights issues, reorganisations, sale of undertaking, mergers and liquidation. The purpose of the notification is to enable the bondholders to decide whether or not to convert. Stock exchange rules may in any event require that certain of these events be notified to the holders of listed securities.

(d) **Listing** The issuer agrees to endeavour to maintain the listing of its shares on the present stock exchange and agrees that the shares on conversion will be listed on all stock exchanges where classes of share capital into which they are converted are listed at conversion.

Taxation

In addition to general taxation aspects relating to bonds, there are certain additional factors that are relevant in the context of an issue of equity-linked bonds.

So far as concerns the issuer, while the interest paid on bonds will normally be a deductible expense in computing its taxable profits, the dividend paid on shares will not normally be so deductible.

For bondholders, taxation aspects in the jurisdiction of the issuer need to be considered:

(a) **Dividends** The treatment of a dividend on shares for income tax purposes may differ from that of interest on bonds – in particular a shareholder may be subject to a withholding tax on his dividend. Unlike bonds, there is of course no grossing-up protection for tax deductions from dividends. The rate of the withholding tax may be reduced by a double tax treaty or convention.

(b) **Gains tax** Gains realised on the disposal of shares or warrants may be subject to gains tax. In the case of convertible bonds, it is important to establish whether conversion will give rise to a potential capital gains tax liability. In some jurisdictions "roll-over relief" may be available, with the result that there is no liability to gains tax on conversion, and the shares issued on conversion are treated as having been acquired at the original acquisition cost of the bonds converted. In the case of the exercise of a warrant, this consideration would not normally arise because the holder would be subscribing new money for the shares and not disposing of his bonds. In computing his gain on any later disposal of the shares the costs of the warrant would normally be added to the cost of the shares.

(c) **Issue taxes** The issue of shares on conversion or subscription may give rise to a liability to pay stamp duty or other duties or taxes in the jurisdiction of the issuer. In eurobond convertibles the issuer generally takes responsibility for stamp, issue and registration taxes in his own jurisdiction relating to the conversion of the bonds and issue of shares but bondholders must pay all such taxes in the locations of the external conversion agents if the conversion notice is presented there, and must pay such taxes if shares on conversions are issued by the bondholder's direction to a third party. Stamp duty may also be payable on the subsequent transfer of shares issued upon conversion or subscription.

9–23

Warrants to purchase bonds

General

9–24 Bonds may be issued with a warrant to subscribe for further bonds at par at a specified interest rate and of a specified maturity. The advantage to the investor is that he has the right to buy bonds at a pre-determined fixed rate so that if rates sink in the meantime, he holds a valuable warrant. These warrants were popular in the late 1970s and early 1980s.

The circular for the original bonds describes the terms of the warrants and of the new bonds. The warrant exercise procedures are set out in a warrant agency agreement between the issuer and a warrant agent. This may contain provisions for meetings of warrant holders. The warrant agent must publicise advance notice reminding warrant holders of the expiry of the option period.

Listing is for the original bonds, the warrants and the new bonds. The warrants can be traded separately from the original bonds.

Securities regulation

9–25 Three securities are involved in the package: the original bond, the warrant and the new bond issued on exercise of the option. Since the warrants are detachable and can be traded separately, they could come into the hands of the public in secondary market trading. Hence the issue of the new bonds might be made to the public and thereby contravene securities regulation, notably the US Federal securities laws. Hence a full lock-up of the warrants and new bonds is usually established.

One technique for achieving this is for the warrants to be represented on issue by a global warrant deposited with, say, a common depository for Euroclear and Cedel. The warrant holders are not entitled to definitive warrants. The subscribers to the warrants will have warrants credited to their accounts with Euroclear or Cedel upon delivery of certificates that the beneficial owner is not a national or resident of the United States. Warrants are transferable only in accordance with the rules and procedures of Euroclear and Cedel for transfers of interests in the global warrant.

On exercise of the option to subscribe for a new bond, the warrant holder is credited with an interest in a temporary global bond which is also deposited with the common depository at the time of the issue of the initial bonds. Definitive bonds are available only after a lock-up period after expiry of the option period against certificates of non-US ownership.

Warrants exercise procedure

A typical procedure is as follows: the warrant holder delivers a form of warrant exercise notice to Euroclear or Cedel prior to the end of the option period five banking days in advance of the exercise date and arranges for his account at Euroclear or Cedel to be debited with the subscription money for the bonds plus an amount equal to interest on the bonds since the last interest payment date (or date of issue of the warrant if earlier). The clearing agent endorses the global warrant with a reduction, endorses the global bond with the increase and credits the new bondholder's account with its share of the global bond. The warrant agent pays the subscription moneys to the issuer.

Normally the issuer can cancel the obligation to issue bonds only if withholding taxes are imposed for which the issuer would have to gross-up under the terms of the new bond.

9–26

Bearer depository receipts

Reasons for bearer depository receipts

In many jurisdictions, direct bond issues by a local entity may not be possible for a variety of reasons, typically: interest on bearer bonds would be subject to a withholding tax; a bond issue would attract a large issue tax or a stamp duty; public issues are prohibited – even to sophisticated investors; bearer securities are prohibited; or a clearing agent may be unwilling to accept securities of a particular type because of the extra administration involved, e.g. bearer units under a unit trust.

9–27

Structure involving depository

One possible solution is to issue the bonds to an intermediary which then issues bearer depository receipts to the investors. This structure has been more usually used for share issues to be traded internationally where the investor deposits his shares with a depository who issues a bearer depository receipt entitling the holder to call for his shares from the depository and in the meantime to be paid income on the shares received by the depository. But the technique can be adopted successfully to pure debt issues.

9–28

The structure is as follows:

1. The issuer issues a debt security to an intermediary financial institution such as a trust corporation or a bank (the "depository") under a deposit agreement. This obligation may avoid the local tax objection or prohibition.

2. The depository issues bearer depository receipts ("BDRs") to investors under the terms of which the holders are entitled to receive principal and interest to the extent principal and interest are received on the security of the issuer deposited with the depository. The depository must be able to issue the BDRs without adverse tax or other consequences.

Documenting the depository arrangements

9–29 There are several ways of documenting the depository arrangements. A common method is a **limited recourse contract**. Under this scheme, the depository holds the deposited obligation in its own right and agrees, as its own unsecured obligation, to pay holders of BDRs amounts equal to amounts received on the deposited obligation. This is similar to a bank sub-participation. The method has the disadvantage that the investor has a double risk – the risk of the issuer and the risk of the depository. If the depository fails, the holders of the BDRs would not be able to look through to the ultimate issuer. The offering circular would have to contain disclosures about the depository (since his credit risk is involved) and there may be applicable filing requirements for the depository if the BDR is a "security" or a "debenture" issued by the depository within the scope of applicable prospectus legislation. Sub-participations are discussed at para 7–18 *et seq*.

Two methods of mitigating the credit risk of the depository will usually not be practicable. Under the first method, the depository could **charge** the proceeds of the deposited obligation as security for its obligations to the holders of the BDRs: but there may be negative pledge, registration and banking regulation objections. Under the second, the depository could agree to **assign** the deposited obligation on the depository's insolvency: but this may (a) fall foul of the original prohibition giving rise to the BDR scheme or (b) constitute a voidable fraudulent preference by the depository if the assignment takes place within the suspect period before the bankruptcy (just the time when the assignment is needed). Sometimes the depository holds amounts **paid** by the issuer on **trust** for receiptholders, i.e. this is a trust of proceeds, not of the original obligation to pay.

Secured issues

Generally eurobond issues are unsecured because:

(a) Eurobond investors prefer issuers who are well-known and who can therefore borrow unsecured.

(b) Investors are not equipped, it is said, to undertake a sophisticated credit analysis of issuers who can only borrow secured; the evaluation of the security itself may be an impediment to marketing the bonds.

(c) If the issuer commonly borrows unsecured, the grant of security may be inhibited by negative pledges in loan agreements or bond issues.

(d) Security is administratively cumbersome, e.g. generally a trustee is required to hold, monitor and enforce the security. Security cannot be enforced piecemeal, e.g. an asset must usually be sold as a whole and not sub-divided between bondholders for the purposes of a sale.

But secured issues of international bonds have been known. The most common are securitisations and repackagings, e.g. secured bonds issued by a single purpose issuer secured on home loan mortgages bought by the issuer from a mortgage institution. In practice, investors rely solely on the rating of the securities granted by a rating agency. Securitisations are described elsewhere in this series of works.

Eurocommercial paper

Introduction

A eurocommercial paper ("ECP") programme is an uncommitted facility whereby the issuer can issue short-term debt securities (i.e. "notes" with a maturity of up to one year) to certain professional dealers at short notice. The terms of each issue must be agreed at the time as there are no commitment fees. Notes are commonly issued two days after each agreement.

Typically, notes issued under an ECP programme are sold at a discount and do not bear interest. The yield to the investor will therefore be the difference between the price paid for the note and the face amount of the note which is payable at maturity. For example, a US$100,000 six-month note which is issued at 95 per cent of its principal amount (i.e. US$95,000) will have an annual yield of 10 per cent when it is redeemed for US$100,000 at maturity six months later. Dealers make their profit by on-selling for more, not out of fees.

Most ECP programmes are multi-currency, multi-dealer programmes providing the issuer with possibilities to tap a wide variety of market opportunities.

Documentation

9–32 The documentation for an ECP programme tends to be fairly standard. Market forms were developed by the Euronote Association. The typical documentation comprises: the notes themselves; a dealer or programme agreement; an issuing and paying agency agreement; a deed of covenant; a deed of guarantee (if it is a guaranteed programme); and an information memorandum which is very short and is up-dated and warranted prior to each issue.

The notes and global notes The notes issued under an ECP programme are usually extremely simple. They comprise a covenant to bearer to pay the principal amount (i.e. the face value) of the note at maturity. As mentioned, the notes are normally non-interest bearing and are issued at a discount. They are issued in large denominations, e.g. US$500,000 each. The normal covenants and protections which one would typically expect for longer-term debt securities (such as a negative pledge provision and events of default) are not included. The rationale for this is that the investor's credit risk is relatively short-term and hence there is no real need for special credit protections.

The notes contain a tax grossing-up clause in normal Eurobond form.

9–33 Apart from these core provisions, there may be provisions which cater for notes denominated in particular currencies. Examples include ECU (where one would expect provisions dealing with how payment will be made if the ECU ceases to be traded as a recognised composite currency) and sterling (where certain legends are required to appear on the face of the note).

Since most noteholders deliver their notes to a euromarket custodian, notably Euroclear and Cedel, where they remain until maturity, and given the cost of security printing definitive notes, the issuer delivers a single typewritten global note, representing all of the notes being issued, to a representative of the clearing systems (the common depository) which holds it until maturity. The common depositary is therefore the legal holder of this bearer instrument. Global notes provide that a holder can require the issuer to deliver definitive notes in full or partial exchange for the global note upon a specified period of notice.

9–34 **Dealer or programme agreement** The dealer or programme agreement is the agreement between the issuer, the guarantor (if there is one) and the dealers appointed under the programme. It sets up the legal framework pursuant to which notes are issued under the programme once the issuer and the dealers have agreed upon the terms of issue. The agreement has four elements: it sets out the timetable and procedures for any new issue; contains the usual representations, warranties and indemnities of the issuer and, where relevant, the guarantor, repeated whenever notes are issued under the programme; and contains usual selling restrictions whereby dealers sell notes to their investors only in circumstances which comply with applicable securities laws.

Issuing and paying agency agreement The issuing and paying agency agreement is a largely mechanical agreement to streamline the arrangements pursuant to which the notes are actually issued into the market and payments are made under them. 9–35

The issuer delivers pre-signed notes to an agent who fills them in and authenticates them when a deal is struck. The agent receives the purchase moneys on behalf of the issuer and pays amounts due on the notes at maturity out of funds provided by the issuer.

Deed of covenant Since the notes are represented by a global note held by the depositary, since the depositary may be unwilling as holder to get involved in any enforcement, and since defaulting issuers are unlikely to comply with the obligation to deliver definitive notes, the issuer enters into a deed of covenant which provides that, if the issuer fails to make definitive notes available in exchange for the global note, the issuer is obliged to pay the amounts due in respect of the notes directly to the accountholders who are credited as holding the relevant notes in the clearing system. In order to prevent a double obligation, the global note itself becomes void. The purpose of this instrument is to replace the existing contractual relationship that the issuer has with the clearing systems with a directly enforceable obligation between the issuer and the relevant accountholders. Under English law, parties named in a deed (even if not specifically named) can enforce it even though they have not signed it. 9–36

There may similarly be a deed of guarantee for the notes.

Euro medium-term note programmes

Generally

These are framework agreements designed to facilitate the quick, cheap and frequent issue of a wide range of debt instruments. The maturity range of notes issued under the programmes can vary from as little as one month to as long as 30 years. 9–37

The main purpose of these debt instrument programmes is to standardise the terms on which an issuer issues securities and consequently to seek to minimise the documentation for issues of notes, and to restrict the cost, time and administration involved in separately documenting each issue. The market can then respond quickly to borrowing requirements or lending opportunities. Further, many of the non-commercial terms on which large issuers of debt securities in the international capital markets borrow tend not to vary greatly.

Documentation

9–38 Some versions are long and complex to cover all the possibilities, while others are short-form. But typical programme documentation will comprise principally:

- a **programme agreement** (sometimes described as a dealer agreement) between the issuer and the proposed dealers in relation to the establishment and maintenance of the programme and, subject to express variation for any particular issue, the provisions which will apply whenever the issuer and one or more of the dealers agree on the terms for a specific issue under the programme;

- an **agency agreement** between the issuer and the agents appointed to service the programme, to which will be scheduled the forms of the notes which can be issued under the programme;

- an **information memorandum** describing the programme, including the terms and conditions which, unless otherwise agreed between the relevant parties at the relevant time, will apply to notes issued under the programme and giving descriptive information about the issuer (complying, if notes under the programme are to be capable of being listed on a stock exchange, with the requirements of the relevant stock exchange); and

- a **trust deed** (if there is to be a trustee).

9–39 When the issuer and one or more dealers agree on the commercial terms of an issue, it is only those commercial terms, and any other matters which are either not contemplated in the programme documentation or which require a variation to the programme documentation, which need to be included in some form of agreed confirmation. This confirmation is documented as a supplement to the information memorandum for the purposes of disclosure to investors and for listing purposes.

There are obstacles. Law and regulation may change, e.g. securities, tax and banking regulation. The issuer may wish to introduce other group issuers or change the dealers. Less due diligence may in practice be carried out in relation to warranties and the information memorandum prior to each new issue.

Usually there is a periodic review of the programme – perhaps by the provision of updated legal opinions and auditors' comfort letters. The documentation may permit dealers to require specific legal or auditors' confirmations or a revision of the information memorandum.

CHAPTER 10

BOND TRUSTEES AND BONDHOLDER MEETINGS

10–1 This chapter reviews a number of international approaches to is the problem of bondholder representation. The fiduciary duties of trustees are reviewed in chapter 11.

Anglo-American bond trustees

Introduction

10–2 The Anglo-American practice for corporate bond issues is to appoint a trustee in respect of the bonds in order to represent the bondholders. In other countries, corporate legislation often establishes bondholder communities which have voting rights in a similar way to shareholders. One may consider first the Anglo-American bondholder trust.

Advantages for bondholders

10–3 The main advantages of a trustee from the point of view of the bondholders include:

Sophisticated monitoring A sophisticated institution is available to monitor compliance and to study financial information provided by the issuer. More detailed (and even confidential) financial information can be furnished to a trustee which the issuer might be reluctant to put on public display for bondholders generally. A trustee is more likely to become aware of an impending default earlier than individual bondholders.

Resources The trustee has the resources to obtain expert advice (at the expense of the issuer).

Unified enforcement If there were a default, individual legal proceedings by the bondholders might be impracticable because of the disproportionate expense and because concerted action in the common interest is impeded by the wide disparity and anonymity of investors.

Default negotiations If the issuer is in financial difficulties, the trustee can as representative negotiate a debt restructuring with the issuer and other creditors and has the necessary expertise and resources to do so. The trustee can recommend courses of action, but cannot commit the bondholders, e.g. to a moratorium or conversion of the bonds into equity, without their consent. But the trust deed may contain provisions for bondholder meetings to vote on modifications: see below. Of course bonds can contain provisions for bondholder voting even if there is no trustee, but in practice matters are facilitated if there is an expert institution to evaluate restructuring plans and to negotiate a solution. But there is a solid argument that the presence of a trustee can sometimes impede payment to bondholders since, in the absence of a trustee, it is difficult for the issuer to negotiate with bondholders and hence the issuer might therefore be obliged to pay them (or go into an insolvency proceeding).

More protective clauses The presence of a sophisticated monitoring institution facilitates the inclusion of protective covenants and events of default in the bond which it might otherwise be impractical to include, e.g. because of their imprecision (such as a prohibition on "substantial" disposals by the issuer) or because their complexity requires expert review, such as a financial ratio. But many trustees will not agree to the inclusion of a "material adverse change" event of default: the default is too vague to monitor, and therefore exposes the trustee to the risk of liability.

Pro rata payment The presence of a "no-action" clause and clauses requiring post-default payments to be made to the trustee for rateable distribution to bondholders ensure that bondholders are paid pro rata without discrimination and that no single bondholder secures a lead in the race to the court-house door. Compare pro rata sharing clauses in syndicated credits.

Corrections The trustee can be given unilateral power to correct manifest errors. In complex bond issues, such as convertibles, a trustee can be vested with power to resolve unforeseen difficulties, e.g. in the operation of an anti-dilution clause.

Advantages for issuers The issuer may also benefit from the presence of a trustee.

10–5 **Protection against "mad bondholder"** The mad bondholder is the bondholder who actually wishes to be paid. If the issuer is in financial difficulties and hopes to achieve a private rescheduling with its main bank and bond creditors, a single bondholder could accelerate, spark off cross-defaults and effectively force the issuer into formal insolvency proceedings – which, even if they were rehabilitative (US Chapter 11, British administration), generally have a disastrous impact on values and goodwill and hence damage the interests of its creditors. Theoretically, provisions for bondholder voting can control this, but in practice, a "no-action" clause (see below) provides a contractual stay on individual acceleration and enforcement while a restructuring plan is negotiated with the issuer. A trustee is essential to administer the "no-action" clause.

Greater flexibility for waivers and modifications Bonds are often long-term and covenants and defaults which were appropriate at the time of the issue may become unduly restrictive or may prohibit a transaction which does not seriously injure the interests of the bondholders, e.g. the grant of security in contravention of the negative pledge. An event of default might occur which, without a trustee, might expose the issuer to an acceleration by a single bondholder, thereby sparking off cross-defaults and resulting in a collapse of the issuer. In these cases a trustee can be given powers either to deal with the matter itself where the interests of the bondholders are not materially prejudiced or to convene a meeting. The trustee can thus shield the issuer from unreasonable action by bondholders and introduce a flexibility not otherwise available.

Representation On a default, the issuer deals with one representative, not a multitude.

Substitution of debtor Modern eurobond practice allows the trustee to approve a substitution of debtor (under the guarantee of the issuer) if this is desirable, e.g. to avoid a new withholding tax on interest.

Disadvantages of trustees

10–6 But there are disadvantages in having a trustee. The presence of a trustee increases costs and documentation, although often not significantly. Sovereign states and their political sub-divisions commonly regard monitoring by a trustee as a slight to their status: the appointment of a trustee of a sovereign bond issue is accordingly rare. And finally, as mentioned, there is a view that anything which facilitates a postponement of the bondholders' rights or a relaxation of the terms of the bonds is prejudicial to the bondholders. On the whole however the consensus appears to be that there must be some mechanism for bondholder representation and voting even if there is no trustee as such.

Trustees may be required by the circumstances of the issue. A trustee is usually necessary in secured issues to hold the benefit of the security in one name. In some jurisdictions – notably in the Franco-Latin group – land mortgages, for example, must be registered in the name of each creditor, as must assignments of the mortgage. It is impracticable to register each bondholder and each transfer.

A trustee is useful in subordinated issues where the junior bondholders must turn over recoveries to the senior creditors: the trustee can receive the recoveries and turn them over.

Mandatory requirements for a trustee

A trustee may be required by statute or by stock exchange regulation. 10–7

In England there is no statutory requirement for a trustee (except in relation to certain land transactions). Freedom of contract reigns.

In the **United States**, the Trust Indenture Act 1939 (as amended by the Trust Indenture Reform Act of 1990) states that it is unlawful for any person, directly or indirectly, to make use of any means or instruments of transportation or communication in interstate commerce or of the mails to offer or sell bonds unless they are covered by a trust indenture which is registered and qualified under the Act: s 306. Broadly, an international bond issue which avoids the prospectus registration requirements of the Securities Act of 1933 will escape this Act since the exemptions are generally co-extensive with those under the 1933 Act. Exceptionally, the 1939 Act does not apply where the bonds are issued or guaranteed by governments, their political subdivisions or instrumentalities since states regard trustees as a slight. The Act does not apply to bonds guaranteed by a US officially-supervised bank. But unlike the 1933 Act, the 1939 Act contains no exemption for exchange offers.

The SEC may on application exempt bonds proposed to be issued by issuers organised under foreign law and in 1990 the SEC was authorised to exempt any transaction from any provisions of the TIA if found necessary or appropriate in the public interest. Trust indentures must be filed with the SEC for screening in a manner similar to registration statements.

Under s 97 of the **Singapore** Companies Act "every corporation which offers debentures to the public for subscription or purchase in Singapore" must provide for the appointment of a "trustee corporation" as trustee for the holders of the debentures. However, the issue can be exempted by ministerial consent and often is in the case of international issues. Foreign government issues are not caught, nor are issues to professional dealers in securities. The rule applies only to offerings "in Singapore". The position in Australia is thought to be similar.

In **Canada** the legislation is similar to the US 1939 Act: see the Canada Business Corporations Act Part VII.

10–8 **Stock exchange rules** Stock exchanges upon which an issue is listed may insist upon the appointment of a trustee. The London and Singapore stock exchanges require the appointment of a trustee for domestic debt issues, subject to waivers in the UK, e.g. for international bond issues. The Luxembourg stock exchange does not require a trustee.

Comparison of trustees and fiscal agents

10–9 A fiscal agent is wholly different from a trustee. First, a fiscal agent is the agent of the issuer and not the bondholders. A trustee on the other hand is a fiduciary representing the bondholders. Secondly, a trustee has fiduciary and monitoring duties, imposed by the trust deed and by law. A fiscal agent generally has no monitoring or other duties to bondholders under the usual form of fiscal agency agreement. The fiscal agent's main duties are:

(a) to make **payments** to bondholders against presentation of bonds and coupons. The issuer puts the fiscal agent in funds one or two business days prior to the due date and the fiscal agent reimburses the other paying agents for payments made by them. If the full amount is not received, the fiscal agent need pay nothing, i.e. does not have to make pro-rata partial payments.

(b) **administrative obligations,** such as the exchange of a global bond into definitive bonds, the publication of notices, acting as depository for the issuer's annual accounts and other financial information for inspection, the effecting of drawings to determine which bonds are to be redeemed on a partial or optional redemption, the cancellation and destruction of redeemed bonds, the replacement of mutilated, lost or destroyed bonds, and the maintenance of records.

Thirdly, a fiscal agent does not hold the debt claims on trust and is not a creditor of the issuer. It is unusual for the fiscal agent to hold servicing funds on express trust for bondholders to protect them against the insolvency of the fiscal agent; the fiscal agent would have to deposit the funds with a separate bank in a segregated account to identify the trust property and this would be administratively inconvenient. But in the US the imposition of a trust upon moneys held by the fiscal agent is required in regulated trust indentures: s 317(b) of the Trust Indenture Act of 1939.

The issuer pays commission to the fiscal agent by way of remuneration.

Paying agents In addition to the fiscal agent, the issuer directly appoints paying agents in convenient centres. These are not generally sub-agents of the fiscal agent, i.e. the fiscal agent does not take the risk of the sub-agents. It is usually a requirement that there is always a paying agent in the country of the currency of the bonds (to protect bondholders against transfer risks – but not in the case of US dollar issues because of US securities regulation objections) and in one other centre. If the bonds are listed, the stock exchange will commonly require a paying agent within its jurisdiction. A spread of paying agents is not merely for convenience of presentation: paying agents may be required to deduct taxes (unless the bondholder produces an appropriate foreign residence certificate) in one jurisdiction (e.g. the UK) but not in another; and payments in one place may be inhibited by exchange controls, documentary taxes or other restrictions.

The bondholder accordingly has the option of presenting at a paying agent in a more accommodating centre.

Legal characteristics of the trust

Divided ownership

Under traditional Anglo-American law, a trust requires (1) identification of the trust property, (2) intention to create a trust, and (3) identification of the beneficiaries in the sense that it must be clear who is a beneficiary when the trust property vests – they do not have to be specifically named and may be a class. The essence of the trust is that the trustee has the legal ownership of the claims and the beneficiaries have the benefit of those claims. This benefit is a proprietary right, i.e. the claim of the beneficiaries is not merely a debtor-creditor claim in contract against the trustee. This has a number of consequences in common law jurisdictions:

(a) **Enforcement** The trustee as the legal owner has status to sue, enforce and petition for insolvency proceedings.

(b) **Holder of trust property** Because the trustee is the legal owner of the trust property, he can be authorised to deal with that property without any burdensome mechanics involving bondholders. The trustee can receive payments after a default and distribute them. In secured issues, the trustee can hold the security and be the registered holder.

(c) **Ownership on insolvency** Since the beneficiaries have a proprietary interest in the trust assets and therefore do not claim from the trustee merely in contract as creditors of the trustee, if the trustee were to become insolvent, those assets would not normally be claimable by the creditors of the trustee: they do not belong to the trustee. This is not important in practice, since trustees of international bond issues are usually independent trust corporations of undoubted credit.

(d) **Wrongful disposals** If the trustee disposes of the trust assets in breach of trust, the beneficiaries generally have a right to trace the property into whosoever's hands it may come, other than a bona fide purchaser for value in good faith. It is their property. Again, this is of little practical importance since trustees are usually responsible institutions.

What is the trust property?

10–12　In an unsecured issue, the trust property vested in the trustee is the issuer's covenant to pay. The issuer covenants directly with the bondholders in the bonds and gives the trustee a parallel payment covenant. Both the trustee and the bondholders are therefore direct creditors of the issuer. Because this is a duplicate covenant, the trust deed provides that payments by the issuer to bondholders via the paying agency arrangements discharge the parallel covenant in favour of the trustee pro tanto. After a default, the trust deed generally provides that the trustee can require the paying agents or the issuer itself to pay the trustee direct which then holds the proceeds for the account of the bondholders.

By contrast, the practice for English domestic debenture issues in sterling (as opposed to eurobond issues) is that the covenant to pay is given only to the trustee for the debentureholders who are issued with stock certificates recording the terms of the covenants in favour of the trustee. Only the trustee is a creditor of the issuer and not the debentureholders.

The reason for the difference is that the international bond market expects a bearer instrument to contain a direct covenant, whereas domestic issues are invariably registered issues where the same expectation is not present.

Civilian attitudes to the trust

10–13　Trusteeship is an established concept in common law jurisdictions such as the United States, England, Canada, New Zealand, Australia and English-influenced countries. It is however a concept foreign to most countries in the Franco-Latin, Germanic, and Scandinavian groups.

Among the main reasons for the Roman objection to the trust were, firstly, the insolvency hostility to *false wealth* – the debtor with many apparent possessions but little property, thereby deceiving creditors into unjustified credit – the trust is secret; and secondly the unpredictability of *priorities* – an asset which a person sells or mortgages may be held in trust for another so that there may be a priority conflict between the undisclosed beneficiary and the buyer or mortgagee.

Common law jurisdictions jettisoned the "false wealth" policy because (a) the trust was too useful, and (b) it was more important to them that one person's property should not be expropriated to pay another person's creditors, than that creditors should be protected against false wealth. This means that in common law countries priorities are much more complicated. There needs to be some means of protecting the safety of commercial transactions from the secret beneficiary. The risks for purchasers/mortgagees is mitigated by the principle that they rank ahead of the beneficiary if they took for value in good faith without notice of the beneficiary's rights. Apart from land transactions (where the purchaser must positively make reasonable title investigations), notice in commercial transactions is usually actual notice or notice of suspicious circumstances which should put the third party on enquiry.

The "false wealth" and priority objections are of little practical relevance to trusts of bond issues. Hence a number of civil code countries have legislated an approximation of the trust into their legal systems for *debenture issues*, e.g. Argentina, Panama, Chile and Mexico (since 1926), probably as a result of British and American investment. See Pasquel, "The Mexican Fideicomiso: The Reception, Evolution and Present Status of the Common Law Trust in a Civil Law Country", 8 *Columbia Journal of Transnational Law* 54 (1969). In Switzerland, the Netherlands, Germany and Luxembourg, there are fiduciary representatives for holders of debt securities, but it appears they are not trustees in the common law sense since they do not hold trust property which is owned by beneficiaries; there is no parallel covenant in favour of the trustee. Hence the objection to "false wealth" overrides. Further, they do not have authority to sue on behalf of bondholders because they are not owners and not creditors of the issuer: but Luxembourg allows this by special statute.

10–14 Luxembourg law provides for a fiduciary representative as well as the more normal civilian bondholder's representative. Following the *Four Seasons Case* in 1971 in which a Luxembourg court refused to recognise a bondholder resolution made under a trust deed authorising the trustee to claim in the bankruptcy of the issuer on behalf of the bondholders, a decree was enacted in 1972 allowing the use of a *fiduciaire representant*. The law does not import the trust concept of holding assets for beneficiaries, but does permit the trustee to represent bondholders in legal actions and insolvency proceedings. Apart from this, the trustee is purely a representative: i.e. "a legal entity charged with representing and protecting the interests of owners of securities by virtue of a trust agreement (*convention fiduciaire*) entered into between such entity and an issuer of such securities, with the consent, albeit tacit, of such owners". The trust agreement can (and must) stipulate the procedures and clauses of the agreement which can be modified. The trustee must not allow conflicts of interest and has monitoring duties: see para 11–8. The Decree appears mainly to supplement the powers and duties of representatives of bondholder communities under existing Luxembourg law: see para 10–33.

Fiduciary duties of trustees

10–15   The fiduciary duties of trustee in this context are reviewed in chapter 11, notably the position relating to:

- conflicts of interest and secret profits
- due diligence by the trustee
- Chinese walls
- exculpation clauses
- trustee's indemnity.

Eligibility to act as trustee or representative

Regulatory requirements

10–16   The general practice in the international markets is for the trustee to be a professional trust corporation except in Germany where the representative is generally the lead manager of the issue.

Where statute imposes an obligation to appoint a trustee, it is also generally provided that the trustee must be a corporation of a specified minimum *financial standing* (to protect bondholders against impropriety by the trustee followed by the trustee's insolvency) and must be *locally incorporated* so as to be subject to the jurisdiction of the courts and to the supervision of a domestic authority who can monitor the trustee's financial standing and fiduciary reputation.

In **England** there are no statutory requirements except that the stock exchange in London, if it requires a trustee, insists upon a trust corporation, i.e. a UK trust corporation satisfying certain (unburdensome) capital tests: see the Trustee Act 1925 s 68. But, because the Stock Exchange can waive a trustee in eurobond issues, foreign trust corporations are often allowed. Both **Canada** and the **United States** require a local trustee for *regulated* issues but in the United States only one of the trustees need be a local trustee corporation under official supervision. But by s 310(a)(1) of the US Trust Indenture Act of 1939 as amended in 1990, the SEC has broad powers to permit foreign entities to serve as sole trustees under qualified indentures. In **Singapore**, the trustee (if required) must be a local public corporation or a foreign public corporation prescribed as such by the Minister of Law. In civilian countries the bondholders' representative must sometimes be a national, e.g. as in France.

While the supervisory and jurisdictional aspects should not be overlooked, nationality requirements can be a nuisance factor in international issues where a foreign trustee may be better suited to the circumstances of the issue.

For trustees who have a conflict of interest, see chapter 11.

Retirement of trustees

The English Trustee Act 1925 confers a statutory power on trustees to resign subject to conditions. The Australian and Singapore corporate legislation do not permit a trustee of a regulated public issue to retire unless a successor is appointed.

10–17

English trust deeds normally provide that the trustee has power to resign without giving reasons and an extraordinary resolution of bondholders may remove the trustee. The power to appoint new trustees is generally vested in the issuer with the approval of an extraordinary resolution of bondholders. If there is no express power, an English court ultimately has a statutory power under the Trustee Act 1925 s 36.

Bondholders' meetings

Generally

Since each bondholder has a separate contract with the issuer, changes to the terms of the bonds could not be achieved outside statutory insolvency or reorganisation proceedings unless every bondholder were to agree. The obstacles in the path of unanimous agreement, especially in the case of

10–18

bearer bonds, will usually be insuperable. Even if all the bondholders could be traced or persuaded to act, a perverse bondholder could set his face against a move in the general interest of the bondholders and thereby force them or the issuer into paying him out preferentially in order to protect their position.

These difficulties are mitigated if the bondholders can pass resolutions which bind dissenting and absent bondholders and also if the bondholders have a representative who has the necessary expertise and resources to recommend courses of action.

Paradoxically, particularly in the case of state insolvency, the absence of a trustee has, in practice, enhanced the ability of bondholders to secure priority of payment because there is no means of bringing pressure to bear on individual bondholders to reschedule or preventing them from suing and thereby disturbing an orderly rescheduling.

Nevertheless in the ordinary case, unless there is some measure of democratic control, an unreasonable or quiescent minority could dictate to the majority and imperil a beneficial arrangement necessary in an emergency or desirable for the common weal.

Main issues for bondholder decision

10–19 The four principal issues are:

1. Restraint on individual bondholder **acceleration and enforcement** while negotiations with the issuer and other creditors take place

2. Ascertaining the views of the bondholders by the requisitioning of **meetings** or otherwise

3. Identifying those **rights which can be overridden** by bondholders' resolutions and those which should be entrenched

4. Protecting **minority rights** against oppressive, discriminatory or otherwise improper conduct by the majority.

The most common circumstances where bondholders' views are required are where the issuer is in financial difficulties or default, where the issuer seeks a relaxation of a covenant or an event of default to permit prohibited transactions to go forward, e.g. a charge in breach of a negative pledge, and where the issuer is merged as part of a solvent reorganisation.

10–20 In practice, the matter is of greatest importance when the issuer is in financial difficulties. The choice faced by creditors is usually to agree a restructuring of bank, bondholder and other debt, e.g. by rescheduling or by conversion of debt to equity, by private agreement; or to apply for a rehabilitation proceeding, e.g. the US Chapter 11, the British administration under the Insolvency Act 1986, or the French *redressement judiciaire* (1985); or to apply for final liquidation.

Both final liquidation and rehabilitation proceedings tend to destroy the value of the borrower's property and its goodwill — few will contract with an insolvent company. Rehabilitation proceedings tend to be very expensive and long drawn-out because all creditors are involved (not just banks and bondholders) and because of court involvement.

Hence a private debt restructuring is almost invariably more protective of the value of the business and creditor recoveries. But a private agreement is not possible unless all creditors of a class agree to be treated equally since no creditor will bear the burden unless his fellows do so as well. If a bondholder chooses to enforce, then the private restructuring is jeopardised.

Most of the leading jurisdictions permit minority bondholders to be bound by a majority vote. But a few (e.g. the US) refuse to allow a bondholder's payment rights to be overridden or impose high quorum on special majorities which are impractical (e.g. 75 per cent of all bondholders, not just those voting), so that in practice the issuer may be forced into a disadvantageous insolvency proceeding, where typically the bondholder's rights can be overridden by a plan approved by majority creditors and the court, e.g. the US Chapter 11 under BC 1978. Often in the United States, Chapter 11 is the only way out if the debtor has significant public debt. France requires unanimity on debt/equity conversions.

Judical rehabilitation proceedings and private debt restructurings are discussed in another work in this series of works on international financial law.

Enforcement by trustees

Acceleration The conventional English eurobond trust deed provides that if an event of default occurs:

> "The Trustee at its discretion may, and if so requested in writing by the holders of at least one-fifth in principal amount of the Bonds then outstanding or if so directed by an Extraordinary Resolution of the Bondholders, shall [accelerate] the Bonds."

Many English eurobond trust deeds also provide that certain defaults, e.g. breach of covenant or defaults relating to subsidiaries, will not be events of default unless the trustee certifies that in its opinion the occurrence of the event is materially prejudicial to bondholders.

The discretion to accelerate without reference to the bondholders is designed to enable quick action to be taken if required. On the other hand if the trustee is not prepared to accelerate on its own initiative then under the usual form there can be no acceleration unless the stipulated percentage of bondholders so demand. The intent is to prevent premature action by a single bondholder prejudicial to the general interest.

The trustee's power of acceleration must be an express authorisation and, where a stipulated percentage is required to accelerate the bonds, then that requirement must be strictly adhered to or the acceleration will be ineffectual: *Re Berker Sportcraft Ltd's Agreements* (1947) 177 LT 420 (English decision); *Maloney v Home Loan & Trust Co*, 97 Ind App 564,186, NE 897 (1933) modified 187 NE 682 (1933).

Where bonds are trading well below par, the pressure on a trustee to accelerate for a technical breach may be intense. If the issuer is otherwise sound, the trustee should consider whether an opportunistic acceleration would serve the interests of the bondholders as a whole as opposed to those who may have bought the bonds speculatively.

In the absence of a trust deed, each bondholder normally has the right to accelerate his own bond but not the whole issue.

Compare syndicated loans, where acceleration is generally controlled by the majority banks.

For a review of a trustee's duty to notify defaults and for exculpation clauses relieving a trustee for maladministration, see chapter 11.

10–22 **Trustee duties on acceleration** Once the bonds have been accelerated, the trustee should have adequate powers to take enforcement proceedings on behalf of the bondholders. English eurobond practice gives the trustee a discretion to enforce on its own initiative but usually establishes that it is not bound to enforce unless directed to do so by an extraordinary resolution of bondholders or in writing by holders of not less than, say, one-fifth in principal amount of the outstanding bonds and in either case only if indemnified against costs and liabilities in connection with the enforcement.

10–23 **No-action clauses** Commonly the bondholders themselves are prevented from taking independent action by a "no-action" clause. This clause is intended (a) to prevent the race of the most diligent with consequent risk of preferential payments to those bondholders who are able to act most quickly, (b) to prevent a multiplicity of suits and (c) to avoid action by a single bondholder which jeopardises the common security or results in conflicting enforcement actions.

The clause states that no bondholder is to be entitled to enforce unless the trustee, having become bound to enforce, fails to do so within a reasonable time, i.e. the rights of the bondholders to take sole action are suspended.

Rights of enforcement are not usually restrained by no-action clauses in syndicated credits – except sometimes in project finance credit agreements.

The courts have scrutinised no-action clauses in relation to enforcement closely and have shown reluctance to allow inhibitions of the fundamental right to sue to recover one's money.

> In the Canadian decision of *Re Imperial Steel Corp Ltd* (1925) 28 OWN 242 (Ont App Div), the required direction from the majority of the bondholders for an enforcement was not forthcoming and the trustee declined to take the initiative himself. *Held*: any bondholder could bring a class action to have the provisions of the trust deed enforced.
>
> In *Shaughnessy v The Imperial Trusts Company* (1904) NB (Eq R 5), the trustee maintained that the bondholders should put up an indemnity and let the trustee bring the action. *Held*: the right to take the proceeding did not depend in any way upon the trustee refusing. It was the absolute right of the bondholder in order to enforce his own security and recover his own debt.

A leading case in France is *Kerr v Societe Pyrennees Minerals* (Cass February 19, 1908, Clunet 1912, 243, affirming Court of Appeals, Toulouse July 18, 1905, Clunet 1906, 451):

> An English company issued bonds secured by a mortgage on French mines. Both the English trust deed and the French mortgage contained a no-action clause. A bondholder sought to foreclose the mortgage contrary to the clause. The court compared the no-action clause in the trust deed with the position in France as between bondholders and their representative and held that it was not contrary to public policy and should be upheld.

In the **United States** no-action clauses have come under statutory attack in the case of regulated trust indentures. Section 316 of the Trustee Indentures Act of 1939 states that the indenture must provide that the right of a bondholder to institute suit for enforcement of payment after the due date is (subject to a limited exemption for interest) not to be impaired or affected within the consent of the holder, i.e. the right of enforcement is entrenched. Apart from the 1939 Act restrictions, the courts themselves have restricted the scope of no-action clauses:

10–24

> In *Perry v Darlington Fireproofing Co*, 76 Ohio App 101, 63 NE 2d 222 (1945), the court said: "If any such restriction is uncertain, obscure or ambiguous, then any such doubt or uncertainty will be resolved against the maker of the bond and in favour of the bearer thereof."
>
> In *Hirschfield v Astoria Associates Inc*, 139 NYS 2d 519 (Sup Ct 1955), a clause limiting the right to sue "for the enforcement of any covenant herein" was construed not to apply to an "obligation" to pay but only to "covenants" not to incur senior mortgage debts, etc.

A number of US cases have held that the no-action clause must be drawn to the attention of the bondholders in the bond itself and that normally a provision that the terms of the trust deed are incorporated in the bond and that the bond is subject to all its provisions is not sufficient. See *Oswianza v Wengler & Mandell Inc*, 358 Ill 302, 193 NE 123 (1934); *Rittenhouse v Lukens Steel Co*, 116 Pa Super 303, 176 Atl 543 (1935); *Cunningham v Pressed Steel Car Co*, 238 App Div 624, 265 NY Supp 256 (1933). See para 8–40.

10–25 **Insolvency proceedings** The trustee should be given power to file claims in bankruptcy or liquidation and to vote in relation to reorganisation proposals so that the trustee can take concerted action on behalf of the bondholders. Without such express delegation these powers may not be implied. Authorisations on these lines are required by s 317 of the US Trustee Indenture Act of 1939.

Representative actions Court rules may allow a bondholder to bring a representative action on behalf of himself and all other members of the class: an example is the English RSC Ord 15, r 2. The detail is complex.

Organisation of bondholders

10–26 Bondholders cannot act in concert nor can a trustee or bondholder's representative ascertain their views unless there is some procedure for the holding of meetings.

Common law jurisdictions do not generally make statutory provision for bondholder meetings, but trust deeds invariably do. In England a trust deed is useful, but not essential, to provide for meetings: these rights can be given by the bond itself, by a fiscal agency agreement or by a deed poll – this is a deed executed by the issuer for the benefit of bondholders and is in effect the English way of creating a third party beneficary contract.

England The rules of the stock exchange in London require that the trust deed (if one is required) for an issue listed on the exchange must provide that a meeting of bondholders is to be called on a requisition in writing signed by holders of at least one-tenth of the nominal amount of the bonds.

North America In the United States and Canada, although there are no statutory provisions for meetings as such, in the case of regulated issues the trustee and the issuer must (subject to safeguards) provide lists of bondholders who have left their names with the issuer for this purpose and it is then up to the bondholders themselves to lobby other bondholders: see s 312 of the US 1939 Act and s 80 of the Canada Business Corporations Act.

Civil code countries In civil code countries, by contrast, statute often enables bondholders representing a proportion of the outstanding bonds to call meetings to vote on matters of common interest: 5 per cent is prescribed in Brazil, France, Germany and Switzerland but others have a higher percentage, with Belgium requiring an improbable 20 per cent.

Issues on which majority can bind minority

Among the matters which statute and practice contemplate as being possible subjects of bondholders resolutions are: postponement, reduction or cancellation of **payments** of principal, premium or interest; the release or creation of **security** or a guarantee for the bonds; **reorganisation** of the borrower, e.g. on a merger or as a result of an insolvency; **conversion** of the bonds into shares or an exchange of the bonds for other securities, again in connection with mergers or as a part of a compromise on insolvency; alteration of the **currency** of the bonds; **waiver** of a covenant or an event of default (e.g. to enable a work-out to proceed); **exoneration of the trustee** from liability so as to enable the trustee to take action which it might otherwise feel unsafe in taking; the appointment of a **committee** to represent bondholders, especially in liquidation and reorganisation proceedings; and **removal of the trustee** or the bondholders' representatives.

10–27

There is no uniformity as to the matters which are considered so fundamental that each bondholder should have a right of veto.

England English eurobond practice is to confer very wide powers upon bondholders meetings but, in order to protect minority bondholders against abuse of majority power, to require high quorums and majorities for fundamental matters, e.g. a vote of three-quarters of bondholders present at the meeting at which a quorum is three-quarters of the outstanding bonds (an almost impossible quorum in the case of bearer bonds). Other matters may be entrenched, particularly an alteration of currency or a reduction or cancellation of principal.

Civilian countries Civilian legislation tends either to confer a general authorisation whereby bondholders meetings can decide matters of common interest or else to list those matters which may be the subject of a resolution: para 10–32 *et seq*.

United States The policy of the US Trustee Indenture Act of 1939 is to protect the rights of individual bondholders under regulated indentures rather than to permit flexibility. Under s 316 of the Act the indenture must provide that the right of a bondholder to receive payment of principal and interest

10-27 BOND TRUSTEES AND BONDHOLDER MEETINGS

on the bonds on the due dates is otherwise not to be impaired or affected without the consent of each bondholder; hence private work-outs are impossible unless *all* bondholders agree. Apart from this, s 316 allows the inclusion in regulated indentures of provisions (i) authorising the holders of not less than a majority in principal amount of the bonds to direct the time, method and place of conducting proceedings or of exercising the trustee's powers or consenting to the waiver of past defaults, and (ii) authorising the holders of not less than 75 per cent in principal amount of the bonds to consent to the postponement of interest payments for a period not exceeding three years. Note that these restrictions apply only to regulated indentures.

Minority protection

10-28 Trust deeds and statutes in most cases confer wide powers on bondholders' meetings so as not to inhibit reasonable action in this or that special circumstance. There might therefore be a corresponding danger of abuse of majority power.

In **civilian countries** corporate statutes usually establish protections against minority oppression. One method is to subject bondholders' resolutions to judicial review. For example, in Japan Com C Art 326 provides that resolutions must be approved by the court and the court will not approve a resolution where (among other things) the resolution has come to be adopted in an improper manner, is markedly unfair or is contrary to the interests of the bondholders generally.

10-29 **English law** Bondholders voting at a general meeting are not bound to disregard their own selfish interests but are entitled to vote in whatever way they think best for themselves.

> In *Goodfellow v Nelson Line* [1912] 2 Ch 324, 333, Barker J said: "The powers conferred by the trust deed on a majority of debenture-holders must, of course, be exercised bona fide, and the Court can no doubt interfere to prevent unfairness or oppression, but, subject to this, each debenture-holder may vote with regard to his individual interests, though these interests may be peculiar to himself and not shared by debenture-holders."

The resolution can be attacked if:

(a) There is unfairness or **oppression**: *Goodfellow v Nelson Line* [1912] 2 Ch 324. Probably there will be unfairness if there is discrimination between lenders or the minority are deprived of an advantage accorded to the majority.

> In *Re New York Taxi-Cab Co* [1913] 1 Ch 1, a resolution was invalidated

because it purported to provide for a distribution otherwise than pari passu between the debenture-holders.

(b) **Secret advantages** are given to one bondholder.

In *British American Nickel Corp v O'Brien Ltd* [1927] AC 369, the resolutions concerned were invalidated because, amongst other things, certain votes had been secured by the promise of issue of stock to a large holder of bonds in order to induce him to assent to the compromise.

(c) The resolution is not strictly within the **terms of the power**. Powers enabling some lenders to bind the others must be strictly complied with and must be framed in clear and explicit terms.

In *Mercantile Investment and General Trust Co v The International Co of Mexico* (1891) [1893] 1 Ch 484 n at 489, CA, the court said: "A power to release mortgaged premises does not include the power to release the company. The power to modify the rights of the debentureholders against the company does not include a power to relinquish all their rights. A power to compromise their rights presupposes some dispute about them or difficulties in enforcing them and does not include a power to exchange their debentures for shares in another company where there is no such dispute or difficulty. A power to compromise does not include a power to make presents."

In *Hay v Swedish and Norwegian Railway Co Ltd* [1889] 5 TLR 460, CA, the trust deed provided that resolutions passed by the requisite majority should be binding on all the debentureholders. No specific powers were inserted. *Held*: the majority had no power to sanction any departure from the terms of the trust deed.

However generally resolutions within the competence of the meeting have been upheld, even if they converted redeemable bonds into irredeemable bonds: *Re Joseph Stocks & Co Ltd* [1909] 26 TLR 41.

Under the **EC Admissions Directive**, undertakings are under a legal obligation to treat holders of pari passu debt securities equally except for certain offers of early repayment: para 15–9.

In the **United States**, the decisions are to similar effect. The present restrictions on the powers of the majority to bind the majority contained in s 316 of the Trustee Indenture Act 1939 have already been remarked upon.

In *Crosthwaite v Moline Plow Co*, 298 Fed 466 (SDNY 1924), the court allowed a reorganisation involving an exchange of security approved by the requisite majority. The court said: "It has been held in this court . . . that it would be most inequitable to allow a small minority of bondholders . . . in the absence of even any pretense of fraud or unfairness, to defeat the wishes of the overwhelming majority of those associated with them in the benefits of their common security, provided the benefits of an equitable readjustment are extended to all classes of creditors or security holders in like manner."

In *Aladdin Hotel Co v Bloom*, 200 F 2d 627 (8th Cir 1953), a modification was permitted by a specified percentage of the bondholders. That percentage extended the maturity by 10 years. A non-assenting bondholder sued the obligor on the bonds. *Held*: the bondholder was bound by the extension and could not sue.

Trustee's unilateral power to waive and modify

10–31 Anglo-American trust deeds often give the trustee unilateral power to waive breaches, to determine conclusively whether a particular act will constitute a default, and to modify the terms of the bonds if the trustee considers that the matter concerned is not materially prejudicial to bondholders, subject to a bondholder resolution to the contrary. Modifications which are formal, technical or made to correct a manifest error are universally allowed. Whether a trustee should use these powers or call a bondholders meeting to sanction a proposal is often a difficult question, e.g. where the trustee is requested to whitewash a substantial disposal by the issuer or a charge otherwise in breach of a negative pledge, or to accept a bank guarantee in lieu of accelerating on default.

Bondholder communities: comparative review

10–32 This section gives examples of corporate statutes in civil code states regulating bondholder communities.

France A 1935 law provides that bondholders of a class of bonds issued by an SA be grouped as a matter of law into an association having legal personality: the *masse des obligataires*. Meetings are convened by the company or by the holders of one-thirtieth of outstanding bonds by value.

A 1966 law limits the matters requiring the unanimous consent of the bondholder to three – an increase in obligations of bondholders, unequal treatment amongst bondholders of the same class, and the conversion of debt into equity.

The 1966 Law otherwise confers wide powers on the *masse* including a power to appoint a representative. The representative may perform ordinary acts of conservation but a meeting must authorise the representative to sue the company or realise security. A 75 per cent majority by value and the approval of the court is required for a consent to an alteration of the company's objects, a compromise of the bondholders' claims, a modification of the security (if any), or a deferment of interest or principal. No resolution may discriminate between bondholders by treating them differently.

However, because the rules regarding meetings of the *masse*, quorum and majority requirements and the qualifications of the representative are not suited to or are impracticable in international issues of bearer securities, and because many international issues by French borrowers were governed by foreign law, a 1967 Law exempted debt issues by French enterprises outside France.

Where the issue is exempt, some French issuers have constituted a *société civile*. This is a type of civil partnership set up by the bond issue documentation and to which all bondholders belong. Typically the document provides for representation of bondholders, the exclusion of individual bondholder action, and bondholder meetings. The *société civile* of bondholders has been recognised by the French courts since 1927.

See Delaume, "Choice of Law and Forum Clauses in Euro-bonds", 11 *Columbia Journal of Transnational Law* 240 (1972); Frederic C Rich, "Are bondholders' rights protected?" *Euromoney*, September 1981, 95.

Belgium and Luxembourg In Belgium and Luxembourg the law is similar: see the Belgian Co-ordinated Laws on Commercial Companies Arts 91–95, and the Luxembourg Commercial Companies Law of 1915 as amended, Arts 86–90.

10–33

In both cases a general meeting of bondholders of an SA may be called by a director or auditors or upon the requisition of the holders of 20 per cent by value of outstanding bonds.

The competence of the meeting includes the release of security, the reduction and postponement of interest, extension of maturity, conversion of bonds into shares, and changes in the purposes of the company. However, these powers lapse in the event of a composition or bankruptcy at which point the powers of the individual bondholder are resurrected. In Luxembourg the list has been held to be exhaustive.

Votes are passed by a three-quarters majority by value of votes cast in Belgium and two-thirds in Luxembourg. However, in Belgium, unless the resolution is supported by at least one-third of the bonds outstanding, the resolution must be approved by the court. Bondholder resolutions for the reduction of security or the appointment of a representative to deal with the company require only a simple majority vote. Resolutions altering the rights of a particular series of bonds are effective only if approved by an appropriate majority of holders of that class at a separate meeting.

Germany The matter is regulated by the Law concerning the Rights of Bondholders (*Schuldverschreibungsgesetz*) of 1899 as amended.

10–34

Bondholders of an AG (except in the case of small bond issues) can appoint a representative who fills a similar representative function to the English trustee for debentureholders. The representative is usually the bank managing the issue. The representative's powers are defined by the resolution appointing him. He may, by a resolution passed by a 75 per cent majority by value at a bondholder meeting, be given exclusive power to enforce the bondholders' rights.

Modifications or surrenders require the same majority, but the principal of the bond cannot be cancelled or reduced without unanimous consent. Other modifications (such as reduction in the rate of interest or postponement of a redemption date) are permitted only if necessary to enable the company to pay its current debts which are due or to avoid bankruptcy.

10–35 **Japan** The provisions for meetings of debentureholders of a Japanese *Kabushiki-Kaisha* (joint-stock company) are contained in ComC Arts 319 to 341. Except as otherwise provided, a meeting of debentureholders may adopt resolutions, with the permission of the court, in respect of any matter which seriously affects the interests of debentureholders. There must be a meeting for each class of debentures.

The issuer, the manager of the issue or 10 per cent by value of holders can convene a meeting.

The court will not approve a resolution if (inter alia) it is adopted in an improper manner, is markedly unfair or is contrary to the interests of holders generally. Discriminatory treatment can be rescinded.

It seems that alterations to the terms of the debentures require a vote of two-thirds or more of holders present representing more than half the debentures.

See also the Secured Bonds Trust Law of 1905 as amended.

10–36 **Switzerland** In Switzerland, the provisions for bondholders' communities are set out in CO Arts 1157 to 1186. See *Swiss Securities Law*, English translation by Swiss-American Chamber of Commerce (1982). If bonds are issued "directly or indirectly by a public subscription under uniform loan terms by an obligor domiciled or having a business establishment in Switzerland" (which would appear to exclude foreign government issues but not foreign companies having a Swiss establishment), the creditors by law form a community of creditors. There is a separate community for each issue of bonds.

These provisions expressly do not apply to bond issues by the Swiss Confederation, Cantons, municipalities or entities established under public law.

The assembly of creditors can appoint a representative who has the powers conferred on him by law, by the terms of the bond or by the assembly. The obligor must pay his costs. Powers delegated to the representative may not be independently exercised by the creditors. If the obligor is in default, the representative can call upon the issuer to provide pertinent information. He can attend board meetings in an advisory capacity if the interests of the bond creditors are involved. The obligor can itself call an assembly and must do so if 15 per cent by value of bondholders or the representative so requests. A moratorium applies to the rights of the creditors on publication of the convocation of the assembly until the resolution is passed. This moratorium can be lifted if the obligor abuses the right.

Two-thirds majority of the principal of the loan (not just the bondholders present) is required for resolutions on moratoriums and waivers of interest and principal (subject to detailed limits), prepayments, grant of prior security for new money, alteration or release of security, alteration or ratios of bonds to share capital, and conversion of bonds into shares. No bond creditor can be bound by a resolution altering his rights on any other matter. He cannot be obliged to make contributions to which he has not consented. The powers of the court under composition proceedings are reserved. Creditors of each community must be equally treated. Preferences to particular creditors of a community are void.

All resolutions must be approved by the court which can refuse approval if, amongst other things, the common interests of creditors are not sufficiently safeguarded, or a resolution passed to prevent a critical situation of the obligor proves not to be necessary, or the resolution has been brought about by improper means. The rights granted to the community of creditors and the representative cannot be excluded or restricted by contract, but the bond terms can make the adoption of resolutions of the assembly more difficult.

Bonds held by custodians

As explained in para 8–37, most negotiable bonds are deposited with custodians, noticably Euroclear in Brussels and Cedel in Luxemburg, who may in turn deposit with sub-custodians in the country of the currency or issuer to collect payment.

If bonds are payable to a trustee and there is no parallel covenant by the issuer to the bondholders, then it is the trustee who is the creditor who is entitled to vote: *Re Dunderland Iron Ore Co* (1877) 6 Ch D 627; *Re Uruguay Rly Co* (1879) 11 Ch D 372.

On general principles, the physical holder of a bond who has the covenant in his favour is the creditor. Hence the entitlement to vote is vested in the custodian or sub-custodian.

Custodians are often very unwilling to become involved in voting on bondholder plans or debt restructurings. There are three solutions:

1. The bondholders could retrieve their bonds from the custodians. This would be expensive.

2. Statute could treat the ultimate benefical owner as the creditor entitled to vote and ignore the custodian. This is the solution adopted in Germany: if bonds are governed by German law and deposited with the *Deutsche Kassenverein*, which is a depository and clearing system, the ultimate owner is treated as the owner: Safekeeping and Purchasing of Securities Act of February 4, 1937, as amended. But few states have adopted this.

3. The bondholders could instruct the custodian as to how their votes are to be exercised and the custodian, as holder, could give the bondholder an open proxy to vote on behalf of the holder. The problem is that the bonds are usually held on a fungible basis and no particular bond is held for a particular bondholder. Hence there must be arrangments whereby the custodian allocates bonds to specfic bondholders. If the bonds are not serially numbered, they can only be allocated by amount.

Best practice is for the trust deed to provide that, where bondholders have deposited bonds with, say, Euroclear or Cedel, the votes are vested in the account-holders in the custodian's books.

Governing law of trust deeds

Contract between issuer and trustee

10–38 The contract between the trustee and the issuer, e.g. the parallel covenant to pay, is no doubt governed by the normal choice of law and conflict rules relating to contracts and negotiable instruments. These are discussed in another work in this series.

Relationship between trustee and bondholders

The relationship between the trustee and bondholders is outside the Rome Convention on the Law Applicable to Contractual Obligations of 1980 (Art 1(2)) but in England is governed by the Recognition of Trusts Act 1987 implementing the Hague Convention on Trusts of 1986. The Hague Convention has been ratified by Italy. This provides that the validity, construction, effects and administration of a trust are governed by the law chosen by the settlor or, in the absence of any such choice, by the law with which the trust is mostly closely connected: Arts 6, 7 and 8. The effect therefore is that, whether the issue is within the scope of the Rome Convention or the Hague Convention, the governing law is dominant. Both have savings for mandatory rules of the forum: see Arts 15 and 16 of the Hague Convention. These may possibly lead to the collapse of the trust on insolvency in countries which do not recognise the trust: para 10–13.

Conflict with bondholder statutes

The terms of a trust deed may collide with a local statute regarding bondholder representatives and communities. 10–39

For example, resolutions duly passed under the trust deed postponing the maturity of principal or accepting an exchange of securities may be invalid under the local statute, e.g. because the resolution dealt with a matter outside the competence of the bondholders' community.

The first question is whether the statute applies to the bond issue in question. Usually the civilian bondholder statutes apply only to issues by local corporations and not, e.g. by foreign governments. Sometimes it is apparent that only issues to the local public are caught, not private offerings or issues abroad. The Swiss rules apply to issues to the public (presumably the Swiss public) by an obligor domiciled or having a business establishment in Switzerland so that a foreign corporation with a local branch and issuing bonds to the public in Switzerland might be caught.

The US Trustee Indenture Act of 1939 (which limits the scope of bondholder resolutions) is exceptional in applying to all non-exempt public issues which (inter alia) involve a use of the US mails or interstate communication (including US telephones or telexes), whether or not the issuer is US or foreign.

The next question is whether contracting-out is possible. The Swiss and US codes prohibit contracting-out. The Luxembourg list of matters on which bondholders can pass resolutions has been held to be exhaustive.

If contracting-out is not permitted the local courts might treat the statute as a mandatory rule of public policy which overrides the governing law.

> In *Chemins de Fer Portugais v Ash* (Cass March 1944, S 1945 I 77, Rev 1940– 46 107) the Court of Cassation refused to enforce, on the ground of public policy, a Portuguese judicial order confirming a plan approved by 91 per cent of the holders of bonds of a Portuguese railway company which waived a gold clause and authorised the obligor to issue preferential bonds.

Most bondholders resolutions are passed in the context of the financial difficulties of the issuer and hence are very similar to insolvency compositions and voting on reorganisation plans. Hence one might expect that attitudes to the recognition of bondholder resolutions will be similiar to the attitudes to the recognition of foreign insolvency compositions. These are briefly reviewed in another work in this series.

Prescriptive jurisdiction

10–40 Where an issue of bonds conflicts with a local statute imposing regulatory or criminal sanctions, no doubt the rules as to prescriptive jurisdiction are brought into play. The United States, Singapore and Australian legislation on regulated trust deeds impose sanctions of this type. For a general discussion of prescriptive jurisdiction in the field of securities regulation, see chapter 20.

Chapter 11

SYNDICATE AGENTS AND BONDHOLDER TRUSTEES AS FIDUCIARIES

Comparison of bondholder trustees and syndicate agents

Generally

This chapter reviews the duties of syndicate agents and bondholder trustees as fiduciaries representing the interests of the banks or bondholders respectively. They are treated together by reason of the similarity of the law and in order to avoid repetition. 11–1

There are a number of similarities between bondholder trustees and bank syndicate agents. Both are representatives of the lenders, not the borrower or issuer. Both are fiduciaries under agency and trust law and therefore subject to fiduciary duties protecting beneficiaries, e.g. no unauthorised conflict of interest, no secret profits, due diligence, no delegation of powers and duties.

Both are unwilling to assume too much risk ("big pocket" liability if the borrower becomes insolvent). Trustee and agency fees are low, and do not reflect risk. A syndicate agent may also be a trustee, e.g. if the loan is secured.

Differences

But there are significant differences. For example, trust law may be stricter than agency law in protecting beneficiaries, although this is doubtful in the commercial context. Syndicate agents act on behalf of sophisticated institutions (so the agent's exemptions are likely to be more effective), but trustees often do not do so (although in practice most international bondholders are sophisticated institutions). Syndicate agents can easily contact the banks for instructions, but this is usually impractical for bondholder trustees (except via cumbersome and expensive bondholder meetings). 11–2

Banks are not willing to delegate discretions to their agent, but wish to manage their loan themselves. Hence syndicate agents have few discretions

11-2 AGENTS AND TRUSTEES AS FIDUCIARIES

and so fiduciary law has less application – their duties are contractual, not powers. But bondholders are less able to manage directly.

Bondholder trustees and trust deeds are subject to much greater statutory and stock exchange regulation than syndicate agents though one may remark that international bond issues are often outside much of the regulation.

Trustees of bond issues are usually independent trust corporations and so problems of conflicts of interest, secret profits and Chinese Walls are less likely to arise. But syndicate agents often have other banking relationships with the borrower and may be the main banker to the borrower.

Conflicts of interests and secret profits

General rule

11-3 Bondholder trustees and syndicate agents are both fiduciaries representing the interests of others. In practice the rules about conflicts of interest are more important in relation to syndicate agents than trustees, since bondholder trustees are often independent trust corporations not carrying on any other business.

It is universally true that a fiduciary must not put himself in a position where his duty to the banks or bondholders conflicts or might conflict with his private interest (self-interest) or a duty to other beneficiaries (divided loyalty).

The reason for the rule is that, where a trustee has discretionary powers, there is a risk that the exercise of the discretions might be polluted by personal interest or muddled by a divided loyalty. The foundation is not actual injury to beneficiaries but the hallowed orison "lead us not into temptation".

The test is probably whether there is a real sensible potentiality of conflict. In *Aberdeen Rly Co v Blaikie Bros* (1854) 1 Macq 461, HL, Lord Cranworth LC said at 471: "It is a rule of universal application that no-one having such duties to discharge shall be allowed to enter into an engagement in which he has, or can have, a personal interest conflicting with or which may possibly conflict with the interests of those whom he is bound to protect." The possibility of the conflict is increased where the fiduciary has large discretionary powers as opposed to clearly defined administrative duties such as a syndicate agent.

> See also: *Bray v Ford* [1896] AC 44; *Parker v McKenna* (1874) 10 Ch App 96; *Regal (Hastings) Ltd v Gulliver* [1942] 1 All ER 378; *Boardman v Phipps* [1967] 2 AC 46.

Examples of potential conflicts

While it is unsafe to generalise and while each set of facts must be analysed on its merits, the following are some more common examples of clashes which either will or might in the particular circumstances result in an offending conflict:

- There are **cross-shareholdings** or **cross-directorships** (self-interest). It would be out of the question for a fiduciary to act as agent or trustee for a borrowing by its subsidiary. The size of the shareholding which might infect the fiduciary's priority will no doubt depend on the facts. In the case of the trustees, US statute puts the threshold at 20 per cent, France at 10 per cent and Singapore at 5 per cent – a bewildering range. If a syndicate bank has shares in the borrower, the calling in of the loan may reduce the value of the shares (divided loyalty).

- The fiduciary **guarantees** the issue. Here the fiduciary is both prosecution and defence (self-interest).

- The fiduciary is a **representative of two loans or issues** of the same borrower in which case both classes of lenders will be competing for the same assets (divided loyalty). English trustees are usually willing to act on issues of the same class (e.g. two unsecured bond issues) but not of a differing class (e.g. one secured and the other unsecured). However the possibility of conflict is perhaps less where one issue is senior and the other junior on account of the limited action which the junior holders can take to protect themselves against the senior holders.

- The fiduciary is also a **private lender** to the borrower (self-interest), e.g. where the trustee is a bank: *Re Dorman, Long & Co Ltd* [1934] 1 Ch 636 (trusteeship by banks criticised). The bank might be tempted to secure the payment of its own loan first, to call for private security or to insist on building up set-offs. The bank might be privy to information which is protected by bankers' confidentiality but which is highly pertinent to the bondholders or other bank lenders. There might be a temptation not to notify defaults, or an inclination to advance more private money to avert a default or not to accelerate the bonds if the acceleration might prejudice the recoverability of the private loan. Experience has shown that a bank lender who is also a trustee severely restricts its freedom of action as lender in the event of default and is exposed to bondholder action if holders go unpaid.

- The fiduciary has **an investment department** which invests securities for customers under discretionary accounts or holds securities under will trusts (divided loyalty). The interests of the fiduciary as a shareholder for the account of its customers and its duties to the lenders or bondholders

11–4 AGENTS AND TRUSTEES AS FIDUCIARIES

could be in conflict. The value of the security might fall if the loans were called in.

– The fiduciary acts as **financial adviser** to a borrower. The advice may be in conflict with the best interests of the lenders or bondholders. Alternatively the corporate finance department may come to know of a default in circumstances imposing a duty of confidentiality. As to Chinese Walls as a protection, see para 11–22 *et seq*.

– A member of the same group as the fiduciary has one of the above relationships with the borrower or issuer. The fiduciary's wish to protect its fellow company may conflict with its duties to lenders or bondholders.

Effect of conflict

11–5 If there is a conflict, then the following results may ensue:

(a) The fiduciary is more vulnerable to **negligence** proceedings: *Mutual Life Citizens Co v Evatt* [1971] AC 793; *Re Dorman Long & Co* [1934] 1 Ch 636, 671. Exculpation clauses are more likely to be outflanked on the ground that the trustee acted in bad faith: *Dabney v Chase National Bank*, 346 US 863 (1953). A defence under the Trustee Act 1925 s 61 or the Companies Act 1985 s 192(1) is less likely to succeed: para 11–30. In the case of bonds, the clause may be attacked as a surprise clause: para 8–40. Rules of law relating to unfair contract terms may come into play.

(b) Circumstances could arise where conflicting duties are imposed so that whatever the fiduciary does, he will be **liable to one party or another**. If the fiduciary inhibits proper performance of his duties, he does so at his own risk. But see *Kelly v Cooper* [1992] 3 WLR 936, PC, discussed below in relation to Chinese Walls: para 11–24.

(c) The fiduciary may be **liable to account for profits** or benefits derived from his conflicting role, e.g. disgorgement of a private loan paid out to a bank trustee ahead of the bondholders: see *Boardman v Phipps* [1967] 2 AC 46.

(d) **Criminal penalties** where a statute outlaws conflicts for public issues of debt securities, e.g. Singapore Companies Act s 93 (very unusual).

Regulatory controls on conflicts

11–6 As to the specific regulation of conflicts, the matter is left to the general law in the case of syndicate agents. For bond trustees the approach differs. Some jurisdictions set out certain deemed (but usually non-exclusive) conflicts which disqualify a trustee from acting under a **regulated** trust deed, e.g. non-exempt debt issues to the public. This is the approach in the United States, Australia and Singapore. Others do not attempt to identify specific conflicts but merely proscribe conflicts generally. This is the approach in England, Luxembourg and France.

In **England** there are no statutory rules regarding conflicts of interest by syndicate agents or trustees. This is partly because of the almost penal attitude of the English courts to fiduciary conflicts and because banks desisted from acting as trustees after some scathing judicial criticism of conflicting roles and of clauses permitting the trustee to act despite a conflict: *Re Dorman Long & Co Ltd* [1934] 1 Ch D 953 at 671.

The Stock Exchange rules for London listings prescribe that the trustee must have no interest in or relation to the company which might conflict with the position of trustee. The rule refrains from elaboration.

In the **United States**, the Trustee Indenture Act of 1939, as amended by the Trustee Indenture Reform Act of 1990, has intervened to prevent a trustee of a **regulated** indenture from acting after a default if there is a material conflict of interest. If there is a conflict, the trustee must resign within 90 days of the default (subject to certain reliefs) but can act till then. If the trustee cannot find a successor, the trustee will be in violation. The Act sets out nine interests which are deemed to be conflicting, e.g. cross-control, being a trustee under more than one indenture for the same obligor (except under certain conditions), being an underwriter of the securities, or if 20 per cent or more of the trustee's voting shares are owned by the obligor and its directors or officers combined (or more than 10 per cent owned by one such person). Only very limited interlocking of boards of directors is allowed. The only conflict prohibited prior to a default is where the obligor or an affiliate of the obligor serves as trustee. It is clear however that the Act does not override the common law responsibilities of a trustee so that these survive parallel to the 1939 Act: *Morris v Cantor*, 390 F Supp 817 (SDNY 1975). The New York Stock Exchange prohibits certain conflicts of interest.

There is also a provision imposing a sharing of receipts when a default is looming. Since 1990, there is a statutory conflict of interest if the trustee is also a creditor of the issuer, apart from incidental creditor relationships, so that trusteeship by banks who are private lenders to the issuer is no longer possible.

> Section 311(a) of the Act (as amended) provides that if the trustee becomes a creditor of the obligor within three months prior or subsequent to uncured defaults, then the trustee must in effect hold in a separate account for the benefit of investors amounts equal to the reductions of the private claims and property received by the trustee against those claims. However, the section is not all powerful since it excludes some creditor claims of the trustee in its private

capacity and furthermore the three-month rule is rather short in the context of many defaults. This conforms to the three month preference period in BC 1978 s 547. On the other hand, as will be seen, case law has intervened to cause a trustee to disgorge private moneys received even outside the three-month period.

Some of the US cases on trustee conflicts of interest seem forceful and might not on the facts be followed in England.

Dabney v Chase National Bank of the City of New York, 98 F Supp 807 (SDNY 1951), reversed 201, F 2d 635 (2d Cir 1953) modifying 196 F 2d 668 (2d Cir 1952), appeal dismissed, 346 US 863 (1953). An action was brought against the trustee in order to restore loan payments which the trustee had received eight years prior to the declaration of bankruptcy of the obligor on the basis that the loan was made when the trustee had knowledge of the borrower's insolvency. The loan had been made and repaid during the trusteeship. *Held*: a trustee must not compete with the interests of investors and must give the bondholders undivided loyalty free from any conflicting personal interest. The trustee had to pay over to the bondholders sums collected by the trustee on its loan to the borrower.

York v Guaranty Trust Co of New York, 143 F 2d 503 (2d Cir 1944) reversed on statute of limitations grounds, 326 US 99 (1945). The bondholders claimed that they had suffered loss by reason of the trustee's inaction. The trustee had enabled the borrower to meet payments of interest by making private loans to the borrower but nevertheless the trustee failed to exercise its powers to commence liquidation proceedings and thereby to prevent further erosion of the assets. Subsequently the trustee proposed a scheme of arrangement involving the exchange of bonds for shares which was not accepted by all the bondholders. *Held*: the trustee's motive for failing to liquidate was its desire to protect its position as a creditor and mere disclosure of the conflict could not exculpate the trustee. It was wilful misconduct and bad faith to occupy conflicting roles. The decision seems odd because liquidation is often the worst way to protect creditor interests.

Dudley v Mealey, 147 F 2d 268 (2d Cir 1945), cert denied 325 US 873 (1945). The defendant bank, which was a trustee under a bond issue, set off amounts owing to it privately against deposits held by it as a bank. *Held*: the trustee should disgorge these sums received by set-off on the basis that the set-off had robbed the bondholders of an asset of the issuer. By becoming a trustee the banker assumed a duty of undivided loyalty and was not free to enter into relations with the borrower which created a conflict of interest.

11–8   In **Canada** the Canada Business Corporations Act prescribes by s 78 that if there is a material conflict of interest between the trustee's role as trustee and his role in any other capacity, then within 90 days after he becomes aware of the conflict the trustee must either eliminate the conflict or resign from office. This provision is based on a similar provision in the US Trust Indenture Act of 1939 s 310 prior to its amendment in 1990.

The **Singapore** Companies Act s 97, deems that the following offend the independence rule for regulated trusteeships of corporate public issues in Singapore: the trustee or a group company holds more than 5 per cent of the voting power of the borrower's shares; the borrower owes money beneficially to the trustee or a group company, subject to a detailed threshold of 10 per cent of the debentures—this effectively rules out bank trustees – and the trustee has guaranteed the debentures.

It is believed that the **Australian** corporate legislation sets out independence tests on similar lines.

The **Luxembourg** 1972 Decree on trustees requires that a *fiduciaire representant* must be independent of the issuer and its controllers and not put itself in a position liable to create a conflict of interest. A non-complying trustee must rectify the position in three months or resign. No examples of conflict are given.

In **France** Decree-Law of 1935 for the Protection of Bondholders similarly proscribes certain conflicts of interest.

In **Spain**, though the relevant law does not specify expressly what is a conflicting interest it is thought that persons whose interests are liable to conflict with those of the bondholders could not be appointed as a common representative.

Solutions for trustee or agent faced with conflict

A number of possibilities can be considered to deal with potential conflicts.   11–9

1. **Consent of beneficiaries** The beneficiary may consent to a conflict of interest. The consent must be fully informed. A beneficiary can relax a duty provided he "fully understands not only what he is doing but also what his legal rights are, and that he is in part surrendering them": *Boulting v Association of Cinematograph Television and Allied Technicians* [1963] 2 QB 606, 636. Note that, unlike syndicate agents, it is usually impracticable for a trustee to obtain the consent of bondholders if the conflict surfaces subsequently.

    As to authorisation in the trust deed, see *Re Llewellin's Will Trusts* [1949] 1 Ch 225; *Brown v IRC* [1965] AC 244; *Boardman v Phipps* [1967] 2 AC 46; *Lindgren v L & P Estates Ltd* [1968] 1 Ch 572; *North and South Trust Co v Berkeley* [1971] 1 WLR 470; *New Zealand Netherlands Society "Oranje" Incorporated v Kuys* [1973] All ER 1222; *Dunne v English* [1874] LR 18 Eq 524.

    It may not be enough for the fiduciary merely to disclose that he has an interest. The stringent rule requires specific disclosures, e.g. in the prospectus. Consent may be limited by the Companies Act 1985 s 192: see para 11–30. Further, even if the bondholder has consented, a conflict may expose the trustee to the risk of closer scrutiny of the trustee's conduct and to allegations of bad faith destroying any exculpatory protection: see para 11–29 above.

As to syndicate agents, in practice, most banks will know that their agent bank has other ordinary banking relationships with the borrower. It is doubtful that the courts would insist that precise details of a normal relationship be disclosed.

English trust deeds contain clauses which purport to sanction certain conflicts of interest. These clauses do not sanction conflicts of interest generally: they merely, for example, (a) allow cross-directorships, (b) allow the trustee or its officers to enter into other financial transactions with the obligor (including banking, insurance or underwriting contracts) or to deal in the bonds or other securities of the borrower, and (c) allow the trustee to act as trustee for another issue of the same borrower. Such clauses are necessary to enable a business trustee to act at all because of the harsh prohibitions imposed on private trustees.

In the **United States** and **Canada** the trustee cannot contract out of the prohibitions on conflicts of interest in the case of **regulated** trust indentures, e.g. one involving a public offering.

11–10   **Authorising clause in syndicate loan agreements** A typical clause in a syndicated credit agreement endeavouring to authorise a syndicate agent to act in conflict is as follows:

"(a) The Agent shall have the same rights and powers hereunder as any other Bank and may exercise the same as though it were not the Agent.

(b) The Agent and its related entities may accept deposits from, lend money to and generally engage in any kind of banking, trust, advisory or other business whatsoever with the Borrower, and its related entities and accept and retain any fees payable by the Borrower for its own account in connection therewith without liability to account therefor to any Bank."

The rules against conflicts are primarily intended to prevent abuse of position and infection or pollution of discretions. Hence they have lesser application where the agent does not have significant powers or discretions to act on behalf of the banks. Many of the cases pertained to situations where the agent enjoyed large discretions and are not necessarily applicable to a syndicated agent with very limited powers to alter the relationship between the borrower and the lending banks. The sophistication of the participants is also relevant. On the other hand, the attitude of the English courts to fiduciaries acting in conflict is stringent.

2. **Resignation** The trustee could resign but this apparent escape is a limited solution because (a) trust deeds often provide that the resignation is ineffective until a successor is appointed and (b) the bondholders lose an informed trustee, perhaps when they need him most.

3. **Contractual exculpation** The fiduciary could insert an exculpation clause. For the efficacy of exculpation clauses, see para 11–29 *et seq*.

4. **Delegation** If the trust deed allows delegation (which it usually does) the trustee could delegate the exercise of discretions where it may be affected by a conflict.

5. **Chinese Wall** See para 11–22.

Secret profits

An aspect of the conflict of interest principle is that a fiduciary must not make a profit out of his position without the informed consent of the beneficiary: see the summary by Lord Denning MR in *Phipps v Boardman* [1965] Ch 992, CA, affirmed sub nom *Boardman v Phipps* [1967] 2 AC 46, HL. The fiduciary must disgorge the secret profit and is liable to be dismissed.

Examples are: secret commissions; remuneration (this must be expressly provided for in the trust deed or loan agreement); and the use of information acquired in its capacity as fiduciary for its own private ends – this would be unusual in the context but an example might be insider trading.

A fiduciary who purchases the bonds for his own account must satisfy the purity tests applying to a purchase by a trustee of trust property or of the beneficiary's interests. Thus a trustee must not purchase at an undervalue or without disclosing price sensitive information in the trustee's possession: *Re Magadi Soda Co* (1925) 94 LJ Ch 217.

Exculpation clauses Both trust deeds and loan agreements generally state that the agent is not bound to account for profits from other businesses with the issuer or borrower.

Due diligence by the fiduciary

Due diligence generally

A fiduciary must act with due diligence and in the best interests of the beneficiaries. A trustee is required "to bring to the management of trust affairs the same care and diligence which a man of ordinary prudence may be expected to use in his own concerns": *Knox v McKinnon* (1888) 13 App Cas 753, 768.

> See also: *Bartlett v Barclay's Bank Trust Co Ltd* [1980] 1 AER 139 at 152 (compare *Speight v Gaunt* (1883) 9 AC 1 (with regard to ordinary trustees); *Riverstone Meat Co Pty Ltd v Lancashire Shipping Co Ltd* [1960] 1 AER 193, 219; *National Trustees Company of Australasia Ltd v General Finance Company of Australasia Ltd* [1905] AC 373, 381; *Re Windsor Steam Coal Company (1901) Ltd* [1929] 1 Ch 151, 164–5.

A distinction must be made between powers and duties. If a fiduciary fails to perform an express **duty**, such as a duty to accelerate if so directed by the specified majority of bonds, the fiduciary is liable to account for breach of trust. If, on the other hand, the fiduciary fails to exercise a discretion or a **power** conferred on the fiduciary, such as a power to call for compliance certificates or to accelerate on its own initiative, the fiduciary is liable only for the absence of due diligence.

Where a fiduciary is invested with a power, such as a power to call for financial information, he cannot ignore it: he must exercise the power when this would be prudent in the interests of the beneficiaries and examine financial information provided.

Approval of documentation

11–14 The extent of the legal duty of a prospective trustee during the documentation stage to check that the terms of the bond protects bondholders is unclear: the trustee is at this point not in office. But considerations of commercial integrity lead trustees to influence documentation which is not consistent with market practice or is seriously defective. It is doubtful that a manager of a syndicated credit has protective duties towards the syndicate in the normal case: the banks see the documents and can be expected to look after themselves. It would be different if the manager misrepresented the effect of legal advice.

Monitoring duties of trustees

11–15 One of the main functions of trustees is to monitor the issuer's financial state so as to forewarn bondholders of impending dangers.

In **England**, there are no express statutory requirements imposing duties on trustees in relation to the monitoring of issuers. English trust deed practice is not to charge the trustee with an investigatory role.

The trustee is largely a passive recipient of information from the obligor, e.g. trust deeds generally provide that the issuer will supply audited financial statements, annual directors certificates of compliance, notices of actual or pending defaults, and such other information as the trustee may request.

Good practice is for the trustee to exercise these powers at appropriate intervals and to review the information.

In the **United States** the Trust Indenture Act of 1939 (on which the **Canada** Business Corporation Act is modelled) requires specific covenants in the trust deed as to the furnishing of information to the trustee, the SEC and bondholders and as to various compliance certificates. Nevertheless the trustee is still more or less passive and is awakened from his sleep only on a default.

The Singapore Companies Act however transforms the trustee of a non-exempt public offering in Singapore into an active watchdog:

11–16

> Section 101 provides that the trustee must exercise reasonable diligence to ascertain whether or not the assets of the borrowing corporation are likely to be sufficient to discharge the debentures as and when they become due. If the trustee is not so satisfied then there are powers to apply to the court or to the relevant Minister for directions. Protective orders can be issued. Further, the trustee must exercise reasonable diligence to ascertain that the issuer is in compliance with the debentures and must do everything that he is empowered to do to cause the borrowing corporation to remedy breaches. If they are not remedied then the trustee may place the matter before a meeting of the debentureholders and submit proposals for their protection. Where the borrowing corporation proposes a compromise or arrangement then the trustee is under an affirmative duty to explain the effect of the compromise or arrangement to the bondholders and, if it thinks fit, to recommend an appropriate course of action.
>
> Section 103 assists the trustee to monitor the issue. The borrowing corporation must every three months lodge a report with the registrar of companies and with the trustee setting out "in detail" any matters adversely affecting the security or the interests of the debentureholders, e.g. defaults, changes in business, intercompany loans and must also notify charges created by it. The borrower must report on progress made towards authorising the purpose of the loan stated in the application of proceeds section in the prospectus and must repay the loan in certain cases where that purpose is not authorised: s 105.
>
> Section 99 of the Act requires the inclusion of a number of covenants: notably a borrowing limit (without stating what it should be) and a provision whereby the trustee has powers of inspection of the accounting and other records of the company as wide as those possessed by an auditor.
>
> If the bonds are listed on the Singapore Stock Exchange there are additional requirements as to the contents of trust deeds including a remarkable require-

ment that the borrowing company must on request in writing by the trustee cause wholly-owned subsidiaries to guarantee the bonds.

In view of all this one wonders how Singapore trustees can be persuaded to come forward to put their heads on the block.

The **Australian** corporate legislation (on which the Singapore Companies Act is modelled) is (or was) almost identical on the above matters.

The **Luxembourg** *fiduciaire representant* must "follow the financial situation of the issuer and its guarantor (if any) and shall carry out any necessary acts for the preservation and protection of the interests of owners of securities": Art 2 of the 1972 Decree in respect of trustees. The representative must "report to the owners of securities when the protection of their interests so requires" and notify the banking authorities of defaults and consequent measures the representative has taken.

In some civil code countries, such as Switzerland, Germany, Italy and Mexico, the bondholders' representative has the power to attend shareholders meetings.

Monitoring by syndicate agents

See the discussion at para 6–26.

Confidential information

11–17 **Confidential information and trustees** A trustee is under a general duty to give beneficiaries all reasonable information about the trust. Modern forms of trust deed provide that a trustee need not disclose information given to the trustee by the issuer in confidence. The preservation of confidentiality enhances the willingness of issuers to disclose information to the trustee to assist in the monitoring of the bonds.

Confidential information received by agent banks An agent bank may acquire notice of a default in confidential circumstances, e.g. through its investment or corporate finance department. Where a bank has a contractual obligation to disclose information received in a conflicting confidential capacity, the bank may be liable to one or the other for breach of duty: but see *Kelly v Cooper* [1992] 3 WLR 936, discussed at para 11–24. The ultimate remedy of resignation may not be commercially attractive. The practical remedy of requiring the borrower to disclose the information to the banks may be resisted. For this reason some banks split off their investment banking and their trustee departments into separate subsidiaries with separate management. Syndicate loan agreements commonly cover the point as follows:

"The Agent need not disclose any information relating to the Borrower of any of its related entities if such disclosure would or might in the opinion of the Agent constitute a breach of law in any jurisdiction or any duty of secrecy of confidence."

As to the efficacy of Chinese Walls in this case, see para 11–22.

Notification of defaults

11–18 The notification of defaults is perhaps one of the most sensitive aspects of an agent or trustee's duty. Where a trustee fails to notify the bondholders of a default of which it should have been aware and the issuer subsequently goes bankrupt, the bondholders may complain that if they had known of the default then action could have been taken to accelerate the bonds and to recover from the issuer before it was too late.

As to syndicate agents, by virtue of its position as agent bank – and often as a bank having a specially close relationship with the borrower – the agent bank may acquire information which discloses the occurrence of an event of default. A syndicate may suffer loss from non-disclosure if, e.g. timely disclosure would have enabled the banks to suspend further borrowings under the loan agreement or to accelerate the loans before it was too late.

In practice, acceleration will often have a disastrous effect on a borrower by putting it out of business and forcing it into usually catastrophic insolvency proceedings. Allegations therefore that the creditors would have recovered more if the default were known may often seem unconvincing, but unhappily hindsight may prevail.

However the duty to notify the defaults, if there is one, gives rise to two main difficulties.

11–19 **What constitutes knowledge of a default?** This problem is acute with big banks with many departments and employees. The main problems which are likely to come up in practice are:

– the degree of **sophistication** expected of an agent or trustee in the discovery of technical defaults involving specialist legal or accounting skills;

– information may be received by a **senior officer** not conversant with the details of the bank's loan agreements and therefore unaware that the information discloses a default – the classic case of split-knowledge – or information may be received by an employee at another **branch** having nothing to do with the bank's loan administration department;

– the information may be acquired **casually**, e.g. on the golf-course:

Société Generale de Paris v Tranways Union Co (1885) 11 AC 20, HL (officer told of facts while at a funeral);

— a bank may have **departments** dealing with corporate finance, interest swaps, foreign exchange, bond issues or dealing in securities. These departments may be dealing separately with the borrower. Whether the information is imputed to the bank as a whole should depend on the circumstances in which the information is received, e.g. officially or casually, and the responsibilities of the person who receives it. Notice to a junior subordinate is not usually notice to the bank but notice to a senior officer or director usually is: see, for example, *Tesco Supermarkets Ltd v Nattrass* [1972] AC 153, HL. Imputation should also depend on the reasonableness of the internal procedures of the bank for the communication of information to the right department. In the "dangerous dog" cases it was held that the mere fact that a servant knew a dog to be dangerous was no evidence of knowledge on the part of the master, where the servant had nothing to do with the care or control of the dog: *Cleverton v Uffernell* (1887) 3 TLR 509; *Colget v Norris* (1886) 2 TLR 471, CA.

As to Chinese Walls, see para 11–22.

11–20 **When should a default be notified?** In bond issues, the notification of a default which is technical or transient or inadvertent could seriously prejudice the bondholders, e.g. by crystallising cross-default clauses in other borrowing instruments of the issuer, inviting a loss of confidence and preventing the issuer from overcoming an embarrassment which may be momentary only. A trustee can properly take these considerations into account.

Indeed this is recognised by both the US and the Canadian Acts. Under s 85 of the Canada Business Corporations Act, it is provided that the trustee must give to the bondholders, within thirty days after the trustee becomes aware of an event of default, notice of the default if continuing at the time the notice is given "unless the trustee reasonably believes that it is in the best interests of the holders of the debt obligations to withhold such notice and so informs the issuer or guarantor in writing". Under the US Trust Indenture Act of 1939 the determination has to be made by responsible officers of the trustee. However in the US the trustee must notify payment defaults.

11–21 **Ostrich clauses** English trust deeds – which are not subject to statutory requirements on this point – sometimes contain a clause on the following lines:

"The Trustee shall not be bound to take any steps to ascertain whether any Event of Default has occurred and until it shall have actual knowledge or express notice to the contrary the Trustee shall be entitled to assume that no such Event of Default has occurred."

Syndicate loan agreements contain more extensive "ostrich" clauses of which the following is typical:

"The Agent shall not be required to ascertain or inquire as to the performance or observance by the Borrower of the terms of this Agreement or any other document in connection herewith. The Agent shall not be deemed to have knowledge of the occurrence of any Event of Default (or event which with lapse of time, notice, or other condition may constitute such an Event of Default) unless the agency department of the Agent, having specific responsibility for this Agreement, has received written notice from a party hereto describing such Event of Default or event and stating that such notice is a 'Notice of Default'. If such department receives such a notice of default, the Agent shall give notice thereof to the Banks."

Key features of this clause are exclusions of monitoring compliance by the borrower; information casually acquired; information which requires expert familiarity with the agreement and the legal implications of complex clauses (the notice must be stated to be a "Notice of Default"); and information received by another branch or department: Chinese Walls – see para 11–22 below. See also clause 18.17 in Form 3 in the Appendix.

"Ostrich" clauses are suspect in practice, e.g. because they may conflict with a duty of reasonable diligence which may be held to be overriding.

Chinese Walls

Generally

Apart from exclusion clauses and disclosure, two other techniques of managing conflicts of interest, secret profits and default notification are: 11–22

1. **Separate legal entities** The bank splits off each of its functions into a separate legal entity. Some of the objections to this are that the separation may defeat the object of economic efficiency achieved by integrating expertise in one house and in any event there may be common directors and common employees which may give rise to leakages of information.

2. **Chinese Walls** A Chinese Wall is an arrangement whereby there are no flows of information between potentially conflicting departments in the same company. The intention is that the information and interests of one department are not known to another. The wall must establish a complete operational and physical separation to prevent flows of infor-

mation between the conflicting departments. The theory is that if one department is not aware of the bank's self-interest stemming from activities in another department, then its discretions will not be polluted. If one department does not know that a duty is owed to another customer which conflicts, then the first department will be able to act with full diligence to its own customer without any inhibition that it is in some way acting deleteriously to the interests of the other customer.

Weaknesses of Chinese Walls

11–23   Some of the disadvantages of the Chinese Wall are as follows:

1. In terms of economic efficiencies, the wall inhibits the advantages of integration, such as pooled expertise, pooled resources and less expense. This is one of the main objectives of "multiple capacity".

2. The wall may inhibit the identification of acute and intolerable conflicts in time, e.g. if the corporate finance arm is acting for the target in a hostile takeover but the syndication arm is financing the offeror.

3. Senior executives and compliance officers in charge of monitoring and managing the business might have to be excluded from certain decision-making and from communicating conflicts to other executives. This may strike at the concept of collective board responsibility and involve a dilution of management control.

4. In practice, the wall may be particularly thin in small firms where there is a higher risk of seepage, e.g. from casual conversations between employees.

5. It might be very difficult for an injured client to prove breaches of the wall: hence the argument is that the wall should not be allowed at all.

6. The wall is overflown if the information is publicly available. For example, if the syndicate agent learns from the newspapers that the corporate finance arm of the bank is engaged in a contested bid, the bank conglomerate may tend to act in a concerted fashion.

Case law on Chinese Walls

11–24   There is very little English case law on the efficacy of Chinese walls.

Three cases show that the law will not usually permit solicitors to erect Chinese walls thereby enabling them to act for clients on opposing sides. The reason for this is the very high standards imposed upon solicitors as officers of the court and fiduciaries. Hence this is a special case which does not necessarily apply to other agents.

In two nineteenth century dangerous dog cases, one servant of the master knew that the dog was dangerous but the other servant did not. The servant who did not know of the dog's dangerous propensities took the dog for a walk and it bit somebody. *Held*: the master was not liable, because the knowing servant had nothing to do with the care and control of the dog: *Cleverton v Uffernell* (1887) 3 TLR 509, *Colget v Norris* (1866) 2 TLR 471, CA.

Against this is *Harrods Bank v Lemmon* [1932] 2 KB 157. An estate agent office of a firm advised a seller on the sale of his house but the building office of the firm gave a bad drainage report on the house to the purchaser, thereby causing the purchaser to reduce the price. *Held*: in these circumstances the firm could be liable to the seller even though the estate agency office and the building office did not know that the firm was acting on both sides.

In *Kelly v Cooper* [1992] 3 WLR 936 (Privy Council on appeal from Bermuda), there was a conflict between an agent's duty to disclose and its duty of confidentiality. Two contiguous properties were sold through the agency of the same estate agents to the same purchaser. The purchaser was Ross Perot (a US presidential candidate) who wanted one big property. He bought one of the properties and if the owner of the second property had known of this, he would have held out for a much higher price. But the estate agent did not tell him because the agent had a duty of confidentiality to the other owner. The owner of the first property claimed damages against the estate agents for breach of their fiduciary duty in failing to disclose to him a material factor bearing on the price of that property, namely that the same person was interested in purchasing both properties.

Held: where a principal instructs an agent to sell his property, a person who to his knowledge acts for other principals selling property or goods of the same description, the terms to be implied into the agency contract include a term permitting the agent (a) to keep confidential information obtained from each of his principals; and (b) to act for other principals selling competing properties even though a conflict of interest might result.

Accordingly, since the plaintiff was well aware that the defendants would be acting also for other vendors of comparable properties and in so doing would receive confidential information from those other vendors, the agency contract between the plaintiff and the defendants could not have included terms requiring the defendants to disclose such confidential information to the plaintiff or precluding them from acting for rival vendors. The fact that the defendants had a direct financial interest in securing a sale of the second property did not constitute a breach of fiduciary duty since the contract of agency envisaged that they might have such a conflict of interest. Note that there was no Chinese Wall.

In certain circumstances an agent may be obliged to disclose all relevant information to its principal irrespective of its source: see *North and South Trust Co v Berkeley* [1971] 1 WLR 470.

Chinese walls are discussed in detail in the British Law Commission Consultation Paper No 24, *Fiduciary Duties and Regulatory Rules*, HMSO 1992, pp 138–162.

Exculpation clauses

Trust deed practice

11–25 In England, the English form of eurobond trust deed conventionally contains a number of specific and general exculpations. They are, however, not nearly as sweeping as those generally accorded to agent banks in syndicated loan agreements. Bank lenders are sophisticated institutions who wish to control their own investments. But bondholders must of course delegate to a representative and the increased duties of the fiduciary carry an increased liability.

Typically, the trustee is permitted to rely on advice of professional advisers, upon compliance certificates given by responsible officers of the issuer and on minutes of bondholders' meetings; is permitted to assume that communications are authentic; is not concerned to enquire as to whether an event of default has occurred; is not responsible for the application of the proceeds of the issue; and can delegate to agents and appoint custodians without being responsible for their actions, provided the trustee exercises reasonable care in their selection.

> See Trustee Act 1925 ss 24 and 25; *Re Vickery* [1931] 1 Ch 572; *Re Lucking's Will Trusts* [1968] 1 WLR 866.

Syndicate agent practice

11–26 Agent banks commonly seek to incorporate in the loan agreement express provisions excluding due diligence, negligence and fiduciary liabilities of the agent towards the syndicate which might otherwise arise. The usual express immunities may be classified as follows:

Limitations of agent's role The agreement limits the scope of the duties and discretions of the agent bank so as to reduce the responsibilities which could give rise to liability, e.g. by providing that the agent bank shall only have those powers and duties specified in the agreement and powers incidental thereto; and by expressly conferring certain powers on each bank rather

EXCULPATION CLAUSES 11–29

than the agent so as to reduce the reliance on the agent. For example the banks or a specified proportion of them may, instead of the agent, have power to grant waivers, approve specified changes to the loan agreement, accelerate on a default or serve notice to cure.

General immunities The agent and its officers, employees and agents may be expressed not to be responsible for any default or omission except in the case of their **gross** negligence or wilful misconduct. 11–27

Specific immunities Specific immunities may state, for example, that the agent bank: is not responsible for any inadequacy in the contractual documents (which may have been negotiated by the agent); may rely without enquiry on notice and other communications (e.g. notices of borrowing) believed to have been sent and signed by the proper persons; may rely on the advice of lawyers and other experts selected by it – this is relevant in particular to the conditions precedent documents furnished by the borrower; and is not liable for any representations inducing the loan agreement.

General effect of exclusion clauses: is there a duty?

There is a difference between a duty which is then limited by an exemption clause and a limited duty. In the case of an exemption clause, the agreement imposes a duty on the agent and the exemption clause seeks to limit liability for breach of that duty. In the case of a limited duty, the agreement negatives the existence of the duty so that there is no need to exclude liability for breach. 11–28

While the line may be hard to draw, the first step is to ascertain the scope of the agent's duties from the express and implied terms of the contract, and the second step is to examine whether an exclusion clause is effective to exclude responsibility for a breach of those duties.

Efficacy of exculpations

Exclusion clauses are everywhere suspect. Under the general English rules an exclusion clause cannot exclude liability for fraud; if the exclusion clause is misrepresented in the bond or prospectus, the trustee may not be able to rely on it; in some jurisdictions (not England), contracts of adhesion are suspect: the trust deed is imposed on a "take it or leave it" basis on the bondholders who have no opportunity to participate in its preparation: see para 8–40. Exclusion clauses are invariably construed against the party relying on them. Thus ambiguities are construed in **favour of the beneficiaries**; the 11–29

International Loans, Bonds and Securities Regulation

exclusion clause must be **specific** if it is to cover fundamental breaches which go to the root of the trustee's duties; exclusion of responsibility, e.g. for **negligence**, must be expressly mentioned – the exclusion must expressly cover the breach in question; and if the exclusion clause nullifies another positive clause the exclusion clause may be ignored on grounds of **repugnancy**. There is much law on these points which can be found in the standard works on contract.

Some US trustee examples are:

> In *Frishmuth v Farmer's Loan and Trust Co*, 95 Fed 5 (SDNY 1899) it was held that mere mechanical reliance on certificates of compliance was not enough. The court indicated that the trustee could not rely upon a certificate of the issuer as to the use of proceeds if the trustee knew or had reason to believe that the proceeds were not to be applied properly. The trustee could not hide behind an ostrich clause.

> In *Starr v Chase National Bank*, NYLJ September 21, 1936, (Sup Ct) p 771, Col 6 (Supreme Court), the trustee, even after it knew of default on the bonds, had received substantial sums from the borrower which it used to pay back its own private indebtedness. It had also failed to attach certain free assets to the borrower which were available to it. *Held*: a trustee has an active duty to attach property available for the purpose where it had actual knowledge of a default. The trustee's conduct constituted bad faith so that reliance could not be placed upon the exculpatory clause.

> On the other hand in *Hazzard v Chase National Bank*, 159 Misc 57, 287 NY Supp 541 (Sup Ct 1936) the trustee escaped. The trustee was permitted by the trust deed to substitute collateral securities on presentation of an earnings statement. The trustee, which was also a private lender to the obligor, allowed a substitution of securities known to an executive of the trustee to be worthless. For this purpose the knowledge of the executive, who had nothing to do with the trustee department but was on the board of the obligor, was imputed to the bank as a whole. The trust deed said that the trustee was not liable except for "gross negligence or bad faith". *Held*: although the trustee had been negligent, neither gross negligence or bad faith had been made out. The court cited approvingly a comment to s 222 of the Restatement of the Law of Trusts stating that: "Although he is not liable for mere negligence, he is liable if he acts or omits to act with reckless indifference as to the interest of the beneficiary." The court launched into a remarkable attack on the trustee and the trust deed in language conveying the hostilities engendered by the dark days of the 1930s. The court observed that the facts of the case showed "how utterly unjust to the investing public is the modern trust indenture. Prospective investors are unquestionably induced to purchase debentures, to a great extent, by the name and prestige of the trustee, which are capitalised by the obligor seeking financing, in order to sell its securities . . . While it is true that our courts have, unrealistically, held purchasers to a knowledge of the terms of the indenture, the fact cannot be avoided that seldom, if ever, is the indenture read by such pur-

chasers. It is, indeed, doubtful whether they understand that they should read it, or whether reading it would lead to comprehension of its significance. Reliance is placed almost completely upon the belief that the experience, power, financial acumen and integrity of the trustee will serve as a protection. The untrained investor unquestionably depends upon the great financial institution named as trustee to supply the skill and the watchfulness and the prudence and the experience which he himself lacks... This indenture was particular vicious... the fee of $1,100 per year in this case was grotesquely exorbitant for the negligible services performed and responsibility undertaken by the defendant. The defendant did not earn its fee either in work or in risk. It would be far better for the bondholder to pay a much larger compensation to the trustee, and be able to insist upon the usual vigilance of a fiduciary." However the court held that the indenture absolved the trustee from liability.

Similarly, specific immunity clauses have been struck out.

In *Richardson v Union Mortgage Co*, 210 Iowa, 346, 228 N W 103 (1933), a clause released the trustee from liability for acts of its agents or employees, provided that they were selected with reasonable care. The clause failed to immunise. "Surely", the court said "the trustee was something more than an employment agency".

Statutory limitations on exclusion clauses

The scope of the exclusion clause may be limited by statute.   11–30
In **England**, the following apply to both trustees and syndicate agents.

Unfair Contract Terms Act 1977 Much of this Act is aimed at negativing exemption clauses in contracts between businesses and consumers where there is an inequality of bargaining power. But some of its terms apply in the purely business context. Under s 2(2) of the Act "a person cannot so exclude or restrict his liability for negligence except insofar as the term or notice satisfies the requirement of reasonableness".

In *Photo Production Ltd v Securicor Transport Ltd* [1980] AC 827, [1980] 1 All ER 556, HL, it was stated that, in commercial matters generally, when the parties were not of unequal bargaining power, and when risks were borne by insurance, Parliament's intention in the Act seemed to be one of "leaving the parties free to apportion the risks as they think fit... respecting their decisions". The principle was followed in *The Zinnia* [1984] 2 Lloyd's Rep 211.

Misrepresentation Act Section 3 of the Misrepresentation Act (as amended by the Unfair Contract Terms Act 1977) provides in effect that exclusions of liability for negligent misrepresentation which are a term of the contract must be reasonable as stated in the Unfair Contract Terms Act 1977.

11–31 The following apply only to trustees:

(a) The **Trustee Act 1925 s 61** provides that the court can exclude a trustee from liability from breach of trust only if he satisfies the stringent test that he "has acted honestly and reasonably, and ought fairly to be excused".

(b) **Section 192 of the codifying Companies Act 1985** (which is paralleled in other English-related jurisdictions such as Australia, India and Singapore) provides that any provision contained in a trust deed for securing an issue of the debentures is void insofar as it would have the effect of exempting a trustee from or indemnifying him against liability for breach of trust where he failed to show the degree of care and diligence required of him as a trustee. However, the trustee can be released by three-quarters in value of the debenture holders at a meeting summoned for the purpose of the release "with respect to specific acts or omissions" but not generally.

In England, Australia and Singapore this provision (or its local analogue) applies to any debenture trust deed, irrespective of whether there has been a public offering. The territorial ambit is not stated, nor is it clear whether the section will override a foreign law trust deed conferring wider exculpations.

Whether consumerist statutes (such as the British Unfair Contract Terms Act 1977) limiting exclusion clauses in contracts generally or consumer contracts would apply to "contracts" in a trust deed is a question of construction of the statute.

In the **United States** the Trustee Indenture Act of 1939 distinguishes between pre-default and post-default liabilities in regulated indentures. The indenture can provide that prior to a default the trustee shall not be liable except for the performance of the specific duties set out in the indenture and that the trustee may rely exclusively upon certificates or opinions concerning the requirements of the indenture provided that he has checked that they do so conform. The indenture can, therefore, exclude certain implied duties of the trustees. However, once a default has occurred then the trustee is converted into an active trustee and a higher degree of devotion is required. The indenture must contain provisions whereby the trustee must exercise in the case of a default the care and skill which a prudent man would exercise under the circumstances in the conduct of his own affairs. However, the indenture may not release a trustee from liability for his own negligence or misconduct except for certain errors of judgment (provided that the decisions are referred to senior management) and certain actions taken in good faith in accordance with a majority direction.

For a brief review of attitudes to exculpation clauses in other countries, see para 8–40.

Indemnity to fiduciaries

Trustees

Under English law (equity and statute), a trustee is entitled to be indemnified out of the trust property for costs and liabilities incurred in the proper administration of the trust. This right of indemnity is a first charge on the trust property. A trustee normally has no right of indemnity against the beneficiaries personally.

English trust deed practice is to provide that the issuer must indemnify the trustee against trustee liabilities; and that, in the absence of this indemnity, the trustee is given an express right of reimbursement out of the trust assets. As a matter of law, this indemnity is limited by the restrictions on exculpations already discussed. Trust deeds do not normally contain an express personal indemnity by bondholders except that, if proceedings are required to be taken, it is usually provided, the trustee can decline to proceed unless indemnified against the costs and liabilities of the action.

Syndicate agents

As to an agent bank's right of indemnity, see para 6–28.

PART II

LEGAL OPINIONS

Chapter 12

LEGAL OPINIONS: INTRODUCTION

Generally

Lawyers involved in international financial documentation commonly play a number of roles. They plan and structure transactions. They draft and negotiate the documentation. They explain and (hopefully) facilitate the transaction and advise on its terms and legal effect. They arrange the closing and the execution of the agreements. And finally they provide a formal legal opinion on the validity of the agreements.

12–1

Naturally lawyers are often called upon to provide other opinions, such as reasoned opinions explaining a point of law, but it is with the formal transaction legal opinion that one is mainly concerned here. The furnishing of this legal opinion is almost invariably a condition precedent to the advance of loans or the bond issue and its terms are settled with as much attention to detail as the contractual documents themselves. These transaction opinions tend to be short standardised letters making customary statements and are to be distinguished from:

- Letters of legal advice or reasoned legal opinions on the law or on points of interpretation, e.g. on the priority of a floating charge, or the incidence of a withholding tax, or the regulatory position, or the ranking of debts on insolvency, or on lender liability. These are explanatory and often supported by citation.

- Legal reports as to the scope and suitability of the terms of a document, e.g. a commentary on a loan agreement or on project contracts, such as a concession or supply agreement.

- Title reports, e.g. as to the title to land which is to be mortgaged to a lender.

Comparison with European notaries

Transaction legal opinions stem from US practice in financial matters and were not customary in Europe prior to the 1970s. The nearest equivalent in Continental European practice was (and is) the role played by the notary, notably in land and ship transactions, who in some countries, especially in

12–2

International Loans, Bonds and Securities Regulation   215

the Germanic and Franco-Latin group, assumes a wide responsibility for authenticating signatures, checking powers and authorisations and confirming legal validity.

For example, in Germany, the notary is an official with legal training who is bound by statute,

> "to ascertain the will of the parties, explain the content of the transaction, instruct the parties about the legal consequences of the transaction, and record their statements clearly and unequivocally. In so doing he should take care that errors and doubts are avoided and that inexperienced and unknowledgable parties are not disadvantaged." (*Beurkundungsgesetz* Art 17)

These systems accordingly provide for a "notarial document" (e.g. German BGB Art 128), a "notarial act" (eg Austrian BGB Art 551) or an "*acte authentique*" (French CC Art 1312). The English public notary is quite different: he typically draws up documents for foreign use. The American notary public is different again: he has little or no legal training and is empowered under state law to record sworn statements, to certify signatories and the like. The above description is taken from Zweigert/Kötz, vol II, p 47. The European Continental notary is traceable back to ancient public scribes who were necessary at a time when most people could not write: in medieval times the main school of notaries was located in Bologna. Their origin helps to explain their wider function as an early form of consumerism, if you like.

12–3   In any event there are some similarities between the old notary and the new US-style transaction opinion flowing partly from a fear of fraud and the desire to obtain independent authoritative confirmation in a formal manner that the agreements were properly entered into. By contrast, English, Germanic and Scandinavian practice dispensed with the documentary formality. Lawyers were (and are) expected to check such matters as due incorporation, powers and authorities and to advise as to legal infirmities. Formal letters were not seen as necessary since these matters were central to their duties and regarded as routine. The difference lies in the accent on formality and paperwork rather than responsibility in substance. Views differ on whether these transaction opinions invite excessive attention to points which do not matter and needless negotiations, or whether they have led to greater focus on the legal checks which should be carried out and on the scope of the lawyer's duty and thereby heightened standards. But whatever view one may hold on desirability, or even utility, transaction legal opinions in financial transactions are so well entrenched globally that they are a standard expectation of laymen and imbued with mystical significance. This of course is a characteristic of all ceremonial rites, and one should not cavil too much at the mortal desire for traditional show.

LEGAL OPINIONS: INTRODUCTION

These chapters on legal opinions indicate one view of good practice. Views about good practice differ and non-observance of good practice does not necessarily connote legal liability for negligence.

What jurisdictions should be covered?

The number of legal systems which impinge on an international loan transaction and which might possibly affect its terms can be legion. They include the laws of the borrower's domicile, the lender's domicile, the place of contracting, the place where payments must be made as the place of performance, the place where any assets covered by the security are situate, the place where the bonds are listed or distributed, the country of the forum, and so on. However in practice many of these legal systems coincide and in any event market practice does not sanction extravagant investigation into the laws of every conceivable jurisdiction which might relate to the transaction, e.g. the laws of all the lenders' countries.

The jurisdictions in relation to which opinions should be obtained depend upon the circumstances, but usually in loan and bond issue transactions there is an opinion as to the jurisdiction of the borrower's domicile and a second opinion as to the jurisdiction of the governing law.

Scope of opinions

While legal opinions are usual, there are limits on their scope.

— Formal legal opinions speak only as to certain narrow and basic legal matters and are not general assurances that the whole transaction is satisfactory from a creditor's point of view. An assurance that an agreement is legally binding in accordance with its terms is cold comfort if those terms are wholly inadequate.

— A legal opinion is an opinion, not a guarantee. A lawyer is not an insurer. In the California case of *Lucas v Hamm*, 56 Cal 2d 583, 591 (1961), cert denied 268 US 987 (1962), the court said that the lawyer must "use such skill, prudence and diligence as lawyers of ordinary skill and capacity commonly possess and exercise in the performance of the tasks which they undertake". Court decisions in many jurisdictions do not impose particularly high standards.

— These legal opinions make certain assumptions, often as to factual matters: para 12–7. The assumptions then become risks for the creditor.

— The legal opinion excludes an opinion on certain key questions, notably validity on bankruptcy. This is a major limitation because it is on bankruptcy that validity really matters. But is it a necessary qualification because short letters of this sort cannot be treatises on the law. A similar comment applies to an opinion as to the application of the governing law or as to the status of security.

- A legal opinion speaks as to domestic law not foreign law. The legal comfort is local not universal: para 12–8.

- A lawyer advises only as to existing law. Law, like life on which it is based, is not absolutely predictable and changes rapidly.

It is obvious then that these opinions do not say much.

But the mere rendering of an opinion which does not say much should not normally limit the lawyer's duty to advise in accordance with his instructions – which often are to advise generally. However the opinion itself may indicate to the client the scope of the lawyer's investigation and focus attention on exceptions, e.g. matters of fact, and in that sense limit the lawyer's duty and draw a boundary around client expectations.

Documents examined

12–6 Opinions list the papers examined by the lawyer, such as the original agreements, the constitutional documents of the borrower, authorising resolutions, incumbency certificates, exchange control consents, process agency acceptances and tax clearances and state that the opinion is based on those listed documents. This procedure does not usually limit the scope of the enquiry unless specifically so stated. In any event, commonly the opinion states that he has examined such other documents, treaties, and rules of law as are considered relevant.

The opinion records other steps taken, notably searches at a commercial or companies registry at which are filed the obligor's constitutional documents, names of office-holders and insolvency, winding-up or dissolution steps and register of charges or security interests. The opinion may note whether the absence of a filing prejudices third parties.

Assumptions

12–7 Many legal opinions are prefaced by a series of assumptions which are as a result excluded from the scope of the opinion.

The main usual assumptions are:

- the genuineness of all signatures;

- the authenticity and completeness of original documents;

- the accuracy of copies;

- that relevant meetings of the boards of directors (and shareholders) have been duly convened and held and that a duly qualified quorum of directors (or shareholders) voted in favour of the resolutions;

- that each agreement referred to in the opinion was duly executed by and constitutes a valid and legally binding obligation, in accordance with its terms, of each party thereto other than the obligors;

- that no additional matters would have been disclosed by a search at the relevant companies or commercial registry or registry of insolvency applications since the carrying out of the various searches;

- that each obligor is not insolvent within the meaning of the relevant insolvency legislation at the time it enters into an agreement opined upon, that each obligor will not be insolvent within the meaning of that legislation in consequence of the agreement or the transactions contemplated thereby, and that no action has been taken for the dissolution or winding-up of the obligor or the commencement of any insolvency proceedings. This assumption recognises that actual insolvency may attract preference doctrines (e.g. the voidability of guarantees or gifts), that commitments after the commencement of insolvency proceedings may be void, that the publication of insolvency proceedings is invariably after the event or inefficient and that, even if published, the commencement may relate back to zero hour on the date of the filing or order;

- that there are no contractual or similar restrictions binding on an obligor which would affect the conclusions in the opinion and that any restrictions in an obligor's constitutional documents would not be contravened by the entry into and performance of the agreements, e.g. a borrowing limit;

- that each of the banks is an authorised banking institution under the relevant banking legislation. This is necessary where loan business requires a licence.

A lawyer should not assume facts which the lawyer knows or suspects to be incorrect.

Qualifications generally

If the law does not justify a "clean" opinion, then any qualifications become a legal risk for the creditor which the creditor needs to weigh up. The law is not a matter for negotiation and insistence on clean opinions based on bargaining power produces false comfort.

12–8

If there are known differences of opinion amongst knowledgeable lawyers on a particular point, a cautionary note may need to be introduced into a favourable opinion.

Opinion as to facts

12–9   Commonly, opinions exclude matters of fact, e.g. "no opinion is given as to matters of fact and it is assumed that there are no facts which would affect the conclusions in this opinion".

This undercuts the value of the opinion, since many matters are mixed law and fact. Still, it has to be said. For example, contracts may be set aside for misrepresentation or if they are actually implemented for some unlawful purpose not known to the lawyer. It is often not practicable to check these matters.

Some opinions do make statements which are primarily factual and are hence prefaced by a qualification as to the lawyer's knowledge of those facts. The preface "we know of" may mean that the lawyer has polled other members of the firm and checked through past files. The preface "after reasonable investigation, we know of" implies such investigation as is reasonable in the circumstances.

The mainstream view is that lawyers should decline to express a view as to matters which are not primarily legal in nature and which are not within the professional expertise of a lawyer, nor should they express a view on matters where the factual review required is impracticable. This view is based on the proposition that it is not for a lawyer to undertake business risk on warranties to be given by the client. Many firms regard general opinions as to (a) the absence of material litigation, (b) "no conflict" with contracts and (c) no apparent falsity in a prospectus as primarily factual, while others regard them as within a lawyer's competence in exceptional cases.

Foreign law

12–10   It is customary to state that the legal opinion is given only as to local law. It is also sometimes assumed that no foreign law (as to which no independent verification has been made) will affect the opinion, i.e. private international law rules are excluded.

The reason is that it is not practicable in a short opinion of this type to set out the rules of private international law – there are too many of them and explanation would lead to a treatise. Rather, the principal lawyer should in appropriate cases advise what foreign jurisdictions should be covered by separate foreign advice. Nevertheless, some legal opinions do contain statements to the effect that the governing law will be applied subject to a public policy exception. This seems simplistic and is not usually recommended: see para 13–36.

Lawyers of one jurisdiction are strictly not competent to opine on the laws of another jurisdiction and are usually prevented by their codes from doing so. The proper course is for the creditor to request opinions from other significant jurisdictions which are given directly to the client.

If a transaction does involve a substantial foreign element, a lawyer should advise his client that the lawyer is not competent to advise and, where appropriate, recommend the taking of foreign legal advice. As to which jurisdictions should be covered, see para 12–4.

In selecting a foreign lawyer, one would expect the selecting lawyer to exercise some basic duty of care in accordance with agency law applying where an agent appoints a sub-agent. But this must depend upon the circumstances, e.g. the degree of client reliance, the practicalities, and the known standards of the jurisdiction concerned. But, having exercised such appropriate duty of care in the selection of the foreign lawyer, a lawyer should not be responsible for defects in the foreign advice unless the lawyer expressly assumes responsibility.

> In *Wildermann v Wachtell*, 149 Misc 623, 267 NYS 840 (Sup Ct 1933), the court stated at 624,842 that a "lawyer should not be held to a stricter rule in foreign matters than the exercise of due care in recommending a foreign attorney".
>
> In *Tormo v Yormark*, 338 F Supp 1159 (DNJ 1975), the court imposed a minimal duty of investigation on a principal lawyer in the selection of a foreign lawyer. The court held that in the particular circumstances the lawyers could rely on the foreign jurisdiction's regulation of the initial and continuing fitness and integrity of its lawyers. The principal counsel is not negligent simply for failing to make enquiries into a foreign lawyer's background.

There may be some duty on the principal lawyer to give appropriate instructions to the foreign lawyer, but beyond this one could not be definitive, e.g. on the degree of investigation, asking the right questions and cross-checking. These matters must turn on the circumstances. Normally one would not expect a principal lawyer to have to supervise the work of a foreign lawyer in a commercially developed country, although principal lawyers often do, especially if the foreign lawyer is clearly inexperienced in the transaction concerned.

It is not usually good practice for a principal lawyer to opine that the foreign lawyer's opinion is in form and substance satisfactory.

Whose lawyers give the opinion?

12–12 The opinion may be given by independent lawyers for the lenders, independent lawyers for the borrower or the borrower's in-house counsel, depending on the circumstances. An opinion of the borrower's independent lawyers or in-house counsel in addition to those of the lender's lawyers is sometimes requested on the ground that borrower's lawyers are more likely to be familiar with the borrower's affairs. Some lawyers object to giving opinions to third parties: they say that this leads to a conflict of interest, discourages candour between client and lawyer and is contrary to their code of ethics.

Good practice dictates that parties should rely on their own lawyers, unless convenience, avoidance of duplication of effort, special knowledge, cost, or some other special reason dictates otherwise.

Although practice differs, requests for a lawyer to give an opinion to the other side's client are discouraged in England. The matter has given rise to considerable differences of opinion amongst bar associations in the United States, in particular as to whether the giving of an opinion to the opposing party is a breach of ethics: see Wilfred M Estey, *Legal Opinions in Commercial Transactions* (1990) Butterworths, p 291 *et seq*. In any event, the client's consent should be obtained and special care taken as regards any opinion disclosing threatened litigation which may be prejudicial to the client's interests as a litigant.

Opinions as to law of borrower's domicile

12–13 Usually the most important foreign legal opinion is that of the lawyer in the country where the borrower is domiciled. One reason is that under traditional conflict rules a number of major aspects of the transaction are determined according to this system of law as opposed to the governing law, e.g. status, powers and authorisations. Another is that, even if the lender's claim is technically valid under the governing law, the courts of the borrower's country, where the claim may ultimately have to be enforced, may apply different rules and recognise local prohibiting legislation which would be ignored by the governing law.

When is the opinion given?

12–14 Ideally the legal opinion from the principal lawyers should be given after all the other conditions precedent to a loan or bond issue are in place. The practical convenience of this is that the lender, through its lawyers, can control the approval of the supporting documentation without inviting dispute as to whether this documentation complies with the "conditions precedent" clause. The clause is not satisfied until the opinion is rendered so that the opinion is the last act, the "signing off" by the lawyers, after which the lender is committed. This procedure is dictated by prudence, but is not followed in appropriate cases.

Persons entitled to rely on opinions

Generally The persons to whom a legal opinion is addressed are entitled to rely upon it. These will usually be the lender under the loan agreement or the managers of a bond issue. This is so even if the addressee is the other party who is also legally represented: see, for example, *Allied Finance & Investments Ltd v Haddow & Co* (1983) NZLR 22 CA. There are several Canadian decisions to the same effect.

12–15

It is unusual for a lawyer to be responsible to persons other than the addressees of the opinion, e.g. to assignees of original banks or sub-participants or to subsequent investors in the bonds. Prudent and common practice is for a legal opinion to state expressly:

> "This opinion is given only to the persons to whom it is addressed and may not be relied upon by any other person. It may not be disclosed to third parties without our prior written consent."

This should not be treated as a disclaimer of liability which is subject to vitiating rules restricting the effect of disclaimers.

Lawyers as "experts"

Consideration should be given as to whether a lawyer is an "expert" within securities legislation imposing liability for negligent misstatements by experts in prospectuses which come within the ambit of the regulation.

12–16

A lawyer is not an expert within s 11 of the US Securities Act of 1933 merely because he participates in the preparation of the registration statement, but he may be in relation to specific matters included in the prospectus as having been opined upon by him, e.g., taxation and exchange control: see *Escott v BarChris Construction*, 283 F Supp 643 (SDNY 1968). Under s 11 there is liability to subsequent investors.

Liability in tort

A liability in the tort of negligence may be owed to third parties to whom the lawyer owes a duty of care. In order to show liability, the third party must normally show (a) that a duty of care was owed to him, (b) that the

12–17

lawyer broke that duty, (c) the third party relied on the opinion, and (d) that the negligence caused the loss, e.g. that he would not have entered into the transaction but for the defective opinion: *Sykes v Midland Bank* [1971] 1 QB 113, CA. Case law in the US (apart from California), England and Canada has shown that it is generally very difficult for third parties to satisfy these tests in this context and liability to third parties is unusual except in the case of fraud or special circumstances. Most of the international case law on lawyer's liability to third parties has arisen in the special context of wills which deprive a third party of an intended benefit by reason of some deficiency in drafting or formal execution, e.g. California, *Biankanja v Irving*, 49 Cal 2d 467, 320 P 2d 16 (1958); Canada, *Whittingham v Crease & Co* (1978) 5 WWR 45, 88 DLR (3d) 353 (BC SC).

In bond issues, names of legal firms advising on a transaction are often printed in bond issue prospectuses, excerpts from their opinion may also be specifically included in the prospectus and the opinions may have to be filed with the local stock exchange. It is sometimes said that the status of a legal firm is used to foster investor confidence in the legal propriety of the transaction.

12–18   In **England** the leading case of *Hedley Byrne & Co, Ltd v Heller & Partners Ltd* [1964] AC 465 extended the tort of negligence for misstatements where a duty of care was owed, and product liability cases have established that a subsequent purchaser is not bound by an exclusion clause in a supply contract between the manufacturer and the retailer. But subsequent case law has excluded liability in the tort of negligence for pure economic loss: *Murphy v Brentwood District Council* [1990] 2 All ER 908, HL.

It is therefore unlikely that in England a lawyer is liable for negligence to subsequent investors to whom an opinion is not addressed, unless perhaps there are special circumstances which give rise to a duty of care. In many cases the question may be forestalled because the subsequent investor may not be able to show that he read the original opinion so as to denote reliance and, if he did, he would have seen the paragraph limiting the persons who can rely on the opinion.

12–19   In the **United States**, the SEC has advocated an enlarged role for lawyers in securities law enforcement and contends that the investing public, as well as the client, relies on the securities lawyer.

> In the case of *SEC v Spectrum Ltd*, 489 F 2d 535 (2d Cir 1973), the court held that an attorney who had prepared an erroneous opinion letter, which was alleged to have been used to sell unregistered securities to third parties, could be enjoined from future violations of the 1933 Act on the basis of his conduct having been negligent. The court noted (at pp 541–2). "The legal profession plays

a unique and pivotal role in the effective implementation of the securities laws. Questions of compliance with the intricate provisions of these statutes are ever present and the smooth functioning of the securities markets will be seriously disturbed if the public cannot rely on the expertise proffered by an attorney when he renders an opinion on such matters." But this was not a liability case.

The US Restatement of Torts states, in effect, that liability for negligent information is limited to those whom the person providing the information intended to reach or influence, either himself or through the recipient of the information: see, e.g. *Biankanja v Irving*, 49 Cal 2d 647, 320 P 2d 16 (1958); *Baer v Broder*, 436 NYS 2d 693 (Sup Ct 1981).

> In the California case of *Roberts v Ball, Hart, Brown & Baerwitz*, 128 Cal Rptr 901, 57 Cal App 3d 104 (CA 1976), the law firm opined that a partnership was a general partnership, allegedly wrongly. It was alleged that the client would, to the firm's knowledge, give the opinion to lenders to induce them to lend money to the partnership which they did. Although the case decided only preliminary matters, the court said that a duty of care would be incurred if it could be shown that the lawyers knew that the opinion would be used to induce lenders to give credit to the partnership.

But the third party will not be able to sue if he did not rely on the opinion. Thus in *First Municipal Leasing Corp v Blakenship*, 648 SW 2d 410 (Tex CA, 1983), the lawyer was not liable because the client completed the transaction before receiving the opinion. In *Goodman v Kennedy*, 556 P 2d 737, 134 Cal Rptr 375, 18 Cal 3d 335 (SC 1976), the lawyer was not liable because there was no evidence that the advice was ever communicated to the plaintiff.

As to express terms limiting reliance to the recipients, the US court said in *SEC v Spectrum Ltd*, 489 F 2d 535, 542 (2d Cir 1973) that "where expediency precludes thorough investigation an attorney can preclude the illicit use of his opinion letter... by a statement to that effect clearly appearing on the face of the letter".

In Germany a decision of the Federal Supreme Court (BGH January 18, 1972, VersR 1972, 441, NJW 1972, 678) held an attorney liable to a lender:

> The lawyer knew that his client was insolvent but nevertheless attested solvency. A lender, as a result, did not ask for security for a loan. *Held*: even though the lawyer did not expressly agree to be responsible for incorrect information, he was liable in damages because he knew that the information would be relied on by the recipient in making important decisions. The court also stressed that this rule applies particularly to an attorney whose statements, in view of his function as an independent agent in the service of the law, carry particular weight and are widely trusted by the public.

Chapter 13

LEGAL OPINIONS: PRINCIPAL CONTENTS

This chapter reviews the main substantive contents of the following legal opinions:

— opinions of foreign lawyers in the jurisdiction of the borrower as to term loan

— opinions on securities regulation and prospectuses

— opinions on security.

There is also a brief comment on the opinion of the principal lawyers advising on a transaction.

For forms of opinion, see the Appendix.

Foreign lawyer's legal opinion

13–1 This section reviews the principal paragraphs covered in an opinion as to the law of the borrower's domicile, apart from the general qualifications and assumptions described in the previous chapter: see para 12–6 *et seq*. These are designed for loan agreements and would have to be adapted to cover financial leases, guarantees and bond issue documentation (trust deeds, fiscal agency agreements, subscription, underwriting and selling agreements). The language is short form only.

Status

13–2 The opinion states:

> The Borrower is a corporation duly incorporated and validly existing under the laws of Ruritania.

Status refers to the legal identity and existence of the borrower and is generally determined by the law of the borrower's place of incorporation.

Due incorporation "Duly incorporated" may involve a review of the corporation laws in effect at the time of incorporation and of the incorporating documents. In English-based countries a certificate of registration from the local registration authority is often conclusive proof of due incorporation: see s 13(7) of the British Companies Act 1985; *Hammond v Prentice Bros* [1920] 1 Ch 201.

The EC First Company Law Directive of 1973 no longer allows the retroactive fictitiousness of companies. Articles 10–12 of the First Directive seek to coordinate national legal provisions concerning the nullity of the company and to limit severely the grounds on which it can be declared. Article 10 of the Directive, which is intended to prevent the defective constitution of companies, represents a compromise between the laws of the original member states. Article 12(1) provides that the nullity of the company can be ordered only by a decision of a court on six grounds. Article 121(1) provides that persons who contracted with the company which has been annulled under the impression that it was validly incorporated receive the same protection provided by Art 3 governing publicity as if the company had acted ultra vires. The nullity of a company entails its winding up but does not affect the validity of any commitment entered into with it: Art 12(2) and (3).

So far as Britain is concerned, the question of the nullity of companies did not arise because the certificate of the Registrar of Companies was conclusive as to formation so it was not possible to call into question matters which occurred prior to or contemporaneously with the registration. However this was not the case in many other member states. For example, in France the theory was that the company was based on contract and registration was merely declaratory and it is possible that even now under French law there may still be grounds for the nullity of companies in addition to those stated in the First Directive law: see Art 360 of the French Law concerning commercial companies of July 24, 1966, as amended. In Germany and Italy it was thought that a company could have been nullified on the basis of formal defects in its constitution.

Although there are differences in the method of implementation of the First Directive, it was implemented in Great Britain in 1972, in Ireland in 1973, in Italy in 1969, in Germany in 1969, in Luxembourg in 1972, in Denmark in 1972 and 1973, in Greece in 1986, in Portugal in 1986 and in Spain in 1989.

In the United States, each state has a statute which provides in substance that the corporate existence begins either upon the filing of the articles of incorporation or the issuance of the certificate of incorporation: see the Revised Model Business Corporation Act s 2.03(a). Most statutes add that acceptance of the Articles or the issuance of the certificate of incorporation is "conclusive proof" that all conditions precedent to incorporation have been complied with, except in suits brought by the state: Revised Model Business Corporation Act s 2.03(b). Thus if the Secretary of State accepts a filing or issues a certificate of incorporation, as the case may be, a de jure corporation is in existence notwithstanding mistakes or omissions in the articles of incorporation. There is much state variation and considerable case law about the liability of promoters and incorporators and about de facto corporations.

In practice, it is thought that only a tiny proportion of companies are not properly formed since incorporation in most countries is a very straightforward matter. Most participants in the international financial markets are established companies. Hence the retrospective fictitiousness of companies is not of great importance.

13–5 **Duly organised** Some legal opinions state that the borrower is "duly organised". This may mean that the company's minimum share capital has been duly paid in, that the management, secretary and statutory auditors have been duly appointed, that the company is entitled to start business and that the company has adopted complying internal regulations.

The phrase is not recommended on three grounds. Firstly, the satisfaction of some of these organisational matters, e.g. payment of the minimum share capital, is in some countries a condition precedent to registration as a company. Secondly, if they are not, the checking of those matters would involve a factual investigation in excess of the benefits. Thirdly, due organisation may extend to asserting that the company has obtained regulatory licences to carry on its business, e.g. a credit business, which would involve a factual investigation into its actual activities, or an assertion that the internal management appointments and procedures are proper – something which is usually irrelevant to third parties.

The phrase may have originated from the fact that in the US the bye-laws of a company are not filed on the public register. Nor are they in Canada.

13–6 **Valid existence** "Validly existing" means that the corporation is not a nullity, is not in liquidation and has not been dissolved, e.g. because of a limited duration charter or as a result of a merger. The absence of liquidation proceedings may be (inconclusively) ascertainable from the corporation's minute book or from the local companies registrar or from certificates issued by the local registration authority. In many countries, the commencement of insolvency proceedings has to be followed by a filing at the commercial or companies or mercantile registry. The public notice inevitably follows the event so that the company's business may be frozen and the management dispossessed of their powers before the notification. The opinion might reflect in the assumptions when the last search was made, whether or not this reflects the up-to-date position and (perhaps) whether third parties may rely on the recorded documents, even if deficient.

Limited duration charters are common in Franco-Latin countries, but not English-based countries.

Doctrines of lifting of the veil of incorporation to impose liability on shareholders do not generally affect the valid existence of the company. The corporate form is unimpaired – all that has happened is that the shareholders are responsible in addition. The likeliest incidence of dissolution might arise in the case of prohibited one-man companies. Contrast consolidation of companies on insolvency where, as a result of inextricable commingling, a group of companies are treated as a single unit and all their assets and liabilities are merged. Consolidation is invariably a court-ordered procedure after formal insolvency proceedings have commenced. The total loss of corporate personality after initial due incorporation is very rare.

Good standing "In good standing" has a special meaning in the United States, e.g. that the borrower has filed its annual report and has paid its corporate franchise taxes, and should be avoided in those other jurisdictions where it is not a term of art. It may be taken to mean that the corporation is financially sound, that it is conducting its operations lawfully or that it has obtained the necessary official licences for its actual business. In the United States "good standing" is proved by official certificates.

Qualification to do business This limb of the opinion sometimes also states that the borrower is duly qualified to do business in all jurisdictions where such qualification is necessary.

Where much of a corporation's business is conducted through branches in foreign countries, the lender may be interested in ascertaining that the business is in fact authorised, whether or not lawfully conducted. Failure to observe local legal requirements as to qualification to do business may result in the corporation being exposed to penalties and its contracts rendered unenforceable. This is especially so in the fields of insurance, banking, leasing and financial services.

The rendering of an opinion in the above form would often require investigation of all places where the borrower does business, e.g. owns or leases land, accepts contracts, or has an office – the links can be very tenuous – and foreign legal advice. The cost of such an investigation would usually be prohibitive compared to the benefit and the results may be inconclusive. The opinion is impracticable in the case of large international corporations.

Other forms of entity Apart from companies, the possible forms of juridical persons or associations are legion and include states, departments of state, provinces, municipalities, co-operatives, mutual companies, partnerships, limited partnerships, loose consortiums bound only by contract, statutory corporations, foundations, trusts, and international organisations.

The key questions are:

- Will the entity be **recognised** in the chosen courts? This is a question for newly-formed states and for international organisations and is discussed in another work in this series on financial law. All states appear to recognise the existence of companies and other entities duly formed under the laws of a foreign state and one has not heard of any exceptions.

- Is the entity a legal or **juridical person**? This means that it owns its assets separately from its shareholders or other owners, is liable for its obligations to the extent of those assets (so that its owners are not liable for them, except exceptionally), and can sue and be sued in its own name.

- Is the entity entitled to **immunity** from suit? Immunity is discussed in another work in this series.

13–10 **Trusts** The Anglo-American trust is not a legal entity but simply a bundle of assets held by a trustee as the legal, nominal, or titular holder for the benefit of the beneficiaries. Hence it is the trustee who is the contracting party, although it may, and commonly does, limit its personal liability to the trust assets. A limit on personal liability must be specific: see *Muir v City of Glasgow Bank* (1879) 4 AC 337 (trustees liable); *Re Robinson's Settlement* [1912] 1 Ch 717 (trustees not liable). Although there are some differences in US states, the main features of the English trust in this context are:

- There appears to be no protection to third parties if the transaction is outside the actual powers and authorities of the trust instrument: creditor good faith or ostensible authority are insufficient. Hence it is necessary to review the trust instrument.

- The creditor reaches the trust assets by subrogation to the trustee's right to be reimbursed out of the assets for obligations duly undertaken by him for the account of the trust. If the trustee has been guilty of a breach of trust, then any liability of the trustee to make good his breach by contributing to the trust assets must be deducted from the claim of the creditor claiming by subrogation to the trustee's right of indemnity. Thus if the creditor's claim is 100, but the trustee has in breach of trust invested trust assets in unauthorised investments and thereby incurred a loss of 100, the creditor has no claim against the trust assets. Hence, unlike breaches of company law by directors, creditors take the risk of the trustee, including for breaches of trust: see, in England, *Re Johnson* (1880) 15 Ch D 548; in the United States, *Mason v Pomeroy*, 151 Mass 164, 168, 24 Ne 202, 7 LRA 771 (1890). But the creditor's right to the assets ranks ahead of the trustee's right: see, e.g. *Re Richardson* [1911] 2 KB 705, CA; *Re ADM Franchise Pty Ltd* (1983) 7 ACLR 987; *Re Blundell* (1890) 44 Ch D 1, CA.

– Outside the regulation of collective investment schemes, there are no general rules protecting the assets for the benefit of creditors, e.g. maintenance of capital, non-payment of dividends out of capital and the like.

– In England, trusts are not wound up under the Insolvency Act 1986 but by a creditor's administration order under RSC Ord 85. The rules are quite different and do not attract the highly developed insolvency regime applicable to companies.

Partnerships The rules for partnerships were highly refined by the end of the nineteenth century in Britain and the United States. Limited partnerships are often used in special situations, e.g. financial leasing in the US or Norwegian shipping companies, usually because the tax treatment of a consortium is more favourable. For example, tax losses or capital allowances are more easily used by the partners. In the case of ordinary partnerships, the usual system is that the partners are personally liable, but (in England at least), the private creditors of the partners have first bite at the private assets, and the business creditors first bite at the partnership assets. In the case of limited partnerships, the limited partners are liable only to the extent of their agreed contribution (like shareholders), and the general partner has unlimited liability. As the general partner is usually a shell limited liability company, this unlimited responsibility is generally academic.

Corporate powers

The opinion states:

> **The Borrower has the corporate power to enter into and perform the Agreement.**

The power of the borrower to enter into the transaction is generally ascertained according to the law of its place of incorporation.

This opinion means that the agreement is not ultra vires, e.g. under its corporate statute or by virtue of a general rule of law of a constitutional nature. It does not mean that the transaction has been authorised or that it is not in conflict with other agreements. The addition of "corporate" powers is intended to exclude such matters as regulatory authorisations for its actual business activities, usury, or other general legal rules about the conduct of its business.

The corporate powers of a corporation or municipality will generally be defined by its constitution (by-laws, certificate of incorporation, memorandum of association, statute or charter) coupled in each case with local corporation laws construed in accordance with local law.

Commonly experienced difficulties are (a) absence of express constitutional powers (is there an implied power?), (b) objections to guarantees which are not for the benefit of the corporation or are not ancillary to an express corporate purpose, and (c) restrictions on the powers of a corporation to issue bonds until its capital stock has been fully paid in or unless it is a public company or if the amount of bonded debt would exceed its paid-in capital. The latter restrictions are internationally on the wane.

States have inherent power to borrow but the powers of the executive may be limited by the constitution, e.g. by requiring specific legislative ratification of loans or guarantee commitments of the state. This is more strictly a matter for authorisation.

Due authorisation, execution and delivery

13–13 The opinion states:

> **The Agreement has been duly authorised by appropriate corporate action.**

This opinion means that the necessary action required by agency law and the constitution of the borrower has been taken to authorise the agreement as a binding commitment of the borrower.

The procedures necessary for the authorisation of the loan are generally a matter for local law of the place of incorporation.

13–14 **Corporations** Corporations often authorise by resolution of their managing body, although specified officials may have general powers to authorise and sign loan contracts. Shareholder approvals may be necessary, particularly where a guarantee is granted, where the directors are subject to an overall borrowing limit, or where security is granted over a substantial portion of assets.

How far the lawyer needs to go in ascertaining that authorising meetings are properly convened by appropriate notice, were attended by a quorum of directors who were all duly appointed and that those voting were not disqualified from doing so by conflict of interest or some other bar will depend upon the rules of the jurisdiction concerned and the requirements of the lender. Such an enquiry could be substantial, e.g. checking back through all corporate records and eliminating conflicts of interest. The lender may be protected by statutory or common law rules to the effect that third parties are not prejudiced by internal irregularities or by defective authorisations where the signatories had ostensible authority to act or by returns filed at the local companies registry office which are conclusive as to those authorised to bind the company.

In most commercial jurisdictions, the tendency is to protect third parties where directors act in breach of constitutional authority: this is aimed at the greater predictablity and safety of transactions (except in the case of direct participation or bad faith) so that third parties do not have to monitor directors: see, e.g. s 7 of the US Model Business Corporation Act and the British CA 1985 s 35 introduced by CA 1989.

Where presumptions in favour of a lender are not comprehensive, the lawyer may only be prepared to give the opinion by assuming the validity of a certified resolution and thereby throwing a degree of factual risk on to the lender.

Other entities Special official approvals may be required for municipalities and governments. Governmental borrowings often require specific sanction by the legislature. Sometimes the borrowing is authorised by general enabling legislation permitting the government to borrow up to a specific ceiling or for specific purposes, e.g. economic development. Difficulties can arise where the borrowing limit is expressed in a domestic currency. Is the conversion made at the date of the authorisation, the date of the loan agreement or the date of the actual borrowing? At what rate of exchange? Further, would the loan be ultra vires if the ceiling is exceeded on actual borrowing (which may be many months after the authorisation is given) even though at the time of signature the loan would not have caused the limit to be exceeded? These problems may be resolved by reference to the constitution of the state concerned.

13–15

Execution and delivery

The opinion states:

13–16

The Agreement has been duly executed and delivered.

The persons authorised to execute will be determined either by the authorising resolution or by the general law. In some countries, the names of those authorised to bind the company are filed at the commercial registry and third parties not on actual notice of an irregularity, are entitled to rely on the public file. This is generally true, e.g. in Austria, Germany, Finland, France, and Switzerland, but not England or Canada, although it is thought that in most cases an uncorrected representation of the names of directors by filing at the relevant registry will create a presumption of authority by holding out in the absence of an irregularity known to the creditor.

Where the agreement is executed by an agent under power of attorney, the powers of the company's directors to delegate and the power of attorney should be checked. Third parties may be protected against revocability of the power by legislation similar to the English Powers of Attorney Act 1971.

The manner of execution may be specified by the constitutional laws of the borrower, e.g. execution under seal and identity of countersignatories. A certificate of genuineness of signatures is usually assumed by the opinion to be correct: para 12–7.

Special formalities may be required, especially for security interests. Examples are notarisation and legalisation.

As to delivery, the lawyer should check that the agreement has been "delivered" so as to complete the contract in accordance with contract law. This will usually only be of practical significance where there are special escrow arrangements.

As to conflict of laws on formalities, see the relevant chapter in another work in this series on financial law.

Legal validity

13–17 The opinion states:

> The Agreement would be treated by the courts of Ruritania as the legally binding obligation of the Borrower enforceable in accordance with its terms.

This is the heart of the opinion. The legality of an agreement is generally a matter for the governing law of the agreement subject to certain exceptions. This opinion addresses the question of the recognition of that validity by the courts of the jurisdiction of the lawyer rendering the opinion.

13–18 **Legally binding** This statement overlaps with others in the opinion. If the agreement is legally binding it must not be void (e.g. on account of an ultra vires rule) or because it is unauthorised or improperly executed or because it conflicts with a rule of law (e.g. illegal purpose or usury rule) or because of the absence of an exchange control consent or because it can be rescinded on account of misrepresentation. On the other hand an agreement could be unauthorised, yet be binding on the ground that third parties are not affected by internal irregularities. There is no real difference between "legally valid" and "legally binding".

"Enforceable" The generally accepted meaning of this term is that the agreement is actionable before a court. An agreement can be legally valid but not enforceable, e.g. because of sovereign immunity, failure to stamp or because of Art VIII 2(b) of the IMF Agreement concerning exchange controls (examined elsewhere in this series of works).

13–19

Because some lawyers think that "enforceable" means "specifically enforceable", the opinion may state that specific performance and other remedies are discretionary and would not necessarily be available. Although debts are enforceable in the sense that they are recoverable without proof of damage or duty to mitigate, covenants such as a borrowing limit may effectively be sanctioned only by an event of default. The better view is that "enforceable" does not mean "specifically enforceable" unless so stated.

> In the Californian case of *Trustees of the Central States v Golden Nuggett Inc*, Case No CV 87 – 2684 – AAH (CD Calif 1987), a purchaser of notes alleged misrepresentation in an opinion that the notes were legal obligations of the vendor enforceable in accordance with their terms. The court said that this remedies opinion was simply an opinion that "a contract does exist which on its face neither violates public policy nor is contrary to law". An opinion is not a guarantee that the document will withstand all forms of attack, nor a warranty that it is enforceable according to its written terms. The court said that to hold otherwise would lead to the abandonment of legal opinions in business transactions.

Bankruptcy qualification A common qualification is that legal validity is "subject to all insolvency, bankruptcy, moratorium, reorganisation or similar laws affecting creditors' rights generally". The bankruptcy qualification is a major inroad on the usefulness of the opinion, because it is on bankruptcy that the creditor wishes its rights to be respected. Yet the qualification is necessary because a short opinion is not a suitable vehicle for explaining bankruptcy laws and indeed advice as to the impact of bankruptcy law would require an extended treatise.

13–20

The main bankruptcy doctrines likely to be relevant (depending on the jurisdiction) include:

13–21

- on bankruptcy, creditors receive only a dividend
- powers of the insolvency representative to disclaim or abandon contracts, subject to the payment of damages
- revocation of preferences. This is especially important in relation to security for pre-existing debt and for guarantees.
- the non-provability of post-insolvency interest
- the conversion of foreign currency claims into local currency and the

likely invalidity of top-up currency indemnity claims attempting to override this rule: para 4–6

- moratoriums on maturities
- compulsory compositions and reductions of debt voted by majority creditors or approved by the court or a cramming-down of creditors on reorganisation plans
- freezes on creditor executions and actions on the commencement of insolvency proceedings
- freezes on winding-up petitions or the opening of judicial rescue proceedings
- limitations on insolvency set-off in some countries (not England), thereby overriding a set-off clause. The ban may be total or may extend only to obligations incurred or acquired in a suspect period. Even if insolvency set-off is allowed, the double-dip contemplated by a pro rata sharing clause may be prohibited: para 6–16 *et seq*. An agreement of the borrower to pay without set-off may be overridden by a mandatory insolvency set-off statute (not that this would normally concern a creditor).
- the hierarchy of debts on insolvency, so that preferential and other debts may rank prior.

It is possible that the qualification is customarily implied. A lender wishing to know the position on bankruptcy, etc. should require some such statement as "enforceable in bankruptcy".

The qualification will usually apply expressly to the whole opinion so as to limit the other statements.

13–22 **Other qualifications** Other qualifications will depend upon the circumstances but will usually qualify the whole opinion and include the following:

- the potential invalidity of penalty interest and, in some countries, interest on interest or post-judgment interest, or clauses providing for compensation for creditor losses in addition to interest
- the potential invalidity of agreements to pay in a specific currency and of top-up currency indemnity clauses for judgments in local currency: para 4–6
- limitations on exculpation clauses, e.g. in favour of a syndicate agent or bond trustee
- limitations on clauses providing for the conclusivity of lender's certificates if arbitrary or manifestly wrong, e.g. certificates as to a rate of interest or increased costs or the amount of the debt itself

- restrictions on wide indemnities for costs of enforcement or litigation. These may be in the discretion of the court.
- the inefficacy of a clause that only waivers in writing are effective. One may waive a waiver clause. This is trivial.
- the invalidity of clauses providing for a stamp duty indemnity
- the invalidity in some countries of restrictions on prepayment
- compulsory grace periods or good faith duties on acceleration or immediate payment on default (not England)
- the revocability of agency, e.g. the syndicate agent or a process agent
- the inefficacy of severability clauses stipulating that void or illegal portions of the agreement are severed and do not affect the validity of the other clauses. An illegal taint may poison the whole agreement, despite such a clause.
- the potential inefficacy of protective clauses in guarantees under rules restricting unfair contracts and the like; these are most unlikely to apply
- the potential invalidity of jurisdiction provisions by reason of court rules of forum non conveniens – this would be rare – and stays on several concurrent proceedings.

Most of these qualifications are minor or arise only in exceptional circumstances and a reasonable lender could not legitimately expect otherwise. Some opinions may state that the qualifications do not substantially detract from the main remedies provided by the agreement. Good practice is to explain any material qualifications to the lender by separate advice if required (which it usually is not in the case of sophisticated creditors).

Additional qualifications may relate to usury; financial assistance by a company for the purpose of the acquisition of its own shares; and covenants not to change the constitutional documents, conflicting with company law mandatory provisions.

"Good faith" qualifications There may be a qualification that the validity and enforcement of the agreement is subject to doctrines of good faith, reasonableness and equitable conduct on the part of the lender. The qualification may be implied.

This qualification is primarily intended to cover cancellation of a commitment to lend because of a technicality, e.g. minor non-fulfilment of a condition precedent, or trivial default or breach of warranty; and acceleration without warning or on account of a triviality.

In England, cancellations and accelerations are enforceable literally, even if the event is trivial. Outside consumer credit, the courts give relief only in cases of extreme economic duress or unconscionability which rarely apply in the commercial context: para 3–54. But in the United States, theories of lender liability have restricted the literal application of credit agreement cancellations and accelerations, and these "good faith" principles have surfaced elsewhere.

13–24 **Foreign law opinions** A lawyer giving an opinion as to the validity of an agreement governed by a foreign law must assume that the agreement is valid in accordance with the foreign law concerned. Technically, he is not able to ascertain what the agreement means under foreign law and, if he opines on the basis that the agreement is governed by his local law, he is opining on a fictional agreement.

This problem is somewhat artificial. While some technical phrases may be terms of art having an idiosyncratic legal meaning in one jurisdiction which the foreign lawyer cannot be expected to be familiar with and although one jurisdiction may imply terms not implied in another, this is exceptional and it is generally obvious what the agreement says and it is generally obvious what the substantive obligations are. The foreign lawyer is saved by an express or implied statement that he speaks only as to local law. For the creditor, there is a technical gap but it is inevitable and not usually important.

A confirmation that a term is "enforceable" does not express an opinion as to what the words mean. Nor does the statement infer that a lender will win any contest.

Official consents

13–25 The opinion states:

> **All consents and authorisations of all governmental and official authorities of or in Ruritania have been obtained for the entry into and performance of the Agreement by the borrower.**

The lawyer should check that any exchange control consent covers not only scheduled payments but also accelerated payments and ancillary payments, such as management and commitment fees, alternative interest rates, tax indemnities, increased costs and expenses. In some countries the exchange control authorities give consent in advance only for scheduled payments and require further application to be made for permission to make accelerated payments. Exchange controls have either been dismantled or are on the way out in many developed countries.

Other official consents for credit transactions are unusual, but may be required by the lender, e.g. a banking licence. Note that the opinion relates only to borrower consents.

Non-conflict with laws, constitution or contracts

The opinion states:

13–26

> The execution, delivery and performance of the Agreement do not and will not conflict with (a) any present law of Ruritania, (b) the constitutional documents of the Borrower or (c) so far as we are aware, any order of any court or authority in Ruritania or any mortgage, contract or other undertaking binding on the Borrower or affecting its assets.

Although there is some overlap, the "non-conflict" statement goes further than the "legally binding" opinion.

As to (a), a law which is violated may stop short of avoiding the agreement but may nevertheless impose penalties on the offending borrower damaging to its credit.

As to (b), the constitutional documents may contain a borrowing limit, breach of which may not prejudice third parties who are not expressly aware of the breach but which may cause defaults under other agreements or give rise to potential dispute as to whether the lenders are in fact affected by the breach.

As to (c), if the loan causes a violation of a term of another contract (such as breach of a borrowing restriction or a negative pledge) the resulting default could have serious consequences for the credit of the borrower if the other parties exercised rights to accelerate their loans or to sue for damages. Many lawyers will not be prepared to give an opinion as to (c) and the giving of such an opinion is not usually good practice. In unqualified form, the investigation would require a legal audit of the material contracts of the borrower and involve questions of fact, e.g. whether a financial ratio or borrowing limit is complied with. An investigation of all court records, even local ones, will usually be impracticable. The opinion may give false comfort.

Litigation

The opinion states:

13–27

> We know of no material pending or threatened litigation, arbitration or administrative proceeding in which the Borrower is involved.

Litigation could seriously affect a company's financial standing, e.g. especially in the patent and anti-trust fields.

"Pending" means that the proceedings have actually commenced. "Threatened" probably means an overt threat evidencing a present intention to sue, but not unasserted possible claims.

Materiality is difficult to determine because it involves an assessment of the validity of the claim (the other side's case has not been heard) and its impact upon the company (which involves a financial judgment).

An investigation to support the opinion would probably include enquiry of the executives most likely to know of litigation and a review of the financial statements, of letters from the client to the auditors, of correspondence files, including those with insurers and of the company's books and records. All of this would substantially add to the expense. The giving of this opinion is not usually good practice for external lawyers and is discouraged by some bar associations, including, probably, the English Law Society.

Stamp duties

13–28 The opinion states:

> **No stamp duties or similar documentary taxes imposed by or in Ruritania are payable in respect of the execution and delivery of the Agreement.**

Stamp duties usually affect admissibility in evidence and do not avoid the obligation. In practice if a stamp duty is not paid then a lender would have to pay it in order to enforce the claims where the borrower is insolvent.

Filings

13–29 The opinion states:

> **No filing, recording or registration with any public or official body or agency in Ruritania is necessary or desirable in relation to the making or performance of the Agreement by the borrower.**

Registration is usually required only in relation to the grant of security but sometimes administrative filings are necessary, e.g. to perfect an exchange control consent or to obtain a tax exemption. The statement relates to the borrower, not the lenders.

Legal form

The opinion states: 13–30

> The Agreement is in proper legal form for enforcement in the courts of Ruritania.

This primarily relates to such matters as notarisation, legalisation and language. Where the foreign courts require compliance with the formalities at the place of contracting, the opinion should assume compliance with those formal requirements.

Taxes

The opinion states: 13–31

> The Borrower is entitled to make all payments required to be made by it under the Agreement without deduction for or on account of taxes, charges or restrictions imposed by or in Ruritania.

An opinion as to withholding taxes is desirable even if the borrower is required by the loan agreement to bear these taxes by grossing-up the franked payment. The tax deduction by the borrower may affect the lender's tax position where tax credits for tax deductions are permissible. Further, a withholding tax on a payment which the borrower has to gross up increases the financial load on the borrower and generally puts the loan out of the question.

Pari passu ranking

The opinion states: 13–32

> The obligations of the Borrower under the Agreement rank and will rank pari passu with all its other present and future unsecured indebtedness.

The implications of this clause are discussed in para 3–27. Usual qualifications in the case of corporations are that liquidation expenses, taxes and certain wages are preferential payments.

A debt may also be subordinated:
- if it is substantially equity;

- under the exclusively US doctrine of equitable subordination;
- on certain rescue proceedings, by super-priority rehabilitation loans;
- by non-formalisation in Spanish jurisdictions;
- to bank depositors and insurance policy-holders in some countries;
- to environmental clean-up expenses.

Many of these will already be covered by the bankruptcy qualification: para 13–20.

A statement that the borrower's obligations will rank pari passu with all its other obligations, secured or unsecured, could not generally be made without qualification since this would involve the lawyer warranting that none of the borrower's assets are the subject of security.

Enforcement of foreign judgments

13–33   The opinion states:

> A judgment obtained in the courts of Kinglandia in respect of the Agreement would be enforced by the courts of Ruritania without re-examination of the merits of the case.

The essence of the opinion is that the local courts will not review the merits of the case. Usual qualifications relate to (a) the necessity to obtain a local *exequatur*, (b) jurisdiction of the court of origin, (c) fair trial without fraud, (d) final and conclusive money judgment for a non-tax non-penalty claim, (e) no conflict with another judgment on the same cause of action, (f) non-conflict with public policy, and (g) sometimes, reciprocity. The question of jurisdiction and reciprocity can sometimes be opined on in advance. The international position is summarised in another work in this series on financial law.

Immunity

13–34   The opinion states:

> The Borrower is not entitled to immunity from suit, pre-judgment attachment or restraint or enforcement of a judgment on grounds of

sovereignty or otherwise in the courts of Ruritania in respect of proceedings against it in relation to the Agreement.

The opinion may be buttressed by a statement that the borrower is subject to civil and commercial law with respect to its obligations under the loan agreement and that the loan is a commercial and private act as opposed to a governmental and public act.

If the opinion is given as to the borrower's country, there will usually be restrictions on the enforcement of judgments against the home state and governmental bodies. Governmental bodies may not be subject to insolvency procedures.

If the opinion relates to suit against foreign governments and state entities, waivers are often effective. Exceptions may include diplomatic, military and central bank assets.

The immunity position is generally a matter for the law of the courts where the action is brought.

Sovereign immunity is reviewed in another work in this series.

No adverse consequences; qualifications to do business

The opinion states: 13–35

> Under the laws of Ruritania the Bank will not be deemed to be resident, domiciled or carrying on any commercial activity in Ruritania or subject to any Ruritanian tax as a result only of the execution, delivery and performance of the Agreement. It is not necessary under the laws of Ruritania that the Bank be authorised or qualified to carry on business in Ruritania for the execution, delivery, performance or enforcement of the Agreement.

The first limb of the statement is primarily intended to cover the possibility that the lender may, by virtue of the loan agreement, become subject to (a) qualification rules requiring local administrative approvals or licences for money-lending, etc., (b) the jurisdiction of the local courts and (c) taxation in the borrower's country. The mere fact of contracting with a local entity might be sufficient to constitute a taxable business in the borrower's country especially where the lending bank has a branch there.

The second limb of the opinion refers to the possibility that qualifications may be required for enforcement.

The statement would often be qualified by an assumption that the agreement is the only transaction carried on by the lender in the country concerned. This is because other activities may constitute a local banking business which requires a banking licence, or an ordinary business which is taxable. There may also be a qualification that the agreement may subject the lender to the jurisdiction of the local courts.

Application of governing law

13–36 The opinion states:

> The choice of the law of Kinglandia as the governing law of the Agreement would be upheld as a valid choice of law by the courts of Ruritania. The chosen law would be applied by such courts in proceedings in relation to the Agreement as the governing law of the Agreement in accordance with and subject to their rules of private international law.

Whether this confirmation can be given depends on such questions as to whether the local laws support complete party autonomy or whether the right is restricted, e.g. to connected systems of law or to non-evasive choices or, in the case of governmental loans, by reason of some variant of the Latin-American Calvo doctrine. For choice of law, see chapter 5. The opinion does not require an essay on the private international law rules of the forum, but would do so if the opinion stated without qualification that the courts would apply the chosen law to the agreement as a whole: it would not be practicable to make such a statement.

It is usually impracticable also to confirm that no foreign law would be applied in priority to the chosen governing law, even if subject to a public policy exception. Advice on any key risks should be the subject of separate advice, if required.

Opinions on bond issues

Securities regulation

13–37 Where the transaction involves the issue of securities the opinion may (in addition to the matters listed in the foregoing section, suitably adapted) also cover the qualification of the prospectus and the bonds for public distribution, any required delivery of the prospectus to a registrar of companies or other authority, or, in the absence of listing or publicisation, the persons to whom the bonds may be offered or sold within the jurisdiction, e.g. only to sophisticated investors as defined. The opinion may also draw attention to the legal regime governing stabilisation of the bonds and to restrictions on cold-calling.

Prospectuses

A lawyer acting in relation to a bond issue sometimes is asked to confirm that certain sections of the prospectus on legal matters are a fair summary of the law, e.g. paragraphs on taxation matters, exchange control, stamp duty or local securities laws. The opinions are particularly important because of the potential liability of issuers and managers to the investing public for misstatements in a prospectus. A lawyer should not normally state that he has no reason to believe that the prospectus is incorrect in any material particular and should never comment on financial statements.

Bond issue opinions commonly state that no opinion is expressed as to whether the prospectus or offering circular contains all the information required by statute or general law or stock exchange rules and that the firm has not investigated or verified the truth or accuracy of the information contained in the offering circular, and has not been responsible for ensuring that no material information has been omitted.

Nevertheless in international equity offerings, a practice has developed of issuing "Rule 10b–5" opinions (see para 17–5) required initially by US underwriters as comfort against their potential liabilities under the US securities legislation. These are heavily qualified opinions which state in substance that nothing came to the firm's attention, in the course of participating in the preparation of the offering circular, which causes them to believe that the offering circular contains a material misstatement or omission. No view is expressed as to financial statements or other financial information.

Opinions on security

Legal opinions as to security are difficult. As a reference point, a warranty by the borrower as to security states in substance:

> The security constitutes a first priority security interest over the assets intended to be covered by the security and is not subject to any prior or pari passu interests. The security is enforceable on the insolvency of the Borrower and against all attaching creditors and other third parties.

It is not generally practicable to give a legal opinion in this form. A short opinion letter is often not a suitable vehicle for legal advice on most security interests, particularly as it would be necessary to cover the title of the borrower to the assets and priority (there can be as many as 16 priority contests), as well as the position on bankruptcy which is when the security is most needed. As mentioned, bankruptcy is usually excluded in formal transaction opinions in any event: para 13–20. An attempt to state the position in relation to all types of assets covered by general enterprise charges, such as the floating charge, would be impracticable.

Points which could be covered without an extended essay on mortgage laws include: corporate powers and authorities; due execution; the position as regards proper form, e.g. deed; and documentary taxes.

The opinion could also state what registration or filing is required in a public bureau in the state concerned to perfect the security interest, but not affirm that other methods of perfection have been completed, e.g. possession of negotiable instruments or cash, or notification to debtors of assignments of claims. Often the opinion could not realistically cover perfection in relation to after-acquired property. Dual registration should be considered, e.g. for land, ships, aircraft and intellectual property, especially if the security is a general floating charge.

13–40 Usually an opinion in relation to general security will state that no opinion is expressed as to the existence of or title to any of the secured assets or as to the priority of the security. Apart from guaranteed registration systems for land, ships and aircraft, it is generally difficult to establish conclusively the title to raw materials, goods, investment securities, receivables, contracts and other intangible assets – at least without an extensive and costly enquiry.

The better way of advising a lender unfamiliar with local security as to the position is by an explanatory letter of advice summarising some key matters on a non-exhaustive basis. Land mortgages are in England often accompanied by a lawyer's report on title.

Legal opinions on security are sometimes given on ship, aircraft and land mortgages (since registers indexed by asset have greater predictability), but on the whole standard letters of opinion on security which cover the essential areas of title, priorities and the position on bankruptcy, have not been developed internationally and, by reason of differences in law and in the type of asset and the complexity and number of legal issues, their development is difficult, at least for general business charges (such as the floating charge over all assets), if they attempt to cover those essential areas. As mentioned, any formal transaction opinion on these areas (beyond powers, authorities, due execution and the like) would normally be so qualified as to be of little value and the creditor would be better advised and better informed as to his position by a general letter of advice. But, as always, there are exceptions.

Opinion of principal lawyers

Generally

The formal legal opinion of the principal lawyers concerned with the preparation of the documents and the overall supervision of the legal side of the transaction is traditionally a briefer letter than the opinion just discussed. The responsibility of the principal lawyer is general and extends beyond a narrow legal opinion. Indeed the main function of this opinion is to act as a final legal check or control point and is not issued until all the other documents are in place and lender and lawyer are satisfied that the commitments can come into force.

13–41

A number of comments on the role of the principal lawyers may be made.

Who is the client?

In syndicated loans there will commonly be a single firm of lawyers acting for the syndicate as a group. Naturally the interests of each syndicate member may differ: for example, some may want tough terms or special funding protections which are not sought by the others. In particular there is a potential conflict between the agent's wish to reduce his duties and the desire of a syndicate to cut down clauses exculpating the agent from liability for errors. Although these theoretical conflicts exist, a lawyer who is expressed to be acting for the whole syndicate is usually justified in taking instructions from and giving advice only to the agent. In the normal case it will be clear that the negotiation of the document has been delegated to a single bank and indeed any other method would be unworkable. In cases of special difficulty a lawyer might feel justified in circularising the syndicate on a particular issue.

13–42

Conditions precedent

It should be made clear that an opinion that the documents furnished as conditions precedent are substantially responsive to the requirements of the agreement means that they appear to satisfy the terms of the particular clause on their face and on the basis of any foreign advice received, not that the conditions precedent are in fact fulfilled. The latter would usually be a matter of foreign law. Further, there is often a general condition precedent that the representations and warranties are true and that no default has occurred: lawyers could not express such a view.

13–43

Expert's opinion

13–44 Some opinions given by the principal lawyers simply state a view that the loan agreement is substantially in order in light of the instructions received or some such approving phrase. This may mean that the validity of the agreement and its provisions are, in the light of the experience of the lawyer as to current market practice, within the range of those which are usually found to be acceptable. It does not mean that everything is all right or that the maximum protections have been achieved, although there is perhaps a danger that it may be understood this way. The phrase does little more than state the lawyer's usual responsibility to his client.

Part III

SECURITIES REGULATION

CHAPTER 14

SECURITIES REGULATION: INTRODUCTION

Summary of regulation

Introduction

Securities regulation is bus timetable law – that is, valid until further notice. Nevertheless it is the oldest branch of consumer protection after usury and gaming laws and, although obscured by a maze of regulation, a general direction may be discerned. The task of these chapters is to distill some of the principles with particular reference to international debt issues, as opposed to equity issues. It is however not practicable in a summary to be accurate or comprehensive as to the rules of the several important jurisdictions and so the adviser must look up exactly what time the bus leaves in any particular case.

14–1

Heads of financial regulation

The main heads of regulation of financial markets are:

14–2

- **Securities regulation**, which is the subject of these chapters.
- **Usury laws** These are not usually important for international finance, except in Islamic countries.
- **Gaming laws** These are still a factor in commercial states, but are usually relevant only to swaps and derivatives.
- **Consumer credit laws** These are not important in our context since they usually relate to credit to individuals and non-corporate consumers, not wholesale markets involving sophisticated institutions. See, e.g. the £15,000 limit and the corporate exemption in the UK Consumer Credit Act 1974.
- **Banking laws** See chapter 22. These require the licensing of banking businesses and the supervision of their financial condition.
- **Insurance laws** These require licensing of insurance businesses and, in

some cases, insurance brokers, e.g. UK Insurance Companies Act 1982 and Insurance Brokers (Registration) Act 1977. Their significance is peripheral in this context, and their import lies in the fact that they may inadvertently control guarantee or surety business (pecuniary loss insurance) or options (premium paid for risk).

- **Exchange controls** These never applied in the United States or Canada and have been dismantled in Western Europe.

- **Borrowing controls** These are laws limiting capital issues in the domestic market and are designed mainly to preserve an orderly market, to discourage the use of the domestic currency (Switzerland), to prioritise the government's access to its own market for government borrowing and to discourage foreign entities from borrowing locally and therefore depleting the pool available to local businesses. An example is the UK Control of Borrowing Order, now virtually defunct. These controls, often not statutory, have been important in Germany, Japan and Switzerland.

- **Fiscal laws** Examples are stamp duties and withholding taxes, which have sometimes been used to discourage borrowings from abroad.

Policies of securities regulation generally

14–3   The law must inevitably intervene to regulate an activity where there is a high risk of abuse. The risk of abuse with securities is accentuated because the property is invisible and intangible and usually represents a share in a complex bundle of assets, e.g. a company, or even a share in a bundle of shares, e.g. collective investment schemes. The property is therefore more difficult to evaluate and the investor is more exposed to imprudent investments or, in extreme cases, to sharp practice or deceit.

Protection of unsophisticated investors One main objective of securities regulation is to protect those in need of protection – chiefly unsophisticated individuals – from improper practices and from themselves. Another is to protect the public against the insolvency of those who take money from the public with a view to paying it back later. There is a risk that the institution may dissipate the money in the meantime and become insolvent with consequent loss to the public and collapse in confidence in the financial system.

Excesses of regulatory regimes

14–4   But other opposing policies are also relevant in implementing a regulatory regime. These include:

- The cost of the regulatory regime. Supervisory agencies have to be set up and their staff paid, either by the state or by levies on the market or both. In 1990 the US SEC employed about 2,400 staff, nearly 40 per cent of them lawyers. Compensation funds must similarly be funded. The institutional cost in relation to the value of securities is probably tiny. The real cost is the hidden cost of compliance by individual firms which is not tiny.

– The risk of inviting over-reliance on regulators so that investors come to assume that the state will bail out banks, insurance companies, investment businesses and even large companies which become insolvent. Hence investors might become careless and imprudent in making credit assessments and effectively seek to pass the risk to the tax payer.

– Over-criminalisation of commercial law and punishment exceeding the crime, e.g. the nullification of a substantial contract merely because an investment firm is unlicensed or because a contract omits a prescribed term which is wholly technical. Hence there is a conflict between the desire to control abuse and commercial liberalism.

– Burdensome and expensive paper-pushing regulation which is inefficient in controlling major abuses, especially deliberate frauds.

– International legal collisions between jurisdictions caused by technicalities as opposed to substantive policy differences – a repeat of the old collisions caused by obsolete documentary formalities for contracts, over-short limitation periods, and usury laws.

– Over-complication of law, leading to over-lawyering of financial transactions, and over-prescription which the ordinary person can neither read nor understand nor keep up with and which loses touch with the original objectives.

– The risk of big pocket liability, i.e. imposing liability on bystanders who were partially involved, if the person primarily at fault is insolvent, e.g. imposition of liability on a regulator of a failed firm or imposition of liability on managers of a bond issue for a misrepresentation by the borrower in a prospectus.

– Over-rigid statutes which do not anticipate legitimate changes in the market.

– The use of the regulatory regime not to protect investors but to shut out access to local financing markets by foreign companies – an illegitimate use of investor protection statutes.

Of course it is all a matter of degree and balance and jurisdictions have their own individual policy approaches.

International approaches

14–5 The differing approaches of jurisdictions appear to be influenced by:

- The size and complexity of their financial markets. For example, a large and sophisticated market may need more controls (more participants, bigger credit exposures) and is better able to afford the costs of a comprehensive regulatory regime. This is true of London and New York. Markets dominated by a few responsible institutions may have a club culture imposing its own moral pressures, as in Germany.

- Moral attitudes, e.g. attitudes to money-lending and those who profit by it and attitudes to speculation. These may run very deep and, by reason of their semi-religious intensity, dictate the shape and colour of the regulatory regime.

- The national historical experience of abuse, especially in recessions which, by reason of insolvencies, expose abuses and generate resentments.

Nevertheless, there is a common core of rules in the developed jurisdictions, e.g. issues of securities to the public are uberrimae fidei, not caveat emptor, the imposition of high fiduciary duties on dealers, and the universal legal contempt for fraud.

The most usual way of alleviating the burdens of a regulatory regime is to restrict its scope primarily to the protection of unsophisticated individuals, as opposed to large wholesale institutions who can better evaluate risks and bear losses. This is consumerism and takes its root in protecting those who most need protection. Examples are exemptions from prospectus rules for issues to sophisticated investors and exemptions from mandatory terms in contracts between investment firms and their clients, e.g. general (as opposed to specific) disclosure of conflicts of interest.

Degree of codification

14–6 One significant policy question is the extent to which a jurisdiction should codify the legal regime.

The general law relating to fraud, misrepresentation, and to fiduciary duties is already extremely potent in the developed jurisdictions so that codification is not the creation of wholly new law, but rather the delineation of existing law and the application of general principles to particular situations. Remarkable illustrations of this are: (1) a comparison of the law of misrepresentation between the natural law and securities law studied at para 17–1 *et seq* shows that the enhancement by securities law is often at the edges, (2) fiduciary law in England is in most cases at least as rigorous as many of the rules appearing in various rule-books, and (3) insider trading law in the United States has been developed by case-law using ordinary fraud principles codified in a very general anti-fraud section without the need for a detailed statute.

The advantages of codification are predictability and accessibility so that the market may know what they have to do. The disadvantages are over-prescription and the disguising of general principles by little black-letter rules so that there is a dual regime and a tendency to treat the little rules as the complete code.

Often a single judicial decision reminding the market of the law can have more impact than mountains of codes and regulations and rule-books. A telling illustration of this was litigation in the 1970s which concerned a syndicate agent's liability for alleged misrepresentation in inviting participants into a shipping loan and which ever since has had an enormous effect on the conduct of managing banks in syndicating loans.

Summary of securities regulation

The chief methods by which securities regulation achieves its objectives of protecting the public against investment losses by reasons of fraud or negligence and against the insolvency of dealers and issuers of securities are:

1. **Licensing of investment businesses** The licensing takes into account the competence, reputation and solvency of the applicant.

2. **Codes of conduct enhancing agency and fiduciary duties** These codify duties of due diligence by agents, avoidance of conflicts of interest, fair dealing practices, disclosure of remuneration and record-keeping.

3. **Sanction of securities crimes** These impose criminal liability for, e.g. fraudulent misrepresentation, false markets and insider dealing.

4. **Disclosure requirements for securities** The cornerstone of securities regulation is disclosure so that an investor can make an informed investment decision. The policies are achieved mainly by:

   – prescribing the information which must be disclosed;

   – publishing of the information, such as by registration with a registrar of companies (English-based jurisdictions), a banking commissioner (Luxembourg and Belgium) or an SEC-type authority (US, Ontario) which may screen the prospectus;

   – continuing disclosure so that a holder of securities is kept informed about the status of his investment and the issuer during the currency of his investment as well as at its inception (achieved mainly by requirements for the production of audited financial statements and by continuing disclosure requirements imposed by securities regulation (US), by company law (most commercial countries) or embodied in a listing undertaking given to the stock exchange);

- by enhancing misrepresentation law, e.g. the onus of proof of due diligence is shifted from the investor to the issuer, absolute liability on issuers in some cases, positive due diligence duty on the part of issuers and their directors, additional liability of those involved other than the issuer, e.g. directors, auditors and other experts and, sometimes, managers, and wider damages and rescission remedies.

5. **Limitation on entities entitled to raise money from the public** In many countries, closely held, small or private companies are prohibited from issuing securities to the public. The rationale is that, since these companies benefit from a more relaxed statutory regime imposing less burdens on family enterprises, they should be prevented from putting the public at risk by inviting public capital. Typical relaxations for private companies are:

- exemptions from audited financial statements and prescribed disclosure at the companies or commercial register;

- no minimum number of members;

- less stringent rules as to the amount or maintenance of share capital;

- no minimum number of directors and no two-tier boards; and

- less red-tape in the observance of corporate formalities.

The object is to allow the use of the corporate privilege (no liability of owners on insolvency) by family and small businesses. In return for this weakening of creditor protections, these companies do not have access to public fund-raising. They have to borrow privately from banks.

6. **Control of the terms of securities** Where money is transferred in exchange for a piece of paper, it is fundamental that the piece of paper should constitute a valid legal claim. By reason of the diversity of types of issue, securities regulation cannot in practice impose standards for the terms of the bonds. In this respect reliance is usually placed upon the advisers to the managers. Regulatory regimes rarely go beyond a requirement for the filing of copies of authorisations, constitutional documents, exchange control consents and (sometimes) legal opinions and leave it to legal integrity, market practice and the risk of liability to control the contractual terms. There is however some limited intervention. Common stock exchange requirements include:

- any drawings must be made by lot;
- there must be provision for the replacement of lost or mutilated bonds;
- prescription periods must be of a minimum duration; and
- (unusually) equal treatment of holders of listed securities (EC regulation).

But the law does not regulate, e.g. events of default or covenants.

7. **Bondholder representation** In order to unite and monitor the interests of scattered bondholders, statute and stock exchange regulation may require the appointment of a trustee or, in civilian countries, a bondholder's representative. Bondholders may be given voting rights by statute or contract. See chapter 10.

8. **Financial supervision of dealers** Securities regulation seeks to protect investors from the insolvency of investment firms who may hold clients' money or clients' securities. The rules are developing and are of rapidly increasing importance. The main limbs are:
   - rules which require investment firms to maintain prescribed levels of capital to protect the client against the risk of insolvency of the institution;
   - rules which require investment firms to segregate client moneys and assets from their own moneys and assets to protect the assets in the event of the firm's insolvency; and
   - investor compensation funds. These are usually central funds out of which compensation is paid, usually subject to an upper limit per claim which usually covers only the small depositor or investor. The fund may be government-funded or (more usually) funded by levies on firms, as in the UK and the US. In the US, the Securities Investor Protection Act of 1970 establishes a fund, financed by annual assessments on brokers and dealers which insures customers against their broker's insolvency up to $500,000 for each account.

Meaning of regulated "securities"

Securities legislation typically requires that those who deal in, manage or advise on investments must be authorised and controls the subscription for or the sale of investments. The modern tendency is to define a security or investment widely. Examples are:

- The definition in s 2(1) of the US Securities Act of 1933 whereby "security" includes:

"any note, stock, treasury stock, bond, debenture, evidence of indebtedness, certificate of interest or participation in any profit sharing agreement . . . investment contract . . . or, in general, any interest or instrument commonly known as a "security" or any certificate of interest or participation in, temporary or interim certificate for, receipt for, guarantee of, or warrant or right to subscribe to or purchase, any of the foregoing". Substantially identical definitions are found in other federal securities and state securities laws.

– The definition in the UK Financial Services Act 1986 Sched 1 Part 1, which contains an eleven point list: see para 18–8.

The effect of a wide definition is to make the entire third estate of property subject to the regulation. There are three main forms of property – land, goods and intangibles – and the scope and amount of intangible property in modern economies is now vast. It includes, for example, all contract rights, such as debt contracts, loans, purchase price credits, bank deposits, money transmission payment orders, bills of exchange and promissory notes. It includes all commercial contracts, e.g. contracts of sale, custodian contracts, transportation contracts, building contracts and equipment lease contracts. It includes leases of land and insurance and reinsurance contracts. It includes licences of intellectual property rights, franchises and distributorships. It includes joint ventures and special cases like timeshare interests.

14–10   It is obviously absurd to endeavour to regulate this entire field. The legislator has therefore used three methods to limit the scope of the regulation:

1. The definition of "security" is limited only to rights generally regarded as investment securities, such as shares or debentures. This was the method of the former UK companies legislation and the result has been an accumulation of case law on what is meant by a "debenture", from which one can glean only that a "debenture" is a debenture. This approach envisages that there will be a certificate of debt – an approach weakened by the fact that many securities are now dematerialised and the holder's entitlement is merely recorded in a register.

2. The second approach is to bring all intangibles within the scope of the regulation and then to carve out those which are not to be regulated. This is the method adopted by the British Financial Services Act 1986 which may help to explain why that piece of legislation has weaknesses. The approach is questionable because all intangible property is caught up in the trammels of the Act so that lawyers have to hunt for some reason why a perfectly legitimate transaction which ought not to be regulated is excluded. Further the legislator tends to be over-fussy in his obsessive attention to anti-avoidance, perhaps without appreciating that it is only necessary to regulate the mainstream and that the general

law, e.g. of fraud or fiduciary duties, is perfectly capable of regulating the outside or odd case.

Typical examples of the UK carve-outs are those for commercial supply contracts, bills of exchange, ordinary commercial debts and ordinary commercial futures contracts which are not for investment purposes. This attempt to distinguish commercial from investment contracts is common.

Thus in *Re Brigadoon Scotch Distrib (Can) Ltd* (1970) 3 OR 714, an Ontario court held that warehouse receipts for Scotch whisky purchased for speculative investment purposes were a regulated security.

In *Pacific Coast Exchange Ltd v Ontario Securities Commission* (1977) 2 SCR 3d 112, the Supreme Court of Canada held that a margin contract for the purchase of bags of silver coins was an investment contract and hence a regulated security.

Other methods of carve-outs are to exempt certain issuers, e.g. banks, insurance companies, governments, international organisations or to exempt transactions based on the contracting counterparty, e.g. whether a private or a sophisticated investor.

One course would be to target the regulated investment specifically as one which satisfies three tests cumulatively, namely, type of investment, investment purpose (not commercial) and offered to the public or a section of the public, and then to target specific securities which should be controlled but which would not be caught by the general definition (such as collective investment schemes). This is often the overall effect, but one has to struggle through immense thickets of technicality to reach that result. The regime does not have to catch everything.

History of securities regulation

This section is intended to give a short overview of the history of securities regulation by way of orientation.

The beginnings

In England the licensing of agents in vendible commodities by the Lord Mayor of the City of London goes back to at least the time of Edward I: agents were required to make an oath to be of good behaviour. In 1697 an Act was passed to "restrain the number and ill-practice of Brokers and Stock-Jobbers". Dealers had to be licensed by the Lord Mayor, to provide a bond of £500, forfeitable for misconduct, to act only as agents (not for own account), and to maintain records of transactions. The Act lapsed in 1704. See Rider, Abrams, Ferran, *Guide to the Financial Services Act 1986* (2nd ed 1989) CCH.

In Britain the risks of investment were high-lighted by the burlesque South Sea Bubble episode in the early eighteenth century. The South Sea Company grandiosely sought to acquire the whole of the National Debt amounting to the then huge sum of £31 million in exchange for holdings of the company's stock as a solid basis upon which to attract moneys for certain dubious operations in the South Sea. Every means was used to get in the holdings, including bribery. Royalty was said to have been involved. The bubble was pricked in 1720. Barnard's Act 1734 outlawed option dealings and short-selling. The stock exchange developed its own code of conduct based on honour. But it was only 170 years later that the foundations were laid for present day prospectus legislation.

The immediate occasion was *Derry v Peek* (1889) 14 App Cas 337:

> The defendant's prospectus stated that the company had the right to use steam or mechanical motive power, instead of horses. This was incorrect because the company's special Act of Parliament made that right conditional on the consent of the Board of Trade which was refused. However, the plaintiff lost the case since he was unable to prove that the defendant had made the misrepresentation knowingly or recklessly.

As a result the Directors Liability Act of 1890 was passed subjecting directors and promoters to civil liability for untrue statements in a prospectus unless they proved they had reasonable grounds to believe that the statements were true. Subsequently the Companies Act 1929 consolidated and strengthened regulation: it required the registration of prospectuses issued to the public, prescribed the information to be disclosed and outlawed securities dealing except by authorised persons. Later the 1929 Act was split into the Companies Act 1948, dealing with company prospectuses, and the Prevention of Fraud (Investments) Act 1939 (later updated in 1958) dealing with the licensing of dealers, a prohibition on issues of circulars relating to securities, the control of collective investment plans and the punishment of fraud. These Acts were overtaken by the baroque Financial Services Act of 1986.

United States in the 1930s

14-12 After the Wall Street crash in 1929, the British Companies Act 1929 was one of the models to which the US legislators turned. On it they built an even more labyrinthine edifice, leading a US court to remark in 1969 that those engaged in securities business are like "characters from some Victorian novels wandering aimlessly on treacherous moors": *H Cook & Co Inc v Scheinman, Hochstin & Trotta Inc*, 414 F 2d 93, 98 (2d Cir 1969).

But the Federal securities legislation of the 1930s also had its own native ancestry. One may commence perhaps with the activities of a Mr J N Dalley, a retired grocer and bank director who was appointed Bank Commissioner after the Populist Party's success in Kansas in the 1910 election. Mr Dalley took it upon himself to introduce an informal system of scrutiny and sent potential investors unsolicited warnings about securities he considered suspect. Not satisfied with this haphazard method, he subsequently instigated the passage of an Act in 1911 which required that no security covered by the Act could be sold in Kansas unless a permit had been issued by Dalley's office. This paternalistic approach was followed by many other states and within the next two years 23 states had enacted regulatory laws and all but six of these were either the same or based upon the Kansas statute. Their constitutionality was finally settled by the US Supreme Court in 1917. These laws can be to referred to as "blue sky" laws: see para 15–6.

However, it was not until 1933 that the Federal legislature enacted a statute implementing a comprehensive system of securities controlling disclosure at the Federal level. The impetus to introduce such a system arose as a result of the Wall Street crash of 1929, the subsequent exposure of some questionable securities practices and a general resentment caused by losses. The Securities Act of 1933 is a disclosure and anti-fraud statute primarily affecting the distribution of securities. It was followed by the Securities and Exchange Act of 1934 which set up a licensing system for dealers, established the Securities and Exchange Commission to monitor securities laws and concerned itself with promotion of fair and equitable trading practices in the securities market.

Thus in the United States today there are twin systems of regulation running in parallel, the federal system and the state system. Compliance with federal regulatory requirements does not relieve an issuer from the necessity of complying with such blue sky regulations as may be in force in the state where the securities are to be sold.

Spread of formal regulation

The regime embodied in the Companies Act 1929, whether in its UK or US form, spread apace. The Japanese were requested to enact the US legislation (although in slimmed-down form) after World War II by the occupation authorities as a condition of the re-opening of the Japanese securities markets. Later Ontario followed the US model but shortened it. South Korea followed Japan. Venezuela and Mexico adopted their own versions.

14–13

Meanwhile the 1929 Act flooded the Commonwealth and the colonies. Australian states took it over and subsequently strengthened it. Malaysia and Singapore have traditionally been influenced by Australian corporate legislation.

Continental Europe

14–14 For long the markets in Continental Europe did not adopt the policies embodied in the UK Companies Act 1929. The great nineteenth century European exchanges had worked out their own ways of doing things and were content with self-regulation. Securities dealers, stock exchanges and banks formed a self-policing club with reasonably high standards and a black ball for disreputable outsiders. In the Netherlands, Switzerland and Germany formal securities regulation was thin, especially in Germany where it was virtually non-existent. On the other hand the francophone states of Belgium, France and Luxembourg instituted their own versions of the SEC although with a greater emphasis on criminal sanctions as opposed to civil actions as a means of deterrence. France originally borrowed its disclosure code from the British Companies Act 1900. All these states avoided the common law legislative habit of detailed legislative particularisation.

Now even in the self-regulated Continental European states, the existing liberalism has had to give way to formal regulation: EC directives have made serious inroads on the old flexible methods.

Chapter 15

SECURITIES REGULATION: COUNTRY SUMMARIES

This chapter is intended to give a bird's-eye view of the regime in a few selected countries or regions prior to a more detailed review of specific topics.   15–1

Sources of law

The usual regime comprises three tiers: (1) special securities statutes, (2) general rules of law (common law, civil code, general statutes) covering, for example fraud and misrepresentation, and the duties of agents and other fiduciaries, and (3) customs and codes which were not legally binding but which market participants are expected to comply with. The exact mix varies from country to country.

United Kingdom

The main UK statute is the **Financial Services Act 1986** and rules made thereunder.   15–2

Authorisation of investment businesses The Act provides that no person may carry on investment business in the United Kingdom unless exempted or authorised, usually by becoming a member of a self-regulatory organisation (SRO): s 3. See para 18–2 *et seq*. Authorised persons are subject to codes of conduct and financial supervision by their self-regulatory organisations. Private investors can claim compensation for breach of these codes: s 62.

Investment advertisements The Act provides that no person may issue an investment advertisement (e.g. an information memorandum or offering circular) in the United Kingdom unless it is issued by or its contents have been approved by an authorised person, subject to exceptions: s 57. There are rules as to the prescribed content of investment advertisements and there is tougher liability for misleading information.

An investment advertisement is widely defined to mean any advertisement likely to lead people directly or indirectly to acquire or dispose of investments. The sanctions for breach are: criminal offence; the investment agreement is unenforceable and money paid is recoverable; and compensation for losses (subject to the court's discretion).

SRO rules on investment advertisements commonly provide that the advertisement must be fair and not misleading and contain prescribed information and risk warnings.

There were exceptions, e.g. where the advertisement is only going to "non-private customers" or where the advertisement is required or permitted by the rules of certain investment exchanges.

15–3 The main exemptions are:

1. No investment is involved, e.g. the investment is not a debenture (this generally excludes bank loans)

2. The advertisement is issued only to the issuer's own members or creditors and only concerns the group's shares or debt

3. The advertisement is issued only to investment professionals, large corporates and trusts

4. The issuer is a UK or foreign government or local authority (municipality), or a central bank or an international organisation of which the United Kingdom or an EC state is a member

5. The advertisement is in the form of listing particulars complying with Part IV of the FSA which requires that the listing particulars contain information prescribed by the Stock Exchange and other documents, as well as announcements required or permitted by the Stock Exchange's listing rules. The stock exchange can exempt information relating (inter alia) to debt securities if disclosure is unnecessary for the prospective investors.

6. The advertisement is a prospectus for unlisted securities on an approved exchange complying with Part V of the FSA. This provides that no person shall issue or cause to be issued any securities for admission to dealings on an approved exchange unless a prospectus containing prescribed information has been approved by the exchange and registered with the Registrar of Companies. Part V was not in force as of August 1994. Until in force, Part III of the Companies Act 1985 regulates prospectuses for unlisted securities.

There is an anti-avoidance provision for advertisements for securities issued to a person with a view to on-selling them.

Cold-calling The Act provides that no unsolicited calls (uninvited personal visits or oral communications) may be made to a person in the United Kingdom or from the United Kingdom to a person elsewhere in relation to investment agreements: s 56.

The sanctions for breach are that the agreement is unenforceable, and money paid is recoverable plus compensation for loss (subject to the court's discretion).

The main exemptions in this context are: (1) no investment is involved; and (2) the call is made only on investment professionals, large corporates and trusts.

Collective investment schemes Collective investment schemes (e.g. unit trusts and other pooled investments) are subject to special controls: s 75 *et seq*. The rules distinguish regulated collective investment schemes and unregulated schemes. Regulated schemes may be publicly marketed in the United Kingdom but are subject to heavy regulation covering: the spread of investments; the disclosure of scheme particulars; constitution; investors' rights to redeem their units; and controls on remuneration taken by the operator of the scheme.

Unregulated schemes (whether UK or offshore) are not subject to any of the above constraints but may not be publicly marketed. They may be marketed to certain categories of professionals, experts and individuals for whom they are judged to be suitable before marketing commences. See s 76 of the FSA, the Financial Services (Promotion of Unregulated Schemes) Regulations 1991 and the Financial Services (Regulated Schemes) Regulations 1991.

Fraud Misleading statements or practices are a criminal offence: FSA s 47.

United States

Securities Act of 1933 No offers and sales of securities may be made unless they are registered with the Securities and Exchange Commission (SEC). This means that a complying registration statement (the prospectus and other documents) must be filed with the SEC: s 5. There are exemptions in the case of (1) offers to knowledgeable private offerees, (2) the absence of a "security" (as in a normal bank loan), (3) certain issues of commercial paper, (4) issues to defined sophisticated investors, (5) secondary market dealings, (6) certain foreign transactions, (7) certain US bank issues,

(8) issues by the US government and by US state and local authorities (but not foreign governments or their subdivisions), and (9) certain exchange offers. Most of those exemptions are hedged about with elaborate conditions.

Fraudulent or deceptive practices in any offer or sale of a security are penalised.

Securities Exchange Act of 1934 This Act ("the 1934 Act"): established the SEC; imposes disclosure and other requirements on publicly held companies; prohibits various "manipulative or deceptive devices or contrivances" in connection with the purchase or sale of securities; restricts the amount of credit that may be extended for the purchase of securities; requires brokers and dealers to register with the SEC and regulates their activities; and provides for SEC registration and supervision of national securities exchanges and associations and other securities agents.

Trust Indenture Act of 1939 This Act (as amended) requires that an indenture covering securities must be qualified under the Act, imposes standards of independence and responsibility on the indenture trustee and automatically incorporates provisions in the indenture for the protection of the security holder.

Unlike the Securities Act of 1933, the Act exempts issues by foreign governments but not exchange offers.

Investment Company Act of 1940 This gives the SEC regulatory authority over publicly owned companies which are engaged primarily in the business of investing and trading in securities – the equivalent of the European collective investment scheme.

Investment Advisers Act of 1940 This establishes a scheme of registration and regulation of investment advisers comparable to that contained in the 1934 Act with respect to broker-dealers but not as comprehensive.

15–6 **"Blue Sky" laws** The above legislation is federal and does not exclude state securities laws, commonly known as "Blue Sky" laws. The term "Blue Sky" laws came into being because, it was said, the country was full of promoters of fraudulent enterprises whose frauds were so barefaced that they would be prepared to sell building lots in the blue sky in fee simple: *Hall v Gieger-Jones Co*, 242 US 539 (1917). These provide for registration of broker-dealers, registration of securities to be offered or traded in the state, and sanctions against fraudulent activity. In the old days a Blue Sky survey was a nightmare because of the bewildering variety of statutes, their curious drafting and the uncertain discretions of the administrators. Now however uniformity has been improved, but not achieved, by the adoption by nearly 40 states of versions of the Uniform Securities Act, originally promulgated in 1956, and revised in 1985 and 1988, although there remains great diversity of language and interpretation. The Act has not been adopted by Arizona, California, Florida, Georgia, Illinois, Louisiana, New York, North Dakota, Ohio, Rhode Island, South Dakota or Texas. In some states it is now merely necessary to file the SEC information with the state administrator and the state registration becomes effective automatically, in the absence of adverse action by the state administrator. The standards of state disqualification vary from the simple fraud standard to such discretions as "not fair, just and equitable" and lacking in "sound business principles" – a merit review. By way of contrast, the SEC does not have power to disapprove securities for lack of merit and indeed it is unlawful to represent otherwise in the sale of a security. The only standard is adequate and accurate disclosure of material facts.

If an issue of debt securities is outside the Securities Act of 1933 and the Securities Exchange Act of 1934, then it will often be outside Blue Sky laws and the Trust Indenture Act of 1939. The anti-fraud provisions of Blue Sky laws are additional to those under the Federal legislation.

Other securities states Other relevant US provisions which affect securities are:

- the Glass-Steagall Act (the Banking Act of 1933) excluding commercial banks from areas of the securities business
- regulations of the Federal Reserve Board which regulate credit for the purchase or carrying of securities
- the Commodity Exchange Act (originally passed in 1922) regulating commodities exchanges
- the Foreign Corrupt Practices Act of 1977 establishing accounting and record-keeping requirements for companies subject to the 1934 Act and also prohibiting bribes to foreign officials
- the Racketeer Influenced and Corrupt Organisations Act of 1974, originally directed at organised crime, but used in suits alleging securities fraud.

Territorial ambit The Federal Securities laws generally apply where there is a direct or indirect use of the United States mails or instruments of transportation or communication or interstate commerce (which includes commerce between any foreign country and the United States). Hence the use of the US telephone, fax or post may attract the securities laws. Substantially the same territorial ambit is to be found in the Securities Act of 1933, the Securities

Exchange Act of 1934, the Trust Indenture Act of 1939, the Investment Company Act of 1940 and the Investment Advisers Act of 1940.

EC Council Directives: summary

15–8 The main EC Directives in the field of securities regulation are:

– Admissions Directive 1979

– Listing Particulars Directive 1980

– Interim Reports Directive 1982

– Prospectus Directive 1989

– Second Mutual Recognition Directive 1990

– Mutual Recognition Directive 1989

– Collective Investment Schemes (UCITS) Directive 1985

– Second Banking Directive 1989

– Investment Services Directive 1993

– Capital Adequacy Directive 1993

EC Admissions Directive

15–9 This is the Council Directive of March 5, 1979, co-ordinating the conditions for the admission of securities to official stock exchange listing (79/279/EEC).

Scope The Directive imposes minimum conditions for the admission to official listings on member state stock exchanges. Member states need not apply the Directive to collective investment undertakings (other than the closed-end type) or to securities issued by member states or its regional or local authorities: Art 1. There are limited exemptions for member state companies governed by "special law" where the securities are guaranteed by a member state or one of its federal states: Art 8. An inroad on self-regulation is contained in the provision that decisions of the competent authorities refusing the admission of the security to official listing or discontinuing such a listing are to be subject to a right to apply to the courts: Art 15.

Legal status As to debt securities, the Directive provides that the "legal position of the undertaking must be in conformity with the laws and regulations to which it is subject" and the "legal position of the debt securities" must be also in conformity with those laws and regulations. The securities must be freely "negotiable" (presumably meaning transferable).

General requirements The Directive sets out conditions as to the minimum amount of the issue, provides that (a) (subject to exceptions) shares relating to equity-linked debt securities must be listed, and (b) that the issuer must ensure that all holders of debt securities ranking pari passu are given equal treatment in respect of all the rights attaching to those debt securities (except for offers of early repayment in accordance with national law).

Information All notices and circulars must be published in the territory of the stock exchange and a paying agent must be located there. The issuer must make available its most recent annual accounts and inform the public as soon as possible of any "major new developments", of any change in the rights of holders of debt securities, of any new loan issues (in particular of any guarantee or security in respect thereof), and, in the case of equity-linked securities, of any changes in the rights attaching to the various classes of shares to which they relate. The issuer must ensure that equivalent information is made available to the market at each of the exchanges where the debt securities are officially listed.

EC Listing Particulars Directive

This is the Council Directive of March 17, 1980, co-ordinating the requirements for the drawing up, scrutiny and distribution of the listing particulars to be published for the admission of securities to official stock exchange listing (80/390/EEC).

Scope The Directive deals with the publication of and prescribed disclosure and screening in relation to prospectuses. The Directive applies to securities to be listed on a member state stock exchange but does not apply to collective investment undertakings (other than of the closed-end type) or to securities issued by a state (which appears to include foreign states) or by its regional or local authorities.

Prescribed disclosure By Art 3 member states must ensure that the admission of securities to official listing on the stock exchange is conditional upon the publication of "an information sheet" (called "the listing particulars") which must contain the information set out in the Directive.

In addition by Art 4 the listing particulars "shall contain the information which, according to the particular nature of the issuer and of the securities for the admission of which application is being made, is necessary to enable investors and their investment advisers to make an informed assessment of the assets and liabilities, financial position, profits and losses, and prospects of the issuer and of the rights attaching to such securities." In other words the EC turns listed issues into contracts uberrimae fidei – full disclosure. This obligation must be incumbent upon the "persons responsible" for the listing particulars. Note the reference to "prospects".

The information must be in "as easily analysable and comprehensible a form as possible". The requirements can be adapted to the issuer's sphere of activity or legal form provided that equivalent information is given: Art 5.

15–11 **Exemptions** By Art 6, the competent authorities may allow partial or complete exemption from the obligation to publish listing particulars in certain cases, including shares issued on exercise of conversion or other rights in equity-linked bonds (provided the shares concerned are listed on the *same* stock exchange – they often are not in the case of eurobond issues), and debt securities issued by certain member state monopoly companies, such as utilities, and by certain member state special statutory corporations formed to raise money to finance production where the debt securities are effectively guaranteed by the state.

Derogations As regards derogations from the prescribed disclosure, Art 7 provides that the competent authorities may authorise omission from the listing particulars of certain prescribed information if they consider that:

"(a) such information is of minor importance only and is not such as will influence assessment of the assets and liabilities, financial position, profits and losses and prospects of the issuer; or

(b) disclosure of such information would be contrary to the public interest or seriously detrimental to the issuer, provided that, in the latter case, such omission would not be likely to mislead the public with regard to facts and circumstances, knowledge of which is essential for the assessment of the securities in question."

This provision reduces the traditional flexibility of European stock exchanges.

Sophisticated investors Article 10 provides that where "the application for admission for official listing relates to debt securities nearly all of which, because of their nature, are normally bought and traded in by a limited number of investors who are particularly knowledgeable in investment matters, the competent authorities may allow the omission from the listing particulars of certain information . . . or allow its inclusion in summary form, on condition that such information is not material from the point of view of the investors concerned". This provision is partly to enable the eurobond market to continue in operation. Note the materiality test.

Credit institutions, state-guaranteed issuers and utilities There are certain relaxations for certain regulated financial institutions and for tap issues by certain regulated credit institutions. Abridgements are possible for state guaranteed issues and for companies set up or governed by a special law or which pursuant to a special law have the power to levy charges on their consumers, e.g. utilities: see Art 17.

Screening Article 18 provides that no listing particulars may be published until they have been approved by the competent authorities. The competent authorities shall approve listing particulars only if they are of the opinion that they satisfy all the requirements set out in the Directive. However the Directive is not to affect the competent authorities' liability which continues to be governed solely by the national law.

Publication By Art 20, listing particulars must be published either (a) by insertion in one or more newspapers circulated throughout the member state concerned or widely circulated therein or (b) in the form of a brochure made available free of charge at specified offices. They must also be published or their place of publication notified in an official publication. All announcements must be communicated to the competent authorities (Art 22) and must indicate where the listing particulars will be published. By Art 21, listing particulars must (with exemptions in favour of properly justified cases) be published within a "reasonable period" before the date on which official listing becomes effective and before any grey market trading of pre-emptive subscription rights. In the case of preliminary prospectuses, Art 21 provides that, if some of the terms of the issue are not finalised until the last moment, the competent authorities may merely require the publication, within a reasonable period, of listing particulars omitting information as to these terms but indicating how it will be given. The information must be published before the date on which official listing starts.

Information to be up-to-date Article 23 states that every "significant new factor capable of affecting assessment of the securities which arises between the time when the listing particulars are adopted and the time when stock exchange dealings begin shall be covered by a supplement to the listing particulars, scrutinised in the same way as the latter and published in accordance with the procedures to be laid down by the competent authorities".

Co-ordination There are provisions for the co-ordination of stock exchange requirements in a single text in the case of an issue in several member states simultaneously.

EC Interim Reports Directive

15-13   The Council Directive of February 15, 1982, on information to be published on a regular basis by companies the shares of which have been admitted to official stock exchange listing (82/121/EEC).

This Directive applies only where *shares* are listed on a member state stock exchange and provides for the form and content of interim reports.

EC Mutual Recognition Directive

15-14   Directive 87/345/EEC amends the Listing Particulars Directive. If applications for listing are made within a short interval in more than one member state then, subject to translation and the addition of purely local information, the listing particulars approved by the competent authorities in one member state must be accepted in other member states, without additional information being required or further approval being needed. Mutual recognition is optional if the authority approving the listing particulars has permitted any of the discretionary derogations or exemptions allowed under the Listing Particulars Directive (unless the member state in which mutual recognition is sought itself recognises the derogations or exemptions) or if the issuer is from outside the European Union.

EC Prospectus Directive

15-15   Directive 89/298/EEC requires a prospectus containing specified information about the relevant issuer and securities to be published when securities are first offered to the public. Where a prospectus is drawn up which also meets the requirements of the Listing Particulars Directive, including scrutiny and approval, then, subject to translation and the addition of purely local information, the Prospectus Directive requires it to be mutually recognised as a prospectus for a public offer of the same securities made simultaneously or within a short interval in another member state, without further information being required or further approval needed. Mutual recognition is, however, optional if the authority approving the prospectus has permitted any of the discretionary derogations or exemptions allowed under the Listing Particulars Directive (unless the member state in which mutual recognition is sought itself recognises such derogations or exemptions) or if the issuer is from outside the European Union.

EC Second Mutual Recognition Directive

Directive 90/211/EEC extends the provisions of Directive 87/345 EEC for the mutual recognition of prospectuses as listing particulars to cases where an application for listing is made in only one member state. 15–16

EC UCITS Directive

This is the Council Directive of December 20, 1985, on undertakings for collective investment in transferable securities. The Directive lays down requirements for publicly marketable EC-wide collective investment schemes, e.g. investment powers and an obligation on the operator to redeem units. The Directive was implemented in the United Kingdom by s 75 *et seq* of the Financial Services Act 1986 and rules made under that Act. 15–17

EC Second Banking Directive

Council Directive of December 15, 1989, confers a "single passport" on EC banks enabling them to carry on banking, mortgage lending, consumer credit, investment business and other financial activities throughout the EC on the basis of their home EC state licence: they do not need separate licences in each EC state in which they operate. Prudential supervision (e.g. capital adequacy) is the responsibility of the home EC state. 15–18

EC Investment Services Directive

The Council Directive of May 10, 1993, confers a "single passport" on non-bank investment businesses enabling them to carry on investment business throughout the EC on the basis of their home EC state licence. Prudential supervision is the responsibility of the home EC state. The Directive was due to be implemented before the end of 1995. 15–19

EC Capital Adequacy Directive

The Council Directive of March 15, 1993, harmonises the capital adequacy requirements for banks and investment firms by imposing minimum capital requirements on investment firms and requiring both banks and non-bank investment firms to meet capital adequacy requirements related to position 15–20 risk (risk of fall in value of investments held), counterparty risk (risk of counterparty default), foreign exchange risk, and large exposure risk, etc.

The Directive was due to be implemented before the end of 1995.

Continental European securities regimes

15–21 Securities regulation in continental European countries has developed at an accelerated pace, mainly in response to EC Directives.

In **Belgium** securities law was formalised in 1989–1990. The Banking Commission is the main regulatory agency, although there are others. In **Denmark** the changes took place in 1990–1992. The main supervisor is the Ministry of Industry although it has delegated much of the work. In **France** the markets are supervised by an SEC-type authority established in 1967 – the *Commission des Operations de Bourse* (COB): there is much statute law and regulation. In **Germany**, changes are underway. In **Italy**, the main EC implementing legislation was the Law of January 2, 1991: the key agency is the *Commissione Nazionale per la Societá e la Borsa* (CONSOB) – also a government agency like the French COB.

In the **Netherlands** the matter is governed by the Securities Act of 1992, supervised by the Securities Board of the Netherlands.

In **Portugal** regulation is by Decree No 142–A/91, supervised by the *Comissão do Mercado de Valores Mobiliários* (CMVM). The equivalent in **Spain** is the Securities Market Act of 1988, Law 24/88 of July 28, 1988, supervised by the National Securities Market Commission (CNMV).

Australia

15–22 Australia is a federal state. Because of doubts about the power of the Commonwealth legislature to pass unified Australia-wide companies and securities industry legislation, the states, with a commendable readiness to sink differences, each agreed to pass their own legislation but to make it uniform. Hence each state and territory has the same Corporations Law based on the consolidating Corporations Act 1989 of the Australian Capital Territory, as amended. But there are still New South Wales companies, Victorian companies, Western Australian companies and there is no Australian company. Strictly, each state only has prescriptive jurisdiction over matters within its constitutional competence, e.g. in the case of stock market manipulation, one looks to the law of the state whose stock market is affected by the manipulation.

The Australian Securities Commission, whose members are appointed by the states, has overall supervisory powers. The law requires a registered prospectus for all offers of securities including secondary offers, public or not, so one has to find an exemption, e.g. minimum purchase price of A$500,000 or offers to professional dealers acting as principals.

Japan

The main statute is the Securities Exchange Law of 1948 as amended, especially by the Financial System Reform Act of 1992. The original legislation was requested by the occupation authorities as a condition of the reopening of the Japanese securities exchanges after World War II. The law emerged as a lopped-down version of the US Securities Act of 1933 and the Securities Act of 1934 combined.

Mutual funds are separately regulated by the Securities Investment Trust Law of 1951, as amended.

The securities which are caught are less comprehensive (but collective investment schemes are covered): non-disclosure liability is less onerous; the Ministry of Finance (through its Securities Bureau) is substituted for the SEC; and the statute omits the US extraterritorial language regulating transactions which involve the use of US mails, telephone or telex; and the absence of federalism permits a unified system without state "blue sky" laws. Apart from all this, the actual implementation of these trimmer rules by the authorities is utterly different. There are of course the usual subordinate regulations and orders. But of overwhelming importance in Japan are the official and unofficial administrative guidances (*gyosei-shido*) made known by the Ministry of Finance. One cannot do anything in Japan without advice on this body of grey non-law.

Still, the black-letter rules are important. Under the Law, no person may solicit an offer from "many unspecified persons" to acquire new securities having "uniform terms" or offer to sell or solicit an offer to buy existing securities having "uniform terms" to or from "many unspecified persons", unless the issuer registers the offering or distribution with the Ministry of Finance by a statement containing prescribed information.

The Ministry of Finance interprets "many" to mean offerees exceeding about 50 in number. Note that this is offerees, not eventual purchasers.

There are exemptions from the registration and disclosure provisions in favour of (amongst numerous others on conventional lines) private offerings (interpreted to mean less than about 50 offerees) and offerings to qualified institutional investors designated by ministerial order where there is little likelihood of the securities being on-sold to the public, an exemption introduced in 1993.

The Securities Exchange law contains expected provisions about continuing disclosure, the licensing and regulation of dealers, fraudulent and manipulative practices, stabilisation (detailed controls and reporting requirements) and criminal and civil liabilities in relation to false or misleading statements. While there have been a celebrated series of criminal prosecutions, civil actions for prospectus misrepresentation are virtually unknown. It is often said that this results from the legendary Japanese aversion to litigation but it must be remembered that litigation is not the only form of relief.

The Law and orders thereunder set out requirements for the contents of registration statements. The Tokyo Stock Exchange has its own rules and, for Japanese companies, there are some thin requirements in the Commercial Code.

Secured bonds must be issued in accordance with the Secured Corporate Bond Law of 1905 as amended under which a quasi-trustee must be appointed to administer the securities. The Law, which is inspired by the US Trust Indenture Act of 1939, stipulates the form of the trust deed which has to be submitted to the Ministry of Finance.

Canada

15–24 Canada has had less success than its federal counterpart in Australia in developing a unified country-wide system of securities regulation. Instead, each of the ten provincial and two territorial governments have their own laws, although the major provinces and territories have agreed to cooperate by "national policies" and other means which, for example, delegate the screening of a prospectus to the province of principal distribution. But there is increasing convergence in mutual recognition and co-operation. The only two codes which have country-wide application are the Federal Criminal Code which prohibits certain securities frauds and the separate federal system of prospectus regulation under the Bank Act for banks operating in Canada.

In practice, the securities codes of Ontario and Quebec are the most important.

Ontario, Alberta and Quebec operate a "closed system": all sales by an issuer of its own securities and certain other sales will require a prospectus unless an exemption is available. A number of other provinces retain the English-based rule that the regulation comes into play only if the securities are "distributed to the public".

New Zealand

15–25 In New Zealand the main statutes regulating securities are the Securities Act 1978, the Securities Amendment Act 1988 and the Securities Regulations 1983. The Securities Act and Securities Regulations regulate the issue of securities to the public. The Securities Amendment Act, amongst other things, contains provisions prohibiting insider trading and requires disclosure by certain security holders. The stock exchange has listing requirements. Collective investment schemes are subject to separate statutes, e.g. the Unit Trust Act 1960.

The Securities Act 1978 legislation requires that all securities which are offered or sold to the public must be offered to the public for subscription in or accompanied by a registered prospectus or an authorised advertisement. The prospectus must be registered with the Registrar of Companies.

Most offers will be offers to the public: see *Robert Jones Investments Ltd v Gardner* (1993) 6 NZCLC 68 514.

Offers to "persons whose principal business is the investment of money or who, in the course of and for the purposes of their business, habitually invest moneys" are exempt as are offers to any other person who in all the circumstances can properly be regarded as having been selected otherwise than as a member of the public: Securities Act 1978 s 3(2).

The Sharebrokers Act 1908 prohibits a person from acting as a sharebroker unless he holds a sharebroker's licence.

Only members of authorised futures exchanges may carry on the business of futures dealers: the Securities Amendment Act 1988.

Traditional English countries

General One guesses that probably about three or four dozen English-based British Commonwealth countries (if not more) have a regime based on the pre-1986 English system. This typically comprises provisions in the Companies Act ("CA") backed by legislation corresponding to the old British Prevention of Fraud (Investments) Act 1958 and its forerunner enacted in 1939 ("PFI").

Australia, Canada, New Zealand, Malaysia and Singapore have their own regime. Zambia has installed a US-style SEC. There is additional legislation in South Africa.

The main features of this system, differing from that prevailing elsewhere, are: (1) the absence of official screening of public prospectuses by a regulatory authority, reliance being placed on stock exchanges for listed securities and the liability risks of managers to ensure adequate disclosure; and (2) codes of conduct for licensed dealers which are not legally binding. Instead reliance is placed on ordinary fiduciary law (which in English-based jurisdictions has a high moral tone) and on the ability of the authorities to withdraw a dealer's licence in extreme cases. The system worked well in Britain for more than half a century of considerable capital-raising in a major financial centre.

15–27 **Companies Act** Commonly under the CA it is in effect unlawful for a company, local or foreign, to issue a prospectus, i.e. an advertisement or other invitation, offering to the public the subscription or purchase of any shares or debentures of the company, or for anybody to issue a form of application for shares or debentures unaccompanied by a prospectus unless, amongst other things, the prospectus contains detailed disclosures prescribed by the Act and is registered with the Registrar of Companies before it is issued. The prospectus does not have to be screened by any authority to check that it complies.

The main exemptions (omitting all-important details) are usually (a) no issue to the public; (b) the issuer is not a "company" in the normal sense of a commercial corporation but is, e.g. a municipality or state; (c) the prospectus is issued to existing security-holders (the prospectus does not have to contain the prescribed information even though securities can be renounced to the public but it has to be registered with the Registrar of Companies); (d) the prospectus relates to securities uniform with securities already listed on the local stock exchange (the prospectus must also be registered with the Registrar of Companies); (e) there are no "shares" or "debentures"; (f) the offer is of listed securities by existing holders in the secondary market (subject to an anti-avoidance provision); (g) the issuer is a foreign company and the prospectus is issued to professional dealers in securities or is received abroad; (h) there is no offer for cash (e.g. as on an exchange of securities); or (j) the issue is listed on the local stock exchange in which event stock exchange disclosure requirements take over (although the prospectus must still be registered at the Companies Registry).

15–28 **PFI** The PFI typically prohibits dealing in securities except by licensed dealers in securities, exempt dealers (mainly authorised banks) and certain others; provides for conduct of business rules by dealers (known as the Licensed Dealers Rules); contains a wide anti-fraud section applying to all types of investment in money or property; restricts the distribution of circulars relating to investments; and provides for the official authorisation of unit trusts. As regards securities offerings, the Act usually prohibits distribution of "circulars" relating to "securities" (as defined) which contain either invitations to acquire or dispose of such securities or information calculated to lead directly or indirectly to the acquisition or disposal of such securities.

Unlike the Companies Act, the PFI: (a) extends to all securities, whether or not of a company; (b) is not limited merely to securities but also to interests in securities, unit trusts and collective investments in other property; (c) is not limited to public issues provided there is a "circular" (this probably includes an information memorandum sent out to several persons); and (d) applies also to dealings in the secondary market.

The usual main exemptions in this context are (in bald summary): (a) consent of the relevant government department (which requires normal disclosure); (b) the "circular" conforms with the CA prospectus disclosure requirements; (c) the circular is distributed by, amongst others, licensed or exempt dealers or stockbrokers (who generally have to comply with disclosure codes); (d) the distribution is to existing security-holders of a company or a subsidiary (not available for collective investments); (e) the circular is distributed to professional dealers in securities (as defined); (f) (usually) the circular is distributed abroad; or (g) the securities are listed on the local stock exchange.

Russia

Legislation The main legislation of the Russian Federation regulating securities is the Regulations for the Issue and Circulation of Securities and for Stock Exchanges in the RSFSR No 78 of December 28, 1991 (the "Regulations").

Other relevant laws and regulations are (apart from the 1994 Civil Code):

– Law of the RSFSR on Enterprises and Entrepreneurship of December 25, 1990

– Instruction of the Ministry of Finance of the RSFSR No 2 dated March 3, 1992, on Rules for issue and registration of securities in the territory of the Russian Federation (the "Instruction")

– Regulations on the Execution and Registration of Transactions Involving Securities (Letter of the Ministry of Finance of the Russian Federation No 53, July 6, 1992)

– Letter of the Ministry of Finance of the Russian Federation No 91 of September 21, 1992, "On the Licensing of Activities of Investment Institutions on the Securities market".

Registration of public offerings A public offering of securities must be preceded by the publication of an offering circular delivered to prospective purchasers and a public notice published in the press. This may not be done until the securities are registered and the prospectus is officially approved by the Ministry of Finance. A private placement does not require delivery of a prospectus to potential investors nor does it require publication of an official notice; the only legal requirement is that of filing an application for registration with and obtaining approval from the Ministry of Finance.

The issuer, any guarantors of the issuer and all investment institutions (underwriters or placement agents) engaged by the issuer are obliged to provide the purchaser with a copy of the prospectus, and will be responsible for the authenticity of the information in the prospectus: Regulations Art 34.

There are no penalties for non-compliance with the publicity requirements.

The Russian Ministry of Finance has the right to declare the issue null and void, to suspend issues or to refuse to register them in cases when issuers or investment companies provide unreliable or incomplete data in the issue prospectus. The Ministry of Finance and its local bodies are responsible for checking the completeness of information in the prospectus, but not its authenticity. They may carry out random checks of prospectus information with the aim of protecting the interests of investors: Regulations Arts 37, 38.

Foreign securities are admitted for circulation in the territory of the Russian Federation only after registration with the Ministry of Finance: Regulations Arts 6, 7.

15–30 **Exemptions** A public offer is an offer to a potentially unlimited number of investors. The Instruction imposes the registration requirement on both public offerings and private placements: Instruction Arts 1 to 3.

No provision prevents the re-selling of securities which were initially privately placed and there are no stipulated hold periods.

There is no express exemption for issues to "sophisticated investors". Issues to investment funds must be registered but the legislation does not provide for any hold periods to prevent seepage into the retail secondary market.

All governments and municipalities are subject to the registration requirements. The Regulations do not provide an exemption for international organisations: Regulations Arts 3, 6.

"Securities" are defined in the Regulations so as not to include bank loans or commercial paper issues.

There is no legislation governing market options and futures.

Licensing of dealers An investment institution may enter the securities market only after obtaining a licence from the Ministry of Finance: Regulations Art 21.

The staff must be qualified, but there is no codified professional code of conduct governing investment institutions, so that resort must be had to general rules of law.

China

15–31 In China official securities exchanges were established in Shanghai in 1990 and Shenzen in 1991 which led to queues of reportedly over one million people fighting to obtain lottery tickets entitling them to participate in the right to apply for shares. The regulatory regime is somewhat inchoate and it remains to be seen how it will develop.

Other countries

The securities markets in most countries are small compared to the United States, Japan, Britain, Continental European countries, Canada and Australia. But most commercial countries have a legal regime governing securities. A few may be mentioned.

Some Latin American countries are influenced by the US approach, though without the extended particularisation and prescription of the US legislation. For example, **Argentina's** supervisor is a federal agency *Comision Nacional de Valores* operating under Law 17,811 which governs the public offer of securities. In **Mexico** securities regulation is the province of the Securities Market Law of 1975 as amended, which is also administered by a federal agency, *La Comision Nacional de Valores*.

In **Finland** securities are governed by the Securities Market Act (1989/495) as amended, administered by the banking authorities. The legislation takes EC Directives into account. **Thailand** has a new Securities and Exchange Act BE 2535 of 1992 setting up a Securities and Exchange Supervision Commission.

In the **United Arab Emirates** and other Gulf states, securities regulation is extremely thin, but the local central banks often impose informal restrictions. In **Saudia Arabia**, the Saudi Regulations for Companies of 1965, as amended, prohibit foreign companies from issuing or selling securities in Saudia Arabia unless the prior approval of the Ministry of Commerce is obtained.

Chapter 16

EXEMPTIONS FROM PROSPECTUS REQUIREMENTS

Introduction

16–1 **Available disclosure** The regulation of public prospectuses for the issue of securities attempts to achieve two objectives:

– Full disclosure in appropriate cases, enforced by tougher civil and criminal sanctions.

– Public availability of the disclosure by registration with an SEC, a companies registry or a banking commissioner, via a stock exchange statistical service, or via newspaper advertisements, or a combination of these, and limitation of marketing material in addition to the prospectus.

Professional market In practice the market for securities is largely a professionals market and indeed eurobond issues are almost invariably only marketed to and held permanently by sophisticated investors – central banks, commercial banks, insurance companies, pension funds, investment funds and, sometimes, large corporates. The members of the public do not buy them, and, in practice, except for a few countries, such as the United States, the number of members of the public who buy securities is quite small, although privatisations are changing this.

Marketing only by means of an approved prospectus A regime which requires a complying prospectus will typically seek to ensure that only the approved prospectus is used for marketing to the public. This generally means that there are restrictions on all other methods of marketing without the prospectus, notably restrictions on announcements in the media, advertisements generally, presentations and mail-shots.

Jurisdictions have different attitudes to incidental publicity designed to awaken investor interest in a forthcoming issue. The United States considers that public announcements to condition the market might constitute an unlawful unregistered prospectus and there are detailed rules as to what is and what is not allowed in respect of pre-issue publicity.

Summary of main exemptions

The main objective of the prospectus requirements is to prevent the marketing of securities to the local public in the regulating state except by means of a complying prospectus, but not to prevent the marketing of securities in other contexts. Hence the regime contains exemptions.

16–2

Typical exemptions are:

- Private offerings

- Offerings to sophisticated investors – the most important for international bond issues

- Offerings by governments, municipalities and certain international organisations

- Deposits with banks

- Syndicated bank loans and participations in bank loans

- Commercial paper issues (but these may be caught by banking regulation restricting the taking of deposits)

- Offerings to existing security-holders or to employees

- Listed securities

- Foreign transactions

- Secondary market trading

- Small transactions (not further considered here).

Notwithstanding an exemption from prescribed disclosure and publicisation, the general law relating to misrepresentation and fraud applies, and issues of securities are effectively uberrimae fidei (full disclosure), not caveat emptor.

The usual exemptions may now be reviewed in more detail.

Exemption for private offerings

It would be impracticable and over-burdensome for the law to impose disclosure and registration requirements on private domestic transactions. Private business would stop. Private transactions are invariably exempt from prescribed disclosure and publication/registration.

16–3

Meaning of public The main criterion used to determine whether an offering is private or public is the number of offerees. In the United Kingdom the "public" is probably 30 to 40 offerees who intend to hold securities for their own account. The Hong Kong consensus is 50. Japan, with its concept of "many unspecified persons", has a threshold of about 50, Switzerland as low as 10. Brazil and Finland suggest 100, Indonesia 50, Luxembourg 50 to 70. A Malaysian case held that nine was enough and a very low number seems to be the approach in New Zealand: *Robert Jones Investment Ltd v Gardner* (1993) 6 NZ CLC, 68, 514.

If the offering is led by a number of managers, then there must be arrangements between the managers whereby they ensure that they individually do not make offers to persons that collectively exceed the limit.

In the case of a multinational offering, one question is whether one tots up all the persons internationally (integration) or whether one can treat each territorial group separately.

In the United States, Ontario, France and Spain the private offerings exemption is effectively limited to knowledgeable investors (and usually limited to 300 in France). This is effectively the result of the attitude in countries like New Zealand where the "public" is a tiny number in single figures. In the United States, s 4(2) of the 1933 Act provides that "transactions by an issuer not involving any public offering" are exempt. This exemption does not depend upon the number of persons to whom the offer is made but rather on whether the class of persons to whom the securities are being offered "need the protection of the Act".

> In *SEC v Ralston Purina Co*, 345 US 119 (1953), an offer was made to key employees of the issuer. *Held*: the offer should have been registered because the employees involved "were not shown to have access to the kind of information which registration would disclose". Thus it is not enough that the offer is made to a small number of people: they must also have access to all material information about the issuer: see, for example, *SEC v Continental Tobacco Co*, 463 F 2d 137 (5th Cir 1972); *Doran v Petroleum Management Corp*, 545 F 2d 895 (5th Cir 1977).

Decisions construing s 4(2) and published SEC interpretations limit the private placement exemptions to a limited number of purchasers all of whom (a) are sophisticated investors with respect to the risks involved, usually institutional investors such as banks, insurance companies and pension funds; (b) are capable of bearing the potential loss of their investment; (c) purchase as principals for investment with no view to further distribution (so that resale restrictions are necessary); and (d) have access to information similar to that which would be included in a prospectus in a registered offering.

Because the availability of this exemption is unpredictable, e.g. it depends on questions of fact such as the degree of sophistication of the offerees, the SEC has adopted two exempting rules:

EXEMPTIONS FROM PROSPECTUS REQUIREMENTS 16-5

– Regulation D (1982) as a "safe harbour" which, if satisfied, will fulfil the requirements of the private placement exemption. This Regulation sets out rules as to the absence of general solicitation or advertising, the number and sophistication of investors (specific institutional investors, theoretically unlimited in number, plus up to 35 other sophisticated investors), sometimes full disclosure, and restrictions on resale (unless registered or exempt).

– Rule 144A which allows sales of eligible securities to large institutional investors without an SEC registration statement if the conditions of the Rule are met.

Prohibited forms of marketing The usual prohibition is on the offers on sales of securities to the public unless the prospectus contains the prescribed information and has been publicised by the prescribed method, with or without prior screening or approval by an authority. 16-4

Prohibited marketing will generally include: (1) sending the non-complying prospectus to members of the public; (2) mass mailing (post or electronic) or telephone campaigns; (3) media advertisements (newspapers, television, journals); (4) other advertising, e.g. posters, notices in shops, offices or public places; (5) home-to-home visits by salesmen, and (6) presentations to potential investors – "road-shows".

Tombstones Most of the developed states allow a "tombstone" advertisement. This is a newspaper advertisement which records the issue and is primarily intended to publicise the managers: it states the issuer, amount, and names of the managers, affirms that the securities have been sold, and maintains that the advertisement is inserted as a matter of record only, i.e. is not a solicitation.

International media Advertisements in newspapers having an international circulation or in television broadcasts beamed to other countries create obvious problems. 16-5

The usual course is not to advertise any non-complying issues, e.g. eurobond issues, and, in the case of prospectuses registered in one state, but not another, to prohibit the managers or underwriters from selling to foreign residents. General press announcements to alert the public to a forthcoming issue and to excite interest are often frowned upon or prohibited.

Cold-calling Many states have specific prohibitions against cold-calling, i.e. unsolicited calls. An example is s 56 of the UK Financial Securities Act 1986. Australia and Brunei prohibit going from "house to house" – a typical share-hawking ban on door-to-door salesmen. Mexico achieves the same effect by prohibiting offers to previously unconnected or unknown persons and Taiwan limits offers to existing active clients. Some states allow unsolicited requests for a prospectus.

16–6 Road-shows The attitude to road-shows varies greatly. These are oral presentations to potential investors by the issuer and the managers to generate interest. The usual pattern is that the road-show must be by invitation only and that the only persons who are invited are eligible investors, e.g. sophisticated investors, and that the number of invitees is not so large as to amount to a section of the public. This is generally true in Canada, France, Germany, Italy, Japan, the Netherlands, Switzerland, the United Kingdom and the United States. The rules in, for example, France and the United States are much more restrictive than the above, but those in Germany, the Netherlands and Switzerland are quite liberal.

In many countries it is not permitted to invite financial journalists if the prospectus has not been approved locally, e.g. Australia, Austria, Belgium, Canada, Denmark, Finland, France, Indonesia, Japan, Portugal, Spain, Thailand and the United States, although this may not be the case in Germany, Italy, the Netherlands and Switzerland. In the United Kingdom, in the case of a complying UK prospectus, only the classes of persons specified in Art 9(3) of the Financial Services Act (Investment Advertisements) (Exemptions) Order 1988 can be invited to attend.

States also vary in their attitudes as to how much information can be given at the road-show in addition to the complying prospectus, given that the principal object is that only the approved prospectus should be the selling document. One approach is to limit the written materials provided at the road-show to the prospectus, to require that any oral presentations should be scripted so as to be consistent with the prospectus and to stipulate that there must be no means of applying for the securities at the road-show itself.

16–7 Resale to public In many states (e.g. the United States, Britain, Australia, Ontario), facile avoidance by the sale of securities privately to the investor who intends to on-sell to the public is prohibited. This is the genesis of the practice whereby private investors must confirm that they intend to hold the securities for their own account: some states specifically prescribe "hold" periods, e.g. the United States, Ontario.

There are two broad approaches. The restrictive approach allows re-sale, with or without an initial hold period, only to sophisticated investors, not members of the public: members of the public need a complying prospectus. The liberal approach is to allow re-sales after a hold period but only through professional intermediaries who are subject to codes of conduct imposing duties of care to clients and duties to ensure adequate disclosure. In practice, bond issues are usually by well-known established issuers subject to substantial on-going disclosure requirements by their stock exchanges, and the consumer market for unregistered unlisted off-market securities is probably small.

The United States adopts the restrictive approach. The effect of the US 1933 Act and rulings thereunder is that the restrictions on the resale of exempt privately-placed securities without a registration statement are lifted in three general cases:

- a detailed exemption known as the "section 4 (1½) exemption" (because it is between s 4(1) and s 4(2)) stipulating broadly similar rules to the private placement exemption which allows offers to sophisticated purchasers having access to information without a general solicitation;

- resale under Rule 144 prescribing hold periods of two or three years, subject to conditions; and resale under Rule 144A to "qualified institutional buyers" (Q1Bs);

- resale outside the US under Regulation S: see chapter 21.

The general result in the United States is to allow a secondary market for privately-placed securities without the necessity for a registration statement but only amongst certain institutional investors. But resales remain subject to the federal anti-fraud rules and state Blue Sky laws.

Exemption for offerings to sophisticated investors

The argument is that sophisticated investors do not need the protection of a regulated prospectus. The "sophisticated investors" exemption is essential for eurobond issues in Europe and appears to be universal there. Key factors are (a) financial knowledge and experience, and (b) ability to bear potential losses.

There are several methods of defining sophisticated investors. The traditional English method, followed by numerous countries based on the English pre-1986 model (e.g. Brunei) is to define them as persons whose ordinary business (or part of whose ordinary business) is to buy or sell securities, whether as principal or agent, i.e. professional dealers, which would normally include institutional buyers and large corporates. Austria refers to institutional investors acting in the scope of their professional or commercial activities; Greece and Germany are similar. The US backstop method is to lay down general tests for financial knowledge, experience and ability to bear losses. Many countries specifically list eligible investors, such as broker-dealers, life insurance companies, public authorities, pension funds, authorised banks, mutual investment funds and the like: Spain, Italy,

16–8

France, Australia, South Korea, the Netherlands, Singapore, Portugal. Others deem a purchaser to be sophisticated if he pays more than a certain (high) amount so as to exclude most ordinary individuals, e.g. A$500,000 in Australia, C$150,000 in Ontario and IR £35,000 in Ireland: this confers certainty and obviates the somewhat difficult task of ascertaining a purchaser's mental equipment and his bank balance. Sometimes all these criteria are used so that an investor who satisfies any one of them is exempt.

In other states, the tests may be cumulative, as in France where in some cases the investors must fall within one of the designated categories of institutions, and not number more than 300, and be existing contacts of the manager, and be acting on their own account.

Where it is permissible to make offers to sophisticated investors within the jurisdiction, often the offers must be from outside the territory in case the offers constitute the carrying out of an unlicensed investment business within the jurisdiction, as in Bermuda and Thailand.

The US position has been traditionally hostile to the "sophisticated investors" exemption and the SEC has insisted that issues to sophisticated investors must also be within the private placement exemption. However, if an issue is initially privately placed, it can then immediately be sold to "qualified institutional investors" under Rule 144A. These are defined so as to include most large professional dealers in securities. Of course there are conditions, but the effect is to allow institutional secondary market trading of unregistered securities initially privately placed.

Exemptions for offerings by governmental and public bodies

16–9   Issues by (or guaranteed by) the **home government** are always exempt. The rationale may be that investors are expected to know about their own country and are not at risk. In any event the home government can print more money in the case of a shortage and should not in any event be bothered with a prospectus when topping-up the national debt. The position tends to be similar for states in a federation, provinces, municipalities and other regional units. See, e.g. the US 1933 Act s 3(a).

Issues by **foreign governments** are often exempt because of comity, and the assumption that investment in foreign government securities is essentially a political decision. Britain, Ontario and France exempt issues by foreign governments, but Japan and the United States do not. Issues by foreign **municipalities** and foreign **public corporations** may fall on either side of the line.

Foreign governments, subdivisions and instrumentalities are specifically exempted from the US Trustee Indenture Act (s 304(a)(vii)), no doubt because foreign states would object to being monitored by a non-sovereign trustee.

Commonly, the main financial **international organisations** are specifically exempted, e.g. the World Bank and the Asian Development Bank.

Exemption for deposits with banks

16–10 Deposits with banks are invariably exempt, either specifically or because they are not within the definition of a "security", "investment" or "debenture". Instead the taking of deposits from the public and soliciting of deposits is controlled by bank regulation: chapter 22.

In the United States, issues by a federal or state regulated bank are exempt under s 3(a)(2) of the 1933 Act because they are supervised officially and this is adequate protection to investors. The SEC extends the exemption to US branches of foreign banks if the foreign supervision is substantially similar, although the question of whether the foreign bank is technically within the Investment Company Act of 1940 would have to be considered. Various other issues of securities by US regulated entities are also exempt, e.g. those of regulated insurance companies: s 3(a)(8).

Exemption for syndicated loans by banks

16–11 An offering will escape the prospectus requirements if there is no "investment", "security" or "debenture" within the legislation.

Despite the width of the definition of "security", "debenture" or "investment", bank loan agreements and information memoranda issued to prospective participants in a syndicated loan will not usually be caught even if the loan is evidenced by notes issued by the borrower, and even if the loan is transferable. Syndicated bank loans are exempt in both the United Kingdom and the United States. See para 16–24 *et seq.*

Exemption for issues of commercial paper

16–12 Normally trade finance transactions escape the prospectus requirements. These include bills of exchange in forfaiting transactions, letters of credit, receivables factoring and acceptance credits. The paper is not usually caught by the definition of "security" or "investment".

One question concerns trade-related issues of commercial paper. The term "commercial paper" includes promissory notes, bills of exchange or other instruments satisfying the statutory definition of a negotiable instrument, e.g. certainty and unconditionality: see Art 3 of the US Uniform Commercial Code which is the US version of the British Bills of Exchange Act 1882. Contrast bearer bonds which are negotiable by usage and are not commercial paper, e.g. because their terms are uncertain and conditional on account of floating rates of interest, events of default, covenants and the like.

In **Britain** bills of exchange are usually exempt, but not promissory notes unless they are for the price for goods or services or moneys borrowed to pay the price: FSA 1986 Sched 1 para 2. An issue of commercial paper may fall within another exemption, e.g. issues to sophisticated investors. But the issue may offend the Banking Act 1987 which prohibits the taking of deposits and which provides only limited exemption for tap issues by anybody other than banks.

In the **United States** market, it was necessary to exempt commercial paper from the Federal securities regulation because of the established commercial paper market financing trade receivables, equivalent in economic purpose (but not structure) to the European à forfait market for trade bills. Under s 3(a)(3) of the 1933 Act, commercial paper is exempt from registration under the 1933 Act as an exempted security if it falls within the following definition:

> "Any note, draft, bill of exchange or bankers' acceptance which arises out of a current transaction or the proceeds of which have been or are to be used for current transactions, which has a maturity at the time of issuance not exceeding nine months, exclusive of days of grace, or any renewal thereof the maturity of which is likewise limited."

Commercial paper usually consists of short-term promissory notes (the average maturity is 15 to 45 days) issued at a discount by sound corporate borrowers to commercial paper dealers who freely market and trade in the notes. The market must, by its nature, be free of selling restrictions. As a practical matter, commercial paper cannot be sold without a rating from one of the major credit-rating agencies such as Moody's Investors Service Inc or Standard and Poor's Corporation. The SEC requires that commercial paper must be of prime quality and rated in one of the two top categories. The SEC also requires that commercial paper is of a type not generally purchased by the public – hence the usual minimum denomination of $100,000.

If the proceeds are not used for "current transactions" but rather, e.g. for fixed assets, the notes will not qualify for the exemption. Because money is fungible, the SEC now has the balance sheet test which compares the amount of commercial paper outstanding with the amount of certain current assets. If the notes do not qualify, e.g. because they are to finance an acquisition, it would be necessary to fall back on some other exemption. For example, if the notes are backed by a letter of credit of a US commercial bank they will be a "security issued or guaranteed by a bank". The private placement exemption is an alternative exemption.

In **Ontario** promissory notes or commercial paper maturing within one year from the date of issue of principal amount of C$50,000 or more are exempt.

Exemptions for issues to existing security holders

Issues to existing security-holders are usually exempt. Existing holders should know about the issuer, e.g. because they receive regular accounts or have the benefit of continuing stock exchange disclosure.

The exemption is important for (1) the reorganisation of an issuer in financial difficulties involving the issue of new securities (such as converting bank loans or bonds into equity shares), and (2) option issues, e.g. convertibles and the issue of warrants to subscribe for equity or debt.

Thus the US 1933 Act s 3 (a)(9) exempts exchanges of securities if no extra payment is involved (but there are special rules for bankruptcy reorganisation securities) and the UK Companies Act 1985 s 56(5)(a) exempts issues to existing shareholders or debentureholders from the prescribed contents requirements for prospectuses.

In the United States there can be difficulties with convertible bonds issued in the euromarkets. It is quite possible that a bond will be acquired by a US person in the secondary market with the result that the shares may be issued in the United States or to a US person even though the initial issue of the bond itself was made and completed outside the US under foreign offering exemptions. Either the issuer must register a "shelf" registration statement or the bond must prohibit conversions by US persons. Similar considerations apply to warrants.

In the United States, there is an additional exemption for judicially approved securities issued in the context of a bankruptcy reorganisation (s 3(a)(7) of the 1933 Act), but registration may be required if shareholders vote on the reorganisation, since they are making an investment decision.

Exemptions for listed securities

Where a security is listed, it may be exempt from statutory prospectus requirements because the prospectus will have to comply with stock exchange disclosure requirements. There is no need for duplication. Nevertheless the prospectus may still have to be registered. In Britain, the implementation of the EC directives on listing generally displaces other disclosure

Exemption for foreign issues

16–15 Issues in and out Two considerations are involved here:

- the extent to which a state seals off the home market from securities initially issued abroad. Securities sold abroad may in secondary market trading be acquired locally;

- the extent to which a state espouses the cause of moral imperialism in protecting the public of foreign states by prohibiting local companies from issuing non-complying prospectuses abroad. Some states seek to disallow their territory from being used as a base for peddling poison to foreigners.

It is usually not possible to issue the prospectus or market the securities publicly in a foreign state unless the prospectus complies and is locally authorised. Except where mutual recognition applies, the sending of a prospectus into a foreign state is universally not allowed and other methods of marketing are also generally not allowed (except to exempt sophisticated investors), e.g. mail-shots, road-shows, advertisement in the media, telephone campaigns and personal visits. This is so regardless of whether the prospectus has been approved and registered abroad and satisfies every known standards of safety and merchantability – a prospectus which has been checked, certificated, verified, fussed over by teams of the most pedantic lawyers and accountants from the most pettifogging countries, screened by the most puritanical regulators in the world, scrutinised by Sherlock Holmes and had incense poured over its forecasts by the priestesses at Delphi. None of that is good enough. The restrictiveness of this attitude is shown by comparing the access of the public to ordinary goods – cars, television sets and bananas. Provided these comply with ordinary standards, they can be sold to the public everywhere. But even here nations restrict imports and countries have sometimes used regulatory standards as a covert means of protecting local markets. Hence it seems clear that in some states the prospectus requirements are in practice used not to protect the public against misrepresentation but to shut out access by foreign enterprises to local savings. Where this happens, they are a cloak for a trade barrier or exchange control. The effect is that states seal off their markets from foreign issuers raising capital from local savings, at least by an initial distribution.

EXEMPTIONS FROM PROSPECTUS REQUIREMENTS 16–16

Of course, in most cases the state has no sinister intent – it has just not updated its securities law from the days of purely domestic transactions. The result is a paper wall.

Problems may be caused by advertisements in international newspapers and journals and via television broadcasts receivable abroad.

Some states permit securities to be sold locally from abroad if the request came from a resident and was unsolicited (as in Argentina) or from an existing client or if the security is sold to a professional intermediary. In each case, the actual sales, if frequent enough, may constitute the carrying on of an investment business locally requiring a local licence.

Issues into the regulated state In the **United Kingdom**, prospectus regulation, regulation of investment advertisements and other marketing restrictions are generally limited territorially to issues "in the United Kingdom", e.g. FSA, ss 57, 76. 16–16

In the **United States**, s 5 of the 1933 Act requires registration of any public offering or sale of a security involving the use of any means of interstate commerce, including commerce between the United States and any foreign country. Interstate commerce includes telephone calls, telex and the use of the post. Almost invariably a eurobond offering will involve interstate commerce in this sense. Any sale into the US would be a contravention. However, since 1964 the SEC has recognised that there is no significant US interest to protect if no US investor is involved. Regulation S, adopted in 1990 and accompanied by a 90-page interpretative release, provides a safe harbour for international bond issues by setting out rules for the exemption of off-shore issues. For the detail, see chapter 21. Regard must also be had to s 12(g) of the 1934 Act which requires companies above a certain size engaged in interstate commerce (which includes communication with foreign states) to register the securities with the SEC under the 1934 Act. These companies are then subject to periodic reporting requirements. The section could catch foreign companies inadvertently if US residents buy their securities. Certain exemptions are available.

Reciprocal recognition Notwithstanding the internationalisation of the securities markets, the progress towards mutual recognition of prospectuses issued in foreign states and approved by the authorities there is still very limited.

Even in federal states, the degrees of harmonisation is not as great as could be expected, e.g. in Canada. In the United States the Uniform Securities Act and the modification of Blue Sky laws have not provided complete mutual recognition. But Australia provides for the adoption by each state of the same securities code: para 15–22.

Internationally, the most important initiatives are the EC directives discussed above, and limited mutual recognition of registrations between the United States and Canada pursuant to 1991 SEC Releases.

Any mutual recognition of registered prospectuses still leaves open the question of mutual recognition of differing exempt transactions, continuing disclosure, stabilisation, and other matters.

In Japan, solicitation in Japan of purchases by outsider dealers is probably prohibited without a Japanese registered prospectus. But there is an exemption for sales of foreign securities which are either foreign listed or subject to foreign disclosure if (usually) they are sold only to Japanese licensed securities dealers or designated financial institutions or are solicited by a Japanese licensed securities dealer: see Art 14–16 of the Ordinance regarding Disclosure of the Status of Corporations.

Australia allows Australian licensed dealers to offer clients foreign securities, subject to conditions including approval of the foreign exchange. In France securities listed on designated foreign exchanges, which reciprocate and which meet certain criteria of investor protection, can be offered in France subject to conditions: Decree of 25 October 1990. Singapore can exempt international securities subject to conditions, notably that they are offered only to sophisticated investors by professional intermediaries and they are listed on a recognised stock exchange: Companies Act s 46(2A) and (2B).

Exemption for secondary market trading

16–17 Securities markets would grind to a halt if every sale of a security had to be preceded by the publicisation of a prospectus. The general theory is that, once a prospectus has been publicised, the investor must rely on continuing disclosure requirements – under company law or a listing code or securities regulation – to assess the security. This however does not resolve the problem of issues which are initially exempt from being on-sold in the secondary market without the benefit of the initial prospectus. This tends to arise in three main cases:

– where the securities were initially privately placed: this is discussed at para 16–7

– where the securities were initially issued to sophisticated investors and were exempt: para 16–8

– where the securities were initially issued abroad and were exempt: para 16–15.

The two main legislative approaches are (a) either to regulate only the primary market and cover the secondary market by the supervision of brokers, or (b) to prohibit all sales of securities without a prospectus and then carve out exemptions for the secondary market.

Australia and the US adopt the second method. In the United States, the 1933 Act in effect requires that all offers and sales of securities require registration unless an exemption is available. Section 4(1) then exempts "transactions carried out by any person other than an issuer, underwriter or dealer". Of course there can be no exemption for direct sales by the issuer since these are in their nature primary offerings. Section 4(4) exempts unsolicited transactions carried out by brokers. Section 4(3) exempts transactions carried out by dealers more than 40 or 90 days after the first offering (subject to qualifications). Hence after the initial primary distribution anybody can buy from broker/dealers who are themselves subject to codes of conduct. That leaves underwriters. These are generally those who purchase direct from the issuer: see s 2(11) of the 1933 Act. Purchasers will generally not be underwriters if they buy in the ordinary course of business without any arrangement to participate in the primary distribution. They can then freely on-sell. But it seems that sales by underwriters in the primary distribution of initially exempt securities are caught unless some other exemption is available, e.g. a sale to sophisticated investors.

Shelf registration

Shelf registration is the registration of a prospectus which is continually updated and which is the basis of a subsequent sale or series of sales without on each occasion incurring the cost and delays of a new registration each time. The object is to enable the issuer to take advantage of market opportunities quickly or to raise capital rapidly when it needs it. This is not strictly an exemption since a prospectus must initially be filed. 16–18

In the United States, Rule 415, adopted in 1985, sets out the conditions for shelf registration: this has been widely used for continuous offerings of medium-term notes.

Due diligence is inevitably required prior to each issue. There may be rules that the financial statements are not out-of-date, e.g. they must be not more than six months old, in which event there is a black-out period.

Guaranteed issues

Sometimes the securities regulation can be escaped on the basis that a guarantee is not a security. Hence the company in a regulated jurisdiction sets up a finance subsidiary in a non-regulated jurisdiction. The finance subsidiary issues the securities which are guaranteed by the parent. The issue of the securities is not regulated, nor is the guarantee. 16–19

Collective investment schemes

16–20 Pools marketed to the public are subject to the toughest regulation. They are seen as the classic South Sea Bubble. The statutory definition of a pool generally covers any form of collective investment in securities or other property whereby investors share with other investors in a plan for sharing the benefits of an enterprise designed to make profits or to enjoy some benefit from securities or other property. They generally include unit trusts, mutual funds and open-ended investment companies. "Open-ended" means that the shares are redeemable, as opposed to "closed-end" where they are not. The advantages of pools is that investors can pool their funds so as to obtain professional management of the combined portfolio and so as to obtain a larger diversification than would otherwise be available. Hence they are a favoured investment medium and a substantial capital-provider for enterprises. The reasons for the statutory suspicion of pools include:

- The security is an investment in an investment (or even in a further investment if the pool itself invests in other pools) so that the investor is not in direct control of the ultimate value, does not have direct voting rights in the underlying securities, relies on somebody else to collect the income, and is completely dependent upon the investment expertise of the pool manager who may, because he is not investing his own money, be inclined to invest in speculative securities or to trade on margin.

- Holders can redeem units, thereby resulting in an uncontrolled reduction of capital.

- History has shown that those managing the pool may be tempted to use it for their own ends, e.g. by buying performing securities for themselves and by dumping poor securities in the pool, by overcharging expenses and fees, by generating excessive commissions for themselves in their capacity as brokers, by churning securities in the fund, and by selling to the pool securities of their related companies which would not otherwise be saleable, or securities the manager has underwritten and cannot otherwise sell.

An important distinction between unit trusts and open-ended investment companies is that (a) company law protections apply to investment companies, e.g. members can exert control in a way that unit holders often cannot, and (b) companies are subject to auditing and registration requirements. In the United Kingdom however, it is not yet possible to establish open-ended investment companies. On the other hand both unit trusts and open-ended investment companies enjoy the same characteristic that investors can redeem their "shares" at net asset value: effectively the pool can purchase its own shares or reduce its capital without the consent of the court or creditors. For this reason, unit trusts and open-ended investment companies are subject to strict regulation. In the United Kingdom, see FSA ss 75 and 76; Financial Services (Promotion of Unregulated Schemes) Regulations 1991; Financial Services (Regulated Schemes) Regulations 1991.

In the **United Kingdom**, s 75 of the Financial Services Act 1986 defines a collective investment scheme as being

16–21

> "any arrangements with respect to property of any description, including money, the purpose or effect of which is to enable persons taking part in the arrangements (whether by becoming owners of the property or any part of it or otherwise) to participate in or receive profits or income arising from the acquisition, holding, management or disposal of the property or sums paid out of such profits or income".

But the arrangements must be such that the participants do not have day-to-day control over the management of the property in question and the collective investment scheme must have the characteristic either that the contributions of the participants and profits or income out of which payments are to be made to them are pooled or that the property in question is managed as a whole by or on behalf of the operator of the scheme.

Since this definition would catch virtually any arrangement whereby two or more people have an interest in some common venture, it is necessary to carve-out the arrangements to which it does not apply. Again the legislative method is to catch everything, however innocent, so that the enquirer has to establish that there is an exemption. Needless to say, the exemptions are not easy to follow.

In the **United States** investment companies and unit trusts are rigorously controlled by the Investment Company Act of 1940 as amended. An investment company cannot publicly (meaning probably not more than 100 security-holders) offer securities in the US unless registered under the Act or exempt. Unhappily the definition of an investment company is so wide (e.g. companies that have more than 40 per cent of their total assets in investment securities – s 3(a)(3)) as potentially to catch companies which are not strictly mutual funds as ordinarily understood, e.g. finance subsidiaries, whose only asset is the on-lending to other group companies, foreign banks, insurance companies or parent companies who only hold the shares of their subsidiaries or companies which have sold assets and invested the proceeds temporarily in short-term securities. In recognition of this problem, the SEC has adopted a number of complex and qualified exceptions in favour of the above classes.

16–22

As to the **European Union** see the UCITS Directive of 1985.

Application of prospectus requirements to international bonds

16–23 International bonds issued outside the United States generally escape securities regulation mainly by use of the near-universal "sophisticated investors" exemption. Because the applicable US exemption is cumbersome, US selling restrictions and compliance with Reg S are essential: for the detail, see chapter 21. The basic requirement for most non-US issuers is that the offering must be an off-shore transaction and there must be no directed selling efforts in the United States. The intent is to avoid *primary* offerings into the United States without a registration statement filed with the SEC, but the rule does not prevent secondary market sales in the US.

In practice, issues of eurobonds by non-US issuers which are not intended for the US market observe the following:

- there is a "lock-up" for 40 days after the closing and the bonds are represented by a global bond deposited with Euroclear or Cedel pending the issue of definitive notes to purchasers (who must certify non-US beneficial ownership);
- the offer documents contain standard form selling restrictions and warnings whereby the bonds are not to be offered or sold in the United States or to US persons;
- prescribed reminders to participants that US selling restrictions apply.

Broadly speaking, these procedures will also satisfy the requirements of tax legislation in the United States (TEFRA) designed to prevent the avoidance of tax. The TEFRA rules seek to prevent primary offerings of bearer bonds in the United States and to encourage the issue of registered securities. For the detail, see chapter 21.

In practice, investors in eurobonds have been reasonably protected by the fact that, if the bonds are listed, they must comply with the disclosure requirements of the applicable stock exchange, by the general law which in effect imposes a disclosure requirement in any event (para 17–9 *et seq*); and by the fact that international bond issuers are generally of high credit standing. International bond investors will normally subscribe only to issues of reputable names they have heard of. But there have been major defaults on eurobonds.

Application of prospectus requirements to loan syndications

16–24 A lead bank mandated to arrange a syndication of a loan will approach other banks in the market to see whether or not they would be willing to participate. Common practice is for banks who express interest to be sent an information memorandum giving financial and other information about the borrower which has been prepared in conjunction with the borrower by the managing bank.

The information memorandum generally contains the term sheet giving details of the loan; details of the history and business of the borrower; details of the management of the borrower; and the borrower's financial statements.

As discussed above, if an information memorandum is a prospectus which is regulated by domestic legislation, then: it must contain prescribed information; it must be registered with a Securities Commission, a Registrar of Companies or some other authority; and the liability for misrepresentation is more onerous.

It will almost invariably be found however that the information memorandum will benefit from an exemption, notably: 16–25

— The circular constitutes a **private** offering and not an invitation to the "public". But the scope of the meaning of public may involve a small group, e.g. 30 or 40 persons: para 16–3.

— It is issued only to **sophisticated investors** or professional investors or experts who can be expected to look after themselves, e.g. banks. In the UK and the rest of Europe the circulation of offering material to sophisticated investors is generally exempt from prospectus requirements. But in the United States, the Securities Act of 1933 and the Securities Exchange Act of 1934 contain provisions which are more restrictive. In particular, offerings to professional dealers and securities in the United States are not exempt and private offerings have to satisfy stringent terms: para 16–18.

— The borrower is a **government** or a government instrumentality or a municipality: para 16–19.

— The participations in the loan agreement do not constitute "**securities**", "**debentures**", or "**investments**" within the securities legislation. As to the United Kingdom, it is considered that a loan agreement is not a "debenture" controlled by the Financial Services Act 1986. This is because syndicated loans are not similar to marketable debentures, even if syndication is by the sale of participation certificates, although there is no directly applicable case law. The United States courts have in effect exempted bank loan agreements and the grant of participations from the scope of the Securities Acts in the normal case by exalting the remedial purpose of the legislation over the literal meaning of the words: see, e.g. *Banco Espanol de Credito v Security Pacific National Bank*, 973 F 2d 51 (2d Cir 1992). The courts have held that Securities Acts are only intended to protect those purchasing securities. Generally, a "note" is not a "security" regulated by the legislation if used in relation to a commercial loan but is a "security" if it represents an investment. See, e.g. *United House Foundation Inc v Forman*, 421 US 837 (1975) following the leading case of *SEC v W J Howey Co*, 328 US 293 (1946).

– The circular is issued externally to **foreigners** and, as a matter of construction, the statute is territorially limited. The FSA controls on investment advertisements apply only to those issued "in the United Kingdom". As to US territoriality, see para 16–16.

CHAPTER 17

SECURITIES REGULATION: MISREPRESENTATION AND NON-DISCLOSURE

Sources of law

The law relating to lies has become somewhat more complicated since the time of Moses and the burning bush. 17–1
  The law on the subject is often multi-layered as follows:

- Traditional general **criminal fraud** by common law or statute, and not limited to securities

- Traditional general rules covering **civil liability** for negligent or innocent misrepresentation in tort or contract by common law or statute and not limited to securities

- Specific statutes relating to **criminal frauds** and **civil liability** for misrepresentation in relation to securities, whether or not a regulated prospectus is involved

- Specific laws relating to misrepresentation in **regulated prospectuses** which must contain prescribed disclosure by statute or a listing code.

Summary of enhanced liability under regulated prospectuses

Specific securities statutes enhance disclosure and liability for **regulated** prospectuses. But ordinary law is often already tough so to that extent the securities statute is a codification of existing rules. 17–2
  There are great variations, but typical features of statutory rules include:

- The prospectus must contain **prescribed** information. This is deemed to be material. Liability for omissions may be civil or criminal or both.

- There is a general duty of **full disclosure** of all material facts (as with insurance policies). This may be the practical effect of the general law in any event: para 17–14.

- There is an express duty of **due diligence**, i.e. a positive duty to make reasonable enquiries. Compare the ordinary law of negligence which is not dissimilar: para 17–9.

- The **onus of proof** for due diligence/no knowledge may be shifted on to the person alleged to have made the misrepresentation.

- There may be **absolute liability** on the issuer, regardless of knowledge. Compare the ordinary law of innocent misrepresentation whereby a misrepresentation attracts liability only if the misrepresentation has become a term of the contract: para 17–9.

- **Contracting-out** may be prohibited. Under the general law judicial antipathies to exculpation clauses often sharply limit contracting-out. But the securities regime is typically more absolute.

- There are express **remedies** of rescission and damages. Compare ordinary law remedies, which are often similar.

- Liability is extended to **persons other than the issuer**, e.g. directors (who might otherwise be able to hide behind their non-executive status), managing underwriters, co-managers, auditors, lawyers, and other experts. Compare the ordinary law relating to criminal aiders and abettors, duties of care in tort, and the fiduciary duties of agents.

- Sometimes there is no necessity to prove **reliance** or inducement, although this feature, found in the United States, is unusual elsewhere.

One may observe that prospectuses for international bond issues and loan syndications are usually exempt from the rules relating to regulated prospectuses: para 16–24. But the ordinary law very readily converts information supplied in relation to a securities or loan transaction into a full disclosure duty (because of the rule that a half-truth is as good as a lie, so that misleading omissions are actionable), and a duty to exercise due diligence (because of the tort of negligence). See para 17–14.

One of the most important questions is the liability of the managers who organise the bond issue or loan syndication because they are usually the only pocket left to pay ("big pocket liability"). A claim against the issuer for misrepresentation does not add much if the issuer is insolvent – the issuer is directly liable for the debt. Jurisdictions differ fundamentally in their attitude to big pocket liability.

Heads of general misrepresentation liability in England

17–3 **General rules of law** In England, there are at least five heads of liability for misrepresentation by rules of law which apply generally and not merely to securities:

1. **Theft Act 1968 s 19** Intentional deceit by an officer of a body corporate to creditors about its affairs.

    In *R v Kylsant* [1932] 1 KB 442, CCA, the prospectus correctly stated the past dividends but omitted to state that dividends had been maintained only by drawing on secret reserves. The result was that the prospectus gave a false impression of the company's financial stability. *Held*: fraud within the precursor to the Theft Act section.

    In *R v Bishirgian* [1936] 1 All ER 586, CCA, the prospectus omitted to point out that the capital was really being raised to finance a huge gamble involving an attempt to corner the world's supply of pepper. *Held*: fraud within the precursor to the Theft Act section.

2. **Fraudulent misrepresentation at common law** Civil liability for damages and rescission where a misrepresentation is made fraudulently, i.e. with knowledge of its falsity or recklessly, not caring whether it is true or false: *Derry v Peek* (1889) 14 App Cas 337, HL. Criminal liability may also result.

3. **Negligent misrepresentation under s 2(1) of the Misrepresentation Act 1967** Civil liability for negligent misrepresentation.

4. **Negligent misrepresentation at common law** The law will imply a duty of care if a party seeking information from a person possessed of special skill trusts him to exercise due care and that person knew or ought to have known that reliance was being placed on his skill and judgment: *Hedley Bryne & Co Ltd v Heller & Partners Ltd* [1964] AC 465 (a case involving a negligent bank credit reference).

    However, case law shows a marked tendency to limit tort liability for economic loss, e.g. the House of Lords decision in *Caparo Industries plc v Dickman* [1990] 2 AC 605 (auditors not liable for company accounts to bidder for the company's shares).

5. **Innocent misrepresentation at common law** The general rule is that no action for damages lies for a mere innocent misrepresentation, i.e. one which is neither fraudulent or negligent: *Gilchester Properties Ltd v Gomm* [1948] 1 All ER 493. But there may be liability if, for example, the misrepresentation has become a term of the contract and there is much case law on this. In bond issues, express warranties as to the offering circular are commonly given only to the managers of the issue, not to the bondholders themselves. If rescission is available for innocent misrepresentation, then the court may award damages in lieu under s 2(2) of the Misrepresentation Act 1967.

Liability under securities statutes In Britain, investor protection statutes enhance the ordinary civil and criminal misrepresentation rules. The following are the main heads:

1. **Misleading statements and practices: s 47 of FSA** False statements, promises or forecasts or concealment of material facts, which are dishonest or reckless and which are for the purpose of inducing a person to enter into an investment agreement, as defined. Misleading practices and conduct for the same purpose are also outlawed. This section will not usually apply to bank syndication offering memoranda.

2. **Listing particulars: ss 150–152 of FSA** Untrue or misleading statements in London listing particulars or omission of prescribed information. Liability applies to the issuer, directors, persons accepting responsibility (e.g. auditors), and persons authorising the particulars (which may include managing banks). There is an exception for foreign international securities. Due diligence defence.

3. **Corporate prospectuses: ss 67–78 of Companies Act 1985** Untrue statements in corporate prospectuses (British or foreign) which are regulated by the Act (not e.g. if not to the public or if within the sophisticated investors exemption). Liability applies to directors and those who authorised the issue of the prospectus. There is a due diligence defence, but no "international securities" exemption. The provisions do not duplicate ss 150–152 of FSA. Criminal liability is possible.

4. **Scheme particulars** Financial Services (Regulated Schemes) Regulations 1991 Untrue or misleading statements in "scheme particulars" (i.e. the prescribed disclosure document for regulated collective investment schemes) or omission of prescribed information.

Heads of misrepresentation liability in the United States

17–5 The United States has a range of legal rules similar to England—some arising from the general law, others directed specifically at the securities markets. The main specifically securities laws are Rule 10b 5, promulgated under the 1934 Act, and ss 11 and 12 of the 1933 Act.

Rule 10b 5 This rule, promulgated under s 10b of the 1934 Act; provides:

"It shall be unlawful for any person, directly or indirectly by the use of any means or instrumentality of interstate commerce, or of the mails, or of any facility of any national securities exchange,

(a) to employ any device, scheme or artifice to defraud;

(b) to make any untrue statement of a material fact or to omit to state a material fact necessary in order to make the statements made, in the light of the circumstances under which they were made, not misleading; or

(c) to engage in any act, practice or course of business which operates or would operate as a fraud or deceit upon any person,

in connection with the purchase or sale of any security."

The section applies to any purchase and sale of any security regardless of whether or not the transaction has been registered and regardless of whether or not the "security" is exempt from certain of the registration provisions of the Act.

Knowledge of the falsity is required but probably recklessness is enough. Negligence is insufficient: *Ernst and Ernst v Hochfelder*, 425 US 185 (1976).

Liability is civil as well as criminal. The civil liability is grounded on a breach of statutory duty: *Kardon v National Gypsum Co*, 69 F Supp 512 Ed Pa (1946). The plaintiff must show that he relied on the statement, but some courts have presumed reliance. See also *Blue Chips Stamps v Manor Drug Stores*, 421 US 723 (1975); *TSC Industries Inc v Northway Inc*, 426 US 438 (1976); *Herman & MacLean v Huddleston*, 459 US 375 (1983). Aiding and abetting liability was severely limited by the US Supreme Court in *Central Bank of Denver v First Interstate Bank of Denver*, No 92–854, April 19, 1994.

Section 11 of the US Securities Act of 1933 Section 11 of the 1933 Act, which applies only to registered offerings, exemplifies the stricter approach to misrepresentation in public securities transactions.

> The section provides that if any part of the registration statement filed with the SEC (which includes the prospectus) when it became effective, contained an untrue statement of a material fact or omitted to state a material fact required to be stated therein or necessary to make the statements therein not misleading, any person (which includes purchasers in the secondary market) acquiring the security may sue (among others) every person who signed the registration statement, directors, experts and underwriters. He does not have to prove reliance, but cannot sue if he knew of the untruth or omission: s 11(a). The term "material" is defined in Rule 405, to mean "matters as to which an average prudent investor ought reasonably to be informed before purchasing the security registered". By s 6 the registration statement must be signed by the issuer, its principal executive officers, its principal financial officer, its comptroller and the majority of its board of directors, except that a security issued by a foreign government or a political subdivision need only be signed by the underwriter of the security. By s 15 controllers of a party liable under s11 are also liable, subject to various good faith and due diligence defences. The liability is joint and several, with rights of contribution (except in case of fraud).
>
> By s 14 the parties cannot contract out.
>
> The issuer has no defence but each other person has a defence if, amongst other

things, he proves that he had, after reasonable investigation, reasonable ground to believe and did believe, at the time the registration statement became effective, that the statements were true and there was no omission. Experts such as accountants, engineers and valuers are responsible only for the portion prepared or certified by them. Persons other than experts do not need to prove reasonable investigation of the accuracy of the expert's statements so that the registration statement is divided into "expertised" and "unexpertised" portions. The standard of reasonableness is "that required of a prudent man in the management of his own property".

The section contains detailed provisions for the calculation of damages. The damages are not "rescission" damages but the difference between the price the plaintiff paid (but not more than the public offering price) and the price at which he disposed of the security or (if he still owns it) its value at the time of suit: see *Beecher v Able*, 435 F Supp 797 (SDNY 1977). The damages are reduced if the decline is attributable to other factors, e.g. general economic depression. In the case of each underwriter (other than those receiving more than a proportionate share of commissions, etc.) damages are not to exceed the total price of the securities underwritten by him and distributed to the public.

Action must be brought within one year of discovery of the misrepresentation but not later than three years from the public offering.

17–7 The first fully litigated decision on s 11 was the celebrated case of *Escott v BarChris Construction Corp*, 283 F. Supp. 643 (SDNY 1968).

BarChris was a small company engaged in the construction, equipping and sale of bowling centres. It filed a registration statement for the sale of $3 million worth of $5\frac{1}{2}$ per cent convertible subordinated debentures in 1962. The plaintiffs brought an action under s 11 against three classes of defendants: the directors, the accountants and the underwriting group. The alleged misrepresentations related inter alia to errors in the accounts, non-disclosure of officers loans, use of proceeds in a manner not disclosed in the registration statement and additional undisclosed business activities. Parts of the registration statement, it was alleged, gave the impression that the bowling industry and BarChris were healthy when in fact they were on the brink of disaster. *Held*: the misstatements were material and that the defendants, not having exercised due diligence, were all liable under s 11.

The court held:

(a) Materiality need not include actual reliance and it was sufficient if the misstatement was one of a material fact which if correctly stated would have deterred or tended to deter the average prudent investor from purchasing the securities in question.

(b) The defence of due diligence advanced by the principal officers or directors was negatived because of their access to the facts. Subsequent decisions have shown that it is almost impossible for executive directors to succeed in a due diligence defence, because of their access to information: see, e.g. *Feit v Leasco*, 332 F Supp 544 (EDNY 1971). They virtually guarantee the accuracy of the prospectus.

(c) The outside directors (who were not participants in the decisions of management) had a duty to verify independently and personally the accuracy of the prospectus and not merely to rely upon what was told to them by the executive management.

(d) Probably directors would be held to standards of due diligence depending on their expertise. For example, a lawyer-director would have a higher investigatory duty than a layman. On the other hand the court declined to treat lawyers as experts for the purposes of the s 11 liabilities.

(e) A new director who had joined the board after the initial registration statement had been filed but before it had become effective was held not to have exercised due diligence by merely checking the company's credit rating and the reputation of its auditors. The court rejected the notion that the new director has any lesser duty than any other director and adopted the reasoning of the English case of *Adams v Thrift* [1915] 2 Ch 21 in which a new director who knew nothing about the prospectus and did not even read it but rather depended on the statement of the company's managing director that it was correct was held liable for the misstatements.

(f) The underwriters' contention that the registration statement was the company's and not theirs and they were entitled to rely on statements made by the company's officers and counsel without independently verifying them was not accepted. The court ruled that, as the underwriters had a common interest in the saleability of the issue, they had responsibilities as to the quality of the investment for the public and did not have a lesser standard of due diligence. They had to do more than merely inquire of the issuer. However the underwriters were permitted to rely on audited figures since s 11 allows reliance on the opinion of experts. In *Matter of Richmond Corp*, 41 SEC 398 (1963) the SEC asserted that by associating itself with a proposed offering, the underwriter impliedly represented that it had made a professional investigation, thereby inducing investors to rely for their appraisal on the underwriter's endorsement of the security.

(g) Apparently no distinction was made for the purposes of s 11 between the duty of the lead manager and that of the subordinate underwriters. In practice it is impractical for each underwriter to perform its own investigation and the effect of this part of the decision is that co-managers have an increased reliance on due investigation by the lead manager.

(h) The court also rejected the due diligence defence of the accountants who had audited the 1960 financial statements and who had carried out the post-audit review three months later for the purposes of the issue. It was found that in the course of the post-audit review the accountant had not followed the programme required by generally accepted accounting standards, e.g. he had not read the latest minutes. The court emphasised the impropriety of sending inexperienced associates to perform the investigation.

17–8 Section 12 of the US Securities Act of 1933 This imposes liability on any person who offers or sells securities by means of any written or oral communication which misstates a material fact or omits a material fact necessary to make the statements made not misleading under the circumstances.

Unlike s 11, this provision applies to misstatements or omissions in any form, in any securities transaction and whether or not subject to the registration provisions of the 1933 Act. All that is required is that there is some use of the mails or facilities of interstate commerce in the course of the transaction: see *Franklin Savings Bank v Levy*, 551 F 2d 521 (2d Cir 1977). The purchaser can only sue the person from whom he bought the security and cannot therefore sue an issuer if the purchaser has bought the securities from an underwriter: see *Collins v Signetics*, 605 F 2d 110 (3d Cir 1979). The sale must be made "by means of" the misleading communication. The purchaser need not show that the communication had a decisive effect on his decision but he must show at least some causal relationship to his decision: *Jackson v Oppenheim*, 533 F 2d 826 (2d Cir 1976). The purchaser does not have to show actual reliance on the misstatement: see *Johns Hopkins University v Hutton*, 422 F 2d 1124 (4th Cir 1970). The seller has a defence if he can establish that he did not know, and in the exercise of reasonable care, could not have known, of the untruth or omission.

The 1934 Act also imposes liabilities for material misstatements or omissions in any documents filed with the SEC under the 1934 Act, subject to a "good faith without notice" defence.

Aspects of general law of misrepresentation

17–9 This section summarises aspects of the general law of misrepresentation, apart from special securities statutes, and compares these aspects to the toughening of the law achieved by securities statutes.

Misrepresentor's knowledge of the misrepresentation

Liability differs according to whether the misrepresentor (1) knew of the falsehood or was reckless (fraud); (2) did not know of the falsehood but did not make reasonable investigation (negligent); and (3) did not know of the falsehood and did make reasonable investigation (innocent misrepresentation);

Knowing or reckless misrepresentation In the case of knowing fraud, there is criminal liability for deceit and civil liability for damages and rescission. Aiders and abettors are liable, e.g. directors and participating managers. There is no contracting-out and no right of contribution from co-delinquents.

Reckless disregard for the truth, i.e. gross sloppiness, is generally enough. In such a case, actual knowledge does not have to be proved: *Derry v Peek* (1889) 14 AC 337, HL.

Securities fraud codes reinforce those rules. Both s 47 of the British FSA and the US Rule 10b-5 treat Nelsonian knowledge or recklessness as equivalent to actual knowledge. Both provisions apply to securities transactions regardless of whether the prospectus has to be registered: para 17-3.

Negligence and due diligence Under ordinary English law, if the misrepresentor believes that the statement is true but fails to check it properly or was negligent, then usually there is no criminal liability but he may incur civil liability for damages. The liability for negligent misstatements in business transactions is well established in English law: *Hedley Byrne & Co Ltd v Heller & Partners Ltd* [1963] 2 A11 ER 575, HL.

17-10

It may be that the standard of due diligence depends upon the circumstances. For example, a circular distributed to sophisticated banks invited to participate in a loan may attract a lesser duty than the distribution of a prospectus to retail investors. But the law on relative truth is unclear.

Securities regulation may impose specific due diligence standards. Section 11 of the US Securities Act of 1933, SRO rules on investment advertisements in the United Kingdom and the rules set out in the London Stock Exchange Yellow Book all effectively require reasonable investigation. The US *BarChris* case (para 17-7) suggests that the extent of investigation required under s 11 to establish a due diligence defence depends on the level of experience of the defendant and his relationship to the issuer: a lawyer-director is likely to be held to higher standards than a non-lawyer non-executive director.

Innocent If a misrepresentor honestly believed the statement was true and is not negligent, then the investor may be entitled to rescission (by law or under a term of the contract) or damages in lieu of rescission under the Misrepresentation Act 1967 or for breach of contract (if a term of the contract).

17-11

Securities regulation may impose absolute liability, e.g. s 11 of the US Securities Act of 1933 imposes absolute liability on the issuer. Effectively the statements in the prospectus become warranted terms of the investment contract which, as is often the case with breaches of absolute contractual terms, give rise to a remedy regardless of due diligence on the part of the defendant. After all, the issuer has the money.

What is a misrepresentation?

17–12 **Non-factual matters** Misrepresentation is not limited to statements of fact. For example, case law in England and the United States has established the following:

– **Statements of intention** Statements of intention, such as the proposed use of proceeds, future capital programmes or dividend policy, are misrepresentations if the representor did not in fact have that intention.

– **Forecasts** A forecast is a misrepresentation if the representor did not actually believe the forecast or if (as will usually be the case) there is an implied representation that there are existing facts which make the forecast reasonable: *Esso Petroleum Co Ltd v Mardon* [1976] 2 All ER 5, CA. Plainly a person making a forecast does not guarantee the forecast since the law accepts the difficulties inherent in prophecy.

> In *Beecher v Able*, 374 F Supp 341 at 348 (SDNY 1974), the court held that "an earnings forecast must be based on facts from which a reasonably prudent investor would conclude that it was highly probable that the forecast would be realised. Moreover, any assumptions underlying the projection must be disclosed if their validity is sufficiently in doubt that a reasonably prudent investor, if he knew of the underlying assumptions, might be deterred from crediting the forecast."

If a forecast is made, it should be short-term and the assumptions upon which it is based should be clearly stated, should be reasonable and, if possible, backed by an expert's review. In bond issue prospectuses in particular, statements as to future prospects should contain hard information only. In project finance, the cash-flow forecasts are long-term. The cash flows state the position which would apply on the basis of stated assumptions, e.g. completion date, market price, inflation, capital costs, operating costs, production profile, recoverable reserves, interest rates and rates of exchange.

17–13 – **Statements of opinion** An opinion is a misrepresentation if it is not in fact held or contains an implication that the opinion is based on facts justifying the opinion: *Brown v Raphael* [1958] 2 All ER 79, CA. Hence opinions of lawyers, auditors or of the directors as to the likelihood of availability of tax or exchange control exemptions may court liability. An opinion expressed as a statement of fact may be treated as such: *Reese River Silver Mining Co Ltd v Smith* (1869) LR 4 HL 64. It should therefore be made clear that opinions are only opinions.

- **Statements of law** These are probably on the same footing as statements of opinion. The classical view that statements of law cannot be misrepresentations (on the basis that everybody should know the law) can no longer be relied upon. The reasons are that statements of law and fact are often intertwined; foreign law is, in England, treated as a matter of fact; and a fraudulent misrepresentation of law is always actionable. In England, misrepresentations as to the law have been held to be actionable in the case of erroneous statements as to the priority of stock, the borrowing powers of a company, the existence of encumbrances on shares and that planning permission exists for a particular use. Many circulars contain numerous statements of law, e.g. as to tax, exchange control consents and corporate authority.

- **Summaries** Summaries of documents (e.g. constitutional documents, guarantees, governmental licences, rights attached to shares, contracts) must be fair and not misleading. In England, an incorrect map has been held to be a misrepresentation. If the summary is misleading, it is not enough to state that the summary is subject to the terms of the document.

- **Omissions** Traditionally, loan and securities contracts are not *uberrimae fidei*, ie there is no duty to disclose everything which is material. Silence is not a misrepresentation. However, in practice this protection is generally unavailable under the ordinary law, because:

    - Once something is said and it is one-sided, there is a misrepresentation. A half-truth is as good as a lie: see *Gluckstein v Barnes* [1900] AC 240, HL. Partial disclosure by omitting the adverse factors is therefore riskier than no disclosure at all. Strictly the non-disclosure rule may be limited only to those omissions which make the actual statement in the prospectus not misleading. In practice, however a prospectus provides so much information that any material non-disclosure will almost inevitably cause one or other actual statement to be misleading.

      In *TSC Industries, Inc v Northway, Inc*, 46 US 438, 449 (1976) it was said that there is a misrepresentation if there was a "substantial likelihood that the disclosure of the omitted fact would have been viewed by the reasonable investor as having significantly altered the total mix of information made available".

    - Non-disclosure can be a misrepresentation if a participant in the transaction stands idly by and allows a person to make a misrepresentation which he knows to be false: *Hardman v Booth* (1863) 1 H & C 803. This may amount to tacit confirmation of the misrepresentation, e.g. if a manager allows an issuer or a borrower to make a misstatement in the circular.

- If a manager has access to inside information, a special duty of disclosure to participants or investors may result from this privileged position: see, for example the New Zealand case of *Coleman v Myers* (1977) 2 NZLR 298 (director's duty to shareholders in sale of shares transaction).

- Regulated prospectuses are invariably subject to a full disclosure duty. For example, s 11 of the US Securities Act of 1933 imposes liability if the registration statement "omitted to state a material fact required to be stated therein or necessary to make the statement therein not misleading". The EC Listing Directive (which is absorbed into UK law) requires prospectuses for EC listed securities to disclose everything material. Section 47 of the UK FSA makes the "dishonest concealment of material facts" in an investment transaction a criminal offence.

True information subsequently becomes false

17–15 If a statement was initially true but subsequently becomes untrue, to the knowledge of the representor before the contract is entered into by the investor, there is under the ordinary law a positive duty to correct this statement. Failure to do so is fraud: *Davies v London & Provincial Marine Insurance* (1878) 8 Ch D 469 at 475.

Some securities codes specifically require the information to be true up to a specific cut-off date, but the rule applies in any event as a matter of general law.

Whether there is a general duty to continue positively to check the information up to the time of contract by the investor is often unclear – does due diligence stop when the offering circular is issued? The cut-off date for s 11 of the US Securities Act of 1933 is when the registration statement becomes effective. The cut-off date under the EC Listing Directive (absorbed into UK law) is governed by Art 23: this requires that every "significant new factor capable of affecting assessment of the securities which arises between the time when the listing particulars are adopted and the time when stock exchange dealings begin" must be covered by a supplement to the listing particulars.

In a bond issue, a change of circumstances before allotment of the bonds should be "stickered" on the final prospectus or otherwise notified to potential investors. The subscription agreement should oblige the issuer to notify adverse changes and to publicise them. In the case of a loan agreement, the syndicate manager should arrange for the borrower to send out a correcting letter to potential participants.

In some circumstances, it seems that the prospectus can continue in force in the after-market so that there would be continuing liability to subsequent purchasers: para 17–20. Whether there is a continuing due diligence duty in such a case is unclear, but in the case of listed securities the matter is usually covered by continuing disclosure obligations.

Access to information

If the circular contains misstatements, it is not enough that the investors had access to the correct information or could have discovered the truth from documents made available for inspection unless the investors did in fact discover the truth: *Redgrave v Hurd* (1881) 20 Ch D 1, CA. Under ordinary law there is no objection to referring to disclosed documents not reproduced in the circular, e.g. available published accounts or to information in a stock exchange's statistical services or at a registration authority provided that the circular itself does not misstate this information.

17–16

Inducement (reliance)

Under ordinary law a representee cannot sue unless he was induced by the misrepresentation to make the investment. He will therefore have no claim if he did not read the circular or knew that the statement was false or if he would have contracted anyway. In England it is enough that a misrepresentation is one of the factors which induced the investors even if it is not the sole reason: *Edgington v Fitzmaurice* (1885) 29 Ch D 459 (misstatement as to use of proceeds).

The argument against the reliance rule in securities transactions is that the listed price at which the investor buys the security is based upon the prospectus being correct. He does not necessarily (and often will not) read the prospectus in detail or at all – even if he is a dealer in the primary market. Further most prospectuses are long and complex and have to be filtered through analysts. It would be unrealistic to insist that the ordinary investor purchasing in the market should have read it and he will often rely merely on what the experts say about the security. Section 11 of the US Securities Act of 1933 recognises these arguments by providing that an investor does not have to prove reliance.

On the other hand, it seems unreasonable that an investor should be able

17–17

to claim if he knew of the error or would have bought the security anyway. The English courts require reliance but will probably assume reliance in many cases unless the defendant can show that the investor did not rely on the misrepresentation.

Materiality

17–18 **Generally** A misrepresentation is material if it may reasonably be regarded by an average prudent investor as influencing him in a decision as to whether or not to invest in a security on the specified terms. In practice, if a misstatement is trivial, the complainant may find it difficult to prove that he was induced to enter into the contract as a result.

> Section 11 of the US Securities Act of 1933 imposes the objective standard of the "the average prudent investor". A fact is material if it is a "fact which if it had been correctly stated or disclosed would have deterred or tended to deter the average prudent investor from purchasing the securities in question": *Escott v BarChris Construction Corp*, 283 F Supp 643 (SDNY 1968).

Standards of information What is the truth? Truth is not absolute. There is much international variation, e.g. on the amount of prescribed information; detail and length; the desirability of forecasts; generally applied accounting principles (GAAP); and segmented analysis of products.

Prescribed information is material If a regulated prospectus fails to contain the prescribed information, the liabilities are often both criminal and civil, regardless of whether the information is in fact material. The prescribed information is deemed to be material: see the British Companies Act 1985 ss 56, 57 and 66; s 11 of the US Securities Act of 1933.

Remedies

17–19 In practice, the remedies against the borrower are of little value if the borrower is insolvent which is when the misrepresentation is usually discovered. The main remedies are:

- **Event of default** Loan agreements usually contain an express event of default entitling the lenders to accelerate the loans for inaccuracy of a warranty as to the correctness of the offering memorandum. A right to damages will not generally add much to the claim for the loan except in the case of limited recourse loans where the claim for damages could override the limitations on recourse. By contrast, prospectus misrepresentation is not usually an express event of default in a bond issue: the warranties in the offering circular are given only to the managers in the subscription agreement.

- **Damages** Invariably the law provides damages for fraudulent or negligent misrepresentation (and sometimes for innocent misrepresentation). In England, the damages are usually "rescission damages", not just the loss resulting from the error. If the investor would not have made the investment, then he is entitled to his whole loss, e.g. the loss of the entire loan if the issuer is completely insolvent or the price he paid less the actual value of the investment: *McConnell v Wright* [1903] 1 Ch 54.

See also *Doyle v Olby (Ironmongers) Ltd* [1969] 2 All ER, CA; New Zealand: *New Zealand Refrigerating Co v Scott* (1969) NZLR 30; Canada: *Parma v G & S Properties Ltd* (1969) 5 DLR (3d) 315.

In the US under Federal law the loss appears to be limited to the position the injured party would have been in if the representation had been true: see *Affiliated Ute Citizens v US*, 406 US 128 (1978) – a Rule 10b-5 insider trading case.

In *Beecher v Able*, 435 F Supp. 397 (SDNY 1977) it was held in a s 11 case that a defendant is not liable for a decline attributable to reasons other than the misrepresentation. Section 11 of the US 1933 Act sets out detailed rules for calculating damages.

- **Rescission** The investor may rescind the transaction, provided he acts as soon as he becomes aware of the misrepresentation. On rescission the injured party is entitled to his money back plus any other losses suffered. But he must not adopt the transaction, e.g. where, after becoming aware of his right, his conduct indicates that he does not propose to rescind, or where he collects interest or votes or attempts to sell the securities.

Who can sue?

Original misrepresentees The persons to whom the misrepresentation is made can sue, e.g. the original lenders under the loan agreement or the original subscribers to the bond issue. Difficulties arise as to whether assignees of a loan or purchasers of a bond in the secondary market can sue, i.e. when does a circular spend its force?

Subsequent purchasers Assignees of a loan and subsequent purchasers of the security can sue if accuracy is warranted in the contract assigned (as in loan agreements, but not bonds); or there is shown to be a duty of care in tort to subsequent purchasers under the *Hedley Byrne* principle (if the representor could reasonably have foreseen that the subsequent purchaser would rely on the circular); or there is an express right under a securities statute.

When does circular spend its force? Once other factors begin to influence the price in the after-market, such as new information from the issuer, or once nobody could reasonably assume that the information is up-to-date, purchasers of the securities thereafter should not be allowed to sue on the basis of the prospectus unless perhaps the prospectus is still dominant.

> Under the US Securities Act of 1933 a purchaser must prove reliance on the prospectus if he buys the security after the publication of an earnings statement by the issuer covering at least 12 months after the effectiveness of the registration statement. This seems a long period for a prospectus to continue to thrive.
>
> In the English case of *Andrews v Mockford* [1896] 1 QB 372, the plaintiff had been sent a copy of a company's fraudulent prospectus but he had not subscribed for any shares. Seven months later, a telegram falsely reporting a gold strike by the company was published. The plaintiff then bought shares in the company in the market. *Held*: the prospectus was intended to induce the plaintiff not only to subscribe for shares but also to buy them in the market thereafter. The prospectus was not exhausted when the plaintiff bought and therefore he could rely on the combined effect of the prospectus and the telegram.

Who can be sued?

17–21 **Ordinary law** The following are potentially liable for a misrepresentation under the ordinary law:

- The **borrower** or **issuer** who made the misrepresentation. But this claim is useless if the issuer is insolvent.

- **Directors** of the issuer if they participated in the tort or undertook express responsibility, e.g. under a listing code. Numerous English cases have imposed liability on directors of a company provided that they directly authorised the tort or participated in its commission: but, contrary to securities regulation, directors not involved would not be caught. The imposition of liability involves a lifting of the veil of incorporation. The claim is also usually of little practical value.

- All those to whom statements in the prospectus are **attributed** and who consented to their inclusion, e.g. auditors, lawyers and other experts.

- All others who **participated** in the misrepresentation, such as the managers: para 17–24 *et seq*. The ease with which liability is visited on others involved reveals a jurisdiction's attitude to big pocket liability.

Securities regulation This usually imposes liability on specific participants in the issue of regulated prospectuses. Examples are: 17–22

- Section 11 of the US 1933 Act: directors, underwriters and experts are jointly and severally liable but an expert is liable only for his own portions and an underwriter's liability is limited to the published offering price of the securities which he underwrote. In the *BarChris* case (para 17–7) the court rejected the suggestion that lawyers involved in helping draft the registration statement were "experts" or that the accountants had "expertised" anything other than their audited financial statements.

- Section 67 of the British Companies Act 1985 imposes liability on those who "authorised the issue of the prospectus": para 17–4.

- Section 152 of the British Financial Services Act 1986 imposes liability on anybody who authorised all or any part of London listing particulars. A directors' "responsibility statement" is required by the London Stock Exchange.

- Article 4 of the EC Listing Directive imposes liability on the "persons responsible for the listing particulars".

A US commentator has observed that it seems that only the postman who mails the fraudulent prospectus and the company which manufactured the paper on which the violating documents are printed will escape liability.

Exclusion of liability As a general rule, where the circular is regulated, e.g. is subject to registration or must contain prescribed information, no contracting-out is possible by those expressed to be liable. 17–23

Outside securities regulation, it is usually not commercially acceptable for an issuer or a borrower (or its directors) to exclude liability, but managers commonly exclude liability.

Directors may take an indemnity from the issuer. The SEC position is that these indemnities are against public policy because they tend to mitigate the sanction of personal liability. See *Globus v Law Research Service*, 318 F Supp 955 (SDNY 1970), affirmed 442 F 2d 1346 (2d Cir 1971).

Misrepresentation liability of managing banks and co-managers

General principles In practice misrepresentation actions tend to be brought only when the borrower or issuer itself is in liquidation or in financial difficulties (when the misrepresentation is discovered) and the claim is therefore made against other persons involved since these may be the only pockets left to pay. The damages would be the loss of the loan. Jurisdictions differ greatly in their attitude to big pocket liability. Those countries which readily 17–24 impose liability on managers are effectively placing a duty on the managers to monitor and police the borrower. They justify this by the argument that the managers profited from the loan by reason of their commissions, a somewhat thin proposition since commissions are tiny compared to the gross amount of the loan and not paid as a fee for due diligence.

In the usual case, those involved in the dissemination of information to solicit participations in a syndicated loan are the borrower, the managing banks and, sometimes, co-managers. In a bond issue, the lead manager usually assists in the preparation of the offering circular.

In both cases, often the co-managers do not directly participate in the preparation of an information memorandum or offering circular and leave this to the lead manager in conjunction with the borrower or issuer. The co-managers are however commonly associated with the information (their names may appear on the cover) and their names will usually appear on invitational telexes to potential bank participants or bond underwriters.

The borrower is primarily liable for statements in a syndication or bond issue information circular. This is the borrower's document and the function of the lead manager is to help the borrower to draft it. It is almost invariably not information emanating from the lead bank.

In both syndicated loans and bond issues, the practice is for the managers to take specific representations from the borrower as to the accuracy of the information in the loan agreement or (in bond issues) in the subscription agreement. But these warranties will be useless if the borrower is insolvent.

Offering material for syndicated loans and international bonds to sophisticated investors are generally not subject to securities statutes applying to misrepresentation in regulated prospectuses. The matter is left to the general law.

17–25 **Heads of liability for lead managers** The liability of the lead manager and co-managers *depends on the facts and circumstances* and also on the general approach of the jurisdiction. In England lead managers of a bond issue or loan may be liable on the following grounds:

- **Active and knowing involvement** If the lead manager *knew* that the statements were false (or was *reckless*), then the misrepresentation is a fraud and the lead manager may be liable as an *aider and abettor* on usual principles of criminal law (in addition to civil liability), e.g. because it held itself out as being partially responsible for the information or stood idly by and allowed the information to go out knowing it was untrue.

- **Tort of negligence** The lead manager may be liable for the tort of negligent misstatement: *Hedley Byrne & Co Ltd. v Heller & Partners Ltd* [1964] AC 465, HL. But a duty of care owed by the lead manager would have to be established and this might be difficult unless it could be shown that the lead manager ought to have known that the participants were relying on the lead manager to check the information. The English courts restrict negligence liability for economic loss (as opposed to bodily injury or death) – see *Caparo Industries v Dickman* [1990] 2 AC 605 (auditors had no duty to potential bidders); *Murphy v Brentwood District Council* [1990] All ER 908 (local building authority had no liability to purchaser of defective house). The policy is to limit extravagant tort liability and to restrict it to the person primarily responsible – the borrower.

— **Agent or fiduciary** The lead manager may be liable if it was acting as agent of the bank participants and failed in the fiduciary duty of due diligence normally imposed on agents. This would depend upon whether the participants expressly or impliedly appointed the lead manager as their agent to prepare the information – this would in practice be unusual. The lead manager will often be an independent contractor, not an agent of anybody. However in one case the court considered that a lead bank had fiduciary duties to potential participants in providing them with information about the borrower.

> In *UBAF Ltd v European American Banking Corpn* [1984] QB 713, [1984] 2 All ER 226, CA, it was alleged that EABC had sent UBAF term sheets and background material about a shipping loan in which they said that the loans were "attractive financing of two companies in a sound and profitable group". UBAF alleged that they lent money to the shipping company in reliance on the representations. Shortly afterwards the borrower defaulted. The judge said:
>
>> "The transaction into which the plaintiffs were invited to enter, and did enter, was that of contributing to a syndicate loan where, as it seems to us, clearly the defendants were acting in a fiduciary capacity for all the other participants. It was the defendants who received the plaintiffs' money and it was the defendants who arranged for and held, on behalf of all the participants, the collateral security for the loan. If, therefore, it was within the defendants' knowledge at any time whilst they were carrying out their fiduciary duties that the security was, as the plaintiffs allege, inadequate, it must, we think, clearly have been their duty to inform the participants of that fact and their continued failure to do so would constitute a continuing breach of their fiduciary duty."
>
> Note that in this case the loan had already been made and EABC sold a portion of its own loan to UBAF.

The lead manager could on the facts be agent of the *borrower* in preparing the information, as opposed to the bank syndicate. An agent is sometimes concurrently liable for a misrepresentation made by his principal if the agent is involved.

Co-managers Co-managers might on *the facts* be liable on one of the above grounds or because they appointed the lead bank as their agent and are liable as principals for the acts of their agent committed in the course of his agency.

Exclusion of liability by loan syndication managers

17–26 **Generally** Because of the risk of liability to those arranging a syndication in connection with information provided about the borrower, managing banks commonly seek to exclude responsibility towards participants. Their position is (a) that participants are sophisticated institutions who should rely on their own credit evaluation rather than that of the managing bank and (b) that the borrower should alone be responsible for information disseminated to raise the loan.

An information memorandum therefore generally states (a) that the borrower alone is responsible for the information, (b) that the information has not been *independently verified* by the manager, (c) that the lead bank is *not responsible* for it, (d) that each recipient of the memorandum should make its own *independent assessment* in deciding whether to participate in the loan, and (e) that banks will *not rely* on the memorandum. This exclusion is commonly buttressed by express clauses on the same lines in the final loan agreement. See the form in the Appendix.

17–27 **Express exclusion of liability** An exclusion clause would not protect a party from criminal liability nor (probably) from civil liability for *fraudulent* misrepresentation. As to *negligent* misrepresentation, the Misrepresentation Act 1967, as amended, in effect requires the exclusion to be reasonable in the circumstances as stated in the Unfair Contract Terms Act 1977. But this applies only if the misrepresentation is a term of the contract – it may become one by virtue of the warranties clause. Also under s 2 of the Unfair Contract Terms Act 1977 an exclusion of negligence in relation to a contract in a notice must satisfy the reasonableness test. *Hedley Byrne* negligence liability in tort can be excluded by contract. Where the information is addressed to sophisticated banks, it may be easier to satisfy the test of reasonableness.

Indemnity from borrower The managing bank may also obtain an indemnity from the borrower in case liability for misstatement rebounds on the manager: this is illusory if the borrower is insolvent, usually the very time when a manager is likely to wish to have recourse to the indemnity.

An indemnity against the consequences of a deliberate commission of a tort is usually unenforceable. On the other hand, an express agreement to indemnify for the consequences of a tort committed innocently or negligently is valid. If this were not the case, motor liability insurance would be impossible.

Exclusion of liability by bond managers

Indemnity from issuer The subscription agreement for a bond issue will usually also contain a specific indemnity from the issuer to the managers in respect of any liabilities, actions or demands which they may incur or which may remain against them as a result of omissions from or inaccuracies in the offering document. As mentioned, this is valueless if the issuer is insolvent.

Disclaimer The managers also minimise their exposure by making it clear in the formal offer document that they are not responsible for the information contained in the offer document relating to the issuer and the eurobonds.

Due diligence procedures An offering circular is both a marketing document and a liability document. The purpose of due diligence is to check that the stated facts are correct and to ascertain whether there are any material omissions. The degree of due diligence depends upon the issuer and the issue. For example, the World Bank, which makes frequent bond issues, has a highly professional staff which assiduously updates prospectus information. On the other hand, due diligence may have to be elaborate in the case of a corporate issuer without much experience entering the market for the first time.

In the ordinary case, the usual procedures for a eurobond prospectus include the following:

– The circular is discussed in detail with senior management in the presence of lawyers and the company's external and internal auditors. A line by line discussion is generally appropriate in the case of first-time issuers. Sources of outside information should be specifically identified. Where management regards information as confidential, e.g. because it might aid competitors or is otherwise sensitive, the lead manager should review the information in confidence privately and assess whether it is material. Management should understand that, although representatives of the underwriters or the lawyers may help in actually writing portions of the prospectus, the officers of the issuer are responsible for it.

- The external auditors produce a "comfort letter" in which they assert the absence of material changes since the last financial statements on the basis of certain specified spot checks and enquiries. For US cases on auditors comfort letters, see, e.g. *Reves v Ernst & Young*, 494 US 56 (1990); *Marine Bank v Weaver*, 455 US 551 (1982); *SEC v W J Howey Co*, 328 US 293 (1946).

- The in-house lawyers of the issuer may be asked to give a carefully hedged opinion as to the accuracy of the prospectus information (apart from the financial statements). External lawyers do not usually comment on factual matters of this sort, although there is a growing practice to the contrary: para 13–38. A review of material contracts is unusual for a bond issue by a major corporate, but may be instigated in other cases. The same applies to debt contracts, an examination of the minutes books and site visits.

- Experts, such as lawyers, accountants or bankers, will comment on statements within the special area of their expertise.

17–30   Eurobond due diligence procedures are often less than those adopted for domestic issues for several reasons: (1) the issuer is commonly listed so that current information is available through stock exchange services pursuant to continuing disclosure requirements; (2) speed of the issue, (3) high credit-standing of the issuer, and (4) sale to sophisticated investors. The checking process for, say, UK domestic issues is painstaking by contrast: the draft prospectus may be set out in the form of verification notes in which each statement must be ticked off by somebody knowledgeable in that particular area of the issuer's business.

Prospectus contents

Strengths and weaknesses of disclosure codes

17–31   Disclosure codes may arise from statute, stock exchange regulation, rules of market associations, and market practice. The object of disclosure is to enable investors to make an informed investment decision, to prevent fraud and to mitigate losses through insolvency. The law therefore steers a middle course between, on the one hand, only controlling fraud and, on the other, intervening to pass on the merits of securities.

The strength of disclosure is that it mitigates fibbing, and it gives security analysts a means of guiding the investing public.

The weaknesses include the following:

- usually only experts can assess the information – it has to be filtered through to the lay investor;
- the past is not necessarily a guide to the future;
- an adverse turn in market conditions, currency exchange rates or interest rates can happen very quickly;
- financial accounts are creatures of art not science and are formulated on a "going concern" basis – values collapse on insolvency;
- prospectuses do not compare the issuer to other issuers: although the degree of competition can be stated, detailed industry comparisons are often impractical;
- disclosure assumes that the investor will be sufficiently informed to make an investment decision;
- there is an avalanche of information which obscures the main points.

These weaknesses are inevitable and it would be wrong to expect too much of a prospectus.

The degree of disclosure varies according to the jurisdiction and, in each jurisdiction, varies according to the issuer (e.g. governmental, commercial, foreign), the type of placement (private or public), the type of security (e.g. debt, convertible, or equity), and the investor (e.g. sophisticated investor or the private individual).

The various disclosure codes show great differences of approach, in particular on the following points:

- **Prescribed contents** All the codes have an umbrella rule that everything material must be disclosed but some of them embark on a detailed list of the items which must be disclosed or considered, e.g. the US SEC and the London stock exchange Yellow Book. The result is a sort of instruction manual for the prospectus writer. The divergences in the detail of these instructions demonstrate the difficulty of prescribing materiality for all classes of issuer.

- **Commercial secrecy** The codes differ in their balance between, on the one hand, the preservation of commercial secrecy and personal privacy, and, on the other, the needs of the investor. Examples are the attitudes to the disclosure of segmented profits, material contracts and management remuneration.

- **Accounting** The codes reflect different local attitudes to accounting principles and practices. For example, some of the main differences between

US generally accepted accounting principles (GAAP) and foreign accounting rules include such matters as: (a) whether cost accounting is on an historical basis so that assets are included on the balance sheet at historical cost (US GAAP) or can be shown at current cost (so that revaluations increase the assets or profits); (b) whether the replacement cost of assets is capitalised and amortised over a number of years (US GAAP) or are expensed as an operating cost; (c) whether goodwill—which is the difference between the purchase price of a business and its net book value—must be capitalised and amortised against income (US GAAP) or can be written off against equity on the balance sheet without impacting an income; (d) whether deferred tax must be accounted for (US GAAP) or whether the tax is accounted for only if it is likely to become payable in the foreseeable future; (e) the entities which have to be consolidated; and (f) the capitalisation of liabilities which are essentially borrowings, e.g. finance leases. But international accounting standards are drawing closer together.

- **Sophisticated investors** Some of the codes recognise a distinction between the information needed for issues targeted to sophisticated investors and those intended for the general public. The US SEC has historically been more reluctant to make this distinction.

- **Debt/equity** Most of the codes distinguish between debt and equity issues and require less information for debt issues. Equity is junior capital and hence is riskier. Equity disclosure applies to convertible bonds.

- **Burdens** The codes exhibit different policy views as to the point at which disclosure becomes over-burdensome without compensating protections for the investors.

Contents of corporate prospectuses

17–33 Set out below are typical heads for an industrial issuer in a full prospectus.

There are often relaxations for offering circulars for international bond issues which are often slim documents, e.g. because the issuer is listed and the information is publicly available by reason of the continuing disclosure requirements of the stock exchange.

The prospectus sets out any responsibility statement, e.g. of directors, states that no person is authorised to give any information or make any representation except as stated in the prospectus, excludes changes since the date of the prospectus (ineffective), and states that the managers may stabilise the issue.

The prospectus will usually cover the following ground:

- Terms and conditions of the securities

- Use of proceeds, e.g. the net proceeds will be used to repay the indebtedness of the issuer and for its working capital requirements. If the proceeds are to be applied for a specific purpose which fails, English law holds that the issuer must immediately repay the money and in the meantime may (but not necessarily) hold it on trust for subscribers so that the money does not fall into the pool available to unsecured creditors if the issuer becomes insolvent: see *Re Nanwa Gold Mines Ltd* [1955] 3 All ER 219; *Gibert v Gonard* (1884) 56 Ch D 439; contrast *Moseley v Cressey's Co* (1865) LR 1 Eq 405.

    Failure to disclose any material purpose for which the funds are being raised may be a misrepresentation. In *R v Bishirgian* [1936] 1 All ER 586, CCA, the prospectus omitted to disclose that the capital was being raised to finance a huge gamble involving an attempt to corner the world supply of pepper. The person responsible was convicted of fraud.

- Debt record, e.g. past defaults

- Capitalisation table. Total capitalisation of the issuer on a consolidated basis, i.e. total loan capital and total shareholding equity, e.g. share capital, reserves and retained profits.

- Summary of earnings. A table for up to five years summarising consolidated and segmented financial data for main products and services. Attitudes to segmented analysis vary greatly, e.g. whether to segment net profits as well as gross turnover, and geographic segmenting as well as product segmenting. The US has stringent requirements.

- Identity and corporate details, e.g. place of incorporation of issuer

- History and business. The detail will naturally depend upon the type of business. Risk factors to be considered include (a) reliance on patents, licences, distributorship agreements, other commercial and financial contracts, raw materials, suppliers and key persons, (b) customer concentrations, (c) risk of obsolescence because of technology changes, (d) position in the industry and degree of competition (this generally has to be generalised because it is impracticable to verify detailed information about other companies), (e) cyclicality of the industry, (f) foreign operations and political risks, (g) risks of governmental regulation, (h) environmental controls and compliance, and (i) financial risks, e.g. foreign exchange fluctuations, interest rates and sources of capital. All the main listing codes (generally or specifically) require information as to some or all of these aspects. The EC Listing Directive is typical in requiring "summary information regarding the extent to which the group is dependent, if at all, on patents or licences, industrial, commercial or financial contracts or new manufacturing processes, where such factors are of fundamental importance to the group's business or profitability".

- Principal products and services
- Principal properties: location, size, tenure
- Main subsidiaries, joint ventures and other investments
- Capital investment programmes
- Research and development
- Management
- Employees
- Auditors report
- Financial statements (between two and five years)
- Taxes, such as withholding taxes in the issuer's country
- Exchange control
- Listing and markets
- Statement that no material adverse change in consolidated financial position since last accounts
- Statement that no material legal or arbitration proceedings are pending or threatened
- Corporate authorisations for the issue
- Documents available for inspection:
    - Material contracts
    - Directors service agreements
    - Constitutional documents
    - Auditors and experts reports and consents
    - Required accounts
    - Issue documents

US-influenced practice is also to include a section entitled "management's discussion and analysis of financial condition" which involves a comparison of recent results, possibly future trends, liquidity, capital resources and planned future commitments.

Contents of bank prospectuses

Banks are frequent issuers in the international capital markets and this section lists typical prospectus headings for the "history and business" paragraphs.

17–34

The SEC has special rules for banks – see the SEC Industry Guides.

Business This will describe the bank's business: lending, securities and underwriting business, foreign exchange, trade, leasing, swaps, investment, advisory, corporate finance, domestic mortgage finance, futures trading, equity investment, export finance, investment management, correspondent banking.

Loan portfolio Breakdown by type of borrower (concentration), geographical area, country risk and degree of concentration in particular industries, e.g. commercial, financial, agricultural, construction; type of credit (term, overdraft, project, trade finance, secured); interest rates (floating or fixed), currency of loans, any insider lending; loan fees.

Guarantees Type, commissions, effect on capital. Other classes of off-balance sheet engagements, such as swaps.

Loan loss experience and reserves This should deal with general reserves and with special reserves against particular loans.

Foreign currency Foreign currency transactions; foreign currency exposure.

Funding Interest-bearing liabilities. Breakdown showing bank and other deposits, maturity, currency and funding costs.

International operations Foreign branches and representative offices. Separate details for domestic operations if the international operations are significant, e.g. exceed 10 per cent.

Banking system and supervision A section on the banking system might describe the operations of the central bank, the types of financial institutions and the supervisory regime (optional according to expected investor familiarity). Details of capital adequacy, liquidity and inspection.

Main risks Experience has shown that the main risks for banks are loans to insiders; too many eggs in one basket; bad credit decisions, sometimes resulting from inadequate separation of credit approval staff from marketing staff; funding or currency mismatch; speculation in areas outside banking, e.g. underwriting bonds, investment in equities, futures and options; and employee frauds. These points should be borne in mind in preparing the prospectus.

Contents of governmental prospectuses

17-35 **Prescribed disclosure** Generally there is no substantive prescription, except by the SEC. The EC Listing Directive is not applicable to states.

Usual headings The format is fairly standardised and is likely to contain information under the headings listed below:

1. Geography and population
2. Constitution and government
3. International relations – membership of international organisations (United Nations, IMF, World Bank) and of regional economic associations, regional development institutions and treaty organisations
4. Economy – gross domestic product for five years by major sectors with a commentary: Investment – five years accounts of national investment by sector with commentary; development plans; economic sectors (details of main areas of economy); and prices, wages and employment
5. Foreign trade – balance of payments, foreign exchange reserves and exchange control
6. Financial system – central bank and other financial institutions
7. Public finance – domestic and external debt obligations, amortisation table, tax system, budgetary system, external debt record. As to the latter, if the issuer has not always paid its external debt when due, it should be stated why not and whether overdue payments were subsequently met. A typical example is suspensions by reason of "trading with the enemy" legislation, wartime legislation or wartime disruption.

Application of proceeds The prospectus provides, e.g. that the proceeds will be added to the consolidated fund or to the state's official foreign exchange reserves to finance the balance of payments or to repay foreign borrowings, or to finance an economic plan or economic development expenditure or for on-lending to financial institutions to fund infrastructure.

Generally, in the case of a sovereign issuer, the use of proceeds for a governmental as opposed to a commercial purpose does not, under most immunisation rules, immunise the transaction since the transaction itself, i.e. borrowing money, is commercial regardless of its purpose, e.g. whether or not it will be spent on a governmental object such as military barracks.

Continuing stock exchange disclosure

All developed stock exchanges require that an issuer keep the holders of the securities informed as to the position of the issuer and matters affecting the securities during the life of the securities. One objective is to prevent a false market where trades are done on the basis of wrong information.

17–36

Continuing disclosure typically covers (1) audited annual financial statements and reports, and also semi-annual and sometimes quarterly reports (as in the US); (2) material events, such as major acquisitions or disposals, changes in management or control or auditors, exceptional losses, and material litigation.

Most exchanges have special arrangements for the protection of confidential matters.

The advantages of continuing disclosure, apart from information to investors, is that it facilitates short-form prospectuses to take special advantage of a market opportunity. All that is needed is to up-date the information publicly disclosed and to provide details of the issue.

The emphasis in London is on prompt notification, general accessibility of the information to the market and the preservation of the strictest secrecy with regard to inchoate developments which are price sensitive, e.g. workouts, major new contracts, and new issues of securities.

Misrepresentation and conflict of laws

Governing law of torts

The claim for breach of duty in relation to a securities transaction could arise under the general civil law rules of tort or delict. Potential examples are (a) breach of statutory duty under a securities statute, (b) misrepresentation, (c) conspiracy and (d) frauds by a dealer, such as insider trading.

17–37

If, say, a Swiss underwriter sells to a Swiss investor in Switzerland bonds issued by a Swiss company under circumstances which do not constitute actionable misrepresentation under the law of Switzerland but do under the law of England, it would seem surprising if, in the event that action were brought in the English courts, the English courts were to impose their own standards of liability on the transaction. If on the other hand an English underwriter, on business for a few days in Switzerland sells English bonds to an English investor also on business in Switzerland, it would seem equally surprising if the English courts were to fail to apply English law to what is essentially an English transaction. However the governing law rules for tort are developing and one can do no more than indicate solutions which courts have followed without attempting to discern a consistent approach.

Broadly speaking, the options are:

(a) the courts can determine liability according to their own law, or

(b) they can apply the law of the territory where the tort took place , or

(c) they can adopt a more flexible approach and apply whichever system of law bears the most significant relationship to the tort.

The rules have been primarily formulated in the context of product liability and motor accident cases, notably injuries to guest passengers, but it would seem that the principles could apply to securities torts.

If the tort rules create uncertainties, a plaintiff may be able to frame his claim in contract, e.g. a contractual claim for misrepresentation inducing a contract as opposed to a tort claim for deceit or negligent misrepresentation.

In practice, a lie is a lie everywhere and so is a careless fib, so that the potential for conflicts is not that great. The real conflicts arise in relation to the liability of managers and underwriters, and in relation to attitudes to court procedures. This is perhaps a uniquely US risk. The litigation risk is exarcebated there by jury trials, the contingent fee system, liberal rules on class actions, a minimal contacts jurisdiction, enhanced pre-trial discovery of documents, and the risk of treble damages. Although many US cases in this area are settled, the mere prospect of having to go through the litigation process oppresses defendants into settling for a compromise sum as the most attractive of the several unattractive options.

Law of the courts (lex fori)

17–38 The lex fori has been abandoned practically everywhere except for the somewhat idiosyncratic rules of England and related jurisdictions. The objection to the application of the lex fori is that it encourages forum-shopping and theoretically enables an investor to sue in those courts whose system of law is more likely to support his claim, provided that he can get those courts to exercise jurisdiction. The success of the claim depends entirely on the courts chosen and not on the centre of gravity of the tort.

Further the rule ignores the merits. As Cardozo J remarked in *Loucks v Standard Oil Co of New York*, 224 NY 99, 120 NE 198 (1918):

> "If a foreign statute gives the right, the mere fact that we do not give a like right is no reason for refusing the plaintiff what belongs to him. We are not so provincial as to say that every solution of a problem is wrong because we deal with it otherwise at home."

Law of the place of the tort

Under this approach, the courts apply the law of the place where the wrong took place. The objections are that (i) given international communications, the place where a misrepresentation takes place may be entirely fortuitous (and even uncertain as where the misrepresentation is made in one country and is acted upon by a purchase of securities in another) and (ii) the mechanical application of the rule offends common-sense where the entire transaction belongs to another country – as in the example given above of a sale of English bonds between two Englishmen temporarily in Switzerland.

17–39

However this doctrine is (or was) almost universally adopted on the Continent of Europe. An example is the French leading case of *Lautour v Guiraud* (Cour de Cassation, Chambre Civile (1948) Dalloz 357):

> An accident occurred in Spain involving two French lorries driven by French drivers as a result of which one of the drivers was killed. Under the law of Spain, the place where the accident took place, the widow could not recover because negligence could not be proved. Under the law of France she could. *Held*: Spanish law applied and recovery was refused.

Where the rule of the law of the place of the tort is followed, as mentioned above there can be difficulties in determining the place where the wrong was committed. For example, is a misrepresentation committed where the document is despatched, where it is received or where it is acted upon (by a purchase)? Some common law jurisdictional cases on this point are cited in para 17–42.

Closely connected law of the tort

The final possibility is that the applicable law of the tort will be that which is most closely connected to the wrong in question. The US Conflicts Restatement adopts this view by providing in s 145 that "the rights and liabilities of the parties with respect to an issue in tort are determined by the local law of the state which, as to that issue, has the most significant relationship to the occurrence and the parties". In determining the most significant relationship one can take into account such factors as the place where the injury occurred, the place where the conduct causing the injury occurred, the domicile, nationality, place of incorporation and place of business of the parties and the place where the relationship, if any, between the parties is centred.

17–40

While undoubtedly this doctrine suffers from uncertainty it nevertheless allows the necessary flexibility to achieve a just result. This flexibility was adopted in the leading New York case of *Babcock v Jackson*, 12 NY 2d 473; 240 NYS 2d 743; 191 NE 2d 279 (1963), [1963] 2 Lloyd's Rep 286:

> New York law was applied to determine the liability of a New York driver towards his New York passenger as a result of an accident in Ontario on a weekend trip from New York. If Ontario law had been applied the injured passenger would not have been able to recover. The court applied the centre of gravity theory to give a remedy under New York law.

English law

17–41 The present English law on the subject does not exclusively follow any of the above theories and is not altogether satisfactory. The two leading cases on the matter are:

> *Phillips v Eyre* (1870) LR 6 QB 1 – action for assault and false imprisonment alleged to have been committed in Jamaica by Governor of the island; *Boys v Chaplin* [1971] AC 356 – motor accident in Malta between Englishmen temporarily stationed in Malta in British armed services: English law applied.

> The effect appears to be that an action in England on a tort committed abroad will succeed:
> (a) if the conduct complained of is actionable as a tort by English domestic law, and
> (b) there is civil liability under the law of the place where the tort took place or, exceptionally, the act is wrongful under the law of the country which has the most significant relationship with the occurrence. See Dicey, chapter 35. At the time of writing, a bill was before Parliament to introduce the "closest connection" test.

Jurisdiction over tort claims for misrepresentation

17–42 **England** The English courts can claim civil jurisdiction over tort claims (subject to the forum non conveniens principle) if (amongst other cases) the damages were sustained or resulted from an act committed within the jurisdiction: RSC Ord 11, r 1(f). This is subject to the European Judgments Conventions discussed in chapter 3.

> In *Original Blouse Co v Bruck Mills Ltd* (1963) 42 DLR (2d) 174, the alleged misrepresentations were made by telephone and letter from a defendant in Quebec to the plaintiff in British Columbia where they were acted upon to the plaintiff's loss. The court in British Columbia held that, for the purposes of jurisdictional rules, the tort had been committed in British Columbia.

> In *Diamond v Bank of London and Montreal* [1979] QB 333, CA, an English

court held that, where misrepresentations are made by telex or telephone by a person abroad to a person in England, the tort is committed in England.

EC and EFTA Under the Brussels Convention of 1968 and the Lugano Convention of 1988, defendants must be sued at their domicile or, in the case of tort, the "place where the harmful event occurred". The doctrine of forum non conveniens does not apply.

United States A series of US decisions have established that, where a foreign investor is damaged by a securities fraud and the investor is a US national, then the US contacts need be minimal only, e.g. preparation of the documents there. On the other hand where the foreign investor is an alien resident, then greater US contact is required. Note that these were mainly cases of alleged *fraud*, as opposed to honest but negligent misrepresentation, so that the exercise of jurisdiction was clearly more justifiable. Some of the cases involved the gigantic IOS fraud of the 1970s and there can hardly be any objection to a court somewhere, anywhere, invoking its sanctions.

17–43

> In *Bersch v Drexel Firestone Inc*, Il 519 F 2d 974 (2d Cir 1975), cert denied, US 96 S Ct 453 (1975), a class action was brought by US citizens resident in the United States, US residents abroad and foreign citizens resident abroad, alleging securities violations in relation to distributions of common stock in Investors Overseas Services Ltd (IOS) a Canadian corporation. Preliminary meetings, including the drafting of some of the marketing documentation and the allegedly misleading prospectus, had been conducted within the United States but the mailing of the final prospectus was done abroad and only a minority of the securities were purchased by US residents. *Held*: the resident Americans could claim. The US citizens resident abroad could also claim on the basis that the "merely preparatory activities" in the United States were enough to support jurisdiction. However the claims of the non-Americans failed.

> See also *Wandschneider v Industrial Incomes Inc* (1971–1972 Transfer Binder) CCH Fed Sec L Rep para 93.422 (SDNY 1972); *Travis v Anthes Imperial Ltd*, 473 F 2d 515 (8th Cir 1973); *Continental Grain (Australia) Pty Ltd v Pacific Oilseeds Inc*, 592 F 2d 409 (8th Cir 1979); *FOF Proprietary Funds Ltd v Arthur Young & Co*, 400 F Supp 1219 (SDNY 1975), *Des Brisay v Goldfield Corpn*, 549 F 2d 133 (9th Cir 1977); *SEC v Kasser*, 584 F 2d 109 (3rd Cir) cert denied 431 US 938 (1977).

> In *Leasco Data Processing Equipment Corp v Maxwell*, 468 F 2d 1326 (2d Cir 1972), Leasco, an American corporation, alleged fraudulent misrepresentations in inducing Leasco through a wholly-owned Netherlands Antilles subsidiary to purchase shares of Pergamon Press Ltd which was a British corporation controlled by a Mr Maxwell. Suit was brought under the fraud Rule 10b-5. It was alleged that misrepresentations were made by telephone calls and by the use of the US mails. The purchase took place in London. *Held*: there was constructive conduct within the United States and the court had subject-matter jurisdiction.

The court also indicated that if all the misrepresentations alleged had occurred in England the court would entertain most serious doubts whether the extraterritorial application of the Securities Acts could be justified.

In *Finch v Marathon Securities Corpn*, 316 F Supp 1345 (SDNY 1970), an English plaintiff brought a Rule 10b–5 case alleging fraud in connection with the purchase of securities of a British company not trading in the US. *Held*: the court had no jurisdiction on the ground that there was no domestic injury of consequence where a foreign plaintiff sought redress against other foreigners for losses sustained from an alleged fraudulent inducement in a foreign country to purchase securities of a foreign corporation. A similar result was reached in *Fidenas AG v Honeywell Bull AG*, 606 F 2d (2nd Cir 1979).

In *Grunenthal GmbH v Hotz*, 712 F 3d 421 (9th Cir 1983), a foreign plaintiff sued foreign defendants for fraud in the sale of foreign securities. There were four meetings, the first three outside the US and the last in Los Angeles where the agreement was signed. The only factual misrepresentation in the US was a repetition of earlier misrepresentations made abroad. *Held*: the representations in the US were "significant with respect to the alleged violations" and "furthered the fraudulent scheme". The court had subject-matter jurisdiction, on the basis that the fundamental purpose of the US securities laws was to achieve a high standard of business ethics in the securities industry: this was consistent with the intent of Congress, as expressed in the anti-fraud provisions of the US securities laws, to elevate the standard of conduct in securities transactions.

CHAPTER 18

SECURITIES REGULATION: REGULATION OF DEALERS

Authorisation of dealers

Licensing of investment businesses

Most developed jurisdictions have a system of licensing of dealers in securities and other providers of investment services. Licences are given on the basis of the service providers' moral probity, financial record, financial integrity, competence and, sometimes, business experience. Investment businesses are then subject to various conduct of business rules designed to protect the investing public and to financial supervision. 18–1

Authorisation in Britain

Generally, the licensing and regulation of investment businesses in the United Kingdom is covered by the Financial Services Act 1986 and regulations made thereunder. 18–2

Section 3 of the FSA provides that no person shall carry on investment business in the United Kingdom unless he is authorised or exempted. Contravention is a criminal offence. Business done by or through an unauthorised person is unenforceable against other party (subject to the court's discretion to enforce).

What is an investment? Investments are defined in great detail in the FSA Sched 1 Part I to mean (subject to detailed qualifications):

- shares
- debentures or acknowledgments of debt (except purchase price credits, cheques, bank deposits, leases and insurances)
- warrants to subscribe for shares or debentures
- depositary receipts
- units in collective investment schemes

- options for investments, currency and precious metals
- futures contracts for investment purposes, excluding ordinary commercial contracts
- contracts for differences (e.g. FT-SE index contracts)
- long term insurance contracts (excluding death and incapacity insurance and reinsurance)
- rights and interests in investments.

18–3 **What is investment business?** An investment business is defined in FSA Sched 1 Part II to mean (in summary):

- dealing in investments (buying, selling, subscribing, underwriting), whether as principal or agent
- arranging deals in investments (excluding, inter alia, deals for oneself, money-lending, arranging finance for deals, and deals by authorised businesses)
- managing investments on a discretionary basis
- advising on the merits of particular investments (excluding advice in the ordinary media but not investment tip-sheets)
- establishing, operating or winding up collective investment schemes, including acting as a trustee.

But there are detailed exclusions relating to the following (Sched 1 Parts III and IV):

- dealing as principal
- corporate group activities and joint ventures
- sales of goods and supplies of services
- employee share schemes
- sale of a body corporate
- trustees
- exclusions for persons without a permanent place of business in United Kingdom and the like.

The most important exclusion is the first of these – dealing as principal. No authorisation is required to buy or sell securities for one's own account unless the buyer or seller is a market maker; or holds himself out as a dealer in securities; or regularly solicits members of the public who are not investment professionals to buy or sell. If this were not the case, then ordinary investors who buy securities from dealers would have to be authorised. Dealing with or through an authorised or exempt person from abroad is exempt.

There is a separate rule for derivatives (i.e. options, futures and contracts for differences): buying or selling derivatives as principal does not require authorisation provided the contract is entered into *with or through* an investment professional. "Through" means as agent or arranged by an investment professional.

Exempted persons The following persons do not need authorisation under the FSA:

- appointed representatives, i.e. persons appointed by authorised persons to market the services of the authorised person: s 44;

- listed money market institutions, i.e. brokers and dealers in short term debt instruments, swaps and other money market instruments subject to Bank of England supervision: s 43. These institutions are regulated by the Bank of England.

Territorial scope Authorisation is required for carrying on an investment business from a permanent place of business in the United Kingdom or if the activities constitute the carrying on a business in the UK: s 1(3). Tax and jurisdiction cases indicate that in unusual cases even single transactions may suffice. Jurisdiction cases show that the place where business is carried on is where the contracts are made (where the acceptance is posted or the fax or telex received): see *Brinkibon Ltd v Stahag Stahl* [1982] 1 All ER 293. See also on carrying on business *Grasinger & Son v Gough* (1896) AC 325; *Greenwood v FL Smidth & Co* (1922) 8 TC 193; *Vogel v R&A Kohnstamm Ltd* [1973] QB 133.

There are various detailed exclusions of foreign transactions in FSA Sched 1 para 27 including a general blanket exception for transactions by UK persons with overseas persons if the overseas person did not solicit the UK person or the overseas person solicited the UK person in a manner complying with the regulatory scheme in the Act (e.g. the exemptions from coldcalling or compliance with advertisement regulations). The general effect therefore is that, if a UK person takes the initiative to do a deal with somebody abroad, the foreign person is not carrying on an unauthorised investment business in the UK, but if the overseas person markets the investment in the UK in an unapproved manner, the business may require authorisation if in the result it is business carried on the UK. But since the contact required to carry on business in the UK is minimal and since international trading is mainly electronic, the reach of the FSA is easily triggered. The position is ameliorated by the fact that deals by an overseas person (not carrying on a UK investment business) through a UK authorised or exempt person do not require authorisation by the overseas persons (Sched 1 para 26(1)), so that persons abroad can deal through UK professional intermediaries.

One may note the EC "single passport" under the Second Banking Directive (for banks) and the Investment Services Directive (for non-banks).

Authorisation in the United States

18–6 The US Securities and Exchange Act of 1934 provides in s 15 that it is unlawful for any broker or dealer "to make use of the mails or any means or instrumentality of state commerce to effect any transactions in, or to induce or attempt to induce the purchase or sale of, any security" (except certain exempt securities) unless the broker/dealer has been registered with the SEC. A foreign exchange dealer using US telephones, telex or post would be within the prohibition. Isolated transactions suffice. A dealer cannot effect US private placings unless he is registered as a broker-dealer under the US Act of 1934.

However a codifying Rule 15 a-6 has restricted the scope of s 15(a) with regard to non-US broker-dealers in certain cases and allows limited activities by foreign broker-dealers in the US. Mutual recognition is on the table.

The giving of investment advice in the United States normally requires registration under the Investment Advisers Act of 1940. Foreign advisers generally establish a US subsidiary if it is desired to give US advice.

Conduct of business

Regulation of conduct of investment business generally

18–7 **Sources of regulation** Securities laws commonly regulate conduct of business in detail. The usual sources of the regulation are variously: securities statutes and rules thereunder, self-regulation by stock exchanges (sometimes under statutory enabling powers), the traditional criminal law, and traditional agency law (due diligence, no conflicts of interest, no secret profits, disclosure).

Retail and business investors Investor protection rules are primarily intended to protect unsophisticated investors, i.e. ordinary members of the investing public. The advanced regulatory codes recognise that it is over-burdensome and paternalist to attempt to protect business investors in all fields. This approach is evidenced by dispensations in the codes of conduct in favour of business investors as regards, for example, specific disclosure of conflicts (as opposed to general disclosure), advice on suitability or risk, segregation of clients' moneys, and cancellation rights. But of course no dispensations are permitted for frauds – misrepresentation, market rigging, insider dealing.

Conduct of business in the United Kingdom

Authorisation is obtained usually by joining a self-regulatory organisation (SRO). There are currently three of these:

– The Securities and Futures Authority (SFA)
– The Investment Management Regulatory Organisation (IMRO)
– The Personal Investment Authority (PIA)

The SROs are themselves subject to supervision by the main UK investment business regulator, the Securities and Investments Board (SIB). SIB prescribes "core" rules applicable to all SRO members. SIB has also laid down ten broad principles of investment business ("honesty and integrity", "due diligence" and the like). In addition to the core rules and principles, each SRO makes "third tier" rules applicable to its members. The SIB and SROs may also issue guidance.

SRO and SIB rules cover such matters as: (1) the permitted scope of business (each investment firm has a business profile which defines the investment activities it may engage in); (2) requirements that individuals engaged in investment business are registered and pass examinations; (3) financial regulations (members have to maintain prescribed levels of capital – see below); (4) segregation of clients' money and imposition of a statutory trust; and (5) conduct of business rules: these cover such matters as customer documents, advertisements, risk warnings, unsolicited calls, obtaining the best price for the customer, contract notes, suitability of the investment, corporate finance exemption, record-keeping, reporting transactions to regulators, conflicts of interest, disclosure of commissions; excessive charges, churning, restrictions on personal account dealing by staff, and other matters. There are substantial dispensations for sophisticated investors so that the rules are mainly consumerist for retail sales. There are also dispensations for "execution-only" and occasional customers. But of course the professionals are not exempt from fiduciary duties imposed by the common law.

Breach of the core rules and third tier rules entitles *private* investors who suffer loss to bring a civil action for compensation: s 62.

There is an Investors' Compensation Fund which compensates investors who suffer loss where an investment business becomes insolvent. This is funded by levies on all investment businesses.

Investment exchanges In the United Kingdom, regulation of investment business is separate from the regulation of dealings on investment exchanges. The investment exchanges, such as the stock exchange, the futures and options exchanges, the petroleum exchange and the metals exchange are separate from the SROs. The investment exchanges regulate dealings on-exchange and the use of exchange facilities. Exchange members will also be members of SROs, usually the SFA. Hence exchange members will usually have two sets of rules to comply with – the exchange rules and the SRO rules. Exchange membership is, unlike SRO membership, not mandatory in the United Kingdom. Investment businesses join exchanges if they want or need to use the exchange dealing facilities.

Conduct of business in the United States

18–9 In the United States, the rules stem primarily from the Securities and Exchange Act of 1934 buttressed by stock exchange rules. Breaches may lead to both criminal and civil sanctions – not just loss of the dealer privilege.

The SEC has delegated powers to self-regulatory authorities supervised by the SEC. These include US stock exchanges and the National Association of Security Dealers created in 1938 to which nearly all registered US broker-dealers belong. The NASD has developed Rules of Fair Practice covering such matters as the business conduct of members, recommendations to customers, charges and commissions, disclosure of prices, conflicts of interest, customers securities and funds, and the like – a complete fiduciary code.

The 1934 Act prohibits fraudulent practices and transactions in the capital markets and those provisions apply to broker-dealers: s 15(b)(3). The 1934 Act also contains rules to protect clients, notably a minimum capital requirement, fiduciary duties (competence, "know the customer" and "suitability" rules), the regulation of short selling, and margin rules.

Protection of client assets

18–10 Many codes oblige dealers to place client's money in a separate trust account at an approved bank (in order to protect investors against the broker's insolvency) and to register and segregate the client's investments (to prevent commingling and a muddled loss of securities). Commonly dealers are prohibited from creating security over their client's securities, e.g. for bank loans, subject to exceptions. At common law this is obviously not allowed.

Obligations to place money in a separate client account at a bank creates difficulties if the money is to be used to pay calls for margin collateral to an exchange. If the intermediary pays the money to a member of the exchange to support the client's dealings, that member commonly must deposit as principal so that, if the member fails, the exchange can set off obligations owed by the defaulting member to the exchange against the margin deposit owed by the exchange. In the result the client's money is used to pay the debt of the defaulting member. The jurisdiction has to decide whether to protect the client or whether to enhance netting: the rationale of netting is discussed elsewhere in this series of works on financial law.

Conflicts of interest generally

Ordinary agency law holds that an agent may not put himself in a position where his personal interest conflicts with his duty to his client; his duty to one client conflicts with his duty to another (divided loyalty); or he takes a secret profit – this is an example of a conflict of interest. 18–11

Securities codes codify these duties. Again, there is a double-layer law – the code and the ordinary law of agency.

Conflicts of interest are particularly acute in the case of financial conglomerates which comprise departments or subsidiaries including a bank financing the issuer, a dealer in securities, a department providing corporate financial advice to the issuer, a manager of unit trusts and pension funds, an investment manager of discretionary accounts, a trustee of will trusts, a trustee of debt or convertible issues, or a syndicate agent bank – each owing duties to the principal or beneficiary, and each potentially in conflict with its own interest or in conflict with the interest of another principal.

Examples of conflicts in financial conglomerates are:

– The underwriting arm may be tempted to dump securities it has underwritten in captive discretionary accounts.

– The proceeds of an issue by the underwriting arm may be used to repay the bank's private loan.

– The corporate finance arm may put pressure on the fund management arm to support its clients by buying its securities or voting in a particular way.

– The corporate finance arm may know of a default under a syndicated loan in respect of which the banking arm is a syndicate manager – an example of divided loyalty.

Generally, there is a potential flow of confidential or price-sensitive information about securities between the broking, investment, banking and trustee arms.

Other examples of conflicts may be cited. If a client orders a sale of a large block of securities, the price may fall, and the broker may be tempted to sell his own securities first. If the client orders a large purchase, the price may go up, and the broker may be tempted to buy first. Codes may provide that the customer's order is to have priority – the priority rule.

Where a dealer buys a line of securities with a view to allocating them amongst clients and himself, he may be tempted to allocate to himself if the price goes up, or to allocate to clients if the price goes down. Rules may provide for the immediate allocation of purchases or sales. These supplement the ordinary law: see, e.g. *Scott & Horton v Godfrey* [1901] 2 KB 726.

Self-dealing and secret profits

18–12 An agent may not secretly sell his own securities to the client or secretly buy the client's securities himself – undisclosed self-dealing.

The antiquity and strength of the objection to self-dealing is evidenced by a 1697 enactment in England which prohibited brokers from acting as principals on pain of perpetual disqualification.

> In *Rothschild v Brookman* (1831) 2 Dow & Cl 188, a purchase of a client's stock by a broker was set aside. In *Lucifero v Castel* (1887) 3 TLR 371, a client instructed his agent to buy a yacht. The agent bought one himself and sold it to the client at a considerable mark-up. *Held*: the agent could recover only what he paid for the yacht. See also *Regier v Campbell-Stuart* [1936] Ch 766 (recovery of undisclosed excess profit); *Nicholson v Mansfield* (1901) 17 TLR 259 (broker charged an undisclosed commission and mark-up: the client could repudiate). But reasonable and undisclosed charges for transfer services have been permitted: *Stubbs v Slater* [1910] 1 Ch 632. An agent cannot avoid the self-dealing prohibition by selling his principal's property to a company controlled by him: *Salamons v Pender* (1865) 3 H&C 639.

The duty is strict as a deterrent – even if the broker buys at the market price: see *Boardman v Phipps* [1967] 2 AC 46 (a trustee case). An agent may not make a secret profit out of his agency, such as a secret mark-up, or buying the securities himself or on-selling at a profit, even if he buys at market price: *De Bussche v Alt* (1878) 8 Ch D 286 (ship). A broker must pass on a volume discount to his principal: *Turnbull v Garden* (1889) 20 LT 218. There is much English case law – see the books on agency.

Managing conflicts

The main methods of managing these conflicts are:

- Informed consent of the beneficiary: this is often impracticable. One question is whether *general* advance consents are enough: see para 11–9.
- Locating the conflicting activities in separate subsidiaries. This may defeat the purpose of the economies achieved by financial conglomerates.
- Chinese Walls, i.e. administrative arrangements to prevent the flow of information between divisions: see para 11–22.
- Excluding liability for conflicts of interest. But exclusions may be restricted by the securities code or by the general law: see para 11–25 *et seq*.

Duties of skill, care and diligence

General fiduciary laws and codes may impose duties of skill, care and diligence by the broker in favour of the client, notably:

- a duty to act promptly on instructions;
- a duty to obtain the best bargain reasonably obtainable;
- a duty to warn clients, or more usually, unsophisticated individual clients, of the risks, especially in relation to futures and options;
- a duty of the broker to familiarise himself with the customer's financial and personal circumstances, so that advice is suitable – the "suitability rule".

In the United States the "shingle theory" holds that a dealer who turns out a shingle as an expert in securities and offers advice to customers violates the anti-fraud provisions of the 1933 and 1934 Acts if he fails to make full disclosure of possible conflicts of interest or other facts material to the customer's investment decision: see *Charles Hughes & Co v SEC*, 139 F 2d 434 (2d Cir 1943) – a case on excessive mark-up by a dealer.

A dealer, anxious to maximise commission, may be tempted to recommend unsuitable securities to a client. The British, American and Australian codes require dealers who recommend securities to have an adequately informed basis for doing so.

> In *Merrill Lynch*, SEA Rel, 14149 (1977) a US securities firm was obliged, on the "shingle theory", to pay US$1.6 million to customers. Sanctions were imposed on 28 salesmen for alleged unsubstantiated recommendations of the

stock of an electronics company. See also *Berko v SEC*, 316 F 2d 137 (2d Cir 1963); *Hanly v SEC*, 415 F 2d 589 (2d Cir 1969).

In England, financial intermediaries are subject to duties of care arising from contract, fiduciary law or agency.

See, e.g. *Solomon v Barker* (1862) 2 F&F 726; *Elderkin v Merrill Lynch, Royal Securities Ltd* (1977) 80 DLR (3d) 313; *Briggs v Gunner* (1979) 129 NLJ 116. But, apart from regulatory rules, the courts have not imposed positive duties to warn customers of unwise or risky investments: *Stafford v Conti Commodity Services Ltd* [1981] 1 All ER 691; *Drexel Burnham Lambert International NV v El Nasr* [1986] 1 Lloyds Rep 356.

Customer agreements

18–15 The code may require customer agreements in writing between the investment firm and the client containing prescribed terms, e.g. description of the services to be rendered, remuneration, disclosure of conflicts of interest and risk warnings. The customer may be entitled to cancellation rights after a cooling-off period. The United Kingdom SRO rules contain provisions to the above effect, but with considerable relaxations in favour of experienced business customers, as opposed to private individuals.

Remedies

18–16 The remedies of injured clients may include: remedies under general fiduciary contracts or tort law for damages for breach of duty, disgorge of secret profits, rescission of contracts; public reprimand; rights to compensation, cancellation and disgorge; injunctions and restitution orders on the initiative of the regulator; criminal sanctions for fraud; investigation by regulatory authorities, involving search and seizure powers; powers of intervention by the regulator, and the institution of liquidation or insolvency proceedings by the regulator; revocation or suspension of investment authorisation, prohibitions on certain activities and disqualification.

All these sanctions are available in the United Kingdom, either by the general law or under the FSA, and most, if not all, are available to the US SEC. The SEC has power to fine.

Margin regulations

18–17 These control the purchase of securities on credit in order (a) to prevent the diversion of credit to speculative securities transactions, and (b) to protect the investing public from overreaching themselves.

In the United States margin regulations made by the Federal Reserve Board under the authority of the 1934 Act limit the amount of credit that may be initially extended on any security, e.g. to 50 per cent of the price. The margin regulations apply to equities and convertible bonds but not debt or US official securities. See Regulations T and X.

In the United Kingdom, the SRO rules regulate the granting of credit by investment firms to fund securities transactions. In certain cases an "adequate credit assessment" must be made of the client by an officer of the investment firm independent of the officer who normally deals with the client.

Cold calling

A dealer "cold calls" a customer where he solicits a security dealing when the customer has not requested the call. Cold calling may be caught under various direct prohibitions (see the British FSA s 56) or by prohibitions on share hawking, as in Australia.

18–18

Financial regulation of dealers

Generally Banks, investment firms and insurance companies are subject to financial regulation which covers such matters as liquidity and capital adequacy. The aim is to prevent insolvency of the regulated firm which causes loss to investors dealing with the firm directly, and which also invites systemic, domino or cascade risk, i.e. the risk that one market participant becomes insolvent and brings down other participants because the first participant fails to discharge its obligations to other participants.

18–19

The structure of financial regulation UK investment businesses are subject to financial regulation by their SRO and (if they are members of an exchange) by their exchange.

18–20

Foreign investment businesses carrying on business in the United Kingdom are generally subject to their home state regulator's financial regulation. The home state regulator shares information with the SRO concerned.

Financial regulation of UK investment firms generally covers the following matters:

1. **The level of capital required** This has a number of components: a minimum level, e.g. £100,000 for most SFA member firms; (b) an element to reflect the annual expenditure of the business, e.g. a quarter of annual expenditure; (c) an element to reflect investments held by the firm for its own account. There are detailed rules for each different type

of investment. The level of required capital reflects the risk of falls in the market value of the investments; and (d) an element to reflect the risk that a counterparty will fail to perform its obligations, e.g. to pay money or deliver securities. This depends on the quality of the counterparty and the number of days for which the obligation is overdue. Netting of bilateral obligations may reduce this exposure.

2. **Permitted forms of capital** Certain types of capital are discounted in assessing capital adequacy, e.g. tangible fixed assets. Other types of capital only count if they are in prescribed forms, e.g. subordinated loan capital must be in the form prescribed by the SRO concerned and cannot exceed four times share capital.

3. **Periodic reporting** Investment firms must report their capital position periodically to their SRO, e.g. SFA firms have to report fortnightly as well as quarterly and annually.

The EC Capital Adequacy Directive, which was due to be implemented at the end of 1995, harmonises capital adequacy requirements for investment firms throughout the European Union.

CHAPTER 19

SECURITIES REGULATION: SECURITIES FRAUDS

Summary

The principal securities frauds are: 19–1

— deceitful misrepresentation or non-disclosure — already reviewed in chapter 17;

— market manipulation and the like — reviewed in this chapter;

— insider dealing — reviewed in this chapter.

Market manipulation

This is the creation of a false market. An example is simultaneous selling 19–2
and buying of the same securities to create an impression of hectic dealing and hence demand ("wash-sales"). The rigging can be achieved through an associate by matching orders or by a syndicate selling the same parcel of securities in the chain ("pools"). The manipulator unloads the securities on the market just before the truth dawns and the price drops.

> In *Scott v Brown, Doering, McNab & Co* [1892] 2 QB 724, brokers and a client agreed to buy shares of a projected company on the stock exchange at a premium to induce the public to believe that there was a real market in the shares and a real premium. *Held*: the contract was illegal.

Corners

Corners are attempts by dealers to monopolise an investment and then to 19–3
sell only at abnormally high prices to those who have contracted to sell to third parties and are therefore desperate to buy. The speculative short seller is forced into a corner. This may be an unlawful manipulation of the market. In *Salaman v Warner* (1891) 65 LT 132; 7 TLR 454, CA, the court

refused to treat this as fraudulent unless there was an actual misrepresentation. See also *Sanderson & Levi v British Mercantile Marine & Share Co, The Times*, July 19, 1899.

False rumours

19–4 Another example of a fraud on a market is spreading false rumours about an issuer and then buying the securities at their depressed price.

The notion of fraud on a market is not new.

> In *R v De Berenger* (1814) 3 M&S 67; 105 ER 536, the accused bought up government bonds at the time of the Napoleonic wars, and then spread rumours in London and Kent that Napoleon was dead and that peace would soon be made. The price of the bonds shot up and the accused sold them, reaping a profit. *Held*: criminal conspiracy. Lord Ellenborough CJ said: "it is a fraud levelled against all the public, for it is against all such as may possibly have anything to do with the funds on that particular day. It seems to me also not to be necessary to specify the persons, who became purchasers of the stock, as the persons to be affected by the conspiracy, for the defendants could not, except by a spirit of prophecy, divine who would be the purchasers on a subsequent day."

In fact, the first English reported case of fraud on a market appears to be in 1369:

> In *Anon* (1369) Jenk 49 (Case xciii); 145 ER 36, an alien spread a false rumour in the Cotswolds that there was a market glut of wool overseas and overseas traders would buy no more. The object was to cause the price to fall. *Held*: criminal falsity. The alien was fined, ransomed and imprisoned. Publishing a falsehood which may occasion detriment to the public, e.g. that the coin is debased, is a crime. *Salus populi est suprema lex*.

This principle of fraud on the market was followed in *A-G v Starling* (1663); 83 ER 1164 regarding a conspiracy to raise the price of pepper. See also *R v Waddington* (1801) 1 East 143; 102 ER 56 where a dealer spread false rumours that the supply of hops was nearly exhausted so as to enhance the price.

Scalping

19–5 A variant is scalping. Scalping occurs where an investment adviser purchases securities for his own account and then publicly recommends the securities. The public buy on the faith of the recommendation and the dealer sells at a profit. In the United States this has been held to be fraud: see, e.g. *SEC v Capital Gains Research Bureau*, 375 US 180 (1963) and *Zweig v Hearst Corporation*, 594 F 2d 1261 (9th Cir 1979): the latter case involved an SEC injunction against a newspaper columnist who recommended shares which he had purchased. The columnist was subsequently held liable to persons who alleged that the price at which they bought securities was significantly affected by his recommendations.

These frauds are controlled by traditional general rules such as conspiracy, obtaining pecuniary advantage by deception, dishonest concealment of material facts, or by specific securities regulation – see, e.g. FSA, s 47; the US Securities and Exchange Act 1934, s 15.

Exemption for stabilisation

Stabilisation is the making of bids or offers by lead managers during the primary distribution to maintain the price: see para 8–22. Strictly it may run counter to market-rigging or insider trading prohibitions. But the need to stabilise prices is a greater priority and hence is commonly permitted. Stabilisation in the United States is governed by Rule 10b-7 under the 1934 Act and in the United Kingdom by SIB rules of some complexity. 19–6

Churning

Churning is the metaphor for excessive transactions on a managed account in order to generate commissions. In the United States it has been held that churning can be a fraud within Rule 10b-5: see, e.g. *Mihara v Dean Witter*, 619 F 2d, 814 (9th Cir 1980). In the United Kingdom, churning is contrary to SRO rules and would constitute a breach of fiduciary duty to the managed account client, but not a criminal fraud. 19–7

Insider dealing

Meaning of insider dealing

Insider dealing occurs where a privileged insider, such as an officer or professional adviser, who has unpublished material price-sensitive information about securities gained by virtue of his relationship with the company, exploits that information to make a profit or avoid a loss by dealing in the securities, the price of which would have been materially altered if the information had been disclosed. 19–8

The classic example is a purchase by a director of shares of a target company which his own company proposes to make an offer for. Another example arises where a director sells securities in his own company on the basis of his inside information that the company is about to announce results showing a material adverse change in financial condition.

Insider dealing is seen as an abuse of an insider's position of trust and confidence and as harmful to the securities markets because outsiders can be cheated by insiders and are not able to deal on equal terms: as a result the ordinary investor loses confidence in the market.

The rules are more important in relation to equities where prices are more sensitive to financial conditions. But the principles could impact upon bonds and of course upon convertibles or other bonds with an equity element.

Insider dealing under the general law

19–9 The general law has proved weak to control insider dealing. The protections available under general law may be summarised as follows:

(a) Where a trader makes an **affirmative misrepresentation** about the security to his counterparty, he may be liable for misrepresentation under normal rules.

(b) Where a trader **omits to disclose** a material factor about a security, he may in exceptional circumstances be liable for non-disclosure. Generally, however, there is no liability for non-disclosure.

(c) Where a trader is in a **special relationship** with his counterparty, e.g. a relationship of agency, trusteeship or other relationship of special confidence, he may thereby incur a duty of full disclosure.

> In *Coleman v Myers* (1977) 2 NZLR 228, directors of a closely-held company acquired shares from the shareholders in circumstances where the shareholders reposed trust and confidence in them. *Held*: the directors were under a full disclosure duty in these special circumstances.

> In *Allen v Hyatt* (1914) TLR 444, the directors were negotiating an amalgamation with another company and induced individual shareholders to give them options to buy shares at par by saying that this would assist negotiations. The directors exercised the options and made a profit. *Held*: the directors were accountable for the profit because they had held themselves out as willing to act as agents in the negotiations and were thus in a fiduciary relationship imposing a duty of full disclosure.

(d) A fiduciary may be liable to account for **secret profits**. Thus where a director buys securities in a target company for which his own company is about to make an unpublished offer, he may be liable to account to his own company for secret profits received from the improper use of fiduciary information. The obstacles here are the bars on derivative actions by shareholders if the company itself decides not to take action against the wrongdoer: see the cases based on *Foss v Harbottle* (1843) 2 Hare 461 in England, and, in the United States, *Burks v Lasker*, 441 US 471 (1979).

These rules however are of little assistance for trades injuring third parties on anonymous stock exchanges. The hall-mark of the insider is that he is completely silent. Silence is not misrepresentation. The counterparty does not know who he is dealing with and is not induced to enter into the transaction by the trader. Unlike a face-to-face transaction, the dealer cannot make a direct enquiry of his counterparty or rely on the normal misrepresentation or non-disclosure rules.

Hence the general law protections against insider dealing on anonymous exchanges are slim. Apart from the above cases, the general rule is that an insider buying securities in his own company does not have to disclose material facts to the shareholder: see, for example *Percival v Wright* [1902] 2 Ch 421.

Specific regulation of insider dealing

Reports of holdings Many jurisdictions require insiders, such as directors, to disclose their shareholding in the company in a public register. The result is that dealings by insiders are known to the public and may be taken as an indication of the insider's view of the company's financial situation. Commonly, however, the disclosure is limited to voting securities (but may include convertibles). Thus the UK Companies Act 1985 requires prompt disclosure of transactions by a director, his close family and interests, and by shareholders with 3 per cent or more of the voting securities of a public company. In Ontario the threshold is 10 per cent of a company's voting securities. The United States has 10 per cent and specified insiders must file statements with the SEC indicating their holdings. Disclosure was introduced in France in 1967 and abandoned in 1970 on account of the deluge of paper.

Reporting does not prevent insider dealing as such and often debt securities are not covered.

Note that these reporting requirements are to be distinguished from those requiring a specified percentage of beneficial shareholdings to be notified – a rule intended to avoid surprise takeovers.

Listing codes Listing codes generally require an issuer promptly to publicise any significant new factors affecting the company's securities and to maintain the utmost secrecy in the meantime.

19–11 **Prohibition on directors' dealing** The United States is somewhat unusual in rendering certain insiders absolutely liable for short-term profits, regardless of whether based on insider information. Section 16(b) of the Securities Exchange Act of 1934 makes insiders (directors, officers and principal shareholders) account to their corporation for any profit received on securities listed on a national exchange which is realised within six months of the acquisition of the security. The insider is liable for these "short-swing" profits regardless of any intention to use inside information to make a gain.

The UK Companies Act 1985 prohibits directors and their families from purchasing options in listed securities of a public company or a related company – this is a blanket criminal prohibition but relates only to options.

Insider dealing codes Finally there are several specific codes directed against insider dealing: see below.

EC Directive on Insider Dealing

19–12 The EC Directive of November 13, 1989, co-ordinating regulations on insider dealing (89/592/EEC) states in the preamble that the smooth operation of the secondary market in transferable securities depends to a large extent on the confidence it inspires in investors and that the factors on which the confidence depends include the assurance afforded to investors that they are placed on an equal footing and that they will be protected against the improper use of insider information.

Article 1(1) states that "inside information" means "information which has not been made public of a precise nature relating to one or several issuers of transferable securities or to one or several transferable securities, which, if it were made public, would be likely to have a significant effect on the price of the transferable security or, securities in question". The Directive applies to "transferable securities" which are defined to be "(a) shares and debt securities, as well as securities equivalent to shares and debt securities; (b) contracts or rights to subscribe for, acquire or dispose of securities referred to in (a); (c) futures contracts, options and financial futures in respect of securities referred to in (a); and (d) index contracts in respect of securities referred to in (a) when admitted to trading on a market which is regulated and supervised by authorities recognised by public bodies, operates regularly and is accessible directly or indirectly to the public": Art 1(2).

The Directive does not apply to transactions carried out in pursuit of monetary, exchange rate or public debt-management policies by a sovereign state, by its central bank or any other body designated to that effect by the state, or by any person acting on their behalf. Member states may extend this exemption to their federated States or similar local authorities in respect of the management of their public debt: Art 2(4).

There are further exemptions in the preambles in favour of market makers, counterparties acting bona fide and stabilisation of new issues or secondary offers.

19–13 By Art 2(1), each member state shall prohibit any person who by virtue of his membership of the administrative, management or supervisory bodies of the issuer, or by virtue of his holding in the capital of the issuer, or because he has access to such information by virtue of the exercise of his employment, profession or duties; possesses inside information "from taking advantage of that information with full knowledge of the facts by acquiring or disposing of for his own account or for the account of a third party, either directly or indirectly, transferable securities of the issuer or issuers to which that information relates".

Where the person concerned is a company, the prohibition applies to the actual persons who take part in the decision to carry out the transaction for the account of the legal person concerned: Art 2(2).

The prohibition applies to any acquisition or disposal of transferable securities effected through a professional intermediary: Art 2(3).

But each member state may provide that the prohibition shall not apply to acquisitions or disposals of transferable securities effected without the involvement of a professional intermediary outside the market defined in Art 1(2).

19–14 Article 3 prohibits tipping. Each member state shall prohibit any person subject to the prohibition laid down in Art 2 who possesses inside information from (a) disclosing that inside information to any third party unless such disclosure is made in the normal course of the exercise of his employment, profession or duties; and (b) recommending or procuring a third party, on the basis of that inside information, to acquire or dispose of transferable securities admitted to trading on its securities markets as referred to in Art 1(2).

Article 4 deals with tippees by providing that each member state must also impose the prohibition provided for in Art 2 on any person other than those referred to in that Article who with full knowledge of the facts possesses inside information, the direct or indirect source of which could not be other than a person referred to in Art 2. These are secondary insiders.

Article 5 defines the markets covered. Each member state must apply the prohibitions provided for in Arts 2, 3 and 4, at least to actions undertaken within its territory to the extent that the transferable securities concerned are admitted to trading on a market of a member state. In any event, each member state must regard a transaction as carried out within its territory if it is carried out on a market, as defined in Art 1(2), situated or operating within that territory.

Article 6 provides that each member state may adopt provisions more stringent than those laid down by the Directive.

Article 7 in effect requires timely provision of information to official stock exchanges and thus to markets so as to reduce the risk of insider dealing.

Articles 8 to 13 deal with enforcement by competent authorities, sharing of information cross-border and penalties.

United States

19–15 The US Federal securities regulation does not have a specific insider trading code. Instead the rules have been developed by case law grafted on to the ubiquitous anti-fraud Rule 10b-5, the text of which is set out at para 17–5. Some of the leading cases are as follows:

Re Cady Roberts & Co, 40 SEC 97 (1961). A broker was told by directors that the dividend would be cut. The broker sold the company's stock for his clients before the information was made public. *Held*: the broker was liable notwithstanding that he had a conflicting duty to do his best.

SEC v Texas Gulf Sulphur Co, 401 F 2d 833 (2d Cir 1968). In this SEC administrative decision, officials and employees of a company made substantial profits in company stock after learning that an unpublicised exploratory drill on the company's property showed promise of extraordinary ore discoveries.

Investors Management Co, 44 SEC 633 (1971). An aircraft manufacturer told a broker/dealer, who was acting as a principal underwriter for a debenture issue, that current earnings would be much less than a previously published forecast. The dealer's underwriting department told the sales department which told major institutional clients who sold large amounts of stock before the information became public. *Held*: the dealer was liable.

Chiarella v US, 445 US 222 (1980). An employee of a financial printing firm handling secret tender offer documents in the course of printing purchased stock of the target companies. *Held*: the employee was not criminally liable under Rule 10b-5. He did not have the status of an insider.

Affiliated Ute Citizens v US, 406 US 128 (1972). Defendants purchased shares of Ute Development Corporation from members of a tribe without telling them that the shares were trading at higher prices in another market. *Held*: they had no right to remain silent. This case shows that, as regards direct dealing, the seller must, under Rule 10b-5, show that the buyer was induced by a failure to disclose material facts.

United States v Newman, 664 F 2d 12 (2d Cir 1981). It was alleged that investment bankers in two firms passed highly confidential information about proposed takeovers and mergers to a broker in another firm who in turn gave the information to two confederates residing outside the United States. On the basis of this information the alleged conspirators purchased and sold stock in the subject companies, reaping substantial gains. *Held*: the broker was successfully prosecuted for aiding and abetting violations of Rule 10b-5.

See also *SEC v Materia*, 745 F 2d 197 (2d Cir 1984) cert denied 105 S Ct 2112 (1985); *United States v Winans*, 612 F Supp 827 (SDNY 1985) affirmed sub nom *United States v Carpenter*, 791 F 2d 1024 (2d Cir 1986).

Other countries

Outside Europe and the United States, insider dealing legislation is now spreading. Examples are:

19–16

Australia:	Corporations Act 1989 ss 1002–1002U (civil and criminal liability)
Canada:	provincial securities statutes imposing both civil and criminal liability
Indonesia:	Decree of the Minister of Finance No 1548 of 4 Dec 1990: criminal but not civil liability
Mexico:	Securities Market Law of 1975, as amended, Art 16
New Zealand:	Part I of the Securities Amendment Act 1988. Liability is civil, not criminal, but the court can impose a penalty.
Philippines:	Revised Securities Act of 1982
Singapore:	Securities Industry Act (Cap 289) s 103 *et seq*. Civil and criminal liability
South Africa:	Companies Act s 440(F)(1)
Thailand:	Securities and Exchange Act BE 2535 of 1992

Main prohibitions

The usual prohibitions are three in number:

19–17

- an insider takes advantage of unpublished price-sensitive information by acquiring or disposing of securities;
- the insider recommends or procures a third party to acquire or dispose of securities;

- an insider discloses inside information (usually with intent) to a third party otherwise than in the proper performance of his office, employment or profession.

This brief survey refers mainly to the EC directives, the US law, and the provisions of the British Criminal Justice Act 1993 ("CJA") implementing the EC Directive in Part V.

19–18 **Insiders** There are three classes of insider: (1) true insiders – such as directors; (2) quasi-insiders – those having privileged access, such as professional advisers, lawyers, auditors and financial advisers; and (3) tippees – those who are given information by an insider.

The difficult question is where to draw the line, especially as regards casual insiders such as the alert financial printer or the capitalist-minded cleaning lady.

The **EC Directive** catches (broadly) directors, shareholders and those having access by virtue of their "employment, profession or duties", including presumably company employees, auditors, lawyers, security analysts, government officials, tax authorities and regulators.

It is unsafe for companies to give research analysts unpublished information about the company, i.e. all information must be publicised first.

In the **United States**, case law has caught officers, employers and brokers but not an employee of a financial printing firm. According to *Chiarella* (see above), the test is not based on a special relationship between the insider and the issuer giving access to privileged information but rather on whether there was a special relationship with the counterparty giving rise to a duty to disclose. In the US both tippers and tippees have been held liable. Some of the US case law has been concerned with the problem of whether an issuer giving information privately to securities analysts could be liable as a tipper if the security analyst then acts on the non-public information.

> In *Elkind v Liggett and Myers*, 635 F 2d 156 (2d Cir 1980), the court held that certain information given by corporate officers to analysts about earnings could reasonably be expected to be used by the tippee for trading advantages – which it was – and therefore the officers could be liable. The court held that a "pre-release review of the reporting of analysts is a risky activity, fraught with danger" because the company has to steer between misleading stockholders by implied approval of analysts reports and tipping. Perhaps the solution is not to comment at all.
>
> In *Re Dirks*, 681 F 2d 824 (DC Cir 1982), a securities analyst was told by a retired middle level employee of the Equity Funding Corporation of America that there was a massive fraud in fictitious insurance policies with the corporation. The analyst confirmed the allegations with specified employees and disseminated the information to institutional investors whom he knew were likely to

and in most instances did sell their holdings. He also informed the outsider auditors and the Wall Street Journal. The SEC found that Dirks had violated Rule 10b–5 because he came into possession of non-public, corporate information from persons he knew were insiders and transmitted that information to persons likely to trade on such information before it became public. However because of his role in revealing the fraud and his efforts to alert the auditors, the sanction was a censure only.

Inside information

19–19 Generally inside information is that which is likely materially to affect the price of securities if it were public. The problem here is drawing a line between specific information and mere hunches based on rumours or guesswork and research or fact-finding on commercial or economic trends or businesses. The EC Directive requires the information to be "precise" and related to a single company or several companies (but not the economy generally).

Another problem is the degree of publication. Information ought to be disseminated to the market before the insider deal, otherwise the insider could publish and then act immediately before the market could absorb the information. The EC Directive merely refers to information which is not "public". The CJA provides that information may be treated as public even though it can be acquired only with diligence or expertise; if it is communicated only to a section of the public; if it can be acquired only by observation; if it is communicated only on payment of a fee; or if it is published only outside the United Kingdom. But information published in accordance with the rules of a regulated market or which can be readily acquired by those likely to deal is public.

US case law has required that the information be not only published but generally disseminated in a medium likely to achieve the widest distribution: *SEC v Texas Gulf Sulphur Co*, 401 F 2d 833 (2d. Cir 1968).

Securities covered by the prohibitions

19–20 Outside the United States, the tendency is to limit the insider trading prohibition to publicly available or listed securities.

There is no such limitation under the US Rule 10b-5 which applies to any purchase or sale of a security, as defined, whether or not listed.

Sometimes the prohibition applies only to corporate securities and not those, e.g. of states, international organisations and the like. Rule 10b–5 of the US is not so limited. As to the coverage of the EC Directive, see para 19–14. The CJA covers debt securities issued by a company or "public sector body" i.e. any government, local authority or central bank and deals effected on a regulated market (defined by regulation). Off-market deals are caught only if they are through a professional intermediary.

Sanctions

19–21 Sanctions may be criminal or civil or both. Any form of sanction runs into the difficulty of identifying the insider and obtaining the necessary discovery, especially if the insider arranged the transaction from abroad through a bank which raises the bank secrecy defence against foreign subpoenas. The CJA creates criminal not civil consequences (maximum of seven years imprisonment). CJA s 63 provides that no contract is void or unenforceable by reason of an insider dealing offence.

A further problem with civil liability arises from the fact that there is no relationship between the insider dealer and his counterparty in the market. It is not practicable to show which counterparty dealt with the insider amongst the many transactions which may have taken place between the time the insider dealt and the time the inside information became public. If the insider were to be liable for losses to all counterparties in the market (e.g. the difference between the price with and without the information) then the liability could be vast and disproportionate to the offence. In the *Texas Gulf Sulphur* case mentioned above it has been estimated that the liability to sellers of the shares was in the region of US$350 million – that is, US$150 million more than the net worth of the corporation.

In the **United States** the courts do not require privity: *Shapiro v Merrill Lynch*, 495 F 2d 228 (2d Cir 1974). All that needs to be shown is that the plaintiff dealt in the same period as the insider dealt. Damages are to be limited to the insider's profit or the loss he avoided: *Elkind v Liggett & Myers*, 635 F 2d 156 (2d Cir 1980).

Damages are available in Australia and Ontario, e.g. the difference between the price of the securities with and without publication of the insider information and there is usually a liability on directors and the like to disgorge profits to the issuer itself. In New Zealand the liability is primarily civil (not criminal) and the maximum liaibility is three times the gains or losses: Part 1 of the Securities Amendment Act 1988.

Conflict of duties

19–22 Where a broker or bank managing a discretionary investment account becomes aware of unpublished price sensitive information, there may be a conflict between his duty not to trade and his duty to act in the best interests of his customer. The prohibition on insider trading is usually overriding.

In *Re Cady Roberts & Co*, 40 SEC 97 (1961), a broker was liable for insider trading on the basis of a tip about a drop in earnings notwithstanding that he had a conflicting duty to sell his clients' holdings of the stock concerned. It seems that in such a case the dealer would also be liable to his clients if the dealer made an affirmative recommendation: *Slade v Shearson, Hammill & Co*, CCH 94, 319 (SDNY 1974). One possible solution is a Chinese Wall between the banking/underwriting department on one side and the investment/advisory/sales departments on the other. A Chinese Wall, if effective, stops confidential information passing from individuals on one side of the wall to individuals on the other side of the wall.

Negative profits

Generally, where an insider holding securities is influenced not to sell because of inside information and thereby avoids a loss, it is impracticable to impose liability because of the difficulty of proving intent to sell which was subsequently doused by the inside information.

In the United States, the plaintiff must have purchased or sold a security. Thus a counterparty has no claim where he refrains from doing anything at all but would have dealt if he had known: *Birnbaum v Newport Steel Co*, 193 F 2d 461 (2d Cir 1952). Therefore a defendant who suffers a loss when insiders sell on unfavourable news and the price falls as a result may have no standing since he did not sell.

Intent

Normally there must be actual knowledge by the insider that he is an insider and that the information is inside information, i.e. the insider dealing must be knowing and deliberate.

Exemption for stabilisation

Stabilisation is essentially insider trading because the managers are dealing in bonds while in the possession of insider information as to market reaction to the original invitations. The main purpose of stabilisation is to even out the market in the primary distribution period so that it reflects the real value of the securities and not speculative dealings. See para 8–22.

In both the United Kingdom and the United States, there are specific exemptions for stabilisation of some complexity. The EC Directive contemplates an exemption.

Territoriality

19-26 A major problem for the control of insider dealing is the territorial scope of the prohibition. If the prohibition is strictly territorial it is a simple matter for the insider to trade from abroad or on a foreign stock exchange – through a dummy company if necessary.

As regards the UK position, the CJA applies (in the case of dealing) where the individual was in the United Kingdom when he did an act constituting or forming part of the offence or where the regulated market or professional intermediary is in the UK. In the case of the offences of disclosing inside information, or encouraging insider dealing, the offence is committed if the individual or the recipient was in the United Kingdom when the disclosure or encouragement took place.

The US Rule 10b–5 applies where the fraud is achieved "by the use of any means or instrumentality of interstate commerce, or of the mails or of any facility of any national securities exchange". Insider dealing abroad may be subject to US jurisdiction if the fraud has an impact on the US securities markets (the "effects" doctrine).

> In *Schoenbaum v Firstbrook*, 405 F 2d 200, modified en banc, 405 F 2d 215 (2d Cir 1968), cert denied 295 US 906 (1969), the American plaintiff was a minority shareholder of a Canadian corporation Banff whose stock was traded on an American stock exchange. He alleged that a Canadian subscriber of Banff shares had conspired with the directors of Banff and used undisclosed inside information to acquire an issue of Banff's securities at a price substantially lower than their true value. In the result he alleged that the value of his holdings was diluted. All the transactions took place in Canada. *Held*: there had been a fraud upon a corporation which had the effect of depriving it of fair compensation for the issue of its stock. This impaired the value of American investments and had a sufficiently serious effect upon United States commerce to warrant assertion of subject-matter jurisdiction for the protection of American investors.

Other exemptions

19-27 The CJA exempts market-makers in certain cases and also has exemptions so as not inadvertently to catch the activities of investment banks advising on take-overs or underwriting securities. Underwriting new securities is generally exempt in the United Kingdom because the securities are not then actually admitted to dealing on a regulated market.

CHAPTER 20

SECURITIES REGULATION: EXTRATERRITORIAL SCOPE

Internationalisation of securities markets

The securities markets are international and investments issued in one country can come to rest practically anywhere else in the world. But securities law is not international with the result that there is bound to be some collision between legal systems.

Some of the chief points of abrasion are:

- unlawful marketing of securities in a regulated state, such as the despatch from one state of an unregistered prospectus into a regulated state: para 16–15 *et seq*;

- the ability of a regulating state to apply its disclosure and misrepresentation rules to foreign issuers and underwriters;

- licensing requirements for foreign dealers and investment advisers who do business (e.g. on the telephone) in regulated states;

- the control of manipulative or fraudulent practices by foreign dealers, such as insider dealing or market rigging;

- margin requirements, i.e. the amount of credit which can be given on the purchase of a security;

- requirements for the appointment of a trustee or bondholders' representative to look after the interests of bondholders located in a regulated state: para 10–7.

There is nothing new about the application of domestic laws to foreign transactions in the economic field. Anti-trust laws, exchange control regulations and economic sanctions are cases in point. The problem with the territorial approach to securities regulation is that, like money, securities know no boundaries and that activities in these intangible assets are carried out by electronic messages sent from anywhere and flashed up on a screen anywhere so that attempts to domesticate them and for states to regulate domestic transactions are bound to present difficulties.

20–1

Territorial scope of criminal statutes

20–2 Each state has power to legislate for the whole world if it wishes to, although enforcement outside the territorial domain will be limited by practical considerations. The first step therefore is to examine whether the statute has express extraterritorial effect, e.g. whether it applies by its terms to conduct abroad or to foreigners. If it does so, then plainly the courts of the regulating state must apply the statute.

Some statutes are specific: thus s 57 of the British Financial Services Act 1986 states expressly that the prohibition on the issue of non-complying investment advertisements applies only where the issue is in the United Kingdom and s 3 states that it is the carrying on of an investment business "in the United Kingdom" which is prohibited without authorisation. But the activities required to carry on business in the UK are minimal so that there have to be carve-outs for legitimate foreign activities.

The Federal securities legislation in the United States generally applies where there is a direct or indirect use of the United States mails or instruments of transportation or communication in interstate commerce. See s 2(7) of the Securities Act of 1933, s 3(a)(17) of the Securities Exchange Act of 1934, s 303(1) of the Trust Indenture Act of 1939, s 2(a)(18) of the Investment Company Act of 1940 and s 202(a)(10) of the Investment Advisers Act of 1940. In each case commerce between any foreign country and the United States is included in the definition of interstate commerce. The definition includes use of the US mails, telephone and telex.

Section 30(b) of the 1934 Act states that, except for evasive transactions, the Act and regulations thereunder do not apply to any person "insofar as he transacts a business in securities without the jurisdiction of the United States", but this exclusion has been emasculated by the courts to vanishing point.

If the statute is silent on territoriality, then the courts apply their own views (which differ) of international law on prescriptive jurisdiction.

Enforcement of criminal statutes

20–3 If a prescriptive statute has extraterritorial effect, the ability of the regulating state to enforce its laws depends on the type of sanction, e.g. whether (a) criminal prosecution, (b) official investigation, (c) administrative process such as revocation of a dealing licence or freezing of the exercise of rights on securities, or (d) official injunctions. Enforcement may depend upon whether the state can get hold of the delinquent by extradition or otherwise. It is a universal rule that no court will enforce the penal provisions on a foreign state so it is generally impossible for a prosecuting authority of one state to bring the case in a foreign state or to enforce a conviction there.

The United States has signed Memoranda of Understanding with a number of foreign states and foreign securities authorities covering such matters as insider trading and the exchange of information. There are MOUs with Brazil, Canada, France, Japan, Mexico, the Netherlands and the United Kingdom. There is much informal cooperation between regulators.

Jurisdiction over civil wrongs

In the case of civil wrongs giving rise to a private remedy, the plaintiff must first establish that the court has adjudicatory jurisdiction over the defendant. The adjudicatory jurisdiction of various states is discussed elsewhere in this series of works on financial law and includes (a) submission or appearance in the action by the defendant (most states), (b) presence of defendant within the state or the carrying on of business by the defendant in the forum state (most jurisdictions), (c) location of assets within the forum state (Germany, Austria, Denmark, Japan, Scotland), (d) nationality of the plaintiff in the forum state (France and Luxembourg), (e) residence of the plaintiff within the forum state (Belgium, the Netherlands and Italy in some circumstances), (f) in contract and tort matters, the establishment of the prescribed nexus between the activity complained of and the forum state.

The position is affected by multilateral jurisdiction conventions, such as that between European Community and European Free Trade Association states (which essentially provide that a defendant domiciled in an EC or EFTA state must be sued in that state).

In addition to personal jurisdiction over the defendant, the United States courts also require subject-matter jurisdiction. This means that the plaintiff's claim must be of a type which the US court can adjudicate and, in securities matters, depends largely on whether the statute applies to the conduct in question. In other states there is often no requirement for subject-matter jurisdiction as such, but the result is often the same.

Principles of prescriptive jurisdiction

The generally accepted international rules defining the ambit of a state's ability to control criminal conduct are its *prescriptive jurisdiction*. The main principles are summarised below. For "poison" read, say, unregistered prospectus, fraudulent prospectus, non-complying prospectus, unauthorised road show, unlicensed dealing or sale of a security to a resident, market rigging or insider trading.

1. **Objective territorial principle** A person manufactures poison in an anti-

poison state and Z in the anti-poison state drinks it. The anti-poison state can punish the manufacturer. The offence and its impact took place entirely within the territory of the anti-poison state: see *The Lotus* [1927] PCIJ, Series A, No 9.

20–6 2. **Subjective territorial principle** A person manufactures poison in an anti-poison state and sends it into a neutral state where a victim drinks it. The anti-poison state can punish the manufacturer. The territory of the anti-poison state should not be used as a base for peddling poison to foreigners.

In *R v Markus* [1974] 3 All ER 705: an individual director of a UK company organised sales amongst German investors of units in a Panama unit trust. The brochure about the unit trust contained false and fraudulent information. The distribution of the brochure took place exclusively in Germany, but each individual investor was asked to send an application form to London and the applications were all processed and dealt with in London. *Held*: the points of contact and activities within the United Kingdom were an essential link in the fraudulent scheme. Markus was convicted for fraud under the then securities anti-fraud statute.

The principle is well established by other cases outside securities law.

In *R v Hornett* [1975] RTR 256, the accused was convicted where documents were forged and uttered in the United Kingdom although with intent to defraud persons abroad. See also *R v Stoddart* (1909) 25 TLR 612 (letters containing false inducements sent abroad but posted in England).

In *Gold Star Publications Ltd v DPP* [1981] 2 All ER 257, HL, obscene magazines were produced in the United Kingdom entirely for export overseas. *Held*: even though their holding might amount to moral imperialism, the UK was not to be used as a source of a flourishing trade in pornography. See also *Treacy v DPP* [1971] 1 All ER 10, HL.

US law adopts similar principles.

In *IIT v Vencap Ltd*, 519 F 2d 1001 (2d Cir 1975) on remand 411 F Supp 1094 (SDNY 1975), the court remarked: "We do not think Congress intended to allow the United States to be used as a base for manufacturing fraudulent security devices for export even when these are peddled only to foreigners."

20–7 3. **Protective principle** A person manufactures poison in a neutral state and sends it into an anti-poison state intending his victim will drink it. The anti-poison state can punish the manufacturer if it can get hold of him. The same principle might apply if the manufacturer does not send the poison into the anti-poison state but some fumes escape into the anti-poison state and excite the victim there. This is known as the "effects" doctrine. The "effects" doctrine becomes increasingly controversial where, for example, the only effect of the poison in the anti-poison state is minimal.

In *R v Baxter* [1971] 2 All ER 359, CA, the accused sent letters from Northern Ireland to pools promoters in England falsely claiming he had won. *Held*: although the message was sent from abroad, it was intended to cause deception within the jurisdiction.

In *R v Oliphant* [1905] KB 67, Lord Alverstone CJ said, "I am unable to draw any distinction between sending information by post or by telephone and giving the same information by direct personal communication in London." Hence, the despatch of fraudulent offering material from abroad into England is a fraud in England because the deception is practised in England.

An extension of the doctrine is that the counselling and procuring of an offence which is committed in England is punishable even though the counselling and procuring take place entirely abroad.

In *R v Millar* [1970] 1 All ER 577, CA, a lorry firm manager in Scotland allowed a driver to take a truck into England with dangerously defective tyres. A tyre burst and third parties in another vehicle were killed. The Scottish manager was convicted of counselling and procuring the offence since he set in motion the agencies by which the crime was committed.

For the United States see, e.g. the insider trading case of *Schoenbaum v Firstbrook* discussed at para 19–26. See also the US cases at para 17–43 regarding the application of US fraud rules to frauds committed abroad.

4. **Nationality principle** A person manufactures poison in a neutral state and poisons a victim who drinks it. The victim is a national of an anti-poison state. The anti-poison state can in some circumstances punish the manufacturer.

5. **Universality principle** A person manufactures poison in a neutral state and poisons a victim in the neutral state. Nobody in an anti-poison state is affected. The anti-poison state can punish the manufacturer where the crime is so dangerous to the international order that it does not matter who punishes the manufacturer so long as he is punished. Examples are international terrorism, hijacking and piracy.

Comment on extraterritorial application

20–9 No sensible person objects to the extraterritorial reach of the law in the case of fraud, lies or cheating in the securities field since these are crimes in all civilised states. Nor does anybody object to a licensing system and codes of conduct for investment businesses operating from a permanent establishment in a particular country, if not excessive. The main problems with extraterritoriality arise where the activity is perfectly legitimate and honest but is caught by a pure technicality or a fine-trigger statute applying if there are only minimal local contacts, or by one state's views of unacceptable behaviour which are purely theocratic and are not shared by other states, or by a desire of the legislating state, not to protect its citizens from a foreign poison, but to seal off its market from foreign fund-raising, i.e. where securities regulation is used as a restrictive practice or counter-measure against tax avoidance. In the United States, there is the additional feature of oppressive lititgation by reason of the factors mentioned at para 17–37, including treble damages.

CHAPTER 21

SECURITIES REGULATION: US SELLING RESTRICTIONS IN EUROBOND ISSUES

Introduction

This chapter is highly technical and is intended for practitioners. It sets out a brief explanation of US securities and tax laws affecting primary offerings of debt and equity outside the US and the various selling restrictions to which those laws give rise. Although equity offerings are occasionally mentioned for the sake of comparison, the discussion below is primarily concerned with issues of debt in the euromarkets by non-US issuers. 21–1

Regulation S

Generally Regulation S was published in 1992 by the SEC which provides guidelines under which offerings of securities can be made outside the United States without registration under the Securities Act of 1933 (the "Securities Act"). The Regulation was intended to clarify, simplify and liberalise the position that existed prior to the adoption of the Regulation. 21–2

Regulation S is a "safe harbour" provision. In other words, if the requirements of Regulation S are satisfied, the participants in the offering, including the issuer, will be protected from liability under the US securities laws in the event those laws are in fact inadvertently breached in connection with the offering. If those laws are deliberately breached, the safe harbour should also protect the participants in the offering who do not participate in and are unaware of the breach, unless the safe harbour is itself lost by that breach.

Fundamental requirements The two fundamental requirements of Regulation S are that the offering must be an "offshore transaction" and that there must be no "directed selling efforts" in connection with the offering in the United States. There may be additional restrictions, depending on the category of the offering. If any one participant in an offering engages in directed selling efforts in the US, the benefit of the safe harbour is lost for all participants. This does not mean that liability will be imposed upon all participants, but only that the potential liability of each participant is greater.

21–3 **Three categories** Regulation S divides offerings of debt (and equity) securities into three categories, Category 1, Category 2 and Category 3.

If Category 1 applies, there are no restrictions other than the two fundamental restrictions mentioned above.

If Category 2 applies, "offering restrictions" apply, namely:

1. a restricted period of 40 days from the later to occur of the closing date and the commencement of the offering;

2. a requirement that the offer documents include certain prescribed selling restrictions and warnings; and

3. a requirement that participants in the offering (those receiving a selling concession or fee in connection with the distribution of the offering), other than those who have already signed the subscription agreement for the bonds (or, e.g. a selling group agreement containing the US selling restrictions), receive a confirmation in a prescribed form to the effect that US selling restrictions do apply.

If Category 3 applies, the Category 2 restrictions apply as well as certain additional restrictions. Only Categories 1 and 2 are relevant for non-US issuers of debt. In certain cases non-US issuers which are US-owned are treated as US issuers (to whom the more restrictive categories apply). This summary deals exclusively with non-US issuers.

21–4 **SUSMI** A non-US non-governmental issuer is a Category 1 issuer in respect of its debt for purposes of Regulation S if the issuer reasonably believes that there is no substantial US market interest ("SUSMI") in respect of its debt securities. There will be SUSMI in respect of its debt securities only if **all three** of the following statements are true:

1. its debt is held by 300 or more US persons;

2. more than US$1 billion of principal of its aggregate outstanding debt is held by US persons; **and**

3. more than 20 per cent of its aggregate outstanding debt is held by US persons.

For the purposes of these tests: "debt" includes non-participating non-convertible preferred stock and asset-backed securities but excludes US commercial paper and other securities issued under the exemption in s 3(a)(3) of the Securities Act; and "US person" means, essentially, US residents and US-organised entities.

If **any one** of the three statements above is **not** true, then there is no SUSMI in respect of the issuer's debt securities, and it is therefore a Category 1 issuer. If all three are true, there is SUSMI, and it is a Category 2 issuer. A common practice is to adopt Category 2 selling restrictions in the offer documents, particularly where there is any doubt as to whether or not SUSMI exists.

Equity offerings The position regarding offerings of **equity** securities by non-US issuers is more complicated and any one of the three categories may apply. Also there is a different test for SUSMI with respect to equity securities of an issuer. It is possible for an issuer to fall into different categories for debt and equity.

Governmental issuers A non-US **governmental** issuer is always a Category 1 issuer for purposes of its debt (and equity) offerings, and therefore in such cases no representation is required from the issuer that there is no SUSMI with respect to the relevant securities. A "governmental issuer" includes an issuer issuing under the guarantee of a sovereign.

Guaranteed issues For guaranteed issues (other than issues guaranteed by a sovereign), if the guarantor is the parent of the issuer, the status of the guarantor determines the applicable category for the purposes of Regulation S. If the guarantor is not the parent of the issuer (again, excluding sovereign guarantors), then the relevant category is the most restrictive category applicable to either the issuer or the guarantor. For example, assuming that, considered separately, the issuer would be a Category 2 issuer and the guarantor a Category 1 issuer, if the guarantor is the parent of the issuer, Category 1 selling restrictions will apply. If the guarantor is not the parent, Category 2 restrictions will apply.

Allotment securities "Allotment securities" are permanently restricted: in other words, they may never be sold directly to US persons even after the expiry of the 40-day restricted period applicable to Category 2 (and Category 3) issues. An "allotment security" is a security which a manager (or other distributor) took on to its books in connection with the offering and which it has not yet sold. Such securities must be sold into the market in order to "season", that is, for the US restrictions to become no longer applicable. Sales by a manager to an affiliate or to another manager or one of its affiliates will not count for purposes of "seasoning". The securities will remain allotment securities, subject to the prohibition on sales to US persons, until such time as they are genuinely sold into the market.

Section 4(3) of the Securities Act

21–6   An additional provision of the Securities Act might affect the activities of euromarket dealers in connection with a eurobond offering, whether or not they are in the management group or any underwriting or selling group. Section 4(3) of the Securities Act provides that no dealer can sell securities into the United States until after the period ending 40 days after the closing date of the offering. Unlike the US selling restrictions described in this chapter, s 4(3) also affects secondary market transactions with US persons.

TEFRA C and D

21–7   **Generally** The Tax Equity and Fiscal Responsibility Act of 1982 ("TEFRA") was introduced, inter alia, to limit tax evasion by US taxpayers. One of the principal purposes of the legislation is to discourage the issue of bearer debt securities in the United States and to encourage US investors to hold debt securities in registered form. The legislation (as supplemented by regulations promulgated by the US Internal Revenue Service (the "IRS")) may be enforced by the IRS by the imposition of sanctions on the issuer or the holder of bearer bonds or both.

There are no TEFRA selling restrictions required in respect of registered debt. There is also an exemption for debt securities with a maturity of 365 days or less – primarily, euro-commercial paper. The TEFRA requirements do not apply to genuine secondary market sales to US persons.

TEFRA requires that:

1. the issuer of bearer bonds must ensure that "reasonable arrangements" are in place to prevent bearer debt securities being sold to US persons in connection with the primary offering;

2. a specified legend be carried on the debt securities (there is an exemption, however, if TEFRA C, as described below, applies); and

3. there must be no payment of interest in the United States.

"TEFRA C" and "TEFRA D" are **alternative** sets of rules published by the IRS, compliance with which ensures that an issue of bearer debt satisfies the "reasonable arrangements" requirement. They are sometimes respectively referred to as the "C Rules" and the "D Rules".

TEFRA C applies to an issue if the securities are issued only outside the   21–8
United States and its possessions by an issuer that does not significantly
engage in **interstate commerce** with respect to the issue either directly or
through an agent, a manager, an underwriter or a member of a selling
group.

The term "interstate commerce" is defined (at some length) in the TEFRA
rules and means essentially any contacts with the US before or after closing
in connection with the **primary** offering of an issue, including negotiation or
any other communication between participants in the issue while one of
such participants is in the US. Genuine secondary market sales to US investors following the primary offering do not constitute "interstate commerce"
(although such sales may violate other US selling restrictions applicable to
the securities or may be subject to other provisions of US law).

The involvement in an issue of a manager which is a non-US subsidiary of
a US entity or a non-US branch of a bank does **not** constitute "interstate
commerce" provided there are no contacts with the US parent or head office
(or other US branches), as the case may be, in respect of the issue.

TEFRA C should only be used if all parties are satisfied that there is no
intention to place any of the securities in the US and that it is unlikely that
there will be any interest in the US in such securities. It can never be used if a
Rule 144A or traditional private placement in the US is being made.

TEFRA D applies to most straightforward issues of bearer debt in the euro-   21–9
markets. TEFRA D provides for a restricted period of 40 days from the closing date of the issue and requires that certification of non-US beneficial
ownership be obtained before definitive securities can be issued or interest
paid to securityholders. It also requires that securities be made available to
investors in definitive form within a reasonable period following the end of
the restricted period. Some side effects of this are that (a) a fully permanent
global security cannot be used for an issue and (b) even issues using a semi-permanent global security should use a separate temporary global security
during the restricted period, to be replaced at the end of the restricted period
by the semi-permanent global security.

The main reason for preferring TEFRA D to TEFRA C (despite the
restricted period and certification requirements of the former) is that
TEFRA D provides a "safe harbour" for the issuer whereas TEFRA C does
not. In other words, if TEFRA D is complied with in connection with an
offering, inadvertent sales to US persons will not result in the imposition of
issuer sanctions. TEFRA C provides no such protection. TEFRA D selling
restrictions are in general not difficult to comply with and the euromarkets
have for some time been accustomed to similar restrictions.

The tax law treatment does not follow the securities law treatment. For
example, a TEFRA D 40-day restricted period will apply (assuming the

relevant securities are issued in bearer form) even where the issuer is Category 1 (and where, therefore, there is no Regulation S restricted period). The definition of "US person" under TEFRA D is much broader than that under Regulation S.

Rule 144A

21–10   Apart from registration of an offering under the Securities Act (an expensive and cumbersome process), there are only two means by which euro-securities can be sold to US persons in connection with a primary offering. One is a traditional US private placement, normally effected under the SEC's Regulation D. The other, introduced in 1991, is Rule 144A, which is intended to be simpler, quicker and less expensive than a traditional private placement.

Rule 144A is a rule published by the SEC under the Securities Act which exempts from the registration requirements of the Securities Act private placements of eligible securities in the United States with large US institutional investors who are "qualified institutional buyers" ("QIBs") under the Rule. Any person other than the issuer may rely on Rule 144A.

The basic procedural requirements are relatively few:

1. The securities must satisfy the eligibility requirement of Rule 144A.

2. The seller must sell only to QIBs and only through a US-registered broker-dealer.

3. The seller must notify the QIB purchaser at the time of the sale that the sale is being made on the basis of Rule 144A.

4. There must be no "general solicitation or advertising" of the offering in the United States.

In essence, securities are eligible for placement under Rule 144A if (a) they are not fungible with securities traded on a US investment exchange or on NASDAQ and (b) the issuer of the securities satisfies the information requirements of Rule 144A. The basic information requirement is that the issuer provide "reasonably current" financial information to each US holder of the relevant securities on demand. There are exemptions from this requirement for sovereign issuers and for issuers who have registered under the SEC's Rule 12g3–2(b), under which a non-US issuer provides to the SEC (in English) only what it makes publicly available in its home jurisdiction.

21–11   In connection with a Rule 144A placement, care is required on two points in particular: (a) whether the issuer is an investment company under the US Investment Company Act of 1940 ("1940 Act"), and (b) the appropriate level of due diligence and disclosure which must be carried out in connection with the US placement.

Regarding (a), if an issuer falls within the wide definition of "investment company" in the 1940 Act and is not registered under the 1940 Act, or does not fall within an applicable exemption, then a sale contract to a US person is subject to rescission by the US person, effectively an unlimited put at the original purchase price to the original seller.

Regarding (b), normally any additional disclosure required for the US investors is (if sufficient information is not already included in the original offering circular) included in a "wrap-around" or supplement to the offering circular prepared specifically for the US placement.

One also needs to consider the Rule 10(b)(6) and 10(b)(7) passive market-making restrictions, although these raise problems primarily for equity rather than debt offerings.

Because of TEFRA, a registered option should be included in a euro-offering of debt where it is contemplated that a portion of the offering will be sold under Rule 144A to US persons. Certain additional selling restrictions may be advisable, particularly if the securities are index or commodity-linked.

The foregoing relates only to US federal (national) law. One may also need to consider the requirements of the State securities (or "blue sky") laws in each state of the United States in which placements will be made or in which prospective QIBs are resident.

Standard form selling restrictions

Standard form US selling restrictions have been developed by practitioners. The eurobond offer documents which require US selling restrictions (or other US-related language) are the invitation telex, the offering circular, the subscription agreement, the section in the trust deed or fiscal agency agreement dealing with exchange for definitive securities and the form of global security (which normally has attached as exhibits the standard form certificates as to non-US beneficial ownership). In addition, the language of the "Payments" section of the terms and conditions of a eurodollar issue is affected by the requirements of TEFRA if the securities are in bearer form.

PART IV

BANK REGULATION

CHAPTER 22

BANK REGULATION: GENERAL PRINCIPLES

Introduction

This chapter is not primarily intended to be a guide on how to set up a bank or to obtain authorisation for an institution seeking to take public moneys. It is intended to give a view of what supervision of authorised institutions is about and what regulatory considerations banks (and, indeed, their customers) need to bear in mind in carrying out transactions. The review is purely orientational.

22–1

Credit businesses

The core business of banks is the taking of deposits from the public in the form of current (or chequeing accounts) or savings accounts and making loans. This business also includes the issue of credit cards, money collections and transmissions, foreign exchange and the issue of guarantees.

22–2

Specialist activities include trade finance (letters of credit, acceptance credits), home mortgage loans, development finance, and sectoral credits, e.g. ship or aircraft finance.

Related credit businesses include:

– factoring and discounting of commercial receivables (trade finance);

– consumer credit;

– equipment leasing;

– investment banking, mainly comprising the arranging and underwriting of issues of debt and equity securities;

– advisory work, e.g. corporate finance advice and investment advice;

– credit reference and data processing;

– trust business, such as will trusts, fiduciary deposits, trusteeship of debt issues, management of portfolios of securities, management of collective investment schemes, and custodianship of securities;

- futures, options and swaps business.

Some or all of these businesses may be carried on through separate subsidiaries.

Authorisation of banks

22–3 The usual prohibition is on the receipt of money from the public in order to finance loans or other credits. In other words, the taking of deposits from the public to finance a banking business requires authorisation, as opposed to carrying on a banking business, whatever that may be. The regulation does not prohibit lending money provided that the loans are not funded by public deposits.

There are many formulations circling round this core concept and, because the prohibition often catches any moneys which are repayable debt and which are used to finance a business, there commonly need to be express exceptions, e.g. for tap issues of debt instruments, advance payments for goods, services or the like (e.g. travel agent and consumer goods deposits), security deposits (landlord's deposits and margin collateral posted to exchanges) and intra-group loans. All these exemptions are available under the UK Banking Act 1987, though often subject to conditions.

Home mortgage companies (US thrifts, UK building societies, European Continental cooperatives) are often subject to a separate authorisation and regulatory system.

The territorial scope is commonly the acceptance of deposits within the regulated territory, regardless of where the banking business is carried on and regardless of where the public depositor is located. Fine distinctions may be made as to whether a deposit credited to an account abroad for the account of the local institution is or is not the acceptance of deposits locally.

The regulation will also typically prohibit the use of the word "bank" or any of its derivatives in a company's name, or representations that the company is carrying on a banking business. Local representative offices of foreign banks may be permitted to use the home name, provided it is made clear that they are only a representative office and not entitled to take deposits.

Finally, the regime will control advertisements or solicitations inviting the public to deposit money.

This system is accompanied by provisions for the licensing of banks, the revocation or restriction of licences, and the establishment of local branches of foreign banks (accompanied often by requirements for the deposit locally of minimum assets to protect local creditors).

Some regimes control the establishment of branches and subsidiaries by authorised banks. In the United States the financial power of banks is restricted by a prohibition on inter-state branch banking under the McFadden Act of 1927, but this may have led to the weakening of banks and the proliferation of small banks (as a result of which there can be thousands of current bank insolvencies there). This system has now been liberalised in some US States. By contrast Europe encourages European-wide banking by virtue of the Second Banking Directive which confers a single European-wide "passport" upon institutions located in and authorised by the competent authorities in a member state as regards the defined types of credit activities.

Restrictions on non-banking activities

Jurisdictions differ greatly as to whether they prevent banks from carrying on businesses which are not core banking and, if they do, how they achieve the control.

Some countries permit universal banks, especially in Continental Europe, but in practice the supervisors may discourage expansion into other activities, especially insurance. In the United States, the Banking Act of 1933 – popularly known as the Glass-Steagall Act – separates commercial banking from investment banking, and there is a similar segmentation in Canada and Japan. The typical prohibition is against underwriting or dealing in securities, with exemptions for temporary investments or investment in not more than a small percentage minority of the listed securities of a particular enterprise, for holdings of securities in the case of realisations (such as the enforcement of share pledges), and for custodian or executorship holdings.

The objective of this separation is variously to prevent conflicts of interest, to reduce the risk that banks will embark on businesses with which they are not familiar and invest depositors' money in risky equity investments instead of "safe" loans, to facilitate financial supervision by the regulators (e.g. by observing the boundary between banking and insurance regulators), and – historically in the US – to limit what was feared to be excessive financial power of banks. To some extent these restrictions are cultural and their precise scope may be controversial, with the result that the detail of the regulation is in constant flux according to the mood of the day.

Financial supervision generally

Banks are supervised to a greater or lesser extent throughout the world, although those in the major financial centres, the EU and larger countries tend to be subject to broadly the same type and degree of regulation in light of the increasing convergence of standards of supervisors. Partly this arises from the desire of the supervisors not to lose a strategic advantage (e.g. a lower capital weighting in one jurisdiction would make it cheaper for a bank to make a loan out of that jurisdiction which gives it a competitive advantage) and partly from the awareness that large-scale financial crises, such as frauds by an international bank, seldom can be contained within one jurisdiction.

The effect is that the financial regulation of banks has achieved a remarkable degree of harmonisation which does great credit to the good sense of central banks and other bank regulators and shows what can be done when the obvious international interdependence and mutuality of interest in regulatory matters is acted upon.

The regulators around the world tend to fall into two categories: (1) central banks, and (2) specialist supervisors. In Germany, the Bundesbank is both central bank and supervisor, as is the Bank of England. However, in the United States, there is a dual banking system with both state and federal banks, regulated by a number of banking supervisors (one for each state) and by the Federal Deposit Insurance Corporation which has overall responsibility for US banks and the protection of depositors' funds. National banks under the National Bank Act of 1863 and organised under federal law are supervised by the Office of the Comptroller of the Currency, the FDIC and the equivalent of a central bank in the US, namely the Federal Reserve System. In practice, US banking regulation is largely federalised, but there is much overlap, leading to complaints that more regulation does not lead to better regulation.

The rationale for supervising banks should always be borne in mind when considering what regulations apply and what the regulator is seeking to achieve. In the United Kingdom, banks are primarily supervised in order to protect the position of depositors with those institutions, i.e. to protect them against a bank insolvency. Other reasons for supervision globally are the stability of internal and international markets and matters related to exchange control.

Methods of regulation of banks differ dependent on the jurisdiction. All commercial jurisdictions now have some sort of statutory framework behind their regulation and many, particularly the Commonwealth countries, are based on the UK's banking legislation. But, whereas some jurisdictions back these primary statutes up with government-made regulations, others, such as the UK, use policy statements to indicate how the regulators interpret the relevant legislation. A good example of the difference between the policy approach and the statutory approach is to be found in the discouragement of banking and insurance company tie-ups. In the United Kingdom this is discouraged by the Bank of England as a policy matter, whereas, in the United States, it is statutorily prohibited.

Main heads of financial supervision

A regulator considering whether a bank continues to meet the authorisation criteria has regard to the following: 22–6

1. Capital adequacy (including own funds)

2. Large exposures

3. Liquidity

4. Systems and controls

5. Ownership and management (including controllers, directors and managers)

6. Foreign exchange risk.

Central banks and other regulators are interested in the measure of risk each institution is undertaking and the amount of capital it holds to absorb losses which can arise from the taking of those risks. Essentially, an institution's capital is there to absorb losses and therefore cushion depositors against those losses. The above measures help to quantify the risks involved in banking transactions and thus to try to ensure that risks are kept within tolerable limits. In some cases a bank's specialisation permits it to operate more risky ratios or against more favourable measures than other institutions which are less experienced or expert in the particular market concerned. This should be borne in mind when dealing with regulators since, by employing the right people and putting the correct systems and controls in place, a competitive advantage may be obtained by virtue of being permitted to operate a lower capital adequacy ratio.

What can never be adequately guarded against through prudential ratios is the problem of fraud which comes from within as well as outside banks. In order to try to minimise this risk regulators thus monitor the systems and controls of banks either by the use of reports by professionals such as accountants (e.g. the reporting accountants regime in the UK) or by teams of inspectors employed by the particular regulator in question (e.g. the FDIC).

Other protections for depositors may include restrictions on the grant of security by banks and depositor compensation funds, as well as special winding-up or rehabilitation procedures in which the regulators may be able to take the initiative or even, as in the United States, take over the management of the bank.

The auditors of a bank must often be specially qualified and have expanded monitoring duties, including the right to report direct to the regulator if anything should be amiss – whistle-blowing.

Capital adequacy

Minimum capital

22-7 In order to be a credit institution and thus accept deposits from members of the public and use those funds for the purpose of making loans, all institutions in the European Union must maintain paid up share capital of ECU 5 million. If they fall below this level then this is one of the grounds on which their authorisation may be revoked. For the great majority of existing banks this is not a hindrance, but the adoption of this policy has sent a clear message that the small deposit-takers which used to exist (particularly in the UK) are no longer to be encouraged to accept deposits from members of the public. Minimum capital requirements apply to banks in most other developed jurisdictions.

Basle Agreement

22-8 Following discussions amongst the major banking regulators at Basle, a set of guidelines for the measurement of a bank's own funds (or capital) and its solvency ratio (or capital adequacy ratio) were drawn up in 1988. These measures were enshrined in the EC Own Funds Directive and the Solvency Ratio Directives. These Directives have now been legislated upon by all member states and so form part of the law of each member state, thus causing banks to operate on a more or less level playing field with respect to the minimum ratio of weighted risk assets to capital which they must maintain.

The rationale behind capital adequacy is that all of a bank's assets receive a risk weighting dependent on the category into which they fall. This weighting is then multiplied by the size of the asset. Once all of the assets have been given a weighting and multiplied by that weighting then the total is measured as a percentage of the "own funds" of the institution, broadly its share capital plus disclosed reserves plus some types of subordinated debt as set out in the next chapter. A bank's own funds can be either in the form of Tier One or Tier Two capital. Tier One is broadly described as permanent while Tier Two is semi-permanent, being reduced in value over time or less certain. A bank can only count the same amount of its Tier Two capital as it has Tier One capital (although banks are not precluded from carrying greater amounts).

Under the Basle convergence principles, as reflected in the Solvency Ratio Directive, the minimum ratio which an institution is permitted to maintain is eight per cent. For example, bank loans to OECD central banks have a zero risk weight. So no capital is required. Residential mortgages have a 50 per cent risk weight, so these are valued at half their nominal amount: in effect the bank must have $4 capital for every $100 lent. Ordinary unsecured loans to the private sector have a 100 per cent risk weight, so that for every corporate loan the bank must have $8 capital for every $100 lent. The effect is that the loans to the private sector are more expensive for the bank than home mortgage loans.

For off-balance sheet assets there are credit conversion factors as set out in the next chapter. The nominal principal amount of the asset is multiplied by a credit conversion factor, the resulting amounts then being weighted accordingly to the nature of the counterparty. An example would be a performance bond (50 per cent credit risk conversion factor) for a principal amount of $100 to a corporate client (100 per cent weighting). The amount of capital required would be $4 as the credit conversion factor for the off-balance sheet performance bond is 50 per cent and the counterparty weighting is 100 per cent, i.e. $\frac{50}{100} \times \frac{100}{100} \times \frac{8}{100}$

Foreign exchange and interest rate related contingencies are also weighted under the Basle system to ensure that all risks which a bank undertakes are taken into account in the capital adequacy measurement. As there is only the risk of replacing the cash flow by entering into another transaction if the counterparty defaults, the method of measurement is different to that mentioned above. For an explanation of the calculation method, see the next chapter. The Basle Committee permits bilateral netting of transactions to allow banks to calculate their risk asset ratio on a net exposure basis where certain specific conditions are met. The requirements for this are also set out in the next chapter.

This does not mean that there is a level playing field for all institutions as national supervisors may permit only the largest or most expert banks to operate at this low minimum ratio of 8 per cent. Other banks involved in riskier business or which are less expert may be asked to maintain a higher ratio. Usually national legislation provides that an institution must operate its business in a prudent manner which then permits the setting of a level below which the bank should not fall. In many countries different levels are adopted to reflect the point at which an institution should attempt to maintain its business and a point at which the supervisor will determine that there has been a breach of the required level and when action might become appropriate. These are sometimes referred to as the trigger and target ratios. A bank should attempt to remain at or above its target ratio, but should never fall below its trigger ratio. To fall in between would normally involve increased monitoring by the supervisor coupled with a warning as to the lack of systems which allowed the breach. In this regard allowances are made for banks which do not operate on-line systems for knowing what credits have been entered into by its branches, but if this is the case then the regulator will wish to know that limits are put in place for each branch or manager concerned so that matters can never get out of hand.

The weightings themselves are worked out by supervisors acting together in assessing the various risks involved. These risks include the insolvency of borrowers from the bank. There might also be currency conversion risks, and settlement risks on foreign exchange transactions. Apart from the national discretions permitted to allow for differences in markets, all weightings are the same on a global basis for the majority of supervisors which work on the Basle method of calculation as set out in the next chapter. This ensures that loan costs for banks (which will usually be passed on to larger borrowers) are broadly kept on a level playing field, thus ensuring there is no competitive advantage to booking a loan in one place rather than another. However, it should be borne in mind that there may be other costs outside the capital adequacy system which will be incurred by booking the loan in one jurisdiction rather than another. In the United Kingdom, for example, the Bank of England charges a cost for all loans made in sterling at a particular balance sheet date in order to fund its supervision. Similar costs are charged in the United States.

Different countries permit their institutions to operate at different levels of capital adequacy. In Germany, for instance, all credit institutions are permitted to maintain the minimum eight per cent capital adequacy level, whereas in the United Kingdom, variable rates are set dependent upon the factors mentioned above.

22–9A   As set out above, the Basle agreement was in place before the EC enacted the Solvency Ratio and Own Funds Directives. In a role reversal, EC-based banks are to be subject to a new Capital Adequacy Directive ("CAD") to be brought into force by member states by December 31, 1995. This is to be closely followed by a regime which was under discussion at Basle in early 1995. Both regimes are likely to follow the same guidelines and, indeed, in order to create the traditional level playing field, this is to be expected.

The CAD expands upon the existing capital adequacy framework by introducing the concept of a banking book for on balance sheet loans, etc., and a trading book for off-balance sheet financial instruments.

Under the Basle regime, loans and other on balance sheet products are all measured for capital adequacy purposes by their credit risk. Under the CAD, these instruments remain in what is now to be termed the banking book and continue to be subject to the same evaluation, i.e. an assessment of risk based on who the borrower is.

Under the CAD regime, all instruments which are traded, subject, inter alia, to a de minimis exemption, form part of the trading book and are subject to credit risk *and* market related risk requirements for capital adequacy purposes.

The banking book and the trading book are mutually exclusive. Financial instruments which are generally held to maturity as investments are not considered to be part of the trading book. This is also the case where instruments are purely purchased to hedge exposures on the banking book. The measurement of off balance sheet instruments in the banking book continues to be carried out, as noted above, by the use of credit conversion factors.

The CAD also deals with the specific capital adequacy measurement of repos and reverse repos, foreign currency risk, interest rate position risk, equity position risk and underwriting where these form part of a bank's trading book. Weightings are worked out by taking into account many different market related risk factors including an instrument's maturity.

The CAD also introduces a Tier 3 element of capital which can be used to calculate the Own Funds, or capital base, of a bank. Tiers 1 and 2 remain unchanged and are as set out above. Up to a specific maximum amount, Tier 3 comprises both subordinated debt with a minimum original maturity of over two years and the daily mark-to-market trading book profits. Unlike Tier 2 capital there is no amortisation of Tier 3 capital as it nears maturity, but it is only repayable with the consent of the supervisor concerned.

The CAD introduces a concept of monitoring whereby supervisors can sanction a financial model used to calculate, inter alia, interest rate sensitivity and option pricing. The use of these models, where recognised, generally results in lower capital requirements.

Liquidity

Many banks in the past have failed through not being able to sustain a run on depositors' funds. The basis of banking is that funds are borrowed short term by the bank from, inter alia, public depositors, and then lent long term or medium-term to borrowers from the bank. It is not always possible, nor would it be wise, for banks to call in their term loans ahead of time. Banking is built on confidence and if borrowers found themselves being called upon to repay early they may lose confidence in the bank concerned. Regulators recognise the need for banks to carry out their traditional business while trying to balance this with the need to maintain adequate liquid funds to repay a percentage of short-term deposits with maturing funds or standby facilities from other market lenders. All supervisors thus maintain liquidity standards which banks are required to meet.

When considering a level of adequate liquid or liquifiable funds which a bank should maintain, supervisors assess, amongst other things, the ability of banks to go into the market to borrow wholesale funds. Regulators take into account the fact that it is when banks most need liquidity that they will be perceived as bad risks and the markets will close to them. Therefore, while this is one element in the melting pot when deciding what ratio to set, more emphasis is placed on matching maturities of maturing assets and liabilities and on committed standby facilities. It may be argued that it is particularly difficult to obtain a committed standby facility without the incorporation of a break clause for material adverse change and so such facilities are virtually worthless in a liquidity sense. Where there is such a clause then regulators may not permit them to be taken into account.

Dependent on the make-up of the deposit base and its historical stability, regulators will usually permit banks to hold less than their maturing liabilities in the form of liquid or liquifiable assets. Contingent liabilities will be taken into account, as will standby facilities. The mismatching of these funds is usually measured on the basis of sight to eight days, eight days to one month, one month to three months and so on. The calculation of liabilities to assets will be measured as a percentage and is likely to be around 8 per cent in the first band, 15 per cent in the second and so on. However, this measure varies greatly for the reasons set out above. The bank may be required to deposit a small percentage of its deposit liabilities with the central bank, e.g. 5 per cent of average demand deposits.

Large exposures

22–11   Large exposures are a risk to banks because of the profound effect on their balance sheets if a large exposure becomes non-performing. The first problem for a bank when a large loan becomes non-performing is that there is an interest rate mismatch. The bank is paying interest on the money it borrowed from depositors or in the wholesale markets, but is not recouping that interest from the loan it has made. It is also possible that any scheduled repayments which were due to be made in a foreign currency but which are not made, can lead to the bank having to cover that exposure by going into the market to obtain the relevant currency to settle the other side of its transaction. This point is looked at below in relation to foreign currency exposures: see para 22–13.

Not only will the bank be short of the interest payments, but it is also likely to be short of capital repayments necessitating another trip to the market to cover the shortfall (again with increased costs). Eventually, should the borrower not recover, the bank will be left with a dividend in the liquidation and will have to write off the loss against profits. While a prudent institution will have made provisions, this loss will damage its profitability. Dependent on the size of the exposure, the magnitude of the damage will be increased. Hence regulators seek to control the size of large exposures which a bank may enter into.

In the United Kingdom a bank may not enter into an exposure over 25 per cent of its adjusted capital base (basically calculated in the same way as for its risk asset ratio) unless it has obtained the prior written consent of the Bank of England to do so. A bank must also notify the Bank of England on a regular basis of the exposures it has entered into which are over 10 per cent of its adjusted capital base. The Bank of England then monitors this information in order to ensure that it is aware of where potential problems could lie ahead for the bank concerned. In collating the data the regulator can also see how many of the banks it regulates have loaned money to a particular borrower.

Banks in the United Kingdom which are sophisticated in foreign exchange dealing or market lending are permitted to incur exposures at present in excess of 25 per cent of adjusted capital base without prenotifying the Bank of England. These exposures can only be to a limited list of market counterparties which must be prenotified to, and approved by, the Bank of England. However, with the implementation of the CAD, these exposures incur the "soft limit" capital requirements if they form part of a bank's trading book and carry heavier capital requirements than before: see para 22–11.

It is not only single exposures which are measured by this system. Exposures to groups of companies are aggregated, as are exposures connected to each other, e.g. loans to directors and their companies. It is often the case that a director will have given guarantees in respect of the company of which he is a director and so the several borrowings are very much entwined. Transactions of different types are also aggregated when measuring exposures to persons, e.g. foreign exchange settlement risk for a company will be aggregated to the mortgage loan made to buy a factory as will the loan made to finance an acquisition. In this way the regulator looks at the borrower and connected persons in order to see what effect its liquidation would have on the bank concerned. Should the risk be deemed too great then the bank may be asked to scale down the extent of its exposure, either by selling the loan to another bank or by asking for security for the loan. Regulators seek to control a bank's actions by requiring that each bank set out its policy on large exposures which should be linked to its method of credit assessment and the overall way in which it conducts its business. This policy is then reviewed by the regulator which can then make suggestions for its improvement to attempt to introduce best market practice wherever possible.

Sectoral exposures are also measured and limited to endeavour to spread the risks a bank enters into among different types of borrower, thus lessening the likelihood that a collapse in one economic sector will lead to a collapse in the bank's loan portfolio.

The regulator will also consider asking the reporting accountants used by it or its own inspectors to consider whether the bank can accurately aggregate its large exposures and then report these to the regulator. In this way the regulator ensures that it is obtaining the correct information it needs to assess the position.

Typically also credits to or guarantees for the benefit of affiliates or related entities of insiders are sharply limited, either by express regulation or by administrative guidelines.

22–11B The CAD sets out "soft limits" which can be applied to banks wishing to run positions in instruments held in their trading book in excess of 25 per cent of the capital base of the bank concerned. Should a bank wish to take advantage of a "soft limit" it must set aside additional capital. The additional capital required is incremental, i.e. it rises proportionately to the amount the exposure exceeds 25 per cent of the capital base: thus the larger the exposure, the greater the risk and the more capital required.

Systems and controls

22–12 The systems and controls of a bank must be adequate for it to continue to be authorised. Regulators will examine the degree of sophistication of financial products in which a bank deals and will then expect that bank to have a sophisticated enough system to cope with such transactions. In many cases the regulator will ask for sight of an institution's management letter from its auditors to consider whether systems and controls are adequate. The management reporting structure and the composition of the board of the institution and, in particular, its audit committee (staffed by non-executive directors) will be assessed. Should a regulator be discontented with the systems and controls, then it will ask for improvements to be made and back this up in various ways. In some jurisdictions it is possible to impose conditions as an institution's continued authorisation, whereas in others the only sanction is to remove that authorisation.

Foreign exchange risk

22–13 Regulators measure the open positions of banks against, in most cases, their own base currency. In the United Kingdom this will be sterling and in the United States, dollars. Institutions are limited to operating daily and overnight positions which it is within their expertise and systems to prudently manage. In this way the regulator takes into account the risk that settlement will not occur, that dealers will lose money on a strategy that has gone wrong, or that the size of the exposure may simply be too large for the institution to cover if it encounters trading difficulties.

Foreign exchange risk is also now measured, as are exposures to all off-balance sheet product risks, in a bank's risk asset ratio, but regulators will still consider it directly by reason of the potential risk of sudden and volatile swings in foreign exchange values.

Ownership and management

Persons who are, or who wish to become, directors, controllers or managers of banks will have to be fit and proper for their individual role. Fitness and properness will be measured on the basis of a person's probity, experience and skill in relation to the particular role to be performed.

22–14

In the case of all EC institutions, a controller is broadly a person who individually or together with his associate(s) controls 3 per cent or more of the shares (whether voting or not) of an institution. There are different standards for different levels of shareholding since greater power can be wielded at higher levels.

In the main, new controllers have to apply to become controllers and be vetted prior to taking up their position. This can often be done on an informal basis in order to avoid strict statutory time limits and a rejection which will then go on record for other supervisors in banking and other areas. The Bank of England recommends this approach.

The standard for directors and managers can be very different to that for controllers as the former are generally involved in actually approving loans, whereas controllers tend to be removed from this day-to-day involvement. This does not mean that the tests are easier for one position rather than another, but it is more appropriate to say that every position is unique and a candidate will be assessed in relation to that particular position. Directors will normally be cleared informally with the supervisor prior to taking up employment, as will managers.

There have been many public examples of dubious personnel escaping the safety net of being deemed fit and proper, but, as this matter is not dealt with publicly, it is not possible to say how many depositors and institutions have been protected against those deemed to be not fit and proper.

CHAPTER 23

BANK REGULATION: BASLE CAPITAL ADEQUACY

Introduction

23–1 This chapter is technical and is intended as a brief tabulated summary of the main provisions of the Basle Agreement of 1988 as amended which was a set of guidelines for the measurement of a bank's capital adequacy and drawn up by the major banking regulators in Basle. The Basle principles are enshrined in the EC Own Funds Directive and the Solvency Ratio Directive and are espoused by most (if not all) of the leading bank regulators in the world. The manner in which capital is compared to exposures is briefly explained at para 22–8 to which reference should be made.

The information in this appendix is derived from the paper "International Convergence of Capital Measurement and Capital Standards" produced by the Basle Committee on Banking Regulations and Supervisory Practices as amended.

The detail of capital adequacy is fast-changing and the latest position should always be checked.

Tier 1: Core Capital

23–2 (a) Permanent shareholders' equity:

  (i) Fully paid up share capital/common stock; and
  (ii) Perpetual non-cumulative preferred shares.

(b) Disclosed reserves

(c) Published interim retained profits

less

(d) Goodwill

and

(e) Current year's unpublished losses

Tier 2: Supplementary Capital

(a) Undisclosed reserves and unpublished current year's retained profits

(b) Asset revaluation reserves

(c) General provisions/general loan loss reserves

(d) Hybrid capital instruments

This heading includes a range of instruments which combine characteristics of equity capital and of debt. Their precise specifications differ from country to country, but they should meet the following requirements:

- they are unsecured, subordinated and fully paid-up;
- they are not redeemable at the initiative of the holder or without the prior consent of the supervisory authority;
- they are available to participate in losses without the bank being obliged to cease trading (unlike conventional subordinated debt);
- although the capital instrument may carry an obligation to pay interest that cannot permanently be reduced or waived (unlike dividends on ordinary shareholders' equity), it should allow service obligations to be deferred (as with cumulative preference shares) where the profitability of the bank would not support payment.

Cumulative preference shares having these characteristics would be eligible for inclusion in this category. In addition, the following are examples of instruments that may be eligible for inclusion: long term preferred shares in Canada, *titres participatifs* and *titres subordonnés à durée indéterminée* in France, *Genussscheine* in Germany, perpetual subordinated debt and preference shares in the United Kingdom and mandatory convertible debt instruments in the United States. Debt capital instruments which do not meet these criteria may be eligible for inclusion in item (e).

(e) Subordinated term debt.

This includes conventional unsecured subordinated debt capital instruments with a minimum original fixed term to maturity of over five years and limited life redeemable preference shares. During the last five years to maturity, a cumulative discount (or amortisation) factor of 20 per cent per year will be applied to reflect the diminishing value of these instruments as a continuing source of strength. Unlike hybrid capital instruments, these instruments are not normally available to participate in the losses of a bank which continues trading. For this reason these instruments will be limited to a maximum of 50 per cent of Tier 1.

Deductions from Total Capital (total of Tier 1 and Tier 2)

23–4 (a) Investments in unconsolidated banking and financial subsidiaries

(b) Investments in the capital of other banks and financial institutions (at the discretion of national authorities)

Limits and Restrictions on Capital

(a) The total Tier 2 supplementary elements (a-e) should not exceed a maximum of 100 per cent of Tier 1 elements.

(b) Subordinated term debt should not exceed a maximum of 50 per cent of Tier 1 elements.

(c) General provisions are restricted to $1\frac{1}{2}$ per cent of risk assets.

Risk weights by category of on-balance-sheet asset

23–5   0 per cent

(i) Cash which includes (at national discretion) gold bullion held in own vaults or on an allocated basis to the extent backed by bullion liabilities

(ii) Claims on central governments and central banks denominated in national currency and funded in that currency

(iii) Other claims on OECD central governments and central banks

(iv) Claims collateralised by cash or OECD central-government securities or guaranteed by OECD central governments

0, 10, 20 or 50 per cent (at national discretion)

(i) Claims on domestic public-sector entities, excluding central government, and loans guaranteed by such entities

Originally the following may be permitted by some regulators to be weighted at 10 per cent.

10 per cent

(i) Holdings of fixed-interest securities issued (or guaranteed) by OECD central governments with a residual maturity of one year or less, and floating-rate and index-linked securities of any maturity issued or guaranteed by OECD central governments.

(ii) Claims collateralised by OECD central government fixed-interest securities with a maturity of one year or less, and similar floating-rate securities of any maturity.

(iii) Holdings of securities issued by non-OECD central governments with a residual maturity of one year or less and denominated in local currency and funded by liabilities in the same currency.

20 per cent

(i) Claims on multilateral development banks and claims guaranteed by, or collateralised by securities issued by such banks

(ii) Claims on banks incorporated in the OECD and loans guaranteed by OECD incorporated banks

(iii) Claims on banks incorporated in countries outside the OECD with a residual maturity of up to one year and loans with a residual maturity of up to one year guaranteed by banks incorporated in countries outside the OECD

(iv) Claims on non-domestic OECD public-sector entities, excluding central government, and loans guaranteed by such entities

(v) Cash items in process of collection

50 per cent

(i) Loans fully secured by mortgage on residential property that is or will be occupied by the borrower or that is rented

Optionally other lending secured on property involving, e.g. housing associations in the United Kingdom, may attract a 50 per cent weighting.

100 per cent

(i) Claims on the private sector

(ii) Claims on banks incorporated outside the OECD with a residual maturity of over one year

(iii) Claims on central governments outside the OECD (unless denominated in national currency – and funded in that currency – see above)

(iv) Claims on commercial companies owned by the public sector

(v) Premises, plant and equipment and other fixed assets

(vi) Real estate and other investments (including non-consolidated investment participations in other companies)

(vii) Capital instruments issued by other banks (unless deducted from capital)

(viii) All other assets

Credit conversion factors for off-balance-sheet items

23–6 The framework for calculating the credit conversion factors for off-balance sheet items takes account of the credit risk on off-balance-sheet exposures by applying credit conversion factors to the different types of off-balance-sheet instrument or transaction. With the exception of foreign exchange and interest rate related contingencies, the credit conversion factors are set out in the table below. They are derived from the estimated size and likely occurrence of the credit exposure, as well as the relative degree of credit risk as identified in the Basle Committee's paper "The management of banks' off-balance-sheet exposures: a supervisory perspective" issued in March 1986. The credit conversion factors would be multiplied by the weights applicable to the category of the counterparty for an on-balance-sheet transaction (see above).

Instruments

Instruments	Credit conversion factors
1. Direct credit substitutes, e.g. general guarantees of indebtedness (including standby letters of credit serving as financial guarantees for loans and securities) and acceptances (including endorsements with the character of acceptances)	100%
2. Certain transaction-related contingent items (e.g. performance bonds, bid bonds, warranties and standby letters of credit related to particular transactions)	50%
3. Short-term self-liquidating trade-related contingencies (such as documentary credits collateralised by the underlying shipments)	20%
4. Sale and repurchase agreements and asset sales with recourse, where the credit risk remains with the bank	100%
5. Forward asset purchases, forward deposits and partly-paid shares and securities, which represent commitments with certain drawdown	100%
6. Note issuance facilities and revolving underwriting facilities	50%

7. Other commitments (e.g. formal standby facilities and credit lines) with an original maturity of over one year   50%

8. Similar commitments with an original maturity of up to one year, or which can be unconditionally cancelled at any time   0%

Member countries will have some limited discretion to allocate particular instruments into items 1 to 8 above according to the characteristics of the instrument in the national market.

Foreign exchange and interest rate related contingencies

The treatment of foreign exchange and interest rate related items needs special attention because banks are not exposed to credit risk for the full face value of their contracts, but only to the potential cost of replacing the cash flow (on contracts showing positive value) if the counterparty defaults. The credit equivalent amounts will depend inter alia on the maturity of the contract and on the volatility of the rates underlying that type of instrument.

Despite the wide range of different instruments in the market, the theoretical basis for assessing the credit risk on all of them has been the same. It has consisted of an analysis of the behaviour of matched pairs of swaps under different volatility assumptions. Since exchange rate contracts involve an exchange of principal on maturity, as well as being generally more volatile, higher conversion factors are proposed for those instruments which feature exchange rate risk. Interest rate contracts are defined to include single-currency interest rate swaps, basis swaps, forward rate agreements, interest rate futures, interest rate options purchased and similar instruments. Exchange rate contracts include cross-currency interest rate swaps, forward foreign exchange contracts, currency futures, currency options purchased and similar instruments. Exchange rate contracts with an original maturity of 14 calendar days or less may be excluded.

A majority of G-10 supervisory authorities are of the view that the best way to assess the credit risk on these items is to ask banks to calculate the current replacement cost by marking contracts to market, thus capturing the current exposure without any need for estimation, and then adding a factor (the "add-on") to reflect the potential future exposure over the remaining life of the contract. It has been agreed that, in order to calculate the credit equivalent amount of its off-balance-sheet interest rate and foreign exchange rate instruments under this current exposure method, a bank would sum:

– the total replacement cost (obtained by "marking to market") of all its contracts with positive value; and

– an amount for potential future credit exposure calculated on the basis of the total notional principal amount of its book, split by residual maturity as follows.

Residual maturity	Interest rate contracts	Exchange rate contracts
Less than one year	nil	1.0%
One year and over	0.5%	5.0%

No potential credit exposure would be calculated for single currency floating/floating interest rate swaps; the credit exposure on these contracts would be evaluated solely on the basis of their mark-to-market value.

23–8 A few G-10 supervisors believe that this two-step approach, incorporating a "mark to market" element, is not consistent with the remainder of the capital framework. They favour a simpler method whereby the potential credit exposure is estimated against each type of contract and a notional capital weight allotted, no matter what the market value of the contract might be at a particular reporting date. It has therefore been agreed that supervisory authorities should have a discretion to apply the alternative method of calculation described below, in which credit conversion factors are derived without reference to the current market price of the instruments. In deciding on what those notional credit conversion factors should be, it has been agreed that a slightly more cautious bias is justified since the current exposure is not being calculated on a regular basis.

In order to arrive at the credit equivalent amount using this original exposure method, a bank would simply apply one of the following two sets of conversion factors to the notional principal amounts of each instrument according to the nature of the instrument and its maturity:

Maturity	Interest rate contracts	Exchange rate contracts
Less than one year	0.5%	2.0%
One year and less than two years	1.0%	5.0% (i.e. 2% + 3%)
For each additional year	1.0%	3.0%

It is emphasised that the above conversion factors, as well as the "add-ons" for the current exposure method, should be regarded as provisional and may be subject to amendment as a result of changes in the volatility of exchange rates and interest rates.

Netting

Consideration was given to the issue of bilateral netting, i.e. weighting the net rather than the gross claims with the same counterparties arising out of the full range of forwards, swaps, options and similar derivative contracts. The Committee was concerned that if a liquidator of a failed counterparty has (or may have) the right to unbundle netted contracts, demanding performance on those contracts favourable to the failed counterparty and defaulting on unfavourable contracts, there is no reduction in counterparty risk. Netting generally is reviewed elsewhere in this series of works on financial law.

23–9

Accordingly, it has been agreed for capital adequacy purposes that:

(a) Banks may net transactions subject to novation under which any obligation between a bank and its counterparty to deliver a given currency on a given value date is automatically amalgamated with all other obligations for the same currency and value date, legally substituting one single amount for the previous gross obligations.

(b) Banks may also net transactions subject to any legally valid form of bilateral netting not covered in (a), including other forms of novation.

(c) In both cases (a) and (b), a bank will need to satisfy its national supervisor that it has:

  (1) a netting contract or agreement with the counterparty which creates a single legal obligation, covering all included transactions, such that the bank would have either a claim to receive or obligation to pay only the net sum of the positive and negative mark-to-market values of included individual transactions in the event a counterparty fails to perform due to any of the following: default, bankruptcy, liquidation or similar circumstances;

  (2) written and reasoned legal opinions that, in the event of a legal challenge, the relevant courts and administrative authorities would find the bank's exposure to be such a net amount under:

   – the law of the jurisdiction in which the counterparty is chartered and, if the foreign branch of a counterparty is involved, then also under the law of the jurisdiction in which the branch is located;
   – the law that governs the individual transactions; and
   – the law that governs any contract or agreement necessary to effect the netting.

  The national supervisor, after consultation when necessary with other relevant supervisors, must be satisfied that the netting is enforceable under the laws of each of the relevant jurisdictions;

(3) procedures in place to ensure that the legal characteristics of netting arrangements are kept under review in the light of possible changes in relevant law.

Contracts containing walkaway clauses will not be eligible for netting for the purpose of calculating capital requirements pursuant to this Accord. A walkaway clause is a provision which permits a non-defaulting counter-party to make only limited payments, or no payment at all, to the estate of a defaulter, even if the defaulter is a net creditor.

23–10 For banks using the **current exposure** method, credit exposure on bilaterally netted forward transactions will be calculated as the sum of the net mark-to-market replacement cost, if positive, plus an add-on based on the notional underlying principal. The scale of add-ons to apply will be the same as those for non-netted transactions as set out in this chapter. The Committee will continue to review the scale of add-ons to make sure they are appropriate. For purposes of calculating potential future credit exposure to a netting counterparty for forward foreign exchange contracts and other similar contracts in which notional principal is equivalent to cash flows, notional principal is defined as the net receipts falling due on each value date in each currency. The reason for this is that off-setting contracts in the same currency maturing on the same date will have lower potential future exposure as well as lower current exposure.

23–11 The **original exposure** method may also be used for transactions subject to netting agreements which meet the above legal requirements until market risk-related capital requirements are implemented, at which time the original exposure method will cease to be available for banks supervised according to the Basle Accord. The conversion factors to be used during this transitional period when calculating the credit exposure of bilaterally netted transactions will be as follows:

Maturity	Interest rate contracts	Exchange rate contracts
Less than one year	0.35%	1.5%
One year and less than two years	0.75%	3.75% (i.e. 1.5% + 2.25%)
For each additional year	0.75%	2.25%

These factors represent a reduction of approximately 25 per cent from those in para 23–10 above. For purposes of calculating the credit exposure to a netting counterparty during the transitional period for forward foreign exchange contracts and other similar contracts in which notional principal is equivalent to cash flows, the credit conversion factors in para 23–8 above could be applied to the notional principal, which would be defined as the net receipts falling due on each value date in each currency. In no case could the reduced factors above be applied to net notional amounts.

Simple example of calculating the net to gross ratio

Transaction	Counterparty 1		Counterparty 2		Counterparty 3	
	Notional amount	Mark to market value	Notional amount	Mark to market value	Notional amount	Mark to market value
Transaction 1	100	10	50	8	30	-3
Transaction 2	100	-5	50	2	30	1
Gross replacement cost (GR)		10		10		1
Net replacement cost (NR)		5		10		0
NGR (per counterparty)	0.5		1		0	
NGR (aggregate)	$\Sigma NR/\Sigma GR = 15/21 = 0.71$					

Proposed Expanded Matrix*

Residual Maturity	Interest Rate	Foreign Exchange And Gold	Equity**	Precious Metals, Except Gold	Other Commodities
Less Than One Year	0.0%	1.0%	6.0%	7.0%	12.0%
One To Five Years	0.5%	5.0%	8.0%	7.0%	12.0%
Five Years Or More	1.5%	7.5%	10.0%	8.0%	15.0%

    * For contracts with multiple exchanges of principal, the factors are to be multiplied by the number of remaining payments in the contract.
  ** For contracts that automatically reset to zero value following a payment, the residual maturity is set equal to the time until the next payment.

Appendix

OUTLINES AND PRECEDENTS

Appendix

OUTLINES AND PRECEDENTS

Part I: Loan Agreements

1. Letter to Mr Al Yx
2. Mandate for a syndicated term loan
3. Syndicated US dollar term loan agreement
4. Interest rate determinations
5. Multicurrency clause in syndicated term loan agreement
6. Exceptions to a negative pledge
7. Exceptions to a prohibition on disposals
8. Modifications to a tax grossing-up clause
9. Modifications to an increased cost clause
10. Confidentiality clause
11. Arranger's disclaimer on syndication information memorandum
12. Outline of sub-participation agreement

Part II: Legal Opinions

13. Foreign lawyer's legal opinion on credit agreement
14. Principal lawyer's legal opinion on credit agreement

Part III: Bond Issues

15. Subscription agreement for a corporate issue of notes
16. Terms and conditions of a fixed rate US dollar note
17. Form of temporary global note for an issue of notes

Appendix: Part I

LOAN AGREEMENTS

1. Letter to Mr Al Yx

(This precedent for a syndicated term loan agreement was originally drafted by the author in 1978 and has been little changed since then).

Mr Al Yx,
The State Mining Co
Ruritania.

Dear Al,

Please pardon me for writing this on the back of an envelope. It's all I had on the plane back to London.

As I said, we and the syndicate can let you have the US$100,000,000 for your big new hole in the ground.

This is how we see the deal:

1. **Send us a telex**

    You can have the money any time up to 12 months from now. Just send us a telex. In good time please, say, five banking days. Big round amounts only, we don't deal in peanuts. We will each chip in our bit and no more.

2. **We've got shareholders too**

    Pay us back our money. Eight equal lots, one every six months starting 30 months from now.

3. **You want out**

    If you want to pay back early, that's fine, but you must call us up 30 days ahead and pay us $\frac{1}{4}$ per cent consolation fee. Big rounded amounts only. Early pay-back means a shorter deal.

4. **Milk of human kindness**

    As I explained to you, we unfortunately have to charge for this money. I congratulate you on beating us down to 1 per cent over LIBOR. Charity runs in our blood.

    We will fix every three or six months at your choice (five banking days again, please). You pay the interest at the end of each period. I hope you took on board my explanation of how we work out interest periods, the 11.00 a.m. (London time) routine, etc. Remember? Anyway, just leave the mechanics to us as we always do it.

If you don't pay on the nail, we can add an extra 1 per cent to the usual rate till you pay up.

5. **That's your problem**

    I know it's very difficult for you to understand, Al, but we don't carry the $100,000,000 around in our pockets. We have to get it elsewhere in London. If we can't, naturally we'll get round a table with you and talk about other ways and means. But if we don't see eye to eye after, say, 30 days, you pay us back. And that's the end. It's too bad that you may not be able to get the money either, that's your problem.

6. **The taxman**

    You pay us in spendable dollars of the US of A at our New York agent, grabbable immediately. And we want the full amount, i.e. you pay the taxman and top up our money.

7. **Extras**

    Cost to us is cost to you plus spread. But we have to face facts. Central banks, taxmen and other like persons are poking their noses into our business. The deal could be more pricey for one of us. Reserves, prettier balance sheets, that sort of thing. You pay us the extra. We will tell you how much and you can't argue. But if any of us ups the cost, then you can take him out.

8. **We don't want to go to jail**

    If our side of the deal runs foul of the law, no more money from the bank affected and you take him out straightaway. Plus the unwinds.

9. **The paperwork**

    You can't have any money until your directors, the central bank and our lawyers have given us their OK the way we like it.

10. **Promises, promises**

    You promise us:

    (i) Your Company is there in good shape.
    (ii) Your Company can do this deal and you, Al, can sign.
    (iii) It's all legal.
    (iv) The authorities have given their thumbs-up.
    (v) No mistakes in your last financials. Things haven't got worse since then.
    (vi) Nobody's suing you for big money.
    (vii) You are sticking by the terms of your other deals.
    (viii) The fact-sheet we sent round about you sets it out like it is.

11. Do's and don'ts

  (a) Don't put your assets in hock.
  (b) If the balloon goes up, we get equal pay-out with your other deals.
  (c) Send us your fiscals within 90 days of year-end.
  (d) Send us other info when we ask for it.
  (e) Dig the hole asap.

12. The plug

Our money back straightaway and not another cent if:

  (i) You don't comply.
  (ii) You have told us a lie.
  (iii) You don't stick by the terms of your other deals.
  (iv) You go bust.
  (v) You vanish.
  (vi) You close up shop or sell out in a big way.
  (vii) Your other creditors move in.
  (viii) We don't like the way things are going for you financially.
  (ix) Your hole in the ground doesn't get dug like you said or fills up with water, etc.

13. No stabs in the back

Al, this bit is between us and the banks.

You, colleagues in the syndicate, appoint us as your leader to run this deal. We are delighted to be of assistance and value your esteemed confidence. But, just to avoid any unpleasant misunderstandings, we have to make some things clear. It's every man for himself. We don't have to tell you what we know: you check it out yourselves. If we have slipped from the very highest standards of veracity in order to get you into this deal, keep your eyes open next time. We can believe everything the lawyers or anybody else tells us. We can do other deals with the borrower and pocket the profit. If it's between us and you, we can look after No. 1. Naturally, we will do what most of you want within reason, but if we foul up, no liability. Sorry.

14. Boiler-plate

You can mostly skip this part, Al, since it's the boiler-plate.

  (a) You will pay us our out-of-pockets, including the lawyers. I much enjoyed eating out in Ruritania at your expense.
  (b) We could lose money if you don't pay when we say. You will see us whole, especially for the unwinds.
  (c) You pay the stamps.
  (d) If we turn a blind eye once, it doesn't mean we'll do so next time.
  (e) We don't have to write it all out here: we can still throw the book at you.

- (f) We can give other banks a slice of the action any time. We can switch to our other offices.
- (g) I'm a lousy linguist and I don't speak Ruritanian, beautiful language though it is. Please help us out with translations.
- (h) If the judge gives us dinarios, etc., you make up the difference.
- (i) If you don't pay, we can grab any money you left with us.

15. **The Rules**

I was most touched by your patriotism, Al, but you must appreciate that if we play by your Ruritanian rules, His Most Majestic Excellency The Sun King of Ruritania can change the rules in the middle of the game. So, if you don't mind, we'll keep to the English rule-book.

16. **The Judge**
- (a) English judge to sort out any problems. Or New York. Or anywhere else we care to name. We can send the invite c/o your offices in London and New York. Don't say it's inconvenient.
- (b) I have to speak in metaphors here. If you park your car on a yellow line, we can give you a ticket. And tow your car away. Even if it's marked CD.

Assuming you like this deal, Al, please say so.

Yours hopefully,

Joe Y. Zed

....

Moneybank

It's OK by me.

Al Yx

....

The State Mining Co.

It's OK by us.

Moneybank	$20,000,000
Manybanks	$20,000,000
Muslimbank	$20,000,000
Moltobanco	$10,000,000
Magnifiquebanque	$10,000,000
Misyomobank	$10,000,000
Meanbank	$8,000,000
Meanestbank	$2,000,000
	US$100,000,000

2. Mandate for a syndicated term loan

To: The Borrower
From: The Arranging Bank

Dear Sirs,

We (the "Bank") would be pleased to endeavour to arrange and syndicate for you (the "Borrower") a syndicated term loan facility on the following summary terms:

1.	**Facility**	Non-revolving term loan facility
2.	**Amount and currencies**	US$100,000,000 or its equivalent in other currencies which are freely available, transferable and convertible and which are acceptable to the syndicate
3.	**Borrower**	The Borrower and any subsidiary of the Borrower incorporated in Ruritania and approved by the syndicate
4.	**Guarantor**	All present and future operating Ruritanian subsidiaries of the Borrower
5.	**Arranger and Agent Bank**	The Bank
6.	**Syndication**	A syndicate of banks arranged in consultation with the Borrower. The Bank reserves the final right to select the syndicate. The Bank proposes to participate to the extent of US$10,000,000. The Borrower will prepare an information memorandum to be used for syndication.
7.	**Underwriting**	The Bank will underwrite the full amount of the Facility.
8.	**Purpose**	General corporate purposes. The loans must not be used to finance the acquisition of companies or businesses.
9.	**Repayment and maturity**	The loans drawn will be repaid by eleven equal semi-annual instalments commencing on the date 24 months after the sign-

		ing of the loan agreement. The loans will be finally repaid in full on the seventh anniversary of the signing of the loan agreement.
10.	**Interest**	The aggregate of: (a) The average (rounded up to four decimal places) of the London interbank offered rates as shown on the appropriate Telerate screen for interest periods of one, three or six months selected by the Borrower or, if the syndicate so agree, twelve months; and (b) A margin of 1 per cent p.a. Interest is payable at the end of interest periods, but not less frequently than every six months.
11.	**Fees**	Front-end fee of [ ] per cent of the facility, payable on the earlier of the date falling 30 days after signing and the date of the first drawing and to be distributed by the Arranger at its discretion. Commitment fee of [ ] per cent payable quarterly in arrears on the undrawn, uncancelled amount of the facility. Facility fee of [ ] per cent payable quarterly in arrears on the uncancelled amount of the facility, whether drawn or not. Agency fee of US$[ ] p.a. payable in advance.
12.	**Commitment period**	The facility will be available for drawing for six months from the date of signing of the Facility in amounts or multiples of $10,000,000.
13.	**Prepayment and cancellation**	The Borrower may cancel the facility in multiples of US$10,000,000 on giving at least 30 days' notice. Prepayments are to be applied to repayment instalments in inverse order of their maturity.
14.	**Covenants**	The loan agreement will include coven-

ants by the Borrower and the Guarantors usual in a facility of this kind, including:
- a negative pledge;
- supply of financial information
- pari passu clause
- restriction on disposals
- no merger or substantial acquisitions or change of business
- group tangible net worth to exceed [ ] at all times
- the ratio of group total borrowings to group tangible net worth not to exceed [ ] at any time;
- the ratio of operating profit (before tax and after adding back borrowing costs) to borrowing costs for each financial half-year to exceed [ ].

15. **Default**

The loan agreement will include events of default usual in a facility of this kind, including:
- cross-default in respect of financial indebtedness of the Borrower, the guarantors and their subsidiaries
- material adverse change
- change of control of the Borrower.

16. **Expenses**

The Borrower will pay all out-of-pocket expenses (including legal fees and expenses) incurred by the Arranger in connection with the negotiation, syndication, documentation and signing of the facility and the costs of any agreed publicity, whether or not the loan agreement is signed.

17. **Governing law**

English

18. **Jurisdiction**

Non-exclusive jurisdiction of the English courts

19. **Documentation**

This offer is subject to the negotiation and signing of a loan agreement and other documentation acceptable to the Bank and the syndicate. The Bank's legal advisers are Messrs Pettifog and Pedant.

The documentation will include provisions usual in a facility of this kind, including conditions precedent, representations and warranties, a tax grossing-up clause, increased costs clause, illegality clause and an alternative interest clause.

20. **Conditions** This offer is subject to the following conditions: (1) there is, prior to the signing of the loan agreement, in the opinion of the Bank, no material change in the syndicated loan markets or in the business or financial condition of the Borrower and its subsidiaries or in national or international financial, economic or political conditions and (2) there is no other syndication of another credit by the Borrower or any of its subsidiaries prior to the signing of the loan agreement.

This offer will remain open until close of business on [   ] at which time it will lapse.

Except for paragraph 16 (Expenses), this offer, on acceptance, is binding in honour only and is not a legally binding agreement. Paragraph 16 is intended to be legally binding.

Please signify your agreement by signing and returning a copy of this letter.

Yours faithfully,

....
For and on behalf of
[the Bank]

We agree to the above

....
For and on behalf of
[the Borrower]

Dated............................

3. Syndicated US dollar term loan agreement

Note: Term loan agreements are discussed in chapters 2 to 5, and syndication in chapters 6 and 11. Subsequent precedents in this Appendix illustrate relaxations of certain of the clauses.

THIS AGREEMENT is dated [   ] between:

1. RURITANIAN COMPANY S.A., incorporated in Ruritania under (Registered No. [   ]) (the "**Borrower**");
2. MONEYBANK as arranger (in this capacity the "**Arranger**");
3. THE FINANCIAL INSTITUTIONS listed in Schedule 1 as banks (the "**Banks**"); and
4. MONEYBANK as agent (in this capacity the "**Agent**").

IT IS AGREED as follows:

1. Interpretation

1.1 Definitions In this Agreement:

"**Affiliate**" means a Subsidiary or a Holding Company (as defined in Section 1000 of the Ruritanian Company Act 1980) of a specified Party or any other Subsidiary of that Holding Company.

"**Business Day**" means a day (other than a Saturday or a Sunday) on which banks are open for business in London and New York City.

"**Commitment**" means the amount in Dollars set opposite the name of a Bank in Schedule 1 to the extent not cancelled or reduced under this Agreement.

"**Commitment Period**" means the period from the date of this Agreement to the Term Date (both dates inclusive).

"**Default**" means an Event of Default or an event which, with the giving of notice, lapse of time, determination of materiality or fulfilment of any other applicable condition (or any combination of the foregoing), would constitute an Event of Default.

"**Dollars**" and "**$**" means the lawful currency of the United States of America.

"**Event of Default**" means an event specified as such in Clause 17.1 (Events of Default).

"**Facility Office**" means the office(s) notified by a Bank to the Agent:

(a) on or before the date it becomes a Bank; or
(b) by not less than five Business Days' notice,

as the office(s) through which it will perform all or any of its obligations under this Agreement.

"**Fee Letter**" means the letter dated the date of this Agreement between the Arranger and the Borrower setting out the amount of various fees referred to in Clause 19 (Fees).

"**Finance Document**" means this Agreement, the Fee Letter, a Novation Certificate or any other document designated as such by the Agent and the Borrower.

"**Finance Party**" means the Arranger, a Bank or the Agent.

"**Financial Indebtedness**" means any indebtedness in respect of:

(a) moneys borrowed and debit balances at banks;
(b) any debenture, bond, note, loan stock or other security;
(c) any acceptance credit;
(d) receivables sold or discounted (otherwise than on a non-recourse basis);
(e) the acquisition cost of any asset to the extent payable before or after the time of acquisition or possession by the party liable where the advance or deferred payment is arranged primarily as a method of raising finance or financing the acquisition of that asset;
(f) leases entered into primarily as a method of raising finance or financing the acquisition of the asset leased;
(g) currency swap or interest swap, cap or collar arrangements;
(h) amounts raised under any other transaction having the commercial effect of a borrowing or raising of money; or
(i) any guarantee, indemnity or similar assurance against financial loss of any person.

"**Group**" means the Borrower and its Subsidiaries.

"**Information Memorandum**" means the Information Memorandum dated [ ] and prepared by the Borrower in connection with this Agreement.

"**Interest Period**" means each period determined in accordance with Clause 8 (Interest Periods).

"**LIBOR**" means the arithmetic mean (rounded upward to the nearest $\frac{1}{16}$th of 1 per cent) of the rates, as supplied to the Agent at its request, quoted by the Reference Banks to leading banks in the London interbank market at or about 11.00 a.m. two Business Days before the first day of the relevant Interest Period for the offering of deposits in Dollars for a period comparable to the relevant Interest Period.

"**Loan**" means, subject to Clause 8 (Interest Periods), the principal amount of each borrowing by the Borrower under this Agreement or the principal amount outstanding of that borrowing.

"**Majority Banks**" means, at any time, Banks:
(a) whose participations in the Loans then outstanding aggregate more than 50 per cent of all the Loans then outstanding; or
(b) if there are no Loans then outstanding, whose Commitments then aggregate more than 50 per cent of the Total Commitments; or
(c) if there are no Loans then outstanding and the Total Commitments have been reduced to nil, whose Commitments aggregated more than 50 per cent of the Total Commitments immediately before the reduction.

"**Margin**" means 1 per cent per annum.

"**Novation Certificate**" has the meaning given to it in Clause 25.3 (Procedure for novations).

"**Original Group Accounts**" means the audited consolidated accounts of the Group for the year ended [ ].

"**Party**" means a party to this Agreement.

"**Reference Banks**" means, subject to Clause 26.4 (Reference Banks), the principal London offices of Moneybank, Markbank and Misyomobank.

"**Repayment Date**" means each date for the payment of a Repayment Instalment.

"**Repayment Instalment**" means each instalment for repayment of the Loans referred to in Clause 6 (Repayment).

"**Security Interest**" means any mortgage, pledge, lien, charge, assignment, hypothecation or security interest or any other agreement or arrangement having the effect of conferring security.

"**Subsidiary**" means a subsidiary within the meaning of section 100 of the Ruritanian Companies Act 1980;

"**Taxes**" means all taxes, withholdings, levies, imposts, compulsory loans and similar requirements.

"**Term Date**" means [the last day of the Commitment period during which the Borrower can draw down borrowings].

"**Total Commitments**" means the aggregate for the time being of the Commitments, being $100,000,000 at the date of this Agreement.

1.2 Construction

(a) In this Agreement, unless the contrary intention appears, a reference to:

(i) an "**authorisation**" includes an authorisation, consent, approval, resolution, licence, exemption, filing and registration;
a "**month**" is a reference to a period starting on one day in a calendar month and ending on the numerically corresponding day in the next calendar month, except that, if there is no numerically corresponding day in the month in which that period ends, that period shall end on the last day in that calendar month;
a "**regulation**" includes any regulation, rule, official directive, request or guideline (whether or not having the force of law) of any governmental body, agency, department or regulatory, self-regulatory or other authority or organisation;

(ii) a provision of law is a reference to that provision as amended or re-enacted;

(iii) a Clause or a Schedule is a reference to a clause of or a schedule to this Agreement;

(iv) a person includes its successors and assigns;

(v) a Finance Document or another document is a reference to that Finance Document or other document as amended, novated or supplemented; and

(vi) a time of day is a reference to London time.

(b) Unless the contrary intention appears, a term used in any other Finance

Document or in any notice given under or in connection with any Finance Document has the same meaning in that Finance Document or notice as in this Agreement.

(c) The headings in this Agreement are for convenience only and are to be ignored in construing this Agreement.

2. The facility

2.1 Facility Subject to the terms of this Agreement, the Banks agree to make Loans during the Commitment Period to the Borrower up to an aggregate principal amount not exceeding the Total Commitments. No Bank is obliged to lend more than its Commitment.

2.2 Severality of a Finance Party's rights and obligations

(a) The obligations of a Finance Party under the Finance Documents are several. Failure of a Finance Party to carry out those obligations does not relieve any other Party of its obligations under the Finance Documents. No Finance Party is responsible for the obligations of any other Finance Party under the Finance Documents.

(b) The rights of a Finance Party under the Finance Documents are divided rights. A Finance Party may, except as otherwise stated in the Finance Documents, separately enforce those rights.

3. Purpose

The Borrower shall apply each Loan for working capital purposes. Without affecting the obligations of the Borrower in any way, no Finance Party is bound to monitor or verify the application of any Loan.

4. Conditions precedent

4.1 Documentary conditions precedent The obligations of each Finance Party to the Borrower under this Agreement are subject to the condition precedent that the Agent has notified the Borrower and the Banks that it has received all of the documents set out in Schedule 2 in form and substance satisfactory to the Agent.

4.2 Further conditions precedent The obligation of each Bank to make any amount available under Clause 5.3 (Advance of Loans) is subject to the further conditions precedent that:

(a) on both the date of the request for a Loan and the date for the advance of the amount:

   (i) the representations and warranties in Clause 15 (Representations and warranties) to be repeated on those dates are correct and will be correct immediately after the Loan is made; and

   (ii) no Default is outstanding or might result from the making of the Loan; and

(b) the Agent has received all other documents, opinions, certificates, consents and assurances as it may reasonably request in connection with the Loan.

5. Drawdown

5.1 Commitment Period The Borrower may borrow a Loan during the Commitment Period if the Agent receives, not later than five Business Days before the proposed drawdown date, a duly completed request substantially in the form of Schedule 3. The undrawn amount (if any) of the Total Commitments shall automatically be cancelled at close of business on the Term Date.

5.2 Completion of requests for Loans A request for a Loan will not be regarded as having been duly completed unless:

(a) the date for the borrowing of the Loan is a Business Day falling on or before the Term Date;

(b) the principal amount of the Loan is a minimum of $10,000,000 and an integral multiple of $10,000,000 or the balance of the undrawn Total Commitments;

(c) the first Interest Period selected complies with Clause 8 (Interest Periods); and

(d) the payment instructions comply with Clause 10 (Payments).

Each request must specify one Loan only, but the Borrower may, subject to the other terms of this Agreement, deliver more than one request on any one day.

5.3 Advance of Loans The Agent shall promptly notify each Bank of the details of the requested Loan. Subject to the terms of this Agreement, each Bank shall make its participation in the Loan available to the Agent on the relevant date for borrowing specified in the request for payment to the Borrower in accordance with Clause 10 (Payments). The amount of a Bank's participation in a Loan will be the proportion of the Loan which its Commitment bears to the Total Commitments on the proposed date for borrowing.

6. Repayment

6.1 Repayment Instalments The Borrower shall repay the Loans in full by 10 approximately equal semi-annual instalments. Each instalment shall have a principal amount equal as nearly as possible to one-tenth of the principal amount of all the Loans borrowed under this Agreement. The first Repayment Instalment shall be repaid 60 months after the date of this Agreement, and subsequent Repayment Instalments shall be repaid at six-monthly intervals from that date. The final Repayment Instalment shall be repaid on the seventh anniversary of the date of this Agreement.

6.2 Designation The Agent shall designate which of the Loans (or which part of the Loans) shall be repaid in order to satisfy each Repayment Instalment.

7. Prepayment and Cancellation

7.1 Voluntary Prepayment The Borrower may, by giving not less than 30 days' prior notice to the Agent, prepay any Loan on the last day of an Interest Period for that Loan in whole or in part (but, if in part, in an integral multiple of $10,000,000). Any such prepayment shall be applied against the Repayment Instalments in inverse order of maturity.

7.2 Voluntary Cancellation The Borrower may, by giving not less than 30 days' prior notice to the Agent, cancel the undrawn amount of the Total Commitments in whole or in part (but, if in part, in an integral multiple of $10,000,000). Any cancellation in part shall be applied against the Commitment of each Bank pro rata.

7.3 Additional right of prepayment and cancellation If:

(a) the Borrower is required to pay to a Bank any additional amounts under Clause 11 (Taxes); or

(b) the Borrower is required to pay to a Bank any amount under Clause 13 (Increased costs); or

(c) interest on a Bank's participation in a Loan is being calculated in accordance with Clause 12.4(c) (Alternative basis for outstanding Loans), then, without prejudice to the obligations of the Borrower under those Clauses, the Borrower may, whilst the circumstances continue, serve a notice of prepayment and cancellation on that Bank through the Agent. On the date falling five Business Days after the date of service of the notice:

1. the Borrower shall prepay that Bank's participation in all the Loans; and

2. that Bank's undrawn Commitment shall be cancelled.

7.4 Miscellaneous provisions

(a) Any notice of prepayment or cancellation under this Agreement is irrevocable. The Agent shall notify the Banks promptly of receipt of any such notice.

(b) All prepayments under this Agreement shall be made together with accrued interest on the amount prepaid.

(c) No prepayment or cancellation is permitted except in accordance with the express terms of this Agreement.

(d) No amount prepaid under this Agreement may subsequently be re-borrowed. No amount of the Total Commitments cancelled under this Agreement may subsequently be reinstated.

8. Interest Periods

8.1 Selection

(a) The Borrower may select an Interest Period for a Loan in either the relevant request for the Loan or, if the Loan has been borrowed, a notice received by the Agent not later than five Business Days before the commencement of that Interest Period. Each Interest Period for a Loan will commence on its drawdown date or the expiry of its preceding Interest Period.

(b) Subject to the following provisions of this Clause 8, each Interest Period will be either an approved duration or an optional duration as so selected under paragraph (a) above. In this Clause 8:

"**approved duration**" means one, two, three or six months; and

"**optional duration**" means 12 months or any other period of more than six months agreed by the Banks.

(c) If the Borrower fails to select an Interest Period for an outstanding Loan in accordance with paragraph (a) above, that Interest Period will, subject to the other provisions of this Clause 8 (Interest Periods), be six months.

8.2 Selection of an optional duration

(a) If the Borrower selects an Interest Period of an optional duration, it may also select an Interest Period of an approved duration to apply if the selection of an optional duration becomes ineffective in accordance with paragraph (b) below.

(b) If:

   (i) the Borrower requests an Interest Period of an optional duration; and
   (ii) the Agent receives notice from a Bank not later than 3.00 p.m. three Business Days prior to the commencement of the Interest Period that matching deposits may not, in its opinion, be available to it in the London interbank market to fund its participation in the Loan for that Interest Period [or it does not agree to the request],

the Interest Period for that Loan shall be the alternative period so specified or, in the absence of any alternative selection, six months. In this event, the Agent shall promptly notify the Borrower and the Banks of the new Interest Period for the Loan.

8.3 Non-Business Days If an Interest Period would otherwise end on a day which is not a Business Day, that Interest Period shall instead end on the next Business Day in that calendar month (if there is one) or the preceding Business Day (if there is not).

8.4 Consolidation Notwithstanding Clause 8.1 (Selection), the first Interest Period for each Loan shall end on the same day as the current Interest Period for any other Loan. On the last day of those Interest Periods, those Loans shall be consolidated and treated as one Loan.

8.5 Coincidence with repayment dates If an Interest Period would otherwise overrun the final Repayment Date, it shall be shortened so that it ends on that Repayment Date. The Agent may also shorten any Interest Period for any Loan (and may redesignate any Loan as two Loans) to ensure that the aggregate principal amount of Loans with an Interest Period ending on a Repayment Date is not less than the Repayment Instalment due on that Repayment Date.

8.6 Other adjustments The Agent and the Borrower may enter into such other arrangements as they may agree for the adjustment of Interest Periods and the consolidation or splitting of Loans.

8.7 Notification The Agent shall notify the Borrower and the Banks of the duration of each Interest Period promptly after ascertaining its duration.

9. Interest

9.1 Interest rate The rate of interest on each Loan for each of its Interest Periods is the rate per annum determined by the Agent to be the aggregate of the applicable:

(a) Margin; and

(b) LIBOR.

9.2 Due dates Except as otherwise provided in this Agreement, accrued interest on each Loan is payable by the Borrower on the last day of each Interest Period for that Loan and also, if the Interest Period is longer than six months, on the date falling six months after the first day of that Interest Period.

9.3 Default interest

(a) If the Borrower fails to pay any amount payable by it under this Agreement on the due date, it shall forthwith on demand by the Agent pay interest on the overdue amount from the due date up to the date of actual payment, as well after as before judgment, at a rate (the "**default rate**") determined by the Agent to be 1 per cent per annum above the higher of:

   (i) the rate on the overdue amount under Clause 9.1 (Interest rate) immediately before the due date (if of principal); and

   (ii) the rate which would have been payable if the overdue amount had, during the period of non-payment, constituted a Loan in the currency of the overdue amount for such successive Interest Periods of such duration (whether days, weeks or months) as the Agent may determine.

(b) The default rate will be determined by the Agent on each Business Day or the first day of, or two Business Days before the first day of, the relevant Interest Period, as appropriate.

(c) If the Agent determines that deposits in the currency of the overdue amount are not at the relevant time being made available by the Reference Banks to leading banks in the London interbank market, the default rate will be determined by reference to the cost of funds to the Agent from whatever sources it may select.

(d) Default interest will be compounded at the end of each Interest Period.

9.4 Notification The Agent shall promptly notify each relevant Party of the determination of a rate of interest under this Agreement.

10. Payments

10.1 Place All payments by the Borrower or a Bank under this Agreement shall be made to the Agent to its account at such office or bank in the principal financial centre of the country of the relevant currency as it may notify to the Borrower or Bank for this purpose.

10.2 Funds Payments under this Agreement to the Agent shall be made for value on the due date at such times and in such funds as the Agent may specify to the Party concerned as being customary at the time for the settlement of transactions in the currency concerned.

10.3 Distribution

(a) Each payment received by the Agent under this Agreement for another Party shall, subject to paragraphs (b) and (c) below, be made available by the Agent to that Party by payment (on the date and in the currency and funds of receipt) to its account with such office or bank in the principal financial centre of the country of the relevant currency as it may notify to the Agent for this purpose by not less than five Business Days' prior notice.

(b) The Agent may apply any amount received by it for the Borrower in or towards payment (on the date and in the currency and funds of receipt) of any amount due from the Borrower under this Agreement or in or towards the purchase of any amount of any currency to be so applied.

(c) Where a sum is to be paid to the Agent under this Agreement for another Party, the Agent is not obliged to pay that sum to that Party until it has established that it has actually received that sum. The Agent may, however, assume that the sum has been paid to it in accordance with this Agreement, and, in reliance on that assumption, make available to that Party a corresponding amount. If the sum has not been made available but the Agent has paid a corresponding amount to another Party, that Party shall forthwith on demand by the Agent refund the corresponding amount together with interest on that amount from the date of payment to the date of receipt, calculated at a rate determined by the Agent to reflect its cost of funds.

10.4 Currency

(a) Amounts payable in respect of costs, expenses, Taxes and the like are payable in the currency in which they are incurred.

(b) Any other amount payable under this Agreement is, except as otherwise provided in this Agreement, payable in Dollars.

10.5 Set-off and counterclaim All payments made by the Borrower under this Agreement shall be made without set-off or counterclaim.

10.6 Non-Business Days

(a) If a payment under this Agreement is due on a day which is not a Business Day, the due date for that payment shall instead be the next Business Day in the same calendar month (if there is one) or the preceding Business Day (if there is not).

(b) During any extension of the due date for payment of any principal under this Agreement, interest is payable on that principal at the rate payable on the original due date.

10.7 Partial payments

(a) If the Agent receives a payment insufficient to discharge all the amounts then due and payable by the Borrower under this Agreement, the Agent shall apply that payment towards the obligations of the Borrower under this Agreement in the following order:

  (i) **first,** in or towards payment pro rata of any unpaid costs and expenses of the Agent under this Agreement;
  (ii) **secondly,** in or towards payment pro rata of any accrued interest due but unpaid under this Agreement;
  (iii) **thirdly,** in or towards payment pro rata of any principal due but unpaid under this Agreement; and
  (iv) **fourthly,** in or towards payment pro rata of any other sum due but unpaid under this Agreement.

(b) The Agent shall, if so directed by all the Banks, vary the order set out in sub-paragraphs (a)(ii) to (iv) above.

(c) Paragraphs (a) and (b) above shall override any appropriation made by the Borrower.

11. Taxes

11.1 Gross-up All payments by the Borrower under the Finance Documents shall be made without any deduction and free and clear of and with-

SYNDICATED US DOLLAR TERM LOAN AGREEMENT

out deduction for or on account of any Taxes, except to the extent that the Borrower is required by law to make payment subject to any Taxes. If any Tax or amounts in respect of Tax must be deducted, or any other deductions must be made, from any amounts payable or paid by the Borrower, or paid or payable by the Agent to a Bank, under the Finance Documents, the Borrower shall pay such additional amounts as may be necessary to ensure that the relevant Bank receives a net amount equal to the full amount which it would have received had payment not been made subject to Tax.

11.2 Tax receipts All Taxes required by law to be deducted or withheld by the Borrower from any amounts paid or payable under the Finance Documents shall be paid by the Borrower when due and the Borrower shall, within 15 days of the payment being made, deliver to the Agent for the relevant Bank evidence satisfactory to that Bank (including all relevant Tax receipts) that the payment has been duly remitted to the appropriate authority.

12. Market disruption

12.1 Absence of quotations If a Reference Bank does not supply an offered rate by 1.00 p.m. two Business Days before the first day of an Interest Period, the applicable LIBOR shall, subject to Clause 12.2, be determined on the basis of the quotations of the remaining Reference Banks.

12.2 Market disruption If:

(a) no, or only one, Reference Bank supplies a rate for the purposes of determining LIBOR or the Agent otherwise determines that adequate and fair means do not exist for ascertaining LIBOR; or

(b) the Agent receives notification from Banks whose participations in a Loan exceed 50 per cent of that Loan that, in their opinion:

   (i) matching deposits may not be available to them in the London interbank market in the ordinary course of business to fund their participations in that Loan for the relevant Interest Period; or

   (ii) the cost to them of obtaining matching deposits in the London interbank market would be in excess of LIBOR for the relevant Interest Period,

the Agent shall promptly notify the Borrower and the Banks of the fact and that this Clause 12 is in operation.

12.3 Suspension of drawdowns If a notification under Clause 12.2 applies to a Loan which has not been made, that Loan shall not be made.

However, within five Business Days of receipt of the notification, the Borrower and the Agent shall enter into negotiations for a period of not more than 30 days with a view to agreeing an alternative basis for the borrowing of that and any future Loan. Any alternative basis agreed shall be, with the prior consent of all the Banks, binding on all the Parties.

12.4 Alternative basis for outstanding Loans If a notification under Clause 12.2 applies to a Loan which is outstanding, then, notwithstanding any other provision of this Agreement:

(a) within five Business Days of receipt of the notification, the Borrower and the Agent shall enter into negotiations for a period of not more than 30 days with a view to agreeing an alternative basis for determining the rate of interest or funding or both applicable to that Loan or any other Loans;

(b) any alternative basis agreed under paragraph (a) above shall be, with the prior consent of all the Banks, binding on all the Parties;

(c) if no alternative basis is agreed, each Bank shall (through the Agent) certify on or before the last day of the Interest Period to which the notification relates an alternative basis for maintaining its participation in that Loan;

(d) any such alternative basis may include an alternative method of fixing the interest rate, alternative Interest Periods or alternative currencies but it must reflect the cost to the Bank of funding its participation in the Loan from whatever sources it may select plus the Margin; and

(e) each alternative basis so certified shall be binding on the Borrower and the certifying Bank and treated as part of this Agreement.

13. Increased costs

13.1 Increased costs

(a) Subject to Clause 13.2 (Exceptions), the Borrower shall forthwith on demand by a Finance Party pay to that Finance Party the amount of any increased cost incurred by it as a result of any law or regulation (including any law or regulation relating to taxation, or reserve asset, special deposit, cash ratio, liquidity or capital adequacy requirements or any other form of banking or monetary control).

(b) In this Agreement "increased cost" means:

(i) an additional cost incurred by a Finance Party as a result of it having entered into, or performing, maintaining or funding its obligations under, this Agreement; or

(ii) that portion of an additional cost incurred by a Finance Party in making, funding or maintaining all or any advances comprised in a class of advances formed by or including its participations in the Loans made or to be made under this Agreement as is attributable to it making, funding or maintaining those participations; or

(iii) a reduction in any amount payable to a Finance Party or the effective return to a Finance Party under this Agreement or on its capital; or

(iv) the amount of any payment made by a Finance Party, or the amount of any interest or other return foregone by a Finance Party, calculated by reference to any amount received or receivable by that Finance Party from any other Party under this Agreement.

[Note: Increased costs are often extended to those affecting the holding company of a Bank.]

13.2 Exceptions Clause 13.1 (Increased costs) does not apply to any increased cost:

(a) compensated for under Clause 11 (Taxes); or

(b) attributable to any change in the rate of Tax on the overall net income of a Bank (or the overall net income of a division or branch of the Bank) imposed in the jurisdiction in which its principal office or Facility Office for the time being is situate.

14. Illegality

If it is or becomes unlawful in any jurisdiction for a Bank to give effect to any of its obligations as contemplated by this Agreement or to fund or maintain its participation in any Loan, then:

(a) that Bank may notify the Borrower through the Agent accordingly; and

(b) (i) the Borrower shall forthwith prepay that Bank's participation in all the Loans together with all other amounts payable by it to that Bank under this Agreement; and

(ii) the Bank's undrawn Commitment shall forthwith be cancelled.

15. Representations and Warranties

15.1 Representations and warranties The Borrower makes the representations and warranties set out in this Clause 15 to each Finance Party.

15.2 Status

(a) The Borrower is a limited liability Borrower, duly incorporated and validly existing under the laws of Ruritania;

(b) each member of the Group has the power to own its assets and carry on its business as it is being conducted.

15.3 Powers and authority The Borrower has the power to enter into and perform, and has taken all necessary action to authorise the entry into, performance and delivery of, the Finance Documents to which it is or will be a party and the transactions contemplated by those Finance Documents.

15.4 Legal validity Each Finance Document to which the Borrower is or will be a party constitutes, or when executed in accordance with its terms will constitute, the Borrower's legal, valid and binding obligation enforceable in accordance with its terms.

15.5 Non-conflict The entry into and performance by the Borrower of, and the transactions contemplated by, the Finance Documents do not and will not:

(a) conflict with any law or regulation or judicial or official order; or

(b) conflict with the constitutional documents of any member of the Group; or

(c) conflict with any document which is binding upon any member of the Group or any asset of any member of the Group.

15.6 No default

(a) No Default is outstanding or might result from the making of any Loan; and

(b) no other event is outstanding which constitutes (or with the giving of notice, lapse of time, determination of materiality or the fulfilment of any other applicable condition or any combination of the foregoing, might constitute) a default under any document which is binding on any member of the Group or any asset of any member of the Group to an extent or in a manner which might have a material adverse effect on the business or financial condition of any member of the Group or on the ability of the Borrower to perform its obligations under this Agreement.

15.7 Authorisations All authorisations required or desirable in connection with the entry into, performance, validity and enforceability of, and the transactions contemplated by, the Finance Documents have been obtained or effected (as appropriate) and are in full force and effect.

15.8 Accounts The audited consolidated accounts of the Group most recently delivered to the Agent (which, at the date of this Agreement, are the Original Group Accounts):

(a) have been prepared in accordance with accounting principles and practices generally accepted in Ruritania consistently applied; and

(b) fairly represent the consolidated financial condition of the Group as at the date to which they were drawn up,

and there has been no material adverse change in the consolidated financial condition of the Group since the date to which those accounts were drawn up.

15.9 Litigation No litigation, arbitration or administrative proceedings are current or, to the Borrower's knowledge, pending or threatened, which might, if adversely determined, have a material adverse effect on the business or financial condition of any member of the Group or the ability of the Borrower to perform its obligations under the Finance Documents.

15.10 Information Memorandum

(a) The information contained in the Information Memorandum was true in all respects as at its date;

(b) the Information Memorandum did not omit as at its date any information which, if disclosed, might adversely affect the decision of a person considering whether to enter into this Agreement; and

(c) nothing has occurred since the date of the Information Memorandum which renders the information contained in it untrue or misleading in any respect and which, if disclosed, might adversely affect the decision of a person considering whether to enter into this Agreement.

15.11 Times for making representations and warranties The representations and warranties set out in this Clause 15:

(a) are made on the date of this Agreement; and

(b) (with the exception of Clause 15.10 (Information Memorandum)) are deemed to be repeated by the Borrower on the date of each request for a Loan and the first day of each Interest Period with reference to the facts and circumstances then existing.

16. Undertakings

16.1 Duration The undertakings in this Clause 16 remain in force from the date of this Agreement for so long as any amount is or may be outstanding under this Agreement or any Commitment is in force.

16.2 Financial information The Borrower shall supply to the Agent in sufficient copies for all the Banks:

(a) as soon as the same are available (and in any event within 180 days of the end of each of its financial years), the audited consolidated accounts of the Group for that financial year;

(b) as soon as the same are available (and in any event within 120 days of the end of the first half-year of each of its financial years), the unaudited consolidated accounts of the Group for that half-year; and

(c) (i) together with the accounts specified in paragraph (a) above, a certificate signed by its auditors setting out in reasonable detail computations establishing compliance with Clause 16.13 (Financial covenants);

   (ii) together with the accounts specified in paragraph (b) above, a certificate signed by two of its senior officers on its behalf setting out in reasonable detail computations establishing compliance with Clause 16.13 (Financial covenants).

16.3 Other information The Borrower shall supply to the Agent:

(a) all documents despatched by it to its shareholders (or any class of them) or its creditors (or any class of them) at the same time as they are despatched;

(b) promptly upon becoming aware of them, details of any litigation, arbitration or administrative proceedings which are current, threatened or pending, and which might, if adversely determined, have a material adverse effect on the financial condition of any member of the Group or on the ability of the Borrower to perform its obligations under this Agreement; and

(c) promptly, such further information in the possession or control of any member of the Group regarding its financial condition and operations as any Finance Party may request,

in sufficient copies for all of the Banks, if the Agent so requests.

16.4 Notification of Default The Borrower shall notify the Agent of any Default (and the steps, if any, being taken to remedy it) promptly upon its occurrence.

16.5 Compliance certificates The Borrower shall supply to the Agent:

(a) together with the accounts specified in Clause 16.2(a) (Financial information); and

(b) promptly at any other time, if the Agent so requests, a certificate signed by two of its senior officers on its behalf certifying that no Default is outstanding or, if a Default is outstanding, specifying the Default and the steps, if any, being taken to remedy it.

16.6 Authorisations The Borrower shall promptly:

(a) obtain, maintain and comply with the terms of; and

(b) supply certified copies to the Agent of,

any authorisation required under any law or regulation to enable it to perform its obligations under, or for the validity or enforceability of, any Finance Document.

16.7 Pari passu ranking The Borrower shall procure that its obligations under the Finance Documents do and will rank at least pari passu with all its other present and future unsecured obligations, except for taxes and employee remuneration and benefits which are mandatorily preferred by law applying to companies generally.

16.8 Negative pledge

(a) The Borrower shall not, and shall procure that no other member of the Group will, create or permit to subsist any Security Interest on any of its present or future assets.

(b) Paragraph (a) does not apply to any lien arising by operation of law in the ordinary course of business and securing amounts not more than 30 days overdue.

(c) If the Borrower creates or permits to subsist any Security Interest on any of its assets contrary to paragraph (a) above, all the obligations of the Borrower under this Agreement shall automatically and immediately be secured upon the same assets, ranking at least pari passu with the other obligations secured on those assets.

16.9 Transactions similar to security The Borrower shall not, and shall procure that no other member of the Group will:

(a) sell, transfer or otherwise dispose of any of its assets on terms whereby it is or may be leased to or re-acquired or acquired by a member of the Group or any of its related entities; or

(b) sell, transfer or otherwise dispose of any of its receivables on recourse terms, except for the discounting of bills or notes in the ordinary course of trading,

in circumstances where the transaction is entered into primarily as a method of raising finance or of financing the acquisition of an asset.

16.10 Disposals

(a) The Borrower shall not, and shall procure that no other member of the Group will, either in a single transaction or in a series of transactions, whether related or not and whether voluntarily or involuntarily, sell, transfer, grant a lease or otherwise dispose of all or any substantial part of its assets.

(b) Paragraph (a) does not apply to:
   (i) disposals made in the ordinary course of business of the disposing entity; or
   (ii) disposals of assets in exchange for other assets comparable or superior as to type, value and quality.

16.11 Change of business The Borrower shall procure that no substantial change is made to the general nature or scope of the business of the Borrower or the Group from that carried on at the date of this Agreement.

16.12 Mergers and acquisitions

(a) The Borrower shall not enter into any amalgamation, demerger, merger or reconstruction.

(b) The Borrower shall not, and shall procure that no other member of the Group will, acquire any assets or business or make any investment if the assets, business or investment is substantial in relation to the Group.

16.13 Financial covenants

(a) In this Clause 16.13:

"**Balance Sheet**" means, at any time, the latest published audited consolidated balance sheet of the Group.

"**Interest Payable**" means all interest, acceptance commission and any other continuing, regular or periodic costs and expenses in the nature of interest (whether paid, payable or capitalised) incurred by the Group in effecting, servicing or maintaining Total Consolidated Borrowings during a financial year of the Group.

"**Operating profit**" means the consolidated net pre-taxation profits (after adding back Interest Payable) of the Group for a financial year of the Group (but before taking into account any extraordinary items).

"**Tangible Consolidated Net Worth**" means at any time the aggregate of:
  (i) the amount paid up or credited as paid up on the issued share capital of the Borrower; and
  (ii) the amount standing to the credit of the consolidated capital and revenue reserves of the Group;

  based on the Balance Sheet but adjusted by:

(1) adding any amount standing to the credit of the profit and loss account of the Group for the period ending on the date of the Balance Sheet to the extent not included in sub-paragraph (ii) above and to the extent the amount is not attributable to any dividend or other distribution declared, recommended or made by any member of the Group;
(2) deducting any amount standing to the debit of the profit and loss account of the Group for the period ending on the date of the Balance Sheet;
(3) deducting any amount attributable to goodwill or any other intangible asset;
(4) deducting any amount attributable to a revaluation of assets after [date of the most recent accounts] or, in the case of assets of a Borrower which becomes a member of the Group after that date, the date on which that Borrower becomes a member of the Group;
(5) reflecting any variation in the amount of the issued share capital of the Borrower and the consolidated capital and revenue reserves of the Group after the date of the Balance Sheet;
(6) reflecting any variation in the interest of the Borrower in any other member of the Group since the date of the Balance Sheet;
(7) excluding any amount attributable to deferred taxation;
(8) excluding any amount attributable to minority interests; and
(9) eliminating inconsistencies between the accounting principles applied in connection with the Balance Sheet and those applied in connection with the Original Group Accounts.

"**Total Consolidated Borrowings**" means at any time the aggregate (without double counting) of the following:

(i) the outstanding principal amount of any moneys borrowed by any member of the Group and any outstanding overdraft debit balance of any member of the Group;

(ii) the outstanding principal amount or the nominal amount of any debenture, bond, note, loan stock or other security of any member of the Group;

(iii) the outstanding principal amount of any acceptance under any acceptance credit opened by a bank or other financial institution in favour of any member of the Group;

(iv) the outstanding principal amount of all moneys owing to a member of the Group in connection with the sale or discounting of receivables (otherwise than on a non-recourse basis);

(v) the outstanding principal amount of any indebtedness of any member of the Group arising from any advance or deferred payment agreements arranged primarily as a method of raising finance or financing the acquisition of an asset;

(vi) the capitalised element of indebtedness of any member of the Group in respect of a lease entered into primarily as a method of raising finance or financing the acquisition of the asset leased;

(vii) any fixed or minimum premium payable on the repayment or redemption of any instrument referred to in sub-paragraph (ii) above; and

(viii) the outstanding principal amount of any indebtedness of any person of a type referred to in sub-paragraphs (i) – (vii) above which is the subject of a guarantee by any member of the Group.

Any amount outstanding in a currency other than Ruritanian francs is to be taken into account at its Ruritanian francs equivalent calculated on the basis of the Agent's spot rate of exchange for the purchase of the relevant currency in the London foreign exchange market with Ruritanian francs at or about 11.00 a.m. on the day the relevant amount falls to be calculated.

(b) All the terms used in this paragraph (a) are to be calculated in accordance with the accounting principles applied in connection with the Original Group Accounts.

(c) The Borrower shall procure that:

(i) Tangible Consolidated Net Worth is not at any time less than RF[   ];

(ii) Total Consolidated Borrowings do not at any time exceed [   ] per cent of Tangible Consolidated Net Worth at that time; and

(iii) the ratio of Operating Profit to Borrowing Costs is not, at the end of each financial year of the Group, less than [   ] to one.

17. Default

17.1 Events of default Each of the events set out in Clauses 17.2 to 17.14 (inclusive) is an Event of Default (whether or not caused by any reason whatsoever outside the control of the Borrower or any other person).

17.2 Non-payment The Borrower does not pay on the due date any amount payable by it under the Finance Documents at the place at and in the currency and funds in which it is expressed to be payable.

17.3 Breach of other obligations The Borrower does not comply with any provision of the Finance Documents (other than those referred to in Clause 17.2 (Non-Payment)).

17.4 Misrepresentation A representation, warranty or statement made or repeated in or in connection with any Finance Document or in any document delivered by or on behalf of the Borrower under or in connection with any Finance Document is incorrect in any respect when made or deemed to be made or repeated.

17.5 Cross-default

(a) Any Financial Indebtedness of a member of the Group is not paid when due; or

(b) an event of default howsoever described (or any event which with the giving of notice, lapse of time, determination of materiality or fulfilment of any other applicable condition or any combination of the foregoing would constitute such an event of default) occurs under any document relating to Financial Indebtedness of a member of the Group; or

(c) any Financial Indebtedness of a member of the Group becomes prematurely due and payable or is placed on demand as a result of an event of default (howsoever described) under the document relating to that Financial Indebtedness; or

(d) any commitment for, or underwriting of, any Financial Indebtedness of a member of the Group is cancelled or suspended as a result of an event of default (howsoever described) under the document relating to that Financial Indebtedness; or

(e) any Security Interest securing Financial Indebtedness over any asset of a member of the Group becomes enforceable.

17.6 Insolvency

(a) A member of the Group is, or is deemed for the purposes of any law to be, unable to pay its debts as they fall due or to be insolvent, or admits inability to pay its debts as they fall due; or

(b) a member of the Group suspends making payments on all or any class of its debts or announces an intention to do so, or a moratorium is declared in respect of any of its indebtedness; or

(c) a member of the Group, by reason of financial difficulties, begins negotiations with one or more of its creditors with a view to the readjustment or rescheduling of any of its indebtedness.

17.7 Insolvency proceedings

(a) Any step (including petition, proposal or convening a meeting) is taken with a view to a composition, assignment or arrangement with any creditors of any member of the Group; or

(b) any order is made or resolution passed for, or any step (including petition, proposal or convening a meeting) is taken with a view to, the rehabilitation, administration, custodianship, liquidation, winding-up or dissolution of any member of the Group or any other insolvency proceedings involving any member of the Group.

17.8 Appointment of receivers and managers

(a) Any liquidator, trustee in bankruptcy, judicial custodian, compulsory manager, receiver, administrative receiver, administrator or the like is appointed in respect of any member of the Group or any part of its assets; or

(b) the directors or a member of the Group requests the appointment of a liquidator, trustee in bankruptcy, judicial custodian, compulsory manager, receiver, administrative receiver, administrator or the like; or

(c) any other steps are taken to enforce any Security Interest over any part of the assets of any member of the Group.

17.9 Creditors' process Any attachment, sequestration, distress or execution affects any asset of a member of the Group and is not discharged within 14 days.

17.10 Analogous proceedings There occurs, in relation to a member of the Group, any event anywhere which, in the opinion of the Majority Banks, appears to correspond with any of those mentioned in Clauses 17.6 to 17.9 (inclusive).

17.11 Cessation of business A member of the Group ceases, or threatens to cease, to carry on all or a substantial part of its business.

17.12 Unlawfulness It is or becomes unlawful for the Borrower to perform any of its obligations under the Finance Documents.

17.13 Ownership of the Borrower Any single person, or group of persons acting in concert, acquires control of the Borrower.

17.14 Material adverse change Any event or series of events occurs which, in the opinion of the Majority Banks, might have a material and adverse effect on the financial condition or operations of a member of the Group or on the ability of the Borrower to comply with its obligations under the Finance Documents.

17.15 Acceleration On and at any time after the occurrence of an Event of Default the Agent may, and shall if so directed by the Majority Banks, by notice to the Borrower:

(a) cancel the Total Commitments; and/or

(b) demand that all or part of the Loans, together with accrued interest and all other amounts accrued under this Agreement be immediately due and payable, whereupon they shall become immediately due and payable; and/or

(c) demand that all or part of the Loans be payable on demand, whereupon they shall immediately become payable on demand.

18. The Agent and the Arranger

18.1 Appointment and duties of the Agent Each Finance Party (other than the Agent) irrevocably appoints the Agent to act as its agent under and in connection with the Finance Documents, and irrevocably authorises the Agent on its behalf to perform the duties and to exercise the rights, powers and discretions that are specifically delegated to it under or in connection with the Finance Documents, together with any other incidental rights, powers and discretions. The Agent has only those duties which are expressly specified in this Agreement, and those duties are solely of a mechanical and administrative nature.

18.2 Role of the Arranger Except as specifically provided in this Agreement, the Arranger has no obligations of any kind to any other Party under or in connection with any Finance Document.

18.3 Relationship The relationship between the Agent and the other Finance Parties is that of agent and principal only. Nothing in this Agreement constitutes the Agent as trustee or fiduciary for any other Party or any other person and the Agent need not hold in trust any moneys paid to it for a Party or be liable to account for interest on those moneys.

18.4 Majority Banks' directions The Agent will be fully protected if it acts in accordance with the instructions of the Majority Banks in connection with the exercise of any right, power or discretion or any matter not expressly provided for in this Agreement. Any such instructions given by the Majority Banks will be binding on all the Banks. In the absence of such instructions, the Agent may act as it considers to be in the best interests of all the Banks.

18.5 Delegation The Agent may act under the Finance Documents through its personnel and agents.

18.6 Responsibility for documentation Neither the Agent nor the Arranger is responsible to any other Party for:

(a) the execution, genuineness, validity, enforceability or sufficiency of any Finance Document or any other document;

(b) the collectability of amounts payable under any Finance Document; or

(c) the accuracy of any statements (whether written or oral) made in or in connection with any Finance Document (including the Information Memorandum).

18.7 Default

(a) The Agent is not obliged to monitor or enquire as to whether or not a Default has occurred. The Agent will not be deemed to have knowledge of the occurrence of a Default. However, if the Agent receives notice from a Party referring to this Agreement, describing the Default and stating that the event is a Default, it shall promptly notify the Banks.

(b) The Agent may require the receipt of security satisfactory to it, whether by way of payment in advance or otherwise, against any liability or loss which it may incur in taking any proceedings or action arising out of or in connection with any Finance Document before it commences those proceedings or takes that action.

18.8 Exoneration

(a) Without limiting paragraph (b) below, the Agent will not be liable to any other Party for any action taken or not taken by it under or in connection with any Finance Document, unless directly caused by its gross negligence or wilful misconduct.

(b) No Party may take any proceedings against any officer, employee or agent of the Agent in respect of any claim it might have against the Agent or in respect of any act or omission of any kind (including gross negligence or wilful misconduct) by that officer, employee or agent in relation to any Finance Document.

18.9 Reliance The Agent may:

(a) rely on any notice or document believed by it to be genuine and correct and to have been signed by, or with the authority of, the proper person;

(b) rely on any statement made by a director or employee of any person regarding any matters which may reasonably be assumed to be within his knowledge or within his power to verify; and

(c) engage, pay for and rely on legal or other professional advisers selected by it (including those in the Agent's employment and those representing a Party other than the Agent).

18.10 Credit approval and appraisal Without affecting the responsibility of the Borrower for information supplied by it or on its behalf in connection with any Finance Document, each Bank confirms that it:

(a) has made its own independent investigation and assessment of the financial condition and affairs of the Borrower and its related entities in connection with its participation in this Agreement and has not relied exclusively on any information provided to it by the Agent or the Arranger in connection with any Finance Document; and

(b) will continue to make its own independent appraisal of the creditworthiness of the Borrower and its related entities while any amount is or may be outstanding under the Finance Documents or any Commitment is in force.

18.11 Information

(a) The Agent shall promptly forward to the person concerned the original or a copy of any document which is delivered to the Agent by a Party for that person.

(b) The Agent shall promptly supply a Bank with a copy of each document received by the Agent under Clause 4 (Conditions Precedent) upon the request and at the expense of that Bank.

(c) Except where this Agreement specifically provides otherwise, the Agent is not obliged to review or check the accuracy or completeness of any document it forwards to another Party.

(d) Except as provided above, the Agent has no duty:

  (i) either initially or on a continuing basis to provide any Bank with any credit or other information concerning the financial condition or affairs of the Borrower or any related entity of the Borrower whether coming into its possession before, on or after the date of this Agreement; or
  (ii) unless specifically requested to do so by a Bank in accordance with this Agreement, to request any certificates or other documents from the Borrower.

18.12 The Agent and the Arranger individually

(a) If it is also a Bank, each of the Agent and the Arranger has the same rights and powers under this Agreement as any other Bank and may exercise those rights and powers as though it were not the Agent or the Arranger.

(b) Each of the Agent and Arranger may:

  (i) carry on any business with the Borrower or its related entities;
  (ii) act as agent or trustee for, or in relation to any financing involving, the Borrower or its related entities; and
  (iii) retain any profits or remuneration in connection with its activities under this Agreement or in relation to any of the foregoing.

18.13 Indemnities

(a) Without limiting the liability of the Borrower under the Finance Documents, each Bank shall forthwith on demand indemnify the Agent for its proportion of any liability or loss incurred by the Agent in any way relating to or arising out of its acting as the Agent, except to the extent that the liability or loss arises directly from the Agent's gross negligence or wilful misconduct.

(b) A Bank's proportion of the liability set out in paragraph (a) above will be the proportion which its participation in the Loans (if any) bears to all the Loans on the date of the demand. If, however, there are no Loans outstanding on the date of demand, then the proportion will be the proportion which its Commitment bears to the Total Commitments at the date of demand or, if the Total Commitments have then been cancelled, bore to the Total Commitments immediately before being cancelled.

(c) The Borrower shall forthwith on demand reimburse each Bank for any payment made by it under paragraph (a) above.

18.14 Compliance

(a) The Agent may refrain from doing anything which might, in its opinion, constitute a breach of any law or regulation or be otherwise actionable at the suit of any person, and may do anything which, in its opinion, is necessary or desirable to comply with any law or regulation of any jurisdiction.

(b) Without limiting paragraph (a) above, the Agent need not disclose any information relating to the Borrower or any of its related entities if the disclosure might, in the opinion of the Agent, constitute a breach of any law or regulation or any duty of secrecy or confidentiality or be otherwise actionable at the suit of any person.

18.15 Resignation of the Agent

(a) Notwithstanding its irrevocable appointment, the Agent may resign by giving notice to the Banks and the Borrower, in which case the Agent may forthwith appoint one of its Affiliates as successor Agent or, failing that, the Majority Banks may appoint a successor Agent.

(b) If the appointment of a successor Agent is to be made by the Majority Banks but they have not, within 30 days after notice of resignation, appointed a successor Agent which accepts the appointment, the Agent may appoint a successor Agent.

(c) The resignation of the Agent and the appointment of any successor Agent will both become effective only upon the successor Agent notifying all the Parties that it accepts its appointment. On giving the notification, the successor Agent will succeed to the position of the Agent and the term "Agent" will mean the successor Agent.

(d) The retiring Agent shall, at its own cost, make available to the successor Agent such documents and records and provide such assistance as the successor Agent may reasonably request for the purposes of performing its functions as the Agent under this Agreement.

(e) Upon its resignation becoming effective, this Clause 18 (The Agent and the Arranger) shall continue to benefit the retiring Agent in respect of any action taken or not taken by it under or in connection with the Finance Documents while it was the Agent, and, subject to paragraph (d) above, it shall have no further obligations under any Finance Document.

18.16 Banks The Agent may treat each Bank as a Bank, entitled to payments under this Agreement and as acting through its Facility Office(s) until it has received not less than five Business Days' prior notice from that Bank to the contrary.

18.17 Chinese Wall In acting as Agent or Arranger, the agency and syndications division of each of the Agent and the Arranger shall be treated as a separate entity from its other divisions and departments. Any information acquired by the Agent or Arranger otherwise than in the capacity of Agent or Arranger through its agency and syndications division may be treated as confidential by the Agent or Arranger and shall not be deemed to be information possessed by the Agent or Arranger in their capacity as such.

19. Fees

19.1 Front-end fee The Borrower shall pay to the Agent for the Arranger a front-end fee in the amount agreed in the Fee Letter. The front-end fee is payable on [   ] or (if earlier) the first drawdown date. The front-end fee shall be distributed by the Agent, on behalf of the Arranger, among the Banks in the proportions agreed between the Arranger and the Banks prior to the date of this Agreement.

19.2 Commitment fee

(a) The Borrower shall pay to the Agent for each Bank a commitment fee computed at the rate of [   ] per cent per annum on the undrawn, uncancelled amount of that Bank's Commitment during the Commitment Period.

(b) Accrued commitment fee is payable quarterly in arrears from the date of this Agreement and on the earlier of the Term Date and the date of full utilisation or cancellation of the Total Commitments. Accrued commitment fee is also payable to the Agent for a Bank on the cancelled amount of its Commitment at the time the cancellation takes effect.

19.3 Agent's fee The Borrower shall pay to the Agent for its own account an agency fee in the amount agreed in the Fee Letter. The agency fee is payable annually in advance. The first payment of this fee is payable on the date of this Agreement and each subsequent payment is payable on each anniversary of the date of this Agreement for so long as any amount is or may be outstanding under this Agreement or any Commitment is in force.

19.4 VAT Any fee referred to in this Clause 19 (Fees) is exclusive of any value added tax or any other Tax which might be chargeable in connection with that fee. If any value added tax or other Tax is so chargeable, it shall be paid by the Borrower at the same time as it pays the relevant fee.

20. Expenses

20.1 Initial and special costs The Borrower shall forthwith on demand pay the Agent and the Arranger the amount of all costs and expenses (including legal fees) incurred by either of them in connection with:

(a) the negotiation, preparation, printing and execution of:

   (i) this Agreement and any other documents referred to in this Agreement; and

   (ii) any other Finance Document (other than a Novation Certificate) executed after the date of this Agreement;

(b) any amendment, waiver, consent or suspension of rights (or any proposal for any of the foregoing) requested by or on behalf of the Borrower and relating to a Finance Document or a document referred to in any Finance Document; and

(c) any other matter, not of an ordinary administrative nature, arising out of or in connection with a Finance Document.

20.2 Enforcement costs The Borrower shall forthwith on demand pay to each Finance Party the amount of all costs and expenses (including legal fees) incurred by it:

(a) in connection with the enforcement of, or the preservation of any rights under, any Finance Document; or

(b) in investigating any possible Default.

21. Stamp duties

The Borrower shall pay and forthwith on demand indemnify each Finance Party against any liability it incurs in respect of, any stamp, registration and similar tax which is or becomes payable in connection with the entry into, performance or enforcement of any Finance Document.

22. Indemnities

22.1 Currency indemnity

(a) If a Finance Party receives an amount in respect of the Borrower's liability under the Finance Documents or if that liability is converted into a claim, proof, judgment or order in a currency other than the currency (the "**contractual currency**") in which the amount is expressed to be payable under the relevant Finance Document:

- (i) the Borrower shall indemnify that Finance Party as an independent obligation against any loss or liability arising out of or as a result of the conversion;
- (ii) if the amount received by that Finance Party, when converted into the contractual currency at a market rate in the usual course of its business is less than the amount owed in the contractual currency, the Borrower shall forthwith on demand pay to that Finance Party an amount in the contractual currency equal to the deficit; and
- (iii) the Borrower shall pay to the Finance Party concerned forthwith on demand any exchange costs and taxes payable in connection with any such conversion.

(b) The Borrower waives any right it may have in any jurisdiction to pay any amount under the Finance Documents in a currency other than that in which it is expressed to be payable.

22.2 Other indemnities The Borrower shall forthwith on demand indemnify each Finance Party against any loss or liability which that Finance Party incurs as a consequence of:

(a) the occurrence of any Default;

(b) the operation of Clause 15.15 (Acceleration) or Clause 28 (Pro rata sharing);

(c) any payment of principal or an overdue amount being received from any source otherwise than on the last day of a relevant Interest Period or other Interest Period as provided for in Clause 9.3 (Default interest) relative to the amount so received; or

(d) (other than by reason of negligence or default by a Finance Party) a Loan not being made after the Borrower has delivered a request for the Loan, or a Loan (or part of a Loan) not being prepaid in accordance with a notice of prepayment.

The Borrower's liability in each case includes any loss of margin or other loss or expense on account of funds borrowed, contracted for or utilised to fund any amount payable under any Finance Document, any amount repaid or prepaid or any Loan.

23. Evidence and calculations

23.1 Accounts Accounts maintained by a Finance Party in connection with this Agreement are prima facie evidence of the matters to which they relate.

23.2 Certificates and determinations Any certification or determination by a Finance Party of a rate or amount under this Agreement is, in the absence of manifest error, conclusive evidence of the matters to which it relates.

23.3 Calculations Interest and the fee payable under Clause 19.2 (Commitment fee) accrue from day to day and are calculated on the basis of the actual number of days elapsed and a year of 360 days.

24. Amendments and Waivers

24.1 Procedure

(a) Subject to Clause 24.2 (Exceptions), any term of the Finance Documents may be amended or waived with the agreement of the Borrower, the Majority Banks and the Agent. The Agent may effect, on behalf of the Majority Banks, an amendment or waiver to which they have agreed.

(b) The Agent shall promptly notify the other Parties of any amendment or waiver effected under paragraph (a) above, and any such amendment or waiver shall be binding on all the Parties.

24.2 Exceptions An amendment or waiver which relates to:

(a) the definition of "**Majority Banks**" in Clause 1.1;

(b) an extension of the date for, or a decrease in an amount or a change in the currency of, any payment under the Finance Documents;

(c) an increase in a Bank's Commitment;

(d) the inclusion of additional borrowers;

(e) a term of a Finance Document which expressly requires the consent of each Bank; or

(f) Clause 28 (Pro rata sharing) or this Clause 24 (Amendments and waivers),

may not be effected without the consent of each Bank.

24.3 Waivers and Remedies Cumulative The rights of each Finance Party under the Finance Documents:

(a) may be exercised as often as necessary;

(b) are cumulative and not exclusive of its rights under the general law; and

(c) may be waived only in writing and specifically.

Delay in exercising or non-exercise of any such right is not a waiver of that right.

25. Changes to the parties

25.1 Transfers by the Borrower The Borrower may not assign, transfer, novate or dispose of any of, or any interest in, its rights or obligations under this Agreement.

25.2 Transfers by Banks

(a) A Bank (the "**Existing Bank**") may at any time assign, transfer or novate any of its rights or obligations under this Agreement to another bank or financial institution (the "**New Bank**"). [The prior consent of the Borrower is required for any such assignment, transfer or novation, unless:

    (i) the New Bank is another Bank or an Affiliate of a Bank; or
    (ii) a Default is outstanding.

However, the prior consent of the Borrower must not be unreasonably withheld or delayed and will be deemed to have been given if, within 14 days of receipt by the Borrower of an application for consent, it has not been expressly refused.]

(b) A transfer of obligations will be effective only if either:

    (i) the obligations are novated in accordance with Clause 25.3 (Procedure for novations); or
    (ii) the New Bank confirms to the Agent and the Borrower that it undertakes to be bound by the terms of this Agreement as a Bank in form and substance satisfactory to the Agent. On the transfer becoming effective in this manner the Existing Bank shall be relieved of its obligations under this Agreement to the extent that they are transferred to the New Bank.

(c) Nothing in this Agreement restricts the ability of a Bank to sub-contract an obligation if that Bank remains liable under this Agreement for that obligation.

(d) On each occasion an Existing Bank assigns, transfers or novates any of its rights or obligations under this Agreement, the New Bank shall, on the date the assignment, transfer or novation takes effect, pay to the Agent for its own account a fee of $500.

(e) An Existing Bank is not responsible to a New Bank for:

SYNDICATED US DOLLAR TERM LOAN AGREEMENT

- (i) the execution, genuineness, validity, enforceability or sufficiency of any Finance Document or any other document;
- (ii) the collectability of amounts payable under any Finance document; or
- (iii) the accuracy of any statements (whether written or oral) made in or in connection with any Finance Document.

(f) Each New Bank confirms to the Existing Bank and the other Finance Parties that it:

- (i) has made its own independent investigation and assessment of the financial condition and affairs of the Borrower and its related entities in connection with its participation in this Agreement and has not relied exclusively on any information provided to it by the Existing Bank in connection with any Finance Document; and
- (ii) will continue to make its own independent appraisal of the creditworthiness of the Borrower and its related entities while any amount is or may be outstanding under this Agreement or any Commitment is in force.

(g) Nothing in any Finance Document obliges an Existing Bank to:

- (i) accept a re-transfer from a New Bank of any of the rights or obligations assigned, transferred or novated under this Clause; or
- (ii) support any losses incurred by the New Bank by reason of the non-performance by the Borrower of its obligations under this Agreement or otherwise.

(h) Any reference in this Agreement to a Bank includes a New Bank but excludes a Bank if no amount is or may be owed to or by it under this Agreement and its Commitment has been cancelled or reduced to nil.

25.3 Procedure for novations

(a) A novation is effected if:

- (i) the Existing Bank and the New Bank deliver to the Agent a duly completed certificate, substantially in the form of Schedule 4 (a "**Novation Certificate**"); and
- (ii) the Agent executes it.

(b) Each Party (other than the Existing Bank and the New Bank) irrevocably authorises the Agent to execute any duly completed Novation Certificate on its behalf.

(c) To the extent that they are expressed to be the subject of the novation in the Novation Certificate:

- (i) the Existing Bank and the other Parties (the "**existing Parties**") will be released from their obligations to each other (the "**discharged obligations**");

(ii) the New Bank and the existing Parties will assume obligations towards each other which differ from the discharged obligations only insofar as they are owed to or assumed by the New Bank instead of the Existing Bank;

(iii) the rights of the Existing Bank against the existing Parties and vice versa (the "**discharged rights**") will be cancelled; and

(iv) the New Bank and the existing Parties will acquire rights against each other which differ from the discharged rights only insofar as they are exercisable by or against the New Bank instead of the Existing Bank,

all on the date of execution of the Novation Certificate by the Agent or, if later, the date specified in the Novation Certificate.

25.4 Reference Banks If a Reference Bank (or, if a Reference Bank is not a Bank, the Bank of which it is an Affiliate) ceases to be a Bank, the Agent shall (in consultation with the Borrower) appoint another Bank or an Affiliate of a Bank to replace that Reference Bank.

25.5 Register The Agent shall keep a register of all the Parties and shall supply any other Party (at that Party's expense) with a copy of the register on request.

26. Disclosure of information

A Bank may disclose to one of its Affiliates or any person with whom it is proposing to enter, or has entered into, any kind of transfer, participation or other agreement in relation to this Agreement:

(a) a copy of any Finance Document; and

(b) any information which that Bank has acquired under or in connection with any Finance Document.

27. Set-off

A Finance Party may set off any matured obligation owed by the Borrower under this Agreement (to the extent beneficially owned by that Finance Party) against any obligation (whether or not matured) owed by that Finance Party to the Borrower, regardless of the place of payment, booking branch or currency of either obligation. If the obligations are in different currencies, the Finance Party may convert either obligation at a market rate of exchange in its usual course of business for the purpose of the set-off. If either obligation is unliquidated or unascertained, the Finance Party may set off in an amount estimated by it in good faith to be the amount of that obligation.

28. Pro rata sharing

28.1 Redistribution If any amount owing by the Borrower under this Agreement to a Finance Party (the "**recovering Finance Party**") is discharged by payment, set-off or any other manner other than through the Agent in accordance with Clause 10 (Payments) (a "recovery"), then:

(a) the recovering Finance Party shall, within three Business Days, notify details of the recovery to the Agent;

(b) the Agent shall determine whether the recovery is in excess of the amount which the recovering Finance Party would have received had the recovery been received by the Agent and distributed in accordance with Clause 10 (Payments);

(c) subject to Clause 28.3 (Exception), the recovering Finance Party shall within three Business Days of demand by the Agent pay to the Agent an amount (the "**redistribution**") equal to the excess;

(d) the Agent shall treat the redistribution as if it were a payment by the Borrower under Clause 10 (Payments) and shall pay the redistribution to the Finance Parties (other than the recovering Finance Party) in accordance with Clause 10.7 (Partial Payments); and

(e) after payment of the full redistribution, the recovering Finance Party will be subrogated to the portion of the claims paid under paragraph (d) above and the Borrower will owe the recovering Finance Party a debt which is equal to the redistribution, immediately payable and of the type originally discharged.

28.2 Reversal of redistribution If under Clause 28.1 (Redistribution):

(a) a recovering Finance Party must subsequently return a recovery, or an amount measured by reference to a recovery, to the Borrower; and

(b) the recovering Finance Party has paid a redistribution in relation to that recovery,

each Finance Party shall, within three Business Days of demand by the recovering Finance Party through the Agent, reimburse the recovering

Finance Party all or the appropriate portion of the redistribution paid to that Finance Party. Thereupon, the subrogation in Clause 28.1(e) (Redistribution) will operate in reverse to the extent of the reimbursement.

28.3 Exception A recovering Finance Party need not pay a redistribution to the extent that it would not, after the payment, have a valid claim against the Borrower in the amount of the redistribution pursuant to Clause 28.1(e) (Redistribution).

29. Severability

If a provision of any Finance Document is or becomes illegal, invalid or unenforceable in any jurisdiction, that shall not affect:

(a) the validity or enforceability in that jurisdiction of any other provision of the Finance Documents; or

(b) the validity or enforceability in other jurisdictions of that or any other provision of the Finance Documents.

30. Counterparts

This Agreement may be executed in any number of counterparts, and this has the same effect as if the signatures on the counterparts were on a single copy of this Agreement.

31. Notices

31.1 Giving of notices All notices or other communications under or in connection with this Agreement shall be given in writing or by telex or facsimile. Any such notice will be deemed to be given as follows:

(a) if in writing, when delivered;

(b) if by telex, when despatched, but only if, at the time of transmission, the correct answerback appears at the start and at the end of the sender's copy of the notice; and

(c) if by facsimile, when received.

However, a notice given in accordance with the above but received on a non-working day or after business hours in the place of receipt will only be deemed to be given on the next working day in that place.

31.2 Addresses for notices

(a) The address, telex number and facsimile number of each Party (other than the Agent) for all notices under or in connection with this Agreement are:

  (i) those notified by that Party for this purpose to the Agent on or before the date it becomes a Party; or
  (ii) any other notified by that Party for this purpose to the Agent by not less than five Business Days' notice.

(b) The address, telex number and facsimile number of the Agent are:

  [   ]

  or such other as the Agent may notify to the other Parties by not less than five Business Days' notice.

(c) All notices from or to the Borrower shall be sent through the Agent.

(d) The Agent shall, promptly upon request from any Party, give to that Party the address, telex number or fax number of any other Party applicable at the time for the purposes of this Clause.

32. Language

(a) Any notice given under or in connection with any Finance Document shall be in English.

(b) All other documents provided under or in connection with any Finance Document shall be:

  (i) in English; or
  (ii) if not in English, accompanied by a certified English translation and, in this case, the English translation shall prevail unless the document is a statutory or other official document.

33. Jurisdiction

33.1 Submission For the benefit of the Finance Parties, the Borrower agrees that the courts of England have jurisdiction to settle any disputes in connection with any Finance Document and accordingly submits to the jurisdiction of the English courts.

33.2 Service of process Without prejudice to any other mode of service, the Borrower:

(a) irrevocably appoints [   ] as its agent for service of process relating to any proceedings before the English courts in connection with any Finance Document;

(b) agrees that failure by a process agent to notify the Borrower of the process will not invalidate the proceedings concerned; and

(c) consents to the service of process relating to any such proceedings by prepaid posting of a copy of the process to its address for the time being applying under Clause 31.2 (Addresses for notices).

33.3 Forum convenience and enforcement abroad The Borrower:

(a) waives objection to the English courts on grounds of inconvenient forum or otherwise as regards proceedings in connection with a Finance Document; and

(b) agrees that a judgment or order of an English court in connection with a Finance Document is conclusive and binding on it and may be enforced against it in the courts of any other jurisdictions.

33.4 Non-exclusivity Nothing in this Clause 33 limits the right of any Finance Party to bring proceedings against the Borrower in connection with any Finance Document:

(a) in any other court of competent jurisdiction; or

(b) concurrently in more than one jurisdiction.

34. Governing law

This Agreement is governed by English law.

This Agreement has been entered into on the date stated at the beginning of this Agreement.

SCHEDULE 1

BANKS AND COMMITMENTS

Banks	Commitments
Moneybank	$20,000,000
Markbank	$20,000,000
Monghongbank	$20,000,000
Moltobanco	$10,000,000
Magnifiquebanque	$10,000,000
Misyomobank	$10,000,000
Meanbank	$8,000,000
Meanestbank	$2,000,000
Total Commitments	US$100,000,000

SCHEDULE 2

CONDITIONS PRECEDENT DOCUMENTS

1. A copy of the memorandum and articles of association, bye-laws and other constitutional documents and the certificate of incorporation of the Borrower.

2. A copy of a resolution of the board of directors of the Borrower:

   (i) approving the terms of, and the transactions contemplated by, this Agreement and resolving that it execute this Agreement and the Fee Letter;
   (ii) authorising a specified person or persons to execute this Agreement and the Fee Letter on its behalf; and
   (iii) authorising a specified person or persons, on its behalf, to sign and despatch all documents and notices to be signed and despatched by it under or in connection with this Agreement.

3. A specimen of the signature of each person authorised by the resolution referred to in paragraph 2 above.

4. A certificate of a director of the Borrower confirming that the borrowing of the Total Commitments in full would not cause any borrowing limit binding on the Borrower to be exceeded.

5. A certificate of an authorised signatory of the Borrower certifying that

each copy document specified in this Schedule 2 is correct, complete and in full force and effect as at a date no earlier than the date of this Agreement.

6. A copy of any other authorisation or other document, opinion or assurance which the Agent considers to be necessary or desirable in connection with the entry into and performance of, and the transactions contemplated by, any Finance Document or for the validity and enforceability of any Finance Document.

7. A legal opinion of Pettifog & Pedant, legal advisers to the Agent, addressed to the Finance Parties, in form acceptable to the Agent.

SCHEDULE 3

FORM OF REQUEST FOR LOAN

To: Moneybank as Agent

From: Ruritanian Company S.A.   Date:[   ]

Ruritanian Company S.A. $100,000,000 Credit Agreement dated [   ]

1. We wish to borrow a Loan as follows:

    (a) Date for borrowing of the Loan: [   ]
    (b) Amount: [   ]
    (c) First Interest Period: [   ]/alternative Interest Period: [   ] Complete only if the requested Interest Period is of an optional duration
    (d) Payment Instructions: [   ]

2. We confirm that each condition specified in Clause 4.2 (Further conditions precedent) is satisfied on the date of this Request.

By:

RURITANIAN COMPANY S.A.
Authorised Signatory

SCHEDULE 4

FORM OF NOVATION CERTIFICATE

To: Moneybank as Agent

From: [THE EXISTING BANK] and [THE NEW BANK]   Date: [   ]

Ruritanian Company S.A. $100,000,000 Credit Agreement dated [   ]

We refer to Clause 25.3 (Procedure for novations).

1. We [   ] (the "**Existing Bank**") and [   ] (the "**New Bank**") agree to the Existing Bank and the New Bank novating all the Existing Bank's rights and obligations referred to in the Schedule in accordance with Clause 25.3 (Procedure for novations).

2. The specified date for the purposes of Clause 25.3(c) is [date of novation].

3. The Facility Office and address for notices of the New Bank for the purposes of Clause 31.2 (Addresses for notices) are set out in the Schedule.

4. This Novation Certificate is governed by English law.

THE SCHEDULE

Rights and obligations to be novated

[Details of the rights and obligations of the Existing Bank to be novated].

[Existing Bank]	[New Bank]
By:	By:
Date:	Date:

[New Bank]

[Facility Office Address for notices]

MONEYBANK as Agent

By:

Date:

SIGNATORIES

Borrower

RURITANIAN COMPANY S.A.
By:

Arranger

MONEYBANK
By:

Banks

MONEYBANK
By:

MARKBANK
By:

MONGHONG BANK
By:

MOLTOBANCO
By:

MAGNIFIQUEBANQUE
By:

MISYOMOBANK
By:

MEANBANK
By:

MEANESTBANK
By:

Agent

MONEYBANK
By:

4. Interest rate determinations

Annual Interest

Three methods are commonly used in calculating annual interest:

1. 365/365: Under this method the rate of interest is divided by 365 and this produces a daily interest factor. The number of days that the loan is outstanding is then multiplied by this daily interest factor. A different amount of interest is charged for months of different lengths. This is the method used for domestic UK sterling loans and is the normal method for domestic finance.

2. 360/360: Under this method each month is treated as having the same number of days (30). Thus, interest for each month is the same. However, for a calendar year the interest is exactly the same as that calculated by using the 365/365 method. This is the method used for international bond issues, except floating rate notes (which apply the next method).

3. 365/360: The third method is a combination of the first two methods. The interest rate is divided by 360 days (30 days for each month) to create a daily factor. The number of days that a loan is outstanding is then multiplied by this daily factor. Thus interest charged for months of different lengths is different and interest charged for a calendar year is greater than interest charged under either the 365/365 or 360/360 methods. This is the method used for eurocurrency loans (including eurosterling).

Formula for Sterling London Interbank Offered Rate

"LIBOR" means the rate quoted by the Bank to leading banks in the London interbank market at or about 11 a.m. (London time) on the first day of the relevant Interest Period for the offering of deposits in UK Sterling for a period comparable to the relevant Interest Period and for the relevant amount.

Telerate formula for London Interbank Offered Rate

"LIBOR" means, in relation to any Advance:
(a) the rate per annum of the offered quotation for deposits in the

currency of that Advance for a period comparable to the relevant Interest Period, which appears on Telerate Page 3750 or Telerate Page 3740, as the case may be, at or about 11.00 a.m. on the day two Business Days before the Interest Period; or

(b) if no such offered quotation appears on the Telerate page 3750 or Telerate Page 3740, as the case may be, the arithmetic mean (rounded upwards, if necessary, to four decimal places) of the per annum rates, as supplied to the Agent at its request, quoted by each Reference Bank to leading banks in the London interbank market at or about 11.00 a.m. on the day two Business Days before the Interest Period for the offering of deposits in the currency of that Advance in an amount comparable to the participation of the Reference Bank in that Advance and for a period equal to the relevant Interest Period. If on any occasion a Reference Bank fails to supply the Agent with a quotation required of it, the rate for which such quotation was required shall be determined from those quotations which are supplied to the Agent.

For the purposes of this definition, "**Telerate Page 3750**" means the display designated as "Page 3750" and "**Telerate Page 3740**" means the display designated as "Page 3740" on the Telerate Service (or such other page as may replace Page 3750 or Page 3740, as the case may be, on that service or such other service as may be nominated by the British Bankers' Association as the information vendor for the purpose of displaying British Bankers' Association Interest Settlement Rates for deposits in the relevant currency). Times are London time.

Reuters Screen formula for London Interbank Offered Rate

"LIBOR" means, in relation to an Advance:

(a) the arithmetic mean (rounded upwards to the nearest $\frac{1}{16}$th of 1 per cent) of the rates appearing on the Reuters Screen LIBP page (in the case of an amount denominated in Sterling) or LIBO page (in the case of an amount denominated in US Dollars), or equivalent successor to such page or other page as appropriate (as determined by the Agent) (the "Reuters Screen") at or about 11.00 a.m. on (or, in the case of an amount denominated in US Dollars, two Business Days before) the first day of the relevant Interest Period in relation to that Advance, as being the interest rates offered in the London Interbank Market for deposits in UK Sterling or, as the case may be, US Dollars, for a period comparable to the relevant Interest Period; or

(b) if less than three relevant rates appear on the Reuters Screen for the purposes of paragraph (a) above or the relevant Advance is denominated in a currency other than Sterling or US Dollars, the arithmetic mean (rounded upward to four decimal places) of the rates, as supplied to the Agent at its request, quoted by each Reference Bank to leading banks in the London interbank market at or about 11.00 a.m. on (or, in the case of an amount denominated in a currency other than Sterling, two Business Days before) the first day of the relevant Interest Period in relation to that advance, for the offering of deposits in the relevant currency for a period comparable to that of the relevant Interest Period.

5. Multicurrency clause in syndicated term loan agreement

Note: For a comment on this clause, see para 2–21.

1. Selection notice

(a) An "**optional currency**" is any freely convertible, readily available and freely transferable currency. "**Dollars**" means US dollars. "**Original Dollar Amount**" of a loan is the amount of a Loan in Dollars if it had been drawn and had remained denominated throughout in Dollars.

(b) The Borrower shall give notice to the Agent, to be received by the Agent not later than 11.00 a.m. (London time) five Business Days prior to the commencement of each Interest Period relative to a Loan, specifying:

  (i) the currency (whether Dollars or an Optional Currency) in which the Borrower wishes such Loan to be denominated for such Interest Period;

  (ii) if the Borrower wishes such Loan to be denominated in more than one currency, the amount in Dollars to be denominated in each such currency (being a minimum of $[   ] and an integral multiple of $[   ] or the balance of such Loan, if more);

The Agent shall promptly notify each Bank of any such notice or of its absence.

(c) If the Borrower fails to give such notice, it shall be deemed to have given a notice specifying Dollars for the Loan concerned.

(d) Each part of a Loan which is to be denominated in a different currency from any other part of such Loan pursuant hereto shall thenceforward be treated as a separate Loan.

(e) The Borrower may not choose a currency if as a result the Loans would be denominated at any one time in more than [three] currencies.

2. Determination of currency

(a) A Loan may be denominated during an Interest Period in an Optional Currency so specified only if no Bank gives a counter-notice to the Agent by 2.00 p.m. (London time) three Business Days prior to such

Interest Period stating that it does not agree such currency. In that event such Loan shall be denominated in Dollars during such Interest Period unless all the Banks agree with the Borrower that such Loan shall be denominated in another Optional Currency for such Interest Period.

(b) The Agent will notify the Borrower and the Banks not later than 5.00 p.m. (London time) three Business Days prior to each Interest Period of the currency in which such Loan is to be denominated for such Interest Period.

3. Revocation of currency

Notwithstanding that a Loan is to be denominated in an Optional Currency for an Interest Period pursuant to the above, if prior to 10.00 a.m. (London time) on the first day of such Interest Period the Agent receives notice from Banks participating in not less than 25 per cent of such Loan that, by reason of any circumstances, it is impracticable for such Banks to fund their participations in such Loan in such Optional Currency during such Interest Period in the ordinary course of business in the London Interbank Eurocurrency Market, the Agent shall give notice to the Borrower and to the Banks to that effect before 11.00 a.m. (London time) on such day. In such event:

(a) in the case of the drawdown of a Loan, the Borrower and the Banks may agree that such drawdown shall not be made;

(b) in the absence of such agreement and in any other case, such Loan shall be denominated in Dollars during such Interest Period except that interest shall be fixed, not at 11.00 a.m. (London time) two Business Days prior to the commencement of the Interest Period, but at 1.00 p.m. (London time) on the first day of the Interest Period; and

(c) in any event, the Borrower shall indemnify each Bank against any loss and expenses which such Bank may certify (such certification to be conclusive) as incurred by it as a consequence of the occurrence of any such event and the operation of this sub-clause 3.

4. Agent's spot rate of exchange

In this Agreement the "Agent's spot rate of exchange" in relation to an Interest Period means the Agent's spot rate of exchange for the purchase in the London Foreign Exchange Market of the appropriate amount of the relevant Optional Currency with Dollars at 11.00 a.m. (London time) two Business Days before such Interest Period.

5. Drawdowns

If a Loan is to be drawn down in an Optional Currency, each Bank will make available to the Agent an amount in such Optional Currency determined by converting into that Optional Currency such Bank's participation in the Original Dollar Amount of such Loan on the basis of the Agent's spot rate of exchange relative to such Interest Period.

6. Change of currency

If a Loan is to be continued during the next Interest Period relative thereto in a different currency from that in which it was denominated during the preceding Interest Period, such Loan shall be repaid at the end of such preceding Interest Period in the currency in which it is then denominated and (subject to receipt of such repayment and subject to the terms of this Agreement) shall be re-advanced forthwith on terms that:

(a) if such Loan is to be denominated in Dollars during such next Interest Period, each Bank will forthwith make available to the Agent its participation in the Original Dollar Amount of such Loan applicable at the beginning of such next Interest Period;

(b) if such Loan is to be denominated in an Optional Currency during the next Interest Period, each Bank will forthwith make available to the Agent each such Optional Currency in an amount determined by converting into that Optional Currency such Bank's participation in the Original Dollar Amount of such Loan applicable at the beginning of such next Interest Period on the basis of the Agent's spot rate of exchange relative to such next Interest Period.

7. Same Optional Currency

(a) If a Loan is to be continued during the next Interest Period relative thereto in the same Optional Currency in which it was denominated during its preceding Interest Period, there shall be calculated the difference between the amount in such Optional Currency of such Loan at the end of the preceding Interest Period and at the beginning of such next Interest Period. The latter amount shall be determined by converting into that Optional Currency the Original Dollar Amount of such Loan applicable at the beginning of such next Interest Period on the basis of the Agent's spot rate of exchange relative to such next Interest Period. At the end of such preceding Interest Period, the Borrower shall repay the difference in such Optional Currency or (as the case may be) at the beginning of such next Interest Period each Bank shall forthwith make available to the Agent its participation in such difference.

(b) If the said Agent's spot rate of exchange applicable to such next Interest Period shows an appreciation or depreciation of such Optional Currency against Dollars of less than 5 per cent when compared with the Original Exchange Rate, no amounts shall be payable in respect of such difference. "Original Exchange Rate" means the Agent's spot rate of exchange used for determining the amount of such Optional Currency for the Interest Period which is the latest of the following:

   (i) the Interest Period during which such Loan was first denominated in such Optional Currency if such Loan has since then been denominated in that Optional Currency;
   (ii) the most recent Interest Period immediately prior to which a difference was required to be paid under this sub-clause 7.

8. Notification of rates and amount

The Agent shall promptly notify the Banks and the Borrower of the Agent's spot rate of exchange (as to which the Agent's determination shall be conclusive) and of Optional Currency amounts hereunder as soon as they are ascertained.

6. Exceptions to a negative pledge

Note: The negative pledge covenant is discussed at para 3–10 *et seq*. Set out below are some possible exceptions from a negative pledge which may be appropriate in a particular case or which may be suggestive of other exceptions. It would be unusual for all of the exceptions to be agreed, and many of the exceptions are themselves unusual and are not recommended for the normal case. From the point of view of banks, the difficulty with exceptions is to ensure that the negative pledge cannot be avoided by the use of an exception for a purpose for which it was not intended. Some of the exceptions overlap.

If a negative pledge does not merely prohibit security, but also prohibits transactions having the effect of security, this may catch various forms of title finance, such as factoring, discounting, sale and repurchase, retention of title, leasing, hire purchase, sale and lease-back, stock borrowing agreements and set-off. In such a case, much wider exceptions would have to be considered by borrowers and these are not illustrated below.

Negative pledge

The Borrower will (and will procure that none of its Subsidiaries will) create or permit to subsist any mortgage, charge, pledge, lien, hypothecation or other security interest upon all or any of the assets of the Borrower or any of its Subsidiaries.

Exceptions to the negative pledge

The foregoing prohibition does not apply to the following:

Consent Security Interests created with the prior written consent of the Majority Banks.

Existing security interests Security Interests in existence at the date of this Agreement and set out in the schedule to this Agreement and securing principal amounts not at any time exceeding $[   ].

Automatic liens Liens arising by operation of law in the ordinary course of business and securing amounts not exceeding $[   ] in total at any one time outstanding for all such liens and not more than 30 days overdue or, if longer, being contested in good faith.

Equivalent contractual liens Liens created by contract in the ordinary course of business of the Borrower or Subsidiary concerned in circumstances where the lien would have arisen by operation of law in the absence of contract and securing amounts not exceeding $[   ] in total at any one time outstanding for all such liens and not more than 30 days overdue or, if longer, being contested in good faith.

Existing security interests on after-acquired assets Security Interests existing on an asset at the time of the acquisition or lease of the asset by the Borrower or a Subsidiary after the date of this Agreement, but only if (1) the Security Interest was not created in contemplation of the acquisition or lease, (2) the principal amount secured by the Security Interest is not increased after the acquisition or lease and (3) the Security Interest is discharged within six months of the acquisition or lease.

Security Interests existing on new Subsidiaries Security Interests existing on the assets of a company at the time it becomes a Subsidiary after the date of this Agreement, but only if (1) the Security Interest was not created in contemplation of the company becoming a Subsidiary, (2) the principal amount secured by the Security Interest is not increased after it becomes a Subsidiary, and (3) the Security Interest is discharged within six months of the company becoming a Subsidiary.

Security Interests existing on merger Security Interests existing on the assets of a company with which the Borrower or a Subsidiary is merged, but only if (1) the Security Interest was existing at the time of the merger, (2) the Security Interest was not created in contemplation of the merger, (3) the principal amount secured by the Security Interest is not increased after the merger, and (4) the Security Interest is discharged within six months of the merger.

Purchase money Securities Interests over assets acquired by the Borrower or a Subsidiary after the date of this Agreement securing not more than 80 per cent of the purchase price of the asset, or a credit to finance not more than 80 per cent of the price, plus commercial interest and costs.

Development Security Interests Security Interests over any asset which is developed or improved by the Borrower or a Subsidiary after the date of this Agreement but only if (1) the Security Interest is to secure finance for the development or improvement concerned, (2) the total principal amount secured by all such Security Interests at any one time outstanding does not exceed $[   ], and (3) the Majority Banks have previously approved the Security Interest, such approval not to be unreasonably withheld.

Taxes Security Interests securing taxes and other governmental levies and arising by statute but only if the taxes and levies are not more than 60 days overdue or, if longer, are being contested in good faith by appropriate measures.

Judgments Security Interests securing judgments which do not constitute an Event of Default.

Court bonds Bonds constituting Security Interests created pursuant to court order as security for costs in connection with litigation or created as a condition of any prejudgment attachment, arrest or injunction sought by the Borrower or a Subsidiary.

Bonds to secure release Bonds constituting Security Interests over cash deposits or marketable investment securities to procure the release from judicial arrest of an asset belonging to the Borrower or a Subsidiary, but only if the arrest is not an Event of Default and the total amount secured by all such bonds does not at any one time exceed $[   ].

Caution money Security Interests over cash deposits not exceeding $[   ] in total at any one time outstanding and required by any real property lessor to the Borrower or a Subsidiary as caution money in respect of the obligations of the Borrower or the Subsidiary under the lease.

Charge-backs Security Interests over any claim owned by the Borrower or a Subsidiary, being Security Interests which are created in favour of the obligor liable on that claim, but only if the obligor is validly prohibited from disposing of the Security Interest.

Clearing houses settlements Security Interests over cash deposits or marketable investment securities in favour of any clearing house or exchange for securities or for futures, options or similar financial contracts or in favour of any bank providing settlement services for the clearing house or exchange, to secure the obligations of the Borrower or a Subsidiary to deliver or pay in settlement, or credits by the bank for the settlement payment, but only if (1) the dealings secured are in the ordinary course of trading, (2) the total amount secured by all such Security Interests does not at any one time exceed $[   ], (3) the Security Interest is required under the standard terms of the clearing house, exchange or bank concerned, and (4) each secured amount is paid within five business days of being incurred.

EXCEPTIONS TO A NEGATIVE PLEDGE

Margin Security Interests over cash deposits or marketable investment securities in favour of any exchange or financial institution by way of margin collateral for dealings in securities, foreign exchange or derivatives in the ordinary course of trading but only if the total value of all such collateral does not at any one time exceed $[   ].

Letters of credit Security Interests over goods, documents of title to goods and related documents and insurances and their proceeds to secure liabilities of the Borrower or a Subsidiary in respect of a letter of credit issued for all or part of the purchase price and costs of shipment, insurance and storage of goods acquired by the Borrower or the Subsidiary in the ordinary course of trading as part of its inventory.

Retention of title Security Interests over goods and their proceeds and arising by virtue of the supplier's retention of title clause to secure only the purchase price of the goods, but only if the goods are inventory purchased by the Borrower or a Subsidiary in the ordinary course of trading.

Bonds Security Interests over cash deposits or marketable investment securities securing the performance by the Borrower or a Subsidiary of bid, tender, advance payment, retention money, maintenance or performance bonds issued in the ordinary course of the contracting business of the Borrower or the Subsidiary, but only if the total amount at any one time outstanding and secured by all such Security Interests does not exceed $[   ].

Official export credits Any Security Interest over any goods to secure liabilities incurred on concessional terms in connection with the supply of those goods, being terms provided by any governmental or other similar export credit agency or official export-import bank or official export-import credit insurer.

Joint venture agreements Any Security Interest over the shares of the Borrower or a Subsidiary in, or debt obligations owed to the Borrower or a Subsidiary by, or its interest in the assets of, any joint venture company, or joint venture association, or partnership or other joint venture to secure liabilities incurred in connection with the joint venture in favour of the other joint venture participants but only if the total principal amount secured by all such Security Interests and at any one time outstanding does not exceed $[   ].

Project finance Any Security Interest created by a Subsidiary over the assets of any capital project of the Subsidiary commenced after the date of this

Agreement (or over the shares of a company carrying out the capital project) to secure credits, lease obligations or other indebtedness to finance the capital project where the financiers' rights of recovery are primarily limited to the assets of the capital project.

Trading debt Security Interests securing sums which are not Financial Indebtedness [see the definition in clause 1 of the Syndicated Term Loan Agreement in this appendix], but only if (1) the sums secured were incurred in the ordinary course of trading of the Borrower or Subsidiary concerned and (2) the total principal amount of the sums secured by all such Security Interests does not at any time exceed $[   ].

Social security Security Interests created in the ordinary course of business in connection with worker's compensation, unemployment insurance and other types of social security.

Intragroup Security Interests created by the Borrower or any Subsidiary in favour of another Subsidiary or the Borrower, but only if the company holding the security (1) is the Borrower or a Subsidiary which guarantees the obligations of the Borrower under this Agreement and (2) remains beneficially entitled to the Security Interest.

Renewals Any Security Interest renewing or replacing those in paragraph [   ] above, but only if (1) the Security Interest secures a principal amount not exceeding that outstanding and secured by the previous Security Interest at the time of the renewal or replacement and (2) the Security Interest is over the same assets.

Substitutions Any Security Interest over assets substituted for those covered by a Security Interest permitted by paragraph [   ] above, but only if (1) the Security Interest secures the same liabilities, (2) the substituted assets are of the same type as the replaced assets, and (3) the substituted assets do not exceed the value of the replaced assets at the time of the substitution.

Free amount Security Interests which secure total principal amounts which do not at any one time exceed $[   ] [or 5 per cent of the Consolidated Tangible Net Worth as defined] or where the book value of all the assets covered by the Security Interests does not exceed 5 per cent of the book value of the Consolidated Net Tangible Assets as defined.

Equal security Any Security Interest if the obligations of the Borrower under this Agreement are at the same time equally and rateably secured by that Security Interest over the same assets (but so that the Majority Banks control its enforcement).

Currency conversions For the purposes of the above limits, sums in currencies other than US dollars shall be converted into US dollars at the prevailing spot rate in the London foreign exchange market from time to time. If a limit would be exceeded by reason only of fluctuations in exchange rates, the limit shall not be deemed to be exceeded for 10 business days after the excess first arises.

7. Exceptions to a prohibition on disposals

Note: Set out below are some illustrations of exceptions to a prohibition on disposals by the borrower in a term loan agreement. See clause 16.7 of the Syndicated Term Loan Agreement in this Appendix. Some of the exceptions are unusual. The clause itself is discussed at para 3–29 *et seq*.

The Borrower shall not, and shall procure that none of its Subsidiaries will, either in a single transaction or in a series of transactions, whether related or not and whether voluntarily or involuntarily, sell, transfer, lease or otherwise dispose of all or a substantial part of its respective assets, except that the following disposals shall not be taken into account:

(a) disposals made in the ordinary course of business of the disposing entity;

(b) disposals from a Subsidiary to the Borrower or to another Subsidiary but, in the case of a disposal from one Subsidiary to another Subsidiary, only if the percentage ownership of the Borrower in the receiving Subsidiary (whether such ownership is direct or indirect through other Subsidiaries) is not significantly less than the Borrower's percentage ownership (whether direct or indirect as aforesaid) in the disposing Subsidiary;

(c) disposals of cash raised or borrowed for the purposes for which it was raised or borrowed;

(d) disposals of investments listed or dealt in on any securities exchange or over-the-counter market (not being investments in any member of the Group);

(e) disposals of property in exchange for (or sale of assets for cash and the application within six months of the cash in the acquisition of) other property comparable or superior as to type, value and quality;

(f) disposals at market value on arm's-length terms for cash payable at the time of the disposal;

(g) leases of assets on arm's-length terms for rentals payable not less frequently than semi-annually;

(h) disposals of obsolete assets for cash;

(i) disposals during any financial year of the Group where the aggregate book value of the property or assets disposed of in that financial year does not exceed 5 per cent of Gross Shareholders' Funds (as defined

EXCEPTIONS TO A PROHIBITION ON DISPOSALS

and as shown in the then most recent audited annual consolidated accounts of the Group);

(j) any disposal if:

    (1) the Borrower delivers to the Bank, prior to the disposal, a certificate of a duly authorised officer of the Borrower certifying that, immediately after the disposal, the Borrower would be in compliance with Clause [   ] (Financial Covenants), together with calculations in reasonable detail evidencing the compliance; and

    (2) in the opinion of the Bank, the disposal will not have a material adverse effect on the credit-standing of the Borrower or on the ability of the Borrower to perform its payment obligations under this Agreement;

(k) any disposals for cash if the net proceeds of the disposal are, immediately on the disposal, applied towards prepayment of the loans.

8. Modifications to tax grossing-up clause

Note: Set out below are modifications to the tax grossing-up clause in Clause 11 of the Syndicated Term Loan Agreement (Precedent 3, above). The clause is discussed at para 4–2 *et seq.*

Clause 11.3   Tax credits

If the Borrower pays any additional amount under Clause 11.1 (a "**Tax Payment**") and a Bank obtains a refund of a tax, or credit against tax, by reason of that Tax Payment (a "**Tax Credit**"), and that Bank is able to identify the Tax Credit as being attributable to the Tax Payment, then the Bank concerned shall reimburse to the Borrower such amount as that Bank determines to be the proportion of the Tax Credit as will leave that Bank (after that reimbursement) in no better or worse position than it would have been if the Tax Payment had not been required. Nothing in this Clause interferes with the right of any Bank to arrange its tax affairs in whatever manner it thinks fit. No Bank is obliged to claim a Tax Credit, or to claim a Tax Credit in priority to any other claim, relief, credit or deduction available to it. No Bank is obliged to disclose any information regarding its tax affairs or computations to the Borrower.

Clause 11.4   UK Banks

If, otherwise than as a result of the introduction of, or change in the interpretation, administration or application by any governmental authority or organisation of, any law or regulation or any practice or concession of the UK Inland Revenue occurring after the date of this Agreement, a Bank,

(a) is not or ceases to be recognised by the Inland Revenue as a bank carrying on a bona fide banking business in the United Kingdom for the purpose of section 349 of the Income and Corporation Taxes Act 1988; or

(b) does not take any interest or acceptance commission received by it under this Agreement into account as a trading receipt of such a business,

the Borrower shall not be liable to pay that Bank under Clause 11.1 any amount in respect of taxes levied or imposed by the UK or any taxing authority of or in the UK in excess of the amount it would have been obliged to pay if that Bank had not ceased to be so recognised by the Inland Revenue or, as the case may be, had taken such interest or acceptance commission into account as a trading receipt of such a business.

Clause 11.5   Mitigation

If circumstances arise, in relation to the Agent or a Bank, which would result in the Borrower being required to pay any additional amount to a Bank under Clause 11.1, then, without qualifying the obligations of the Borrower under that Clause, the Agent or the Bank concerned shall endeavour to take such reasonable steps (in consultation with the Borrower) as may be reasonably open to it to mitigate or remove those circumstances or the effect of those circumstances, including (without limitation) the transfer of any office through which the Agent performs its agency functions under the Finance Documents or the Bank's Facility Office to another jurisdiction or the transfer of its rights and obligations under this Agreement to another bank or financial institution acceptable to the Borrower, unless, in the opinion of the Agent or that Bank, as the case may be, such steps might be prejudicial in any way to the Agent or that Bank or would be contrary to its policies as to booking location.

Clause 11.6   Transfers

[The assignment and transfer clause would provide that the Borrower is not to be under a greater liability under Clause 11.1 in the case of an assignment, change of facility office or novation by a Bank, than it would be in the absence of the transfer. The greater liability should be tested only at the time of the transfer, so that, if subsequent taxes are imposed, the transferee is not limited to the position of the transferor.]

9. Modifications to an increased cost clause

Note: The following are possible exceptions to the increased cost clause in Clause 13 of the Syndicated Term Loan Agreement (Precedent No 3 above). The clause is discussed at para 4–5.

Clause 13.2 General exclusions

Clause 13.1 does not apply to any increased cost:

(a) compensated for by the operation of Clause 11 (Taxes); or

(b) attributable to any change in the rate of tax on the overall net income of a Bank (or the overall net income of a division or branch of the Bank) imposed in the jurisdiction in which its principal office or Facility Office for the time being is situate; or

(c) resulting from the implementation by the applicable authorities having jurisdiction over that Finance Party or its Facility Office of specific capital adequacy requirements officially announced prior to the date of this Agreement to the extent clearly ascertainable from the announcement, but not more stringent requirements on or after the date of this Agreement; or

(d) arising solely by reason of a Bank's unreasonable delay in notifying the Agent of its right to make a demand under Clause 13.1 (Increased Costs) after it has become aware of and is able to ascertain the amount of its claim.

Clause 13.3 Mitigation

If, in respect of the Agent or any Bank, circumstances arise which would, or would upon the giving of notice, result in the Borrower being required to pay any additional amount to a Bank under Clause 13.1 (Increased costs), then, without qualifying the obligations of the Borrower under that Clause, the Agent or that Bank, as the case may be, shall endeavour to take such reasonable steps (in consultation with the Borrower) as may be reasonably open to it to mitigate or remove those circumstances or the effect of those circumstances, including (without limitation) the transfer of (in the case of the Agent) any office through which it performs its agency functions under the Finance Documents or (in the case of a Bank) its Facility Office to another jurisdiction or the transfer of its rights and obligations under this Agreement to another bank or financial institution acceptable to the Borrower, unless, in the reasonable opinion of the Agent or that Bank, as the case may be, such steps would be prejudicial in any way to the Agent or that Bank or would be contrary to its policies as to booking location.

Clause 14.4   Transfer

[The transfer clause would provide that the Borrower is not to be under a greater liability under Clause 13.1 in the case of an assignment, change of facility office or novation by a Bank then it would be in the absence of the transfer. The greater liability should be tested only at the date of the transfer, so that, if subsequent increased costs arise, the transferee is not limited to the position of the transferor.]

10. Confidentiality clause

Note: Set out below is a clause in a loan agreement – or more typically a project finance agreement where there is a greater premium on confidentiality – whereby the Banks agree to keep the transaction and information supplied in connection with the transaction confidential.

Confidentiality

A Bank may not disclose:

(a) this Credit Agreement; or

(b) any information which that Bank has acquired under or in connection with this Credit Agreement,

(together "**Confidential Information**") to any person.

Exceptions

Notwithstanding the above, a Bank may disclose Confidential Information:

(a) with the prior written consent of the Borrower;

(b) to the officers and employees of that Bank or to lawyers and accountants retained as professional advisers to that Bank, provided that they are first made aware of the terms of this Clause;

(c) to its affiliates or any person with whom it is proposing to enter, or has entered into, a transfer, participation or other agreement in relation to this Agreement but only if that person has first entered into a confidentiality undertaking, in favour of the Borrower and the relevant Bank, substantially in the scheduled form [on the lines of this Clause];

(d) which at the time of disclosure is in the public domain otherwise than by reason of a breach by the relevant Bank of this Clause;

(e) which the Bank is in its reasonable opinion required by any law or regulation or subpoena or legal process to disclose;

(f) if an Event of Default or pending Default has occurred or the disclosure is in connection with the protection or enforcement of the relevant Bank's rights under this Agreement;

(g) to any banking or other official regulatory or self-regulatory body or authority pursuant to its request;

(h) in connection with any offering of securities by the Bank or its affiliates pursuant to disclosure requirements or in order to prevent any false market or insider dealing in relation to securities, or otherwise where required by any stock exchange or securities regulation or rule;
(i) for the purposes of:
   (i) obtaining any authorisation, approval or consent, or making any filing, registration or notarisation; and
   (ii) paying any stamp, registration or similar tax or charge in any relevant jurisdiction in respect of this Agreement;
(j) to the Agent Bank or another Bank under this Agreement; or
(k) if the disclosure would be permitted as an exception to the banker's duty of confidentiality under English law.

11. Arranger's disclaimer on syndication information memorandum

Note: A bank arranging a syndication generally excludes responsibility for any information memorandum prepared in relation to the syndication: See para 6–5 *et seq*. Set out below is a typical disclaimer.

Important Notice

[   ] (the "**Company**") has mandated Moneybank (the "**Arranger**") to arrange the credit facility outlined in this Information Memorandum and to distribute this Information Memorandum on the Company's behalf to potential participants in the facility.

The Company is solely responsible for this Information Memorandum and confirms on page [   ] of this Information Memorandum that it has taken all reasonable care to ensure that all statements of fact contained in this Information Memorandum are true and accurate in all material respects and do not omit anything likely to render that information materially misleading, and that all forecasts in this Information Memorandum are reasonably based.

The Arranger does not make any representation or warranty, express or implied, as to the accuracy or completeness of the information set out in this Information Memorandum or that it will remain unchanged after the date of this Information Memorandum. The Arranger has no responsibility for the information or for any inaccuracy in the information or for omissions, whether by reason of negligence, gross negligence or otherwise except where the employees of the Arranger concerned with this syndication actually know of the inaccuracy or omission and it is material. The Arranger does not undertake to review the financial condition or affairs of the Company or any of its subsidiaries or affiliates at any time or to advise any participant in the facility of any information coming to its attention at any time. The Arranger has not independently verified, or carried out any due diligence in relation to, any of the information contained in this Information Memorandum.

The Arranger does not accept any responsibility for the legality, validity, effectiveness, adequacy or enforceability or any documentation in relation to the facility.

This Information Memorandum is not a recommendation by the Arranger

ARRANGER'S DISCLAIMER ON SYNDICATION

that any recipient of this Memorandum should participate in the facility. Each potential participant should determine its interest in participating in the facility based upon such investigations as it deems necessary for the purpose.

This Information Memorandum is made available to potential participants in the facility on the strict understanding that it is confidential subject to and in accordance with the banker's duty of confidentiality under English law. No recipient of this Information Memorandum may disclose the document or any information in it to any person not previously approved in writing by the Arranger.

The Information Memorandum is submitted to selected banks specifically with reference to the proposed facility and may not be reproduced or used in whole or in part for any other purpose.

12. Outline of sub-participation agreement

Note: The following is an outline summarising the main terms of a typical sub-participation agreement. See chapter 7 for a discussion.

1. The Bank grants the Participant a participation in the loan evidenced by the loan agreement from the effective date (falling at the end of the interest period for the loan to avoid broken funding costs).

2. On the effective date the Participant will pay the amount of the participation to the Bank and will subsequently pay to the Bank its share of subsequent advances when the Bank is to make those advances under the loan agreement.

3. If and when the Bank applies an amount received from the borrower towards the borrower's obligations under the loan agreement, the Bank will pay the Participant a sum equal to the Participant's proportion of that amount in the currency received. Payments to the Participant are conditional on receipts by the Bank from the borrower. Allocation to principal, interest, and other amounts. Receipts include receipts by set-off, but not:
   - receipts which must be redistributed under the pro rata sharing clause in the loan agreement;
   - receipts which are blocked or received in a non-transferable currency.

4. Bank account, currency and funds of reciprocal payments. Participant will pay without set-off or deduction.

5. The relationship between the Bank and the Participant is debtor-creditor. The Bank does not transfer or assign any rights under the loan agreement, or hold them or their proceeds on trust for the Participant.

6. The Bank may exercise or refrain from exercising rights under the loan agreement or rights of set-off, or enforce or not enforce the loan agreement and vary or waive its terms without responsibility to the Participant, but will not agree to reduce or extend the maturity of payments. Bank will administer the loan agreement with the same care as it usually exercises in relation to its loans, and has no other duty of care to the Participant.

7. The participation is at the entire risk of the Participant. The Bank is not responsible for non-performance by the borrower or for the validity or

sufficiency of the loan documentation, and makes no representation as to the financial condition of the borrower. The Bank has no fiduciary obligations to the Participant and may engage in other transactions with the borrower without duty to account. The Participant will make its own investigations of the borrower's credit and not rely on the Bank. The Bank will not monitor the status of the borrower.

8. The Bank will forward to Participant documents received by the Bank from the borrower under the loan agreement if entitled to do so.

9. The Bank's obligations are subject to all applicable laws and regulations, including the right to deduct any withholding taxes that are levied.

10. Each party represents its power and authorities, and the legal validity of its obligations under this agreement.

11. The Bank need not pay the Participant until the Bank is satisfied that it has received the corresponding amount from the borrower. If the Bank does pay, but does not receive, the Participant will repay plus interest.

12. If the Bank must repay any amounts, by reason of preference or otherwise, the Participant will repay its share.

13. If as a result of financial difficulties or exchange controls, the borrower becomes subject to any rescheduling or reorganisation of any of its debt or a composition or plan involving the loan (including a conversion of the loan into shares or other securities of the borrower or another person and including a substitution of debtor) which is accepted by at least 50 per cent of the creditors of the class concerned (a "**general debt restructuring**"), the Bank may participate in the general debt restructuring, will not be obliged to account to the Participant in respect of any novation or roll-over of the loan or any conversion under the general debt restructuring, and will endeavour to give the Participant the benefit of its share of the reorganised debt, shares or other securities on the same terms mutatis mutandis as this agreement. The Participant will pay to the Bank its share of new loans made by the Bank in connection with the general debt restructuring if 75 per cent of the creditors of the class concerned participate in the new loans pro rata. Assignment to Participant of its share of restructured debt or securities on request if Bank entitled to assign.

14. Miscellaneous: the Bank may set off against Participant; no assignments by either party; not a partnership; confidentiality; notices; each pays own costs; Participant will reimburse its share of enforcement expenses; governing law; jurisdiction.

Appendix: Part II

Legal Opinions

13. Foreign lawyers' legal opinion on credit agreement

To: The Agent Bank and the Banks

Dears Sirs,

We have acted as your Ruritanian legal advisers in connection with (1) a Credit Agreement (the "**Credit Agreement**") dated [   ], between [   ] (the "**Borrower**"), the Banks and the Managers (each as defined therein) and [   ] as Agent for the Banks (the "**Agent**") under which the Banks have agreed to make available to the Borrower a credit facility of $100,000,000.

We have examined originals or copies of such corporate records of the Borrower, governmental authorisations or orders, certificates of public officials and of representatives of the Borrower and other documents as we have deemed relevant and necessary as the basis of our opinion. [These may be specified, e.g. Board resolutions.]

We have relied upon the certificates and other documents referred to above and have not independently established their accuracy. On [   ] we carried out a search of the Borrower's file at the Mercantile Registry in Dracula City. This search does not necessarily reveal the up-to-date position.

In giving this opinion, we have assumed:

(a) the genuineness of all signatures;

(b) the authenticity and completeness of all documents submitted to us as originals;

(c) the conformity to original documents of all documents submitted to us as copies and the authenticity and completeness of the original documents;

(d) that each meeting of the board of directors [and shareholders] of the Borrower stated to have been held has been duly convened and held and that in each case a duly qualified quorum of directors [or shareholders] voted in favour of the resolutions;

(e) that each agreement referred to in this opinion was duly executed by and constitutes a valid and legally binding obligation, in accordance with its terms, of each party thereto other than the Borrower;

(f) that all certificates and other documents on which we have expressed reliance remain accurate and that no additional matters would have been disclosed by a company search at the Mercantile Registry if carried out since the carrying out of the search referred to above;

(g) that the Borrower is not subject to insolvency proceedings and no application has been made or resolution passed for such insolvency proceedings;

(h) that there are no contractual or similar restrictions binding on the Borrower which would affect the conclusions in this opinion and that any restrictions in the Borrower's Articles of Association would not be contravened by the entry into and performance of the Credit Agreement.

Based upon the foregoing and subject to the qualifications set out below and subject to matters not disclosed to us and to matters of fact which would affect the conclusions set out below, we are of the opinion that, so far as the present laws of Ruritania are concerned:

(a) **Status** The Borrower is a corporation duly incorporated and validly existing under the laws of Ruritania.

(b) **Powers and authority** The Borrower has the corporate power to enter into and perform the Credit Agreement and the transactions contemplated thereby and has taken all necessary corporate action to authorise the entry into and performance of the Credit Agreement and the transactions contemplated thereby.

(c) **Due execution** The Credit Agreement has been duly executed and delivered by the Borrower.

(d) **Legal validity** The Credit Agreement constitutes a legal, valid and binding obligation of the Borrower enforceable in accordance with its terms and would be so treated in the courts of Ruritania; the Credit Agreement is in proper form for its enforcement in such courts.

(e) **Non-conflict with laws** The entry into and performance of the Credit Agreement and the transactions contemplated thereby do not and will not violate (i) any present law or regulation of or in Ruritania or (ii) the constitutional documents of the Borrower.

(f) **Consents** All authorisations, approvals, consents, licences, exemptions, filings, registrations, notarisations and other requirements of governmental, judicial and public bodies and authorities of or in Ruritania required or advisable in connection with the entry into and performance by the Borrower, and the validity and enforceability of the Credit Agreement and the transactions contemplated thereby have been obtained or effected and are in full force and effect.

(g) **Pari passu** The obligations of the Borrower under the Credit Agreement rank at least pari passu with all its other unsecured obligations.

(h) **No immunity**:
- (1) the Borrower is subject to civil and commercial law with respect to its obligations under the Credit Agreement;
- (2) the entry into and performance of the Credit Agreement by the Borrower constitute private and commercial acts;
- (3) neither the Borrower nor any of its assets enjoys any right of immunity from set-off, suit or execution in respect of its obligations under the Credit Agreement.

(i) **Taxes on payments** All amounts payable by the Borrower under the Credit Agreement may be made free and clear of and without deduction for or on account of any taxes imposed, assessed or levied by Ruritania or any authority thereof or therein.

(j) **Stamp notices** No stamp or registration duty or similar taxes or charges are payable in Ruritania in respect of the Credit Agreement.

(k) **Enforcement of foreign judgments** A judgment obtained in the courts of England or the state courts of or federal courts in the State of New York in respect of the Credit Agreement would be enforced by the courts of Ruritania without re-examination of the merits of the case. [For usual qualifications, see para 13–33.]

(l) **No adverse consequences; qualifications to do business** Under the laws of Ruritania neither the Agent nor any Bank will be deemed to be resident, domiciled or carrying on any commercial activity in Ruritania or subject to any Ruritanian tax as a result only of the entry into and performance of the Credit Agreement, or the transactions contemplated thereby. It is not necessary under the laws of Ruritania for the entry into, performance or enforcement of the Credit Agreement that the Agent or any Bank be authorised or qualified to carry on business in Ruritania.

(m) **Application of proper law** The choice of English law as the governing law of the Credit Agreement would be upheld as a valid choice of law by the courts of Ruritania and applied by such courts in proceedings in relation to the Credit Agreement as the governing law of the Credit Agreement.

The qualifications to which this opinion is subject are as follows:

1. This opinion relates only to Ruritanian law and it is assumed that no law of any other jurisdiction affects the conclusions in this opinion.

2. This opinion is subject to all insolvency and other similar laws affecting the rights of creditors.

[For other possible qualifications, see the final paragraphs of the next opinion.]

Note: The internal lawyers of the Borrower giving an opinion may be prepared to add the following paragraphs:

1. [Instead of para (e) in the above opinion] **Non-conflict with laws** The entry into and performance of the Credit Agreement and the transactions contemplated thereby do not and will not violate (i) any present law or regulation or (so far as I am aware after due enquiry) any official or judicial order, of or in Ruritania, or (ii) the constitutional documents of the Borrower, or (iii) (so far as I am aware after due enquiry) any agreement or document to which the Borrower or any of its subsidiaries is a party or which is binding upon any of them or any of their respective assets, nor result in the creation or imposition of any security interest on any of their respective assets pursuant to the provisions of any such agreement or document.

2. **No default** (So far as I am aware after due enquiry) no event has occurred which constitutes a material default under or in respect of any agreement or document to which the Borrower or any of its subsidiaries is a party or by which the Borrower or any of its subsidiaries may be bound (including, inter alia, the Credit Agreement) and no event has occurred which, with the giving of notice, lapse of time, determination of materiality or other conditions might constitute a material default under or in respect of any such agreement or document.

3. **Litigation** So far as I am aware after due enquiry, no litigation, arbitration or administrative proceedings are at present current, pending or threatened, which might if adversely determined have a material adverse effect on the business, assets or financial condition of the Borrower or those of any of its subsidiaries.

14. Principal lawyers' legal opinion on credit agreement

To: The Agent Bank and the Banks

Dear Sirs,

We have acted as legal advisers in England to [   ] (the "**Agent**") in connection with (1) the Credit Agreement (the "**Credit Agreement**") dated [   ] between [   ] (the "**Borrower**"), the banks and financial institutions therein referred to (the "**Banks**"), the Managers therein referred and the Agent, under which the Banks have agreed to make available to the Borrower a credit facility of US$100,000,000.

We have received instructions from and participated in discussions with the Agent about the provisions contained in the Credit Agreement.

We have examined and relied on a copy of the opinion dated [   ] of Pettifogo and Pedantissimo, Ruritanian legal advisers to the Agent and the Banks.

For the purposes of giving this opinion, we have assumed the power and authority to execute and the due execution and delivery of the Credit Agreement by the parties thereto and that, so far as the laws of any jurisdiction other than England are concerned, and in particular the laws of Ruritania, the Credit Agreement is the valid and legally binding obligation of the Borrower.

We have also assumed:

1. the authenticity and completeness of all documents submitted to us as originals;
2. the conformity to original documents of all documents submitted to us as copies and the authenticity and completeness of the original documents; and
3. that there are no contractual or similar restrictions binding on the Borrower which would affect the conclusions in this opinion.

Based upon the foregoing and subject to the qualifications set out below and subject to matters not disclosed to us and to matters of fact which would affect the conclusions set out below, we are of the opinion that, so far as the present laws of England are concerned:

1. The Credit Agreement constitutes the legally binding obligations of the Borrower in accordance with its terms.

2. The execution, delivery and performance by the Borrower of the Credit Agreement does not and will not violate in any material respect any provision of any present English law or regulation applicable to companies generally.

3. The Borrower is not immune from suit or execution in the courts of England as regards the Credit Agreement, except for certain diplomatic immunities.

4. No authorisations, approvals, consents, filings, registrations, notarisations or other requirements of or with governmental, judicial or public bodies and authorities of or in England are required by the Borrower in connection with the performance, validity or enforceability of the Credit Agreement.

5. It is not necessary or advisable to file, register or record the Credit Agreement in any public place or elsewhere in England and Wales.

6. No stamp, registration or other similar duties are payable in England in respect of the execution or delivery of the Credit Agreement.

The qualifications to which this opinion is subject are as follows:

1. This opinion relates only to English domestic law and it is assumed that no law of any other jurisdiction affects the conclusions in this opinion.

2. This opinion is subject to all insolvency and other laws affecting the rights of creditors.

3. Certain of the obligations may be qualified by the non-conclusivity of certificates, doctrines of good faith and fair conduct, invalidity of unreasonable exculpations of liability, equitable remedies and other matters, but in our view these qualifications would not defeat your legitimate expectations in any material way. [The legal opinion may set out a list: see para 13–22. Some of these are either trivial or remote, and most would not surprise reasonable expectations.]

This opinion is given for the sole benefit of the Banks which are the original parties to the Credit Agreement and may not be relied upon by or disclosed to any other person.

Yours faithfully,

Appendix: Part III

BOND ISSUES

15. Subscription agreement for a corporate issue of notes

Note: These agreements are discussed at para 8–18 *et seq*. This issue is to be listed in London and constituted by a trust deed.

MEGACORP S.A.

U.S.$100,000,000

10 per cent. Notes due 2005

SUBSCRIPTION AGREEMENT

To: City Finance Limited
      Zurich International plc
      Investor Markets Limited
      (the "Managers")

c/o City Finance Limited
      [Address]   24th February, 1995

Dear Sirs,

MEGACORP S.A. (the "Issuer") proposes to issue US$100,000,000 10 per cent. Notes due 2005 (the "Notes", which expression where the context admits shall include the Global Note (as defined below)). The Notes will be in bearer form in the denomination of US$1000 each and will be constituted by a Trust Deed (the "Trust Deed") between the Issuer and The Legal Debenture Corporation plc as trustee (the "Trustee") substantially in the form of the draft signed for identification by Messrs. Pettifog & Pedant with such changes as may be approved by City Finance Limited (the "Lead Manager") on behalf of the Managers.

We wish to record the arrangements agreed between us for this purpose:

1. Subscription

Subject to the terms and conditions of this Agreement the Issuer agrees to issue the Notes and the Managers jointly and severally agree to subscribe and pay for the Notes on the Closing Date (as defined below) at a subscription price of 99.75 per cent of the principal amount of the Notes (the "Subscription Price", being the issue price of 100 per cent less the selling concession of 0.25 per cent of the principal amount).

2. Closing

The net subscription money in respect of the Notes, namely the sum of US$99,425,000 (representing the Subscription Price, less the amount of the commission specified in clause 4 and less the amount mentioned in clause 5) will be paid by the Lead Manager on behalf of the Managers to the Issuer at 10.00 a.m. (New York City time) on 1st March, 1995 or at such other time and/or date as the Issuer and the Lead Manager on behalf of the Managers may agree (the "Closing Date") in New York same day funds against delivery of a temporary global note (the "Global Note") representing the Notes, in the form provided in the Trust Deed to a common depositary for Morgan Guaranty Trust Company of New York, Brussels office, as operator of the Euroclear System, and Cedel Bank, société anonyme.

3. Undertakings

The Issuer undertakes with the Managers that it will:

1. on or before the Closing Date execute the Trust Deed;

2. on or before the Closing Date execute a paying agency agreement (the "Agency Agreement") substantially in the form of the draft signed for identification by Messrs. Pettifog & Pedant with such changes as may be approved by the Lead Manager on behalf of the Managers; and

3. bear and pay any stamp or other duties or taxes on or in connection with the issue and delivery of the Notes and the execution and delivery of this Agreement, the Trust Deed and the Agency Agreement and any value added tax payable in connection with the commission or other amounts payable or allowed under this Agreement and otherwise in connection with the transactions envisaged by this Agreement.

4. Commission

In consideration of the agreement by the Managers to act as the agents of the Issuer in relation to the issue of the Notes and to subscribe and pay for the Notes as provided above, the Issuer shall pay to the Managers a combined management and underwriting commission of 0.30 per cent of the principal amount of the Notes. The Managers shall be entitled to deduct such commission from the subscription money as provided in clause 2.

5. Expenses

The Issuer shall bear and pay all costs and expenses incurred in connection with the printing, checking and initial delivery of the Notes (including the delivery of Notes in definitive form in exchange for the Global Note), the printing and distribution of the Offering Circular dated 24th February, 1995 (the "Offering Circular") the printing and production of all other documents connected with the issue and distribution of the Notes, advertising, the listing of the Notes on The International Stock Exchange of the United Kingdom and the Republic of Ireland Limited (the "London Stock Exchange") and the arrangements for signing this Agreement and shall also pay the remuneration of the Trustee and the expenses incurred by it, including the fees of its legal advisers.

In addition, the Issuer agrees to pay to the Managers the amount of up to US$25,000 in respect of legal, travelling, telex, telephone, facsimile, postage and other costs and expenses incurred and to be incurred by the Managers in connection with the preparation and management of the issue and distribution of the Notes. The Managers shall be entitled to deduct such amount from the subscription money as provided in clause 2.

6. Representations and Warranties

1. As a condition of the obligation of the Managers to subscribe and pay for the Notes the Issuer represents and warrants to the Managers as follows:

    (a) that the consolidated balance sheets of the Issuer and its subsidiaries (the "Group") as at 31st December, 1993 and 1994 and the consolidated profit and loss accounts of the Group for the three years ended 31st December, 1994 appearing in the Offering Circular were prepared in accordance with the requirements of law and with accounting principles generally accepted in Ruritania consistently applied and that they give a true and fair view of the consolidated financial condition of the Group as at the dates as at which they were prepared and of the results of their operations and changes in financial condition for the three years ended 31st December, 1994 and that there has been no material adverse change or any development involving a prospective material adverse change in the consolidated condition (financial or otherwise) of the Group since 31st December, 1994 except as disclosed in the Offering Circular;

(b) that the Offering Circular contains all material information with respect to the Group and that the statements contained therein relating to the Group and to the use of the proceeds of the issue of the Notes are in every material particular true and accurate and not misleading and that there are no other facts in relation to it the omission of which would in the context of the issue of the Notes make any statement in the Offering Circular misleading in any material respect and that all reasonable enquiries have been made to ascertain such facts and to verify the accuracy of all such statements;

(c) that the Offering Circular contains all the information required by section 146 of the Financial Services Act 1986 (the "FSA") and otherwise complies with the listing rules made by the London Stock Exchange under the FSA (the "Listing Rules");

(d) that the issue of the Notes and the execution of this Agreement, the Trust Deed and the Agency Agreement by the Issuer have been duly authorised by the Issuer and that upon due execution, issue and delivery the same will constitute legal, valid and binding obligations of the Issuer enforceable in accordance with their respective terms subject to the laws of bankruptcy and other laws affecting the rights of creditors generally;

(e) that the execution and delivery of this Agreement, the Trust Deed and the Agency Agreement and the issue and distribution of the Notes and the performance of the terms of the Notes, this Agreement, the Trust Deed and the Agency Agreement will not infringe any law or regulation and are not contrary to the provisions of the constitutional documents of the Issuer and will not result in any breach of the terms of, or constitute a default under, any instrument or agreement to which the Issuer is a party or by which it or its property is bound;

(f) that no member of the Group is involved in any litigation or arbitration proceedings relating to claims or amounts which are material in the context of the issue of the Notes nor so far as the Issuer is aware is any such litigation or arbitration pending or threatened;

(g) that all consents and approvals of any court, government department or other regulatory body required by the Issuer for the execution and delivery of this Agreement, the Trust Deed and the Agency Agreement and the issue and distribution of the Notes and the performance of the terms of the Notes, this Agreement, the Trust Deed and the Agency Agreement have been obtained and are in full force and effect;

(h) that no event has occurred which would constitute (after the issue of the Notes) an event of default under the Notes or which with the giving of notice or the lapse of time or other condition would (after the issue of the Notes) constitute an event of default;

(i) that neither the Issuer, its affiliates (as defined in Rule 405 under the US Securities Act of 1933 (the "Securities Act")) nor any persons (other than the Managers) acting on its or their behalf have engaged or will engage in any directed selling efforts (as defined in Regulation S under the Securities Act) in respect of the Notes; and

(j) that the Issuer, its affiliates and any person (other than any Manager) acting on its or their behalf have complied with and will comply with the offering restrictions requirement of Regulation S under the Securities Act.

2. The Issuer undertakes to indemnify the Managers and their directors, officers, employees and controlling persons (each an "Indemnified Person") against any losses, liabilities, costs, claims, actions, damages, expenses or demands which any of them may incur, or which may be made against any of them, as a result of or in relation to any actual or alleged misrepresentation in, or actual or alleged breach of, any of the above representations and warranties or in connection with any actual or alleged inaccuracy in or actual or alleged omission from, the Offering Circular and will reimburse any such person for all costs, charges and expenses which they may pay or incur in connection with investigating, disputing or defending any such action or claim. Each Indemnified Person shall give prompt notice to the Issuer of any action commenced against it in respect of which indemnity may be sought under this Agreement. The Issuer may participate at its own expense in the defence of the action. If it so elects within a reasonable time after receipt of the notice, the Issuer may assume the defence of the action with legal advisers chosen by it and approved by the Indemnified Person defendant in the action, unless the Indemnified Person reasonably objects to the assumption on the ground that there may be legal defences available to it which are different from or in addition to those available to the Issuer. If the Issuer assumes the defence of the action, the Issuer shall not be liable for any fees and expenses of the legal advisers of the Indemnified Person incurred thereafter in connection with the action. In no event shall the Issuer be liable for the fees and expenses of more than one legal adviser or firm of legal advisers of the Indemnified Person in connection with any one action or separate but similar or related actions in the same jurisdiction arising out of the same general allegations or circumstances. Neither the Issuer nor the Guarantor shall be liable to indemnify any Indemnified Person for any settlement of any such action effected without the consent of the Issuer (the consent not to be unreasonably withheld or delayed).

3. The Issuer undertakes with the Managers that it will forthwith notify the Lead Manager on behalf of the Managers of any material change affecting any of the above representations and warranties at any time before payment is made to the Issuer on the Closing Date and that it will take those steps which may be reasonably requested by the Lead Manager to remedy and/or publicise the material change. Upon any material breach of any of the above representations and warranties or any change rendering any of the above representations and warranties inaccurate in a material respect coming to the notice of the Managers before payment being made to the Issuer on the Closing Date, the Managers shall be entitled (but not bound) by notice to the Issuer to elect to treat such breach or change as (except as otherwise specifically provided) releasing and discharging the Managers from their obligations under this Agreement.

4. The above representations, warranties and indemnity shall continue in full force and effect notwithstanding:

   (a) the actual or constructive knowledge of any Manager with respect to any of the matters referred to in the representations and warranties of the Issuer; or

   (b) the completion of the arrangements set out in this Agreement for the subscription and issue of the Notes.

7. Listing

1. The Issuer shall, if it has not already done so, make an application for the Notes to be listed on the London Stock Exchange. In connection with such application, the Issuer shall endeavour to obtain the listing as promptly as practicable and the Issuer shall furnish any and all documents, instruments, information and undertakings that may be necessary or advisable in order to obtain or maintain the listing.

2. The Issuer confirms that the Offering Circular has been approved by the London Stock Exchange as listing particulars and shall ensure that they are delivered to the Registrar of Companies for registration.

3. If after the preparation of the Offering Circular for submission to the London Stock Exchange and before the commencement of dealings in the Notes following their admission to the Official List:

   (a) there is a significant change affecting any matter contained in the Offering Circular whose inclusion was required by section 146 of the FSA or by the Listing Rules or by the London Stock Exchange; or

(b) a significant new matter arises the inclusion of information in respect of which would have been so required if it had arisen when the Offering Circular were prepared,

the Issuer shall give to the Lead Manager full information about the change or matter and shall publish supplementary listing particulars (in a form approved by the Lead Manager) as may be required by the London Stock Exchange, and shall otherwise comply with sections 147 and 149 of the FSA and the Listing Rules in that regard.

8. Conditions

This Agreement and the respective rights and obligations of the parties to this Agreement are conditional upon:

1. there having been, as at the Closing Date, no event making any of the representations and warranties contained in clause 6(1) untrue or incorrect in any material respect on the Closing Date as though they had been given and made on such date;
2. the delivery to the Managers and the Trustee on or before the Closing Date of:
   (a) legal opinions in such form and with such contents as the Lead Manager and the Trustee may reasonably require from Pompous & Sons, legal advisers to the Issuer, from Dracula & Dracula, legal advisers to the Managers and the Trustee in Ruritania, and from Pettifog & Pedant, legal advisers to the Managers and the Trustee in England; and
   (b) a certificate signed by a duly authorised officer of the Issuer to the effect stated in paragraph (1); and
   (c) any reports and confirmations from the auditors of the Issuer as the Lead Manager may reasonably require;
3. the Notes being admitted to the Official List of the London Stock Exchange, subject only to the issue of the Notes on or before the Closing Date; and
4. the execution of the Trust Deed and the Agency Agreement by the parties thereto on or before the Closing Date.

In the event that any of the foregoing conditions is not satisfied on or before the Closing Date, this Agreement shall (subject as mentioned below) terminate and the parties hereto shall (except for the liability of the Issuer in relation to expenses as provided in clause 5 and except for any liability arising before or in relation to such termination) be under no further liability arising out of this Agreement, provided that the Lead Manager on behalf of the Managers may in its discretion and by notice to the Issuer waive satisfaction of any of the above conditions or any part of them.

9. Responsibility for sales

The Issuer shall have no responsibility in respect of the legality of the Managers or other persons offering and selling the Notes in any jurisdiction or in respect of the Notes qualifying for sale in any jurisdiction.

10. Managers' Undertakings and Warranty

Each of the Managers undertakes that it will observe and perform the following provisions:

1. (a) Each Manager understands that the Notes have not been and will not be registered under the Securities Act and may not be offered or sold within the United States or to, or for the account or benefit of, US persons except in accordance with Regulation S under the Securities Act or pursuant to an exemption from the registration requirements of the Securities Act. Each Manager represents and agrees that it has offered and sold the Notes, and will offer and sell the Notes (i) as part of their distribution at any time and (ii) otherwise until 40 days after the later of the commencement of the offering and the Closing Date, only in accordance with Rule 903 of Regulation S under the Securities Act. Accordingly, each Manager further represents and agrees that neither it, its affiliates nor any persons acting on its or their behalf have engaged or will engage in any directed selling efforts with respect to the Notes, and it and they have complied and will comply with the offering restrictions requirement of Regulation S. Each Manager agrees that, at or prior to confirmation of sale of Notes, it will have sent to each distributor, dealer or person receiving a selling concession, fee or other remuneration that purchases Notes from it during the restricted period a confirmation or notice to substantially the following effect:

"The Securities covered hereby have not been registered under the US Securities Act of 1933 (the "Securities Act") and may not be offered and sold within the United States or to, or for the account or benefit of, US persons (i) as part of their distribution at any time or (ii) otherwise until 40 days after the later of the commencement of the offering and the closing date, except in either case in accordance with Regulation S (or Rule 144A if available) under the Securities Act. Terms used above have the meaning given to them by Regulation S."

Terms used in this subparagraph (a) have the meanings given to them by Regulation S.

(b) Each Manager agrees that, except to the extent permitted under US Treas. Reg. section 1.163–5(c)(2)(i)(D) (the "D Rules"), (i) it has not offered or sold, and during the restricted period will not offer or sell, Notes in bearer form to a person who is within the United States or its possessions or to a United States person, and (ii) it has not delivered and will not deliver within the United States or its possessions definitive Notes in bearer form that are sold during the restricted period.

(c) Each Manager represents and agrees that it has and throughout the restricted period will have in effect procedures reasonably designed to ensure that its employees or agents who are directly engaged in selling Notes in bearer form are aware that such Notes may not be offered or sold during the restricted period to a person who is within the United States or its possessions or to a US person, except as permitted by the D Rules.

(d) Each Manager which is a United States person represents that it is acquiring the Notes in bearer form for purposes of resale in connection with their original issuance and that if it retains Notes in bearer form for its own account, it will only do so in accordance with the requirements of US Treas. Reg. section 1.163–5(c)(2)(i)(D)(6).

(e) Each Manager agrees that, with respect to each affiliate that acquires from it Notes in bearer form for the purpose of offering or selling such Notes during the restricted period, it either (i) repeats and confirms the representations and agreements contained in subparagraphs (b), (c), and (d) above on its behalf or (ii) will obtain from such affiliate for the benefit of the Issuer the representations and agreements contained in subparagraphs (b), (c) and (d) above.

(f) Terms used in subparagraphs (b) to (e) above have the meanings given to them by the US Internal Revenue Code and regulations thereunder, including the D Rules.

2. Each Manager represents and agrees that:

(a) it has not offered or sold and will not offer or sell in the United Kingdom by means of any document any Notes prior to application for listing of the Notes being made in accordance with Part IV of the FSA, other than in circumstances which do not constitute an offer to the public within the meaning of the Companies Act 1985;

(b) it has complied and will comply with all applicable provisions of the FSA with respect to anything done by it in relation to the Notes in, from or otherwise involving the United Kingdom; and

(c) it has only issued or passed on and will only issue or pass on in the United Kingdom any document received by it in connection with the issue of the Notes, other than any document which consists of or any part of listing particulars, supplementary listing particulars or any other document required or permitted to be published by the listing rules under Part IV of the FSA to a person who is of a kind described in Article 9(3) of the Financial Services Act 1986 (Investment Advertisements) (Exemptions) Order 1988 or is a person to whom the document may otherwise lawfully be issued or passed on.

3. The Notes may not be offered or sold to the public in Ruritania.

4. No action has been taken by the Issuer or any of the Managers that would, or is intended to, permit a public offer of the Notes in any country or jurisdiction where any such action for that purpose is required. Accordingly, each Manager undertakes that it will not, directly or indirectly, offer or sell any Notes or distribute or publish any offering circular, prospectus, form of application, advertisement or other document or information in any country or jurisdiction except under circumstances that will, to the best of its knowledge and belief, result in compliance with any applicable laws and regulations and all offers and sales of Notes by it will be made on the same terms.

5. Without prejudice to the generality of paragraph (4), each Manager agrees that it will obtain any consent, approval or permission which is, to the best of its knowledge and belief, required for the offer, purchase or sale by it of Notes under the laws and regulations in force in any jurisdiction to which it is subject or in which it makes such offers, purchases or sales and it will, to the best of its knowledge and belief, comply with all such laws and regulations.

6. No Manager is authorised to give any information or to make any representation in connection with the offering or sale of the Notes other than those contained in the Offering Circular.

7. Each Manager undertakes to indemnify the Issuer, each of the other Managers and their respective directors, officers, employees and controlling persons against any losses, liabilities, costs, claims, actions, damages, expenses or demands which any of them may incur or which may be made against them arising out of or in relation to or in connec-

tion with any unauthorised action by that Manager, failure by that Manager to observe any of the above restrictions or requirements or the making by that Manager of any unauthorised representation or the giving or use by that Manager of any information which has not been authorised by the Issuer or any of the other Managers. The provisions of clause 6(3) with respect to the conduct and settlement of actions shall apply mutatis mutandis to this indemnity.

11. Stabilisation

If the Managers, or any of them, in connection with the distribution of the Notes offer Notes in excess of the aggregate principal amount to be issued or effect transactions with a view to stabilising or maintaining the market price of the Notes at levels other than those which might otherwise prevail in the open market, they shall not in doing so be deemed to act as agents of the Issuer. The Issuer will not as a result of any action taken by the Managers, or any of them, under this clause be obliged to issue Notes in excess of the aggregate amount of Notes to be issued under this Agreement, nor shall the Issuer be liable for any loss, or entitled to any profit, arising from any excess offers or stabilisation.

12. Termination

Notwithstanding anything contained in this Agreement, the Lead Manager on behalf of the Managers may by notice to the Issuer terminate this Agreement at any time before the time on the Closing Date when payment would otherwise be due under this Agreement to the Issuer in respect of the Notes if, in the opinion of the Managers, there shall have been such a change, whether or not foreseeable at the date of this Agreement, in national or international financial, political or economic conditions or currency exchange rates or exchange controls as would in their view be likely to prejudice materially the success of the offering and distribution of the Notes or dealings in the Notes in the secondary market and upon the notice being given the parties to this Agreement shall (except for the liability of the Issuer in relation to expenses as provided in clause 5 and except for any liability arising before or in relation to such termination) be released and discharged from their respective obligations under this Agreement.

13. Notices

Any notice or notification in any form to be given by the Managers to the Issuer may be given by the Lead Manager on behalf of the Managers and may be delivered in person or sent by telex, facsimile or telephone (subject in the case of a communication by telephone to confirmation by telex or facsimile) addressed to:

MEGACORP S.A.
[Address]
Telex Number: [   ]
Facsimile Number: [   ]
Attention of: [   ]

Any such notice shall take effect, in the case of delivery, at the time of delivery and, in the case of telex, at the time of despatch.

14. Law and jurisdiction

This Agreement is governed by, and shall be construed in accordance with, English law. The Issuer hereby agrees for the exclusive benefit of the Managers that the courts of England are to have jurisdiction to settle any disputes which may arise out of or in connection with this Agreement and that accordingly any suit, action or proceedings (together referred to as "Proceedings") arising out of or in connection with this Agreement may be brought in such courts. Nothing contained in this clause shall limit any right to take Proceedings against the Issuer in any other court of competent jurisdiction, nor shall the taking of Proceedings in one or more jurisdictions preclude the taking of Proceedings in any other jurisdiction, whether concurrently or not. The Issuer hereby appoints Process Agent Limited at its registered office for the time being in England to accept service of any Proceedings on its behalf.

15. Miscellaneous

1. Time shall be of the essence of this Agreement.
2. The heading to each clause is included for convenience only and shall not affect the construction of this Agreement.
3. This Agreement may be executed in any number of counterparts, all of which, taken together, shall constitute one and the same agreement and any party may enter into this Agreement by executing a counterpart.

Please confirm that this letter correctly sets out the arrangements agreed between us.

SUBSCRIPTION AGREEMENT

Yours faithfully,
MEGACORP S.A.
By:

We agree to the foregoing.

For: City Finance Limited

By:

For: Zurich International plc
         Investor Markets Limited

By:

16. Terms and conditions of a fixed rate US dollar note

Note: Bond and note issues are discussed in chapters 8 to 11. See especially para 8–39 *et seq*. This issue is constituted by a trust deed.

The US$100,000,000 10 per cent. Notes due 2005 (the "Notes", which expression shall in these Conditions, unless the context otherwise requires, include any further notes issued pursuant to Condition 16 and forming a single series with the Notes) of MEGACORP S.A. (the "Issuer") are constituted by a Trust Deed dated March 1, 1995 (the "Trust Deed") made between the Issuer and The Legal Debenture Corporation p.l.c. (the "Trustee") as trustee for the holders of the Notes (the "Noteholders") and the holders of the interest coupons appertaining to the Notes (the "Couponholders" and the "Coupons" respectively). The issue of the Notes was authorised by a resolution of the Board of Directors of the Issuer passed on 16th February, 1995. The Notes are on issue listed on The International Stock Exchange of the United Kingdom and the Republic of Ireland Limited (the "London Stock Exchange"). The statements in these Conditions include summaries of, and are subject to, the detailed provisions of and definitions in the Trust Deed. Copies of the Trust Deed and the Agency Agreement dated 1st March, 1995 (the "Agency Agreement") made between the Issuer, the initial Paying Agents and the Trustee are available for inspection during normal business hours by the Noteholders and the Couponholders at the principal office for the time being of the Trustee, being at the date of issue of the Notes at [address of the Trustee] and at the specified office of each of the Paying Agents. The Noteholders and the Couponholders are entitled to the benefit of, are bound by, and are deemed to have notice of, all the provisions of the Trust Deed and the Agency Agreement applicable to them.

1. **Form, Denomination and Title**

1. The Notes are in bearer form, serially numbered, in the denomination of US$1,000 each with Coupons attached on issue. Title to the Notes and to the Coupons will pass by delivery.

2. The Issuer, any Paying Agent and the Trustee may (to the fullest extent permitted by applicable laws) deem and treat the holder of any Note and the holder of any Coupon as the absolute owner for all purposes (whether or not the Note or Coupon shall be overdue and notwithstanding any notice of ownership or writing on the Note or Coupon or any notice of previous loss or theft of the Note or Coupon).

2. Status

The Notes and the Coupons are direct, unconditional and (subject to the provisions of Condition 3) unsecured obligations of the Issuer and (subject as provided above) rank and will rank pari passu, without any preference among themselves, with all other outstanding unsecured and unsubordinated obligations of the Issuer, present and future, but, in the event of insolvency, only to the extent permitted by applicable laws relating to creditors' rights.

3. Negative Pledge

So long as any of the Notes remains outstanding, the Issuer will not create or permit to be outstanding any pledge, mortgage, charge or other security interest for the benefit of the holders of any Relevant Indebtedness (as defined below) upon the whole or any part of the property or assets, present or future, of the Issuer or any of its Subsidiaries to secure (a) any payment due in respect of any Relevant Indebtedness, (b) any payment under any guarantee of any Relevant Indebtedness, or (c) any payment under any indemnity or other obligation relating to any Relevant Indebtedness without, in any such case, at the same time according to the Notes either the same security as is granted to or is outstanding in respect of such Relevant Notes or such guarantee, indemnity or other like obligation or such other security as shall be approved by the Trustee or by an Extraordinary Resolution (as defined in the Trust Deed) of the Noteholders.

For the purposes of this Condition 3:

"**Relevant Indebtedness**" means bonds, debentures, notes or other similar securities of the Issuer or any other person with a stated maturity of more than one year from the creation thereof which:

(i) are by their terms payable, or confer a right to receive payment, in any currency other than Ruritanian dollars, or are denominated in Ruritanian dollars and more than 50 per cent of the aggregate principal amount thereof is initially distributed outside Ruritania by or with the authorisation of the issuer thereof, and

(ii) are for the time being, or are intended to be, quoted, listed, ordinarily dealt in or traded on any stock exchange or over-the-counter or other similar securities market; and

"**Subsidiary**" means a subsidiary as defined in section 100 of the Ruritanian Companies Act 1985.

4. Interest

1. The Notes bear interest from and including 1st March, 1995 at the rate of 10 per cent per annum, payable annually in arrear on 1st March (each an "Interest Payment Date"). The first payment shall be made on 1st March, 1996. Each Note will cease to bear interest from and including its due date for redemption unless, upon due presentation, payment of the principal in respect of the Note is improperly withheld or refused or unless default is otherwise made in respect of payment in which event interest shall continue to accrue as provided in the Trust Deed.

2. When interest is required to be calculated in respect of a period of less than a full year, it shall be calculated on the basis of a 360-day year consisting of 12 months of 30 days each and, in the case of an incomplete month, the number of days elapsed.

5. Payments

1. Payments of principal and interest in respect of each Note will be made against presentation and surrender (or, in the case of part payment only, endorsement) of the Note, except that payments of interest due on an Interest Payment Date will be made against presentation and surrender (or, in the case of part payment only, endorsement) of the relevant Coupons, in each case at the specified office outside the United States of any of the Paying Agents.

2. Payments will be made at the specified office of any Paying Agent outside the United States, at the option of the holder, by US dollar cheque drawn on, or by transfer to a US dollar account maintained by the payee with, a bank in New York City, subject in all cases to any fiscal or other laws and regulations applicable in the place of payment, but without prejudice to the provisions of Condition 7.

   Notwithstanding the foregoing, payments will be made at the specified office in the United States of any Paying Agent, and (if no such appointment is then in effect) the Issuer shall appoint and maintain a Paying Agent with a specified office in New York City at which payments will be made, (a) if (i) the Issuer shall have appointed Paying Agents with specified offices outside the United States with the reasonable expectation that the Paying Agents would be able to make payment at the specified offices outside the United States of the full amount payable with respect to the Notes in the manner provided above when due, (ii) payment of the full amount due in US dollars at all specified offices of the Paying Agents outside the United States is illegal or effectively precluded by exchange controls or other similar restrictions and (iii) the payment is then permitted under US law and/or (b) at the option of the relevant holder if the payment is then permitted under US law without involving, in the opinion of the Issuer, adverse tax consequences for the Issuer.

3. Each Note should be presented for payment together with all relative unmatured Coupons, failing which the full amount of any relative missing unmatured Coupon (or, in the case of payment not being made in full, that proportion of the full amount of the missing unmatured Coupon which the amount so paid bears to the total amount due) will be deducted from the amount due for payment. Each amount so deducted will be paid in the manner mentioned above against presentation and surrender (or, in the case of part payment only, endorsement) of the relative missing Coupon at any time before the expiry of 10 years after the Relevant Date (as defined in Condition 7) in respect of the relevant Note (whether or not the Coupon would otherwise have become void pursuant to Condition 8) or, if later, five years after the date on which the Coupon would have become due, but not thereafter.

4. A holder shall be entitled to present a Note or Coupon for payment only on a Presentation Date and shall not, except as provided in Condition 4, be entitled to any further interest or other payment if a Presentation Date is after the due date.

"**Presentation Date**" means a day which (subject to Condition 8):

(a) is or falls after the relevant due date or, if the due date is not or was not a Business Day in New York City, is or falls after the next following such Business Day; and
(b) is a Business Day in the place of the specified office of the Paying Agent at which the Note or Coupon is presented for payment and (unless the second following paragraph applies, in the case of payment by transfer to a US dollar account in New York City as referred to above) in New York City.

"**Business Day**" means, in relation to any place, a day on which commercial banks and foreign exchange markets settle payments in that place.

If a Note or Coupon is presented for payment at a time when, as a result of differences in time zones, it is not practicable to transfer the relevant amount to an account as referred to above for value on the relevant Presentation Date, the Issuer shall not be obliged so to do but shall be obliged to transfer the relevant amount to the account for value on the first practicable date after the Presentation Date.

5. The names of the initial Paying Agents and their initial specified offices are set out at the end of these Conditions. The Issuer reserves the right, subject to the approval of the Trustee, at any time to vary or terminate the appointment of any Paying Agent and to appoint additional or other Paying Agents provided that it will at all times maintain a Paying Agent having a specified office in New York City and at least two other Paying Agents having specified offices in separate European cities approved by the Trustee, one of which, so long as the Notes are listed on the London Stock Exchange, shall be London or such other place as the London Stock Exchange may approve. Notice of any termination or appointment and of any changes in specified offices will be given to the Noteholders promptly by the Issuer in accordance with Condition 13.

6. Redemption and Purchase

1. Unless previously redeemed or purchased and cancelled as provided below, the Issuer will redeem the Notes at their principal amount on 1st March, 2005.

2. If the Issuer satisfies the Trustee immediately before the giving of the notice referred to below that (a) as a result of any change in, or amendment to, the laws or regulations of Ruritania or any political sub-division of, or any authority in, or of, Ruritania having power to tax, or any change in the application or official interpretation of the laws or regulations, which change or amendment becomes effective after [date of subscription agreement], on the occasion of the next payment due in respect of the Notes the Issuer would be required to pay additional amounts as provided or referred to in Condition 7, and (b) the requirement cannot be avoided by the Issuer taking reasonable measures available to it, the Issuer may at its option, having given not less than 30 nor more than 60 days' notice to the Noteholders in accordance with Condition 13 (which notice shall be irrevocable), redeem all the Notes, but not some only, at their principal amount together with interest accrued to but excluding the date of redemption, provided that no notice of redemption shall be given earlier than 90 days before the earliest date on which the Issuer would be required to pay the additional amounts were a payment in respect of the Notes then due. Prior to the publication of any notice of redemption pursuant to this paragraph, the Issuer shall deliver to the Trustee a certificate signed by two Directors of the Issuer stating that the requirement referred to in (a) above will apply on the occasion of the next payment due in respect of the Notes and cannot be avoided by the Issuer taking reasonable measures avail-

able to it and the Trustee shall be entitled to accept the certificate as sufficient evidence of the satisfaction of the conditions precedent set out above, in which event it shall be conclusive and binding on the Noteholders and the Couponholders.

3. The Issuer or any of its Subsidiaries may at any time purchase Notes (provided that all unmatured Coupons appertaining to the Notes are purchased with the Notes) in any manner and at any price. If purchases are made by tender, tenders must be available to all Noteholders alike.

4. All Notes which are (a) redeemed or (b) purchased by or on behalf of the Issuer or any of its Subsidiaries will forthwith be cancelled, together with all relative unmatured Coupons attached to the Notes or surrendered with the Notes and accordingly may not be reissued or resold.

5. Upon the expiry of any notice as is referred to in paragraph (2) or (3) above the Issuer shall be bound to redeem the Notes to which the notice refers at the relative redemption price applicable at the date of such redemption together with interest accrued to but excluding the redemption date.

7. Taxation

1. All payments in respect of the Notes by the Issuer shall be made without withholding or deduction for, or on account of, any present or future taxes, duties, assessments or governmental charges of whatever nature ("**Taxes**") imposed or levied by or on behalf of Ruritania, or any political sub-division of, or any authority in, or of, Ruritania having power to tax, unless the withholding or deduction of the Taxes is required by law. In that event, the Issuer will pay such additional amounts as may be necessary in order that the net amounts received by the Noteholders and Couponholders after the withholding or deduction shall equal the respective amounts which would have been receivable in respect of the Notes or, as the case may be, Coupons in the absence of the withholding or deduction; except that no additional amounts shall be payable in relation to any payment in respect of any Note or Coupon:

    (a) to, or to a third party on behalf of, a holder who is liable to the Taxes in respect of the Note or Coupon by reason of his having some connection with Ruritania other than the mere holding of the Note or Coupon; or

    (b) to, or to a third party on behalf of, a holder who would not be liable or subject to the withholding or deduction by making a declaration of non-residence or other similar claim for exemption to the relevant tax authority; or

(c) presented for payment more than 30 days after the Relevant Date except to the extent that a holder would have been entitled to additional amounts on presenting the same for payment on the last day of the period of 30 days assuming that day to have been a Presentation Date.

2. In these Conditions, "**Relevant Date**" means the date on which the payment first becomes due but, if the full amount of the money payable has not been received in New York City by the Principal Paying Agent or the Trustee on or before the due date, it means the date on which, the full amount of the money having been so received, notice to that effect shall have been duly given to the Noteholders by the Issuer in accordance with Condition 13.

3. Any reference in these Conditions to any amounts in respect of the Notes shall be deemed also to refer to any additional amounts which may be payable under this Condition or under any undertakings given in addition to, or in substitution for, this Condition pursuant to the Trust Deed.

8. Prescription

Notes and Coupons will become void unless presented for payment within periods of 10 years (in the case of principal and five years (in the case of interest) from the Relevant Date in respect of the Notes or, as the case may be, the Coupons, subject to the provisions of Condition 5.

9. Events of default

1. The Trustee at its discretion may, and if so requested in writing by the holders of at least one-fifth in principal amount of the Notes then outstanding or if so directed by an Extraordinary Resolution of the Noteholders shall (subject in each case to being indemnified to its satisfaction), give notice to the Issuer that the Notes are, and they shall accordingly forthwith become, immediately due and repayable at their principal amount, together with accrued interest as provided in the Trust Deed, in any of the following events ("Events of Default"):

   (a) if default is made in the payment of any interest due in respect of the Notes or any of them and the default continues for a period of seven days; or

(b) if the Issuer fails to perform or observe any of its other obligations under these Conditions or the Trust Deed and (except in any case where the Trustee considers such failure to be incapable of remedy when no continuation or notice as is hereinafter mentioned will be required) the failure continues for the period of 30 days (or such longer period as the Trustee may permit) next following the service by the Trustee on the Issuer of notice requiring the same to be remedied; or

(c) if any Indebtedness for Borrowed Money of the Issuer or any of its Principal Subsidiaries becomes due and repayable prematurely by reason of an event of default (however described) or the Issuer or any of its Principal Subsidiaries fails to make any payment in respect of any Indebtedness for Borrowed Money on the due date for payment or any security given by the Issuer or any of its Principal Subsidiaries for any Indebtedness for Borrowed Money becomes enforceable or if default is made by the Issuer or any of its Principal Subsidiaries in making any payment due under any guarantee and/or indemnity given by it in relation to any Indebtedness for Borrowed Money of any other person; or

(d) if any order is made by any competent court or resolution passed for the winding up or dissolution of the Issuer or any of its Principal Subsidiaries, save for the purposes of reorganisation on terms approved in writing by the Trustee; or

(e) if the Issuer or any of its Principal Subsidiaries ceases or threatens to cease to carry on the whole or a substantial part of its business, save for the purposes of reorganisation on terms approved in writing by the Trustee, or the Issuer or any of its Principal Subsidiaries stops or threatens to stop payment of, or is unable to, or admits inability to, pay, its debts (or any class of its debts) as they fall due, or is deemed unable to pay its debts pursuant to or for the purposes of any applicable law, or is adjudicated or found bankrupt or insolvent; or

(f) if (i) proceedings are initiated against the Issuer or any of its Principal Subsidiaries under any applicable liquidation, insolvency, composition, reorganisation or other similar laws, or an application is made for the appointment of an administrative or other receiver, manager, administrator or other similar official, or an administrative or other receiver, manager, administrator or other similar official is appointed, in relation to the Issuer or any of its Principal Subsidiaries or, as the case may be, in relation to the whole or a part of the undertaking or assets of any of them, or an encumbrancer takes possession of the whole or a part of the undertaking or assets of any of them, or a distress, execution, attachment, sequestration or other process is levied, enforced upon, sued out or put in force against the whole or a part of the undertaking or assets of any of them and (ii) in any case (other than the appointment of an administrator) is not discharged within 14 days; or if the Issuer or any of its Principal Subsidiaries initiates or consents to judicial proceedings relating to itself under any applicable liquidation, insolvency, composition, reorganisation or other similar laws or makes a conveyance or assignment for the benefit of, or enters into any composition or other arrangement with, its creditors generally (or any class of its creditors) or any meeting is convened to consider a proposal for an arrangement or composition with its creditors generally (or any class of its creditors).

PROVIDED, in the case of any Event of Default other than those described in subparagraphs (a) and (d) (in the case of a winding up or dissolution of the Issuer) above, the Trustee shall have certified to the Issuer that the Event of Default is, in its opinion, materially prejudicial to the interests of the Noteholders.

2. For the purposes of these Conditions:

(a) a Principal Subsidiary of the Issuer at any time shall mean a Subsidiary of the Issuer (inter alia):

(i) whose gross revenues attributable to the Issuer (consolidated in the case of a Subsidiary which itself has Subsidiaries) or whose total assets (consolidated in the case of a Subsidiary which itself has Subsidiaries) represent not less than 10 per cent of the consolidated gross revenues attributable to the shareholders of the Issuer, or, as the case may be, consolidated total assets, of the Issuer and its Subsidiaries taken as a whole, all as calculated respectively by reference to the then latest audited accounts (consolidated or, as the case may be, unconsolidated) of the Subsidiary and the then latest audited consolidated accounts of the Issuer and its Subsidiaries; or

(ii) to which is transferred the whole or substantially the whole of the undertaking and assets of a Subsidiary of the Issuer which immediately before the transfer is a Principal Subsidiary of the Issuer; or

(iii) which has outstanding any notes, bonds or other like securities which are quoted, listed or dealt in on any recognised stock exchange or securities market and/or of which the Trustee is trustee,

all as more particularly defined in the Trust Deed.

A report by the Auditors of the Issuer that in their opinion a Subsidiary of the Issuer is or is not or was or was not at any particular time or throughout any specified period a Principal Subsidiary of the Issuer may be relied upon by the Trustee without further enquiry or evidence and, if relied upon by the Trustee, shall, in the absence of manifest error, be conclusive and binding on all parties; and

(b) "Indebtedness for Borrowed Money" means any present or future indebtedness (whether being principal, premium, interest or other amounts) for or in respect of (i) money borrowed, (ii) liabilities under or in respect of any acceptance or acceptance credit or (iii) any notes, bonds, debentures, debenture stock, loan stock or other securities offered, issued or distributed whether by way of public offer, private placing, acquisition consideration or otherwise and whether issued for cash or in whole or in part for a consideration other than cash.

10. Enforcement

1. The Trustee may at any time, at its discretion and without notice, take such proceedings against the Issuer as it may think fit to enforce the provisions of the Trust Deed, the Notes and the Coupons, but it shall not be bound to take any proceedings or any other action in relation to the Trust Deed, the Notes or the Coupons unless (a) it shall have been so directed by an Extraordinary Resolution of the Noteholders or so requested in writing by the holders of at least one-fifth in principal amount of the Notes then outstanding, and (b) it shall have been indemnified to its satisfaction.

2. No Noteholder or Couponholder shall be entitled to proceed directly against the Issuer unless the Trustee, having become bound so to proceed, fails so to do within a reasonable period and such failure shall be continuing.

11. Substitution

The Trustee may, without the consent of the Noteholders or Couponholders, agree with the Issuer to the substitution in place of the Issuer (or of any previous substitute under this Condition) as the principal debtor under the Notes, the Coupons and the Trust Deed of another company, being any Subsidiary of the Issuer, subject to (a) the Notes being unconditionally and irrevocably guaranteed by the Issuer, (b) the Trustee being satisfied that the interests of the Noteholders will not be materially prejudiced by the substitution, and (c) certain other conditions set out in the Trust Deed being complied with.

12. Replacement of notes and coupons

Should any Note or Coupon be lost, stolen, mutilated, defaced or destroyed it may be replaced at the specified office of the Paying Agent upon payment by the claimant of the expenses incurred in connection with the replacement and on such terms as to evidence and indemnity as the Issuer may reasonably require. Mutilated or defaced Notes or Coupons must be surrendered before replacements will be issued.

13. Notices

All notices to the Noteholders will be valid if published in a leading English language daily newspaper published in London or such other English language daily newspaper with general circulation in Europe as the Trustee may approve. Any notice shall be deemed to have been given on the date of publication or, if so published more than once or on different dates, on the date of the first publication. It is expected that publication will normally be made in the Financial Times. If publication as provided above is not practicable, notice will be given in such other manner, and shall be deemed to have been given on such date, as the Trustee may approve.

14. Meetings of noteholders, modification, waiver and authorisation

1. The Trust Deed contains provisions for convening meetings of the Noteholders to consider any matter affecting their interests, including the modification by Extraordinary Resolution of these Conditions or the provisions of the Trust Deed. The quorum at any meeting for passing an Extraordinary Resolution will be one or more persons present holding or representing a clear majority in principal amount of the Notes for the time being outstanding, or at any adjourned meeting one or more persons present whatever the principal amount of the Notes held or represented by him or them, except that at any meeting, the business of which includes the modification of certain of these Conditions and certain of the provisions of the Trust Deed, the necessary quorum for passing an Extraordinary Resolution will be one or more persons present holding or representing not less than two-thirds, or at

any adjourned meeting not less than one-third, of the principal amount of the Notes for the time being outstanding. An Extraordinary Resolution passed at any meeting of the Noteholders will be binding on all Noteholders, whether or not they are present at the meeting, and on all Couponholders.

2. The Trustee may agree, without the consent of the Noteholders or Couponholders, to any modification (subject to certain exceptions) of, or to the waiver or authorisation of any breach or proposed breach of, any of these Conditions or any of the provisions of the Trust Deed which is not, in the opinion of the Trustee, materially prejudicial to the interests of the Noteholders or to any modification which is of a formal, minor or technical nature or to correct a manifest error.

3. In connection with the exercise by it of any of its trusts, powers or discretions (including, without limitation, any modification, waiver, authorisation or substitution), the Trustee shall have regard to the interests of the Noteholders as a class and, in particular but without limitation, shall not have regard to the consequences of the exercise of its trusts, powers or discretions for individual Noteholders or Couponholders resulting from their being for any purpose domiciled or resident in, or otherwise connected with, or subject to the jurisdiction of, any particular territory and the Trustee shall not be entitled to require, nor shall any Noteholder or Couponholder be entitled to claim, from the Issuer or any other person any indemnification or payment in respect of any tax consequence of any such exercise upon individual Noteholders or Couponholders except to the extent already provided for in Condition 7 and/or any undertaking given in addition to, or in substitution for, Condition 7 pursuant to the Trust Deed.

4. Any modification, waiver or authorisation shall be binding on the Noteholders and the Couponholders and, unless the Trustee agrees otherwise, any modification shall be notified by the Issuer to the Noteholders as soon as practicable thereafter in accordance with Condition 13.

15. Indemnification of the trustee

The Trust Deed contains provisions for the indemnification of the Trustee and for its relief from responsibility, including provisions relieving it from taking action unless indemnified to its satisfaction.

16. Further Issues

The Issuer is at liberty from time to time without the consent of the Noteholders or Couponholders to create and issue further notes or bonds either

(a) ranking pari passu in all respects (or in all respects save for the first payment of interest thereon) and so that the same shall be consolidated and form a single series with the outstanding notes or bonds of any series (including the Notes) constituted by the Trust Deed or any supplemental Deed or (b) upon such terms as to ranking, interest, conversion, redemption and otherwise as the Issuer may determine at the time of the issue. Any further notes or bonds which are to form a single series with the outstanding notes or bonds of any series (including the Notes) constituted by the Trust Deed or any supplemental Deed shall, and any other further notes or bonds may (with the consent of the Trustee), be constituted by a Deed supplemental to the Trust Deed. The Trust Deed contains provisions for convening a single meeting of the Noteholders and the holders of notes or bonds of other series in certain circumstances where the Trustee so decides.

17. Governing law and submission to jurisdiction

The Trust Deed, the Notes and the Coupons are governed by English law.

The Issuer has in the Trust Deed irrevocably and unconditionally waived and agreed not to raise any objection which it may have now or subsequently to the laying of the venue of any Proceedings in the courts of England and any claim that any Proceedings have been brought in an inconvenient forum and has further irrevocably and unconditionally agreed that a judgment in any Proceedings brought in the courts of England shall be conclusive and binding upon the Issuer and may be enforced in the courts of any other jurisdiction. Nothing in this Condition shall limit any right to take Proceedings against the Issuer in any other court of competent jurisdiction, nor shall the taking of Proceedings in one or more jurisdictions preclude the taking of Proceedings in any other jurisdiction, whether concurrently or not.

The Issuer has in the Trust Deed irrevocably and unconditionally appointed Process Agent Limited at its registered office for the time being as its agent for service of process in England in respect of any Proceedings and has undertaken that in the event of it ceasing so to act it will appoint such other person as the Trustee may approve as its agent for that purpose.

17. Form of temporary global note for an issue of notes

MEGACORP S.A.

U.S.$100,000,000

10 per cent. Notes due 2005

This temporary Global Note is issued in respect of the US$100,000,000 10 per cent. Notes due 2005 (the "**Notes**") of MEGACORP S.A. (the "**Issuer**"). The Notes are issued subject to and with the benefit of an Agency Agreement (the "**Agency Agreement**") dated 1st March, 1995 between, inter alia, the Issuer and London Bank, N.A. as Fiscal Agent (the "**Fiscal Agent**"). The Notes are issued subject to and with the benefit of the Conditions of the Notes (the "**Conditions**") set out in the Agency Agreement.

1. Promise to pay

Subject as provided in this temporary Global Note, the Issuer, for value received, promises to pay the bearer upon presentation and surrender of this temporary Global Note the sum of US$100,000,000 (one hundred million US dollars) or such lesser sum as is equal to the principal amount of the Notes represented by this temporary Global Note on 1st March, 2005 or on such earlier date as the principal amount of this temporary Global Note may become due under the Conditions and to pay interest on the principal sum for the time being outstanding at the rate of 10 per cent per annum from March 1, 1995 payable annually in arrear on 1st March in each year until payment of the principal sum has been made or duly provided for in full together with any other amounts as may be payable, all subject to and under the Conditions.

2. Exchange for definitive notes and purchases

The definitive Notes to be issued on exchange will be in bearer form in the denomination of US$1,000 each with interest coupons ("**Coupons**") attached.

Subject as provided below, definitive Notes will only be issuable after the date (the "**Exchange Date**") which is 40 days after the closing date for the Notes.

This temporary Global Note may be exchanged for duly executed and authenticated definitive Notes without charge and the Fiscal Agent or such other person as the Fiscal Agent may direct (the "**Exchange Agent**") shall deliver, in full or partial exchange for this temporary Global Note, an aggregate principal amount of duly executed and authenticated definitive Notes with Coupons attached equal to the principal amount of this temporary Global Note submitted for exchange. Notwithstanding the foregoing, no definitive Notes will be so issued and delivered unless there shall have been presented to the Exchange Agent a certificate from Morgan Guaranty Trust Company of New York, as operator of the Euroclear System ("**Euroclear**") or Cedel Bank, société anonyme ("**Cedel**") substantially in the form of the certificate attached as Exhibit A.

Any person who would, but for the provisions of this temporary Global Note and of the Agency Agreement, otherwise be entitled to receive a definitive Note shall not be entitled to require the exchange of an appropriate part of this temporary Global Note for a definitive Note unless and until he shall have delivered or caused to be delivered to Euroclear or Cedel a certificate in substantially the form of the certificate attached as Exhibit B (copies of which form of certificate will be available at the offices of Euroclear in Brussels and Cedel in Luxembourg and each of the Paying Agents named in the Agency Agreement).

Upon (a) any exchange of a part of this temporary Global Note for a definitive Note or (b) receipt of instructions from Euroclear or Cedel that, following the purchase by or on behalf of the Issuer or any of its subsidiaries of a part of this temporary Global Note, part is to be cancelled, the portion of the principal amount of this temporary Global Note so exchanged or to be so cancelled shall be endorsed by or on behalf of the Fiscal Agent on Part 1 of the Schedule to this temporary Global Note, whereupon the principal amount of this temporary Global Note shall be reduced for all purposes by the amount so exchanged or cancelled and endorsed.

3. Benefits

Until the entire principal amount of this temporary Global Note has been extinguished in exchange for definitive Notes, this temporary Global Note shall in all respects be entitled to the same benefits as the definitive Notes for which it may be exchanged, except that the holder of this temporary Global Note shall only be entitled to receive any payment on this temporary Global Note on presentation of certificates as provided below.

4. Payments

Payments in respect of Notes for the time being represented by this temporary Global Note shall be made to the bearer only upon presentation by Euroclear or as the case may be, Cedel, to the Fiscal Agent at its specified office of a certificate, substantially in the form of the certificate attached as Exhibit A, to the effect that Euroclear or as the case may be, Cedel, has received a certificate substantially in the form of the certificate attached as Exhibit B.

Upon any payment in respect of the Notes represented by this temporary Global Note the amount so paid shall be endorsed by or on behalf of the Fiscal Agent on Part II of the Schedule to this temporary Global Note. In the case of any payment of principal the principal amount of this temporary Global Note shall be reduced for all purposes by the amount so paid and the remaining principal amount of this temporary Global Note shall be endorsed by or on behalf of the Fiscal Agent on Part II of the Schedule to this temporary Global Note.

5. Authentication

This temporary Global Note shall not become valid or enforceable for any purpose unless and until it has been authenticated by or on behalf of the Fiscal Agent.

6. Governing law

This temporary Global Note is governed by English law.

IN WITNESS whereof this temporary Global Note has been executed on behalf of the Issuer.

MEGACORP S.A.

By:
....

Dated 1st March, 1995

CERTIFICATE OF AUTHENTICATION

This is the temporary Global Note
described in the Agency Agreement
By or on behalf of
London Bank, N.A. as Fiscal Agent
(without recourse, warranty or liability)

....

THE SCHEDULE

PART I

EXCHANGES FOR DEFINITIVE NOTES AND CANCELLATIONS

The following exchanges of a part of this temporary Global Note for definitive Notes and cancellations of a part of the aggregate principal amount of this temporary Global Note have been made:

Date of exchange or cancellation	Part of the aggregate principal amount of this temporary Global Note exchanged for definitive Notes	Part of the aggregate principal amount of this temporary Global Note cancelled	Remaining principal amount of this temporary Global Note following exchange or cancellation	Notation made by or on behalf of the Fiscal Agent
	US$	US$	US$	

PART II

PAYMENTS

The following payments in respect of the Notes represented by this temporary Global Note have been made:

Date of payment	Amount of interest paid	Amount of principal paid	Remaining principal amount of this temporary Global Note following payment	Notation made by or on behalf of the Fiscal Agent
	US$	US$	US$	

EXHIBIT A
MEGACORP S.A.
US$100,000,000

10 per cent. Notes due 2005

(the "Securities")

This is to certify that, based solely on certifications we have received in writing, by tested telex or by electronic transmission from member organisations appearing in our records as persons being entitled to a portion of the principal amount set forth below (our "**Member Organisations**") substantially to the effect set forth in the Agency Agreement, as of the date hereof, [   ] principal amount of the above-captioned Securities (i) is owned by persons that are not citizens or residents of the United States, domestic partnerships, domestic corporations or any estate or trust the income of which is subject to United States federal income taxation regardless of its source ("**United States persons**"), (ii) is owned by US persons that (a) are foreign branches of US financial institutions (as defined in US Treasury Regulations section 1.165–12(c)(1)(v)) ("**financial institutions**") purchasing for their own account or for resale, or (b) acquired the Securities through foreign branches of US financial institutions and who hold the Securities through such US financial institutions on the date hereof (and in either case (a) or (b), each such US financial institution has agreed, on its own behalf or through its agent, that we may advise the Issuer or the Issuer's agent that it will comply with the requirements of section 165(j)(3)(A), (B) or (C) of the Internal Revenue Code of 1986, as amended, and the regulations thereunder), or (iii) is owned by US or foreign financial institutions for purposes of resale during the restricted period (as defined in US Treasury Regulations Section 1.163–5(c)(2)(i)(D)(7)), and to the further effect that US or foreign financial institutions described in clause (iii) above (whether or not also described in clause (i) or (ii)) have certified that they have not acquired the Securities for purposes of resale directly or indirectly to a US person or to a person within the United States or its possessions.

If the Securities are of the category contemplated in section 230.903(c)(3) of Regulation S under the Securities Act of 1933, as amended, then this is also to certify with respect to such principal amount of Securities set forth above that, except as set forth below, we have received in writing, by tested telex or by electronic transmission, from our Member Organisations entitled to a portion of such principal amount, certifications with respect to such portion, substantially to the effect set forth in the Agency Agreement.

We further certify (i) that we are not making available herewith for exchange (or, if relevant, exercise of any rights or collection of any interest)

FORM OF TEMPORARY GLOBAL NOTE

any portion of the temporary global Security excepted in such certifications and (ii) that as of the date hereof we have not received any notification from any of our Member Organisations to the effect that the statements made by such Member Organisations with respect to any portion of the part submitted herewith for exchange (or, if relevant, exercise of any rights or collection of any interest) are no longer true and cannot be relied upon as of the date hereof.

We understand that this certification is required in connection with certain tax laws and, if applicable, certain securities laws of the United States. In connection therewith, if administrative or legal proceedings are commenced or threatened in connection with which this certification is or would be relevant, we irrevocably authorise you to produce this certification to any interested party in such proceedings.

*Dated

[Morgan Guaranty Trust Company of New York,
Brussels office, as operator of the
Euroclear System] [Cedel Bank, société anonyme]

By ....
Authorised Signatory

* To be dated no earlier than the date to which this certification relates, namely (a) the payment date or (b) the date set for the exchange of the temporary Global Note for definitive Notes.

EXHIBIT B

MEGACORP S.A.

US$100,000,000

10 per cent. Notes due 2005

(the "Securities")

This is to certify that as of the date hereof, and except as set forth below, the above-captioned Securities held by you for our account (i) are owned by person(s) that are not citizens or residents of the United States, domestic partnerships, domestic corporations or any estate or trust the income of which is subject to United States federal income taxation regardless of its source ("United States person(s)"), (ii) are owned by US person(s) that (a) are foreign branches of US financial institutions (as defined in US Treasury

Regulations section 1.165–12(c)(1)(v)) ("financial institutions") purchasing for their own account or for resale, or (b) acquired the Securities through foreign branches of US financial institutions and who hold the Securities through such US financial institutions on the date hereof (and in either case (a) or (b), each such US financial institution hereby agrees, on its own behalf or through its agent, that you may advise the Issuer or the Issuer's agent that it will comply with the requirements of section 165(j)(3)(A), (B) or (C) of the Internal Revenue Code of 1986, as amended, and the regulations thereunder), or (iii) are owned by US or foreign financial institution(s) for purposes of resale during the restricted period (as defined in US Treasury Regulations section 1.163–5(c)(2)(i)(D)(7)), and in addition if the owner of the Securities is a US or foreign financial institution described in clause (iii) above (whether or not also described in clause (i) or (ii)) this is further to certify that such financial institution has not acquired the Securities for the purposes of resale directly or indirectly to a US person or to a person within the United States or its possessions.

If the Securities are of the category contemplated in section 230.903(c)(3) of Regulation S under the Securities Act of 1933, as amended (the "Act"), then this is also to certify that, except as set forth below (i) in the case of debt securities, the Securities are beneficially owned by (a) non-US person(s) or (b) US person(s) who purchased the Securities in transactions which did not require registration under the Act; or (ii) in the case of equity securities, the Securities are owned by (x) non-US person(s) (and such person(s) are not acquiring the Securities for the account or benefit of US person(s)) or (y) US person(s) who purchased the Securities in a transaction which did not require registration under the Act. If this certification is being delivered in connection with the exercise of warrants pursuant to section 230.902(m) of Regulation S under the Act, then this is further to certify that, except as set forth below, the Securities are being exercised by and on behalf of non-US person(s). As used in this paragraph the term "US person" has the meaning given to it by Regulation S under the Act.

As used herein, "**United States**" means the United States of America (including the States and the District of Columbia); and its "**possessions**" include Puerto Rico, the US Virgin Islands, Guam, American Samoa, Wake Island and the Northern Mariana Islands.

We undertake to advise you promptly by tested telex on or prior to the date on which you intend to submit your certification relating to the Securities held by you for our account in accordance with your documented procedures if any applicable statement herein is not correct on such date, and in the absence of any such notification it may be assumed that this certification applies as of such date.

This certification excepts and does not relate to [   ] of such interest in the above Securities in respect of which we are not able to certify and as to which we understand exchange and delivery of definitive Securities (or, if relevant, exercise of any rights or collection of any interest) cannot be made until we do so certify.

We understand that this certification is required in connection with certain tax laws and, if applicable, certain securities laws of the United States. In connection therewith, if administrative or legal proceedings are commenced or threatened in connection with which this certification is or would be relevant, we irrevocably authorise you to produce this certification to any interested party in such proceedings.

*Dated

By ....
Qualified Account Holder

* To be dated no earlier than the fifteenth day before the date to which this certification relates, namely (a) the payment date or (b) the date set for the exchange of the temporary Global Note for definitive Notes.

SELECT BIBLIOGRAPHY

Articles from the journals are not listed in this bibliography. The main English journals on international finance include *International Financial Law Review* (Euromoney), *Journal of International Banking Law* (ESC Publishing Ltd/Sweet & Maxwell), and *Butterworths Journal of International Banking and Financial Law*. Bibliographies referring to the article literature may be found in many of the works listed below. In the main, this list only includes works which contain comparative or international law and not standard works on the domestic law of a jurisdiction.

1. General works

The following works contain discussions of term loans and bond issues and related topics together with conflicts of laws so far as it relates to international finance.

Cresswell, Blair, Hill, Wood	*Encyclopaedia of Banking Law* (1982–) looseleaf, Butterworths
Penn, Shea and Arora	*The Law and Practice of International Banking* (1987) Sweet & Maxwell
Ravi Tennekoon	*The Law and Regulation of International Finance* (1991) Butterworths
Frank Graaf	*Euromarket Finance: Issues of Euromarket Securities and Syndicated Eurocurrency Loans* (1991) Kluwer. Contains useful lists of legal articles.

A classic work is by Georges H Delaume, *Legal Aspects of International Lending and Economic Development Financing* (1967) Oceana. See also:

Norbert Horn (ed)	*The Law of International Trade Finance* (1989) Kluwer.
Kheng Koh (ed)	*Current Developments in International Banking and Corporate Financial Operations* (1989) Butterworths/National University of Singapore

Joseph J Norton	*International Finance in the 1990s: challenges and opportunities* (1993) Blackwells
David Pierce et al (eds)	*Current Issues of International Financial Law* (1985) National University of Singapore
R S Rendell (ed)	*International Financial Law: lending, capital transfers and institutions* (2nd ed 1983) Euromoney

2. Term loans and syndicated loans

See the works listed under **General works** above. See also:

Peter Gabriel	*Legal Aspects of Syndicated Loans* (1986) Butterworths.
Stanley Hurn	*Syndicated loans: a handbook for banker and borrower* (1990) Woodhead-Faulkner
R P McDonald	*International Syndicated Loans* (1982) Euromoney
Tony Rhodes	*Syndicated Lending: practice and documentation* (1993) Euromoney

3. International bond issues

See the works listed under **General works** above. The following may also be consulted:

FG Fisher III,	*Eurobonds* (1988) Euromoney.
Roger McCormick & Harriet Creamer	*Hybrid Corporate Securities: International Legal Aspects* (1987) Sweet & Maxwell
Terence Prime	*International Bonds and Certificates of Deposit* (1990) Butterworths.
G Ugeux	*Floating Rate Notes* (1985) Euromoney

4. Securities regulation

The literature on securities regulation in the form of domestic books and articles in the legal periodicals is substantial. There are a few compilations of country reports which, by reason of the volatile nature of securities regulation, quickly become out of date. Note especially:

Harold Bloomenthal (ed)	*International Capital Markets and Securities Regulation;* 5 vols 1982, up-dated, Clark Boardman Callaghan. Reports cover more than a dozen countries and include some general surveys.
Euromoney	*International Securities Law* (1992). Reports cover 22 countries.
Euromoney	*Issuing Securities,* IFLRev Supplement, March 1993. Brief country reports.
Roy M Goode (ed)	*Conflicts of Interest in the Changing Financial World* (1986) Institute of Bankers and Queen Mary College, University of London
Francis W Neate	*Developing Global Securities Market* (1987) Graham & Trotman/IBA
Rosen	*International Securities Regulation* (1986–) Oceana

5. Banking regulation

Marc Dassesse	*EC Banking Law* (2nd ed 1994) Lloyds of London Press

6. Legal opinions

Gruson, Hutter, Kutschera	*Legal Opinions in International Transactions* (2nd ed 1989) Graham & Trotman
Wilfred M Estey	*Legal Opinions in Commercial Transactions* (1990) Butterworths

Both works contain extensive bibliographies, lists of articles and bar association guidelines.

LIST OF RESEARCH TOPICS

This list contains a list of topics which could be considered for a research thesis or a shorter article. The topics relate to the areas covered by this book. Research topics in relation to the areas covered by other books in this series on international financial law will be found in the volume concerned.

The selection is based on relative originality and usefulness. Topics which have already been extensively covered by the legal literature are not included. In many cases there is an existing literature on the listed topics, but further work is considered worthwhile to develop what has already been achieved or to explore a new approach. It is possible that some of the listed topics may not be at all original and the author is simply unaware of the work which has already been done. If the chosen titles do not appeal, it is hoped that they will be suggestive of those which do. Some of the titles are no more than pointers which would have to be developed into a proper topic.

The author would be very glad to receive a copy of any essays which may be written and which are derived from this list.

Chapters 2 to 11: Term loans and bond issues

- History of the syndicated loan in the nineteenth and twentieth centuries
- Financial covenants in corporate loan agreements and bonds
- Force majeure in loan agreements, bonds and financial trading contracts
- The flight from bond negotiability: depositories and clearing systems
- Comparative anti-dilution clauses in convertible bonds
- Comparative law of bondholder trustees (including conflict of laws)
- Comparative law of bondholder communities and bondholder democracy (including conflict of laws)
- Conflicts of interest and financial agents: common law, Germanic and Napoleonic approaches
- Chinese walls in comparative law
- Exclusion clauses in financial contracts
- Drafting styles for financial contracts

Chapters 12 and 13: Legal opinions

- Comparison of the role of notaries with that of lawyers rendering transaction opinions: history and context
- Transaction opinions on security interests

Chapter 14 to 23: Securities and bank regulation

- International history of securities regulation
- Codification of securities regulation: international survey
- What is a "security?" – international classifications of regulated securities
- Comparative law of exemptions from filing and disclosure requirements for prospectuses
- The "sophisticated investors" exemption in securities regulation: comparative law
- Comparative disclosure codes
- Duties of full disclosure in commercial and financial transactions
- Forecasting in prospectuses and bank syndication memoranda
- History of "fraud on a market": market manipulation, false rumours and insider dealing
- Self-regulation in securities law: international survey
- Criminalisation of securities law
- Burdens and benefits of securities regulation: the balance sheet
- International harmonisation of securities regulation
- Big pocket liability in securities law
- Comparative law of conduct of business by securities dealers
- Comparison of consumer and wholesale protections in securities regulation
- Bank regulation and bank insolvency
- To what extent does securities regulation codify the ordinary law (e.g. misrepresentation, fiduciary duties)?
- International securities regulation and freedom of capital

INDEX

All references refer to paragraph number

Acceleration. *See* **Events of default**
Africa. *See also* **Nigeria; Zambia**
  state insolvencies, 1–8
Agency
  agent bank of syndicate. *See* **Syndicate agents**
  participations, 7–3
Alberta. *See* **Canada**
Appropriations
  term loans, 2–25
Arbitration
  condition precedent, 5–60
  decision ex aequo et bono, 5–62
  delay, 5–62
  enforcement, 5–61
  expenses, 5–62
  expert adjudication, 5–59
  finality, 5–58
  jurisdictional disputes, 5–62
  New York Convention on the Recognition and Enforcement of Foreign Arbitral Awards 1958, 5–61
  privacy, 5–59
  procedure, 5–60
  public contracts, 5–61
  suitability for financial contracts, 5–57
Argentina. *See also* **Latin America**
  debenture issues, 10–13
  securities regulation, 15–32
Asia and Pacific. *See* **Australia; China; Hong Kong; India; Indonesia; Japan; Korea (South); Malaysia; New Zealand; Pakistan; Philippines; Singapore; Thailand**
Assignments clause
  generally, 4–9
  protections for borrower, 4–10

Australia. *See also* **English-based countries**
  bondholder trustees
    monitoring duties, 11–16
    retirement of, 10–17
  cold calling, 16–5, 18–18
  eligible investors, 16–8
  exculpation clauses, 11–31
  insider dealing, 19–16
    damages for, 19–21
  prescriptive jurisdiction, 10–40
  prospectus
    foreign issues, 16–16
    private offerings
      cold calling, 16–5
      resale to public, 16–7
      road-shows, 16–6
    reciprocal recognition, 16–16
    secondary market reading, 16–17
    sophisticated investors, 16–8
  securities regulation, 15–22
    history, 14–13
    insider dealing, 19–16
  share hawking, 18–18
  state immunity, 5–64
  trust deeds, 10–40
  trusts, attitudes to, 10–13
Austria
  conflict of laws, 5–8
  insolvency set-off, 4–11
  long-arm jurisdiction, 5–38
  Lugano Convention 1988, 5–39
  New York Convention on the Recognition and Enforcement of Foreign Arbitral Awards 1958, 5–61
  notarial acts, 12–2
  prospectus
    road-shows, 16–6
    sophisticated investors, 16–8

International Loans, Bonds and Securities Regulation

Bank regulation
  authorisation of banks, 22–3
  capital adequacy. *See* **Capital adequacy**
  controls. *See* systems and controls, *infra*
  credit businesses, 22–2
  financial supervision
    generally, 22–5
    main heads of, 22–6
  foreign exchange risk, 22–13
  generally, 1–15, 22–1
  large exposures, 22–11
    Capital Adequacy Directive and, "soft-limits", 22–11A, 22–11B
  liquidity, 22–10
  non-banking activities, restrictions on, 22–4
  ownership and management, 22–14
  restrictions on non-banking activities, 22–4
  systems and controls, 22–12

Banking laws
  generally, 14–2

Basle Agreement 1988
  capital adequacy, 7–37, 22–8 to 22–9, 23–1 to 23–11
  generally, 1–8

Bearer bonds. *See* **Bonds**

Bearer depository receipts
  documentation, 9–29
  limited recourse contract, 9–29
  reasons for, 9–27
  structure involving depositary, 9–28

Belgium
  bondholders' meetings, 10–33
  Brussels Convention 1968, 5–39
  Euroclear. *See* **Euroclear**
  insolvency set-off and, 4–11
  long-arm jurisdiction, 5–38
  prospectus, road-shows, 16–6
  securities regulation, 15–21
    history, 14–14
  state immunity, 5–64

Bermuda. *See also* **English-based countries**
  sophisticated investors, 16–8

"Big pocket" liability
  bondholder trustees and syndicate agents, 11–1, 17–2

"Blue Sky" laws
  generally, 15–6, 16–7, 16–16

Boiler-plate clause
  generally, 4–13

Bond issues. *See also* **Bonds**
  advance of funds, 8–5
  bearer depository receipts. *See* **Bearer depository receipts**
  equity-linked issues. *See* **Convertible debt**
  euro-medium term note programmes
    documentation, 9–38 to 9–39
      agency agreement, 9–38
      information memorandum, 9–38
      programme agreement, 9–38
      trust deed, 9–38
    generally, 9–37
  eurobonds. *See* **Eurobonds**
  eurocommercial paper. *See* **Eurocommercial paper**
  generally, 1–11
  legal opinions
    prospectuses, 13–38
    securities regulation, 13–37
  meaning, 1–11
  prospectus. *See* **Prospectus**
  secured issues, 9–30
  securities regulation, legal opinions, 13–37
  special types of issues, 9–1 *et seq*
  syndicated loans compared
    advance of funds, 8–5
    covenants, 8–11
    currency conversion, 8–6
    detailed comparison, 8–3 to 8–14
    disclosure requirements, 8–3
    documentation, 8–4
    events of default, 8–12
    forum, 8–14
    governing law, 8–14
    interest, 8–6
    investors, number and anonymity of, 8–2
    issue mechanics, 8–2
    main differences, 8–1 to 8–2
    margin protections, 8–8

INDEX

Bond issues—*cont.*
  syndicated loans compared—*cont.*
    modification, 8–13
    payments and equality, 8–9
    prepayments, voluntary, 8–7
    prescription, 8–14
    repayment, 8–7
    transfer, 8–13
    transferability, 8–2
    voluntary prepayment, 8–7
    waiver of immunity, 8–14
    warranties, 8–10
  trustees. *See* **Bondholder trustees**
Bondholder communities. *See*
  Bondholders' meetings
Bondholder trustees
  advantages
    bondholders, for, 10–3
    issuers, for, 10–5
  Anglo-American bond trustees, 10–2 *et seq*
  approval of documentation, 11–14
  "big pocket" liability, 11–1, 17–2
  bondholders' meetings. *See*
    Bondholders' meetings
  Chinese Walls
    case law, 11–24
    conflicts of interest, 11–11
    disadvantages, 11–23
    generally, 11–22
  confidential information and, 11–17
  conflicts of interest
    accounting for profits, 11–5
    Chinese Walls, 11–11
    consent of beneficiaries, 11–9
    contractual exculpation, 11–11
    criminal penalties, 11–5
    cross-directorships, 11–4
    cross-shareholdings, 11–4
    delegation, 11–11
    effect of, 11–5
    examples, 11–4
    fiduciary acts as financial adviser to borrower, 11–4
    fiduciary guarantees issue, 11–4
    fiduciary has investment department, 11–4
    fiduciary is also private lender, 11–4
    fiduciary is representative of two loans or issues, 11–4

Bondholder trustees—*cont.*
  conflicts of interest—*cont.*
    general rule, 11–3
    liability of fiduciary, 11–5
    negligence proceedings, 11–5
    regulatory controls on, 11–6 to 11–8
    resignation, 11–11
    solutions, 11–9 to 11–11
    Stock Exchange rules, 11–6
  defaults, notification of. *See*
    notification of defaults, *infra*
  disadvantages, 10–6
  documentation, approval of, 11–14
  due diligence
    approval of documentation, 11–14
    confidential information, 11–17
    duties, 11–13
    generally, 11–13
    monitoring duties, 11–15 to 11–16
    notification of defaults. *See*
      notification of defaults, *infra*
    powers, 11–13
  eligibility, 10–16 *et seq*
  enforcement by
    acceleration, 10–21
      trustee duties on, 10–22
    insolvency proceedings, 10–25
    no-action clauses, 10–23 to 10–24
    representative actions, 10–25
  exculpation clauses
    conflicts of interest, 11–11
    efficacy of, 11–29
    general effect of, 11–28
    practice, 11–25
    secret profits, 11–12
    statutory limitations, 11–30 to 11–31
  fiduciaries, as, 11–1 *et seq*
  fiduciary duties, 10–9, 10–15
  fiscal agents compared, 10–9 to 10–10
    paying agents, 10–10
  generally, 10–1, 11–1
  indemnity, right of, 11–32
  insolvency proceedings, 10–25
  issuer, contract with, 10–38
  legal characteristics of the trust. *See* **Trust**
  mandatory requirements, 10–7
  stock exchange rules, 10–8

Bondholder trustees—*cont.*
meetings. *See* **Bondholders' meetings**
monitoring duties, 10–9, 11–15 to 11–16
no-action clause, 10–4, 10–23 to 10–24
notification of defaults
generally, 11–18
ostrich clauses, 11–21
what constitutes knowledge, 11–19
when default should be notified, 11–20
organisation of bondholders, 10–26
powers, 11–13
regulatory requirements, 10–16
relationship with bondholders, 10–38
representative actions, 10–25
retirement, 10–17
secret profits, 11–12
stock exchange rules, 10–8
syndicate agents compared
conflicts of interest. *See* conflicts of interest, *supra*
differences, 11–2
generally, 11–1
secret profits, 11–12
trust, characteristics of. *See* **Trust**
trust deed. *See* **Trust deed**
unilateral power to waive and modify, 10–31

Bondholders' meetings
comparative review, 10–32 to 10–36
generally, 10–18
main issues for bondholder decision, 10–19 to 10–20
final liquidation, 10–20
rehabilitation proceedings, 10–20
majority powers, 10–20, 10–27 to 10–28
minority protection, 10–27, 10–28 to 10–30
oppression, 10–29
resolution outside terms of power, 10–29
secret advantages, 10–29
unfairness, 10–29
no-action clauses, 10–23 to 10–24
organisation of bondholders, 10–26
trust deeds, 10–26

Bonds. *See also* **Bond issues**
bearer bonds
anonymity, 8–31
defences of issuer, 8–35
notification to issuer, 8–31
payments on, 8–52
prescription clause, 8–54
priorities, 8–34
registered bonds compared, 8–31 to 8–35
set-offs, 8–35
title, 8–33
transfer, 8–32
bearer depository receipts. *See* **Bearer depository receipts**
clearing systems, 8–37 to 8–38
Cedel, 8–37, 10–37
custodians, 1–14, 8–37, 10–37 to 10–38
Euroclear, 8–37, 10–37 to 10–38
convertible bonds. *See* **Convertible debt**
covenants, 8–11, 8–42
deep discount bonds, 8–46
disclosure requirements, 8–3
documentation, 8–4
equity-linked bonds. *See* **Convertible debt**
events of default, 8–12, 8–55
acceleration, 8–55
enforcement, 8–55
face of, 8–39
fiscal agency, incorporation of, 8–40
foreign bonds, 1–13
form and transfer, 8–41
forum, 8–56
governing law, 8–56
interest, 8–6
deep discount bonds, 8–46
fixed rate, 8–6, 8–44
floating rate, 8–6, 8–45
swaps, 8–46
zero coupon, 8–46
investors
character of, 8–2
number and anonymity of, 8–2
issues. *See* **Bond issues**
listing of
advantages of, 8–24

Bonds—*cont.*
listing of—*cont.*
disadvantages of, 8–25
stock exchanges, 8–23
margin protections, 8–8
marketing and distribution
impact day offerings, 8–16
issue procedures, 8–21
London eurobond issues. *See*
London eurobond issues
methods, 8–15 to 8–16
preliminary prospectus offerings, 8–16
private placements, 8–15
stabilisation, 8–22
maturities, 1–14
negative pledge, 8–11, 8–43
negotiability
bearer and registered bonds compared, 8–31 to 8–35
English law of, 8–29 to 8–30
governing law of, 8–36
meaning of, 8–28
notices, 8–56
pari passu clause, 8–11, 8–42
paying agents, 8–53
payments
bearer bonds, 8–52
and equality, 8–9
paying agents, 8–53
perpetual bonds, 8–48
prepayment, 8–7
prescription, 8–14
contractual alterations, 8–54
generally, 8–54
statutory periods, 8–54
redemption
bullet, 8–47
early redemption for tax, 8–50
early voluntary redemption, 8–49
perpetual bonds, 8–48
purchase of bonds by issuer, 8–51
registered bonds
bearer bonds compared, 8–31 to 8–35
defences of issuer, 8–35
notification to issuer, 8–31
priorities, 8–34
set-offs, 8–35
title, 8–33
transfer, 8–32

Bonds—*cont.*
repayment, 8–7, 8–47 to 8–51
tax considerations, 8–26 to 8–27
terms of, 8–39 *et seq*
transferability, 8–2
trust deed, incorporation of, 8–40
trustees. *See* **Bondholder trustees**
types of, 1–13 to 1–14
waiver of immunity, 8–14, 8–56
warranties, 8–10
warrants to purchase
generally, 9–24
securities regulation, 9–25
warrants exercise procedure, 9–26
Borrowing controls
generally, 1–15, 14–2
Brazil
bondholders' meetings, 10–26
MOU with United States, 20–3
prospectus, private offerings, 16–3
Britain. *See also* **England; English-based countries**
bank regulation, large exposures, 22–11A
Brussels Convention 1968, 5–39
collective investment schemes, 16–20, 16–21
definition, 16–21
dealers
authorisation of, 18–2 to 18–5
exempted persons, 18–4
investment business
defined, 18–3
exclusions, 18–3
investments, defined, 18–2
self-regulating organisations, 18–8
territorial scope, 18–5
conduct of business, 18–8
investment exchanges, 18–8
Investment Management Regulatory Organisation (IMRO), 18–8
Personal Investment Authority (PIA), 18–8
Securities and Futures Authority (SFA), 18–8, 18–9
SROs, 18–8, 18–9
financial regulation structure
generally, 18–20

Britain—*cont.*
  dealers—*cont.*
    level of capital required, 18–20
    periodic reporting, 18–20
    permitted forms of capital, 18–20
  EC First Company Law Directive, 13–3
  insider dealing. *See* **Insider dealing** generally
  large exposures, regulation of, 22–11A
  MOU with United States, 20–3
  New York Convention on the Recognition and Enforcement of Foreign Arbitral Awards 1958, 5–61
  nullity of companies, 13–3
  open-ended investment companies, 16–20
  prospectus
    collective investment schemes, 16–20, 16–21
    commercial paper issues, 16–12
    foreign government offerings, 16–9
    listed securities, 16–14
    private offerings, 16–3
      resale to public, 16–7
      road-shows, 16–6
    syndicated bank loans, 16–11
  securities regulation
    authorisation of investment business, 15–2
    cold calling, 15–4
    collective investment schemes, 15–4
    dealers. *See* dealers, *supra*
    fraud, 15–4
    history, 14–14
    investment advertisements, 15–2
    SRO rules, 15–2
  state immunity, 5–64
  syndication, 1–5
    informational material, 6–7
  tax considerations for bonds, 8–27
  unit trusts, 16–20
Brokers. *See* **Dealers**
Brunei
  prospectus
    cold calling, 16–5
    sophisticated investors, 16–8

Brussels Convention on Jurisdiction and the Enforcement of Judgments in Civil and Commercial Matters, 1968. *See* **European Judgments Conventions**
Bustamente Code
  generally, 5–8

Canada
  Alberta, securities regulation, 15–24
  bondholder trustees
    conflicts of interest, 11–8, 11–9
    monitoring duties, 11–15
    notification of defaults, 11–20
    regulatory requirements, 10–7, 10–16
  bondholders' meetings, 10–26
  insider dealing, 19–16
  legal opinions, 12–18
  London eurocurrency market and, 1–6
  MOU with United States, 20–3
  Ontario
    insider dealing, damages for, 19–21
    prospectus
      foreign government offerings, 16–9
      private offerings, 16–3
        resale to public, 16–7
      sophisticated investors, 16–8
    securities regulation, 15–24
  preliminary prospectus offerings, 8–16
  prospectus
    foreign issues, 16–16
    reciprocal recognition, 16–16
    road-shows, 16–6
  Quebec, securities regulation, 15–24
  securities regulation, 15–24
    insider dealing, 19–16
  trusts, attitudes to, 10–13
Capital adequacy
  Basle Agreement 1988, 7–37, 22–8 to 22–9, 22–9A, 23–1 to 23–11
  Capital Adequacy Directive (CAD), 15–20, 18–20
  banking book, 22–9A
  calculation of Own Funds, 22–9A

INDEX

Capital adequacy—*cont.*
  Capital Adequacy Directive (CAD)—*cont.*
    large exposures, "soft limits", 22–11B
    monitoring under, 22–9A
    repos, 22–9A
    reverse repos, 22–9A
    trading book, 22–9A, 22–11A, 22–11B
  minimum capital, 22–7
  participations, 7–37 to 7–40
Capital markets. *See* **Eurocurrency markets; London eurocurrency market**
Cedel
  Eurocommercial paper, 9–33
  generally, 8–37, 10–37 to 10–38
  warrants exercise procedure, 9–26
Central banks
  bank regulation. *See* **Bank regulation**
  state immunity. *See* **State immunity**
  state loans, 1–18
Central and Eastern Europe. *See also* **Hungary; Poland; Russia**
  state insolvencies, 1–8
Channel Islands
  Brussels Convention 1968, 5–39
Chile. *See also* **Latin America**
  debenture issues, 10–13
China
  securities regulation, 15–31
Chinese Walls
  bondholder trustees, 11–11, 11–22 to 11–24
  case law, 11–24
  conflicts of interest, 11–10, 11–11, 18–13
  disadvantages, 11–23
  generally, 11–22
  syndicate agents, 11–11, 11–22 to 11–24
Choice of law
  alternative choices, 5–18
  centre of gravity, 5–16
  choice of law clause, 5–2 *et seq*
    terms of, 5–2
  depeçage, 5–19
  evasive choice, 5–14
  express choice of applicable law, 5–9 to 5–13

Choice of law—*cont.*
  factors influencing, 5–3
  freedom of choice, 5–9
  implied choice, 5–16
  incorporation of law, 5–20
  insulation, 5–4 to 5–5
    limits on, 5–6
  international rules, summary, 5–16
  law of the forum, 5–16
  no express choice, 5–15
  no foreign element, 5–13
  optional choices, 5–18
  party autonomy, 5–9
  policy interests, 5–16
  public international law, 5–22
  renvoi, 5–21
  Rome Convention 1980. *See* **Rome Convention**
  scope of applicable law, 5–23
  state contracts, 5–17
  summary of international rules, 5–16
  Switzerland, 5–11
  tacit choice, 5–16
  United States, 5–10
  variation of governing law, 5–12
Churning. *See* **Securities fraud**
Clearing systems
  Cedel, 8–37, 10–37 to 10–38
  custodians, 1–14, 8–37, 10–37 to 10–38
  Euroclear, 8–37, 10–37 to 10–38
  generally, 8–37 to 8–38
Cold calling
  generally, 15–4, 16–5, 18–18
Collective investment schemes
  advantages, 16–20
  open-ended investment companies, 16–20
  prospectus, 16–20 to 16–22
  securities regulation, 15–4
  unit trusts, 16–20
  United Kingdom, 16–20, 16–21
  United States, 16–22
Conflict of laws
  choice of law. *See* **Choice of law**
  England. *See* **England**
  misrepresentation. *See* **Misrepresentation and non-disclosure**
  United States. *See* **United States**

International Loans, Bonds and Securities Regulation

INDEX

Conflicts of interest. *See also* **Secret profits**
bondholder trustees. *See* **Bondholder trustees**
Chinese Walls, 11–10, 11–11, 18–13
consent of beneficiaries, 11–9, 18–13
dealers. *See* **Dealers**
exculpation clauses, 11–10, 11–11, 18–13
New York Stock Exchange rules, 11–7
securities regulation. *See* **Securities regulation**
syndicate agents. *See* **Syndicate agents**
Consumer credit law
generally, 1–15, 14–2
Convertible bonds. *See* **Convertible debt**
Convertible debt
advantages
access to investors, 9–6
deferred equity financing, 9–6
generally, 9–5
maturity, 9–6
terms, 9–6
anti-dilution provisions
case law on dilution, 9–16
generally, 9–14 to 9–15
no adjustment on dividend payments, 9–18
warrant issues, 9–17
bonds with share warrants attached, 9–3
compulsory takeover offers, 9–12
conversion premium, 9–2
conversion price, 9–2
covenants of issuer
availability of sufficient shares, 9–22
listing, 9–22
notification, 9–22
ranking of shares, 9–22
exchange controls, 9–13
exchange rate, 9–7
foreign investment restrictions, 9–12
generally, 1–14, 9–2
issue of shares at a discount, 9–9
legal aspects, 9–9 *et seq*
listing, 9–4
loss of conversion privilege, 9–8

Convertible debt—*cont.*
meaning, 1–14
mergers and spin-offs, 9–21
pre-emption rights, 9–10
securities regulation, 9–11
stock exchange limits, 9–13
takeovers, 9–12, 9–19 to 9–20
taxation
dividends, 9–23
gains tax, 9–23
generally, 9–23
issue taxes, 9–23
Corners. *See* **Securities fraud**
Covenants
amalgamations and mergers, 3–35
bonds, 8–11, 8–42
breach of, remedies for, 3–8
change of business, 3–35
consents, 3–35
damages for breach, 3–8
disposals, 3–29 to 3–30
exclusions, 3–31
reasons for, 3–29
equity-linked bonds
availability of sufficient shares, 9–22
listing, 9–22
notification, 9–22
ranking of shares, 9–22
events of default. *See* **Events of default**
financial covenants
dividend limitation, 3–32
generally, 3–32
information, 3–34
interest cover, 3–32
leverage ratio, 3–32
minimum net worth, 3–32
tests, 3–33
functions of, 3–6 to 3–7
generally, 2–1, 3–5
guarantee limits, 3–35
injunction restraining breach, 3–8
maintenance of status, licences and franchises, 3–35
negative pledge. *See* **Negative pledge**
objectives of, 3–6 to 3–7
pari passu clause, 3–27 to 3–28, 8–11
remedies for breach, 3–8
specific performance, 3–8

Covenants—*cont.*
  syndicated loans, 8–11
Custodians
  bonds, 1–14, 8–37, 10–37 to 10–38
  Cedel, 8–37, 10–37 to 10–38
  Euroclear, 8–37, 10–37 to 10–38
  Eurocommercial paper, 9–33
  objects of, 8–37
  securities, 8–38

Damages
  breach of covenant, for, 3–8
  insider dealing, for, 19–21
  misrepresentation, for, 17–19
Dealers
  authorisation of. *See also* **Britain; United States**
    licensing investment businesses, 14–7, 18–1
  cold calling, 18–18
  conduct of business
    Britain. *See* **Britain**
    generally, 18–7
    retail and business investors, 18–7
    sources of regulation, 18–7
    United States. *See* **United States**
  conflicts of interest
    generally, 18–11
    managing conflicts, 18–13
    secret profits, 18–12
    self-dealing, 18–12
  customer agreements, 18–15
  duties of skill, care and diligence, 18–14
  financial regulation
    generally, 18–19
    structure, 18–20
  financial supervision, 14–8
  fraud. *See* **Securities fraud**
  insider dealing. *See* **Insider dealing**
  licensing investment businesses, 14–7, 18–1
  margin regulations, 18–17
  protection of client assets, 18–10
  regulation of, 18–1 *et seq*
  remedies for clients, 18–16
  secret profits, 18–12
  securities fraud. *See* **Securities fraud**
  self-dealing, 18–12

Deep discount bonds. *See* **Bonds**
Default indemnity
  generally, 4–7
Denmark
  Brussels Convention 1968, 5–39
  EC First Company Law Directive, 13–3
  long-arm jurisdiction, 5–38
  prospectus, road-shows, 16–6
  securities regulation, 15–21
Depeçage
  choice of law, 5–19
Directors
  lender liability, 3–9
  liability for misrepresentation, 17–21
  prohibitions on dealing, 19–11
Disposals. *See* **Covenants**
Drawdown of loans
  generally, 2–2, 2–10
"Duly organised"
  meaning, 13–5

Eastern Europe. *See* **Central and Eastern Europe**
England. *See also* **Britain**
  acceleration, 3–54
  agent for service of process, 5–31, 5–52
  arbitration laws, 5–58
  bondholder trustees
    acceleration, 10–21
    bondholder, relationship with, 10–38
    Chinese walls, 11–24
    conflicts of interest, 11–6, 11–9
    exculpation clauses, 11–30
    monitoring duties, 11–15
    no statutory requirements, 10–7, 10–16
    notification of defaults, 11–21
    ostrich clauses, 11–21
    retirement of, 10–17
    stock exchange rules, 10–8
  bondholders' meetings, 10–26
    majority powers, 10–27
    minority protection, 10–27, 10–29
    oppression, 10–29

England—*cont.*
bondholders' meetings—*cont.*
resolution outside terms of power, 10–29
secret advantages, 10–29
unfairness, 10–29
conflict of laws, 4–8, 5–8
choice of law, 5–2
evasive, 5–14
insulation, 5–4, 5–5
long-arm jurisdiction, 5–15
no-express choice, 5–15
party autonomy, 5–9
state contracts, 5–17
contractual shortenings, 8–54
covenants, 3–46
exculpation clauses, 11–30
extortionate credit bargains, 2–18
floating charge, 3–46
forum non conveniens, 5–55
illegality, 4–8
insolvency set-off, 4–11
judgment debts, 2–18
judicial districts, 5–2
judicial jurisdiction, 5–55
legal opinions, 12–18
legal systems of, 5–2
listing of bonds, 8–25
long-arm jurisdiction, 5–38
misrepresentation
conflict of laws, 17–41
jurisdiction over tort claims, 17–42
due diligence, 17–10
fraudulent misrepresentation, 17–3
general rules of law, 17–3
heads of general misrepresentation, 17–3
inducement, 17–17
innocent misrepresentation, 17–3, 17–11
Misrepresentation Act 1967, 17–3, 17–11
negligence, 17–3, 17–10
reliance, 17–17
securities statutes
corporate prospectuses, 17–4
generally, 17–4
listing particulars, 17–4
misleading statements and practices, 17–4

England—*cont.*
misrepresentation—*cont.*
scheme particulars, 17–4
Theft Act 1968, 17–3
negative pledges
automatic security clause, 3–24
scope and efficacy of, 3–23
security covered, 3–12
title finance, 3–14
negotiability of bonds, 8–29 to 8–30, 8–33, 8–34, 8–35
negotiablity of bonds, notification to issuer, 8–31
nullity of companies, 13–3
partnerships, 13–11
public notaries, 12–2
security over future assets, 3–24
specific performance, 2–8, 2–9
stock exchange, 8–25
syndicate agents
Chinese Walls, 11–24
conflicts of interest, 11–6
statutory limitations on exculpation clauses, 11–30
syndicated loans, 1–5
term loans, application of proceeds, 2–13
trusts, attitudes to, 10–13
usury, 2–18
English-based countries
insolvency set-off, 4–11
limited duration charters, 13–6
securities regulation
Companies Act, 15–27
generally, 15–26
PFI, 15–28
sophisticated investors, 16–8
trusts, attitudes to, 10–13
Equity-linked bonds. *See* **Convertible debt**
Eurobond market
origins of, 1–12
Eurobonds. *See also* **Bond issues; Bonds**
meaning, 1–13
US selling restrictions in. *See* **United States**
Euroclear
Eurocommercial paper, 9–33
generally, 8–37, 10–37 to 10–38
warrants exercise procedure, 9–26

542   Wood: *Law and Practice of International Finance*

INDEX

Eurocommercial paper (ECP)
  documentation, 9–32 to 9–33
    dealer or programme agreement, 9–34
    deed of covenant, 9–36
    issuing and paying agency agreement, 9–35
    notes and global notes, 9–32
    generally, 9–31
    yield to investor, 9–31
Eurocurrency
  meaning, 1–6
Eurocurrency markets. *See also* **London eurocurrency market**
  generally, 1–9
Eurodollar
  generally, 1–6
European Judgments Conventions
  alternatives to domicile, 5–42
  basic principles, 5–40
  concurrent and related actions, 5–47
  consumer contracts, 5–44
  contracting out, 5–49 to 5–53
    limits on, 5–52
  countries covered, 5–39
  courts, non-Convention, 5–41, 5–50
  defendants, non-Convention, 5–48
  exclusive jurisdiction, 5–43
  forum non conveniens, 5–45, 17–42
  generally, 5–39
  insurance contracts, 5–44
  jurisdiction over tort claims, 17–42
  mutual recognition and enforcement of judgments, 5–54
  non-Convention courts, 5–41, 5–50
  non-Convention defendants, 5–48
  protective measures, 5–46
European Union
  Admissions Directive, 10–29
    comment, 15–9
    general requirements, 15–9
    generally, 15–9
    information, 15–9
    legal status, 15–9
    scope, 15–9
  Brussels Convention. *See* **European Judgments Conventions**
  Capital Adequacy Directive (CAD). *See* **Capital adequacy**

European Union—*cont.*
  collective investment schemes, 16–22
  First Company Law Directive, 13–3
  Insider Dealing Directive, 19–12 to 19–14
    classes of insider, 19–18
    exemption for stabilisation, 19–25
    inside information, 19–19
    securities covered by prohibition, 19–20
  Interim Reports Directive, 15–13
  Investment Services Directive, 15–19
  judgment conventions. *See* **European Judgments Conventions**
  Listing Particulars Directive
    co-ordination of stock exchange requirements, 15–12
    credit institutions, 15–11
    derogations, 15–11
    exemptions, 15–11
    generally, 15–10, 15–15
    information to be up-to-date, 15–12
    prescribed disclosure, 15–10
    publication, 15–12
    scope, 15–10
    screening, 15–12
    sophisticated investors, 15–11
    state-guaranteed issuers, 15–11
    utilities, 15–11
  Lugano Convention. *See* **European Judgments Conventions**
  Mutual Recognition Directive, 15–14
  Own Funds Directive, 22–9A
  Prospectus Directive, 15–15
  Rome Convention 1980. *See* **Rome Convention**
  Second Banking Directive, 15–18, 22–3
  Second Mutual Recognition Directive, 15–16
  securities regulation, 15–8 *et seq*
  Solvency Ratio Directive, 22–9A
  tort claims jurisdiction, 17–42
  UCITS Directive, 15–17, 16–22
Events of default
  acceleration, 3–8, 3–54, 8–55, 10–21 to 10–22, 17–19
  aircraft loans, 3–53
  bonds, 8–12, 8–55

Events of default—*cont.*
change of control, 3–50
classification of defaults
  breach of other obligations, 3–40
  breach of warranty, 3–41
  generally, 3–38
  non-payment, 3–39
creditor processes, 3–45
cross-default, 3–42
  express limitations, 3–43 to 3–44
effect of, 3–37
enforcement, 8–55
financial leases, 3–53
generally, 1–4, 2–1, 3–5
government loans, 3–52
guaranteed loans, 3–51
insolvency
  actual insolvency, 3–47
  proceedings, 3–46
liquidation proceedings, 3–46
material adverse change, 3–3, 3–48 to 3–49
  effect of clause, 3–49
notification of, 11–18
"poison pill", 3–50
project loans, 3–53
remedies for misrepresentation and, 17–19
ship loans, 3–53
state loans, 3–52
subsidiaries, 3–51
syndicated loans, 8–12
warranty, breach of, 3–3, 8–12
Evergreen warranty
generally, 3–3, 8–10
Exchange controls
convertible debt, 9–13
generally, 1–15, 14–2
Exclusion clauses. *See* **Exculpation clauses**
Exculpation clauses
bondholder trustees. *See* **Bondholder trustees**
conflicts of interest, 11–10, 11–11
secret profits, 11–12
syndicate agents. *See* **Syndicate agents**
trust deeds, 11–25
Execution and delivery
generally, 13–16

Extraterritoriality
criminal statutes
  enforcement of, 20–3
  Memoranda of Understanding (MOU), 20–3
  territorial scope, 20–2
internationalisation of securities markets, 20–1
jurisdiction over civil wrongs, 20–4
prescriptive jurisdiction
  generally, 20–5
  nationality principle, 20–8
  objective territorial principle, 20–5
  protective principle, 20–7
  subjective territorial principle, 20–5
  universality principle, 20–8

False market. *See also* **Securities fraud**
creation of, 19–2
False rumours. *See* **Securities fraud**
False wealth
trusts and, 10–13
Faroe Islands
Brussels Convention 1968, 5–39
Finland
Lugano Convention 1988, 5–39
New York Convention on the Recognition and Enforcement of Foreign Arbitral Awards 1958, 5–61
prospectus
  private offerings, 16–3
  road-shows, 16–6
securities regulation, 15–32
Fiscal agents
administrative obligations, 10–9
agent of issuer not bondholder, 10–9
bondholder trustees compared, 10–9 to 10–10
bonds, 8–40, 10–10
commission, 10–9
duties of, 10–9
euro-medium term notes, 9–38
eurocommercial paper, 9–35
paying agents, 8–53, 9–35, 10–10
payments, 10–9
remuneration, 10–9

INDEX

Fiscal laws
  generally, 14–2
Forum non conveniens
  European Judgments Conventions, 5–45
  judicial jurisdiction, 5–55
Forum selection
  insulation, 5–27
France
  acceleration clauses, nullified on insolvency, 3–54
  acte authentique, 12–2
  bondholder trustees
    conflicts of interest, 11–8
    generally, 10–32
    no-action clauses, 10–23
  bondholders' meetings, 10–26, 10–32
  bonds, notification to issuer, 8–31
  Brussels Convention 1968, 5–39
  choice of law, 5–2
  contractual shortenings, 8–54
  domicile, election of, 5–34
  due incorporation, 13–3
  eligible investors, 16–8
  eurocurrency market, 1–9
  insolvency set-off and, 4–11
  legal opinions, 13–3
  long-arm jurisdiction, 5–38
  MOU with United States, 20–3
  nullity of companies, 13–3
  prospectus
    foreign government offerings, 16–9
    foreign issues, reciprocal recognition, 16–16
    private offerings, 16–3
    road-shows, 16–6
    sophisticated investors, 16–8
  redressement judiciare, 3–28
  securities regulation, 15–21
    history, 14–14
  state immunity, 5–64
  super-priority moratorium loans, 3–28
Franco-Latin countries
  land mortgages, registration of, 10–6
  limited duration charters, 13–6
  notaries, 12–2

Franco-Latin countries—*cont.*
  security over future assets, 3–24
  trusts, attitudes to, 10–13
Fraud. *See* **Securities fraud**
Gaming laws
  generally, 1–15, 14–2
Germanic countries
  notaries, 12–2
  trusts, attitudes to, 10–13
Germany
  bank regulation, 22–5
  bondholder trustees
    generally, 10–34
    monitoring duties, 11–16
  bondholders' meetings, 10–26, 10–34
  bonds, notification to issuer, 8–31
  Brussels Convention 1968, 5–39
  contractual shortenings, 8–54
  custodians, 10–37
  EC First Company Law Directive, 13–3
  fiduciary representatives, 10–13
    regulatory requirements, 10–16
  insolvency set-off, 4–11
  long-arm jurisdiction, 5–38
  notarial document, 12–2
  notaries, 12–2
  nullity of companies, 13–3
  prospectus
    road-shows, 16–6
    sophisticated investors, 16–8
  securities regulation, 15–21
    history, 14–14
  state immunity, 5–64
  trusts, attitude to, 10–13
Gibraltar
  Brussels Convention 1968, 5–39
"Good standing"
  meaning, 13–7
Government loans. *See* **State loans**
Greece
  Brussels Convention 1968, 5–39
  EC First Company Law Directive, 13–3
  insolvency set-off and, 4–11
  New York Convention on the Recognition and Enforcement of Foreign Arbitral Awards 1958, 5–61

Greece—*cont.*
 prospectus, 16–8
 sophisticated investors, 16–8

Hague Convention on Trusts 1986, 10–38
Hong Kong. *See also* English-based countries
 eurocurrency market, 1–9
 prospectus, private offerings, 16–3
Hungary. *See also* Central and Eastern Europe
 conflict of laws, 5–8

Iceland
 Lugano Convention 1988, 5–39
Illegality clause
 generally, 4–8
Increased costs clauses
 generally, 4–5
India
 exculpation clauses, 11–31
Indonesia
 insider dealing, 19–16
 prospectus
  private offerings, 16–3
  road-shows, 16–6
Insider dealing
 affirmative misrepresentation, 19–9
 classes of insiders, 19–18
 codes, 19–11
 conflict of duties, 19–22
 EC Directive on, 19–12 to 19–14, 19–18, 19–19, 19–20
 exemption for stabilisation, 19–25
 general law, under, 19–9
 inside information, 19–19
 intent, 19–24
 listing codes, 19–10
 main prohibitions, 19–17 *et seq*
  securities covered by, 19–20
 meaning, 19–8
 negative profits, 19–23
 omitting to disclose, 19–9
 prohibition on directors' dealing, 19–11

Insider dealing—*cont.*
 reports of holdings, 19–10
 sanctions, 19–21
 secret profits, 19–9
 special relationships, 19–9
 stabilisation, exemption for, 19–25
 territoriality, 19–26
 United States, 19–15
Insolvency
 law, 1–16 to 1–17
 state insolvency, 1–8
Insulation
 forum selection, 5–27
 governing law, 5–4 to 5–5
 limits on, 5–6
Insurance laws
 generally, 14–2
Interest
 bonds, 8–6, 8–44 to 8–46
 deep discount bonds, 8–46
 fixed rate, 8–6, 8–44
 floating rate, 8–6, 8–45
 post-insolvency, 2–18
 substitute basis clause, 2–19 to 2–20
 swaps, 8–46
 term loans, 2–16 to 2–18, 2–20
 zero coupon, 8–46
Investment businesses. *See* Dealers
Investment Management Regulatory Organisation (IMRO)
 generally, 18–8
Ireland. *See* Republic of Ireland
Italy
 bondholder trustees, 11–16
 bonds, notification to issuer, 8–31
 Brussels Convention 1968, 5–39
 EC First Company Law Directive, 13–3
 eligible investors, 16–8
 Hague Convention on Trusts 1986, 10–38
 insolvency set-off, 4–11
 nullity of companies, 13–3
 prospectus
  road-shows, 16–6
  sophisticated investors, 16–8
 securities regulation, 15–21
 state immunity, 5–64

INDEX

Japan
arbitration laws, 5–58
bondholder communities, 10–35
bondholders' meetings, 10–35
  minority protection, 10–28
bonds, notification to issuer, 8–31
choice of law, 5–2
insolvency set-off, 4–11
London eurocurrency market and, 1–6
long-arm jurisdiction, 5–38
MOU with United States, 20–3
New York Convention on the Recognition and Enforcement of Foreign Arbitral Awards 1958, 5–61
prospectus
  foreign government offerings, 16–9
  foreign issues, 16–16
  private offerings, 16–3
  road-shows, 16–6
  reciprocal recognition, 16–16
securities regulation, 14–13, 15–23

Judgment debts
generally, 2–18

Judicial jurisdiction
agent for service of process, 5–31, 5–34
arbitration. *See* **Arbitration**
Brussels Convention. *See* **European Judgments Conventions**
civilian practice, 5–34
domicile, election of, 5–34
European Judgments conventions. *See* **European Judgments Conventions**
exclusive jurisdiction clauses, 5–35
forum non conveniens, 5–55
international jurisdiction rules
  generally, 5–36
  long-arm jurisdiction, summary, 5–38
  universal bases of jurisdiction, 5–37
jurisdiction clauses, 5–24 *et seq*
  exclusive jurisdiction clauses, 5–35
  multiple jurisdiction clauses, 5–35
  short-form, 5–24

Judicial jurisdiction—*cont.*
lis alibi pendens, 5–56
Lugano Convention. *See* **European Judgments Conventions**
mailing of process, 5–32
multiple actions, 5–56
multiple jurisdiction clauses, 5–35
process
  agent for service of, 5–31
  mailing of, 5–32
purposes of forum selection
  additional forum, 5–26
  European Judgments Conventions, 5–30
  foreign recognition, 5–30
  forum and governing law, 5–28
  forum non conveniens, 5–30
  generally, 5–26
  immunity, 5–29
  insulation, 5–27
  standards of the courts, 5–29
restrictions on, 5–55 *et seq*
venue, 5–33

Judicial rehabilitation proceedings
generally, 10–20

Korea (South)
bonds, notification to issuer, 8–31
eligible investors, 16–8
prospectus, 16–8
securities regulation, 14–13
sophisticated investors, 16–8

Latin America. *See also* **Argentina; Chile; Mexico; Panama; Venezuela**
Bustamante Code, 5–8
conflict of laws, 5–8
securities regulation, 15–32
state insolvencies, 1–8

Legal opinions
assumptions, 12–7
bond issues
  prospectuses, 13–38
  securities regulations, 13–37
borrower's domicile, opinions as to law of, 12–13

International Loans, Bonds and Securities Regulation   547

Legal opinions—*cont.*
  contents of
    bankruptcy qualification, 13–20 to 13–21
    corporate powers, 13–12
    due authorisation, 13–13
      corporations, 13–14
    due incorporation, 13–3 to 13–4
    "duly organised", 13–5
    "enforceable", 13–19
    execution and delivery, 13–16
    filings, 13–29
    foreign judgments, enforcement of, 13–33
    foreign law opinions, 13–24
    foreign lawyer's legal opinion, 13–1 *et seq*
    "good faith" qualifications, 13–23
    "good standing", 13–7
    governing law, 13–36
    immunity, 13–34
    legal form, 13–30
    legal validity, 13–17
      bankruptcy qualification, 13–20 to 13–21
      "enforceable", 13–19
      foreign law opinions, 13–24
      "good faith" qualifications, 13–23
      legally binding, 13–18
    legally binding, 13–18
    litigation, 13–27
    no adverse consequences, 13–35
    non-conflict with laws, constitution or contracts, 13–26
    official consents, 13–25
    pari passu ranking, 13–32
    partnerships, 13–11
    qualification to do business, 13–8, 13–35
    stamp duties, 13–28
    status, 13–2
    taxes, 13–31
    trusts, 13–10
    "validly existing", 13–6
  documents examined, 12–6
  European notaries compared, 12–2 to 12–3
  facts, as to, 12–9
  foreign law, 12–10 to 12–11
  foreign lawyer's, 13–1 *et seq*

Legal opinions—*cont.*
  generally, 1–19, 12–1
  jurisdictions covered, 12–4
  lawyers giving opinions, 12–12
  liability. *See* reliance and liability, *infra*
  notaries compared, 12–2 to 12–3
  principal lawyers, of
    client, identifying, 13–42
    conditions precedent, 13–43
    expert's opinion, 13–44
    generally, 13–41
  qualifications, 12–8, 13–20 to 13–21
    bankruptcy qualification, 13–20 to 13–21
    foreign law, 12–8
    "good faith" qualifications, 13–23
    opinions as to facts, 12–9
  reliance and liability
    generally, 12–15
    lawyers as "experts", 12–16
    tort liability, 12–17 to 12–20
  scope of opinions, 12–5
  security, on, 13–39 to 13–40
  timing, 12–14
Lender liability
  covenants, 3–9
  generally, 2–8
Lifting the veil
  generally, 13–6
Limitation. *See* **Prescription**
Lis alibi pendens
  generally, 5–56
Listing of bonds
  advantages, 8–24
  disadvantages, 8–25
  equity-linked bonds, 9–22
  stock exchanges, 8–23
Loan sales and transfers. *See* **Participations**
London eurobond issues
  documents, 8–18
  bonds, 8–20
  fiscal agency agreement, 8–20
  global bond, 8–20
  managers' agreement, 8–19
  offering circular, 8–18
  prospectus, 8–18
  selling agreements, 8–19

London eurobond issues—*cont.*
  documents—*cont.*
    subscription agreement, 8–18
      market disruption, 8–18
      subscription, 8–18
      warranties, 8–18
    trust deed, 8–20
    underwriting agreements, 8–18
  structure, 8–17
London eurocurrency market
  generally, 1–6
  intermediation, 1–7
  loans to lesser developed countries, 1–7
  origins of, 1–7
  petrodollar explosion and, 1–7
  recycling, 1–7
  state insolvencies, 1–8
Lugano Convention on Jurisdiction and the Enforcement of Judgments in Civil and Commercial Matters 1968. *See* **European Judgments Conventions**
Luxembourg
  bondholder trustees
    conflicts of interest, 11–8
    monitoring duties, 11–16
  bondholders' meetings, 10–33
  bonds, notification to issuer, 8–31
  Brussels Convention 1968, 5–39
  Cedel. *See* **Cedel**
  EC First Company Law Directive, 13–3
  fiduciary representative, 10–13, 10–14
  insolvency set-off and, 4–11
  listing of bonds, 8–25
  long-arm jurisdiction, 5–38
  prospectus, private offerings, 16–3
  securities regulation, 14–14
  stock exchange, 8–25
  trusts, attitude to, 10–14

Malaysia
  securities regulation, 14–13
Market manipulation. *See* **Securities fraud**
Materiality
  events of default, 3–40, 3–41
  misrepresentation, 17–18

Materiality—*cont.*
  warranties, 3–3
Memoranda of Understanding (MOU)
  United States, 20–3
Mergers. *See also* **Takeovers**
  convertible debt, 9–21
Mexico. *See also* **Latin America**
  bondholder trustees, 11–16
  debenture issues, 10–13
  insider dealing, 19–16
  MOU with United States, 20–3
  New York Convention on the Recognition and Enforcement of Foreign Arbitral Awards 1958, 5–61
  prospectus, cold calling, 16–5
  securities regulation, 14–13, 15–32
    insider dealing, 19–16
Middle East. *See* **Brunei; Saudi Arabia; Turkey; United Arab Emirates**
Misrepresentation and non-disclosure
  absolute liability, 17–2
  access to information, 17–16
  bond managers
    exclusion of liability
      disclaimer, 17–28
      due diligence procedures, 17–29
      eurobonds, 17–30
      indemnity from issuer, 17–28
  borrower, liability of, 17–21
  co-managers' liability, 17–25. *See also* lead managers' liability, *infra*
  general principles, 17–24
  conflict of laws
    close connected law of the tort, 17–40
    English law, 17–41
    governing law of torts, 17–37
    jurisdiction over tort claims, 17–42 to 17–43
    law of the place of the tort, 17–39
    lex fori, 17–38
  continuing disclosure, 17–36
  contracting-out, 17–2
  director liability, 17–21
  due diligence procedures, 17–10, 17–29 to 17–30
  enhanced liability under regulated prospectuses, summary, 17–2

International Loans, Bonds and Securities Regulation

Misrepresentation and non-disclosure—cont.
forecasts, 17–12
heads of general misrepresentation. *See* **England; United States**
inducement, 17–2, 17–17
information, access to, 17–16
innocent misrepresentation, 17–11
intention, misstatements of, 17–12
issuer, liability of, 17–21
knowing misrepresentation, 17–9
law, misstatements of, 17–13
lead managers' liability. *See also* co-managers' liability, *supra*
   active and knowing involvement, 17–25
   agent or fiduciary, 17–25
   general principles, 17–24
   generally, 17–25
   tort of negligence, 17–25
materiality
   generally, 17–18
   prescribed information, 17–18
   standards of information, 17–18
meaning of misrepresentation
   forecasts, 17–12
   misstatements of intention, 17–12
   misstatements of law, 17–13
   misstatements of opinion, 17–13
   non-factual matters, 17–12
   omissions, 17–14
   summaries of documents, 17–13
   true facts become false, 17–15
misrepresentor's knowledge of the misrepresentation, 17–9
   due diligence, 17–10
   innocence, 17–11
   knowing or reckless misrepresentation, 17–9
   negligence, 17–10
misstatements of intention, 17–12
misstatements of law, 17–13
misstatements of opinion, 17–13
negligence, 17–10
non-factual matters, 17–12
omissions, 17–14
opinion, misstatements of, 17–13
participants in, liability of, 17–21
prospectus contents
   bank prospectuses, 17–34

Misrepresentation and non-disclosure—cont.
prospectus contents—*cont.*
   corporate prospectuses, 17–33
   disclosure codes
      accounting, 17–32
      burdens, 17–32
      commercial secrecy, 17–32
      debt/equity, 17–32
      government prospectuses, 17–35
      prescribed contents, 17–2, 17–32
      sophisticated investors, 17–32
      strengths and weaknesses, 17–31 to 17–32
reckless misrepresentation, 17–9
reliance, 17–2, 17–17
remedies
   damages, 17–19
   events of default, 17–19
   generally, 17–19
   rescission, 17–19
sources of law, 17–1
stock exchange, continuing disclosure, 17–36
summaries of documents, 17–13
syndication managers' liability
   exclusion of
      express, 17–27
      generally, 17–26
      indemnity from borrower, 17–27
      information memorandum, 6–8
true facts become false, 17–15
who can be sued
   exclusion of, 17–23
   ordinary law, under
      borrower, 17–21
      directors, 17–21
      generally, 17–21
      issuer, 17–21
      participants, 17–21
   securities regulation, 17–22
who can sue
   circular spends force, when, 17–20
   original misrepresentees, 17–20
   subsequent purchasers, 17–20
Multicurrency clauses
generally, 2–21
Multiple actions
generally, 5–56
Multiple jurisdictions. *See* **Judicial jurisdictions**

Negative pledge
  automatic security clause, 3–24 to 3–27
  bonds, 8–11, 8–43
  generally, 3–10
  governing law, 3–13
  purposes of clause, 3–10
  scope and efficacy of, 3–22
  security covered
    exclusions, 3–17 to 3–26
    generally, 3–12
    interpretation, 3–13
    subsidiaries, 3–16
    title finance, 3–14 to 3–15
  term loans, 3–10 to 3–26
Netherlands
  Brussels Convention 1968, 5–39
  eligible investors, 16–8
  fiduciary representatives, 10–13
  insolvency set-off, 4–11
  long-arm jurisdiction, 5–38
  MOU with United States, 20–3
  prospectus
    road-shows, 16–6
    sophisticated investors, 16–8
  securities regulation, 15–21
    history, 14–14
Netherlands Antilles
  Brussels Convention 1968, 5–39
New York Convention on the Recognition and Enforcement of Foreign Arbitral Awards 1958, 5–61
New Zealand. *See also* **English-based countries**
  prospectus, private offerings, 16–3
  securities regulation, 15–25
    insider dealing, 19–16, 19–21
  trusts, attitudes to, 10–13
Nigeria
  New York Convention on the Recognition and Enforcement of Foreign Arbitral Awards 1958, 5–61
Norway
  Lugano Convention 1988, 5–39

Norway—*cont.*
  New York Convention on the Recognition and Enforcement of Foreign Arbitral Awards 1958, 5–61
Notaries
  generally, 12–2
Novations. *See also* **Participations**
  appropriation of payments, 7–32
  generally, 7–2
  guaranteed loans, 7–31
  management, 7–34
  recourse to seller, 7–33
  rescheduling clause, 7–34
  secured loans, 7–31
  set-off, 7–30
  solicitation, 7–30
  substitution certificates, 7–29
  syndicated loans, 8–13
  transaction, 7–28
  transfer of obligations and benefits, 7–30

Ontario. *See* **Canada**
Ostrich clauses
  generally, 11–21
Overdrafts
  term loans compared, 2–1

Pacific. *See* **Asia and Pacific**
Pakistan
  state immunity, 5–64
Panama. *See also* **Latin America**
  debenture issues, 10–13
Pari passu
  bonds, 8–11, 8–42
  covenants, 3–27 to 3–28, 8–11
  legal opinions as to, 13–32
Paris Club
  generally, 1–8
Participations
  agency, 7–3
  assignment
    appropriation of payments, 7–14
    generally, 7–2
    guaranteed loans, 7–13, 7–24
    loan agreement
      benefit of, 7–8
      restrictions in, 7–7

Participations—*cont.*
  assignment—*cont.*
    management, 7–17
    notice to debtor, 7–10
    recourse to seller, 7–15
    rescheduling and new money clause, 7–16
    secured loans, 7–13, 7–24
    set-off, 7–11
    solicitation, 7–12
    transaction, 7–6
    transferability of lead bank's obligations, 7–9
  capital adequacy, 7–37 to 7–40
  guaranteed loans, 7–13
  methods, 7–2
  novations. *See* **Novations**
  reasons for loan transfer, 7–1
  risk participations, 7–2
    benefit of loan agreement, 7–36
    transaction, 7–35
  secured loans, 7–13
  securities regulation, 7–41
  securitisations, 7–2
  set-off, 7–5, 7–11, 7–23, 7–30
  sub-participations, 7–2
    appropriation of payments, 7–24
    double-risk, 7–19
    guaranteed loans, 7–24
    loan agreement
      benefit of, 7–22
      obligations under, 7–22
      restrictions, 7–21
    management, 7–27
    purpose of, 7–20
    recourse to lead bank, 7–24
    rescheduling and new money, 7–25 to 7–26
    secured loans, 7–24
    set-off, 7–23
    solicitation, 7–23
    transaction, 7–18
  terminology, 7–3
Partnerships
  legal opinions, 13–11
Paying agents. *See also* **Fiscal agents**
  generally, 8–53, 9–35, 10–10
Payment
  bearer bonds, 8–52
  fiscal agents. *See* **Fiscal agents**
  paying agents, 8–53, 9–35, 10–10

Payment—*cont.*
  payments by borrower clause, 2–22 to 2–24
  place of, 2–23
  time of, 2–24
Personal Investment Authority (PIA)
  generally, 18–8
Philippines
  insider dealing, 19–16
  New York Convention on the Recognition and Enforcement of Foreign Arbitral Awards 1958, 5–61
Poland. *See also* **Central and Eastern Europe**
  New York Convention on the Recognition and Enforcement of Foreign Arbitral Awards 1958, 5–61
  state insolvency, 1–8
Pools. *See* **Collective investment schemes**
Portugal
  Brussels Convention 1968, 5–39
  EC First Company Law Directive, 13–3
  eligible investors, 16–8
  prospectus
    road-shows, 16–6
    sophisticated investors, 16–8
  securities regulation, 15–21
Prepayments
  bonds, 8–7
  syndicated loans, 8–7
  term loans, 2–15
Prescription
  bonds, 8–14, 8–54
  contractual alterations, 8–54
  statutory periods, 8–54
  syndicated loans, 8–14
Prescriptive jurisdiction. *See* **Extraterritoriality; Securities regulation; Trust deeds**
Private debt restructuring
  generally, 10–20
Pro rata sharing
  set-off, 6–17
  syndicate loan clauses, 6–16 to 6–18, 8–9

Project finance
   "build-operate-transfer" projects, 1–10
   essence of, 1–10
   generally, 1–10
   loan syndications, 16–24 to 16–25
   privatisation and, 1–10

Prospectus
   advertisements, tombstones, 16–4
   available disclosure, 16–1
   bank deposits, 16–10
   bank prospectuses, 17–34
   collective investment schemes, 16–20 to 16–22
   commercial paper issues, 16–12
   corporate prospectuses, 17–33
   disclosure codes. *See* **Misrepresentation and non-disclosure**
   EC Prospectus Directive, 15–15
   exemptions from requirements, 16–1 *et seq*
   summary, 16–2
   existing security holders, 16–13
   foreign issues
      issues into the regulated state, 16–16
      issues in and out, 16–15
      reciprocal recognition, 16–16
   government prospectuses, 17–35
   governmental and public bodies, 16–9
      foreign governments, 16–9
      foreign municipalities, 16–9
      foreign public corporations, 16–9
      international organisations, 16–9
   guaranteed issues, 16–19
   international bond issues, 16–23
   international organisations, 16–9
   legal opinions as to, 13–38
   listed securities, 16–14
   London eurobond issues, 8–18
   marketing only by means of approved prospectus, 16–1
   misrepresentation and non-disclosure. *See* **Misrepresentation and non-disclosure**
   pathfinder prospectus, 8–16

Prospectus—*cont.*
   preliminary prospectus offerings, 8–16
   private offerings
      cold calling, 16–5
      generally, 16–3
      international media, 16–5
      meaning of public, 16–3
      prohibited forms of marketing, 16–4 *et seq*
      resale to public, 16–7
      road shows, 16–6
      tombstones, 16–4
   professional market, 16–1
   red herring prospectus, 8–16
   road-shows, 16–6
   secondary market reading, 16–17
   shelf registration, 16–18
   sophisticated investors exemption, 16–8
   syndicated loans, 16–11, 16–24 to 16–25
   tombstones, 16–4

Quebec. *See* **Canada**

Redemption. *See* **Repayment**
Registered bonds. *See* **Bonds**
Repayment
   bonds, 8–7, 8–47 to 8–51
   bullet repayment, 2–14, 8–47
   early redemption for tax, 8–50
   early voluntary redemption, 8–49
   instalments, by, 2–14, 8–47
   perpetual bonds, 8–48
   purchase of bonds by issuer, 8–51
   syndicated loans, 8–7
   term loans, 2–14
Republic of Ireland
   Brussels Convention 1968, 5–39
   EC First Company Law Directive, 13–3
   prospectus, 16–8
   sophisticated investors, 16–8
Reserve requirements
   meaning, 1–7
   US banks, 1–7

Revolving loan
  meaning, 1–9, 2–2
Road-shows
  generally, 16–6
Rome Convention (Rome Convention on the Law Applicable to Contractual Obligations 1980)
  alternative choices, 5–18
  Brussels Protocol 1988, 5–7
  depeçage, 5–19
  express choice of applicable law, 5–9
  freedom of choice, 5–9
  generally, 3–13, 4–8, 5–7, 5–16
  no foreign element, 5–13
  renvoi, 5–21
  variation of governing law, 5–12
Russia. *See also* **Central and Eastern Europe**
  securities regulation
    exemptions, 15–30
    legislation, 15–29
    licensing of dealers, 15–30
    registration of public offerings, 15–29

Saudi Arabia
  securities regulation, 15–32
Scalping. *See* **Securities fraud**
Scandinavia. *See also* **Denmark; Finland; Norway; Sweden**
  insolvency set-off, 4–11
  tort claims jurisdiction, 17–42
  trusts, attitudes to, 10–13
Secret profits. *See also* **Conflicts of interest**
  bondholder trustees, 11–12
  dealers, 18–12
  exculpation clauses, 11–12
  insider dealing, 19–9
  syndicate agents, 6–24, 11–12
Securities clearance systems. *See* **Custodians**
Securities fraud
  churning, 19–7
  corners, 19–3
  false rumours, 19–4
  generally, 15–4
  insider dealing. *See* **Insider dealing**

Securities fraud—*cont.*
  market manipulation, 19–2
  scalping, 19–5
  stabilisation, exemption for, 19–6
  wash-sales, 19–2
Securities and Futures Authority (SFA)
  generally, 18–8, 18–9
Securities regulation
  agency duties, codes of conduct, 14–7
  banking laws, 14–2
  "Blue Sky" laws, 15–6, 16–7, 16–16
  bondholder representation, 14–8
  codes of conduct, 14–7
  codification, 14–6
  cold calling, 15–4, 16–5
  collective investment schemes, 15–4
  countries summaries 15–1 *et seq. See also* under individual countries, *e.g.* **United States**
  dealers. *See* **Dealers**
  disclosure requirements, 14–7
  excesses of regulatory regimes, 14–4
  extraterritoriality. *See* **Extraterritoriality**
  fiduciary duties, codes of conduct, 14–7
  fraud. *See* **Securities fraud**
  generally, 1–15, 14–1
  history, 14–11 to 14–14
  international approaches, 14–5
  investment advertisements, 15–2
  licensing of investment business. *See* **Dealers**
  limitation on entities entitled to raise money from the public, 14–7
  meaning of securities, 14–9 to 14–10
  misrepresentation and non-disclosure. *See* **Misrepresentation and non-disclosure**
  policies
    generally, 14–3
    protection of unsophisticated investors, 14–3
  prospectus. *See* **Prospectus**
  protection of unsophisticated investors, 14–3
  sanctions for securities crimes, 14–7
  securities, meaning of, 14–9 to 14–10
  securities fraud. *See* **Securities fraud**
  sources of law, 15–1

INDEX

Securities regulation—*cont.*
  summary of, 14–1 *et seq*, 14–7 to 14–8
  terms of securities, control of, 14–8
  unsophisticated investors, protection of, 14–3
  US selling restrictions in Eurobond issues. *See* **United States**
  warrants to purchase bonds, 9–25
Securitisations
  generally, 7–2
Set-off
  bearer bonds, 8–35
  insolvency set-off, 4–11
  participations, 7–5, 7–11, 7–23, 7–30
  pro rata sharing, 6–17
  registered bonds, 8–35
  term loans, 2–26, 4–11
Singapore. *See also* **English-based countries**
  bondholder trustees
    conflicts of interest, 11–8
    monitoring duties, 11–16
    regulatory requirements, 10–16
    retirement of, 10–17
    stock exchange rules, 10–8
  eligible investors, 16–8
  eurocurrency market, 1–9
  exculpation clauses, statutory limitations on, 11–31
  insider dealing, 19–16
  prospectus
    foreign issues, 16–16
    reciprocal recognition, 16–16
    sophisticated investors, 16–8
  securities regulation
    history, 14–13
    insider dealing, 19–16
  state immunity, 5–64
  trust deeds, 10–40
South Africa
  insider dealing, 19–16
  long-arm jurisdiction, 5–38
  securities regulation
    generally, 15–26
    insider dealing, 19–16
  state immunity, 5–64

Spain
  bondholder trustees, conflicts of interest, 11–8
  Brussels Convention 1968, 5–39
  EC First Company Law Directive, 13–3
  eligible investors, 16–8
  insolvency set-off and, 4–11
  pari passu clauses, 3–27
  prospectus
    private offerings, 16–3
    road-shows, 16–6
    sophisticated investors, 16–8
  securities regulation, 15–21
Specific performance
  covenant, of, 3–8
Stamp duty
  equity-linked bonds, 9–23
  legal opinions, 13–28
State immunity
  waiver of
    generally, 5–64
    principles of, 5–65
    terms of clause, 5–63
State insolvency
  generally, 1–8
State loans
  events of default, 3–52
  generally, 1–18
Stock exchanges. *See also* **Bonds**
  advantages of listing, 8–24
  continuing disclosure, 17–36
  disadvantages of listing, 8–24
  equity-linked bonds, 9–4
  generally, 8–23
  rules for bondholder trustees, 10–8
Substitute basis clause. *See* **Interest**
Swaps
  interest swaps, 8–46
Sweden
  long-arm jurisdiction, 5–38
  Lugano Convention 1988, 5–39
  New York Convention on the Recognition and Enforcement of Foreign Arbitral Awards 1958, 5–61
Switzerland
  bondholder communities, 10–36
  bondholder statutes, 10–39

International Loans, Bonds and Securities Regulation

Switzerland—*cont.*
  bondholder trustees, monitoring duties, 11–16
  bondholders' meetings, 10–26, 10–36
  conflict of laws, 5–8, 5–11
  fiduciary representatives, 10–13
  insolvency set-off, 4–11
  Lugano Convention 1988, 5–39
  New York Convention on the Recognition and Enforcement of Foreign Arbitral Awards 1958, 5–61
  prospectus
    private offerings, 16–3
    road-shows, 16–6
  securities regulation, history, 14–14
  state immunity, 5–64
Syndicate agents
  acceleration, 6–27
  agency duties, paying, 6–21
  agent of bank not borrower, 6–22, 11–1
  approval of documentation, 11–14
  authority of, 6–20 to 6–21
  banking duties, 6–21
  "big pocket" liability, 11–1, 17–2
  bondholder trustees compared
    conflicts of interest. *See* **conflicts of interest**, *infra*
    differences, 11–2
    generally, 11–1
    secret profits, 11–12
  Chinese Walls
    case law, 11–24
    conflicts of interest, 11–11
    disadvantages, 11–23
    generally, 11–22
  conditions precedent duties, 6–21
  confidential information and, 11–17
  conflicts of interest, 6–24
    accounting for profits, 11–5
    authorising clause in syndicate loan agreements, 11–10
    Chinese Wall, 11–11
    consent of beneficiaries, 11–9
    contractual exculpation, 11–11
    criminal penalties, 11–5
    cross-directorship, 11–4
    cross-shareholdings, 11–4
    delegation, 11–11

Syndicate agents—*cont.*
  conflicts of interest—*cont.*
    effects of, 11–5
    examples, 11–4
    fiduciary acts as financial adviser to borrower, 11–4
    fiduciary guarantees issue, 11–4
    fiduciary has investment department, 11–4
    fiduciary is also private lender, 11–4
    fiduciary is representative of two loans or issues, 11–4
    general rule, 11–3
    liability of fiduciary, 11–5
    negligence proceedings, 11–5
    regulatory controls on, 11–6 to 11–8
    resignation, 11–11
    solutions, 11–9 to 11–11
  contractual duties, 6–23
  default duties, 6–21
  defaults, notification of. *See* notification of defaults, *infra*
  discretion, exercise of, 6–25, 11–2
  documentation, approval of, 11–14
  due diligence, 6–24
    approval of documentation, 11–14
    confidential information, 11–17
    duties, 11–13
    generally, 11–13
    monitoring duties, 6–21, 6–26
    notification of defaults. *See* notification of defaults, *infra*
    powers, 11–13
  exculpation clauses
    conflicts of interest, 11–11
    efficacy of, 11–29
    general effect of, 11–28
    general immunities, 11–27
    limitation of agent's role, 11–26
    practice, 11–26
    secret profits, 11–12
    specific immunities, 11–27
    statutory limitations, 11–30
  fiduciaries, as, 6–24, 11–1 *et seq*
  functions of, 6–21
  generally, 6–4, 6–19, 11–1
  indemnity, right of, 6–28
  monitoring duties, 6–21, 6–26
  notification of defaults, 11–18

INDEX

Syndicate agents—*cont.*
  notification of defaults—*cont.*
    generally, 11–18
    ostrich clauses, 11–21
    what constitutes knowledge, 11–19
    when default should be notified, 11–20
  powers of, 6–20, 11–13
  receipt of notices, 6–21
  removal of, 6–29
  repayment, 8–7
  scope of authority, 6–20 to 6–21
  secret profits, 6–24, 11–12
Syndicate agents
  advance of funds, 8–5
  agent bank. *See* **Syndicate agents**
  assignment, 8–13
  bond issues compared. *See* **Bond issues**
  complex project security arrangements, 8–2
  covenants, 8–11
  currency conversion, 8–6
  default interest, 8–6
  democracy. *See* syndicate democracy, *infra*
  disclosure requirements, 8–3
  documentation, 8–4
  events of default, 8–12
  functions of lead bank, 6–3
  generally, 1–5
  history, 1–5
  information memorandum, 6–5
    international regulation of information memorandum, 6–6
    misrepresentation liability, 6–8
  interest, 8–6
  investors
    character of, 8–2
    number and anonymity of, 8–2
  issue mechanics, 8–2
  mandate, 6–2
  margin protection, 8–8
  meaning, 1–5
  misrepresentation liability
    exclusion of liability by managers, 17–26 to 17–27
    information memorandum, 6–8
  modification, 8–13
  multicurrency options, 8–2

Syndicate agents—*cont.*
  novations, 8–13
  payment of loans to borrower, 6–14
  payments by borrower, 6–15
  payments and equality, 8–9
  prepayment, 8–7
  prescription, 8–14
  principles of, summary, 6–4
  pro rata sharing clauses, 6–4, 6–16 to 6–18, 8–9
  prospectus exemptions, 16–11, 16–24 to 16–25
  relationship between syndicate members, 6–9 *et seq*
  revolving credit, 8–2
  several commitments, 6–4
  severality of bank commitments, 6–9 to 6–10
  sophisticated investors, 8–2
  standby facility, 8–2
  syndicate agents. *See* **Syndicate agents**
  syndicate democracy, 6–4, 6–11 to 6–13
    majority powers, 6–11 to 6–13
    validity of, 6–13
    no-action clauses, 6–13
  term sheet, 6–2
  transfer, 8–13
  warranties, 8–10

Taiwan
  cold calling, 16–5
Takeovers. *See also* **Mergers**
  convertible debt, 9–12, 9–19 to 9–20
Taxation
  bonds, 8–26 to 8–27
  convertible debt
    dividends, 9–23
    gains tax, 9–23
    generally, 9–23
    issue taxes, 9–23
  early redemption for tax, 8–50
  grossing-up clauses
    drafting, 4–4
    generally, 4–2
    return of tax credits, 4–3
Term loans
  agreement to lend, 2–2
  application of proceeds, 2–11 to 2–13
    unlawful purpose, 2–12

Term loans—*cont.*
  appropriations, 2–25
  assignments, 4–9 to 4–10
  boiler-plate clause, 4–13
  cancellation, 2–15
  choice of law clause. *See* **Choice of law**
  conditions precedent, 2–3 to 2–9
    remedies
      bank default, for, 2–8
      borrower default in borrowing, for, 2–9
      to each loan separately, 2–5 to 2–7
  covenants. *See* **Covenants**
  currency indemnity, 4–6
  default indemnity, 4–7
  disaster clauses, 2–19
  drawdown of loans, 2–2, 2–10
  events of default. *See* **Events of default generally**
  financial terms, 2–1 *et seq*
  force majeure clauses, 2–19
  generally, 1–4, 2–1
  illegality clause, 4–8
  increased costs clauses, 4–5
  interest, 2–16 to 2–18, 2–20
  jurisdiction clause. *See* **Judicial jurisdiction**
  "lines of credit" compared, 2–1
  margin protections, 4–2 *et seq*
  multicurrency option, 2–21
  negative pledge. *See* **Negative pledge**
  overdrafts compared, 2–1
  payments by borrower, 2–22 to 2–24
    place of, 2–23
    time of, 2–24
  prepayments, 2–15
  repayment, 2–14
  revolving loan, 2–2
  set-off, 2–26, 4–11
  substitute basis clause, 2–19 to 2–20
  tax grossing-up
    drafting, 4–4
    generally, 4–2
    return of tax credits, 4–3
  waivers 4–12. *See also* **Waivers**
  warranties. *See* **Warranties**
Thailand
  insider dealing, 19–16

Thailand—*cont.*
  prospectus
    road-shows, 16–6
    sophisticated investors, 16–8
  securities regulation, 15–32
  insider dealing, 19–16
Trust. *See also* **Bondholder trustees**
  attitudes to, 10–13
  divided ownership
    enforcement, 10–11
    generally, 10–11
    holder of trust property, 10–11
    ownership on insolvency, 10–11
    wrongful disposals, 10–11
  false wealth and, 10–13
  legal characteristics of, 10–11 *et seq*
  property, 10–12
Trust deeds
  bondholder statutes, conflict with, 10–39
  bondholders' meetings, 10–26
  contract between issuer and trustee, 10–38
  contracting out, 10–39
  exculpation clauses, 11–25
  generally, 8–40
  governing law of, 10–38 *et seq*
  prescriptive jurisdiction, 10–40
Trustees. *See* **Bondholder trustees**
Turkey
  conflict of laws, 5–8
  state insolvency, 1–8

United Arab Emirates
  securities regulation, 15–32
United Kingdom. *See* **Britain**
United States
  arbitration laws, 5–58
  bank regulation
    authorisation of banks, 22–3
    restrictions on non-banking activities, 22–4
  "Blue Sky" laws, 15–6, 16–7, 16–16
  bondholder trustees
    conflicts of interest, 11–9
      New York Stock Exchange rules, 11–7
    regulatory controls, 11–7
    exculpation clauses, 11–29, 11–31

United States—*cont.*
  bondholder trustees—*cont.*
    monitoring duties, 11–15
    no-action clauses, 10–24
    notification of defaults, 11–20
    regulatory requirements, 10–7, 10–16
  bondholders' meetings, 10–26
    majority powers, 10–20, 10–27, 10–29
    minority protection, 10–30
  bonds, notification to issuer, 8–31
  collective investment schemes, 16–22
    investment companies, 16–22
    unit trusts, 16–22
  conflict of laws, 5–8, 5–10
    choice of law
      express choice of applicable law, 5–10
      jurisdictions, 5–2
      New York General Obligations Law, 5–10
      renvoi, 5–21
      state contracts, 5–17
    misrepresentation, jurisdiction over tort claims, 17–42
  corporate rehabilitation, 3–28
  dealers
    authorisation of, 18–6
    conduct of business, 18–9
    insider dealing. *See* insider dealing, *infra*
    National Association of Security Dealers, 18–9
  exculpation clauses, 11–29
    statutory limitations on, 11–31
  Federal Reserve
    Regulation D, 1–7
    Regulation Q, 1–7
    Regulation S, 16–16, 16–23
  forum non conveniens, 5–55
  insider dealing
    classes of insider, 19–18
    damages, 19–21
    exemption for stabilisation, 19–25
    generally, 19–15
    inside information, 19–19
    prohibition on directors' dealing, 19–11
    reports of holdings, 19–10
    sanctions, 19–21

United States—*cont.*
  insider dealing—*cont.*
    securities covered by prohibitions, 19–20
    territoriality, 19–26
  investment companies, 16–22
  legal opinions, 12–2, 12–3, 12–5
    contents of, due incorporation, 13–4
    "in good standing", 13–7
    liability in tort, 12–19 to 12–20
  London eurocurrency market and, 1–6
  long-arm jurisdiction, 5–38
  Memoranda of Understanding, 20–3
  misrepresentation, 17–5 to 17–8
    conflict of laws, jurisdiction over tort claims, 17–42
    due diligence standards, 17–10
    innocence, 17–11
    reliance, 17–17
  negative pledges
    automatic security clause, 3–26
    scope and efficacy of, 3–23
    security covered
      interpretation, 3–13
      subsidiaries, 3–16
  New York Convention on the Recognition and Enforcement of Foreign Arbitral Awards 1958, 5–61
  New York General Obligations Law
    choice of law, 5–10
    forum non conveniens, 5–55
  notary public, 12–2
  open-ended investment companies, 16–21
  prospectus
    bank deposits, 16–10
    collective investment schemes, 16–22
    commercial paper issues, 16–12
    existing security holders, 16–13
    foreign government offerings, 16–9
    foreign issues
      reciprocal recognition, 16–16
      registration of, 16–16
    listed securities, 16–14
    pre-issue publicity, 16–1
    preliminary prospectus offerings, 8–16

United States—*cont.*
prospectus—*cont.*
private offerings, 16–3
cold calling, 16–5
resale to public, 16–7
road-shows, 16–6
secondary market reading, 16–17
shelf registration, 16–18
sophisticated investors exemption, 16–8
syndicated bank loans, 16–11
reserve requirements, 1–7
Securities and Exchange Commission (SEC), 15–5, 15–6, 16–3, 16–10, 16–12, 16–23
securities regulation
"Blue Sky" laws, 15–6, 16–7, 16–16
brokers, 18–6
Commodity Exchange Act, 15–7
dealers. *See* dealers, *supra*
extraterritoriality
civil wrongs, 20–4
criminal statutes, 20–3
Memoranda of Understanding (MOU), 20–3
prescriptive jurisdiction, 20–6
Federal Reserve Board regulations, 15–7
Foreign Corrupt Practices Act 1977, 15–7
Glass-Steagall Act (Banking Act 1933), 15–7, 22–4
history, 14–12
Investment Advisers Act 1940, 15–5, 15–7
Investment Company Act 1940, 15–5, 15–7
Racketeer Influenced and Corrupt Organisations Act 1974, 15–7
Securities Act 1933, 15–5, 15–6, 15–7
misrepresentation liability, 17–6 to 17–8
due diligence standards, 17–10
innocence, 17–11
reliance, 17–17
Securities Exchange Act 1934, 15–5, 15–6, 15–7
misrepresentation liability, 17–5, 17–8

United States—*cont.*
securities regulation—*cont.*
Securities Exchange Act 1934
dealers, conduct of business, 18–9
selling restrictions in Eurobond issues
Regulations S
allotment securities, 21–5
equity offerings, 21–4
fundamental requirements, 21–2
generally, 21–2
governmental issuers, 21–4
guaranteed issues, 21–5
offerings of debt categories, 21–3 to 21–4
SUSMI (no substantial US market interest), 21–4
Rule 144A, 21–10 to 21–11
Securities Act, Section 4(3), 21–6
standard form selling restrictions, 21–12
TEFRA C, 21–7, 21–8
TEFRA D, 21–7, 21–9, 21–12
territorial ambit, 15–7
Trust Indenture Act 1939, 15–5, 15–7
state immunity, 5–64
super-priority moratorium loans, 3–28
syndicate agents, exculpation clauses, 11–29, 11–31
syndicated loans, 1–5
tax considerations for bonds, 8–27
Tax Equity and Fiscal Responsibility Act 1982 (TEFRA), 8–27
C Rules, 21–7, 21–8
D Rules, 21–7, 21–9, 21–12
interstate commerce, 21–8
securities regulation, 21–7, 21–8, 21–9
transaction opinions. *See* legal opinions, *supra*
trust deeds
conflict with bondholder statutes, 10–39
contracting out, 10–39
prescriptive jurisdiction, 10–40
trusts, attitudes to, 10–13
Uniform Securities Act, 15–6

INDEX

United States—*cont.*
  unit trusts, 16–20
Usury laws
  generally, 1–15, 2–18, 14–2

"Validly existing"
  meaning, 13–6
Veil of incorporation
  generally, 13–6
Venezuela. *See also* **Latin America**
  securities regulation, 14–13

Waivers
  clauses limiting, 4–12
  implied, 4–12
  sovereign immunity, of
    principles of, 5–65
    state immunity, 5–64
    terms of clause, 5–63
  term loans, 4–12

Warranties
  bonds, 8–10
  breach of, 3–3, 8–12
  commercial warranties, 3–1
  evergreen warranties, 3–3, 8–10
  generally, 3–1
  group tests, 3–3
  legal warranties, 3–1
  materiality tests, 3–3
  negotiation points, 3–3
  no express warranties, 3–4
  objectives of, 3–2
  syndicated loans, 8–10
  term loans, 3–1 to 3–4
  usual, 3–1
  validity of performance, as to, 3–3
Wash-sales. *See* **Securities fraud**

Zambia
  securities regulation, 15–26